THE FIRST RESORT OF KINGS

RELATED TITLES FROM POTOMAC BOOKS

Envoy to the Terror:
Gouverneur Morris and the French Revolution
by Melanie R. Miller

Napoleon's Troublesome Americans:
Franco-American Relations, 1804–1815
by Peter P. Hill

The Open Society Paradox:
Why the Twenty-First Century Calls for
More Openness—Not Less
by Dennis Bailey

THE
FIRST RESORT
OF KINGS

AMERICAN CULTURAL
DIPLOMACY IN THE
TWENTIETH CENTURY

RICHARD T. ARNDT

Potomac Books, Inc.
Washington, D.C.

Library of Congress Cataloging-in-Publication Data
Arndt, Richard T., 1928–
    The first resort of kings : American cultural diplomacy in the twentieth century /
Richard T. Arndt. — 1st ed.
        p.   cm.
    Includes bibliographical references and index.
    ISBN 1-57488-587-1 (alk. paper)
    1. United States—Relations.   2. Cultural relations—History—20th
century.   3. Diplomats—United States—History—20th century.   4. United States.
Dept. of State—History—20th century.   5. United States Information Agency—
History—20th century.   6. Educational exchanges—United States—History—20th
century.   I. Title.

E744.5.A82   2005
327.73′009′04—dc22   2004060190

Printed in Canada on acid-free paper that meets the
American National Standards Institute Z39-48 Standard.

Potomac Books, Inc.
22841 Quicksilver Drive
Dulles, Virginia 20166

First Edition

10 9 8 7 6 5 4 3 2 1

Dedicated to the memory of Carl Bode, Cleanth Brooks, Phillips Brooks, Robert R. R. Brooks, Frank E. Brown, John L. Brown, Jacob Canter, Martin C. Carroll, John K. Fairbank, Wilma Fairbank, Albert Giesecke, Albert Harkness, Charles Rufus Morey, Howard Lee Nostrand, Leon Picon, Lois W. Roth, John Slocum, Frank M. Snowden, Theodore A. Wertime, Wayne A. Wilcox , Robin W. Winks, Laurence Wylie, T. Cuyler Young, and scores of other departed CAO colleagues who, in tending the orchards of American education and culture abroad, managed once, in another country, to convey a little of the national style, grace, and genius.

CONTENTS

Introduction: An Academic Mole

I know of no profession which must more sorely try the souls of its practitioners than yours.

—George Kennan, to a Cultural Attaché, 1982[1]

IN 1961, HUNDREDS OF YOUNG PEOPLE left comfortable careers to see what they could do for their country. I was one of them. An academic late-bloomer on track to a life as a tweedy academic focused on French literature of the eighteenth century, I took leave from Columbia University to join the US Information Agency (USIA), almost as a lark. Of USIA I knew only that John F. Kennedy had appointed national media hero Ed Murrow as director. My colleagues teased me about joining the Foreign Legion. They were as ignorant as I about the scores of university figures who, beginning in 1942, had leapt from their campuses to jump-start a formal American diplomacy of cultures, improvising yet succeeding beyond all reasonable expectations and thereby helping shape the image of the U.S. abroad for generations to come.

My case turned out differently. I fell in love—the only phrase that fits—with cultural diplomacy and stayed with the practice for a quarter of a century, clinging to my identity and style as a university don and returning to other campuses after retirement. This book reports, among other things, on those years.

Beyond the romance of foreign service and the murky word "information" buried in USIA's name, I had no idea what I was joining. Following an accidental path, I had stumbled onto one of the better-kept secrets of American life, already in 1961 obscured by much smoke and not a few mirrors. I was assigned apprentice-style to the cultural office of the US embassy in Beirut, in ancient Phoenicia, adjoining the great missionary-founded American University, the AUB. There I encountered the diplomatic world and discovered within it a lesser-known underworld, dedicated solely to the educational and cultural dimensions of relations between nations.

Without realizing it, I was a product of that underworld. In the first contingents of Fulbright students going to France, Italy, and Britain in 1949, I received a letter signed by Eleanor Roosevelt appointing us all "ambassadors for America." In Dijon, I began explaining inexplicable America to others. After Dijon, where I courted a Burgundian wife, I taught American students at Columbia the joys of discovering a foreign language and culture, forged links between my university and France, shepherded French visitors around New York, and fathered two bilingual children. The Fulbright program, my French-born and French-trained teachers at Princeton and Columbia, my international students, my contributions to overseas university relations, and my thirst for things French—it never crossed my mind that all this was part of the Franco-American cultural relations that had begun with Ben Franklin in Paris and were abetted by more formal means beginning in 1923. Dozens of US bilateral cultural links had been forged, in a cooperative public-private US effort, supporting broadly defined and very long-range foreign policy objectives. Beguiled by the challenge, delighted by the daily discoveries of learning a new language and culture, intrigued by exotic life-styles, curious about the functioning of embassies, I suddenly found myself apprenticed to the guild of cultural diplomats. Forty-odd years later, I am still learning, as this book will show.

Certainly I kept one foot in the university world, assuming imminent return. As it seems in retrospect, I had become a self-appointed but unwitting mole, burrowing into government service, a spy for the university world, embedded with the cultural services of US diplomacy. Tunneling deep, I kept and added to my university friends. Unlike most moles, I did without the perks: there were no secret bank accounts, no handler to tell me what to do, nor anyone who seemed much interested in anything I learned. But there it was: for twenty-four years, I managed to maintain an academic persona, approximately true to the abiding values of universities, while working within the bureaucracy of USIA and the State Department. Only in early 1986 did I return, earlier than planned, to a campus.

It was a profession few Americans encounter. Quietly, invisibly, indirectly, my cultural colleagues and I spent our lives representing American education and intellect, art and thought, setting foreign ideas about America into deeper contexts, helping others understand the workings of the peculiar US version of democracy, combatting anti-Americanism at its taproots, linking Americans and foreign counterparts, helping the best Americans and foreign students study somewhere else—in short, projecting America, warts and all.

Our work as cultural diplomats carried out in a natural and free-flowing style that, without its being altogether clear to us, sought to extend the natural outreach of a highly communicative and friendly nation and a remarkably successful democracy in the culture of which education played a central role. Americans had assumed since the early decades of their republic that sharing with others was a fundamental duty; the idea flowed from the distinctive American idea of stewardship, fed mainly by churches of all persuasions. With perhaps too little thought to the ultimate results, we cultural officers were opening thousands of tiny windows into other societies, in some cases piercing thick walls. In the dramatic Soviet case, the light that filtered through these ragged apertures touched off the implosion of an empire, as world-shaking as the US educational and cultural diplomatic effort that three decades earlier helped transform two detested wartime totalitarian enemies—Germany and Japan—into trusted friends and pillars of world democracy.

The cultural office of an embassy is a unique perch from which to view the world. With time, my new viewpoint reshaped my view of history. Reflecting on humankind as a cultural diplomat, I came to understand that, if war in Hugo Grotius's phrase was the "last resort of kings"—*ultima ratio regum*—then cultural diplomacy was surely the first. Cardinal Richelieu knew more than most about such things; he first inscribed the phrase on French artillery in 1628, where until 1764 it reminded the world of France's last-resort options; at the same time, France's kings deployed a more systematic form of cultural outreach than any ruler had tried since Alexander of Macedon and his Roman students. Two millennia earlier, Alexander's successor in Egypt might have engraved the Greek equivalent of Grotius on his soldiers' shields, had he known him; instead, the great library he built in Alexander's Egyptian seaport needed no inscription: it was designed as Hellenism's first resort—the Greeks rarely failed to offer the peaceful option first, as before them earlier humans had sought to do through elaborate diplomatic protocols of gift-giving.[2]

My move in 1961 set me to watching human interaction between nations as a meeting of cultures; I began to see the extraordinary impact the American republic had had on the world since Franklin's trip to Paris. Walking the campus of the AUB or of Robert College in Istanbul, it seemed to me that every country in the world had been touched, informally and formally, superficially or in depth, in one way or another, by US private and public educational activities overseas, just as every country has been affected by what they knew of the US founders' attempt to build a durable democratic system out of the political ideas of the past. The formal US cultural diplomacy I practiced was put in place in 1938. Its designers were modest in their aspirations; they aimed at little more than the facilitation of self-generating educational relations between America and the world, in the certainty that, through fair weather and foul, such relations over time would serve US interests in building a peaceful, productive, and democratic world.

The year 1938 capped six years of hard labor by Sumner Welles and his team. Cultural diplomacy entered the Department of State, after a century and a half of private vigor and governmental permissiveness. For those who knew more history than I, 1938 reflected a natural American attempt to adapt millennia of human practice. From the start, the American designers had a few ironclad principles: first, to avoid any trace of propaganda; second, to stand clear of intelligence-gathering; and third, to minimize disruption of fragile foreign cultures. The designers avoided propaganda because the idea and the word had been poisoned, most recently by the Soviets, Italy's Fascists, the Nazis, and the Japanese, so that to Americans "propaganda" meant the governmental Big Lie. There was another subtext: diplomacy itself was suspect. The designers knew the old definition of a diplomat—an honest man sent abroad to lie for his country. They worried that any nation's propaganda was doomed to fail on two counts: as "foreign" activity and as the Big Lie.

American internationalists feared too that imposing the US model on foreign cultures would inevitably backfire. Thus to project US education the educators had to be sensitive, flexible, and adaptive listeners. Cultural diplomats, like educators, had to set up shop somewhere beyond suspicion. In projecting their cultures, groups and nation-states from the beginning of history had insisted on balance, on "exchanges," on reciprocity, and on bidirectional flow. Preaching, whether by cleric or layman, was out of the question in the postcolonial world.

The idea of rejecting propaganda recurs throughout the writings of the 1930s in all the Allied nations. In England as in the U.S., sour memories remained from Allied lies in World War I. Americans aware of growing US power also worried about seeming interventionist. The rise of totalitarian propaganda and aggressive interventions by the Axis and the USSR had shocked the world. In parallel with the French (1923) and the British (1934), the U.S. decided in 1938 on a course of truth, rejecting counter-propaganda even in response to Axis lies. The Allied nations determined to exchange truths.

The advent of hot war brought other demands: Elmer Davis and his Office of War Information (OWI—"information" first served as the American euphemism for "propaganda" in 1917) stuck to white and grey propaganda; the black version was passed off to "Wild Bill" Donovan's Office of Strategic Services (OSS). Cultural relations were still intact when in 1942 wartime pressures and the energetic Nelson Rockefeller began muddying the waters. After the war, especially after Fulbright's visionary plan for global exchanges was in place, the culturalists wanted to follow a parallel but decidedly separate path from information. Then in 1953 much of the cultural dimension of US diplomacy was thrust, under protest, into the new USIA. Until the end of the twentieth century, the idea of an independent American cultural diplomacy gradually eroded. With the death of USIA in 1999, the very existence of cultural diplomacy was imperiled. This book tries to tell that story.

• • •

No complete telling of this story has been attempted.[3] Millions of Americans have participated in formal and informal educational and cultural outreach, yet few have seen the whole picture. Cultural diplomacy is ill-understood because it is complex, proliferant, and multi-tasked. It is also reticent—its successes are most often invisible. On the information side, self-congratulatory American books on USIA—or on Public Diplomacy, as it has been called since 1978—line the shelves. But the rare book on cultural diplomacy, revealing concepts, patterns, and values, too often dips into the denser language of the university world.

Universities and governments march to different drums. Jacques Barzun named his university "The House of Intellect."[4] There in the 1950s dwelt the teachers and the scholars, men and an occasional woman, who lived the life of the mind, the life of learning. Great US research universities like Columbia provided a refuge for scholars who opened themselves to students, conveying a little history, a few core ideas, some approximate values, perhaps a skill or two, and providing the experience of thinking things through under the critical eye of a cultivated intelligence; the scholar-teachers projected a certain intellectual style; they provided analytic tools to help young people understand their world. Eager undergraduates were exposed to masterful teachers who had given their lives to the pursuit of new truths in some sector of the world's knowledge. This was the undergraduate experience.

Fewer Americans passed on to graduate studies, so most of us remember college as a time of growth and social trial-and-error; knowledge was measured by the "courses" one took. But those who remained on for graduate school and headed toward teaching careers, followed another path. They first won slow acceptance from their former teachers as colleagues; they cultivated intellectual curiosity, independence of mind, and a luxurious approach to time; they learned to be principals, working on their own rather than as agents for others' causes. As apprentice-scholars, they worked on what interested them; they treated knowledge critically, rejected dogma, dismissed ideology, and practiced tolerance, even of error as Jefferson insisted. The humanists in particular delighted in exceptions, more interesting than rules, while the social scientists looked for new rules to counter old intuitions. Such attitudes were not designed for the world of large organizations.

One element of my own university life did prepare me for cultural diplomacy. At Columbia, faculty members were expected to respect all three roles of an American university—scholarship, teaching, and service—but to excel in only two. Lionel Trilling called Columbia a "cloister on the half-shell"; I was one of the half-shelled. I was too young and, in retrospect, too modest to plunge into the kind of scholarship which assumes the making of contributions; instead, after teaching, I focused on service, contributing to student life through undergraduate activities like French theater, helping build overseas study programs, developing language-teaching methods and technology, and helping administer my department. This turned out to be tolerable equipment for government, if not comparable to the social science–based training provided by the schools of public policy. But at least it was more useful than what most humanist-educators were given.

Once in USIA, there was no time for reading. I had to build on my strengths; I entered as a committed university animal, one who persisted in seeing the world as an educational challenge, responsive to the therapy of education. Government work consumed only a little of each day, leaving substantial after-hours time. From my first week in Beirut, thanks perhaps to the nearby American University, I saw the university world as my focus; in Lebanon the AUB was a model and a storehouse that strengthened US intellectual relations well beyond Lebanon. To say that the government's views did not always coincide with mine will surprise no one—the theme of tensions between these two sets of values will recur throughout what follows. But for my first decade with USIA the tensions did not slow me down.

Entering government in the summer of 1961, a half-shelled intellectual found little that was familiar. In Washington, after a decade and a half in the rarefied world of two American research universities and a year in a French provincial bastion of Old World humanism, I was unprepared for the shock of mediocrity. USIA's six-week training session grouped two overlapping teams of thirty "lateral-entrants," highly selected we were told. Most of the sixty were well over thirty-two years of age, by the era's regulations, and allegedly experienced in some area "of interest" to USIA and its work. In fact, most came from journalism or public relations backgrounds, with a scattering of secondary or undergraduate educators, or from domestic political work—one from a trade union, one from public policy advocacy, one from non-university military history. I was alone in representing a research university. Among us, eight at most spoke a foreign language with any proficiency (one spoke seven). More than half had left their futures behind. Some had trouble with alcohol, some were shedding families, some were in full career crisis—it was more like the Foreign Legion than my Columbia friends had suspected.

The training tailored to this odd audience was pallid: we read no books, only handouts and an occasional article. The main fare was speakers—USIA officers—who paraded past us for one- or two-hour meetings; a sound US historian graced the permanent staff. Of the speakers, only four provoked memorable critical discussion; the rest are forgotten. There was much USIA puffery: in August 1961, USIA had its eighth birthday, but its staff made it sound venerable. Part of me was ready to leave on the next Greyhound, but curiosity and inertia kept me in place—my economic status required a steady job, but there was no shortage. My salary had been calibrated just one hair's breadth above my Columbia pay, with various allowances; it was easier to stay.

Besides, I had drawn an intriguing assignment. Postings provided the first day's excitement: we were each given a slip of paper slightly larger than the fortune in a Chinese cookie, with the name of a city scribbled in pencil. That year new posts were opening up all over Africa; Francophones like myself assumed we would be sent there. No one questioned assignments—one of our best, a crack reporter and polyglot from Minneapolis, was assigned to nearby Toronto; he asked why and found himself reassigned to war-threatened Elizabethville in the eastern Congo. My chit was a heart-stopper: it read "B-E-R-U-I-T." It took the better part of that first morning to realize that "Beruit" was a clerk's misspelling of Beirut.

Such errors were one of the everyday indignities inflicted on us by tyrannical bureaucratic gatekeepers who controled life issues like payroll, housing, security, shipping, travel, and food supplies. Only in the field, in the embassy "family," would life settle down—the Beirut embassy was a single collegial body of Americans bent on the welfare of their own. Washington instead was filled with danger signs as dreary as USIA's buildings, such as the courtly indifference of State's foreign service officers. In six weeks, sixty American USIA trainees with little in common and even less intellectual stimulation began finding ways to collegiality.

It is an odd fact that few cultural diplomats agree with each other on what they saw and did in their careers. We talk of our work, present and past; and we marvel, on reflection, at how little we shared unless we happened to be together at the same time in the same country. Cultural officers live unique moments, then generalize from their experience; but each experience is invariably *sui generis*, affected by time, place, functions, and the minds around them. In time, Tehran in 1968 was neither the city of 1958 nor that of 1978; in place, the Latin American hands shared little with Eastern European or Japanese or African veterans; in terms of people, Arthur Hartman's Paris embassy in the 1970s was not that of Pamela Harriman or Felix Rohatyn in the 1990s. Describing cultural diplomacy as it actually takes place at ground level irresistibly recalls the shopworn fable of the blind men and the elephant—one feels a tree, another a snake, another a brush, another a flapping sail, another an ivory prong. The total picture of the US cultural diplomatic elephant can only be seen at a distance, in space and in time. That is another goal of this book.

In my case, the larger conceptual picture began to take shape relatively early, less from the guidance of colleagues than from the proximity of the AUB and its faculty, who welcomed me as a colleague. It was the beginning of a forty-year dialogue between foreign and US university friends in the various US and foreign universities which I came to know. Revisiting my experience in 1971–72 during a USIA-funded mid-career fellowship in manpower economics, I began to see patterns. The distillate took clearer form during seven years with scholar-colleagues, undergraduates and graduate students at the University of Virginia and at George Washington University. Retired USIA colleagues were helpful after shedding the service's subtle constraints. Admittedly my understanding of a quarter-century in government is incomplete; I shall surely discover new ironies. But today, this is how it seems.

Rereading the chapters which follow, it came clear to me that I owe various kinds of debts, real and virtual, to hundreds and perhaps thousands, debts for which none of my creditors should be blamed. Diplomats and academics of all callings helped, but to my historian friends I seem to owe the most. At the end of my life, I have come to think in historical rather than political terms, looking to Braudel rather than Machiavelli; I have found the historians' brand of humanism most consistently useful in explaining what I saw. I have come to believe that only the study of yesterday can shed light on today and that only the study of others can help us to understand ourselves. Yet this book is not history and does not pretend to be. In many of the world's languages, "story" and "history" share a single word—which Edmund Morgan has called "hi-story." The following is more story than history. It covers part of a lifetime, trying to capture one man's effort over five decades, beginning in 1949 in France, to bring US and foreign intellectuals together. It tries to depict my struggle to understand how the U.S. sought, with occasionally enlightened government support, to forge enduring and self-sustaining links with the minds and intellectual institutions of the rest of the world, in the midst of constant political clash, endless seeking, and restless new conflicts.

What follows is a set of snapshots, insights into the peculiar mix of vivid highs and dismal lows in my experience of cultural diplomacy. Memory fades, people disappear, pain and joy recede, the world changes—albeit less than is claimed—but a great deal remains. My papers, shipped around five posts abroad and to several American cities, are not the orderly files of a scholar but driftwood from the river which ran through my in-box.

As well as story in history, this book is a memoir, relating twenty-four years in cultural diplomacy and an equal time in observation and reflection before and after. But it is a memoir in which I have tried to stay out of sight. Apropos of Edmund Wilson, Louis Menand noted that historical research is "an empirical enterprise and history writing an imaginative one. We read histories for information, but . . . we want the information in order to acquire the ability to understand the information"; historians, he says, seek to convey "the sense of what life was like when we were not there to experience it."[5] That is what I have tried to do here.

As for my former colleagues, I suspect few will agree with much of what I say. But if these memories strike an occasional spark from their minds or a few pages of disagreement, or if they provoke further reflection by my historian friends and their students and their students' students, picking up from my starting point, then my debt to them will have been paid. I shall surely be accused of naiveté by revisionists, realists, structuralists, deconstructionists, and others, not to mention my beloved USIA colleagues—propagandists, unidirectional informationists, and even cultural allies. I remind them that I am not ignorant of what goes on in other parts of the real forest, including the clandestine world; nor do I ignore the underside of the American Century and the ironies flowing from the rise of the reluctant hegemon; nor am I as naive as I may sound about change in US political process. It is rather that I am committed to laying out a basic framework for considering cultural diplomacy and its achievements, in the terms in which its principal agents and actors lived and saw it. Like a late beloved clergyman friend, I choose to preach my convictions and not my doubts.

The foggy spots in my vision of a quarter-century recur mainly in the fast-moving story of the last two decades, leading up to the end of USIA, the formation of a new structure in State geared to Public Diplomacy, an independent Voice of America (VOA), and the bare survival of the educational and cultural function in Washington, with a disastrously reduced field structure. In these years, there are more questions than answers; charitably, I believe the votes are not all in. We shall need a dozen books following this one to begin to fill out the story of the formal US experience of cultural diplomacy at the end of the twentieth century.

As the years have moved on, fellow practitioners and scholar-colleagues remind me that my itinerary has been idiosyncratic. Knowing this, I have tried at least to be readable and clear. Yet, I have learned to my sorrow that the very act of writing makes experience less true. This book in short can do no more than blaze a faint trail through the underbrush, in the hope that others may some day widen it.

● ● ●

A word on semantics, acronyms, and abbreviations. In a little-known field of public policy, readers will need guideposts. The language and special vocabulary of the American cultural diplomats over time have become a conceptual shorthand. Jargon accumulates in a profession which lives by words, in a craft practiced by few, especially in the ingrown and self-referential USIA. I shall try to help, but beg the reader, like any newcomer to government work, to accept this fact. For acronyms, I shall decode them at first use and elsewhere when it seems important. But some shorthand is better learned at the start.

The mysteries begin with the word "culture" and the phrase "cultural relations," adopted by the French in 1923 when they founded the world's first separate cultural office in a foreign ministry. Archibald MacLeish, then Librarian of Congress, wrote that "cultural relations are not something you have: they are something you read about having. Generally they are something you read about having with considerable reluctance" (1940). After heading State's cultural diplomacy, his view changed little: "Cultural relations is not a bad name in itself; on the contrary, it has all the attributes of gentility and virtue. It is also . . . a boring phrase" (1947).[6]

MacLeish knew, *pace* Anglo-Saxon mistrust, that in most of the world's languages "culture" denotes the highest values to which humankind can aspire. The Greeks all but invented the idea yet had no word for it, coming no closer than *ethos*, or as Werner Jaeger would have it, *paideia*. The Romans used *cultura* for farming, extending it to the nurture of minds, as in Cicero's *culturus animae*. For the Romans, *cultus* denoted a group with common beliefs; for national cultures, the Romans used a word for which history found other uses—*nationes*. Public philosopher Charles Frankel[7] listed culture's multiple meanings in common parlance—the arts, the culture of minds (i.e., education), the dead traditions retarding development, the harmless areas on which diplomats can agree when all else fails, and the anthropologist's meaning—that which distinguishes any group from any other. American political scientists—excepting those who study the Far East—have spent five decades arguing whether the notion of political culture had relevance, whereas historians and sociologists use the phrase routinely. Samuel Huntington legitimized the word "culture" in 1992 and dramatized the dangers in his book *The Clash of Civilizations*, in the text using "culture" and "civilization" more or less interchangeably. In 2000 he coedited a collective book entitled *Culture Matters*.[8]

Recent American usage has lionized—and trivialized—the word, modified by various adjectives—e.g., the corporate culture, women's culture, sports culture, drug culture, the culture of fear. For two decades, the U.S. has been involved in "culture wars." Since 9–11, the US public, obsessed with "why they hate us," has used culture as an ill-defined determinant, focused on the militant element in Islam. A disorienting misuse of the word equates "culture" with "the arts"; a White House conference late in the Clinton years was dedicated to "cultural diplomacy" but in fact treated arts diplomacy, which never drew more than 2 percent of US formal cultural diplomatic budgets. Even experienced US diplomats, especially European hands, fall into this trap.[9]

Most thoughtful cultural diplomats use "culture" as the anthropologists do, to denote the complex of factors of mind and values which define a country or group, especially those factors transmitted by the processes of intellect, i.e., by ideas. "Cultural *relations*" then (and its synonym—at least in the U.S.—"cultural *affairs*") means literally the relations between national cultures, those aspects of intellect and education lodged in any society that tend to cross borders and connect with foreign institutions. Cultural *relations* grow naturally and organically, without government intervention—the transactions of trade and tourism, student flows, communications, book circulation, migration, media access, intermarriage—millions of daily cross-cultural encounters. If that is correct, cultural *diplomacy* can only be said to take place when formal diplomats, serving national governments, try to shape and channel this natural flow to advance national interests. Given its earlier history, it is amazing that US diplomacy for five decades did this through broadly planned but carefully unregimented interventions like the Fulbright Program, forging binational linkages and, it is assumed, enhancing lives everywhere. Before, in its first century and a half, the US government permitted, facilitated, tolerated, and occasionally abetted cultural diplomatic interventions— but rarely funded them. US governmental minimalism allowed foreign information programs—except from the Soviet Union—fairly free play in the U.S. and pointedly followed diplomatic protocols abroad. A laissez-faire policy of free-flowing, two-way cultural relations, without government support or intervention, was a conscious early American choice. In 1938, responding to Latin American requests, State foresaw handling no more than 5 percent of the total work, coordinating, supplementing, and facilitating natural private flows of people and knowledge—and even this facilitative style of cultural diplomacy raised protests from traditionalist US diplomats.

Even the word "diplomacy" cannot be taken for granted. In our sense, it denotes not a product, nor US foreign policy, but a process, a technique, and if I dare say, a culture. Cultural diplomats first of all are practicing diplomats who deal with a sector of society uniquely theirs, the domain of intellect; they must therefore juggle the values of both worlds. Any diplomat represents his or her country, advises the ambassador, builds networks with foreign notables, negotiates agreements, and administers staff. Cultural diplomats do the same, but with a special sector of the political culture, the host country's educational system, its intellectuals, and its artists.[10]

The words "policy" and "cultural policy" also present problems. How cultural diplomacy relates to foreign policy has been debated since 1938, when founding director Ben Cherrington defended a purist definition, seeing cultural affairs as totally apolitical; by 1943 it was obvious that the word "policy" was misleading and that cultural diplomacy had obvious political impacts; in fact, there were many meanings to "policy." The new consensus: cultural diplomacy primarily served broad US interests, those of the longer-range—peace, projection of democracy, economic cooperation over time. Consider the example of school curricula: foreign secondary schools rarely concern embassies—students, unless they collect in mobs, will not soon shape political decision-making. Yet students grow older, and the textbooks that molded them may contain tenacious anti-American biases. That said, reshaping curricula is a long-range goal; it can only be tackled by cultural diplomacy, with host-country cooperation, and perhaps only by multilateral cultural diplomacy, with few expectations for at least a decade. On the other hand, clumsy cultural meddling in schools for short-range tactical purposes can only counter-produce: expecting a cultural program to change school curriculum or to influence a parliamentarian's vote is like assuming all Stanford graduates will vote for the same presidential candidate.

"Cultural policy" is avoided in US life, but overseas it implies a planned approach to maximizing broad US interests, in the world of education and intellect. By carefully selecting exports and imports, sound US cultural policy in a foreign country aims at fostering, correcting, strengthening, and where necessary initiating cultural and educational links with the U.S.

Diplomatic titles can also be difficult. "Cultural attaché" reflects a special language: in world usage, "attachés" are "attached" to embassies but not necessarily part of them. Foreign cultural officers may be cultural attachés, cultural counselors, or cultural ministers, in ascending order of diplomatic rank. Within US diplomacy, they are called simply cultural affairs officers or CAOs. In all cases, the title obscures the CAO's first commitment: education.

The CAO's boss, in US practice since 1917, is the public affairs officer or PAO, who heads a field post called USIS for US Information Service—both terms were borrowed from the military. The information officer (IO) was long the CAO's coordinate colleague under the PAO—the US model contrasts with world practice in placing both culture and information in a single office. The three workaday acronyms—PAO, IO, and CAO—will recur unavoidably in this text. For mnemonic purposes, the reader may appreciate a limerick with which CAOs amuse their friends (it assumes a Latinate pronunciation, i.e., pow for PAO, cow for CAO, and yo for IO):

> A wise and engaging old PAO
> Had a IO and a spirited CAO;
> To keep them together,
> He'd talk of the weather,
> Their kids, and the rise of the Dow.

Acronyms are inescapable. More than most, this book begs tolerance. The reader must accept both that UNESCO will replace the United Nations Educational, Scientific, and Cultural Organization and that cultural affairs officers will be called CAOs. Letter-clusters for names, like FDR, JFK, LBJ, or GWB, or for institutions, like USIA-USIS, VOA, NSC, FBI, or CIA, are common and recognizable. But long-dead government bodies like OWI (Office of War Information), USOE (US Office of Education, which was first in Interior, then in Health, Education, and Welfare, and now in the Department of Education) or AID (Agency for International Development, the last of a dozen acronymic permutations), and nongovernmental organizations (NGOs) like IIE (Institute of International Education), ACLS (American Council of Learned Societies), ACE (American Council on Education), NAS (National Academy of Sciences), or ALA (American Library Association) will live in these pages for the most part in their acronymic forms.

•   •   •

This book proceeds through a roughly chronological narration of the growth of formal American cultural diplomacy—its prehistory before 1776, its informal use by unofficial Americans before World War I, its distortion in the hands of Wilson and his propagandist George Creel, its formal adoption in 1938 by the Department of State, its wartime confusions, and the various twists and turns that brought it to a last-gasp moment of hope in 1978 and thence to accelerated decline. From time to time, we shall step out of chronology to look, first, at snapshots of US cultural diplomats at work, and then at a few of the products which US cultural diplomacy put in place around the world.

The golden years of cultural diplomacy began to fade four decades ago. Today the cultural dimension of diplomacy has been slashed, its independence compromised, its values blurred, its human resources driven away, its budgets strangled, and its honest servants befuddled by misguided reorganizations and meretricious rhetoric. Members of an underinformed Congress have turned their backs on the issue, whether because they, like Senator Helms, see it as an outmoded weapon of the cold war, or a minor component of psychological warfare, or a lavish "giveaway," or a total irrelevancy. Meanwhile the sharp rise in foreign non-understanding has become a national nightmare. Yet few have suggested that a crippled cultural diplomacy might have anything to do with either cause or cure. Cultural diplomacy's decline has thus passed unnoticed, leaving a nation baffled by its apparent defenselessness against the cultural onslaught of an enraged Islamic fragment.

To foreigners, US neglect is no secret. The outside world has watched cultural diplomacy's steady decline, for example, in the closing of the global network of USIS libraries and cultural centers, in cutting off thoughtful periodicals like *An Mahal* for the Arab-speaking world or *Dialogue* for the world, in ending support to fine and performing arts exports in 1994, in the decline of excellence in the Fulbright Program, and in America's recently ended nineteen-year boycott of UNESCO. Asked why nations engage in cultural diplomacy, German Parliamentarian Walter Picard once gave a simple answer: "Why? Because it is what decent nations do" (1980).[11] Such foreign friends today conclude sadly that it is precisely US decency which has come into question, that the U.S., swamped with real and imagined domestic concerns, has lost interest in the world outside its borders. This book may help explain how this loss of faith and trust came to pass and what it implies.

Yet the loss could be repaired. A decent cultural diplomacy costs amazingly little, a shadow of the cost of one wing of fighter aircraft. The American national style still enshrines the values of stewardship, generosity, and volunteerism. Human quality, the base on which cultural diplomacy rests, is not expensive in a country where citizens have always been eager to share. By understanding how, why, and at what cost America discarded cultural diplomacy, we may have a chance of bringing it back to life. I would argue that little matters more.

No single author, certainly not this one, can depict the enormous talent and dedication that hundreds of thousands of free citizens of the new American republic, whether as missionaries or as Fulbrights or as CAOs, brought to their daily transactions over the last two centuries. Let this begin their story.

CHAPTER ONE

Cultural Diplomacy from the Bronze Age to World War I

> It is by opposing reason to emotion and setting up the will for peace against [war] that peoples succeed in substituting alliance, gift and commerce for war, isolation and stagnation.
>
> —Marcel Mauss, 1925[1]

THE RICH EARLY HUMAN PATTERNS of cultural diplomacy lie beyond the reach of any summary. Those who have written on the cultural forms of diplomacy have long alluded to early historical episodes, but few have related these closely to practices in later eras. The question deserves volumes on its own.[2] For our purposes, a few selective glimpses into three thousand years of history, lingering here and there, will remind us that the well-read American Founders, however gifted, did not invent the diplomacy of cultures. For at least three millennia before them, cultural diplomacy had been the first resort of kings.

Recorded since the Bronze Age, cultural diplomacy has been a norm for humans intent upon civilization. By the third millennium B.C.E., diplomacy had evolved, in parallel with language, to permit cooperation between large groups. Moving beyond rituals and ceremonies, chants and dance, language conveyed ideas and permitted forward planning, self-awareness, and reflection. While brute force could still destroy civilization, diplomacy tried to preserve it by linking cultures to cultures.

Diplomats were the king's surrogates. They carried messages, and the best of them also brought back learning. Wise adaptive cultures like the Persians and the Greeks eagerly assimilated foreign information and technologies. They were Arnold Toynbee's "Herodians," who fared better than closed-minded and bullying "Zealots" like the Assyrians or the Chinese of the later T'ang.

Early diplomacy meant relations not between nation-states but between cultures. Adaptive language-cultures, defining themselves over time by custom, then adopted rules, codified them, and turned them into laws, designed to minimize disputes and maximize cooperation. Rules sprang from the metaphors of family: fatherhood defined dominance, equals were "brothers," and migratory tribes around the globe still boast of hospitality in welcoming "a cousin off the plains," in the classic Arab greeting.

Ritual and ceremony helped measure time and mark seasons. Raymond Cohen notes of Bronze Age intergroup relations that "ceremony was of the essence, enacting man's reverence for the gods, exalting the king over his subjects, sanctifying the conclusion of treaties."[3] Groups exchanged first gifts, then information, then goods and people, including mates; they sent their children to live with neighbors to learn about and from them, a process known among the Celts as fosterage—such "exchanges" are as old as time. When trade succeeded raid, plunder, and tribute gave way to tariffs and duties.

By the third millennium, the cities of Sumer had learned to bake cuneiform codes into resistant ceramic, used predominantly to support commerce. History was born when humankind was able to capture and retrieve memory, ponder the past, and reflect before acting. Chronicles recorded only the big news—not the humdrum of peace but the tragic failures of war. The armies at Troy, fighting over elusive cultural concepts like Honor, surpassed chronicle thanks to Homer. The clay tablets of Egyptian Amarna imply long-established patterns of human cooperation; these "letters" show extensive and structured diplomacy between Egypt and trading satrapies like Mittani, Hatti, Elam, Ugarit, and Egypt's Canaanite vassals. They exchanged awe-inspiring gifts, children, experts, marriage partners, goods, and services, all regulated by precise protocols.

Mauss first identified the pattern of gift-making, real and metaphoric, which runs through human history. Like those presented to the infant Christ by the ambassadorial Magi, those sprinkled throughout Homer, and those used to buy Manhattan Island, gifts were the diplomat's opening, a form of sociopolitical currency and a pledge of honor. They were as diverse as "sacks of gold, fine clothing, furniture, jewelry, ornaments, cosmetics, timber, slaves, horses and chariots," recorded Cohen of the Amarna period.[4] In their records, the golden statues of Mittani exemplify the process of gift-making. The marriage of an Egyptian prince and a Mittanian princess sealed Egypt's protection of this minor satrapy against Hittite encroachment. With the marriage came Egypt's promise of two life-size gold statues to flank the Mittani palace entrance. But when the Pharaoh died, responsibility shifted to his son Ikhenaton, who sent gilded wood instead. For seventeen years, between 1350 and 1334 B.C.E., the Mittani expressed dismay. Gilded wood was not enough to proclaim the protector's power.

Before the birth of writing, people and their knowledge were treasures, hence the most precious of gifts. Political brides, or hostages like the mythical Theseus in Crete, were both diplomatic coin and cultural conveyors. Sons and daughters of prominent families were sent abroad. Even slaves, it must be understood, were not always debased day-laborers. In Persia, the slaves who built the great monuments were "juridical persons," many of whom "were in an even more favored position than freed workers."[5] In Egypt, Joseph, an assimilated slave, achieved the highest rank, by his wits alone. As families stretched across borders, common laws grew up to meet new needs.

New technologies—in agriculture, architecture, weaponry, shipping, and crafts—could be transmitted only by individuals. While Assyrians slaughtered their prisoners, the wiser cultures valued human skills and found ways to put them to use. More than conduits for knowledge, exchanges had political purpose: Egypt's exchangee-hostages guaranteed good behavior on both sides; after their return they were channels to their former hosts. Gifts passed from equal to equal and from strong to weak; when they moved from weak to strong, they were easily corrupted into tribute, as in the later centuries of T'ang China.[6] The poisoned gifts of mythology—the apples eaten by Eve and Snow White—were breaches of trust, as was the Trojan Horse, discrediting Greek honor so permanently that we still mistrust "Greeks bearing gifts."

After living amidst the Persians, Herodotus translated this enemy culture into a form which his Periclean compatriots could absorb. Alexander, defeating Darius in 332 B.C.E., admired Persia enough to build his empire on Persian elements, including skillful diplomacy. The great Macedonian ingeniously manipulated powerful cultural symbols. Where he found cooperation, he set up peaceful satrapies to fill out his Hellenist vision and arranged cross-cultural marriages for himself and his captains; he absorbed local styles into Greek spectacles, theater, games, and architecture; he left symbolic buildings everywhere; he embellished coins with cultural, imperial, and kingly symbols; he absorbed foreigners into his army and civil administration, into education and the arts. The confident, resilient, subtle Alexander trekked over hundreds of miles of harsh desert to sacrifice to the Egyptian god Zeus Ammon at Siwa. Instead of having to conquer Egypt, he found himself acclaimed Pharaoh and could launch the Hellenization of the East. The tenacious and assimilative empire he created, bound together by its culture, eventually absorbed every other race and group. Ideas and people came from all over—Jews, Syrians, North Africans, Greeks. In the end, even the conquering Romans were Hellenized.

To re-center his empire, Alexander balanced might with mind. Around 300 B.C.E., his successor in Alexandria, the Seleucid Ptolemy I Soter, created a magnificent tool of cultural politics and diffusion, the world's greatest public-access library, modeled on that of Alexander's teacher Aristotle, and one of the first recorded private collections.[7] Culture in fact was power: with the library and its adjoining Museum, a center for scholars like Euclid, Alexandria overtook Pergamum and Athens to become the major center of learning in the Mediterranean world.

Cultural interchange meant a complex and balanced give-and-take of learning and teaching, export and import, weakness and strength, humility and self-confidence. The Greeks' ethical code *paideia* set the tone of a diplomacy in which humility, modesty, and respect for others were key ideas.[8] Approaching other cultures as learning opportunities, the Greeks continually refreshed their minds and launched a golden age of literature, art, science, and philosophy.

Intellect mattered. While earlier groups had stolen sacred fire, new leaders literally competed for scholars and poets. Philip of Macedon lured Aristotle away from Athens to his court. Theater and mass spectacles served political purposes, forged the group's identity, and, according to Aristotle, kept public passions in check. The Greeks sent their best men—poets and philosophers—abroad as ambassadors, especially when Greek power began to wane.[9] Having drawn from earlier civilizations, they gave freely to others.

There was no grand plan for diplomacy, only a mindset and applied intelligence. Assimilating prisoners of war rather than slaughtering them, building temples or staging spectacles rather than razing cities—these were multivalent political moves, both reflecting and reshaping the world around the Greeks. They understood that humans live on, learn, grow, change, and remember the past. Well-treated prisoners and slaves were human investments—Epictetus, Aesop, and the Roman Terence were only some of Rome's famous slaves. Self-generating migration leveled out labor surpluses and skill shortages. Balancing the humility of learning with the arrogance of teaching was the ultimate genius of *paideia*.

After Greece, it was Rome's turn. Triumphant Rome was absorbed by Greek culture, as it took over the Hellenized world. The earlier agrarians on the lower Tiber knew they were surrounded by superior cultures—the Greeks, the Carthaginian-Phoenicians, and closer neighbors like Etruria, whose Tarquin kings ruled Rome in the sixth century B.C.E. In time these groups would give way, but in the beginning Rome looked up to the Etruscans. Having absorbed Greek craftsmen and ideas, the older nation reached out generously to Rome, encouraging intermarriage and the exchange of sons and daughters. When the Romans needed information, trade stimulation, or societal bridging, the human groundwork was already laid. When relations turned sour, the human investments found other purposes: Roman armies conquered Etruscan lands in the early third century B.C.E. with the help of an Etruscan exchangee who led them through the Ciminian mountains.[10] As assimilationist Rome spread, it absorbed: taking Antioch, the Romans brought back a Syrian prisoner who, after two decades of education and nurture in Rome, was sent back to rule Antioch as Pius Antiochus. Ex-slave Terence wrote Rome's greatest comic plays; historian Polybius, a Greek captive, was Rome's historian-apologist; stoic philosopher Seneca was Spanish; Plutarch, a Greek living in Rome well after Augustus, wrote his paired biographical *Lives* to prove Rome the natural heir of Greece. Romans like the emperor Tiberius studied in Rhodes, Athens, or Alexandria. The Hellenistic world was one.

Libraries, storehouses of knowledge, kept their place of honor. Abroad, Antony restocked Alexandria as a gift to Cleopatra. At home, the Romans turned to civic education: the library for public education founded by Trajan in 113 A.D., with separate sections for Greek and Latin texts, had twenty-eight branches by 400 A.D. Cooperative public-private philanthropy provided new forms of cultural power: in Plutarch, Shakespeare's source, Marc Antony read Caesar's will, which left his open lands and orchards to the populace as parks; the urban conservationist and philanthropist Caesar understood cultural power.[11]

Under Augustus, intellect reigned, as he exploited the arts to create a new Golden Age. Working closely with his friend Maecenas, mythic founder of large-scale philanthropy, he supported writers and poets, including Vergil—whose *Aeneid* provided Rome's mythic identity. At his death, Maecenas willed his wealth back to Augustus—public-private cooperative philanthropy was already at work.[12]

Highly organized, disciplined, and technologically superior, Rome reached outward with architecture as its compelling symbol: temples, theaters, public buildings, triumphal arches, and hydrotechnological miracles surrounded the Mediterranean and reach as far north as German Trier. Rome festooned itself with architectural booty, symbols of outreach, like the giant Egyptian obelisks around today's Eternal City. Augustus's cultural politics made Rome the capital of the known world, but his city was dotted with symbols of other cultures so that citizens of distant domains might feel at home there.[13] Rome was a mosaic of tough-minded and cooperative but semi-independent cultural units. New learning was its heart, knowledge its strength, and openness to new ideas its engine of growth.

Rome fell when its civilization took survival for granted, allowing the brute power of the barbarians to overwhelm the city and its people. Learning went underground. In the so-called Dark Ages few realized that brutality was not the only way. North of the Mediterranean, learning hid in fortified monasteries, libraries bolted their doors, schools disappeared. Further south, Islam grew strong. Haroun al-Rashid and his son Caliph al-Ma'mnun located their capital in Baghdad and crowned it with their own library, the Bayt al-Hikmat or House of Wisdom, where among its holdings Greek literature was preserved in Arabic translation.[14] Drawing their intellectual style from Persia, the Muslims were a civilizing force, absorbing Greek cosmopolitanism as they reached from the Atlantic to China.

In parallel, history's greatest cultural diffusion had been in process for seven centuries, as ideas emanating from Hellenized Jews and Greeks in Palestine spread out to christianize Europe, ever respectful and adaptive of other cultures. Early Christian diffusion was the outreach of an idea, a culture, and a faith; only later, in competition with the sword of Islam, did political and military might take precedence.

In the ninth century, the idea of a politics of culture posited a single Christian empire, holy and Roman, the dream of the Germano-Frankish Charlemagne. The attempt to reconstitute Rome took its most cosmopolitan form in the thirteenth century when Frederick II, Holy Roman Emperor (1194–1250), took over Europe, revived ancient practice, and pursued cultural power as no one had since the fall of Rome.[15]

Frederick merits a pause. Called the Anti-Christ by some and relegated to the Inferno as a heretic by Dante, he was called by his contemporaries *stupor mundi et immutator mirabilis*, wonder of the world and marvelous man of change, because they thought him capable of containing the world's knowledge and moving human life ahead. By 1220 he had moved the seat of the empire from Aachen to Greater Greece, as the south of Italy is still called. He reached out from his capital in Foggia to the trans-Mediterranean south.

The Two Sicilies—present-day Sicily and southern Italy—were already a meeting-ground for Greek, Latin, Hebrew, and Arab culture. Frederick brought the world's greatest scholars, speaking Latin as their common language, to work together and to serve his vision. Knowledge was still being recovered through retro-translations begun by scholars like the Arab Avicenna in Córdoba, whose great Jewish successor Maimonides left Córdoba in 1148 to become physician in Cairo to the court of Saladdin. These scholars were part of Frederick's study; he broadened their mobility and reached out to their students.

The scholar-poets came first—in fact, Frederick was himself a poet. Poetry was a way for him to articulate, comprehend, reconceptualize, and envision the changing world. He saw the Arabs of the southern littoral as the missing piece of his empire. Eschewing force, he negotiated with the Sultan, ignoring Pope Gregory's orders to lead a Crusade against the Arabs and instead planting seeds of the mind. The Arabs, in their admiration for learning, accepted and adopted this "baptized Sultan." Such diplomacy soon earned him the crown of Jerusalem.

At home, the ideas of architecture, economics, medicine, public health, education, and agriculture were his activist tools of change. His new university in Naples welcomed international students. He was launching what would become the Renaissance. In a time when life was brutish and short, Frederick was building a dialogue of cultures and civilizations. But he could not do it alone. He died in 1250, at fifty-six, worn down by harassing enemies.

The greatest individual cultural diplomat of history had no throne. Three centuries after Frederick's total power, the Jesuit Matteo Ricci, with nothing but his mind, learning, and faith in his vision, opened China to the West.[16] Between 1583 and 1610, this second-generation Jesuit almost single-handedly persuaded China to look West. He came from a modest but learned background—his father was a pharmacist in Macerata, in the mountains northeast of Rome, where Jesuits had founded a seminary. Graduating to Rome, Ricci studied amidst polyglot colleagues under inventive scientists like the German Christopher Clavius, mathematician-astronomer and author of the Gregorian calendar.

First-generation Jesuit Alessandro Valignano, principal of Ricci's seminary, had served with Francis Xavier in Japan. He invited Ricci to the Portuguese enclave of Goa in 1573 and soon sent him on to Macao, south of Canton. The orders Valignano gave Ricci are a paradigm for cultural diplomats: set an example with a service-oriented life, learn the world's most difficult language for use at the highest social and intellectual levels, bring Western ideas into harmony with Chinese thought, and overcome xenophobia by sharing learning. In 1583 Ricci entered China.

His tools were cultural. For his dress, he chose the grey robes of the Buddhist holy men. For gifts, he used a prism to trigger discussions of optics and a portrait of the Virgin, drawn in the Western perspective unknown to the Chinese. He soon switched his Buddhist garb to the robes of the revered Graduates, or Confucian scholars, and began translating the first Chinese books ever into Latin and Western texts—often from memory—into Chinese. His message reached well beyond the limits of his voice. To earn the acceptance of the Graduates, he underwent a daunting examination of his trained memory. He recited poems chosen at random from an anthology that he first read that day. Then, to allay suspicions that he had memorized the texts beforehand, he invited each of his ten examiners to produce fifty Chinese ideograms. After brief study, he recited all fifty in order, then repeated them backward. This was a feat of memory that his generation, which included men like Aquinas, considered a natural part of intellect.[17] His performance for the Graduates was also theater, which has always been a useful adjunct of cultural diplomacy. Overnight Ricci became the Wise Man from the West.

Moving on to Peking, Ricci gave the emperor the reliable prism and portrait, plus two novelties: a clock which struck the hours[18] and a clavichord. The emperor was impressed with his gifts. The clock and clavichord required ongoing care, so Ricci and his team could enter the palace at will to tend the clock and to teach the palace eunuchs to play the clavichord. Collegial dialogue began during these palace visits, and mistrust finally vanished when Ricci helped the astronomers, who regulated Chinese life, to recalibrate their instruments. Soon the Jesuit published his famous world map with China's position correctly shown for the first time. The map was a modern triumph of the ancient Chinese art of xylography, or woodcut-printing, in six panels that stood as tall as a man. Ricci assembled and translated books, including Euclid, into Chinese—instant classics—under his Chinese name Li (for Ricci) Mahtou (for Matteo). He saw everyone who came to his door until his death in 1610. His well-tended tomb in Peking stands in a courtyard surrounded by Communist Party headquarters, but his true memorial, the opening of China to a benign West, was soon discarded. His zealous and impatient successors in diplomacy committed every mistake he had carefully avoided; by the end of the eighteenth century, European missionaries were expelled from China.

Like Frederick, who mobilized cultural power in the service of nation-building, Francis I (1496–1547) envisioned a new France a century before Ricci. Pulling France together into a single nation-state, Francis institutionalized the import of culture through diplomacy. Literally transporting the Renaissance from Italy to latecomer France, Francis created a new nation, and in less than two centuries France would lead the world, primarily through its cultural power. In his own way, Francis brought Charlemagne's and Frederick's dreams to reality in the form of a universalist Christian empire.

As a child, Francis sat at the feet of Leonardo da Vinci, a frequent guest of his family. Three years of captivity in Italy taught Francis that his rough-hewn land needed a stronger cultural base. Unlike the Churchmen, he saw no threat in the rebirth of classical learning and was ready to vest intellectual responsibility in individual conscience. His first step, only decades after the invention of movable-type printing when the book was an exciting new technology, was to buy every book that came out of Venice's busy printshops. He sent Guillaume Budé, France's leading classical scholar, as ambassador to Venice, then followed him with four other scholar-poets, the last being the great printer-publisher Etienne Dolet. Together they built the Royal Library, now the Bibliothèque Nationale.

Architecture came next. The Italian Sebastiano Serlio, challenged to adapt classical architecture to French needs, brought in painter Rosso Fiorentino and the younger Primaticcio. Serlio helped expand Francis's Louvre. His books on architecture were soon accepted as textbooks. Italian artists, including Benvenuto Cellini and architects like Guarini, worked in France. Another kind of artist, exemplified by the verses of Pietro Aretino, fed the less sedate side of Francis's taste and the exuberant side of French literature. Agents like Primaticcio bought and commissioned paintings in Rome and Florence. Diplomatic gifts streamed in once rulers like the Medicis learned of Francis's passion for painting. The paintings that rulers received or bestowed on each other were more than gifts—they often contained coded messages beyond language for specific diplomatic purposes.[19]

Language was a national obsession—French had barely begun to take its modern form. One member of the famous Pléïade group of poets, the young scholar-poet Joachim Du Bellay, lived as a diplomat in his uncle's embassy in Rome in 1553. He had already published his *Defense and Illustration of the French Language* in 1549, arguing that a vernacular literature for France could only arise if the French reached back to the classical essence. The militarist title of the *Defense* fed France's persistent obsession with propagating the French language abroad.[20]

For Francis, education was the key to his hopes for France. The Church, fearing the classical revival, had to oppose educational expansion, so Church control over the university was firm. Francis believed that the Church-controlled universities were hindering France's modernization; with Budé he founded the Collège de France, bypassing religious authority. The Collège, an alternate center of intellect, sheltered the classical revival. As French students flowed abroad to foreign universities, foreigners were welcomed in France. A "student hostel" for foreigners called the Collège des Quatre Nations opened in Paris; Strasbourg by the eighteenth century counted two hundred Russians among its foreign students—all part of a cosmopolitan remake of France's mind and mien. The same cultural strategy was carried on by Henry IV and two powerful Cardinal princes, Richelieu and Mazarin, who was himself an Italian import. Francis's grand plan had become a French habit.

By the second half of the seventeenth century, France reached the peak of its cultural power. Louis XIV, the Sun King, began his efforts to radiate and project French intellect. French books, hand-copied newsletters, and gazettes moved around Europe. More important were France's extraordinary human representatives beaming France's light to the far corners of the globe. French jurists joined Wolff and Grotius in elaborating a universal legal system, after the peace of Westphalia in 1648.

The Jesuits, exporters of high-quality education, were the unacknowledged overseas arm of the court. They came from or were trained by the educated elite. They managed a global educational network which was never rivaled; even the nineteenth-century British empire was more intent on training its human resources than on education.

French universalism beamed outward, like the metaphor of the Sun King. The verb *rayonner*, to radiate or shine out in rays, persists in the history of French cultural diplomacy, through Bonaparte, De Gaulle, and their successors in our times. Reaching beyond import, Louis XIV established the first foreign academy in Rome in 1677 to train French artists. Nicolas Poussin (1594–1665) spent most of his life in the Eternal City as an informal cultural adjunct to the embassy, helping compatriots see the great models, commissioning and buying paintings and sculptures, overseeing artists' training, and advising the embassy. The new Academy filled the gap his death left. Soon the idea of an academy in Rome would be imitated by dozens of other nations, including the U.S. in 1896.

France's formal diplomats came from the same intellectual elite as the Jesuits—and all were Jesuit pupils. The brilliant elite trod a delicate line: it was easy to slip from *rayonner* into *éblouir*, from shining to dazzlement. By the eighteenth century, France's diplomatic messengers were in fact dazzling the world with the nation's cultural achievements. France's Jesuits reasserted and expanded the country's role as protector of Christianity, renewing the treaty of protection for Christians which Francis had contracted with Suleiman the Magnificent. In Syria the descendants of the Crusaders who remained behind in the eastern Mediterranean, especially in the Mount Lebanon area, were sheltered by France. To them, Louis XIII sent the Jesuit François Le Clerc du Tremblay, famous as Le Père Joseph, whose name still graces the St. Joseph University and schools all over Lebanon.

France's lay intellectuals went abroad as well, quietly serving the court. Essayist Montaigne, like the Dutch painter Rubens, carried diplomatic messages for their monarchs and brought back ideas. In 1649 Descartes traveled to Holland, necessarily with court approval, then resided until his death at the court of the learned Queen Christina of Sweden. A century later a friend to both the Encyclopedists and the court, Cardinal de

Bernis, represented France in Rome as Ambassador. Voltaire at the court of Frederick the Great played a wily diplomatic role. The French court utilized Diderot's long journey to Russia, where he served as advisor to Catherine the Great in St. Petersburg on the planning of Russia's first university.[21]

Post-revolutionary France, when Bonaparte had restored order and installed a rationalized, disciplined, and slightly more democratic version of the monarchy, carried on virtually without a break, as vigorously universalist as the *ancien régime*. Napoleon casually imported booty to fill his newly-nationalized museum; paying the minimal prices offered to conquerors, his agent Vivant Denon drove hard bargains and sent to the Louvre long wagon-trains loaded with art. It was a free-booting era, condoning official and unofficial archeological and artistic pillage on grounds that the works would be destroyed if left in place.

In exchange, Napoleon exported French ideas and institutions. French cultural diplomacy tried to lure Egypt away from the British orbit and into a functioning relationship with France by educational and scholarly gifts, including schools and institutes still in place. In Italy the means of diplomacy were the same but the purposes different: from his Corsican viewpoint, Bonaparte saw France and Italy as a continuum. His agents set up Italy's administrative, educational, and judicial systems and founded elite-training institutions like the Scuola Normale in Pisa. Through the years, France never wavered in its univeralist goals and remained deeply committed to education and culture, blending import and export. Education and culture were harnessed and managed for the purpose of enhancing, magnifying, and reinforcing French power.

●   ●   ●

This was part of the background that the well-read new Americans might have known as they set about designing an American style of democracy and an appropriate diplomacy. Adept students of history, they read everything available with different eyes: their experience as former subjects helped them understand power from the underside, committing them to tolerance and an early form of pluralism—Jefferson and Franklin saw themselves as settlers sharing a vast new continent with its earlier residents. When Franklin and Jefferson took on their make-or-break assignments in Paris, they had few resources beyond their wits, but their minds were well prepared.[22]

Franklin, at the Boston Latin School, learned how to learn, then dropped out and never stopped learning; Jefferson's classical studies at William and Mary stayed with him for life. Like Montaigne, these men read for practical ends, applying what they read to what they saw around them. This was especially useful in Paris, where American diplomatic practice began. Franklin's ingenuity—more, his genius—won French support for the American war of liberation; Jefferson opened trade channels and purchased the American West. Speaking French after a fashion and learning by trial and error, these men set two distinct styles for formal US diplomacy—Franklin leading from his worldwide scientific reputation, his wit, his guile, and a touch of theater, and Jefferson, from his hands-on experience of shaping democracy, impeccable diplomatic behavior, wise political counsel, intellectual curiosity, and shrewd eye for France's landholdings. On the informal side, they were joined—and plagued—by a man who rarely admitted error, their undisciplined friend Thomas Paine, who exemplified a third style, that of the unofficial American enthusiast. Paine's words would later find echoes in private American zeal around the world. Taken together, Franklin, Jefferson, and Paine sketched out three styles of US cultural diplomatic behavior: wily exuberance, public prudence, and private zeal.

The first of these, the colorful Franklin managed his Paris miracle by cultural means.[23] After two frustrating decades in London, he played the cultural card in France. His unique personal diplomacy was aimed at the entire French nation, but the real target was Louis XVI, who, with a handful of advisors and intellectual go-betweens, had the power to help the new nation. Four decades later the French historian Capefigue called Franklin one of the great charlatans, adding ruefully that "in France charlatanry worked!"

Franklin, no landed aristocrat, early became what he wanted to be, not an aristocrat but a gentleman, perhaps the hardest-working of his century. In London at length as agent for four American colonies, he failed to convince the British to foster a cooperative Commonwealth but built his reputation as a world-class scientist. His diplomacy in London was unsuccessful, but his routines were thorough: he befriended American writers and artists, recruited new Americans like Paine, and generally represented American interests. Cultural tactics, including a chess match with Lord Howe's sister, helped him convey the colonists' position—to no avail.

Diplomats, especially those with talent, are improvisers, inventing things as they go along. Franklin's behavior with the French totally reversed his London style. He arrived with an impressive reputation—John Adams would begrudgingly admit that Franklin was better known in France than Voltaire. In contrast to his London reticence, in Paris he became a famous *salonnier*.

Like the French, Franklin was a universalist. At twenty-five he had written about "forming the virtuous and good men of all nations into a regular body, to be governed by suitable and wise rules," an idea reiterated in his *Autobiography* and developed by Immanuel Kant (1724–1804) in his thoughts on world governance and perpetual peace. With the French, Franklin wisely concealed his universalist mindset, explaining that he had come to study science. This earned him distance, respect, and freedom to behave in a manner closed to the more punctilious Jefferson, the confrontational Adams, and the undisciplined Paine. His adopted role required talent, enormous good humor, self-confidence, shrewd calculation, and an iron will.

Turgot and Beaumarchais had broached the subject of helping the rebels, and the anglophobe Foreign Minister Vergennes agreed that the French should give the colonies aid, as his secret messenger told Franklin in London. Other mediator-friends weighed in—intellectuals like Dupont de Nemours, biologist Buffon, philosopher Condorcet, and economist Quesnay, leader of the Physiocrats. Even Franklin's lady-friends helped—each led a vital salon. Freemason Franklin frequented the powerful Masonic Order in France, comprising an impressive selection of France's best minds. Overwhelmingly, the common people knew Franklin—his face was more familiar than the moon, he confessed in mild embarrassment to his sister; in fact, he found a Franklin fad in full sway when he arrived. Condorcet understood: "He knew that he did not represent his country with the Ministry, so much as he represented it with the nation."

His Parisian persona was a diplomatic decision, reversing his behavior in London. He nurtured his new image through graceful social discourse and unfailing wit. He chose his clothes and lifestyle carefully, living frugally—albeit in a dignified house. He dressed in brown homespun without wig, and in the colder months he wore a beaver hat like Rousseau's and carried a crab-apple staff to help move his gout-ridden legs, tapping into two French myths: Rousseau's noble farmer and Voltaire's Quaker. Wearing the bifocals he had invented, he held his tongue when praised not for his genius but for his thrift in putting up with cracked lenses. Presented at Versailles, he wore brown velvet, appearing without wig as Citizen Franklin, to Louis's delight. He bowed to the king, but not too deeply.

With inexhaustible energy, as he wrote Paine, he tried "to live as if I was to live always." His vast correspondence touched every field. He helped the Duc de la Rochefoucauld publish the constitutions of all thirteen American colonies. He recruited friends to the American cause and officers to its army—Lafayette, Von Steuben, Pulaski, and Kosciusko. He helped Parmentier popularize the newly imported potato, which he saw as a solution to world hunger; the great chemist Lavoisier helped him procure gunpowder; in Nantes, he helped a young English-student, later Citizen Genêt, gadfly to Secretary of State Jefferson; letters reached him from the chemist Marat and the lawyer Robespierre; he advised French publishers about the US book market; founder of the University of Pennsylvania, he tried without success to raise funds for Dartmouth and Brown. Virtually without staff, his casual style concealed a mastery of detail. Adams missed the point and thought Franklin lazy.

The diplomat's job demanded shrewd cultural sensitivity. In 1783 Jefferson's Tuscan friend Filippo Mazzei convinced Franklin that America's Catholics should depose their nonresident British bishop. Although the American clergy had its own candidate, Franklin proposed his Jesuit friend John Carroll, founder of Georgetown University. Vergennes and the young Talleyrand helped Franklin meet the papal nuncio. Nominating Carroll, he reminded the envoy that the American Congress played no role in religion—Rome faced its first diplomatic negotiation in the West with a pointedly secular state. Nervous about the revolutionary Protestants, Rome finally agreed, yielding to its own desire to annoy the British. Carroll was named Bishop in 1784.[24]

In the diplomatic derby, Franklin was running against a thoroughbred: the brilliant Lord Stormont, who had the advantage of reading virtually all of Franklin's mail and watching every move he and the French made. Franklin plunged ahead unperturbed; he could disregard spies, he said, because he practiced transparent diplomacy—speaking for most cultural diplomats, he tried "to be concerned in no affairs that I should blush to have made public." At last he skewered Stormont on an invented French verb: *stormonter*, to exaggerate or lie. Even the humorless Jefferson admired "those *bons mots* with which he used to charm every society."

Adams never understood Franklin's "frivolity," but the explanation was simple: Franklin enjoyed French life and was effective for that very reason; *joie de vivre* was his trump-card. The famous story in which Mme Helvétius interrupted the Adamses' call on Franklin by mopping up her dog's piddle with her shift scandalized the New Englanders; so did the rumor that Franklin had proposed marriage to this fading widow of one of France's great philosophers. They could not know what Mme Helvétius represented in France, any more than they could see the hidden messages under Franklin's light touch. Adams argued for confronting the French with their duplicity, but Franklin insisted on engagement.

Printer-publisher Franklin knew that the printing press could magnify his voice. He was relentless in his writing. In a biting Swiftian satire, he concocted a letter from an imaginary Iroquois chief to the British, presenting a bill for thousands of scalps, including children's. He knew the press—most importantly books and pamphlets—from the inside. The "newspapers" to which he referred in a 1782 letter to Richard Price were little more than undernourished weekly gazettes of no interest.[25]

Franklin was sixty-nine and in poor health when he reached Paris, but he thrived on his work: "I am here among a people that love and respect me, a most amiable people to live with," he wrote to his grandson. He worked for a single cause, his country. He behaved as a suppliant, against Adams's advice: "A diplomat, seeking help from the only real ally his country can count on, simply cannot afford anger. Franklin never once forgot this. Adams never understood it," commented David Schoenbrun, who found a corroborating memo in the Foreign Ministry files, written by an unknown top-level official, proving that Franklin's style worked: "This [the American nation] is a people already civilized by its understanding and which, having acquired its political independence, is about to choose for itself the legislation that is to establish its identity for all time. The history of the world, perhaps, shows no spectacle more interesting, and the political stage has never, perhaps, presented an event, the consequences of which are more important and widespread in the general condition of the globe."[26]

US universalism underlay Franklin's views, but he knew the idea would challenge universalist France. He took a respectful attitude, almost coquettish, toward France. America, he believed, should expect to be wooed, not beg for alliances "but wait with decent dignity for the applications of others."[27] He was less cautious at home. To Congress in 1777 he wrote: "Tyranny is so generally established in the rest of the world, that the prospect of an asylum in America, for those who love liberty, gives general joy and our cause is esteemed the cause of all mankind. . . . We are fighting for the dignity and happiness of human nature." As Jefferson thought, and Paine hoped, the "infectious disease of freedom" was running loose; with his crab-apple cane, Franklin limped daily through the Paris minefield.

No man could have been more different from Franklin than his successor Jefferson, who in turn probably never had a harder job than succeeding Franklin. He knew Franklin's wizardry could not be replicated, so he set out to plow his own furrow. More than anyone else, he shaped formal US diplomatic practice and early French-American economic relations. Coming to Paris directly from Virginia, he represented not the nation Franklin had imagined but a genuine new republican state. Facing mythic illusions in France, the Americans had hard realities to confront and few promises to make. Trade was the key: Jefferson wanted to break the British stranglehold on commerce and persuade France to fill the gap. Representing a penniless, inexperienced, and divided new nation, he preached the future.

Jefferson had no small talk, nor an iota of the theatrical; but wisely he knew it. He looked ahead, behaving, structuring his work, and living like a polished diplomat. Yet ideas came first—he too founded a university. With Lafayette, Jefferson helped draft the Declaration of the Rights of Man; the two then set to work on a post-revolutionary constitution for France, choosing Pennsylvania's as their model. He invited Lafayette and the Patriots, a group of moderate political figures, to his home, where they debated the issues while he sat silent—the French called his passive guidance and uplift "eloquent silence."

He was "the primary conduit for the Franco-American cultural exchange," notes Joseph Ellis, listing Jefferson's contributions to France in agriculture, natural science, botany, and constitutional government, in exchange for borrowings and purchases.[28] He kept work and play apart. As devoted to the arts as his predecessor, he played his violin in private. He commissioned Houdon to sculpt portraits of Washington, Frankln, and himself, and he helped the successor generation of new American painters like John Trumbull. But this, like his romance with Maria Cosway, was diversion and recreation more than a means to penetrate the French mind.

Widespread service to his countrymen was his routine. His range of friends was narrower and more selective than Franklin's, his writings were fewer. Yet he made sure that his friend Mazzei's four-volume work on the U.S. was published and reviewed by no less than Condorcet. Like Franklin, he focused on books and literary journals, subject to the same laws of censorship but freer than the "newspapers"—he knew the French government feared intellect less than it feared the masses. As Dumas Malone noted, "there was little he could really do about the newspapers, and for this reason it was fortunate that they were relatively unimportant."[29] Pouncing on any book which mentioned America, he went to great lengths to correct giants like Abbé Raynal and Buffon, working from memory since he had few books at hand. With the French press, Jefferson was indulgent, as befits an accredited minister; he was less so with British journalism.

Jefferson and Franklin read French well, but both spoke it badly, with atrocious accents. Franklin could exchange repartee, but Jefferson's weakness in French restrained him. Spending more time at home than Franklin, he apparently did little to improve his ability with the language. Universalist Jefferson wanted to see the world knit together through the exchange of goods, services, people, and ideas. Like his beloved friend Madison, he believed that "the free system of government we have established is so congenial with reason, with common sense, and with a universal feeling that it must produce approbation and a desire of imitation, as avenues may be found for truth to the knowledge of nations." For Jefferson, two ingredients were central: freedom and trust. Urging Harvard president Joseph Willard to help strengthen French scholarship in North American natural history, he pleaded for free inquiry: "Liberty is the great parent of science and virtue; . . . a nation will be great in both in proportion as it is free." His passion for books ran him into serious debt. Today Jefferson's gifts to France can be found in various museums in Paris, as one finds analogous French gifts at Monticello.

Jefferson believed democratic constitutionalism could serve as an example to the world, not in the abstract but in precise terms. In March 1789, answering Madison, he expressed hopes about US-style constitutions abroad: "The example of changing a constitution by assembling the wise men instead of assembling armies will be worth as much for the world as the former examples we have given them." He saw the inevitable collision between French universalism and its American nephew, but dreamed of a post-nationalist world in which the virtuous and the talented would rule and in which members of the disciplines and professions would relate, across national lines, more closely than they did to countrymen and neighbors outside their professions: "The societies of scientists . . . form a great fraternity spreading over the whole earth."

His short-range goals were trade and politics; his long-range focus, healthy and resilient relations; his tools, culture and ideas. He spoke for US intellect in Paris more generally than Franklin, and the French valued his special experience as a founder of a new democratic republic; they looked to him for the ideas behind US institutions and involved him in moderating discussions between political leaders. Franklin had projected American ideas and values before the U.S. was born; Jefferson updated and deepened the discourse. In all, he managed his own small miracle—he succeeded Franklin.

Citizen Tom Paine was another matter.[30] While Franklin and Jefferson spoke French poorly, Paine never bothered to learn it at all. Jefferson had guided the enigmatic Paine through a year in London, where Paine—who never took US citizenship—served with distinction as acting US mission chief. But the two epitomized opposite kinds of universalism: Jefferson never doubted he was serving the US national interest, while Paine never aimed at less than the good of humankind, as he made clear in 1796: "A revolution in the state of civilization is the necessary companion of revolution in the system of government." R. K. Webb, in his book on Harriet Martineau, got to the core of the man when he said Paine was "not really interested in America at all but in certain abstract propositions which America could prove." In time he and Jefferson drifted into irreversible estrangement.

Alcohol was Paine's crutch and his downfall. On his first trip to Paris in 1781, seeking to patent his ingenious design for a wrought-iron bridge, his behavior wore Franklin's patience thin. He returned to Paris from London after 1789 as the famous author of *The Rights of Man* and took it as his due when the post-revolutionary Assembly voted him an honorary citizen of France, elected him to the Assembly, and appointed him to the committee drafting France's first constitution. But he was in well over his head; he knew little about parliamentary process, less about France, and no French. Siding with moderate liberal constitutional monarchists centered around the Girondins, he worked with Condorcet on the constitution. Louis XVI was condemned to death by a single vote of the Assembly, despite Paine's courageous negative vote and speech. Later Paine argued pertinently for a commuted sentence for the King but found his wisdom undone by Marat. He continued his perilous interventions in the Assembly, defending Francisco Miranda, the Venezuelan deputy to General Dumouriez at Valmy. Released in 1795, Miranda returned home where, as "Precursor" to Bolívar, he remained a staunch friend to the U.S.

For Paine, all but the axe fell in December 1793 when he was dragged off to Luxembourg prison. There his noble behavior outlasted cruel pressures and serious illness. He was rescued after ten months by the newly arrived minister James Monroe. Paine repaid Monroe's generous post-prison hospitality by grossly overstaying his welcome, finally moving to the home of his publisher on the Parisian outskirts. There, through recurrent bouts of alcoholism, he wrote and tinkered. Another universalist, Bonaparte himself paid a surprise visit to thank him for *The Rights of Man*, which he said he kept under his pillow. But little was left for Paine in Paris, and he returned to the U.S. in October 1802, too advanced in his habits to change. He had gone to France as a private citizen and busied himself in persistent meddling; meanwhile his incendiary publications were touching off revolutionary thinking everywhere in the world.

Paine, the enigma of the American eighteenth century, "had known virtually every important figure in the world in Europe, France, and the U.S. during his lifetime. Yet not one publicly praised him after his death," noted his biographer.[31] Except for his years of good behavior in London, he was far from a diplomat; rather he was a visionary, weaving his dreams into powerful, enduring words that changed the world. When the new nation he had envisioned became a status quo power, with Paine's old friend Jefferson as its chief executive, Paine was left behind. He died in 1809, with only poet-diplomat Joel Barlow as a friend.

Paine's potent words about revolution and the freedom-loving image American political culture had acquired spread around the world. With Paine as America's prophet, expectations of the new nation soared. Consul Nathaniel Hawthorne in Liverpool discovered that America had become the haven for all stateless souls. Historian George Bancroft, later minister to Bismarck, echoed Paine when his British colleague, clad in the gilt and feathers of an ambassador, twitted him for his plain black undertaker's suit: "Sir, I *am* an undertaker," he answered, "an undertaker for the monarchies of Europe."[32] After the world-targeted private diplomacy of Paine, expectations of the U.S. as the fount of revolution still plague the nation.

Other formal diplomatic envoys followed, culled by definition from a tiny educated US elite. Like France's ambassadors, these were men of high distinction—citizen-diplomats: literary figures like Washington Irving, Hawthorne, Lowell, Howells, and Bret Harte; less-remembered intellectuals like writers Joel Poinsett, Barlow, John Hay, George Perkins Marsh, and Thomas Nelson Page; art historians like James Jackson Jarvis; historians Bancroft and John Lothrop Motley; and future president James J. Buchanan. While there were no women, black intellectuals were serving abroad by the end of the century. In 1898 McKinley appointed Charlotte city councilman J. T. Williams as consul to Sierra Leone. Richard Theodore Greener, first black graduate of Harvard in the class of 1870, went to Bombay, then Vladivostok, staying with the service until 1905; his daughter, under the name Belle da Costa Greene, was art advisor and close friend to both J. P. Morgan and Bernard Berenson. And James Weldon Johnson, poet and editor, held minor posts in Venezuela and Nicaragua in 1906–12. All these envoys were intellectuals. In the early American style, diplomats came from the educated class; when abroad, they could move easily between intellect and action.

Part of their reporting was cultural. Poinsett described the cultural, scientific, and educational development of Latin America in ways similar to what Jefferson asked Lewis and Clark to describe in the US West. Paine's friend Barlow in Paris helped free hostages from the Barbary Corsairs, launching half a century of US naval presence in the eastern Mediterranean and quiet support to public diplomats, private missionary-educators, and the former military officers and engineers helping build Egypt, Palestine, Turkey, Greece, and Bulgaria.[33] Formal envoys tolerated private behavior and even joined it: Max Gallo reports that four of Europe's greatest revolutionaries—Garibaldi, Mazzini, Herzen, and Ledru-Rollin—attended a London dinner given by American Consul Charles Sanders for his minister, future president James J. Buchanan.

Missionaries quickly learned that they were first of all educators. They staked out a different kind of American cultural and educational presence abroad, reaching out early from their haystack in Williamstown, Massachusetts. The American colleges in Beirut, Istanbul, and later Cairo, and secondary schools like Aleppo College, were only the most visible of hundreds of missionary schools. Staffed by the Student Volunteer Movement, the nineteenth-century precursor to the Peace Corps, the missionary schools drew their funding from the collection plates of thousands of churches and from fund-raising tours by their directors, traveling by train and horseback. These American educators consciously distinguished their behavior from Europe's missionaries, providing practical education for development, teaching in the local language, creating written forms of language where necessary, and designing type-fonts for their printing presses; they pioneered in women's education and medicine, tending to the health of all God's creatures.

In Lebanon Daniel Bliss, legendary founder of the American University (AUB), competed with the successors of Jesuit Père Joseph. Setting out periodically for the hills of Lebanon, by mule, he would announce plans to "found two schools." When asked why two, he pointed out that once his was in place the Jesuits would quickly found another. In Latin America the arrival of US missionaries was delayed by dogged Catholic resistance; but with scholars as US envoys and with the cultural responsibility implied by Monroe's Doctrine of 1823, the Inter-American Movement nonetheless grew in importance, predicated on hemispheric cooperation and mutual respect; the missionaries followed. Beneath, on the US side, lay the illusion that the American model could be translated to serve the Spanish and Portuguese colonies.

Dedicated individuals went abroad as well, some as children of Paine, men and women of passion who felt compelled to work for justice in the spirit of cultural internationalism. Diplomats tolerated these scholars, philanthropists, and zealots, even when they stirred local pots. Margaret Fuller went to Rome as a foreign correspondent then joined Italy's revolution. Henry Steele Olcott fought British colonial educators to save Buddhist culture in Ceylon and Asia. Howard Baskerville went from Princeton to Tabriz and died fighting the Turks for Persia's independence. Morgan Shuster tried to retrieve Iran's finances from the British and Russian stranglehold. Ernest Fenollosa and Edwin Morse, hired by Japan's Meiji modernizers, set out to teach philosophy and science in Japan's leading university and stayed to save an entire artistic heritage "for the good of humankind," in Fenollosa's words. On the unoccupied northern island of Hokkaido, a team of Americans led by William S. Clark, president of the Massachusetts Agricultural College in Amherst, took the land-grant college idea abroad and founded the University of Sapporo. Archeologists explored Latin America and the Holy Land in the Near East under the benign gaze of Commodore David Porter, moved from command of the Mediterranean flotilla to serve as minister to the Sublime Porte in Constantinople.

Of these forgotten individual educator-expatriates, none is more surprising than Albert Giesecke in Peru.[34] Born in 1885, he was invited to Peru in 1908 to help modernize the school curriculum, and then asked to take over the rectorship of the University of Cuzco high in the Andes. At age twenty-four, he rebuilt the faculty and student body, while indulging his curiosity about pre-Columbian archeology—in 1909 he showed Hiram Bingham the route to Machu Picchu. In 1923 he took over responsibility at the Ministry of Education in Lima for all Peruvian education. Only in 1931 did this remarkable American retire and agree to serve as advisor to the US embassy; without the title, he was the first US cultural attaché in US history. In 1942 he was named CAO and remained at the embassy into the 1960s.

At home American scholar-administrators, goaded by Emerson, were overcoming inhibitions about learning from the Old World. Daniel Coit Gilman at Johns Hopkins and Andrew White at Cornell built the American research university on the basis of what they and tens of thousands of Americans had learned abroad, most often at Humboldt's great university in Berlin. In the US colleges each American scholar-teacher of foreign culture—like Longfellow—was a personal cultural diplomat, a tiny chip in the mosaic of American internationalist learning and culture. After the Civil War, an enlightened Congress recognized that US higher education could only be built with European help; the US Office of Education (USOE) would stimulate and channel the private flow of scholars and students.

The role of the US military abroad in education, science, and development is little known. Its help to formal goverment cultural outreach began early in the nineteenth century and deserves its own chapter. Military cross-cultural sensitivity supported foreign development, US commerce, and the brief US experiment with empire. Commodore Matthew Calbraith Perry in 1821 led a flotilla transporting freed slaves back to Africa; they called their country Liberia, for freedom, and its capital Monrovia, for James Monroe. They were following the lead of British abolitionist Granville Sharp, who made a similar trek three decades earlier to Sierra Leone, capital Freetown. In 1853 the same Commodore Perry made a different kind of cultural history, sailing his Black Ships into Japan. Standing by his side was the twenty-year veteran China missionary S. Wells Williams, later secretary to the U.S. Legation in Shanghai and founding chair of Chinese studies at Yale. Perry opened the door for another educator, Shanghai-merchant Townsend Harris (1804–78). Harris persuaded Secretary Seward to name him the first US minister to Japan. The new minister was dropped ashore near Yokohama by a merchant ship and took up residence in Tokyo in 1855; he quickly persuaded the Japanese that the U.S. was a better trading partner than Europe. The British historian Longford later wrote of Harris that no foreigner had ever so quickly attained influence over an Asian people: His "services were not exceeded by any in the entire history of the international relations of the world." New York City honored its self-educated son, member of the board of education and founder of the city's university system, by giving his name to its fast-track boys' school.

The military's intellectual role in Latin America was extensive, even before Panama, thanks to the Monroe Doctrine. Early on Congress permitted US military staff to be loaned to foreign governments to provide technical assistance. The Navy in 1838 surveyed the southern tip of the continent, carrying on the work of Humboldt. Navy teams explored the upper Amazon in 1851 and the Rio de la Plata in 1853. In 1867 the Smithsonian Institution, founded in 1846 by a British donation, explored the upper Amazon. Dom Pedro II of Brazil welcomed teams from Harvard, Cornell, Indiana, and Stanford to build science education and research. Archeologists John Lloyd Stephens, Ephraim Squier, and Hiram Bingham were given temporary US diplomatic titles, partial funding, and government scientists to help in their expeditions. Latin American activity was a natural consequence of the US commitment to the Inter-American Movement. Its first conference in the U.S. took place in 1885 and lasted six months, with its Latin delegates traveling everywhere courtesy of the Pennsylvania Railroad.[35]

After the Spanish-American War, Latin friendship was more ambivalent. In the former Spanish colonies of Cuba and Puerto Rico, the US military managed education, as a colonial power. Gen. Wheeler, with the cooperation of US universities, railroads, and Army transport ships, started a flow of students to the U.S.—by 1900 fifteen hundred Cuban and Puerto Rican students were studying in the U.S. Another general, Leonard B. Wood, with Harvard president Eliot—who raised an astonishing $70,000 in support—triggered the movement in Cuba by sending 1,450 teachers in Army transport ships for a six-week tour of the U.S., beginning with a seminar at Harvard and ending with a call on President McKinley.

Similar colonialist cultural assistance to the Philippines, delayed by the perceived need to crush former ally and insurgent Emilio Aguinaldo, was extensive. After MacArthur's brutal victory, Governor William Howard Taft brought American advisors and teachers to organize the school system, manage the islands' finances, and shape the judiciary. His friend Daniel Burnham, architect and designer of Washington's Mall and the Chicago waterfront, remade Manila's waterfront, while Mrs. Taft designed the city's public gardens. A new generation of Americans—including Morgan Shuster and Arthur Millspaugh, both later heroes in Iran—

practiced the nascent American art of colonial administration in the Philippines.[36]

Former military officers also reached abroad as unemployed soldiers. Naval hero John Paul Jones in 1788 helped build Catherine the Great's fleet. Dozens of former Civil War officers worked in Turkey and Egypt, where they were led by General George Stone—known as Stone Pasha, Chief of Staff of the Egyptian Army—in building coastal defenses, arms factories, and schools for the Egyptian army; meanwhile the daring Colonel Purdy mapped Egypt's southern frontier. Cavalry Gen. Philip Sheridan went to Berlin as military attaché; he rode with the Prussian army to the outskirts of Paris in 1870, provoking a wave of anti-American rumors inside the besieged city.[37] Invited to brief Prussia's chiefs of staff on Civil War tactics, Sheridan found Bismarck in the audience; as he described Sherman's and Grant's ruthless tactics, Bismarck is said to have left the room in anger, muttering that this was not war but barbarity.[38]

In Italy in 1908–09 we can catch a glimpse of the ingenious patchwork of diplomatic-military-private cooperative voluntarism and its cultural ramifications, thanks to a book by Naval Attaché Reginald Belknap.[40] When earthquakes devastated Messina and Reggio, Milan Consul Bayard Cutting went immediately to survey the scene. With Minister Lloyd Griscom and Belknap, he organized US residents in relief committees, visited the disaster area, and administered unofficial and official US contributions. The Red Cross arrived quickly; Congress appropriated $800,000 for building materials, the Navy provided shipping, and its petty officers supervised construction of three thousand "cottages," housing eighteen thousand people; Belknap reported the job done in four months. The Messina colony, with streets named after Presidents Taft, "Rosvelt," and the American supervisors, included a hospital, a church, schools, and a hotel. Italy's King and Queen and Minister Griscom attended the opening, and Theodore Roosevelt visited. The Boston Belknaps, Philadelphia Griscoms, and New York Cuttings raised private funds. As for the Italian workers, they experienced America's work culture and complained they had never worked so hard in their lives. Belknap noted wistfully that certain of the cottages, flanked by mulberry trees, looked as though they belonged in a New England village. Perhaps they did: with no experience of maintaining wooden constructions, the new residents watched their homes decay. Today only a stone bridge, called "Il Ponte Americano," remains.

The government cash contribution in Italy was justified by Congress as disaster relief, an early form of American outreach first approved in 1815 for earthquake relief in Venezuela to help Paine's friend Francisco Miranda. Sporadic examples of Congress's assistance, often in shipping surplus food products, predated US foreign philanthropy and government aid. Private philanthropy abroad, a form of national cultural outreach, supported the growth of powerful private-sector organizations, like the American branch of the Red Cross. With the rise of the great fortunes, large-scale philanthropy took more concrete shape, still reflecting the Protestant idea of stewardship but moving from collection plates to the checkbooks of titans. By the end of the nineteenth century, America's private overseas outreach, facing larger challenges, needed institutional backing. The philanthropic movement soon moved overseas, extending American generosity and stewardship, and the national instinct for helping God's children everywhere through intellect, education, and a little prayer.

Successful Americans, in contrast to the wealthy of Europe, were driven by the idea of stewardship to give back to the earth what God had given them.[41] Andrew Carnegie, believing it indecent to die wealthy, was first to practice overseas corporate philanthropy, beginning in his native British isles and then internationalizing science and law. Rockefeller went a step further and initiated his pathfinding family foundation, persuaded by ex-missionary Frederick Gates that good works meant good business because the overseas educators, expanding the middle class in the developing world, were laying the groundwork for modern needs like railroads and electricity. In the American Midwest, the service clubs—Rotary (1905), Lions (1915) and Kiwanis (1917)—soon turned international and were joined by others; by the year 2000, these three alone reached into more than 190 countries. With a membership totaling close to three million, they were making vital contributions in public health, focusing on the elimination of specific diseases: polio (Rotary), blindness (Lions), and iodine deficiency (Kiwanis).

The philanthropists and the service organizations like Rotary and the Red Cross based their approach on the missionary-educators and worked in a binational mode. Their experience fed John Hay's dedication to binationalism. Hay, Secretary of State under Roosevelt and Taft, turned binationalism into a national value and created the basic style of formal US cultural diplomacy by recycling the Boxer Indemnities. China had been forced, after the Boxer Rebellion of 1898–1900, to pay crippling indemnities to the West; in 1904 Hay convinced Congress to turn over the funds to a Chinese-US board, to permit Chinese study in the U.S. After 1918 the idea spread: Belgium and later Finland channeled war debt repayments into exchanges; Hoover in 1923 failed to persuade Congress to channel all US military debt into scholarships for the world. When Fulbright in 1947 finally succeeded in globalizing the idea, Hay and Hoover were his models. The Boxer grants prospered until their suspension by the Communists in 1949: by 1926 there were fourteen hundred Chinese students in the U.S., more foreign students than from any nation; returnees were already catalyzing change in Chinese life. Binationalism defused the many threats attributed by wary nations to American educational gifts; it ensured that the intellectual movement would be two-way, and it guaranteed the host nation a voice in administration.

Chinese students, once in the U.S., contributed to US area studies programs, like S. Wells Williams's at Yale. By 1938 the first major chore of

State's new Division of Cultural Relations would be to sort out and support stranded Chinese students. The needs of foreign students, meanwhile, were challenging the norms of US education. While America was sending its elite abroad for education, it was receiving thousands at home, in a rough balance, notwithstanding the hostility and racism of US immigration laws.

Just as the Civil War had ended the benificent US naval presence in the eastern Mediterranean, the healthy organic outreach from the new republic was suspended during America's first experience of European conflict as the impact of total war brought everything to a halt.

• • •

After this race through three millennia of history, it is time to look in detail at the way informal US cultural diplomacy developed after the Allied victory in World War I. In less than two decades, it was obvious that the US government had to devise a formal role, if only as a response to the cultural implications of the world leadership it had reluctantly accepted.

CHAPTER TWO

Total War and Its Aftershocks, 1917–1932

A brief season of war has deeply changed our thought and has altered, it may be permanently, the conditions of our national life.

—Woodrow Wilson, 1898[1]

WAR CAME TO EUROPE three years before the U.S. recognized its interests in joining. On both continents, World War I marked a great divide. For Europe, the impact of a new style of warfare—in which conscripts filled the trenches, in which civilians were as endangered as soldiers, in which an entire continent and its colonies were totally engaged, in which devastatingly efficient weaponry was used without mercy, in which juggernaut tactics destroyed everything in war's tracks, and in which every fiber of the belligerents strained to meet war needs—changed the European world. Lord Grey, watching the lights go out, knew things would never again be the same.

For the U.S. the impact was different. Already the Spanish encounter of 1898 had ignited cautious enthusiasm in Woodrow Wilson, who saw that it had perhaps permanently changed "the conditions of our national life" and initiated courses in the Princeton curriculum to prepare students for the "governance of tropical dependencies." Princeton's Edwin Kemmerer was key among the global economists Emily Rosenberg calls "financial missionaries to the world."[2] The late Warren Zimmerman pointed out that Americans like Roosevelt, Lodge, Hay, Root, and Admiral Mahan were putting together the ideology of "a world movement," as Roosevelt put it, in which victory over Spain would be only the "first great triumph," succeeded by business and education.[3] Entrance into the all-out European war, however reluctant and tardy, thrust America onto the world stage, leaving in the dust the Monroe Doctrine's reciprocal pledge not to intervene in European affairs. While democratic conscription provided America's soldiers, the percentage of the population directly involved was small and casualties minor compared to the bloodletting in Europe. Overall, the nauseating warfare of 1917–18 touched few Americans.[4]

Wilson's universalist and over-ambitious pledge "to make the world safe for democracy" enlisted US interventionism in a global cause; in Wilson's definition of "democracy" there ran an ethnocentric streak. Wilson had two ideas; neither respected other national realities: one was a worldwide "democracy" under a body that he assumed would be compatible, or be made compatible, with US interests and hence would be attractive to Americans; the other was interventionism, e.g., teaching Latin Americans "to elect good men."

In the ghastly war years 1914–18, America's latecomer role had an adventurous derring-do quality about it—jaunty heroes like Eddie Rickenbacker and "Wild Bill" Donovan rode to national fame, business power, and wealth. And the US military kept its century-old pact with culture: the American Expeditionary Force had a strong soldier-education component; it brought black regimental marching bands like the 369th Infantry's famous Harlem Hellcats whose polyrhythms touched off France's passion for jazz.[5] Remnants from soldier-education programs launched the American Library in Paris, a private overseas US library without precedent. France acceded to Pershing's request to set up a conservatory for US band musicians, soon to evolve into Nadia Boulanger's famous Fontainebleau school for American artists, musicians, and architects.

The Great War put an end to the American dream of self-containment. Manifest Destiny had overflowed its unassailable base in the Western Hemisphere. Americans allowed themselves to be convinced the U.S. had purer motives, less cumbersome bureaucracies, better organization, richer resources, harder workers, more generous hearts, a more democratic system, and fewer national blindspots than others. At their best, most Americans agreed, Americans were not only different, they were better.

Exceptionalism, messianism, Manifest Destiny, whatever it is called, came to the fore when the U.S. leapt to the status of a world power almost without knowing it, without the polity's willing it, and with no clear sense of the costs. In support, government's expansion and its inevitable encroachment on American life were underway. For better or for worse, the American Century had begun.

War plus big government raised questions about the intellectual side of US outreach: how to handle information, the role of US education abroad, the wisdom of communicating with foreign populations over the heads of friendly governments. In wartime, with the outside world roughly divided into friends, enemies, and neutrals, these were multidimensional questions.

So they were for the other Allies. In France, the changes of 1914 were abrupt and extensive. Deadly war for survival called forth sacrifices and new energies—most fighting took place on French soil. The French strategy of cultural outreach, four centuries in the making, was sorely tested. Long dominated by intellectuals, educators, scholars, and universities in league with Jesuit missionaries, the diplomacy of culture was an ingrained French habit; but departures from tradition were acceptable in wartime because of the conviction that, after the emergency, things would naturally revert to sacred norms.

As the French doggedly staved off the Germans, every thought focused on survival. Overseas schools and colleges, longterm investments, carried on as schools must; but they were unabashedly mobilized by France and utilized to persuade the elites of neutral or allied countries to support France in its hour of need. Since embassies were known to lie, the Quai d'Orsay risked destroying centuries of nurture by asking the schools and the semi-private Alliances Françaises to distribute Paris news bulletins.

The Quai's cultural division, divided into Catholic and non-Catholic sections, was led by the Catholic poet-diplomat Paul Claudel, and legendary pianist Alfred Cortot was called upon to head a new office sending performing artists around the world. In 1916 Claudel moved to Brazil, where Bourbon France had established a center for fine arts in 1816, as ambassador. Claudel's cultural staff included a young composer from Aix en Provence, Darius Milhaud, who paid his respects to Brazil with his dance suites *Saudades do Brazil* and befriended Brazilian artists like young street musician Heitor Villa-Lobos. The Claudel-Milhaud era convinced Brazil that Paris was its cultural capital.[6]

In France Verdun's taxicabs stopped the German advance and trench warfare took over. The Quai regulated information flow, whether through press, books, films, or the arts; France, without apology, practiced thought-control, serene in the assumption that things would right themselves after the war.

In the U.S., Wilson's first concern was domestic: he needed popular support for the war. The timid US experience of propaganda, after Tom Paine's example, began during the Civil War, yet soldiers' mail was still uncensored. America's entry into the Great War, after Wilson's 1916 campaign boast that he "kept us out," posed a dilemma. Harold Lasswell in his postwar theory of propaganda noted that for Wilson "the waywardness of individuals," as Wilson called the casual American style, had to be forged into wartime discipline, hopefully within the law. Wilson, with no precedent except Washington's use of Paine's and Lincoln's experiments had to persuade the American people to send their sons to die for France. US propaganda began at home.

Wilson's instincts were universalist and hence expansionist. In 1899, glimpsing the inevitability of US world power, he heard Whitelaw Reid, owner-editor of New York's *Herald Tribune* and ambassador to France, urge America's universities to help govern the new US empire. When the Spanish-American War reached Wilson's Princeton, he exulted as if over a footrace: "The nation has broken out of its shell and bids fair to run a momentous career." Around him, the debate raged, as it did in other universities; against stiff faculty opposition, Princeton agreed to prepare its students for a world in which America would exercise some kind of overseas administrative responsibility. Wilson's antagonist Dean Andrew West called the war in the Philippines an "embarrassment," but in 1900 the university offered its first course in colonial administration, "The Expansion of Europe," which was renamed "The Government of Tropical Dependencies" in 1908. When Edwin Kemmerer, a student of Cornell's Jeremiah Jenks and disciple of Charles Conant, left Cornell to join the

Princeton faculty in 1912, he took up the first US chair in international economics, from which he trained a generation of American "financial missionaries," as Emily Rosenberg calls them. Wilson, eager to place Princeton "in the nation's service," saw the U.S. entering a new world "where the nations are rivals and we cannot live or act apart." Frankly accepting US interdependence and perhaps US hegemony as well, he believed US universities should help staff a unique, liberal—and surely better—American-inspired world order.

As president, Wilson used the excuse of war to justify strengthening the executive: new conditions "furnished the necessity of a foreign policy and gave to the executive of the Nation a national character." His biases look quaint today: e.g., southern Europeans were less reliable than the French and British; or, Americans must train the "undisciplined" Filippinos. America's mission strayed from helping less-fortunate brethren to seeking an effective style of international power. The key lay in pulling "wayward" Americans into line, and Wilson aimed propaganda—under his direct management—at US citizens. Lasswell's first purpose for propaganda: to mobilize hatred of the enemy at home.

Americans faced no territorial threat. By contorted nationalist logic, US schools discontinued German-language classes, even though every third or fourth American was German in origin. Disciplining individualist Americans, getting the hill folk of the Tennessee mountains to lay down their lives for France, was expedient and presumably temporary. In Europe *raison d'état* was hedged by powerful and resilient national cultures, but some Americans feared that US culture, bent by propaganda, might snap back less readily to prewar norms.

Enter America's "first minister of propaganda," George Creel. For years a row of photos of former directors graced the wall at USIA leading to the director's office. Though Creel died well before USIA was born in 1953 and had left government work in 1919, his photo, in a high Calvin Coolidge collar, led the others. The Midwestern journalist and sometime poet played a role in Wilson's campaign, and six months before entering the war Wilson asked Creel to form the Committee for Public Information (CPI). In its two years of existence CPI changed America as much as the war itself, and in the postwar years its offshoots helped transform the US mind. CPI put in place a formal mix of government cultural, informational, and propagandistic diplomacy, touching every element of US life.

In 1939 two scholars looked hard at CPI, in partial response to Creel's immodest book *How We Advertised America*. Mock and Larsen in *Words That Won the War* [7] analyzed the Creel experiment, especially its domestic side. As they saw it, and as various CPI veterans, including public relations theorist Edward L. Bernays, reported, Americans had been exposed to a Creel-generated "1917 temper." In their balanced critique, Mock and Larsen saw CPI sympathetically: "A consensus of good people" worked with CPI, and through them CPI "did its work so well that there was a burning eagerness to believe, to conform." Admitting that words *had* won the war, Mock and Larsen offered one excuse for the excesses of CPI: things might have been worse.

Creel's decision to use the word "information" in CPI's name was no accident; he chose "information" expressly to avoid "propaganda"— which Creel agreed was a fatally poisoned synonym for "purposeful lying." Whether the euphemism fooled enemies or reassured Americans is not clear. In war the finer distinctions are overlooked, truth being the inevitable first casualty.

In European and non-European languages, "propaganda" today is sometimes a synonym for advertising, while "information" is often teamed with "intelligence." In 1942 America's first spymaster, "Wild Bill" Donovan, chose the title "Coordinator of *Information*," only later agreeing to split his office into the Office of Strategic Services (OSS), for black or deceptive propaganda, and Elmer Davis's Office of War Information (OWI), for the white or grey variants. "Information" entered common US usage after 1917; it was the core of USIA's name for all but three of its forty-six years (1953–99).

Part of the taint of "propaganda" in Protestant America came from its Church origins. The Latin gerund was chosen by Gregory XV, founder of Propaganda Fide, which both spread the faith and defended it against perceived enemies. Enlightened early Jesuits like Alessandro Valignano and Matteo Ricci were proud to find shelter under its umbrella. But memories of Spanish and Portuguese conversion by the sword and of the Inquisition darkened the term. America needed another word, even before Stalin, Mussolini, Hitler, and the Japanese poisoned "propaganda" beyond repair. "Propaganda" in any language predicates some kind of lying as a legitimate tool of political power. Americans accept advertising, publicity, and public relations as harmless "white" lies and do so more readily than citizens of other nations; yet they are uncomfortable with lies. Creel did not need Orwell to warn him about propaganda when he devised CPI's name.

CPI's alumni would found two great American industries, advertising and public relations, both legitimized forms of lying. Books by Creel and Bernays, who biographer Larry Tye called the "father of spin," were devoured by Stalin, Mussolini, Goebbels, and the Japanese. Creel himself boasted about "advertising America" but was ambivalent about his work: at Stanford University in 1930, he warned a student organization headed by Edward R. Murrow that CPI had lied to their parents and urged that they not be fooled again.

However American in its style, CPI in 1917 set out under the banner of information to commit propaganda, at home and abroad. Its four-man governing committee represented colossal power: In the chair, Creel was Wilson's personal representative, joined by the three Secretaries of State, War, and Navy. Wilson was ultimately in charge. When young CPI propaganda analyst Walter Lippmann reported from Paris to Wilson's assistant, Colonel House, on the misbehavior of a Wilson crony from a

Trenton newspaper, Wilson vented his fury not at the boor but at Lipp-mann: "I am very jealous in the matter of propaganda. I want to keep the matter of publicity entirely in my own hands." Under Wilson's sharp eye, Creel had broad freedom to find his way, invent his tactics, and design his strategies. With a modest Washington staff and a brigade of overseas representatives, this "public relations" counselor to the US government took over the premises of the Carnegie Endowment for World Peace, which Nicholas Murray Butler had abandoned for the duration.

CPI made all kinds of little-recognized history, almost without know-ing it. It ran like a circus, recalled participants. Amidst the fun and games, an unprecedented mobilization of national talent was taking place for both domestic and foreign consumption. Creel recruited university schol-ars, made films, set up exhibits, issued labor publications, sent regular window displays to 650 US business offices abroad, invented the "hand-out" for public information, developed pictorial publicity, propaganda cartoons, and memorable posters, lined up historians and intellectuals, coopted labor leaders, and adapted a raft of other practices unknown before 1917.

Its Speakers Division, headed by Arthur Bestor of the Chatauqua pub-lic lecture circuit, organized talks—including an incredible 75,000 "Four-Minute Man" episodes wherever people gathered. It shaped immigrant publications, telling the news from CPI's viewpoint. It recruited the best New York commercial artists led by Charles Dana Gibson, and persuaded them to contribute posters; the cost of the entire CPI art division over the committee's life span came to $13,000. Major writers were brought in: Samuel Hopkins Adams, Booth Tarkington, Mary Roberts Reinhardt, John Erskine, and Rex Beach, to name a few. Movie stars Theda Bara, Douglas Fairbanks Jr., and Mary Pickford carried on extensive Liberty Bond drives. Hollywood moguls like Griffith, Fox, Loew, Zukor, and Selz-nick played along, producing *The Kaiser, The Beast of Berlin* while sup-pressing films already "in the can." The 1916 Thomas Ince film *Civilization* showed Jesus and President Wilson on the side of peace, then a year later was recut to make Jesus come out in favor of the war. Tin Pan Alley produced patriotic songs. Pressed by Johns Hopkins political scientist and Princeton president Wilson, Guy Stanton Ford, president of the University of Minnesota and a Humboldt alumnus, organized schol-ars for lectures and produced hundreds of pieces of "popular scholar-ship," distributed by the millions. Respected academics wrote widely distributed pamphlets, like future Princeton Dean Christian Gauss's *De-mocracy Today*. Columbia historian James T. Shotwell recruited historians like Frederick Jackson Turner, J. Franklin Jameson, Waldo Leland, and Dana Carlton Munro to do their bit for their country, while Samuel Gompers lined up the labor unions. The list of respected American parti-cipants in CPI's work was dazzling.

The darker side of the picture rested on a simple and now familiar assumption: "loyal" Americans do not question government slogans in wartime. Under three pieces of legislation, the so-called Alien and Sedition Acts, which were passed by a complaisant Congress, more than two thousand questioners of Wilson-Creel orthodoxy were jailed or deported by Attorney General Alexander Palmer—the last prisoner was not released until 1923. The Espionage Act of June 1917, the Trading with the Enemy Act of October 1917, and the so-called Sedition Act of May 1918 were upheld by a unanimous Supreme Court decision in 1919. In 1920 Harvard Law School's Zachariah Chafee was all but dismissed when his book attacked this legislation; young colleagues Dean Acheson and Archibald MacLeish, future shapers of US cultural diplomacy, defended his cause. At the Supreme Court, Justices Brandeis and Holmes deplored the assault on freedom.

Creel said he despised censorship. To sugarcoat the irreducible needs he saw, he instituted the idea of self-censorship, placing the responsibility for restraint on the editors themselves. In fact, since "irresponsibility" was severely punished, self-censorship was a convenient misnomer, noted Emily Rosenberg.[8] In fact Creel was not fully in control. He could not prevent the War Department from banning books, including antiwar and pacifist works by writers like Ambrose Bierce or Henri Barbusse and writers of the left like Norman Thomas. At home CPI distributed misinformation and censored books, periodicals, and films, created and placed unattributed media products, helped pass questionable legislation, and issued the fake Sisson Papers purporting to document Lenin's connivance with the Germans. The military routinely censored soldiers' mail, and the government controled all "war information." Americans accepted these changes and more, as they began to learn the joys of conforming.

Abroad, the freewheeling CPI helped embassies put in place the first national effort to shape foreign images of the U.S. CPI's ideas, attitudes, and administrative structures would carry over into US cultural and informational diplomacy in the years to come. Concealing its more sensitive activities, CPI rolled out a jumble of the classic tools of propaganda, as they have developed since 1917, and a few more, to boot: it distributed publishable political cartoons to US and foreign newspapers; arranged for wounded American soldiers of Italian origin to recuperate in Italian hospitals; organized speaker tours by "patriotic American socialists" to sell the war effort to foreigners on the left; opened "reading rooms"—the first US governmental public-access libraries abroad; set up free English-language schools all over Latin America; and made sure friendly newspapers had enough newsprint to operate. Neither friends nor enemies missed these innovations in diplomatic tradition or failed to see the analogies with British and French activities. CPI was inventing an American style of propaganda justified by war and inspired by its Allies.

CPI's foreign outposts were called US Information Service (USIS) posts and they were headed by a public affairs officer (PAO); both titles were adopted from military practice. A new and very public US presence abroad, with no historical precedent, appeared suddenly in the capitals of the Allied and neutral world. The most interesting experiments took place in the neutral nations, especially those in Latin America, where CPI set out to keep host nations away from the enemy and, with luck, to persuade them to help the U.S.

CPI's overseas improvisations made for a confusing model—they used whatever definitions came to hand. To informational diplomats, CPI bequeathed a passion for improvisation, a love of action, and a distaste for theory. The model for cultural relations was a muddle of good and bad, but clearly culture was a major tool. Outstanding intellectuals had consented to help CPI under Wilson's leadership; but the overall CPI model was based on the newer idea of "spin"; scholars invited to play the game had to work hard to keep things honest.

In the 1930s Sumner Welles reopened the question of cultural diplomacy, explicitly rejecting the CPI model; but in 1942 the unfocused energies of Nelson Rockefeller flowed directly back to CPI—his family's public relations advisor was CPI veteran Ivy Lee. The cultural relations planners of 1933–38 tried to keep propaganda out of it; they reached back instead to other American values, arguing that cultural relations, like higher education, required intellectual independence and integrity. They envisioned an essentially educational diplomacy, based on ideas, truth, knowledge, and the free interplay of all three.

Mock and Larsen knew this: they expressed explicit concern about State's Division of Cultural Relations, warning that the new office needed "only the stimulus of increased international excitement to push it into frank continuation of the work begun by the CPI." Their balanced treatment of CPI notwithstanding, they saw the danger in its methods.

CPI's scholars and educators worked within a media-oriented organization, blending journalism, advertising, and public relations. The effectiveness of media in the U.S. and especially in non-English-speaking and semiliterate foreign countries depended on reducing things to simple terms, with visual aids when possible. CPI's university educators had no illusions about what they were doing, but they hoped their academic values might counterbalance those of the advertiser-journalists. Mock and Larsen concluded that CPI was bigger than the scholars; in the end, it brought a sea change to Americans, for whom "the tossing about of symbols became a substitute for an intellectual transaction." Henceforth, "people thought together and thought in stereotypes." Welles's concerns in 1938 were understandable. So was Nelson Rockefeller's impatience with Welles's distinctions.

Latin America was the emblematic case.[9] In 1914–17 the southern continent offered fertile ground for the Central Powers to stir up anti-gringo residue from the Mexican and Spanish-American Wars. Germany had been investing in cultural relations with Latin America with heavy migration to Latin America, since Humboldt's explorations at the end of the eighteenth century, and by 1817 they had built a science institute in Brazil.[10] Commerce naturally followed closely behind. In Latin America Germany offered an alternative to Britain, a country despised after Wellington had humiliated Catholic Spain. Nazi Germany, with fewer compunctions than the French about exploiting its established cultural networks, assigned "cultural attachés" in its embassies to carry out hard propaganda and espionage.

The U.S., long handicapped in Latin America by its minimalist approach to government and a troublesome history of interventionism, was not lacking in resources. Late-coming American missionary-educators had done good work, and the sporadic but recurrent successes of the Inter-American Movement during the last century had built good will. No one knew this better than CPI's Latin American chief Edward L. Bernays, a sophisticated version of P. T. Barnum. In his prewar life he had been a press agent for Enrico Caruso and the Russian Ballet.[11] The Father of Spin believed that Wilsonian idealism and US commercial interests could make common cause: economic and social development were the first needs, and once a middle class began to emerge, business could take over. Bernays convinced key US corporations, including Ford, Remington, Swift, Standard Oil, and International Harvester, to open their outposts to CPI; others joined and became CPI branches, flag-flying agents of the US government. As commerce moved closer to power, the inter-American focus turned to economics. Corporate-government cooperation was moving toward the corporate style Nelson Rockefeller would find so congenial. Henry Ford, after a failed experiment to produce his own rubber in Amazonia, had a similar idea; Iriye sums up his thinking thus: "In the postwar world, capital, technology, productivity, and efficiency, not armed force, [will] define national and international affairs."[12] Creel himself saw only part of this shift: He boasted of "a vast adventure in salesmanship, the world's greatest adventure in advertising." Soon it was even harder to separate government from business.

Under CPI, films—the vastly popular Hollywood silents—were shown widely, opening new markets for US cinema. CPI's daily Latin American wireless output, traveling via US Navy signals, marked the beginning of overseas shortwave broadcasting, took the first steps toward the Voice of America, and extended US commercial networks. At home, scholars and intellectuals flocked to CPI. Labor unions helped persuade foreign counterparts that this was the "People's War." Free English-teaching classes were set up across Latin America. Reading rooms for US publications sprouted everywhere. In Mexico alone there were seven centers with small libraries, registering 30,000 students in two years. PAO Robert Murray, an enlightened journalist from the *New York World*, saw his work for CPI as education, the sounder the better. There was no need for propaganda in Mexico, because the local press was hungry for solid information. Murray's schools taught English as well as more general subjects including—suprisingly—French. CPI was giving grateful Mexicans what they needed: learning opportunities which might lead to a better life. The enlightened and principled Murray was not alone; fine professionals from various parts of the intellectual world joined CPI to provide the learning opportunities needed. They were American individuals, not soldiers; they were committed, generous, and independent-minded citizens doing what they thought best.

At the Great War's end, Murray was stunned by the under-informed Congress's brutal cut-off of CPI, and he fought to retain his educational programs. But the legislators had permitted CPI only as a weapon of war, and they had had enough of the high-riding Creel. The committee's sudden end eliminated any possibility of continuing its best practices. The Mexican program vanished overnight, a decision lamented by students of Mexican-US relations to this day: "In those final weeks of the CPI, the idealistic members of the staff asked themselves if, after all, they had won their fight for the mind of mankind," wrote Mock and Larsen. And Mexicans got the point: the gringos were wonderful friends—in foul weather.

Creel operated at stratospheric levels. Wilson's 1917 letter, probably drafted by Creel, to the outward-bound CPI chief in neutral Spain instructed him to "abstain from intrigue and to carry out an honest educational mission in a frank and open way." But despite these sensible, high-minded instructions, USIS Spain was soon doing what it wanted, under the ductile argument that German propaganda required strong counter-measures. Spanish branches of companies like Singer lent their show-windows and newspapers were helped to obtain scarce newsprint—provided they ran CPI's stories. Some editors were corrupted more directly—bribed with cash or advertising; writers were paid to defend the U.S., and American residents were mobilized by a weekly *American News*. Creel's journalists ran a media campaign, with strong commercial ties, based on controled information.

With targets like proud Spain, Creel's men faced more complex agendas than anticipated. During the war, CPI was already looking ahead to the postwar era, lining up support for the US positions that would be argued at Versailles. In Europe there were cross-cultural problems as well. The CPI propaganda effort in Italy was headed by the distinguished political scientist Charles E. Merriam of the University of Chicago, later president of the American Political Science Association; he entertained a visiting sub-cabinet official who charmed Romans and Neapolitans alike—the young Franklin Delano Roosevelt. Merriam's team encountered an unforeseen problem: to win the peace, his deputy wrote, Americans had to worry about more than the Germans, they had "first to conquer the Old World's 2,000 years and more of governmental traditions and class and political prejudices." Populist American irritation with traditional Europe, reaching back to John Adams and Tom Paine, reflected a universalism the rough edges of which few Americans understood. CPI might have followed the lead of enlightened friends of Italian culture like George Perkins Marsh, James Jackson Jarvis, Charles Eliot Norton, and Bernard Berenson; instead it approached Rome as though it were Wichita. Wise Italians began to suspect that the "other Americans" were not entirely civilized, that US-Italian cultural entente would be swamped by the generous, carefree, get-on-with-it world of American media and business. Americans saw the Europeans' reactions as uninformed, arrogant, or old-fashioned.

Creel swirled the scholars and the advertisers into one omelette, to win the war—and to serve the ends of US power. His team felt free to override carefully forged diplomatic protocols, to neglect local laws, to mix business and education, to disregard foreign governments, and to aim their words beyond government at the citizenry. As the war drew toward its end, USIS directors around the world were ordered to publicize Wilson's Fourteen Points. Creel, with Wilson at Versailles until the treaty was signed, carried on as though he were still managing CPI. While Britain and France saw Versailles as an opportunity for frank discussion and merging interests in search of consensus, Creel and Wilson instead pushed the hard sell; Creel pointed out that England had Reuters and France had Havas, so the U.S. needed a comparable worldwide media capability. Suddenly US embassies had full-time press offices, issuing more than just news. In Britain the Tories all but declared war over America's attempt to "sell" Wilson's views. Even Bernays criticized Creel on this point. He believed that the most serious opposition to Wilson's ideas resided at home and that Creel had failed to organize a domestic support campaign; hence Versailles was Creel's failure as much as Wilson's.

Bypassing foreign governments overrides long-standing diplomatic protocols; the consensus put in place by the Congress of Vienna saw bypassing as a breech of national trust. Franklin had successfully bypassed government in France, but he had done so with infinite guile; so had Lincoln, but only in the case of his famous but futile letters to the English millworkers—a lone action that provoked Foreign Office fury. Today's notion of Public Diplomacy takes such bypassing as a given—"it worked in the case of the Soviet implosion, so why not?" goes one dubious analogy. Public Diplomacy, in assuming bypassing to be an American entitlement, ignores the lessons of 1919. Americans had learned with the Spanish war that war's first casualty was truth, but what lay ahead in 1917, and again in 1938, was no skirmish with an exhausted imperial power, it was unimaginable total war. The crisis, in Creel's mind, justified almost anything.

Creel's language could soar to Biblical heights: one critic accused him of wanting to convert the world to a "Gospel of Americanism According to Creel." Emily Rosenberg argues that Creel, lured down one of universalism's dangerous byways by limitless power, saw truth as a flexible commodity. Believing fervently in "facts," he thought his truths to be truer than the truths of others; he needed only to "tell America's story to the world" and everything else would fall into place. Abroad it should have been obvious to anyone, as it was to Robert Murray in Mexico, that foreign elites were only interested in the US story up to a point; their deeper and more enduring hunger was for sophisticated and substantial knowledge, for US partnership in analyzing and attacking common problems, and—both to understand and to imitate—for insights into how the U.S. made its decisions, into American values and ideals, into America's best practices.

Creel boasted that during the war there was more freedom at home than in Europe and Mock and Larsen agreed, noting in 1939 that "France and England have become, at least for the time being, 'totalitarian democracies.'" They suggested readers "ask themselves what may happen if America is sucked into the maelstrom"; they warned of pervasive censorship: "American resistance to repressive measures may not be great." In the end, reflecting on America's first "ministry of propaganda," they warned against another CPI. Creel had overlooked the variability of cultural resilience: in the postwar period, Europe's political cultures returned to their approximate earlier shape, but American culture had yet to find itself. Even postwar Britain and France did not completely return to "normal"—for one thing, both nations pledged they would never do propaganda again. In the U.S. the abrupt end of CPI cut off discussion of the question of propaganda and the advertisers proceeded to legitimize the idea. Abroad the German, Russian, Italian, and Japanese totalitarians studied Bernays and Creel and planned how to do it better, unfettered by US scruples. They carried propaganda to new heights and poisoned the word forever.

All this was forgotten by those who enshrined Creel on USIA's wall sixty years later. Creel boasted of fooling the US public without considering Lincoln's warning about fooling the public *all* of the time. A more recent historical analysis glossing the CPI impact pointed to the danger: any "order or organization supposed to embody the absolute principles of Right, the universal interests of humankind, tends to render any opposition to it unhuman or criminal." Hence, concludes Anders Stephansson, "the extraordinary fury of domestic repression, public and private, legal and extralegal, that took place in the United States once the country had entered the [first] war. . . . Neither the experience of the Second World War nor even of the McCarthyist 1950s compares to the repression of domestic dissent during World War I."[13]

CPI's legacy persisted. After the first war Americans were increasingly involved in—and shaped by—a structure larger than themselves, loosely called "government." The conflicted and sometimes angry postwar period of the twenties would be mythologized by a new American literature, epitomized by John Dos Passos's *USA*. CPI intellectuals like Shotwell and Merriam kept their balance and returned to their universities, while others championed cultural internationalism and its diplomatic extension. But with Creel, Paine's reductionist sloganeering had won out over the humane dialogues of Jefferson and Franklin, who exchanged ideas from the base of intellectual integrity and mutual respect and who instinctively adapted to the foreign context, establishing trust by being truthful. Both believed that Americans needed fear nothing from an idea, even a lie or an error, "so long as reason was left free to combat it." But for Paine and Creel, stirring rhetoric in service to a cause banished inconvenient truth. Exchanging ideas in search of truth is not the same as telling America's story *our* way. Before 1917, Americans expected no interference in the exchange of ideas. Afterwards, things were less simple.

• • •

Europe and the U.S. went their separate ways after the Great War, but the two continents had come permanently closer. A devastated Europe began the sad business of rebuilding its infrastructures and replacing a generation of its youth, while in America there was no war damage and comparatively fewer casualties.

For the prehistory of cultural diplomacy, things had changed on both sides. Postwar Europe reverted quickly to historic practice but faced subtle differences, including the decay of the colonial system. In America the idea of cultural diplomacy was erased with the rest of CPI.

As usual, the case of France is a benchmark. The exhausted nation remained committed to the life and leadership of the mind; France's political-cultural consensus and its Jacobin *dirigiste* bureaucracy looked again to cultural power as a worthy companion to political and economic strength with little legislative interference. One lone parliamentarian in 1918 pleaded for dynamic action, replacing the classic metaphor of cultural radiance with "penetration": intellectual institutions were "foci of propaganda," "weapons in the hands of public power." But one Député did not make a nation.[14]

French stepped up its cultural programs with the U.S. America's debt to Lafayette's France had been paid during the war in the US mind; now Americans expected generosity in return. They also expected to be treated as equals. But the long underground rivalry between the two universalist powers was aggravated by perceptions of France's duty to show gratitude, and insouciant Yankee tourists and well-heeled expatriates, soon exasperated the French, as they basked in the glow of US prosperity and a powerful dollar.[15] The French reached out: pianist Alfred Cortot performed all over America, in small cities as well as large. And the culturalists of the Quai d'Orsay, skillful, patient, and urbane, had more than music up their sleeves; they targeted American universities and specifically their French departments. They sent dazzling scholars to US universities, many of whom found permanent jobs in America. The study of French in schools and colleges soon outranked all other languages; the French cultural mission made thousands of gifts to university libraries and opened new opportunities for American study in France. Booming US universities were delighted with French *rayonnement*; they had welcomed writers Jean Giraudoux and André Tardieu at Harvard before 1910, and now giants like Henri Hauser, Gilbert Chinard, Henri Peyre, and André Morize built impressive US careers.[16] Hispanist Maurice Edgar Coindreau joined the Bryn Mawr, then the Princeton, faculty in the 1920s. Thanks to his student James Burnham, he discovered the new American novel and became France's translator of record for the US novel. Jean Hytier, after helping found universities in Tehran and Algiers, settled at Columbia in 1946. Women too were involved: Germaine Brée, after spending the war in Algiers, taught at Bryn Mawr then chaired the French department at New York University.

The honorary dean of this cultural expeditionary force was Yale's Peyre, a generous and voluble man from Provence who was famous for carrying on thoughtful conversations while tending to his correspondence and for correcting typos and factual errors, in green ink, in library periodicals. He spent the rest of his life at Yale, teaching generations of students, building the country's premier department of French studies, welcoming and placing French intellectual imports, shaping other departments of French, and strengthening professional associations. He is an unsung hero of France's cultural diplomacy in the U.S.

To the humanists of the Quai, the French language was imperiled by the growth of English and its market-driven energies. Joining in the trend by training a bilingual France was not an option. Instead the nation dug deeper defenses and pushed hard for French-language teaching abroad; the "private" Alliances Françaises (1880) were generously funded. The overseas classes were France's way of protecting its cultural identity and independence while subsidizing cultural outreach. Export of French performing artists grew, and the overseas religious schools took a step back from proselytization; the "Lay Mission" funded secular supplements like Beirut's Faculty of Letters at the Jesuit St. Joseph university. "Instituts," university extensions, were opened in obvious cities like Florence (1910), Barcelona and Naples (1919), Zagreb (1924), Amsterdam (1933), Lisbon and Stockholm (1937), Kyoto and Chile (1938). Cultural agreements linked France to Austria, Denmark, Iran, Romania, and Sweden.

In 1923 French cultural diplomacy came out in the open in a government office named "Cultural Relations," aimed openly at "the intellectual expansion of France abroad." It was the first office for cultural diplomacy in the world's history. Its funding, doubled during the war, quadrupled by 1938 when it drew down a fifth of the Quai's budget with unmeasured contributions from other ministries like Education. Between the wars this nation of 40 million souls was supporting 120 fully-funded university professors, three hundred university instructors, and 130 teachers in foreign universities and schools. Embassies and cultural institutes in the 1930s were peopled by young intellectuals soon to achieve fame, men like Claude Lévy-Strauss, Michel Foucault, Roland Barthes, and Hubert Beuve-Méry, founding editor of Le Monde. The diplomats came, as always, from the peak of French intellect, with writers like Giraudoux,

Claudel, Alexis Léger (St. John Perse), Roger Peyrefitte, and Paul Morand. Their chief was Philippe Berthelot, the presumed model for the Giraudoux character "who knew by heart the first lines of the *Odyssey*, the last lines of Rilke, and everything in between." At the Quai, cultural staff between 1914 and 1939 ballooned from two to twelve—many more than the comparable US office in 1938. Healthy growth of public-private cooperation was stunted by the Popular Front's decision that only government should be trusted to allocate national resources.[17]

Nazi strength raised the stakes. In 1934 the British agreed with the French that they should fight the lies of Axis propaganda by exchanging truth and founded the British Council. In 1936 French and British cultural missions reported well-funded but heavy-handed Axis propaganda abroad, and shared this information with Washington. Mussolini, Hitler, Salazar, and Franco were all firmly in power, and hundreds of European intellectuals were already in prison, in flight, or in their graves. In Europe culture was still power: it had not held back two German invasions of France, but it had helped France survive those invasions, reason enough to pursue this different kind of war.

England's British Council was founded on this belief. The British, reluctant to deal with overseas cultural relations and education because of class attitudes and mistrust of the word "culture," held angry memories of wartime propaganda. Writer-diplomat Harold Nicolson, a veteran of Versailles, blamed the anti-culture mindset on national arrogance, called propaganda "damnable lies" and pushed for cultural relations. Frances Donaldson, in her fifty-year history of the Council (1984), attacks the smug conviction that British genius, "unlike that of lesser countries, spoke for itself." She adds: "Skepticism about the value of spreading such intangibles as language, literature, the arts and civilized values was almost as complete as the French belief in it."[18] The British mistrusted culture but like the French they knew that cultural relations was an indispensable field for diplomacy.

Creel's British counterpart, Lord Northcliffe, had raised hackles. Lloyd George appointed his press baron friend Director of Propaganda to Enemy Countries—and to the home front. One of his team, the talented multilingual Australian Rex Leeper, repelled by Northcliffe's blunderbuss approach, sought another way. The British Council resulted from Leeper's uphill fight of more than a decade. Britain's leading scholar of cultural diplomacy, J. M. Lee, says the original idea—a Council for Relations with Other Peoples—was cleverly reshaped by Leeper's "sleight-of-hand." Council funding, like university funding, was handled through an arm's-length Grants Commission.[19]

Abroad, there were more imitators of France than of Britain. Pre-Mussolini Italy set up Dante Alighieri Societies around the world. Weimar Germany was even more active because of its vigorous private sector; with its freestanding but government-funded Goethe Institute rooted in the universities, Weimar's private Heidelberg Exchange Service began exchanging students with America in 1922, then became the American-German Student Exchange. In 1927–28, the German cultural internationalist industrialist Adolf Morsbach visited seventy American universities, hoping to generate two-way exchanges; whether blinded by his pride in German universities or convinced that US universities could not yet be expected to provide appropriate training for Germans, he returned with little to show—in 1930 there were still fewer than 130 annual US-German university exchanges. Another private German exchange, the *Werkstudenten* or student-interns was run by the YMCA and funded by German Carl Duisberg and US banker Paul Warburg; it exchanged close to two hundred students annually. Individual Americans of course continued the century-old practice of study in German universities.[20]

At loftier levels, informal and formal German cultural diplomats were at work. Albert Einstein traveled for the Foreign Office in the early 1920s, closely watched by a government which had a high interest in keeping him German. He graced the board of the League of Nation's Committee on Intellectual Cooperation (CIC), forerunner of UNESCO, but he could not spark a German branch. The ironies of a Jew traveling for Germany did not escape him: "Funny people, these Germans," he wrote in 1925. "I am a stinking flower for them and still they keep putting me in their buttonholes."[21] His friend and CIC successor Fritz Haber, another prominent Jewish scientist, served as roving ambassador for Weimar; he founded the Japan Institute in Berlin. Both men were imbued with Humboldt's faith in science as the "conciliator of nations."

In time the totalitarians converted this activity to the needs of power, abusing cultural channels to carry their messages. Italy, Spain, Portugal, and Germany reached out to emigrants and to their former colonies. The USSR worked through national communist parties. Iriye contrasts Japan's Society for International Cultural Relations with the liberal British Council, both founded in 1934: by a single authoritative decision, Japan produced rigid and powerful monothematic propaganda—the Japanese had studied Creel, Bernays, and Northcliffe.

In US political circles, anti-internationalism was in spate. Congress's rejection of CPI foreshadowed the Senate's 1920 vote against the League of Nations. The world watched the US retreat into isolationism, with no countermove to support educational or cultural affairs from Congress. Herbert Hoover saw the value of US government involvement; managing American war relief to Europe, he left two Boxer-style binational educational foundations in Belgium and Finland funded by debt repayments; his wartime deputy H. Alexander Smith in the Senate would cosponsor the 1948 legislation completing the Fulbright Program. As Secretary of Commerce in 1923, Hoover proposed—two decades before Fulbright—a global binational exchange program, funded from debt reflows, of up to $100 million in any one country; he made no headway with an inward-looking Congress.

Reacting to government inaction, the US private world in 1919 began two decades of remarkable cultural internationalist growth.[22] On the one hand, some CPI alumni, joining missionary sons as they entered public life, had glimpsed a new approach to foreign relations. On the other, the university world craved overseas links and knew help would not come from government. During the quarter-century of peace between the two world wars, the U.S. launched a major internationalist expansion without government help, the first step in transforming standoffish US world power into a new, benign style of global hegemony—the American Century was taking shape.

The great foundations stretched abroad. Carnegie's wonderfully American approach to philanthropy, at home and overseas, relied on deeds rather than words; it shared costs and decisions binationally; and it focused on causes upstream rather than present needs. Beginning with cultural gifts to the country of his birth, Carnegie quickly turned institutional. His contributions to libraries in England flowed through the American Library Association (ALA); his endeavors spun off similar institutions supporting science, scholarship, and international law around the world. Merle Curti concluded that the United Nations, international law and arbitration, and the World Court could not have come into existence without the Carnegie Endowment's research, public information, and periodical, *International Conciliation*.

US universities were beginning to expand the study of other nations and regions, looking for ways to conceptualize such study in social scientistic terms; the new field of international relations was beginning to take shape. Carnegie's legatees aided the global spread of science and the international movement of scholars. A plaque in a building on Paris's Boulevard St. Germain, today housing part of France's Ministry of Education, reminds passersby that it long served as Carnegie's hospitality center in Paris for foreign scholars.

The Rockefeller Foundation went further. To combat the wariness provoked by its mythic name, the staff followed Carnegie and practiced a style built on an American version of *paideia*—discrete, tactful, and modest. Like all the early foundations, at home and abroad, it walked the educator's tightrope, stretched between giving and receiving. Nations are not comfortable confessing to needs they cannot meet themselves, thus direct donations require sensitive handling; philanthropists understand that gratitude can be demeaning. Binationalism, in John Hay's Boxer formulation, was the defining idea of US philanthropy.

In China Rockefeller worked with Boxer alumni. Under the leadership of Wicklyffe Rose, who had helped the foundation eradicate hookworm in the American South, Rockefeller reached out in public health around the world, assisting key schools in Beirut (AUB), Singapore, Bangkok, the South Pacific, and Beijing. In 1914 Rockefeller's China Medical Board began building Western medicine in China, supplanting nearly a century of medical missionary heroes.

As foundations stepped in, individual funders faded: John King Fairbank, arriving in Beijing in 1932, watched the modest College of Chinese Studies, a missionary product, face the "sagging support of mission boards, whose trainees were growing fewer."[23] Still, millions of recipients abroad read US foundation support as a modern-day outgrowth of the missionary message: disease and other natural or man-made problems were neither inevitable nor predestined, but manageable by applied intelligence and human effort. This idea could only be conveyed by patient and genuine exchange, honest learning, and individual example. Binationalism as a national habit, if not quite a "policy," had emerged as a unique way of attacking problems by joint action while minimizing fears of US power.

At home dozens of US private institutions sprang to life to manage exchanges: beyond Carnegie and Rockefeller, there were the Guggenheim Foundation and the Commonwealth Fund, among others. There were various youth exchange programs, like the Committee on Friendly Relations among Foreign Students, founded in 1922. International relations clubs around the country received books and publications from Carnegie. Student volunteers still went overseas to teach.

In the seminal year 1919, four central US mediating institutions of international education came to life. Stephen Duggan's Institute of International Education (IIE), with a startup $30,000 grant from Carnegie, managed international university interchange; Charles Homer Haskins's American Council of Learned Societies (ACLS) linked American academic disciplines in the humanities and social sciences to the International Academic Union in Brussels; the International Federation of University Women in London, founded by Barnard College Dean Virginia Gildersleeve, opened the network of US university-educated women to the world; and Georgetown University's School of Foreign Service opened its doors, borrowing IIE's Duggan as a commuting lecturer to get through its first year. Smaller organizations were starting up, e.g., various bilateral "friendship" associations, like Henry Goddard Leach's Swedish-American Society, Nels Poulsen's American Scandinavian Foundation, and Edward Bok's Netherlands-America Foundation.

The fine arts deserve their own chapter. After the war came a time for building the great American collections of European and world art. Andrew Mellon was collecting the paintings which would launch the National Gallery in Washington; J. P. Morgan's successors—the Havemeyers, the Rosenwalds, and others—were filling New York's Metropolitan Museum. Samuel Kress, after building an empire on the basis of five-and-ten cent stores for middle America, exercised his sense of stewardship by acquiring and distributing art both to major national collections and to the smaller cities that had supported his stores, donating fine art to dozens of provincial museums. Like Kress, Mellon brought art to democracy, insisting that Washington's National Gallery allow free entrance in perpetuity, that it never bear his name, and that it never allow government to fund acquisitions. His son Paul would spend his years adding hundreds of paintings to the collection, helping build the celebrated East Wing, and filling Yale's Museum of British Art. The Mellon Foundation, with a broader agenda, contributed in other ways, for example, expanding the literary canon by translating the world's treasures.

Abroad, offspring of Ernest Fenollosa were helping to save other national artistic heritages. Bernard Berenson was awakening Italy to the glories of its art from his Florence base, and Arthur Upham Pope was in and out of Persia; both were awakening their host nations to their priceless heritages. Support to art preservation and postwar restoration of monumental buildings in Europe was undertaken by US foundations: the palaces of Versailles and Fontainebleau and cathedrals, including Reims, St. David, St. Giles, Lincoln, and Gloucester, were saved. Kress, as a pendant to his acquisitions, funded training for American and European art historians, curators, and preservationists; built professionalism in the international museum world; and helped restore architectural monuments in Italy. US archeologists, following Stephens, Squier, Bingham, and US biblical scholars in the Near East, were surveying the world. In France Arthur Kingsley Porter, the only foreigner included in a 1915 French mission behind enemy lines to assess damage to monuments, was a legend; his student Kenneth J. Conant spent his life helping the French uncover and rebuild the great Burgundian Abby of Cluny. In Iraq Yale's Frank Brown was beginning his career in Near Eastern archeology at Dura-Europa; by the end of the 1930s he would serve as Syria's Director of Antiquities, then become the first US CAO in Beirut during the second war.

Private gifts also went to foreign universities. The Eastmans funded dental faculties in universities like Rome's, and there were chairs in American Studies at Oxford and Cambridge. French industrialist Charles Kahn set up a chair in American Studies at the Collège de France, as well as another in International Relations at the University of Wales in Aberystwyth. In Palestine the Hebrew University grew out of gifts from American Jews. Rockefeller built and managed foreign student housing, in the U.S. and abroad, in the form of International Houses.

In rejecting the League of Nations, Congress had also spurned its impressive cultural component, the CIC, father to UNESCO's national commissions. James Shotwell saw the League's intellectual activities as indispensable for Americans, both in terms of connecting with the rest of the world and in cooperating on global projects. Mobilizing the private world from his base at Columbia, Shotwell founded the private American Committee on Intellectual Cooperation, which linked with national CICs around the world. In parallel, Albert Giesecke's teacher and Shotwell's friend Leo S. Rowe, heading the Pan American Union (PAU, later OAS) in Washington, formed a CIC for Latin America.

Globally oriented American intellectuals, many descended from the missionaries, were moving into place. Missionary-sons Hiram Bingham and Karl Mundt were in Congress; ex-missionary Arthur Hummel was building the East Asia collection for the Library of Congress, and his son would soon begin a distinguished diplomatic career, part of it in cultural affairs; and there were dozens of others, including missionary-educators T. Cuyler Young and missionary-sons like Edwin Reischauer and Robert Goheen, following the path of S. Wells Williams by teaching in US universities, working with government or the foundations, or simply—like Pearl Buck—doing what they could.

Universities had been teaching public administration to citizen-administrators for two decades. Pendleton's 1885 legislation had throttled down the spoils system for four decades; now trained professionals were needed. By 1921 Georgetown's School of Foreign Service had graduated its first class, recycling B.A.s into government and foreign service; by 1924 Congress, with the Rogers Act, decided to professionalize the foreign service. A decade later Rockefeller began luring graduates into government careers through public service internships.

US universities were accepting growing numbers of foreign students. Teachers in US overseas schools and colleges were helping channel gifted foreign students to the U.S. With more foreign students, support needs grew. The Committee on Friendly Relations among Foreign Students was started by the Mott family in 1911 as an offshoot of the YMCA, and it quickly became the premier institution for helping foreign students in the U.S. In 1915 it published its first statistical directory, then in 1919 a formal census, *The Unofficial Ambassadors*. By 1921 it was reporting sixty-nine hundred foreign students in the U.S., led by 1,443 Boxer-funded Chinese. By 1930 it counted ten thousand such invisible exports of American education, twice the number of Americans abroad.[24] By 1920, three decades of European-trained American returnees were in place, eager to give back to the Old World what they and their fathers had received there. Although fewer Americans were signing up to teach in mission schools, more Americans were studying abroad: in the century before 1900, fifteen thousand Americans had studied abroad; by 1900 about two thousand graduates were going abroad every year. American exports in education were coming closer to balancing imports.

In New York IIE was switchboard and clearinghouse, thanks to the charismatic Duggan, who had been internationalized by service with the American Council on Education and by years in immigrant education. This quintessential internationalist taught political science and education at Townsend Harris's flourishing City College of New York. Preaching that "today's foreigner is tomorrow's neighbor," Duggan caught public attention. During a long discussion over dinner with his friend Nicholas Murray Butler, President of Columbia, and former Secretary of State Elihu Root, head of the Carnegie Endowment, surely instigated by Duggan and probably pressed on Butler by Shotwell, he raised the idea of IIE. With a grant of $30,000, the Institute was soon in full operation. With Duggan shuttling to Georgetown for teaching, it is perhaps no accident that Congress soon set up a special foreign student visa.

Duggan's IIE ran on a shoestring. He and ten staffers occupied the sixteenth floor of a narrow loft building just west of Fifth Avenue on 45th Street. Within a dozen years, without government support, IIE "had become the representative of nearly all the official agencies of foreign countries having to do with international cultural relations."[25] It was an "unofficial educational embassy," wrote Duggan's deputy Edward R. Murrow. Its early boards included every major American internationalist, from Jane Addams to Henry Morgenthau, and covered every corner of American intellect and politics, from New York Governor Franklin D. Roosevelt to Tennessee Senator Cordell Hull. Duggan saw US cultural diplomacy as a national responsibility; he soon understood that, properly executed, it exceeded the grasp of the private world. Duggan's older son Laurence, after Exeter, Harvard, and a tour at IIE, joined State in 1930 and soon caught the attention of FDR's Undersecretary of State Sumner Welles.

Duggan's third son was adoptive. Edward R. Murrow had headed a loose organization of student governments from four hundred colleges across the U.S. called the National Student Federation of America (NSFA) which set out after World War I to strengthen its international outreach. NSFA's "foreign relations office," i.e., its international political division, was launched in 1925 at a conference addressed by Norman Thomas, Clarence Darrow, and Henry Stimson. At its fifth congress in January 1930, at Stanford University, keynoter George Creel confessed to CPI's lies, and Murrow, delegate from Washington State College at Pullman, never forgot it. Moving east to study college administration at Columbia's Teachers College, he took with him NSFA's international office. Shortly thereafter Duggan lured him into IIE.[26] For one of his first jobs he had to persuade the paranoid Soviets to host a Moscow seminar for US students in the summer of 1934. His unsuccessful efforts in this case earned him a thick FBI file. With Einstein at Princeton, Murrow was soon helping hundreds of refugee scholars escape Europe and relocate in the U.S.; it was a new migration of European scholars, he said, resembling "the expulsion of the Jews from Spain in 1492, the Huguenots' forced exit from France, and the migration of Greek scholars to Italy after the fall of Byzantium."

Soon, says Murrow biographer Sperber, Murrow convinced the nascent CBS radio system to produce a weekly half-hour broadcast built around Duggan called *The University of the Air*, for which Murrow provided exclusive interviews with world figures; CBS then added *Last Week Abroad*, with Duggan as lecturer. In the fall of 1935 Murrow moved on to CBS as Director of Talks, but he never entirely left education or his dream of presiding over a liberal arts college.

IIE, coordinating educational relations with other nations, handled both individual exchanges and problems, including Europe's intellectual exodus. Latin America was a natural focus. First Duggan's son Laurence, then Murrow surveyed US cultural cooperation with Latin Americans; thus IIE was the obvious partner when State set out to design cultural relations with neighbors to the south.

US exchanges in the arts and literature were growing. A Lost Generation, including Archibald MacLeish, had haunted Paris; the Guggenheim Foundation was stirring the mix by enabling writers, like Thomas Wolfe, and black artists, like poet Countee Cullen, to share in the excitement of Europe. Tourists were no longer grand: they came now from the middle class, like students and scholars; they were ex-doughboys and businessmen, men and women, old and young. Sinclair Lewis's Sauk City lay far behind.

These changes owed little to government, other than to general but unintentional help, from Morrill's Land-Grant Act of 1863 to the emergence of the USOE in 1867 to the income tax laws of 1913. On the contrary, the US political mood, as reflected by Congress, still looked inward. Two nationalist and conservative postwar presidents knew that America's business was little more than business; they saw foreign policy, if they saw it at all, as a way to augment foreign sales. The 1928 victory of Republican internationalist Herbert Hoover changed nothing; his party was not ready for the internationalism he knew firsthand—his pre-Fulbright proposal of 1923 died an early death.

Historians Merle Curti and Akira Iriye, from different viewpoints and generations, both see the period between the world wars as a historical high in American private internationalism, despite the onrush of economic disaster and totalitarianism. As though to protest Congress's rejection of the League, the US intellectual world struck out on its own. Cultural internationalism had come to life, even if the news had not reached America's legislators. From their New York base, Butler, Duggan, Shotwell, Root, and others, by travel and by radio, talked and wrote about the inevitability of international interdependence. The Catholic Church, culturally internationalist by definition, encouraged the preaching of young stars like Fulton J. Sheen and discouraged the angry isolationism of Father Coughlin, notes Iriye.[27] New groups promoted the study of international affairs: the Council on Foreign Relations, the Foreign Policy Association, the Foreign Affairs Forum, the Institute of Pacific Relations, and in Denver Ben Cherrington's Foundation for the Advancement of the Social Sciences. Individual universities were reaching abroad: Tufts' Fletcher School of Law and Diplomacy, in addition to training students for diplomacy, nurtured connections with Weimar Germany.

Among the early ethnic bilateral associations, relations with Africa were a special case. There the history of US missionary-educators began early in the nineteenth century at Fourah Bay College in Sierra Leone, with the first black graduate of Amherst College. In the 1920s James Hardy Dillard's commission surveyed black-white contact in Africa, then convinced foundations, like Phelps-Stokes and Jeanes, to support mission-schools, e.g., Adams College in South Africa. Black Americans led by men like Ghana-born J. E. K. Aggrey and T. J. Jones also worked toward better lives for Africans. Dialogue, not top-down teaching, was the theme for cultural diplomacy in Africa. But divisions in the American black community, not unlike those in the Irish and Jewish worlds, interfered with the success of efforts: W. E. B. Dubois and Booker T. Washington clashed, and the ambitious dreams of Marcus Garvey caused dismay.

In time coordination among private agencies became imperative. For-ward-looking private institutions recognized how long it would take to build informal structures to support the needs of world interaction. The key, in the case of the U.S., was coordinated public-private action; but bringing in the government required patience because Congress stood in the way. Iriye sees the 1920s as a burst of global activity before the storms of economic disaster, the disruptive decline of colonialism, and the rise of totalitarianism—which he notes is a twisted form of cultural interna-tionalism serving expansionist goals. In the U.S., internationalist educa-tors expected neither government assistance nor constraint after World War I. Obvious difficulties lay ahead.

A few US statesmen of vision, led by Sumner Welles, knew the time for government coordination, hopefully through mild supplementation, was at hand. Welles saw the wisdom of avoiding perceptions of govern-ment interference; he also knew coordination would take years of patient domestic constituency-building in a very provincial America.[28] The coop-erative efforts of private and public sectors, with enlightened help from business, soon proved to be a defining characteristic of US outreach as binationalism. Thanks to the universities and the corporate world, public and private foreign policy were coming closer. The potent combination would reshape the very notion of diplomacy.[29]

Abroad and at home, the easy years of open-door cultural relations were ending and an early domestic backlash to growing US international-ism had begun. As US political, economic, and business power invested in education and as interested parties began to replace the disinterested activities of the missionary-educators, foreign politicians exploited re-sentments. The outside world was taught first about "global capitalism" then about "Americanization"—today's "globalization." Giesecke could not protect Hiram Bingham from nationalist harassment in Peru: in 1915 having given the nation its national treasure, Machu Picchu, he was ha-rassed by agitators with the unanswerable question: "What is in it for the Americans?" Dumping crates of unsorted potsherds at their feet, Bingham abandoned archeology forever. That same year an identical question was posed to relief-director Herbert Hoover by the German commandant of occupied Brussels; Hoover icily declined to answer and told him no Ger-man could possibly understand. Lenin however, inspired by Marx, an-swered with a slogan. A great deal was in it for the Americans, public or private, because they were master-exploiters, bent upon global domina-tion through economic power.

Buried in the 1915 episodes in Lima and Brussels is the phrase "the Americans." Neither US relief-workers nor scholars nor mission teachers could separate themselves, in foreign minds, from the perceived actions of US government and corporations, whatever distance they kept. The outside world did not understand the mystery of the US public-private divide. Where governmental presence was minimal, private educators were left to function in their own patient style. Hoover and Bingham as well had only minor support from government, but they were not patient men—explanation and gentle persuasion over time might, in both cases, have produced different results. Financial advisor Arthur Millspaugh was endlessly patient in Tehran in 1923 and made a huge contribution to Iranian independence. But in 1942, during his second attempt to organize Iran's finances, the U.S. was no longer neutral, and he saw US policy dictated by its wartime alliances with Iran's historic enemies the British and the Russians. As US power grew on an international level it crowded in on the private world and as American government and business became more visible, public and private spheres blurred in foreign minds. It was easy to generalize, seeing "the Americans" lurking behind all activities.

The early missionary-educators assumed that large-scale private educational efforts overseas, impacting deeply on foreign social and political life, could take place outside politics and commercial interests; but by the 1920s they began to feel naive. With foreign audiences, the apolitical expectations raised by the mythic American Santa Claus were beginning to dispel. The special generosity, the pluralistic sensitivity, and the selfless sharing of nineteenth-century Americans reaching out to the world had filled "reservoirs of good will" everywhere. A helping hand to less fortunate brethren, in a framework of prosperous stewardship, had worked wonders, but at the same time it had sown its share of illusions. By 1918 commercial advantage, once seen as a potential by-product of cultural relations, began to look like its concealed purpose—just as successor generations of the Hawaii missionaries looked more exploitative than Hiram Bingham's grandfather had. And commerce caught congressional attention.

Americans too were raising questions. Curti writes that American doubts were increasing regarding US diplomacy's role during the depression of the 1930s. Churches could not keep up their efforts, and stewardship moved slowly into corporate boardrooms. The Great Depression led Americans to reexamine US foreign contributions; there was anger at foreign "ingratitude," at the myth of the American Santa Claus, at foreign ambivalence, and at foreign corruption. In the political world, "handout" and "giveaway" were sneer-words, and the negative epithet "do-gooder" could kill.

Congress's habit of providing food for disaster relief only when it might reduce US surpluses supported this perception. Random congressional generosity had provided relief aid for foreign disasters beginning in 1812. But even Hoover used disaster relief as systemic political pressure, to manipulate elections in Hungary and Poland. The sword of politics cut two ways. Faced with famine in a devastated postwar Russia, the Bolshevik threat provided Congress with a handy excuse to let Russians starve to death. After the Chilean earthquake of 1939, at the peak of the Good Neighbor Policy, a typically vigorous US government–private-corporate coalition set to work, but Congress declined the $1 million requested as a "hand-out" to a country that was not paying its debts. Congress then redoubled its peevishness by denying a recovery loan. In ironic contrast, Japan's 1923 earthquake evoked a larger private American contribution than had ever been raised before—Curti suggests this donation was prompted by US guilt over racist immigration restrictions.[30]

As the realities of postwar cultural relations crowded in, the generosity once lodged in the national self-image shrank. In US ethnic communities fissures had begun to widen: the Jewish community split on Zionism; the Irish-Americans debated Ireland's future; the black community divided on Africa; and many Italian- and German-Americans were mesmerized by Mussolini and Hitler. Critics of overseas engagement were asking tough questions, and the internationalists found no easy answers. The new generation of educated and skilled internationalist professionals wondered whether the missionary-educators had been doing as much as they thought. In the 1920s AUB resident Bayard Dodge downplayed any hint of colonialist paternalism, insisting that the goal of the university was not conversion, either to Christianity or to the American way of life, but fuller lives for the area's people. The traditional top-down model—transferring knowledge from the industrialized West to the developing world—was giving way to a search for cross-fertilization, to strengthening local cultures, and to sustainable modernization.

Social scienctists analyzed other cultures, pointing out dangers in clumsy cross-cultural communication. Educating an Arab or an African to American standards, for example, might not be best for the student; besides, while opportunities for education may blossom, they may not always produce the intended result. Grim Carnegie Endowment studies on poor whites in South Africa raised educational dilemmas. Several foundations supported a 1945 survey by anthropologist Bronislaw Malinowski; in Curti's summary, he said, "Western education in Africa had too often laid the basis for roles which many Africans could not play."[31] Education had raised unrealistic expectations and trained misfits; watching tribal bonds weaken all over Africa, Malinowski noted that the U.S. preached universal brotherhood abroad but failed to carry it out at home. Philosopher John Dewey, in his several visits to China and Turkey to develop school curricula, saw an America eager to assist but not to invest—a new form of paternalism.

Rethinking missionary-education challenged the fundamental tenets of the teachers—and provided ammunition for nationalist demagogues abroad. At the same time, the new skepticism provided a chastening context for State's cultural planners, as they set out cautiously to design an American cultural diplomacy worthy of the American nation.

CHAPTER THREE

Designing Cultural Relations, 1932–1940

> To be an American is an excellent preparation for culture. We have exquisite qualities as a race, and it seems to me that we are ahead of the European races. . . . We can deal freely with forms of civilization not our own, can pick and choose and assimilate and in short (aesthetically etc.) claim our property wherever we find it.
>
> —Henry James, 1867

AFTER A CENTURY AND A HALF of a Constitution-grounded mindset that allowed US government to decline dealing with culture and education, the creation in 1938 of an office in the Department of State specifically charged with that function ranked as a major moment, widely reported at the time by radio and newspapers. Like the Morrill Act and the USOE in the immediate aftermath of the Civil War, the 1938 decision grew from larger events, guided by the determined vision of a few men at the top—Cordell Hull, Sumner Welles, the two Duggans, and ultimately Franklin D. Roosevelt.

The European crisis of 1930 is usually credited as the trigger of the creation of the Division of Cultural Relations, but it was neither the initial nor the only stimulus. France's diplomacy had already gone into high gear in 1923, capping centuries of quasi-formal activity, as part of its recovery from the first war, and Britain's later decision to open international avenues for cultural diplomacy soon followed. In the U.S., activist thinking in government, with the exception of Hoover's halfhearted efforts in 1923, began with the New Deal. The rise of Fascism heightened interest in foreign affairs and was later exploited by the designers to awaken a slumbering Congress before finally war took over. US cultural diplomacy in fact was first intended to respond to Latin America.

While few legislators had ever thought about the idea of formal cultural outreach, informal cultural activities abroad without government encouragement were a US habit. Europe's growing insistence on bringing a cultural dimension to diplomacy was well known to the newly professionalized US diplomats. Latin Americanists like Sumner Welles were particularly alert to this trend because nations in the southern hemisphere had been pleading for cultural links with the U.S. since the days of Precursor Francisco Miranda. American diplomats, alongside their collegial friends, the missionary-educators, watched French and British education in their colonies; and they saw as well the foreign children of Paine inciting third-world cultures against their colonial masters. Given the prosperous American pluralist democracy and the outreach that Emily Rosenberg called "spreading the American dream,"[1] it was plausible to think the public sector, equally intent on spreading American pluralist democracy, might lend a little no-strings help.

By 1932 the Great Depression and darkening world politics were already squeezing US private support. Educators with overseas agendas were among the first to recognize political and economic warnings: they turned to the corporations, then to the new foundations for funding. But in the early 1930s, some believed, the job had outgrown even these means of support, and new needs for coordination and risk-analysis arose; it was government's turn to strengthen foreign cultural relations.

How much Roosevelt knew about the details is not certain, but he was no stranger to the idea of cultural diplomacy. The idea of a formal overseas projection of America, flowing back to John Hay, Woodrow Wilson, Herbert Hoover, and the values of cultural internationalism, must have occurred to him long before 1932. He had visited Italy for CPI during the First World War; as Assistant Secretary of the Navy, he knew of the military's enlightened educational stance, as well as the Navy's role in governing CPI and in lending its communications links. He had watched Congress destroy CPI, and had seen Hoover channel war debts into exchanges.

Diplomacy's need for a formal cultural dimension was more firmly anchored in the ideas of his social service–oriented wife Eleanor, of her childhood friend Sumner Welles, and of FDR advisor Harry Hopkins, a product of the Social Gospel movement. Welles in particular saw hemispheric affairs as a changing and organic challenge, unlike the geopolitical chess games of Europe. He had seen, under Harding, Coolidge, and Hoover, especially in the Mexican mission of ambassador Dwight Morrow, the wisdom of reversing Theodore Roosevelt's interventionist reading of the Monroe Doctrine. Welles knew the Boxer Indemnities and understood the value of the binational approach; he knew of Hoover's idea of recycling foreign debt reflows into student exchanges. If Roosevelt did not know the details, Welles as the president's advisor on Latin America did.

Welles and journalist-friend Drew Pearson were immersed in Roosevelt's first campaign; they drafted a global US foreign policy for FDR before the nominating convention in 1932, but insider Cordell Hull edited out all but "two pallid phrases"[2]—foreign affairs was certainly not a winning plank that year. Barely visible in the platform, the remains of their draft nonetheless impressed FDR enough to trigger the Good Neighbor Policy. He wanted an early and visible shift of policy toward the southern continent honoring the special relationship spelled out by Monroe, and he understood the value of respecting the Latins' high regard for culture. Latin American leaders like Francisco Miranda and Simon Bolívar, US statesmen like John Quincy Adams and William Henry Seward, and educators like Horace Mann and his Argentine friend Domingo Faustino Sarmiento had seen inter-American intellectual relations as crucial to both sides. The humiliating annexation of Texas and the Spanish-American War reminded Latins that gringos pursued their own interests; those two defeats heightened Latin American pleas for student exchanges, bilateral scholarship, geographic exploration, library development, botanical and zoological research, mapping, archeology, and missionary schools. All this moved forward steadily during the nineteenth century, despite the natural resistance of Latin America's Catholic establishment and the prevailing disdain of the continent's elitist pseudo-Europeans toward the blunt, easy-going *Norteamericanos*. Welles's cautiously balanced bidirectional decisions of 1938 spelling out the political framework of cultural relations with Latin America were implicit in the rest of the world from the outset, and Latin America was his roadmap.

Neighborliness was the theme. Roosevelt's first inaugural address in 1933 pledged the U.S. to "the policy of the good neighbor—the neighbor who resolutely respects himself and, because he does so, respects the rights of others—the neighbor who respects his obligations and respects the sanctity of his agreements in and with a world of neighbors." In the inter-American context, this statement heralded a new look; one corner of the policy triangle was cultural relations.

While Welles had major inputs, the language of the first inaugural address was finally polished by Cordell Hull. Hull, a crusty Tennessee Senator and fervent advocate of lower tariffs, had little foreign experience. He was comfortable neither with Welles nor with the Good Neighbor idea, but he knew FDR favored both and his dream of lowering tariffs was built into the foreign affairs package. Below Welles in the drafting chain was Laurence Duggan, a new entrant to State out of Harvard via IIE; he was "shy, bespectacled, quietly brilliant," Murrow's biographer notes, and "ultra-liberal" in the words of his admiring friend and once-deputy Ellis Briggs.[3] Roosevelt's inaugural reflected Welles's version of Wilson's idea that the U.S. existed "not to serve ourselves but to serve mankind."

Beneath the rhetoric lay strategic realities. The southern Atlantic was protected only by the British fleet. In economic terms Latin America was a magnet for American investment and a giant market that business had barely begun to probe. But European competition was high: not only Spanish, Portuguese, and British, but Italian, German, and Japanese trading companies were increasingly active—the Soviets alone showed no interest. Immigration from both pre-Axis Italy and Germany into Latin America had been heavy.

Latin perceptions of US culture, its high culture by definition, were split. Though parts of the Latin middle class had been shaped by Methodist and Presbyterian missionaries and by the US experiences of men like Miranda and Sarmiento, its tiny European-oriented elite tended to deprecate the rough-hewn Yanqui. Efforts to adopt US constitutional models had not loosened the iron grip of Roman law or the French Church–derived administrative system; centralized government was rooted deep in Latin political culture. To Anglo-Saxons, this disorderly tradition seemed to favor an attraction to proto-fascist discipline and a great enthusiasm for the military similar to that in the cultures of Turkey, Iran, China, and Japan at the beginning of the century. Fascist-oriented Latin governments did not in fact come into existence until the 1940s in Argentina and Bolivia. An attempted right-wing coup in Uruguay was turned aside. In Chile and Brazil German immigrants and military explored closer ties with the Nazis and the Krupp empire.

The U.S. had experience with military governance. Its military had governed its short-lived post-Spanish empire with some success, and thanks to Theodore Roosevelt's energies and sleight of hand, it had redrawn frontiers and engineered the Panama Canal. Dominican strongman Trujillo, trained by occupying US marines and supported by US ambassador Avra Warren, had reigned successfully since 1930 over his island republic, a key forward defense point for the Caribbean and the new canal. Welles himself as ambassador in Cuba had not opposed the rise to power of Fulgencio Batista. Perón's Argentina leaned to the right. To Latin American regimes, the totalitarians seemed plausible models.

Roosevelt wanted better relations with Latin America after years of neglect and random interventionism. While he preferred to deal with democratic governments, he was a realist. His pragmatic friend Hull was a southern politician. In the House he had shaped income and inheritance taxes, then moved to the Senate, where he was thought of as presidential material. In contrast was Sumner Welles, Assistant Secretary for Latin America in 1932, a Groton-Harvard professional diplomat's diplomat. He was imposed on Hull by FDR and soon became Hull's Undersecretary, deputy at that time. Welles was sophisticated, complex, clear-minded, Europeanized, and keenly intelligent. Emblematic of his intellectual reach and his idea of cultural diplomacy is a definition of "culture" he gave in 1942 that was worthy of the French: he said he took "culture in its broadest sense, as the composite of all that men do to make their common life richer and more satisfying."[4]

Welles's alter ego was Laurence Duggan, domestic-service officer in State, who had been in the Latin American bureau only since 1930. Duggan knew Latin America from his two years at IIE and from his father's long experience. He too was an architect of neighborhood.

FDR's first inaugural, blending Hull's push for lower tariffs and Welles's political expertise on the southern continent, did not electrify US voters. But for the southern continent, it was an exciting and radical shift. "The money changers have fled from their high seats in the temple of our civilization. We may now restore the temple to the ancient truths"[5]—FDR's words were read in the south as an apology for high-handed US economic domination.

While Hull, Welles, and FDR worked hard at the neighborly approach, reaching across the nation by rail and by radio to proclaim the new stance, Hull worried about his former colleagues in a recalcitrant Congress. It was no time to ask for funding; to combat the depression, Roosevelt had already been given more than anyone believed possible. Hull, moreover, feared the internationalist assumptions of the Good Neighbor Policy; he worried that a wary nationalist Congress would see Wilson in the shadows. Yet "the hemisphere's backyard"—a phrase which horrified Latin Americans—was as safe a subject as any on which to begin America's education on cultural diplomacy.

On Pan-American Day a month later, Roosevelt spoke to the PAU. Its director Leo Rowe, the Wharton School economist who sent Giesecke to Peru, was an unofficial member of FDR's Latin American "brain trust." Duggan, surely with the help of Rowe and with Wellesean touches, drafted FDR's talk to the union proclaiming cultural internationalism as a means of closer North-South links. Among the qualities of a respectful good neighbor, Roosevelt cited "mutual understanding, and, through such understanding, a sympathetic appreciation of the other's point of view." Never pretending that understanding implied agreement, FDR spoke of building an international structure. In 1933 this was a fresh thought; Fulbright would make mutual understanding the rationale for his program. Later, overuse and the clinging assumption that love must follow understanding would make the phrase a target for gibes by disingenuous congressmen, hawkish unidirectional informationists, and "realist" politicians like Acheson. As Fulbright later put it, in his pithy southern style, understanding was "a helluva lot better than mutual *mis*understanding."

State was small—only 750 officers, Briggs remembered. The professional foreign service had only come into existence in 1924; career diplomats by the 1930s held about two-thirds of the embassies, throttling back the haphazard political appointments of the past. In 1933 State still had only two top-level professional staffers for Latin America below Welles, with numerous diplomats in the field learning by the day. Under Duggan was Warren Kelchner, foreign service class of 1929 and Ph.D. in Latin American studies, who had published a book on Latin American relations with the League. Rowe, the guru of FDR's Latin American brain trust, was a shadow-member of the team with intimate access to every nation in the southern hemisphere and an office three blocks from State and the White House.

Welles persuaded Hull to revive the Montevideo Inter-American Conference, which State under Hoover had let drop after the Havana meetings of 1928.[6] In December 1933 Montevideo was the perfect forum for declaring the US intention to engage with Latin America, after US rejection of the League, and for committing the U.S. to a balanced economic policy. At Montevideo US delegates announced two dramatic commitments: tariff reform and nonintervention. Soon the high-handed Platt Amendment, which had asserted US dominion over Cuba, was abrogated, lifting a weight from US relations with the South; in 1934 the last US troops left Haiti. Tariff reductions began. The new line was beaming out to the world. The U.S. had adopted the diplomatic criteria of friendship and respect.

Montevideo, like all inter-American meetings, had strong cultural dimensions. The U.S., having painted itself into a corner for half a century by rejecting the idea of federal participation in cultural relations, now reversed its claim that American education and culture were solely concerns of the separate states and the private world. Rowe's PAU, taking its cue from the League, had already formed its League-related CIC for Latin America, paralleling Shotwell's in New York. Rowe's CIC gathered eighteen leading American scientific and technical organizations and became the principal cultural-educational interface between the U.S. and the South.

In February 1934 Hull reported on Montevideo at the National Press Club, announcing "a new day in the political, economic, peace, and cultural affairs of this hemisphere."[7] National reaction was lively. No one missed the serious side of Hull's remarks—and no congressman complained. In New York Mayor LaGuardia soon renamed Sixth Avenue "the Avenue of the Americas."

The style of the policy shift was gradual, so as not to upset a paranoid Congress or arouse Latin fears of exploitation or intervention. Meanwhile American experts, at least those employed by the military, were moving south on loan to Latin governments. Given the number of countries in Latin America, the early results seem minor—a few visitors here, a few there—but the door was open and the pace was accelerating.

The Chaco War between Bolivia and Paraguay wound down in 1934, with discreet help from ambassador Spruille Braden in Chile, ending an episode that reinforced the US view of Latin America as a hotbed of destabilizing military adventurism. In Europe, Asia and Ethiopia were threatening, war was on the horizon. Americans were deferring foreign study, and economic depression was already slowing the US universities' capacity to absorb foreign students. Exhortations by Welles and others to universities and foundations soon made some difference, but it was a sacrifice for universities with budget problems. Moreover Latin American foreign students were not always up to academic speed. Welles's team proposed public-private binational committees in the embassies to smooth the way.

Welles never hesitated to associate FDR's name with the good neighbor idea. In New York, capital of cultural internationalism, he called on Nicholas Murray Butler, longtime president of Columbia University, progenitor and head of the Carnegie Endowment, cofounder of IIE, Shotwell's friend, and 1931 Nobel Peace Prize co-laureate with Jane Addams of Hull

House. Welles persuaded Butler to press IIE for more university fellowships.

As the months passed, it was tempting to wave the flag of Axis incursions and other short-term policy considerations to sway Washington skeptics. The increase in German and Italian "cultural" activities troubled both the British and FDR. Still no one in Washington wanted another CPI. Welles, in keeping with the British and the French, argued against propaganda and for a broad but gradual cultural approach, pitched to mutual understanding and binationalism. State polled embassies on questions like German and Italian immigration, foreign investment in schools, scientific interchange, and German bilingualism. The first results were inconclusive. The embassies did not yet see a problem; some even reported that clumsy Axis tactics had already backfired.

The British and French decision for a cultural approach was compelling, and the senior Duggan and Rowe urged avoiding the slightest hint of propaganda. Welles too favored a long-range cultural approach to mutual understanding, through balanced exchanges; the transparency of its processes would unmask Axis propaganda. In the fall of 1937 a second State field survey showed totalitarian propaganda to be a more serious concern. Laurence Duggan, looking back a decade later, said his office saw the German presence in Latin America not as an incursion but as activist economic and political "softening."[8] Others saw immediate danger in a region peopled with German and Italian immigrants that was already too inclined to seek order in authority.

Welles's team appealed to the universities to reach out in a natural and organic way, with minimal government involvement and in strictly educational terms. Sensitive to national egos and the technical problems involved in educational exchanges—Latin American students tended to be ill-prepared and weak in English and educational flows would predictably move more heavily to the north—they devised binational policies and strategies which would shape the Division of Cultural Relations in 1938. The word "exchanges" was a pledge to bilateral balance and reciprocity.

After the success of Montevideo, State called for an off-schedule inter-American conference, preceding the Lima Conference of 1938, to address the need for inter-American coalitions, e.g., to head off border disputes. The special conference would take place in Buenos Aires in December 1936. Montevideo had been useful for broadcasting the new US policy, and now Welles wanted to spell out action agendas and operational details under a revealing theme, "the Maintenance of Peace," which implied the resolution of international disputes. Welles was moving from non-interventionism to hemispheric solidarity; henceforth, an attack on one country was to be an attack on all.

At Buenos Aires the awe-inspiring list of cultural and educational resolutions was treated with full respect by the North Americans. America's premier diplomatic historian, Yale's Samuel Flagg Bemis, was famously skeptical about international factors beyond narrowly defined national interests; now he saw Buenos Aires as a major step, the moment in which "the U.S. assumed leadership in cultural matters."[9] Even where national interests do not coincide, new-convert Bemis maintained, the cultural approach to diplomacy can "assist understanding and soften enmity."

Public opinion in the North and South conditioned the discussions. US policy-shapers, skirting a resurgent CPI, called for broader cultural understanding, to be stimulated by patient exchanges. At home State launched a quiet US campaign in educational and intellectual circles. Hull instructed State's agenda-drafters for Buenos Aires to propose facilitation of student and teacher exchanges. Welles passed the ball to Rowe and the senior Duggan; in mid-June their draft circulated inside government, among private US educators, and in selected Latin countries.

Another player had joined the team: John Studebaker, FDR's Commissioner of USOE, then located in the Department of the Interior. Studebaker was a small-town Iowan who had worked his way through college as a union bricklayer, studied with John Dewey at Columbia, and returned to become Iowa's superintendent of schools. From 1934 until 1948 he was a key Washington discussant of cultural relations. USOE had begun life after the Civil War. One of its first goals had been to strengthen American universities through guidance to US study abroad; under Studebaker, USOE shifted its attention to secondary education. The commissioner was deeply committed to Pan-Americanism, and it was natural for him, without insisting, to volunteer USOE as the logical administrative home for foreign educational outreach. While no one was thinking that far ahead, no in-principle objection to Studebaker's suggestion was heard. Studebaker could not foresee how significant the question would soon become.

To build a US constituency, the Buenos Aires delegation was representative and, in fact, studded with stars. Even Rowe led his own PAU delegation to Buenos Aires. Only one historical figure was absent: Hull failed to enlist his friend Ben Cherrington, generalist, political activist, and director of international studies at the University of Denver. Aboard ship, the delegation was joined by the eloquent, authoritative Samuel Guy Inman, sixty-eight, missionary-educator and minister of the Disciples of Christ. Inman, with extensive Latin American experience, was Shotwell's friend, professor of history at Columbia, the founder-editor of *Nueva Democracía*, an early theorist of international relations, and a zealous promoter of Pan-Americanism. Unfortunately Inman believed he had been asked by Hull—and perhaps he had—to "shepherd" the exchange proposal through the conference.[10] As shepherd, he pressed the shipboard delegation to reach beyond undergraduates to the needs of university scholars, graduate students, and secondary teachers.

The US draft-treaty, approved unanimously by the conference, was a long activist shopping list, calling for the exchange of publications, professional librarians, art exhibits, and educational films; revision of textbooks to reduce hostile presentations of "other countries"; radio for peace; "reading rooms"; protection of intellectual properties; conferences of educators; private-sector cooperation; and press relations. Propaganda was not mentioned.

Back in Washington, Hull and Welles met disastrous news. In their absence Acting Secretary Walton Moore, a seventy-seven-year-old isolationist crony of Hull, had neglected to dissuade Congress from passing the far-reaching Neutrality Act, aimed at the Spanish Civil War: It was now unlawful to provide assistance, even humanitarian, to either side of an armed conflict abroad. In one legislative stroke, the great tradition of US generosity in foreign disasters was wiped away; even the Red Cross was powerless, and US volunteers in the Republican Army's Lincoln Brigade suddenly became outlaws.

Still Hull and Welles were delighted with Buenos Aires, and they set out to publicize its accomplishments. Treaties for maintaining peace, liberalized trade policy, and expanded cultural relations sprang to life. In early 1937 the *New York Times* reported Hull's words: the new cultural policies were "designed to control the governments from within by building public opinion in this hemisphere on the friendship and understanding of the common people." This was not peace-through-understanding but rather the "peaceful adjustment" of controversies by parties who understood each other.[11] Roosevelt pressed for rapid Senate ratification of the Buenos Aries resolutions. J. M. Espinosa, arriving in State a decade later, concluded that the December 1936 conference marked "the first time that a means of developing cultural relations with other countries had been incorporated into the formal policy of the US government."[12]

Inman believed he would head State's cultural relations division. He set out on the lecture circuit, promoting support for the Buenos Aires resolutions and hinting that he could take a measure of credit for them. His parallel letter-writing campaign, undertaken against State's advice, advertised the Nazi threat to the hemisphere. In his effort to sway US audiences, Inman underestimated Welles's passion for anonymity. Told to muzzle Inman, Duggan wrote him that the press was all too ready to inflate such fears, and that business, mistrusting nationalism whether of the right or left, was nervous; the U.S., he wrote, needs "real cultural relations that cannot be accused of being propaganda." Inman's stock plummeted in State.

After Buenos Aires the structure and location of cultural relations mounted in pertinence. Studebaker's offer of USOE as a home for educational exhanges was still open; Kelchner drafted an acceptance of the offer, and Studebaker budgeted $16,000 for the program. Suddenly Welles awoke to the obvious: cultural relations could not be located anywhere but in State because international law lodged responsibility for all foreign conventions and treaties in ministries of foreign affairs. Welles spelled it out, Kelchner and Duggan fell into line, Studebaker agreed, and Kelchner scrapped his draft acceptance. Meanwhile, Welles broadened the US cultural function beyond Latin America to the world; restated and reinforced, global reach would never be challenged.

If location in USOE was closed, cultural diplomacy's structural problems remained. A tempting model was the British Council, funded by government but operating under the public-private Grants Commission. The American designers needed to involve the gigantic US private intellectual world, but Welles still wanted minimal diplomatic and foreign policy control. Definitions therefore were left tentative; Laurence Duggan believed time would spell things out as Americans and foreign audiences experienced "the real activities of the division." He did not pass up the opportunity to decry propaganda: the "division would not engage in competitive propaganda but would endeavor slowly, carefully and meticulously to construct solid foundations for cultural interchange." Even the British might refer to "cultural propaganda" or "true propaganda," but for Welles's team the very word "propaganda" was banned by a broad consensus, including State, USOE, the White House, and private advisors.

Another academic had joined Duggan's staff in the Latin American office: Richard Pattee, Professor of Latin American History at the University of Puerto Rico, an authority on US–Latin American cultural relations. Three decades after his arrival, Pattee remembered wheels spinning in the small office; he found a half-cooked idea fomented by the two Duggans, which "meant a vast amount of fumbling and uncertainty for a long while."[13]

With no authorized funding, the style was daily improvisation. For example: Pan-American Airways had agreed to provide free travel for selected US and Latin students, so Duggan's office undertook to persuade the US Maritime Commission to press for shipboard passage as well and earned a contribution from the Grace Lines. Proposals flooded in, some wise, some trivial, some premature. Duggan's team was begging funding from private sources, e.g., to hire two American professors for São Paolo's thriving missionary school, Mackenzie College (founded in 1886).

In February 1938 Duggan's office was trudging toward the creation of the new division, three months away. Sharing plans with embassies and consulates worldwide, Duggan solicited reactions. Responses were cautiously positive, although one dyspeptic respondent in Tangiers noted that the idea of exchanges was absurd, since Moroccan education had produced no one worth exchanging.[14] Respondents noted that hostile propaganda had begun to damage the US image.

The new division was announced to the private intellectual world at a conference in State on 23 May 1938, attended by dozens who paid their own way for the then-lengthy trip to Washington. The conference was designed to inform, while formulating practical ways to work together in "the desirability, if not the necessity, of closer cultural cooperation." A premature resolution in the House of Representatives had already proposed an office in State as follow-up to Buenos Aires. It was superseded by two pieces of legislation: one established a Division of Cultural Relations and the other a Division of International Communications, to cover Buenos Aires proposals about radio.

The meeting attracted a hundred or more of the right names, a balance of government and private sector. On the government side the stars were Hull, Welles, Assistant Secretary for Latin America George Messersmith, Cecil Jones for the Librarian of Congress, Earl Bressman for Agriculture Secretary Henry Wallace, USOE's Studebaker, and State's progenitors. Leo Rowe spoke for the Latin American viewpoint. On the private side were Frederick Keppel, head of the Carnegie Endowment; George Finch representing Nicholas Butler; John Merriam, head of Washington's science-oriented Carnegie Institution; David Stephens, vice president of the Rockefeller Foundation; Frank Aydelotte, head of the Guggenheim Foundation; Isaiah Bowman, president of the Johns Hopkins University; Laurence Vail Coleman, head of the Association of Museums and a Smithsonian veteran who had worked with Giesecke in Peru in 1928;[15] historian Waldo Leland, head of ACLS; Carl Milam, like Leland, a Duggan advisor and head of ALA; Charles A. Thomson, head of the Foreign Policy Association; and the senior Duggan representing IIE. No one missed the point: they knew they were present at some sort of creation.

State opened the meeting by announcing the new Division of Cultural Relations as a response to Buenos Aires that would extend binational policies to the world. It would "rely on the private sector as the major partner in developing policies."[16] The division's goals were educational: to meet Buenos Aires commitments, strengthen private efforts in Latin America, disseminate information about US culture in Latin America, and increase US knowledge of Latin America. A private advisory committee to the division would be established, called the General Advisory Commission (GAC). Would there be cultural attachés? Messersmith argued there should not: the abuse of the title by Germany and Italy had tainted its utility; besides, foreign service officers from the educated US elite already represented the best in US culture. Seriously underestimating workloads, Messersmith would delay field assignments for four years.

Participants, all from the East Coast, agreed that full university cooperation was the indispensable core. State asked the universities to take responsibility for establishing academic priorities. Rowe proposed that IIE, outside politics, would be the ideal clearinghouse for university selections. American-sponsored schools, competing with the well-heeled Germans and Italians, needed help. Foreign library collections needed materials to support American studies; foreign librarians needed training in basic library services. Book translations and low-cost books and periodicals were vital. The U.S. needed library materials for the study of Hispanic and other cultures. English teaching was a serious global need. Exhibits of fine art should be developed with assistance from the museum world.

Messersmith announced a pertinent coincidence: Congress that same week had authorized expanding the loan of government technicians beyond US military personnel to foreign countries. Welles saw an opportunity to expand his overseas forces in this authorization and set up an Inter-Departmental Committee on Cooperation (ICC), a cornucopia that allowed thirty-seven hundred exchanges to take place between 1938 and 1948 with Latin America alone. Financial considerations were not mentioned by conferees, who were expected to help Hull make the case for educational exchange in Congress.

At the meeting, Welles first proposed his famous 5 percent bargain: no more than 5 percent of overall activity, he said, would come from the government, leaving 95 percent to the private world. Summing up, the no-nonsense Messersmith decried propaganda: "We are not trying to make . . . counter-propaganda. We are interested in the broad basic problem of developing the really friendly relations between this country and our neighbors."[17] Two days later Messersmith pried a start-up budget out of Congress: $27,920 to cover five professionals and three support-staff. In the glow of the meeting's success, no one noticed serious absences. There were no invitees from Congress, from the Bureau of the Budget, or from the White House, nor strictly speaking was there any direct representative of business.

The participants were hard-headed men supremely aware of ominous events in Europe and Asia, and yet the Axis threat was not mentioned. They insisted on designing a cultural internationalist instrument to spread what Ninkovich called "the liberal ecumene." Behind their decisions lurked American suspicions of elitism, foreign outreach, overseas responsibilities, the free circulation of information, advertising, "propaganda," the power of education to lift all boats, business as a benign force for development, and scholars as bureaucrats. The nation was discussing a way of handling formal cultural relations with the rest of the world. Some underlying questions led back to the absent Creel: the nature of "truth" and "facts," conformism, private-public separation, the relationship of culture to policy, and the dangers of distributing propaganda.

The U.S. had joined the Anglo-French decision to answer Axis and Soviet Big Lies not by more propaganda but by a diplomacy of truth. Participants understood that the natural growth of cultural activity abroad would add a new dimension to foreign policy; some assumed it might even add a dimension to America's position in the world.

The May 1938 meeting made it clear that the government would merely facilitate inernationalism, not initiate it. Overlooking Tocqueville's warning that "a democracy can only with great difficulty regulate the details of an important undertaking, persevere in a fixed design and work out its execution in spite of serious obstacles," the conferees moved ahead to plan an optimistic cultural diplomacy. US democracy was trying to find a foreign policy stance compatible with the independence of intellect. Philip Coombs wrote two decades later that "the time had now arrived when the nation's educational and cultural strengths must come to the support of its international position. The debate was over how best to accomplish this without destroying the very values which national policy sought to preserve."[18]

On July 27 State's Division of Cultural Relations came into formal being, and the work began. The planners, leaving room for flexibility, vested a great deal of decision-making authority in the universities in expectation of a give-and-take over time. No one on either side of the public-private divide thought for a moment of going it alone: it was to be governmental cooperation with the private world, dividing the work 95–5.

The planners permitted the onrushing war to be neither motivation nor excuse; propaganda was out. Key planners believed they were forging a critical tool for shaping America's role in the world. In 1940, from his desk in the Library of Congress, Archibald MacLeish wrote words that would ring clear a half-century later: "In a divided world in which the real issue of division is the cultural issue, cultural relations are not irrelevancies. They are everything."[19]

MacLeish, a friend of the Duggans, knew it was impossible to separate Welles's ideas on cultural diplomacy from Laurence Duggan's—for a decade, Duggan drafted Welles's entire output on the subject. Duggan's deputy, the sharp-minded iconoclastic diplomat Ellis O. Briggs, outlined Duggan's central position admiringly in his memoirs. From Briggs, Welles, MacLeish, and everyone who knew him, Duggan earned unflinching devotion.

In 1932 no one, with the possible exceptions of the senior Duggan and Shotwell, had the slightest idea what a formal US cultural diplomacy might look like. As late as the summer of 1938, Hull wrote, "Frankly we don't know how it should be done."[20] Architect Duggan could enlist the best intellectuals in America; he was in touch with individuals, institutions, international bodies, and through Rowe, officials of two dozen Latin countries. Having bitten off a sizable mouthful, he kept any doubts to himself. But the pledges of Buenos Aires were crushing. In 1940 MacLeish, looking beyond the war, expressed his concern: the U.S. had undertaken to present "convincing proofs of the creativeness and vitality of our culture. To fail would be disastrous." He noted that "these commitments have been given without adequate assurances beforehand of the cooperation of those whose cooperation is essential—the handful of true artists and true scholars who alone can enable us to perform these promises; without proper guarantees against the interference of the mediocrities and vulgarities . . . whose interference would make our promises ridiculous."

In April 1940 Duggan touched similar themes using the major instrument of mass information in the 1940s, the radio talk: "Seeds sown years ago and carefully nurtured . . . are now bearing fruit," he said. California had set up the first course on Latin American history and institutions in 1895; in 1940 there were nearly one thousand across the nation. In 1919–23, sixty-six new books on Latin America were published; in

1934–38 there were over six hundred. The growth mirrored the division's intentions, the vigor of its private partners, and its style of dynamic gradualism. Yet MacLeish had doubts: "If the present white-hot zeal is followed by the chill of indifference and casualness, the friendly relations now so earnestly talked about might be set back for generations," he said.

For relations with Congress, Duggan was on the sidelines, relying on Hull and Roosevelt himself. The immediate problems inside State, where there was skepticism—some of it caustic—consumed his time. Messersmith, selectively helpful, was gentler than old-line diplomat Loy Henderson, who exemplified the qualities that earned the foreign service its reputation for arrogance: Henderson saw culture as the camel's nose in State's tent. Duggan's friend, fellow 1930 entrant George V. Allen, soon to emerge as a key player, considered the whole idea of cultural diplomacy experimental. Briggs was agnostic on the question, exemplifying State's ambivalence. Thirty years later he remembered a running debate with Duggan, the kind of give-and-take that in the open American style often makes for sound decisions. The conservative Latin Americanist, admiring Duggan's compassion for other nations, saw it as the obverse of his deep respect for US interests. He warned Duggan, who had not lived abroad, that he was overgenerous when it came to Latin America. Duggan's sympathy for the "downtrodden," as Briggs put it, reflected the demotivating injuries of colonial history.

To Briggs, Duggan and his friend Adlai Stevenson were intellectual brothers who missed the real point—that Latin Americans were simply second-rate, "inferior raw material." He noted, "I agreed with Larry that in terms of hemisphere development, the destruction of indigenous cultures, followed by the colonial heritage of exploitation, had produced too high a proportion of 'downtrodden' for society to sustain indefinitely. . . . [but] I doubted then, and still do, whether certain of the Good Neighbors were capable of learning to dominate the instruments of representative democracy; . . . the intellectuals of Latin America seemed to me to be, with a few notable exceptions, rather a seedy lot."[21] One imagines the lively clash of Briggs's determinist racism and Duggan's tolerant and patient style of engagement. Briggs's lifelong admiration suggests that Duggan was able to win over tough opponents.

Briggs had an operational concern: he doubted that Americans of stature could be recruited. "The problem is to attract an American cultural wizard of sufficient magic to impress foreign intellectuals, and then to fit his sleight of mind to embassy operations."[22] While soon proved wrong, his point underlined opposing views of the human potential for growth, Hobbes versus Locke, Hamilton versus Jefferson, the realist-determinist versus the educator. Yet in their interaction the two men were blades of a pair of shears, cutting a true line. Duggan saw an American capacity for contributing to positive change abroad through education; Briggs thought the U.S. should accept no such responsibility: since cultural diplomacy probably could not be done, it should not be tried. The grumpy

Briggs admitted the division's usefulness—in Duggan's natural exploratory style—and the two men agreed on gradualism.

At this point, we must break off our story for a glimpse of the future. Briggs, at the end of his life, knew Duggan had had a brief flirtation with the Soviet Union, probably motivated by his faith in education and his perception of Soviet backwardness. In 1936 Duggan shared information with an agent of the newly recognized Soviet Union. Raw documents from one of Moscow's KGB archives, published in part and out of context by Allen Weinstein and Alexander Vassiliev,[23] show that Duggan was involved from 1936 to 1939 in low-grade leaks to Soviet agents. The files reveal bottomless and almost comic Soviet ignorance about the U.S., inducing one to imagine Duggan's instinctive American compulsion to enlighten a potentially useful ally. His Soviet handlers persistently complained to Moscow that Duggan gave them nothing of interest; they were looking for information on Europe, and he provided nothing more useful, for example, than standard biographical notes on Lawrence Steinhardt, named ambassador to the USSR. Subject to further revelations, the leaks seem trivial.

By March 1938 Duggan was having second thoughts and insisted on a three-month pause. In 1939 a second break in communications lasted five months. The Nazi-Soviet nonaggression pact of August 1939 and reports of Stalin's purge trials were changing the views of many Americans. Duggan debated questions about the Communists heatedly with his contacts, rejecting their claims that purge victims were Trotskyist subversives. The agents' twisted reporting to Moscow laboriously explained why the investment in Duggan was paying no dividends. In October 1939 Duggan broke off contact permanently. KGB files say he and his handler parted "good friends," continuing to meet from time to time; his "good friends," reporting to their bosses, wrote him off as one more Trotskyist.

Duggan's ambivalence was obvious: he consistently refused payment and respected none of the basic conventions of espionage; for example, he maintained open and casual relations with more serious Soviet sources, including Alger Hiss and Noel Field. In 1940 a persistent Soviet tried to reopen dialogue, and Duggan arranged to meet him at the very public Cosmos Club, across the street from the White House. There Duggan reaffirmed the break. In 1942 an agent tried again, was rebuffed, and reported to Moscow that Duggan was a "100 percent American patriot." The Soviets agreed blackmail would not work but surely worried about what Duggan knew.

FBI reports reached Adolph Berle, director of State's security; Weinstein and Vassiliev say Duggan's house was searched by US counterintelligence. Welles reminded Duggan that, at his level, "Marxist books" were not suitable for his library. Later Berle and Welles, like Briggs, publicly affirmed their faith in Duggan. Historians, perhaps in the context of further archival material, may evaluate the leaks more carefully. But nothing can change an unfortunate fact. During twenty-six months in 1936–39, Duggan passed documents to the Soviets.

Duggan's questionable relationship with the USSR would not concern our story if it had ended in 1939. Welles resigned from State in the fall of 1943, after an alcoholic indiscretion exploited by political enemies. His patron gone, Duggan soon resigned as well, shocking the division staff—he was their friend, leader, guide, and memory. He moved to the UN Relief and Rehabilitation Administration, then to the Carnegie Endowment, directed by his Harvard friend, Alger Hiss—little suspecting that in the the later 1940s friendship meant guilt.

In 1947 Duggan was recruited by his adoptive brother, Ed Murrow, to replace his father at IIE. There he launched full-time into private cultural diplomacy. Settling into his office high over West 45th Street, he knew things in Washington had taken a turn for the worse. The House Un-American Activities Committee, known by its queasy acronym HUAC, was following leads provided by Whittaker Chambers.

The dogged KGB gumshoes did not give up. They fantasized that Duggan in State had been inhibited by fear and that now he could shed constraints. They imagined that IIE was a useful channel for bringing in Soviet "illegals" as students. An imaginative report to Moscow branded IIE a creature of the State Department, "actively used by American intelligence in its work of preparing and sending agents to all the countries it is interested in." They proposed the absurd theory that Duggan might help spot talent in State, legalize their operatives, and provide information on how "American intelligence uses student exchanges in its work against us."[24] A Soviet visitor to IIE was observed by the FBI on 1 July 1948. Duggan's grace shines through the agent's report: after explaining the work of IIE, he gently ushered his guest to the door. Four days later Duggan failed to return a Soviet phone call.

In December 1948 HUAC told retiree Welles that Duggan was under suspicion, but as his biogapher noted, Welles rejected the insinuations "with contempt."[25] A questionable source, citing Chambers, had told HUAC that Duggan was one of six communists in the State Department; Chambers publicly disavowed the story—adding gratuitously that, although he had never met him, Duggan was "pro-communist." With this kind of flimsy evidence, the FBI talked with Duggan in New York on 11 December. Slightly more sophisticated than their Soviet analogs, the FBI had a thick file on Ed Murrow, from his battles with Soviet bureaucracy in the early 1930s.

On 20 December 1948, Laurence Duggan dropped to his death from his sixteenth-floor IIE office. "When his body was found around 7 P.M. he was wearing one overshoe. The other was later found in his office, along with his hat, coat, Christmas cards, letters referring to future engagements, and an airplane ticket to Washington for the next day," wrote

Welles's son. Late that same evening, acting HUAC chairman Karl Mundt hastily pulled together a press conference, with only young Californian Richard M. Nixon at his side, to tell the press that Duggan had been "linked to communism." Asked how many other such were still in State, Mundt said he would reveal the names of the others "as they jump out of windows."

Ed Murrow was grief-stricken. Seeking reactions for his 21 December lead story on CBS radio, he called Welles, who declared passionately that Duggan was a loyal patriot—an opinion shared by the KGB. To Murrow, Welles hinted at "foul play." Murrow's grim radio report blamed HUAC: "The members of the committee who have done this thing . . . may now consult their actions and their consciences," he said—to the consternation of his sponsor, Campbell's Soup. A *Times* editorial of 21 December accused Mundt of attacking a man "whose body was hardly cold."

Prominent people all over the U.S. paid tribute. On Christmas Eve the *Herald-Tribune* carried a poem of outrage by MacLeish. Evoking a passage from the jurist Learned Hand, often cited by Ed Murrow, the first line of the poem laid out MacLeish's fears for his country: "God help that country where informers thrive!"

Murrow and MacLeish assumed that Duggan was hounded to his death, but Briggs and Welles claimed foul play—the KGB had every reason to liquidate Duggan. Welles telegraphed New York's Mayor William O'Dwyer to demand a full investigation, but the police, examining Duggan's office and the floor-to-ceiling window behind his desk, concluded it was an accident caused by his struggle with an overshoe.

Duggan's death remains a mystery. While Welles and Briggs assumed murder, Arthur Schlesinger, less certain, follows Weinstein and Vassiliev in believing that this "romantic," in their words, "fell or jumped." But Schlesinger also notes Welles's support and that of fiercely anticommunist Adolph Berle. Evoking Duggan's stern stand against the Soviet party line in the Bolivian coup of 1934, Schlesinger wondered "what impulses of idealism may have inextricably entangled this decent man with the harsh machinations of Stalinist tyranny." Duggan was realist enough to impress the hard-heads—Welles, Berle, Briggs, Stevenson, George Allen, and even Schlesinger. Paul Nitze, self-styled "unregenerate cold warrior," late in life, considered Duggan a total patriot, although perhaps a bit "soft on communism," but he added that Duggan's beautiful wife was "a fellow-traveler."[26]

In Soviet reports his relations with his handlers were casual, disarmingly indiscreet, civilized, and of little consequence. Giving little, he refused even the most minor gift; the Soviets never attempted to compromise him. In principle, he had established an ideal position from which, when the time might come, he could promote useful dialogue with the USSR. However incautious, Duggan's dealings with the USSR were those of a cultural diplomat.

Stephen Duggan lived out his shattered life for two more years. Mac-Leish, back at Harvard, was disheartened, like other cultural internationalists. The country had entered the soon-to-be-named McCarthy era, which MacLeish knew would damage US capacity for unfettered civil discourse, render intellect suspect, demonize and demoralize the foreign affairs community, and severely damage the growth of intellect in government and in cultural diplomacy. Mundt and McCarthy, with sharp hindsight, wanted to taint anything that Roosevelt and his team had accomplished and had no compunctions about destroying lives and careers.

Laurence Duggan had reason to be proud: he lived to see the birth of the greatest step taken up to that point towards an American cultural diplomacy, Senator J. William Fulbright's program of exchanges (1946–47). Indeed Duggan played a vital role in its launching. Appointed to the first Fulbright oversight board, the Board of Foreign Scholarships (BFS), he offered IIE's services to administer the Fulbright Program and immediately resigned when BFS accepted. To ratchet up the tiny IIE operation, he asked New York foundations to fund a crash effort to get US Fulbright students and scholars into the field a year earlier than seemed possible. As many as a thousand Americans thus went abroad in the fall of 1949 instead of 1950, thanks to Duggan.[27]

His death and the destruction of his reputation by Mundt's committee shattered the morale of the tiny division and its friends. Working out details of the new Fulbright Program, the Senator and the BFS went on the defensive and exercised special care in building impregnable defenses against the know-nothings who regularly surfaced in US political life. Duggan's death was a harbinger of the breakdown of the humanist internationalist consensus shaped between 1919 and 1938, the political soil out of which an American cultural diplomacy had sprung.

Returning to our chronology and the summer of 1938, Ben Cherrington, an amiable giant from Denver and the very opposite of Duggan, set about building the house that Duggan designed. In 1938 the division needed a political leader, someone who could define concept and mission, work by trial and error toward priorities and policies, develop programs and products for the field, and build a constituency in Congress and in the nation. Ben Cherrington was not Hull's first choice—he wanted Samuel Guy Inman, who had left another job to prepare for this assignment. But Inman's career as a missionary in Latin America had left enemies; detractors alleged that he had an "animus against the Catholic Church" and a "lengthy record of hostility to Latin American catholicism."[28] Welles had other reasons to reject Inman: He was unhappy with Inman's display of self-importance after Buenos Aires.

Cherrington was a colorful internationalist academic and a deep-dyed politician, the total Westerner. A Nebraskan, he had begun his graduate work at Berkeley, where he coached the football team in spare moments; he then traveled east for an Ed.D. at Teachers College, Columbia, where he mixed with men like Dewey, Shotwell, Inman, and the senior Duggan. He was Student Secretary for the international YMCA and then he headed Denver's new Social Science Foundation. He spent twenty-five years with the university, served briefly as chancellor, and was a perennial candidate for governor of Colorado. His friendships in the East notwithstanding, his Western origins reassured Congress—he was nominated for division chief by his friend Colorado Senator Edward Costigan.[29]

Visiting Washington to call on Hull before taking the job, he met a few friends in Congress. In New York he visited Stephen Duggan but missed MacLeish at *Fortune*. At State he recalled hearing Hull lay out a dozen issues and themes. First was the secretary's fear of Axis propaganda, less for its inroads than for its reinforcement of Latin stereotypes about US cultural inferiority. Second came the need for flexibility in shaping the division. Third, propaganda was absolutely rejected; Hull wanted to put Creel behind him: "We are clear about one matter: we do not wish to follow the example of the totalitarian States. Whatever we do must conform to procedures and standards long established in our American democracy." Fourth came improvisation: "This is an entirely new venture for our government. There are no precedents to guide us."[30]

Cherrington accepted the job on a one-year contract, pleading irreducible responsibilities in Denver; he would, in fact, renew for a second year, then return to Denver. From there, he would chair the division's General Advisory Commission on Cultural Relations (GAC), until 1948, commuting monthly via the no-frills air transport of his day. The limits on his commitment to the enterprise were costly—the Division of Cultural Relations needed careful seeding and cultivation over time.

In State Cherrington had a small staff and a smaller budget. He learned to augment both, while getting the most out of his gifted team. His strengths lay outside government; he convinced prominent intellectual and academic leaders to travel regularly to Washington. The key— requiring no additional staff at first—was the GAC. In his hands, it was an executive, not an advisory, body. GAC's first membership shows its high aspirations, its total educational focus, its continuity with the planners of the 1930s, and its potential for linking State with the US cultural and intellectual world. Its members included USOE's Studebaker, accepting responsibility for publicizing the program to the universities and for screening university applicants; Stephen Duggan; ALA's Carl Milam; Inman; George N. Shuster, president of Hunter College; and Shotwell, who knew about the line dividing scholarship from propaganda, having organized historians for CPI. Two key advisors declined GAC membership, pleading conflicting interests: Leo Rowe, as head of an association of foreign states; and Charles Thomson of the Foreign Policy Association, who had already agreed to join the division as Cherrington's deputy. The high level of GAC membership made it a strong mediating group between government and the universities, relevant foundations, professional associations, the PAU, and through two CICs the multilateral cultural and educational office of the League of Nations.

GAC set up two subcommittees: one for students and professors, charged with the basic design of exchanges and another for foreign students in the U.S. The exchanges subcommittee represented institutions as impressive as GAC's: for science, the private National Research Council; for education, USOE's Office of Higher Education; for social sciences, the Social Sciences Research Council; for the humanities, the Washington-based ACLS under Waldo Leland; for the Guggenheim Foundation, director Henry Allen Moe, Aydelotte's successor; for scholarship, three US historians of Latin America—Goucher's Mary Williams, Bryn Mawr's Charles Fenwick, and the division's Richard Pattee.

GAC represented the world of intellect and culture, provided protection against State interference, and reached out to constituencies with all the power that Cherrington, Hull, and Roosevelt could lend. It helps to remember, in our time of lightning communications, that its members under wartime conditions communicated among themselves and with Washington by telephone, telegram, letter, and carbon copy; they traveled to Washington by train, five or six hours from New York; and Cherrington shuttled from Denver every month in unpressurized DC-3s.

In June Hull sent Cherrington an amazing four-page letter, surely drafted by Duggan and Pattee and approved by Welles—Cherrington referred to a similar document as a "composite of Hull-Welles-Thomson-Pattee-Cherrington." In the letter Hull lamented the fact that the US government, since its beginnings, had deliberately left to the private sector "what should at least in part have been its responsibility." Cherrington would not therefore *initiate* exchanges but build on what existed and "stimulate cultural interchange" with Latin America, which was prepared for new US efforts by the Good Neighbor Policy. Two-way flow was taken for granted. The new office would help communicate abroad "the spiritual and intellectual values in this country," but it must also enable Americans to understand the culture of other countries.

Hull's letter, a defining document of US cultural diplomacy, anticipates everything that US cultural diplomats—or any nation's cultural diplomats—would do or want to do in the ensuing four or five decades. The tasks mandated stretched well beyond the means of the division's resources: implementing the Buenos Aires conventions; increasing private support for unoffical exchanges; encouraging small US overseas libraries; helping enlarge national library collections; fostering book translations and cheap editions; and assisting binational centers (BNCs). In Hull's four dense pages, propaganda is not mentioned.

More daunting charges were added only a week later in a press release which noted that long-range intentions were global. The release added to the division's tasks preliminary study of the process of cultural exchange; maintenance of sound relations with embassies; interagency coordination in Washington and the field; maintenance of intellectual relations with foreign embassies in Washington; maintenance of relations with the PAU's CIC; expansion of contacts with educational and cultural organizations in the U.S.; and implementation of all cultural treaties.[31]

Populists Hull and Cherrington, spurred on by the ultimate populist vice president Henry A. Wallace, wanted to reach foreign populations below the elites: "The relations among our nations must not rest merely on the contacts between diplomat and diplomat, political leader and political leader, or even between businessman and businessman. They must rest also on contacts between teacher and teacher, between student and student, upon the confluence of streams of thought. . . . This is not a task for government alone but for all of us, the teachers, the men of science and learning." It was an enormous assignment, even as aspirations. In the context of longstanding world practices, no single item was in fact unfamiliar; Hull's letter spelled out what any nation's cultural diplomacy sooner or later must try to cover.

By the time Cherrington took up his charge in September, supportive mail was pouring in from constituents everywhere. Non-understanding came in as well. The first warning came from Welles's friend Drew Pearson, coauthor of the Good Neighbor idea; having mistaken its purpose for propaganda, he thought the division was moving too slowly. Welles deftly explained that Cherrington's staff provided details about the program, and Pearson became a dogged defender.

Propaganda remained the unspoken enemy. Welles pointed out in a national radio broadcast that the administration intended first to support the private world; at little cost, it would contribute to domestic growth and foreign affairs, and after the war it would grow—analogous offices in other countries managed large and fruitful programs. Admitting that foreign counterparts, especially in wartime, relied on propaganda, he reiterated the division's intention to avoid it at all costs; in any case, with its tiny staff, "it is obvious that this is not a propaganda agency." He closed with the pledge that the office would enrich human life.[32]

Welles and Duggan added staff. Charles Thomson came aboard as deputy, and an available foreign service officer just back from Paris, Edward Trueblood, was secunded. Welles insisted Cherrington visit Latin America. The two agreed on a single extended trip, to exchange ideas and think things through. Delegated to the December Inter-American Conference in Lima, Cherrington left Washington after only sixty days for a three-month trip. The conference began with a welcome by co-delegate Albert Giesecke, now advisor and unofficial CAO to the US embassy.

At home the division kept busy. First, it coordinated cooperative exchanges funded elsewhere via the Interagency Coordinating Committee (ICC); second, it cooperated with USOE to exchange students, teachers, and professors under the Buenos Aires Convention; third, it added three GAC subcommittees, for publications, translations, and films; fourth, it began building links between US universities and educational institutions and foreign counterparts; fifth, it coordinated all US government entities working abroad in education and culture.

The Hull mandate reached well over the horizon, miles beyond the division's grasp, but it was a sound road map. The mood was can-do and expansionist, as Hull wanted. One day a six-man Afghan delegation showed up unannounced to study the American police. Sending them off for a morning of sightseeing, staff got busy, and on their return that afternoon, each had been placed with a local police department. (There is no record of how the language problem was solved.) Without budget, the division staff leaned on available institutions in the sleepy capital and its suburbs; Washington's legendary cultural desert was quickly overharvested.[33]

Welles had shrewdly seized on Congress's decision to extend government personnel loans. He became a steely chairman of the ICC. With representation at the undersecretary level, ICC serviced loans of all government employees to other nations. Welles saw the potential in this idea: for one thing, Latin America had been turning for technical expertise to the Axis, which was eager to oblige. The "technical" fields were limitless: economic development, education, road building, geodetic surveys, library management, public health, water-resource management, dam building, and financial management, like that Morgan Shuster had provided for Haiti, the Philippines, and Iran three decades earlier. With ICC in 1938 came the birth of the technical assistance or training function of US cultural diplomacy, which was taken over in 1948 by Point IV-AID. Welles nailed down ownership and the division took charge, so that ICC exchanges were soon the center of its work. The division convinced Congress to allow foreign technicians to work in US agencies as well, and its bidirectional mode put the division on the prewar Washington map. ICC grew quickly, from coverage of eleven agencies to twenty-eight in 1944. In 1948 the division reported on its first decade: seventeen hundred Americans had gone abroad and two thousand foreigners had worked in the U.S.

ICC's two-way flow was misleading. It was in fact a one-way program: "teachers" moved south and "learners" north. But the division ducked the problem: it had established coordinative, authoritative, and non-threatening relationships with every US overseas-related agency in Washington and could broaden its mandate at will. It was now in a position to mold foreign requests to broader educational purposes. The outgoing American technicians, all "teachers" in one sense or another, made the division aware of foreign needs through reporting. The division had become, by Welles's initiative, the US government's technical assistance arm. The bonus: the understanding generated by two-way flow.

With this unanticipated injection of ICC power, the division suffered its first name-change, becoming the Division of Scientific and Cultural Cooperation. Congress in 1939 allocated ICC $370,000 and added an additional third for the division's general needs—half of the requested

$1 million. The green eyeshades in Congress were still skeptical, but the division had two irresistible claims: the successes of ICC and Buenos Aires.

In Lima Cherrington learned, with Giesecke at his elbow. Amid fears of impending war, the Lima Conference brought to life the mutual defense understanding between the U.S. and the South. It renewed the cultural resolutions of Buenos Aires and added thirty-six more. Cherrington followed with visits to all but two of the South American countries.

With his thinking fine-tuned and his commitment bolstered, Cherrington returned to State to kick off a division-wide discussion of goals. In March a draft budget request sought support for ICC plus $270,000. But Congress was beginning to fret about the division's demands. Cherrington notched up the throttle, asking for broad authority for the "stimulation and support of private exchange activities of all types" in the interests of "mutual understanding" as always. The private world helped in every way: Leland's ACLS linked the division to the humanities-based universities; USOE upgraded language and cultural studies in US schools and arranged short-term summer schools for Spanish; the division funded special travel for American students and "professionals," including journalists, doctors, dentists, and lawyers. To help Latin American students in the U.S., the division stimulated English teaching and hospitality; universities were urged to spread foreign students around the country rather than bunch them in a few centers. In the arts, things were also moving. For performing artists already traveling south under commercial management, facilitation and top-offs were offered.

By September 1939, with Cherrington's first year coming to an end, machinery for receiving foreign exchangees was in place—but there was little fuel; stateside cooperation had to be begged. Reviewing US college-admission practices, the division pleaded for closer cooperation between USOE, IIE, and hundreds of universities. Industrial fellowships were launched in Chile and Peru with companies like Grace, Dupont, GE, and Ingersoll-Rand. Ten Chilean engineers visited plants in the US northeast. Summer industrial, medical, and public health internships were introduced. USOE persuaded the American Council on Education (ACE) to ship university catalogs to all embassies. Hospitality for foreign visitors was provided by volunteer groups. With ICC growing, culturally oriented government agencies like the Smithsonian and the Library of Congress were forging intellectual links. Publications flowed in both directions; educational films, although designed for US audiences, went abroad.

The founders defined the division's work with three active verbs: *stimulate, facilitate,* and *coordinate.* Speaking to educators in November 1939, Hull sounded Jeffersonian: "This is not a task for government alone but for all of us: the teachers, the men of science and learning throughout the New World." With the same group, Welles dwelt on the junior-partner role of the government; the division was "a clearinghouse, a coordinating agency, whose purpose it is to collaborate in every appropriate way without trespassing upon and much less supplanting your activities." Again, Congress or staff were not involved in these meetings. And reluctance to admit that Americans needed to learn about others was feeding the division's natural ICC tilt—toward unidirectional information flow.

Funding grew steadily from the 1939 base of $500,000, but staff remained thin, with Congress regularly braking its growth; Congress declined for example to authorize an officer for radio affairs and refused a prescient request for an officer to cover "women's affairs"; it disapproved two roving high-prestige Cultural Counselors, traveling out to the field from the U.S. Resident cultural attachés for the field were also declined by Congress.

In August 1939 the principle of exchanges beyond the Buenos Aires Convention was accepted by Congress—without funding. Cherrington had always argued for gradual growth, but Congress had its own definition of gradualism. It was time for Cherrington to educate Congress, but Congress showed little interest in learning. Long-neglected needs were growing with startling speed, as world events pressed in.

Cherrington was building a national constituency. In October and November 1939 the division held four major conferences on cultural relations. More than a thousand prominent Americans, paying their own way, gathered in Washington to discuss exchanges in education, art and music, publishing and libraries, and medicine. ACLS, the New York Public Library, and PAU contributed to conference costs, making the division's expenditure for all four conferences an implausible $100. Shotwell's CIC, with Carnegie help, prepared the basic conference paper, a survey of US intellectual activities with Latin America.

As word of the new program trickled out, the division found welcoming ears among the national cultural leadership, who hoped Washington might help. Cherrington accepted all speaking invitations. To Welles in May 1940, he reported momentum. The budget had risen to $768,000 by July.

Cherrington was about to depart from State when the fall of France stunned Washington. Suddenly war was no longer unthinkable. But life went on as usual in the future-oriented division. Cherrington reaffirmed his decision to leave, turning things over to Charles Thomson while retaining the GAC chair. No thought seems to have been given to recruiting another politically skilled Cherrington; in the program the gradualist stress on the neutrals and on the postwar era was firmly in place.

A preoccupied Roosevelt was impatient. Certain now that war was on the way, he found the division's slow pace frustrating, failing to see that it had been built for postwar security and exchange, not wartime propaganda.

Cherrington's constituents were beginning to be heard in Congress. Division policy was sound, even allowing for the crypto-unidirectionalism embodied in ICC exchanges. But Thomson was not charismatic like Cherrington; he could not run the division, build constituencies, and charm money out of Congress all at the same time. In the White House the tiring FDR delegated oversight of the division to Vice President Wallace, a passable speaker of Spanish. The antielitist Wallace, former Secretary of Agriculture, was an enthusiast who insisted on reaching "the people." He too echoed Jefferson, speaking on Pan-Americanism in October 1939: "Our task, in collaboration with the twenty American republics, is to do a first-class job of laying a foundation for democracy in this hemisphere—for the kind of democracy that will conserve our soil and people for thousands of years to come." Wallace maintained a cultural realist viewpoint, eschewing idealism: "I do not wish to obscure the fact that an Old World upset by Communism, Fascism, and Nazism is bound to have the most serious repercussions. . . . The day will inevitably come when these systems will bring the utter misery which is inherent in them. Then it will be up to us in the New World, in a sensible, practical fashion and not in a premature idealistic way, to help."[34] With years of turmoil ahead, Wallace spoke as a profound cultural internationalist, concerned about people and their environment. But his populist passion raised problems for the division, which was constrained by limited budgets to work through elites.

Cherrington had kicked off a debate on cultural affairs and foreign policy that continued for two years in the GAC. The founders had built a mechanism to nurture cultural internationalism for decades to come, but they had underestimated Congress's skepticism, State's foot-dragging, presidential impatience, and the confusions of imminent war. Duggan, Cherrington, MacLeish, and Wallace knew perfectly well what was happening in Europe. But they put a higher value on looking ahead, building intellectual cooperation for the longer term, and thinking about the postwar years; they were building a structure of peace for the interdependent world they saw over the horizon.

They mistimed their journey and the international context. They could not have anticipated the lightning successes of Hitler and the Japanese; they underestimated the polycentric tactics of Roosevelt; and they were unprepared for the everyday disruptions of congressional politics. Fervent people of sharp but shorter vision arrived in Washington after Cherrington left and imposed the "wartime departures from tradition" superbly outlined by Ninkovich.[35] A towering leader, even Cherrington himself, might have balanced short and long-range issues; without him, the waters were roiling.

The specific product that war pressed on the division was the very propaganda the founders dreaded. Twenty years later Philip Coombs recalled the hostility of the American people and Congress toward "the dirty business of propaganda."[36] Thomson came up with a deft defense in 1942: "The technique of propaganda is generally similar to advertising; it seeks to impress, to 'press in.' The technique of cultural relations is that of education, . . . to 'lead out.' . . . The goal of cultural relations is something deeper and more lasting, the creation of a state of mind properly called 'understanding.' Understanding endures. It is a thing of the mind, rooted in knowledge and the conviction that is born of knowledge."[37] The distinction was clear, for those who cared to listen: both propaganda and cultural relations were necessary, but they were different—even contradictory—functions. Cherrington had said it: if propaganda was needed, it should be done by another agency.

When Cherrington returned to Denver, Japan was already deep into China; the invasion of Poland had begun a year earlier; France and England were at war with Germany; and in June 1940 France fell and Hitler held continental Europe. US involvement was obvious and inevitable. State entered the maelstrom of war with a cultural program superbly designed, conceived, and staffed for peace. The division, first without Cherrington, then without Welles and Duggan, would survive and prove its gradualist point. But it grew harder, in the swirling waters, to see the competition.

CHAPTER FOUR

Nelson Rockefeller and Other New Boys, 1940—1945

Whether we intended to do so or not, we have now undertaken . . . through official agencies to present . . . convincing proofs of the creativeness and vitality of our culture. To fail would be disastrous.

—A. MacLeish, 1940

THE DESIGNERS OF THE Division of Cultural Relations had built a mechanism to nurture American cultural internationalism for the rest of the century. Cherrington returned to Denver in 1940, leaving Charles Thomson in charge. Recruited from the Foreign Policy Association, he had been the perfect deputy. Cherrington still hovered over the division, as chair of the GAC. Thomson was CEO but Cherrington chaired the board.[1]

The division had lost a redoubtable champion who had barely found his stride when Cherrington left. The tiny office needed a full-time political leader like Cherrington who could maintain touch with, educate, and stroke Congress, someone who could fight off agency predators, deal as an equal with the heads of giant US institutions, weave spells from public platforms, and call in presidential artillery when needed. Instead, the division got a fine administrator and a monthly touch of the room-filling chairman.

While this internal shift was taking place, two kinds of new boys were about to descend on Washington in response to the war. The first to arrive on the scene, only six weeks after Cherrington left, was Nelson A. Rockefeller. No one connected the arrival and departure, not even FDR, who lured the young millionnaire with the vaguest of titles. FDR wanted a Republican by his side during the coming crisis. He had followed Welles's Latin American vision for eight years and was wary of "information"; he had also lived through the Creel years and feared putting such power in the hands of one man. Still, CPI's activism, in retrospect, made the Hull-Welles State Department look sluggish.

Rockefeller knew what he wanted better than FDR did. Like Creel, he insisted on working out of FDR's office, and he kept cabinet officers like Cordell Hull informed only when he wanted. He coveted Latin America for his own ends. Oblivious to precedent, he soon upended Welles's careful planning, as Ninkovich has shown. A point man for activism, he had no patience for learning what had already been achieved. He disregarded the division's elastic capacity to grow and do more, ignored the sound base on which it had been built, spurned ideas like reciprocity and binationalism, considered coordination a meaningless word, and did things his way. At various points, Welles tried reasoning with him, but Rockefeller was impatient with "office-boys," as he called FDR's son James; he responded only to Welles's power plays.

Knowing that FDR had made up his mind, and perhaps already aware that Rockefeller would agree to anything then forget it, Welles set about dealing with the bull in State's china shop. Unfortunately, he could not change a salient fact: the gradualist cultural component, despite superb building, patient constituency-building, and steady field progress, had little spectacular to report.

FDR, Dutchess County squire and ex-governor of his state, liked New Yorkers. He imported various New York wizards besides Rockefeller. In the summer of 1940 two of these touch on our story: James Forrestal and his young colleague Paul Nitze, both from the investment bank Dillon, Reed, and Company. Forrestal would soon get the job he craved, Secretary of the Navy, but while he waited, Roosevelt handed him the Rockefeller hot potato. Forrestal was to bring Rockefeller aboard, reshaping an earlier job description designed by Rockefeller and tailored to his energies. It had been brought to the president by advisors Anna Rosenberg and Beardsley Ruml, with help from Harry Hopkins. Forrestal set out to tame Rockefeller.

Grandson of the world's wealthiest man and second son to John D. Rockefeller Jr., the creator of modern philanthropy, Nelson had less going for him than it might seem.[2] He had missed being number one in a family that prized primogeniture. His school years proved him an ordinary student, hyperactive, dyslexic, and too small for major athletics. What he lacked in intellectual discipline, he made up for in vigor and drive; he did well in minor athletics and managed Dartmouth's football team. His gregarious nature, the ability to listen when he wanted to, the drive to excel, and the boistrous energy of a man with few doubts marked him throughout his life. After attending the liberal Lincoln School, he went to Dartmouth College, where he spent most of his time in the study of art and in extracurricular activities; he received regular tutorials from Dartmouth President Hopkins, a friend of the family.

The young graduate obediently followed older brother John D. III into his father's office, where he glimpsed life at the top from a variety of boards, which were of interest to his father but not to him. Gently breaking loose, he spent the 1930s in various entrepreneurial activities in New York, culminating in the building of the Rockefeller Center complex and in his mother's pet project, the Museum of Modern Art (MoMA).

His experience with the republics to the south, whose effusive bearhug style delighted him and shaped his manner, began during a two-month honeymoon trip around the continent in the spring of 1937. With his bride and entourage, he was received everywhere by Standard Oil executives and provincial governors, who sheltered the party from the sight of poverty. He was already known on the continent as "El Principe de la gasolina," the Oil Prince. In Peru, guided by the embassy's resident-educator-archeologist Albert Giesecke, he learned of the Peruvian government's inability to preserve and analyze a hundred or more pre-800 A.D. bundles from the tombs at Paracas. To convince Peru's president to do the job, he wrote a check.

He returned a year later to Venezuela, wearing a different hat. Having invested in Creole Petroleum, a Standard subsidiary, he decided to familiarize himself with the new company, learning slightly more Spanish and wandering about the oil fields. This time he encountered the underside and was struck by the ugly gap between managers and workers, much as his father had been shocked by the 1915 Ludlow Massacres. But unlike his father he lost no sleep over it. Another surprise came from Mexico's President Lázaro Cárdenas, whom he visited in an honest-broker attempt to get agreement between the expropriation-minded Mexican and the oil companies. But his charm had no effect on the committed Cárdenas, who was cloaked in national dignity and honor; the Mexican's passionate intransigence taught the self-confident thirty-year-old that he could not necessarily charm, arbitrate, or buy off tough antagonists.

Like his father, Rockefeller had seen the contradictions of power; unlike his father, who after the Ludlow incident declined to succeed his father, Nelson set about fixing things. Back home, the third-generation millionaire addressed a meeting of three hundred officials of New Jersey Standard warning that, unless the executives exercised corporate responsibility to "reflect the best interests of the people," their businesses would be taken away.[3] Creole Petroleum adopted education, medical assistance, public works, and other standard features of the Rockefeller Foundation program; reversing its image, it became a good corporate citizen, albeit too late to ward off expropriation.

Rockefeller leapt at a Venezuelan business venture: a first-class hotel for Caracas. The Avila, designed by his friend Wallace K. Harrison, an architect from the Rockefeller Center project, was built by Rockefeller's Fomento Venezolano (Venezuelan Development) and backed by a broad spectrum of investors, primarily oil companies plus Nelson and his brothers. A success as an architectural landmark, the Avila had a painful six-year startup before moving permanently into the black.

A generation younger than Henry Ford, Nelson had understood that responsible profit-oriented industries abroad would do well to practice corporate stewardship. Business could achieve what philanthropy had, while doing something that philanthropy could not—generating permanent jobs for thousands. Singer and Eastman had charted the corporate waters and now Big Oil was coming aboard, as Rockefeller pressed for socially sensitive investment in human development and job creation.

Nelson inherited his father's habit of surrounding himself with superb advisors. He needed them first to do his homework, then to curb his impetuous improvisations. Harrison was his indispensable deputy. His Washington connection was Anna Rosenberg, unofficial member of FDR's early brain trust. His economist was Beardsley Ruml, former Dean of Social Sciences at the Rockefeller-founded University of Chicago. Ruml, father of the pay-as-you-go withholding tax, was close to White House counselor and Social Gospel product Harry Hopkins.

Rockefeller's first priority upon entering FDR's administration was corporate-government partnerships throughout Latin America; but he also had a second agenda, having heard a lot about public relations and CPI from his family's advisor Ivy Lee, a distinguished CPI veteran. Rockefeller and Ruml showed Hopkins their plan to buy up surpluses generated by the closing of European markets, reduce tariffs, work with business for hemispheric investment and development, and refinance the subcontinent's external debts. A critical part of this plan was an advisory council of business executives. In parallel, the government would augment its diplomatic presence and initiate "a 'vigorous program' of cultural, educational and scientific exchange."[4] Hopkins signed on, but he could only open the door in June 1940, when military and economic threats focused Roosevelt's mind on the vulnerable southern hemisphere.

Nowhere in Cary Reich's meticulous biography of Rockefeller's early years is there an indication that the Coordinator was aware of burgeoning cultural exchange with Latin America, either in its missionary-educator beginnings, in State's labors of the preceding eight years, or in the Boxer model of binational and reciprocal sensitivity around which Welles, Duggan, and Cherrington had centered discussion. Nor does it seem to have occurred to him that a cultural outreach program limited to a single part of the globe was a contradiction in terms. For him, nothing was ever too complicated: Latin American exchanges had to be "initiated," the sooner and the more the better; and money was the means of initiation. The problem lay in his deeper purposes: he saw only unidirectional flows of information about the U.S. tied to development. Before USIA coined its motto, he wanted to "tell America's story" to the Latin Americans.

Action on the nomination of Rockefeller, compared to Washington's natural pace and the six-year gestation of the division, moved like quicksilver. Ruml and Rockefeller met Hopkins on Friday, 14 June. On 15 June Roosevelt's memo to State, Agriculture, Treasury, and Commerce urged action. On 17 June Hull, Welles, Henry Wallace, Hopkins, and Secretary of the Treasury Morgenthau met, repressed their annoyance at the memo's insouciant neglect of the past, and answered. On 18 June their cautious response reached the president, who immediately created a federal trading corporation for foreign surpluses. Rosenberg had to remind FDR about the indispensable high-level business advisory committee which was key to Rockefeller's plan.

Forrestal was immediately named as the head of the new body, to

Rockefeller's dismay. Ignoring his lack of interest in Latin America, FDR wanted Forrestal to smooth out the Rockefeller assignment before he moved on to Navy. Forrestal went into high gear, most significantly launching a secret program with Pan-American Airways to build a chain of airstrips all over Latin America and Africa for war supply when it might be needed. Meanwhile Nitze, son of a distinguished German-born philologist at the University of Chicago, was boning up on Latin America. Nitze and Forrestal set about designing "Forrestal's" job.

To the young millionaire, it looked as though FDR's right hand had forgotten his left. Forrestal and Nitze however, realized they were designing a job Rockefeller could handle. The cabinet memo of 18 June had counter-proposed that the Coordinator report not to the president but to the cabinet, but Nitze defended Rockefeller's idea of an office outside the cabinet structure. No fans of Rockefeller, he and Forrestal were doing FDR's bidding; they needed time to placate State and build consensus. They invited Rockefeller to spend a week or two in Washington "trying things out," but he declined. Instead, in early July, the three probed matters over a five-hour dinner at the F Street Club. The proposal was simple: while developing airstrips to eliminate the threat of Axis domination of local airlines, Rockefeller's office would initiate "a propaganda offensive . . . to counter a relentless Axis media blitz."[5] There were no nuances.

Forrestal's short list of potential directors placed Rockefeller third; but FDR was keen on his token Republican. On 26 July he invited the thirty-two-year-old to chair a joint government-private commission on Latin America, asking for a stronger stress "on the cultural and propaganda side of wartime diplomacy."[6] FDR and his drafter were unaware of any contradiction in the two words.

On 16 August Rockefeller was appointed Coordinator for Inter-American Affairs. The job description, wiser than the draft, omitted propaganda. The new office would coordinate "the *cultural* and *commercial* relations of the nation" with Latin America—another odd verbal marriage that never had been explicit before. Rockefeller added the phrase "to help national defense,"[7] completing the muddle. It was the kind of free-for-all he liked; he never moved far from this conflation of culture, commerce, defense, and implicit propaganda, except to add another dangerous noun: intelligence.

Welles and Duggan set to work to tame, educate, and contain the Co-ordinator but State's barons were less diplomatic. They barely concealed their outrage at Rockefeller's job, which to them meant an alternate Department of State for Latin America. As Ellis Briggs remembered it, "The appointment . . . astonished me. So did the news that he had been given $5 million with which to make friends, with a job description that, to the extent it was intelligible, appeared to duplicate the functions of State."[8]

From the viewpoint of cultural diplomacy, this sixty-day merry-go-round was not entirely a catastrophe, but it might have been, without Welles and Duggan. Rockefeller's presence forced the redefinition of eight years of consecutive discussion, involving hundreds of US and foreign educational and intellectual institutions. Now, the division faced a dynamic, activist, and competitive "partner," who geared his work toward imminent war; the cultural focus on the long range had become a by-product of a higher cause. The Coordinator's job description had another hidden flaw: it was wide open to intelligence and secret agreements, like the Pan-American airstrips. Rockefeller was soon wooing J. Edgar Hoover.

Rockefeller's idea was benign corporatism, heavily stressing economics and business—"commerce and culture," as he called it. The effects of this vision were embodied in what became known in Latin America as the *servicios*, entities created within a host government, with local staffing, to work with—or under—US technicians toward agreed-upon goals. These predecessors of the get-it-done Agency for International Development (AID) approach took the ICC technical assistance experience a step further, moving from training to action. The idea was guided binationalism in the paternalist mode: The *servicios* were in fact, Briggs noted, a way to let Americans run things.

Rockefeller's direct line to FDR and his devil-may-care ability to spend his own and others' money allowed him to hire the best. Bypassing personnel regulations, he used salary top-offs, arm-twisting, and private reimbursement. This gave him unprecedented—and unreplicable—human and financial flexibility in government. His name guaranteed access to top-level talent, as well as easy loans from the family's Chase Bank.

Rockefeller's style tended toward a hard version of the soft sell, but his concepts were unclear. For the culturalists, wedded to the long view, he was rocking the boat. For Forrestal, Nitze, and ultimately Roosevelt, the war came first. Propaganda had been rejected by Hull and Welles, but now it moved closer to the center; for Rockefeller culture was only a word. Despite Welles and Duggan, Creel had returned.

Rockefeller was committed to art and education, so long as it did not interfere with more important things. He knew that good culture was good propaganda; but in his haste propaganda became the end, culture the means.

At first, he did little coordinating. He launched an enormous range of activities, ruling tightly over all of them. "Coordination," for him, was not a gentle act of leadership through quiet knowledge and discreet persuasion; instead it was a defensive tactic, "the art of keeping all balls in the air without losing one's own," he said. From the beginning he failed to understand—and none of his high-powered staff could convince him—that it was wiser to cooperate with State than fight it. State's cultural division already had put in place a strong, meticulously defined, and expansible structure for exchanges, heartily supported by US and Latin American intellectuals; the division had made coordination of other agencies' work part of its routine, thanks to Welles's ICC. But Rockefeller's overwhelming style repelled the professionals, and his unorthodox activism destabilized a division committed to gradualism. Tough-minded diplomats in State found Rockefeller's charm eminently resistible, from Welles and Acheson to Spruille Braden and Briggs. USIA historian Lawson, writing twenty years later, judged him a "potpourri of arrogance, ignorance, and inexperience," citing an unnamed diplomat—sounding suspiciously like Briggs—who wrote: "With uninfectious enthusiasm he operated a duplicate Latin American Bureau, peddling the taxpayer's largesse and generating confusion."

Designed to last beyond the war, the division's facilitative approach could have activized and expanded without difficulty—as the British and French cultural services had. Instead the tiny office was outhustled and outshone by the Rockefeller rodeo; worse, it was increasingly ignored, first by Roosevelt and ultimately by Congress. To Rockefeller's credit, once his team glimpsed the advantages of working with Welles's team, he turned over generous slices of his funding to the division. But he never saw that full cooperation might have produced the very things he wanted and that they might have lasted longer.

One close Rockefeller advisor, Dean Robert Caldwell of MIT, quickly understood what the division represented and tried to move the two bodies closer. The Coordinator's five sectors of responsibility, perhaps as drafted by Caldwell, paralleled the division's. Cherrington asked Caldwell to join his GAC.

Rockefeller wanted to do things never done before, and he wanted to do them his way. He was drawn to the Forrestal-Nitze tactical stress, captivated by the idea of combining growth and profit, and lured by the comforting assumption that State could do nothing right and would prefer—as he saw it—to do nothing at all. His first call was on Vice President Henry Wallace, with whom he arranged to play tennis every day at 6 A.M.

He paid another early visit to the FBI's Hoover, who with his Latin American chief Percy Foxworth accepted the invitation to cooperate. Rockefeller blithely offered Hoover cover assignments for FBI agents throughout the southern hemisphere, precisely as the Nazis had done. His first joint project with the FBI aimed at "purifying" US businesses in Latin America. After a three-man team led by Foxworth traveled south to measure the extent of Axis commercial penetration into US business, Rockefeller accepted their report uncritically and announced publicly that precisely seventeen hundred employees of US firms in Latin America were Axis agents. Letters signed by him went to the home-offices of these American firms, suggesting they "voluntarily" fire these people. Only General Motors's Alfred Sloan was outraged enough to resist, but even Sloan soon folded under the Coordinator's smiling blackmail: purge, or we let it be known that GM refuses to fire "known Nazis." A second FBI blacklist entered more delicate terrain, targetting Latin American–owned businesses: this time there were precisely eighteen hundred Axis-related firms; now, "compliance was no longer voluntary."[9] Forrestal was delighted, and Rockefeller had made a friend in Hoover. Others, at home and abroad, were horrified. The Coordinator ignored the dissonance: speaking to a House committee, he referred darkly to the "flood of insidious Axis propaganda."

In Reich's reading of the records, the Coordinator overlooked all crushed toes, duplication, and counter-productivity; his new team was too busy to worry about hurt feelings among the office-boys. To tame him, Welles sent Duggan, whose younger brother Stephen Jr. had been Rockefeller's classmate at the Lincoln School. The gentle yet incisive Duggan began the process of calming things down.

Then Rockefeller handed Welles the perfect excuse to go over his head to FDR: a madcap episode, not untypical, that involved Rockefeller's campaign to buy Latin American newspaper space, at lavish rates in thousands of dailies, for promoting US tourism with eye-catching supplements—good general propaganda, he said. Newspapers supporting the Axis were included in the program because they might be lured to the US side. Reaction was swift. Latin editors immediately saw through the obvious attempt to buy propaganda space and were outraged; they derided the idea because visiting the U.S. was impossible when all transportation was committed to the war effort and because the trip would cost middle-level workers in South America most of their annual salary.

Welles convinced Roosevelt to come down hard. FDR signed Welles's draft letter, which spelled out Welles's clear authority over Rockefeller—but behind the scenes, notes Reich, the president encouraged Rockefeller to continue. FDR's letter insisted that State be kept informed, so Welles named Duggan State's principal link to the Coordinator's office, while Welles himself met weekly with Rockefeller. Soon Rockefeller transferred some of his cultural activities to the division. The new Joint Committee on Cultural Relations included Thomson and Rockefeller's alter ego Wallace Harrison; it was chaired by ACLS's Waldo Leland, who covered the academic sector. Thanks to Duggan and Thomson, Welles and the Coordinator kept uneasy peace for the next two years.

Rockefeller lost no momentum over the contretemps, which to him were trivial. Soon he proposed that field committees of private Americans be set up in each Latin American country—an idea mentioned in Hull's letter. In Rockefeller's model these committees would answer not to State but to him. He slipped the idea past an under-informed FDR, and from then on, there were two official American missions in most Latin countries, one reporting to Hull in State and a second "private" group, led by business, reporting to Rockefeller.

The Coordinator was frying larger fish than the division, with long-range plans of his own. He had a sizable budget and the best staff in Washington; he had his name and his money behind him. His ubiquitous activities, even in retrospect, defy summary. Promoting "his" programs everywhere, never failing to depict the "insidious penetration" of the Axis, wedding "culture" to every word he could, he deployed his power to remarkable effect. In the nonprofit sector, for example, his connections in the arts led to tours by Dartmouth pal Lincoln Kirstein and his "Ballet Caravan," by left-of-center sculptor Jo Davidson to do portraits of Latin American presidents, and by a MoMA show of contemporary US art in ten cities. With a few personal checks, he launched archeological expeditions in seven different countries. At field level the unidirectional flow of artistic and intellectual ventures was impressive. Like Creel, of course, he was setting a style which could not possibly outlive him, but that was no concern of his. As in the CPI era, it was obvious to Latin Americans that the foul-weather gringo friends were at it again.

With modern art, he had unknowingly stumbled into a congressional minefield. MoMA's exclusive focus on contemporary and abstract art raised know-nothing hackles, including those of a Missouri senator named Harry Truman. With a little patience and flexibility, Rockefeller might have worked things out with Congress; instead, the traveling MoMA show damaged the cause of overseas art exhibits for decades to come. Performing arts events were less controversial. Partial assistance from government to traveling performers had begun under the division, and now with more support, they became a standard, if erratic and one-way, US instrument.

State's professionals grumbled. Briggs in Cuba "was soon on the receiving end of messages emanating from the Coordinator, whose staff included a number of young men who had tried to get into the Foreign Service but had failed to do so." He was not the only diplomat who thought Rockefeller, with hard work, might have made a decent vice consul.[10]

In sectors where profit might be generated, Rockefeller was inventive. He plugged American corporations into a vast underdeveloped market, mingling government funds and personal connections. He worked out a plan for US railroads to help upgrade the Mexican system. He worked with radio and the communications industry. For Hollywood and films, he hired his millionnaire friend Jock Whitney, who installed his man in the famous Hays Office, home of Hollywood self-censorship, to make sure that Latin Americans were depicted favorably. With Chase's guaranteed loans in hand, Whitney convinced Walt Disney to make two Latin-friendly films, *Saludos Amigos* and *The Three Caballeros*. He helped the budding Mexican film industry and arranged American investment in Mexican feature films if they passed his criteria.[11] On the curtailing side, Whitney managed to make sure that films he thought unrepresentative were not exported south, including—incredible as it seems to us now— Frank Capra's classic *Mr. Smith Goes to Washington*. The impact of US films and newsreels was massive in a continent eager for the new medium— "even the State Department was impressed," noted Reich.

In the print media, with the assistance of Henry Luce and the editors of *Life*, Rockefeller started a Latin American look-alike, *En Guardia*. In two months the magazine's circulation reached 200,000, then moved past half a million. The Germans paid it the compliment of publishing an imitation, *De Guardia*, which did poorly. *Reader's Digest* began publishing editions in Spanish and Portuguese. Under the supervision of ALA's Carl Milam, three major American libraries were set up in Latin America, led by the flagship Benjamin Franklin Library in Mexico City; Creel-like reading-rooms sprang up everywhere.

In radio, success was spectacular and profitable. Rockefeller persuaded William Paley of CBS to put together La Cadena de las Americas, a Latin American radio network which began with sixty-four stations in eighteen countries and grew from there; CBS provided the network with shortwave transmissions for rebroadcast and a daily fifteen-minute newscast. He subsidized the World Wide Broadcasting Foundation, which operated two of twelve US stations broadcasting in the South.[12] Rockefeller was generating jobs and wealth, at home and abroad.

Some of his ventures were mad; one abandoned project tried to connect the Amazon with the Orinoco by a canal the size of six Panamas; another scheme involved building a fleet of wooden transport ships and had disastrous results. The most successful project was the Institute of Inter-American Affairs, inspired by Wyckliffe Rose's public health work with the Rockefeller Foundation; it fostered investment throughout Latin America in public infrastructure—sanitation, public health, road-building, and the like.

Welles finally squelched Rockefeller's openness to intelligence. In the only display of terse anger that ever sullied their friendship of convenience, Welles issued a steely instruction to end his ill-concealed relations with the FBI immediately, reminding him that even the slightest scent of intelligence, in the high-strung and paranoid Latin American context, would destroy everything they had achieved. Rockefeller agreed and dashed on ahead.

Jumbling the words "commerce," "information," and "propaganda" and linking them to "culture," Rockefeller's disruptive ventures were a mixed bag: they were transformational, as Ninkovich has shown, yet they set dangerous precedents. They were less catastrophic than they might have been because his activities in the field were managed by men and women with a fairly clear idea of the boundaries, a sense of what Latin Americans would accept, and an understanding that Axis actions were not to be imitated. The game was slowly moving to "information," but the culturalist approach was far from dead, especially in field posts. In 1943 the Coordinator's flamboyant claims of success to Congress, impossible to prove or disprove, delighted the normally dour legislators. But his success abroad raised warning flags. As the war moved toward its end, with his friend Wallace cheering from the sidelines, the whole effort began to look to Congress like a Latin American extension of the New Deal. The war mode concealed harder questions: was the program's lavish style sustainable? Were its priorities straight? Were the expectations he raised advantageous to the U.S., immediately and over time? Could cultural affairs in good faith share quarters with propaganda?

When the Coordinator began at last to coordinate rather than usurp division functions, the division expanded. By late 1943, as the war passed from defense to offense, many of Rockefeller's cultural and educational activities were flowing through the division—10 percent of the Coordinator's budget, or over $3 million—leaving $27 million, of course, for Rockefeller. The division's quadrupled budget did not come without strings—Rockefeller was buying into their operations. It was no longer a question of stimulate-coordinate-facilitate. Now, with greater aggregate budgets including its ICC partners' contributions, the division was reluctantly sliding toward activism, unidirectionalism was daily more dominant, and quality control was weakening.

In the field the business committees and the USIS posts worked more closely than they had, as commerce and government cooperated. The theoretical binational overlay of the development-oriented *servicios* was only convenient window dressing, but the scholarship process, built around embassy Committees on Study and Training, was honest binationalism, managed by representatives of both nations' academic worlds. In January 1945, when new director MacLeish absorbed the Coordinator's functions into the division—and Rockefeller was put in charge of State's Latin American affairs—much that was positive had already been assimilated into the division. But the initial premises had blurred.

Few left a mark on US informational and cultural diplomacy like Rockefeller's, especially on the future USIA's activities and on the yet-unborn idea of Public Diplomacy, an accidental, ill-defined and contradictory mix of cultural relations and propaganda, vaguely resembling public relations. In the free, easy and well-funded early 1940s, the Coordinator and his gifted team invented virtually every tool USIA would ever use, *pace* Creel: he brought the arts into every US embassy, and he made US libraries abroad a global expectation. At the same time, no one bears more responsibility for breaking down the finely-wrought distinctions, none of them accidental or capricious, between cultural relations and unilateral information, or between cultural diplomacy and psy-warfare and propaganda, or between private commerce and the public function. Only educational exchanges, especially after their Fulbright component lent strength, managed to avoid Rockefeller's stamp.

• • •

After 1942 there were new boys in town besides Rockefeller. Some immediately wanted cultural tools for their own causes and casually appropriated what they wanted—Roosevelt's polycentric tactics encouraged such proliferation, and none of these tools were copyrighted. Welles argued that—by law—anything the government did abroad in education or training had to pass through State, but when he left State in 1943, ICC's central coordinative power slowly oozed away—State, in fact, held only a mandate based on Welles's reading of international law, and it was soon challenged.

Four large-scale men who would shape cultural diplomacy arrived in Washington between 1939 and 1943, two supporters and two predators. The first in chronology, named Librarian of Congress in 1939, was a friend: Archibald MacLeish. The next two—the colorful Col. "Wild Bill" Donovan and Elmer Davis—would poach freely on the cultural-informational function from their newfound platforms. The fourth arrived last in 1943 as a newly elected young member of Congress, driving his family to the capital from Arkansas for a stay that lasted more than four decades: former president of the University of Arkansas J. William Fulbright.

Turning to the predators Donovan and Elmer Davis, Donovan, a hero of World War I, came first. He, like the Coordinator, had the outlines of a big job and total control in his mind; he proceeded to carve out more than FDR foresaw. Told at the outset that his principal work was to be propaganda, he called himself the Coordinator of Information (COI), a title that would have astonished even Creel, since in this case the word "information" clearly included "intelligence." When Davis entered the scene, Donovan had to shift to a blander name, the Office of Strategic Services (OSS), melding psychological warfare with derring-do covert operations. OSS would mutate into the CIA in 1947.

The founders of US cultural diplomacy, following the French and the British, had set out explicitly *not* to do propaganda, but Donovan, clearly, had no such inhibitions. Not surprisingly, he instantly clashed with Rockefeller over responsibility for propaganda in the south. Rockefeller won, keeping Donovan out of Latin America. Suddenly the Coordinator realized Welles could be a useful friend.

All three men were challenged in turn by Elmer Davis, a respected Midwestern news-broadcaster with an equally imprecise mandate. Staying out of Latin America, Davis soon came to terms with Donovan about splitting COI: Donovan's OSS moved over to make room for Davis's Office of War Information (OWI). At Harvard, young Austrian scholar Walter Roberts was recruited by historian William Langer for his unique research and analysis group in COI; Roberts remembers the almost random division of COI, at the recommendation of British advisors Mark Abrams and Leonard Miall, who came to Washington to make sure COI worked closely with the BBC. Because Abrams and Miall were concerned only about Europe, Rockefeller never heard their two major points: (1) separate information from intelligence, and (2) never mix white or "true" propaganda with black or the unattributed variety. Donovan agreed to go black, while Davis would deal with whites and greys; Rockefeller stayed with Latin America. In the haphazard division of COI, Roberts went with OWI to New York to analyze German propaganda and guide US radio response, a prelude to a distinguished career in USIA and broadcasting.

Research and analysis stayed in OSS, where Langer's extraordinary team of scholars, a platoon or two of the best historians in America, set to work understanding the enemy. Overall, the division of functions was random. OSS—rather than OWI—was given, over the heads of Welles and Rockefeller, a mandate to monitor all foreign broadcasts, so that the Foreign Broadcast Information Service (FBIS), which might have become the "Ears of America," remains to this day an open subsidiary of the CIA.

OWI handled US propaganda, the kind aimed at allies and neutrals, as well as information flow within the U.S. The Rhodes scholar and highly trusted CBS newsman Davis held nothing approaching Creel's power; indeed he faced impressive competition and constraints. He also had more scruples than the CPI director. He chose a powerful deputy who had spent the 1930s as chief information officer for the Department of Agriculture, future-educator Milton Eisenhower. With a small army of media professionals, Davis hammered out OWI's role in tough fights with Donovan and Rockefeller. To no one's surprise, OWI drew heavily on CPI experience, good and bad.

OWI for a brief moment absorbed MacLeish and his Office of Facts and Figures (OFF), founded at the president's request as an independent long-range think-tank, with a stable of brilliant intellectuals like Lasswell, Schlesinger, McGeorge Bundy, and Adlai Stevenson. MacLeish and OFF focused on thinking about the war, explaining war goals to Americans, reflecting on the US postwar role, and preparing the nation for the responsibilities of war's aftermath. Their tools were public pronouncements and speeches for the White House and other agencies. MacLeish smelled trouble as soon as OFF moved inside OWI. Named OWI's assistant director for policy development, he asked that OWI accept, as a continuing function, that his office serve as a catalyst for US thinking about the war and the aftermath. But he rammed into a stone wall in Davis and Eisenhower, who decreed that OWI would handle the news and only the news. MacLeish resigned and returned to the Library of Congress, OFF disbanded, and its staff scattered, some into OWI and others into OSS. From the library, MacLeish did occasional speechwriting—and regular bartending—for FDR.

MacLeish had known Welles, the Duggans, Thomson, and Cherrington for years. As senior editor of *Fortune*, Henry Luce's carriage-trade business magazine, he was part of the New York internationalist group. In 1940 his farseeing article on cultural diplomacy appeared in *The Nation*. From the Library, with the help of ALA's Milam, he had always kept close tabs on the division.

One other player remained above the fray but managed, from his position, to add to the confusion: the well-intentioned Vice President Wallace, tennis partner of the Coordinator. The overworked FDR had delegated oversight of the division to him, perhaps because he spoke passable Spanish. Wallace's populism and enthusiasm brought a new ripple of disarray to the division, as he disregarded the limitations of minimal budgets and challenged its bare-bones, trickle-down focus on national elites. Wallace on the subject of reaching "the people" found an audience in Rockefeller. The unusual vice president, with clear native brilliance, was seen by much of Washington as an enigmatic eccentric; Rockefeller instead considered him the only conceivable successor to FDR. As the president's representative on Cherrington's GAC, Wallace naturally stressed the war effort. But he also introduced three problematic objectives: first, waving aside costs, he wanted division programs to reach the masses; second, he assumed that economic and social development in the poor nations was a US responsibility; and third, he wanted the division to take responsibility for the *substantive* content of mass-oriented information tools like radio and films. These targets were beyond the division's reach, but they suited Rockefeller.

All this Potomac maneuvering was turning attention away from the division, Cherrington, Thomson, and long-range planning. OSS, OWI, and the Coordinator brought benefits to the division along with costs. The most important of the benefits was a resolution of the field representative problem. The new agencies overlooked Messersmith's earlier veto and recruited outstanding American area scholars for the USIS posts. Noteworthy academic figures immediately showed up on OSS and OWI payrolls around the world with the title of PAO or CAO: sinologist John King Fairbank in Chungking, Middle East archeologist Frank E. Brown in Beirut, Sanskritist Norman Brown in Delhi, and Iran missionary-scholar T. Cuyler Young in Tehran, to mention only a few.[13] It was a noteworthy consensus: OWI, OSS, the Coordinator, and the division all agreed that distinguished academics, like Langer's team in Washington, were needed in the field. These pioneer CAOs helped define the job.

Like CPI, OWI felt free to use intellectuals often. In London, Ferdinand Kuhn's division for British affairs brought in anthropologist Margaret Mead to smooth the rough edges caused by the GI presence; with her British scholar-husband Gregory Bateson, she toured US military camps in 1943 and published, in US and British magazines, "The Yank in Britain." Columbia historian Allan Nevins wrote a survey of US history for use in British schools and later, prefaced by the US ambassador, his *Brief History of the U.S.* PAO London Herbert Agar's office had three branches: news, a reference library, and "the slow media"—this was the informationists' name for education and cultural affairs.[14]

Roosevelt had jerry-rigged the ultimate Rube Goldberg machine for cultural diplomacy and placed it in the hands of strong ego-driven men. Few nations could have survived such misorganization and few could have commanded such talent. Wallace pressed for reaching "the people." OSS, with its highly academic research and analysis division under Langer, scholars in the field, and analysis of foreign broadcasting, handled black propaganda and clandestine operations with the military. OWI's informational activities, more discreet at home than Creel's, fed controled information to allies and neutral nations. The Coordinator was king in Latin America for everything: economic and commercial development, white and grey propaganda, the US image in the southern continent, and some intelligence. Meanwhile the embattled division in State was gradually expanding two-way exchanges with Latin America through ICC, and a growing global exchange program aimed at the long range. Needless to say, overlap was rife.

The chaos was not visible to the casual observer, nor probably to any but the most perceptive field participants. USIS posts collected available resources with civility, worrying no more than Washington about ideas. From the division's viewpoint, sacred definitions worked out over a decade were being trampled, while its staff hung on valiantly. For Rockefeller, culture was only a word but the division lived by clear definitions.

Two sacred ideas came under attack from several directions: balanced two-way flow, and the university model. Rockefeller, OWI, and OSS were unidirectional and media-based. The Welles-Duggan-Cherrington idea of dialogue, binationalism, and balanced learning drew on the university ideal. The influx of people from the media and from advertising, given their predominance in the field as PAOs, meant that the model was shifting from the university toward a refined form of public relations. Having graduated to permanence as a continuing agency, the division watched the "real" world—in fact, the false world of wartime—using culture as a tool rather than a purpose.

• • •

In Washington, the war had upset planning. But in the field, USIS posts wanted money, people, and programs. The division worked in Latin America, with token activities in China, South Asia, the Near East, and a few neutral countries. Since Congress had declined to consider a separate cultural field budget for the division, OWI owned the field posts. The field scholars and the division saw each other as natural allies, but the division had little formal say over the academics in the cultural positions abroad. OWI ran the show, collegially but firmly, and the division lent support.

The USIS enclaves, with predictable collegiality, had no trouble working closely with the Coordinator's private committees: Americans, being American, worked as a family, doing the best they could in apparent harmony. A more restrained version of CPI had come back to life, bigger, arguably better, certainly better funded, and more extensive, but this time, Washington direction was scattered in at least four agencies. On-the-ground officers overlooked the details, so long as they got the goods. Foreign audiences too, seeing impressive activity by "the Americans," had little idea whether the money came from OWI, OSS, the Coordinator, State, the foundations, or the Mission Board.

Welles and the uncoordinated Coordinator found relative peace, faced with outside pressures, but Rockefeller's unrelenting exuberance still made boundary management a nightmare. In his regular meetings with Welles and Duggan, Rockefeller always agreed on boundaries, but things had to be hammered out anew every day. Ultimately the decisions were not based on structure and concept but on persistent energy. Still, Welles and Rockefeller made common cause. Welles had not foreseen that the tools of cultural diplomacy would tempt others. The understaffed division could not resist; it needed the money and personnel that Congress refused. The professional publicists among the newcomers puffed their agencies and made them look glamorous. The more reticent division resisted such high-ego show-and-tell. At the top, an ailing president stirred the pot when it suited him. He had divided Creel's power and eliminated one danger, but his tactics kept a talented team off balance.

Available money calls tunes and corrupts ideas; so it did with the division. After careful beginnings, with budgets inching up from half a million, money—more perhaps than could wisely be spent by the small staff—now flowed through the division into the field. Cherrington, Welles, and later Fulbright insisted on gradualism in what they controled. MacLeish, another gradualist, knew what serious commitments the division would bequeath to the future; he also knew the difficulty of recruiting and involving honest American scholars, intellectuals, and artists. Fulbright, who after 1946 kept the division on an even keel for almost thirty years, saw gradualism as a matter of honesty. In the field the slow growth would not frighten anyone or destabilize any economies; at home, learning to spend the money well would surely set a permanent US postwar style for global cultural outreach.

The eager Coordinator kept the division happy by sharing his budget, while deploying his usual mix of private funds, easy loans, and outside talent. Congress's squeeze on division budgets had stunted the program, but Rockefeller shifted $3 million and sixteen personnel slots to the division. Duggan, with Thomson's three-man Joint Committee for Coordination, smoothed things over inside State; dining at the giant's table, the division seemed to grow stronger.

Still, it fell short of the founders' plans. Espinosa, who did not arrive in the division until 1947, reported the veterans' sense of diminishment—Rockefeller's office dwarfed the division. Backed into defensiveness, the division did things for which it was unready, and its bureaucratic power faded with Welles's and Duggan's departures in 1943. Except for Cherrington's GAC, the division was on its own.

Rockefeller's budget in 1941 began at $3.5 million and by 1945 had soared to $30 million. Beyond generous federal budgets and private means, his unprecedented freedoms—guaranteed loans, easy contracting, alliances with competent private bodies, and freewheeling personnel practices—meant he could hire and fire anyone he pleased. He channeled government funds through the big foundations themselves, e.g. for

"Inter-American Fellowships"—an early example of government-funded corporate philanthropy. In service to and cooperation with Welles's vision, their joint power would have been world-shaping, but Rockefeller never managed to see Welles as anything but a useful enemy.

The division's output grew impressively. A review of the years 1938–48 listed more than three thousand division exchanges, thirty-seven hundred ICC government-to-government exchanges, and another three thousand for the Coordinator[15]—nearly ten thousand exchanges by the end of 1948, roughly one thousand per year in only forty countries, roughly 25 per country each year.[16] For the purposes of a comparison, thirty years later at a high point, in 180 countries, the average per country did not exceed twenty-eight.

The division's core values had been distorted by World War II, as Ninkovich concludes in his fine chapter on "departures from tradition." Welles's 5-percent bargain had been overtaken by the activists. The division was funding, initiating, and acting. Soon "the private sector was beginning to relinquish its former primacy in funding and policymaking."[17] What once seemed discreet, dignified, respectful, and binational had gone dynamic, and the division was more ready to serve short-range US purposes.

In the prewar spring of 1941, writer Thornton Wilder, in a long and tough-minded report on a trip to Colombia, Ecuador, and Peru, attacked the principal danger he saw in the US approach: unidirectionalism. He urged Americans to *earn* Latin American respect; he wanted to "prepare" in Latin American minds a favorable view of US disinterestedness, of the US commitment to democracy and its defense, and of US cultural maturity; he wanted Americans to stop preaching and listen. Writer-editor Erwin Canham, member of the GAC, came to the same conclusion: the division's work was far too improvisatory.[18] In the fears of these perceptive participant-intellectuals, who knew perfectly well that truth was war's first casualty, cultural diplomacy might be its second. They were comfortable with the division's original plan of presenting a sense of US continuity and honesty, while calming fears of the American behemoth.

From Wilder's strict viewpoint, the Oil Prince was the wrong man for the job. Welles, knowing that empires generate ambivalence and hatred, tried to set the U.S. on a different course in Latin America; he tried to reduce historic mistrust over time and to reshape Monroe's unacknowledged hegemonic vision. But well-intentioned energies, in Rockefeller's case based on the assumption that bonds would grow naturally from US-owned commerce, were rocking the boat. Unidirectional information—propaganda—was his way of expanding the American dream. In the North, Americans had swallowed the new arts of advertising, and other nations would too; only a few spoilers—like Wilder and Canham, and Mock and Larsen in their CPI study—foresaw problems. In the field ingenious Americans were handling both unidirectional and bidirectional information, both cultural relations and propaganda; they did so with little concern for the blood feuds in Washington.

Field representation had been assured, for the moment. Accepting a share of the responsibilities on Hull's endless list, embassy staff burdens grew; even Messersmith knew special hands and minds were needed. The specialized staff in place doing the cultural work in Latin America was led in the field by three bosses: the PAO, the ambassador's team, and the Coordinator's freestanding local committees. The CAO was already "the man in the middle," as Frankel would call him. The media dubbed them "contact men," or people who help reporters get the story.[19]

The embassies were headed by newly professionalized diplomats, many of whom mistrusted "unfocused activity." But cultural work, by its very nature, was unfocused: at its best, it was exploratory, trial-and-error, sometimes even playful.[20] Some embassies were delighted to turn such things over to local committees. Ellis Briggs believed until the end of his life that government should never have gone into cultural work in the first place.

The new cultural attachés mounted remarkable activities. In the field program the slow pace—e.g., academic process—clashed with eagerness to get things done. The division insisted on quality and reflected the educator's conviction that every educational experience is a unique, potentially life-changing moment requiring careful design. But OWI was already asking field posts to measure performance quantitatively, by the numbers of "locals" moving north, Americans moving south, and books circulated by the library. Reciprocity was easy to overlook: staging Kirstein's Ballet Caravan was hard enough without worrying whether the host-nation would ever send a ballet company to the U.S. So the Welles team stretched "reciprocity" to mean a relatively balanced two-way flow of people, infomation, and cultural goods, knowing that US student interest in Latin America would never match rising Latin student interest in the U.S.

Among the nonacademic grants, the "leader" program—short-term grants, three months in the early days, for foreign visits to the U.S.—had already swung toward unidirectional values and political utility. Despite the division's efforts to balance the program's unilateral direction, foreigners continued to come to the U.S. to learn while Americans went abroad to teach. Short-term visits had been taking place since 1938— actually since 1885, if we remember the inter-American conference that year during which two dozen delegates traveled all over the U.S. by special train. By "leaders," the division meant not only politicians but men and women at the top of their sciences, disciplines, universities, or professions. As for return visitors from the U.S., who were implicitly supposed to represent this same broad array of fields, they were far fewer. Wallace and his friend Louis Rabaut (D-Minn.), czar of the House Appropriations Committee responsible for the division's budget, made matters worse by insisting that exchanges include practical and technical fields like public health, agriculture, engineering, and secondary-school teaching. Embassies resisted these technical professionals, looking for political professionals instead. After the war, with tighter budgets and steady pressures for visible impact, the design of a cultural program with long-range political usefulness would slowly mutate into a political program with dwindling educational value. As early as 1944, the political by-product was becoming the primary message.

Other field realities, beyond division control, had impact on the total program: e.g., the visa policy dictated by Congress. When the communist Chilean poet Pablo Neruda or the Italian Socialist Pietro Nenni or the Catholic and Gaullist philosopher Jacques Maritain were denied visas or grants during or after the war, the U.S. threw away opportunities to educate powerful world voices and prove to skeptics that US hospitality was not restricted to those who agreed with US policy.[21] Efforts to separate social democrats and socialists from communists met know-nothing resistance from mythic figures like California Senator Knowland, for whom "it was all the same goddam thing."

Retuning its wartime work to compete with Rockefeller-generated expectations, the division adopted an up-tempo slogan: "solidarity of democratic morale in the hemisphere." The slogan became a theme that skewed the program even further toward tactical political goals. First, it was difficult to persuade Americans to define "democratic" in ways that covered more than the unique US version. Second, world curiosity about the unique American democratic synthesis ran doubtlessly deep, but foreign nations had other things on their minds. Third, explaining US democracy—like adapting the US Constitution—was impossible without understanding comparative legal systems and national histories. Without such background, lectures on US democracy soon wore thin. Finally, the imposition of a single theme, in a program originally designed to "educate," or open dialogue on all subjects, was another step toward unidirectionalism.

Tight funding brought its own distortions. With high Latin demand for serious US study, the underbudgeted division agreed to provide travel grants for those admitted on their own to US universities, which stretched finances, encouraged foreign educational investments, helped sort out the best, and stimulated US university cooperation. But the idea overlooked the fact that control over selection, and hence the quality of students, was weakened. Moreover such travel grants went only to the wealthy.

The splendid libraries were reciprocal only in the sense that, through internships, they taught professional librarianship. Creel's reading rooms had moved to another level when Rockefeller had built three ALA-designed libraries of excellence, sparked by Mexico City's Franklin Library—headed by New York Public Library director Harry Lydenberg. Dozens of expanded reading rooms in Mexico were staffed by ALA professionals and stocked by ALA criteria. After the war, staffing and book selection would gradually be taken over by USIA.

Binational centers (BNCs), many of them, like the Chilean-American Cultural Institute, left over from CPI, raised other problems. Their governance had never been easy—nothing binational is. The Coordinator knew the word "binational" raised sensitive questions when applied to a fully funded US operation. He clumsily tried to conceal US government funding from his local committees by channeling funds through Waldo Leland's ACLS, but the ruse fooled only Americans. State, again urged by Messersmith, limited new BNCs, on grounds they would open doors for Axis "friendship societies." But Rockefeller's committees brushed the policy aside and new BNCs cropped up all over the southern hemisphere, with no thought as to how they would survive after the war. As with the libraries, once Washington paid the piper, it wanted to call the tune; and the compliant BNCs, with US directors, saw no problem, drifting into comfortable subsidy.

The new field activities were impressive, but they chipped away at the ideal of two-way dialogue. By 1944 much division activity focused on interpreting and projecting—or advertising—the U.S. abroad. Any idea of educating Americans about foreign cultures was mothballed; there was a war to be won and no time for frills. Even Rockefeller, a fervent advocate of US learning, had his own ideas about what such learning entailed. The division's original plan had been to move people in both directions, so that they would both learn and teach, but Rockefeller's purposes followed ICC's: teach foreigners, whether here or there. Shorter-term exchanges began outnumbering the longer stays which permitted learning in depth. The promote-America slant, especially natural in neutral countries, revealed an inherently competitive streak as American enthusiasts found themselves comparing America unfavorably with Britain and France.

Unbalanced exchanges, undirectionalism, and non-reciprocity bothered only the division. In the early Rockefeller wave, Ninkovich saw US cultural programs reversing "traditional conceptions of the legitimate role of governmental cultural activities—whether of the national interest or of the liberal universalist variety, both of which emphasized reciprocity and the primacy of the private sector in policy and administration." He saw a split between the Coordinator's "aggressive national security arrangements" and the division's "traditionally informal approach." Congressional onlookers saw ineptitude on one side or the other. Foreign audiences saw "the Americans" up to their usual games.

None of this was as clear as hindsight makes it seem; any USIS field program is an unreadable mosaic of daily events, individual interactions, available resources, and opportunity. Especially in 1942–45, the field program was being improvised, invented, and reinvented. In State skeptics, activists, and gradualists watched a handful of people doing too much. Activities were dropped into the Washington funnel and sorted out in the field, where the PAOs did the best they could with what they got. With control scattered in four separate agencies, not even Roosevelt was in charge. In the confusion, propaganda continued its drift toward center stage. In one way or another, they were all "telling America's story to the world," in the one-way version of dialogue to which proud and loquacious Americans were already over-inclined.

Division leadership sought to reconcile these tensions in a long discussion kicked off by Cherrington's GAC, thoroughly portrayed by Ninkovich. One group argued that good cultural relations is good propaganda in and of itself; propaganda may be a natural by-product of good relations, but it is never wise to say so. Wordsmith Charles Thomson distinguished "instructive" information from "destructive," contrasting America's "true propaganda"—the British oxymoron spawned during the battle for the Council—with the destructive lies of the Axis. He noted that cultural relations educated, or "led out," while propaganda impressed or, "pressed in." Hitler had told the world that the strength of the totalitarian state lay in its power to "force those who fear it to imitate it" and everyone knew the dangers of playing by Axis rules for propaganda; they thus tried to hold to their vision for sound cultural interchange. But the softer version of propaganda made palatable by US advertising professionals seemed less fearsome.[22]

The great debate had begun on the question of how cultural affairs contributed to US policy. When concerned diplomats asked whether the division's work contributed to foreign policy, easy-going Cherrington, inclined to the purist side, at first brushed the point aside: "It must be cultural exchange for its own sake and not serve ulterior motives," he said in 1940.[23] But the question persisted: if exchanges were part of foreign relations, then perhaps they were part of foreign *policy*? Was foreign policy an "ulterior motive"? What *kind* of foreign policy was meant? These questions, to which the Coordinator was impervious, nagged at concerned minds in the division.

The debate gathered strength, and the GAC carried it to the private world. Cherrington hewed to purism: the division must pursue the goal of long-range understanding; if propaganda must be done, he said, another agency should do it. Welles similarly stressed the long-range "nurture and conservation of cultural values during the period of belligerency . . . and reconstruction"; after that, time would tell. The GAC, including Rockefeller's humanist advisor Robert Caldwell, weighed in: cultural interchange was "a means of strengthening resistance to attacks on intellectual and cultural freedom and of reenforcing moral unity among free people"; thus exchange promoted human welfare. Perhaps foreign *policy* was the wrong beacon, said Caldwell, but he was comfortable with foreign *relations*.

Cherrington, turning to the university world for help in 1943, hired Yale historian Ralph Turner. Turner took Caldwell one step further by dividing foreign policy into short, middle, and long time frames. His paper "The Permanent Cultural Relations Program as a Basic Instrumentality of American Foreign Policy," based on the idea of *permanent* cultural relations, reframed the question. Turner called for active guidance to change, in other societies, through bilateral exchanges. The cultural program had "a definite obligation as one of the basic instrumentalities for modifying international relations and attitudes and for maintaining a better stabilized world order." He predicted that "our leadership in international action in the cultural field will be as decisively necessary" as in politics and economics.[24] Long before France and Japan formally came to the idea in 1978 and 1980, Turner envisioned a three-legged stool for international relations; education/culture would join politics and economics in equal partnership.

State, outside of the division, was impressed enough to ask Turner for three separate memos: a comparative study of cultural relations programs in other countries; a study of existing international intellectual, scientific, and cultural organizations, with suggestions for multilateral organizations after the war; and a long-term US approach to postwar cultural relations. With Welles sharpening his points, Turner's memos caught the naïve in the division by surprise. In the postwar world, fifty years before Huntington, he argued that cultural factors would necessarily move from periphery to center, shaping the overall politics of nations; therefore cultural relations *must* be an instrument for "implementing" US foreign policy.

This impressed State's realists but was strong medicine for Cherringtonians. In the GAC, only Grayson Kefauver, Stanford Dean of Education, accepted the idea of cultural relations as a *necessary* dimension of foreign policy—because the world was shrinking. Staffer Harley Notter redefined "policy": the "policy" of any state toward another encompassed *all* relations between the two peoples; therefore a cultural program *had to* be part of it. Turner agreed, suggesting focus on the longer-range end of the political-cultural continuum for three purposes: to "form a climate of mutual understanding"; to support free exchange of ideas and information for the cultural advancement of Americans and the world's people; and to foster "a peaceful, secure and cooperative world-order, through exchanges." Thomson restated Turner's idea: decent cultural relations can build a sound world order over time, so the U.S. can "pursue as goals the free exchange of ideas and information, and a peaceful, secure, and cooperative world order." This was a convincing and far-reaching synthesis.

The internal debate was targeted at Rockefeller, OWI, State's unidirectional informationists, and its nationalist-isolationists; it aimed at those seeking cultural support for short-term foreign policy; it targetted the naive among Division staff, State officers, and the universities. The Turner synthesis was the first formal US theory of bilateral cultural relations.

Turner was also asked to reopen the question of multilateral cultural affairs, slumbering since the US rejection of the League. He saw that bilateral relations could be carried on between any two nations only up to a point, so that multilateralism might be a better way of dealing with certain local sensitivities. What elements then needed action by the world community? Cherrington, from Denver in September 1941, had already alerted the division to "the reconstruction of the scientific, educational and other cultural phases of European life." In the spring of 1943 Turner followed up this lead with a trip to wartime London, where the Allied ministers of education for Europe had been meeting regularly to plan for the postwar period. In London, Turner saw precisely the right foundation for a postwar multilateral cultural organization. Back in Washington, he urged a formal US delegation be sent to the 1944 meetings and Welles agreed. The division made a prescient choice, asking a young congressman from Arkansas to chair the delegation. The committed internationalist J. William Fulbright took crucial time away from his senatorial election campaign to chair a delegation that included MacLeish. The Europeans, delighted by the US presence, paid Rhodes Scholar Fulbright—who like MacLeish had lived four years in Europe—the highest of compliments, inviting him to chair their meetings. Fulbright's career as an international activist shifted into higher gear, and UNESCO was in gestation.

●   ●   ●

By the war's end, the global reach of the division and its interagency relations were healthy, furthered by OWI and OSS scholars in field posts. Fairbank in China labored for the Library of Congress. In the Near East, the division helped the American University of Beirut, Robert College in Istanbul, the American University in Cairo, and other US schools through the Near East College Association and the Near East Foundation. A Turkish-English dictionary and an Arabic-language history of the U.S. were subsidized. The Phelps-Stokes Fund channeled help to Liberian education. In Afghanistan the departure of German and Japanese teachers and technical assistants opened the door for US missionary-educators. Books and materials flowed to Iran, Morocco, and Ethiopia.

Despite dozens of indications to the contrary, cultural diplomacy was growing, even if it sometimes looked like a field of weeds.

CHAPTER FIVE

MacLeish's Moment, Spring 1945

> In a divided world in which the real issue of division is the cultural issue, cultural relations are not irrelevancies. They are everything. And in such a world a cultural defeat is a defeat on the one front on which defeat cannot be accepted.

> —A. MacLeish, 1940

BATTLES OF IDEAS, at least as defined by scholars and intellectuals, are not normal Washington fare, but struggles for budgets, turf, and mandates are a US entitlement, guaranteed by the Constitution. As the discussion about cultural diplomacy whispered up and down the corridors of the federal government, impressive activities in the field were under way. When the Japanese attacked Pearl Harbor, State already had a coherent structure, a talented staff, and a nascent program in place; and in early 1942, with the help of OWI and OSS, cultural specialists or CAOs began moving into field jobs.[1]

In 1943 Welles's successor Edward Stettinius came to State from the corporate world; he had little understanding of and less concern for the issues of culture versus information. He managed by name change: first, he renamed the division to focus on Cultural Cooperation, keeping two branches, one with sixty-six staffers for Science, Education, and Art, and the other with thirty-one for Information. Soon he "reorganized" again, placing both branches under an Office of Public Information (OPI), directed by OWI's John Sloan Dickey, who had supported Elmer Davis and Milton Eisenhower in OWI against MacLeish's plea for projective thinking. When Cherrington called down university protests because of this second shift, Stettinius quickly slid the cultural branch's name back to Cultural Relations, but kept the division under OPI. By the end of 1944 the cultural contingent had grown to seventy-one persons, information to forty-three. At the same time, OWI had over twelve thousand.[2]

In January 1945 Stettinius took over as Secretary of State. Probably on FDR's orders, he put both branches under an Assistant Secretary for Public and Cultural Affairs (no longer Cultural *Relations*). The functions had together climbed, for the first time, to State's third level. The assistant secretary wearing the double hat was Archibald MacLeish.

In 1939 MacLeish had left his senior editorship at *Fortune* to serve as Librarian of Congress; there he rejuvenated an institution which had sagged badly under the forty-year reign of his predecessor. The first major non-governmental intellectual to grace the Librarian's office, he established a tradition which has lived on. From his desk, this longtime friend of Stephen Duggan had closely followed the division since its birth. Seven years later, sworn in as assistant secretary, he stood alongside two men he had known for years: Nelson Rockefeller, already causing heartburn in the Latin American bureau, over which FDR had placed him, and MacLeish's closest friend Dean Acheson, fellow soldier in the Zachariah Chafee wars at Harvard, who would soon rise to undersecretary.[3]

Upon entering State MacLeish immediately convened a special advisory group for long-range planning, to prepare an agenda for the Senate Appropriations Committee. Cosmetic editing shifted the three active verbs that once conveyed the division's mission: facilitate-stimulate-coordinate became implement-facilitate-supplement—a harmless change at first glance. Facilitation remained but slipped to second place; and supplement seemed more activist and direct than stimulate, hinting that MacLeish intended to initiate more programs. The serious change was the addition of implement, asserting an active division, and the disappearance of coordinate, perhaps already reflecting de facto erosion of Welles's ICC under Stettinius. Certainly MacLeish intended to maintain the division's role as the coordinative center for government's overseas educational activities, but with this change of language it seemed to slip off center.

From his Library, MacLeish had stepped into a lesser job. One can only guess that he wanted the assistant secretary position and asked FDR for it, perhaps negotiating a few unspoken conditions. Statements to Congress during confirmation hearings might explain his interest. He told Congress that "the cultural relations of the government are its most important foreign relations."[4] If FDR stood behind him, then he must have approved his task force's forthright recommendation, with peace in sight, that MacLeish absorb three wartime agencies: the Coordinator's office, OWI, and OSS.

Hull had pressed Cherrington to bite off more than he could chew on the assumption that funds and staff would follow; but in time of war the funding had gone to these other agencies. By regrouping them, MacLeish could capture, reorient, and refocus cultural relations funding as no one else could have.

With the war in its last phase, he was trying to channel its leftover impetus in the right direction. US ignorance about the costs of new global commitments, a Congress of nonbelievers, and clashing Washington egos were only some of the obstacles he faced. But MacLeish had been thinking ahead for years, and he had a healthy respect for his own ability to get things done. In State few saw as he did the potential of a uniquely American cultural diplomacy for US foreign policy; he knew it would be a hard road and that the predators had not yet left town.

Cultural diplomacy had just barely survived wartime change. Entering a tumultuous eight-year period leading to the formation of USIA in 1953,

MacLeish's bureau was coping with old promises and new threats. One can only guess that Roosevelt, with the rallying effect of war dispelled, was persuaded to keep cultural diplomacy alive by his friend MacLeish, who knew that a few promising legislators like Fulbright would stand with him. Yet the vulnerability of the original idea, even before wartime distortions, was obvious to anyone aware of the reigning cynicism of Washington or the gathering anti–New Deal backlash. Elevated to assistant secretary, one of a handful at the third level of State's hierarchy, MacLeish inherited, in principle, a stronger copy of Welles's coordinative mantle. He would provide a thoughtful concept for managing all ongoing programs with a small but committed high-caliber staff.

As part of the bargain, MacLeish had accepted a third job—whether out of naiveté or some farsighted plan is not clear—to handle State's public relations. (No one knew in 1945 that sixty years of experience would prove it impossible to do both jobs well.) There is a faint hint that MacLeish hoped to lure his friend Adlai Stevenson, a former staffer at OFF, into covering the public relations role. Doubtless MacLeish knew what the job entailed. At *Fortune* he had lived at the heart of the media world and knew the consuming nature of the work, and he realized that public relations rested on premises opposite from those of cultural relations. Whatever his thought-process, the self-confident lawyer-poet-statesman accepted the job.

Well-intentioned businessman Stettinius did not have Welles's skills as a global strategist. The former chief of both of US Steel and General Motors had coped with educational and cultural affairs by dividing and renaming that branch. He put Dickey, a hard-nosed trial lawyer and future president of Dartmouth College, in charge because Dickey spoke a language Stettinius understood. Planting Dickey in OPI was a symbolic step toward bringing OWI closer to cultural affairs, but with OWI in charge: OWI staff outnumbered the division's by forty times or more. MacLeish grasped this bramble under a new rubric—assistant secretary for public and cultural affairs—which he must have devised himself.

An unusual public servant, MacLeish was first a serious and committed intellectual, a major American poet trained to the lawyer's rigor; he combined a statesman's leadership style with an intellectual's independence and a poet's gift for words. Seen as the consummate Easterner, he came, in fact, from a suburb of Chicago, via Hotchkiss and Yale, where he played football and made Skull and Bones. He fought in World War I, studied law at Harvard, stayed on there to teach, then moved to Paris where he polished his poetic skills and learned passable French alongside friends in the Lost Generation. From Hotchkiss forward, he was first of all a poet who would win three Pulitzer prizes and the Presidential Medal of Freedom.

At the same time, his work with the Luce empire had brought him close to the world of business; he knew the nation's economic and political leaders and understood their concerns. In New York he knew the Columbia internationalists and Stephen Duggan. Justice Felix Frankfurter was mentor both to MacLeish and his friend Acheson. His European experience, his commitment to internationalism, his lawyer's acumen, his intellectual prominence, and his ability to listen equipped him in a unique way for his job in State.

MacLeish wrote scripts for radio dramas and admired the communications techniques pioneered by serious intellectuals like Duggan and Murrow. In late 1941, he was the principal speaker at William Paley's testimonial dinner for Murrow, who was on leave from London. Murrow had destroyed "the superstition of distance and time, . . . the ignorant superstition that violence and lies and murder on another continent are not violence and lies and murder here," he said. MacLeish touched too on domestic concerns: "Some in this country . . . did not want the people of America to hear the things you had to say, . . . did not wish to remember that the freedom of speech of which this country is so proud is freedom to hear . . . the dangerous truth as well as the comforting truth."[5] MacLeish's private quest was not unlike Murrow's: make information and education compatible and collegial, with the highest standards, then open wider access. Both men wanted to support and strengthen citizen education and the free exchange of ideas.

FDR was safely reelected, and MacLeish knew he had the president's support. As FDR's legate, he had called for a national discussion of the war's purposes and aftermath, a mission he had tried to build into OWI. Regarding cultural and informational programs, he asked, should they persist after the war? If so, should they work together or separately, bilaterally or multilaterally, and at what level of activity and budget? He knew the good and bad about the disastrous 1919 cut-off of CPI. Cultural relations were as vital to peace as to war; in impressive company, he had been thinking about the postwar peace for a decade.

MacLeish knew all players. He had known both Duggans for years. With Fulbright and Ralph Turner, he was a delegate to the 1944 London education meetings. His friend Cherrington chaired the GAC and was available monthly. ALA chief Milam, close friend of the Library, was a designer-founder of the division. A MacLeish article in the *ALA Journal* in July 1942 saw overseas libraries as part of "an intellectual offensive." He also knew the Coordinator, alas too well. He had excoriated Rockefeller with his grating satire "Frescoes for Mr. Rockefeller's City" after the young art lover authorized destruction of Diego Rivera's murals in Rockefeller Center. He had worked on radio projects with his friend actor-director Orson Welles and deplored Rockefeller's shabby treatment of the man. He knew Latin America well, in different ways but surely better than the Coordinator.[6] MacLeish and Rockefeller, when they parted ways, had agreed to live in their different worlds, but life had brought them back together. Rockefeller was a corporatist nationalist wearing an internationalist necktie; but MacLeish was a profoundly committed cultural internationalist who had lived, fought, and published abroad, one who knew the corporate world better than most.

He had a feel for Congress, having nourished the growth of Congressional Reference at the Library. In confirmation hearings for the librarianship, he had faced down a hostile committee—his employers, after all—with a refreshingly straightforward approach; Congress agreed it was lucky to get him. Once there, he had performed miracles. In 1945 hearings for the job in State, he was similarly open, asserting that education and culture were the core of US foreign affairs and among its "most important foreign relations." In world history no one had dared articulate such an idea, particularly before a hostile and under-informed legislature. Beginning a long-range educational campaign with Congress, he took control by commanding attention. As Roosevelt had labored to convince legislators that intellect was a factor of good government, MacLeish tried to bring intellect and culture nearer to the center of foreign affairs.

Without the focus of war, his path was harder. Tackling State's public relations, he now had to carry issues to the American public not as subjects for discussion but as policy to be defended. His bureau was caught up in both daily political tussles and long-range nonpolitical questions; three-quarters of Dickey's time went into getting out news, speeches, and position papers. A major priority in 1945 was to persuade Americans of the wisdom of joining the UN.

The old division had achieved its highest rank ever in the era when there were few Assistant Secretaries and no Deputy Secretary. As a lawyer, he agreed with Welles's principle that State must coordinate anything educational or cultural which government touched abroad. With presidential backing, care, patience, and the acute listening which typified him, MacLeish took on the job of absorbing the three wartime agencies.

Merging the Coordinator's office was relatively easy. The division had already adopted many of its parts, and both agencies used the same field staff. Wallace Harrison, left in charge by Rockefeller, worked well with division head Charles Thomson. Rockefeller's gifts, including the libraries, were relatively easily to accept, if harder to sustain. The panoply of vigorous activities he had devised, overlapping those of OWI, brought a certain amount of confusion; but MacLeish, with a precise sense of direction, knew how to clarify.

OWI was a tougher nut. It employed almost thirteen thousand, in contrast with the division's three hundred. The new combined ceiling for both, mandated by the Budget Bureau, was fixed at three thousand; this meant firing ten thousand people. Beyond sheer numbers, many OWI language-proficient staff, political refugees from Europe's left and right, looked suspicious to provincial elements in Congress. MacLeish was mulling an idea for reshaping OWI, which he would only spell out in 1947. Having managed a business magazine of ideas, he believed that the media and the corporate world, properly approached, motivated, and refocused, could help education and culture grow, and in turn be enriched by the interaction. If journalists write the first draft of history, MacLeish was a second-draft man—*Fortune* by any standards was an intellectual magazine. Further he had managed a large-scale research capability at the Library and a high-powered think-tank in OFF; for him, thorough research and high-quality information underlay good policy formation, whether in education, government, or business. MacLeish had the broad vision, personal stature and magnetism to lead OWI to a different place.

OSS was the tough nut, and MacLeish wisely put it on a back burner. There were elements of interest in OSS: its broadcast monitoring could add sharp ears and shrewd analysts to the Voice of America; and Langer's research and analysis branch could help understand other cultures, tailor US output, and engage intellect abroad. MacLeish approached OSS and Donovan with unhurried respect.

He renamed his office in a straightforward manner, courteously putting information first: the Office of International Information and Cultural Affairs (IICA). In addition to five geographic area offices, it had five operational divisions: two—Exchanges and Libraries—came from the old division; and three—Publications, Radio, and Motion Pictures—from OPI. Cultural components were outnumbered three-to-two, and cultural staff by an order of ten. MacLeish had to bring together not so much two agencies as two separate worlds. Ideas like ICC coordination or the facilitation of others' work meant nothing to OWI's output-oriented activists. The remains of the original division had to function as an independent entity, with close private connections; meanwhile he had to absorb a self-styled dynamo office, swarming with people and money. Culture was led by a few overworked university people; information, by too many underemployed media people.

Arthur Schlesinger Jr., veteran of both OFF and OWI, divided his OWI colleagues into two groups: the thoughtful writer-intellectuals and the talkative public relations–advertisers. The public relations talkers won out from the start, he reported. Domestic division chief Gardner "Mike" Cowles, for one, did not like the "writers." Schlesinger wrote, "We were doubtless an irritating group, accustomed to our independence and resistant to being treated like hirelings. Mike preferred public relations types, trained to please not themselves but the men who paid them. . . . OWI now suffered from a plague of advertising men."[7] In 1945 the media men who had run OWI assumed they would run MacLeish's bureau, but they did not quite get the idea behind the division; Welles's proposal to let the private world take the lead baffled the get-it-done OWI veterans. As a result, MacLeish headed a contradictory, unbalanced, contentious, and schizophrenic bureau.

Records of his discussions with Fulbright on subjects like unprecedented US power and its use after the war have not come to my attention, but talks must have taken place. Fifteen years after MacLeish, Fulbright saw the over-riding postwar question in the assistant secretary's terms when he wondered "whether this nation is prepared to accept the permanent and inescapable responsibilities of having become a major power. . . . Our national purpose is a process to be advanced. . . . That process is the defense and expansion of our democratic values, the furtherance of which rests ultimately on the wisdom, the maturity of judgment, and the moral fiber of a society of free individuals" (1961). The question was not *whether* the U.S. was to be the world's hegemon but rather, what *kind* of hegemon. John Hay and the culturalist founders had bequeathed to MacLeish the idea of binationalism; he did not miss the point that theirs was a uniquely American path to honest bilateral exchanges. MacLeish and Fulbright both called for a modest but gradually growing set of bilateral exchanges, managed binationally, covering all fields of education, with the US and foreign educational world centrally involved. MacLeish knew the Boxer precedent as well as Fulbright, who in two years would extend it to the world.

One question that fell through the cracks was the issue of field staffing and, by implication, the structure of USIS posts, still wedded to the 1917 model. The success of the field posts went unchallenged, but most USIS staff were on OWI's payroll. No one had yet voiced the thought that would become USIA's mantra: that culture and information, living together with apparent success in the field, by definition had to share quarters in Washington. MacLeish wanted both under his thumb, but everything about him indicated that he intended to treat them as equals, not declare one subservient to the other. For the moment, he overlooked Cherrington's separatist argument—that culture and information had to live in two separate houses if the integrity of both sides was to be guaranteed at home and abroad.

Propaganda was not a word he used, although it was by now a fact of Washington life and would shortly get a giant boost from Josef Stalin. The "psy-war" temptation, for the moment at least, was actively resisted by MacLeish, who was totally focused on building structures of peace. The issue was not whether to do propaganda—all nations must. Rather, with "black" propaganda consigned to clandestinity, planners like MacLeish saw dangers in the theory that the American style of "white" or "true" propaganda was fully compatible with US values and appropriate to a nation at peace, as alleged by the informationists. He considered "true propaganda" a hilarious oxymoron. The war, legitimizing the lighter hues of propaganda, led some to forget that peace would have to be waged by other means. Cherrington and MacLeish, well before the cold war, feared info-prop's relentless absorption of cultural affairs.

MacLeish, like Fulbright, was not cowed by the university world. He did not find in it the same all-inclusive model that Cherrington and the Duggans had. For him, the university was only one part of the American mind. After years of thriving inside the Luce empire, he approached intellect by redefining "information." His unusual access to the top levels of the business and media worlds inclined him to see information, as well

as the universities, as a powerful instrument for public education—
Fortune had taught him respect for business intellect. MacLeish in 1945
was seeking to redefine "information" as an extension of education and
intellect. This populist-seeming patrician had deep respect for the people,
having been shaped by not only Hotchkiss, Yale, and Harvard but also
the Chicago suburbs, the US Army, Paris, and *Fortune*. His synthesis was
Jefferson's: given adequate information, citizens will make the right
choices.

Living at a time when information transmission was beginning to
change the nature of the learning process, he was as fascinated by the
public media as Duggan, Murrow,and Columbia internationalists like
Shotwell, Butler, and Dewey had been in their search for effective ways
of educating a democratic citizenry. At *Fortune*, in his radio-writing, at
the Library, and in OFF, MacLeish had learned to work with the media.
As a public intellectual, he wanted to project, in his unique voice, the
high ideals of the American world which, as Librarian of Congress and
unofficial dean of US intellectuals, he had come to represent. Sharing
quarters with "information" for MacLeish was, therefore, less a threat
than an opportunity—provided he was in charge. Defeated once by
Davis, Eisenhower, and Dickey in the battles of the Potomac, he bore
them no malice; but he had a broader vision.

MacLeish was one of the most fertile and farsighted minds in the history of US cultural diplomacy. But in his brief moment in office, he left
no book on the subject, only fragments. Of these, none was more pro-
phetic than his first article in *The Nation* in February 1940, five years before
he took office in State.[8] Singling out Cherrington and Thomson, he began
by twitting the phrase "cultural relations" while stressing its honesty and
seriousness: "It stands for the realization of informed persons that the
present struggle of the propagandas . . . is a struggle for something more
than markets." The Axis "flank attack on the culture of the North American democracies in Latin America was perhaps not a flank attack at all
but the principal engagement." The appropriate US response, he said, was
a decent cultural relations program, striving "to persuade the artists and
intellectuals . . . that a North American culture exists, that it is a culture
worthy of admiration, and that the substitution of a different cultural
influence in the Americas might be the substitution of a worse."

Cultural diplomacy was a long road, "an undertaking as difficult as it
may be dangerous"—difficult because Latin America had already formed
deeply etched impressions of US culture from what they had seen of US
business, commerce, and military incursions, dangerous because the
structure of cultural diplomacy was fragile. Reversing foreign ignorance
and prejudice was only possible over time: "Whether we intended to do
so or not, we have now undertaken . . . through official agencies to present . . . convincing proofs of the creativeness and vitality of our culture. To
fail would be disastrous." The risk was high because these international
cultural "commitments have been given without adequate assurances be-

forehand of the cooperation of those whose cooperation is essential—the handful of true artists and true scholars who alone can enable us to perform these promises." There were no "guarantees against the interference of the mediocrities and vulgarities . . . whose interference would make our promises ridiculous." Looking well beyond the designers of State's cultural experiment, he foresaw conflicts which would not come clear until the end of his century.

After taking office, his thought can be reconstructed from three other fragments in 1945: his blueprint for German recovery, his introduction to *The Cultural Approach* of 1947, and his contribution to a State Department administrative review that appeared in the fall of 1945.

First, German recovery. Few remember that MacLeish, as much as any one man, was the intellectual architect of the US cultural diplomatic victory in West Germany. Chairing a task force convened in May 1945 and lasting into 1947, he designed a policy for rebuilding Germany, which would serve as well in Japan. The policy, shaped in the "Long-Range Policy Statement for German Reeducation" (SWNCC 296/5), launched one of US cultural diplomacy's greatest educational achievements. Published in June 1946 then renewed the following year,[9] the task force document made education the indispensable base of reconstruction: "The reeducation of the German People can be effective only as it is an integral part of a comprehensive program for their rehabilitation. The cultural and moral reeducation of the nation must, therefore, be related to policies calculated to restore the stability of a peaceful German economy and to hold out hope for the ultimate recovery of national unity and self-respect." This task force called for "reconstruction of German cultural life," assuming that the work "must in large measure be the work of the Germans themselves" and noting that "the Nazi heritage of Germany's spiritual isolation must be overcome by restoring as rapidly as possible those cultural contacts which will foster the assimilation of the German people into the society of peaceful nations."[10]

MacLeish was perhaps the only American who could use the word "culture" at the highest levels of political-military policy and make it stick. Henry Kellermann, central participant in German reorientation and author of the indispensable history of the initial German cultural programs, knew the task force memo may have sounded "presumptuous to some and unrealistic to others" but concluded that, even if MacLeish did not manage to make education the supreme goal of Allied or US policy, the statement made it "an 'integral' all-pervasive part of rehabilitation directly linked to political and economic reform." Another remarkable American, Gen. Lucius Clay, soon took over as High Commissioner in Germany (HICOG), with an understanding of MacLeish's gift. Clay appointed Indiana University president Herman B Wells to head the reorientation effort, and Wells helped turn MacLeish's idea into reality.[11] Thanks to MacLeish, Clay, and Wells, German reorientation was a triumph of cultural and educational diplomacy.

The reorientation cost far more than MacLeish had called for. His memo recommended a manageable commitment of resources, more compatible, as it turned out, with what the British and the French allocated and more sustainable over time. The US reorientation program in Germany, like its Japanese equivalent, was instead carried out in the lavish Rockefeller style, fed generously by military surplus sales and German contributions. It proved—for better and for worse—a contagious model for the future USIA, many top officers of which came out of German or Japanese reorientation. German reorientation was not, in fact, replicable, yet it offered an illusory model for programs everywhere, most recently in Iraq. Expectations, both by Germans and the American participants, were inflated as the program soared well beyond SWNCC recommendations. One builder of German reorientation, for example, was the famous Shepard Stone, who during the rest of his career with the Ford Foundation and the Aspen Institute would try to apply reorientation's lessons to the intellectual dimensions of the cold war.[12]

The second insight into MacLeish's thinking comes from his introduction to The Cultural Approach: Another Way in International Relations, which appeared in the spring of 1947. Assigned by MacLeish early in 1945 to two of his IICA staffers, Ruth McMurray and Muna Lee, the book grew from Turner's 1943 idea of surveying the cultural programs of other leading nations. It is the world's first major book in the then-unnamed field of cultural diplomacy. Lee, brought into IICA by MacLeish, was a Mississippi poetess and the wife of Puerto Rican president Muñoz Marín; she and MacLeish had collaborated on a 1944 series of radio dramas about the discoverers of America.

The book went to press in the summer of 1946 with a six-page introduction by MacLeish, reflecting his close reading of the manuscript. Although his message for Americans was implicit rather than prescriptive, this text was the most coherent and influential statement about a peacetime cultural diplomacy ever articulated, including in France.

In his introduction, MacLeish defended the cliché cultural relations, which denotes the idea that "the world's hope for peace, which is another way of referring to the world's hope of survival, is directly dependent upon the mutual understanding of peoples." (Poet MacLeish was good at saying things in a single sentence. In London for the meetings planning UNESCO that same fall, he and Clement Attlee crafted the organization's famous motto: "Since wars begin in the minds of men, it is in the minds of men that the defenses of peace must be constructed.") Introducing Approach, MacLeish unveiled his new definition of "information." Playing with the word, he reversed Creel's operational euphemism. Instead of concealing propaganda, information, with its positive function, would enable education to serve the nation and all of humankind. At the threshold of a new communications era, which he understood better than most, MacLeish imagined the benefits that the global media might bring to the world if used to educate, not obfuscate; to teach, not spin; to tell whole, not partial truths. He attacked "traditionalist" foreign ministries, by implication State and perhaps his friend Acheson, for ignoring international communications. Cultural relations gave nations unprecedented power to correct negative foreign images, he wrote. Thanks to the British Council, for example, "no literate European will ever again refer to the English as a nation of shopkeepers." He concluded: "Foreign Offices are offices of international understanding, the principal duty of which is the duty to make the understanding of peoples whole and intelligible and complete. Until the practice accords with the duty the work will be inadequately done." For the U.S., it was a national responsibility to make its educational and spiritual resources available to other nations.

This unique statement voiced MacLeish's hope for America, in the years after the devastation of Europe; he wanted America, the storehouse and protector of Western culture, to share its intellectual wealth with the world.

A third insight into MacLeish comes from an improbable place and concerns the structure of cultural relations inside State, hence in US foreign policy. In September 1945 State issued a major review of the organization of the State Department in view of postwar needs, signed by an administrator named McCarthy.[13] Although MacLeish left State in July, his impact in this document—which had to have been researched in the spring—was obvious. First, the report recommended that IICA handle its own relations with Congress, instead of entrusting them to the State Department office just vacated by Acheson. This was a vital job, which the overworked Welles and even the focused Acheson had done badly, demanding the kind of long and careful education of Congress which MacLeish clearly intended but had no time to do. Second, the McCarthy report insisted that cultural diplomacy, distinct from information, be maintained in peacetime. The value of such diplomacy had been demonstrated and cultural relations were now an integral part of US foreign relations, as they were for all the great powers; now, cultural relations had to do more than survive, the office had to expand. Third, the report urged defining bilateral cultural elements *before* shaping the multilateral UNESCO's mandate, so that the two would mesh. Fourth, it called for better State coordination with other US government agencies, in both technical expertise and substance, with State managing legal, managerial, and foreign relations questions. Finally, it asserted boldly that cultural relations would play a vital role in helping carry out US national aspirations. One suggestion touched German and Japan reorientation: it recommended a special office in State, directed by a high-prestige American, to govern all activities in the Occupied Areas, including Austria.

This provocative survey had MacLeish's hand all over it. To the extent that it conveyed a general State attitude, it showed that the division had earned a significant place there by 1945. Together with the other two documents we have seen, the McCarthy report described cultural relations as a rich, flexible and coherent component of the foreign policy apparatus and recommended gearing up to do more and better.

Much lay ahead: the UN and UNESCO were on the horizon; in two years the Fulbright Program would be in place, then the Marshall Plan and Point IV, the CIA, the Smith-Mundt supplement to Fulbright, the cold war, its Korean offshoot, and German-Japanese reorientation. In 1945, with the McCarthy mandate in place and under the right leadership, the new bureau of cultural relations stood on the threshold of great achievements. Only MacLeish might have showed Washington how to make it work. He took on the burden of cultural diplomacy in 1945 as a life commitment, in the style of the American intellectual world he had come to represent; he saw cultural relations as part of that high and far-reaching sector of foreign policy Turner had identified, concerned with fostering democracy, freedom of information, exchange of ideas, free markets, and healthy educational growth everywhere.

The ideal was not to be. On 12 April 1945 Roosevelt died and MacLeish was devastated. As custom dictates, he resigned the next day. He remained in office through July, when after three months of silence his resignation was accepted by Harry Truman and his new Secretary of State James Byrnes. Truman had no idea what MacLeish represented; and MacLeish's friend Acheson—who had managed to earn Truman's trust—seems to have done nothing to keep his best friend on the team. In fact, Acheson had always been openly skeptical about cultural relations and wary of his friend's vision, noted his biographer James Chace; in January 1945 he had even quietly asked Dickey to help curb "some of MacLeish's enthusiasms," as Chace put it.[14] By August MacLeish was gone, overlooked by a president who had no idea what he was discarding.

• • •

While the U.S. was debating behind sealed doors whether to continue its investment in cultural affairs, Europe—less encumbered by democratic process—was leaping back into the game. Postwar Europe, where culture maintained its traditional value, was facing questions of survival with huge rebuilding problems and shortages of food and fuel, but cultural diplomacy's role was unquestioned. The U.S., with nothing of its own to rebuild, had always helped others to do so; private contributions were on their way overseas and public help was not far behind. Meanwhile handsome US military cemeteries sprouted all over Europe, sad, beautifully maintained symbols of US commitment.

Both victors and vanquished in Europe, in contrast to the U.S., quickly expanded cultural diplomacy. Overwhelming demands on their national budgets did not dissuade European nations from raising even higher the priority of cultural rebuilding and its projection abroad. Cultural outreach, for Europeans, was a key to national identity and pride; it was a symbol of a renewed global presence and it had implications for intellectual employment.

Each country approached its cultural diplomacy differently. Austria, technically speaking an enemy power for the U.S., quickly devised an ingenious cultural policy to help the world overlook the war years, exporting costly cultural products like the Vienna Opera and Philharmonic, the Vienna Boys Choir, the Lippizaner Stallions, and dozens of solo musicians. The goal, as an unsympathetic Austrian put it, was to convince the world that Brahms and Beethoven were Austrians, but that Hitler was German. Sweden had a different problem: having sat out the war as useful brokers and rescuers, the Swedes worried about their nonengagement; they launched a nonprofit private-public association in 1945 called the Swedish Institute, modeled on Weimar's Goethe Institute and France's *Instituts*. West Germany, in like manner, revived its academic Goethe Institutes and began sending out musicians to ease memories of the Nazi years. Former enemy Italy, now classified as a "cobelligerent," tried to refloat its Dante Alighieri Society outposts around the world but was stymied in the U.S. when the Attorney General listed it as a subversive organization. In Great Britain the British Council picked up its work; ambivalence about culture plus austerity kept budgets spare, barely enough to keep the Council alive; yet it maintained offices in most countries in the world.

France took its usual lead, with more panache but under more difficult circumstances.[15] June 1940 and the German occupation had shattered the nation's infrastructure and self-confidence. As part of De Gaulle's tactics of restoring French morale, France turned once again to cultural diplomacy and *rayonnement*. With the novelist, art critic, and adventurer André Malraux as advisor, De Gaulle pressed France's comparative advantage in culture and mobilized French education. Its internationalist agenda had a distinctly national flavor, in part because of insistence on expanding the use of the French language and in part because France's intellectuals were trained to dazzle. The problems of defeated France were deeply cultural: it had suffered humiliation at the hands of a detested enemy, one which rejected the life of the freely inquiring mind and placed power in the hands of a semiliterate lower middle-class.

Worse, part of the French population had cooperated: the *Milice*, Vichy's internal police force, was more vicious than the Gestapo. Pétain's surrender left a deep scar: he saw Vichy as the only chance for France's survival, but his underlings had other ideas so that Vichy merely slowed the relentless German attempt to take over France's soul. In Vichy's Foreign Ministry, the head of cultural relations was Jean Marx, in charge at the Quai since 1933; within months he was expelled on racial grounds. Other staff, like Suzanne Borel—later the wife of Georges Bidault—took to the *maquis*. Valiant bureaucratic survivors tried to keep money flowing to the overseas schools, but the institutes in Europe that sprouted after the first war were closing their doors; in more remote cities like London,

Cairo, and New York, the institutes turned themselves over to Free France. A New York institute, renamed the Free University, slowly evolved into an important US university, the New School. In Marseille two Americans—Varian Fry and Vice-Consul Hiram Bingham IV, son of the archeologist-Senator—were rescuing thousands of Europe's intelligentsia, bypassing Vichy regulations. Such intellectual refugees were guided to homes in American universities by IIE's Stephen Duggan and Ed Murrow.

After the Allied invasion of North Africa, Vichy lost what little empty civility and perfidious protection it had bought. Foreign private support founded new Free French institutes in Mexico City and Buenos Aires, while the St. Joseph University in Beirut and the French law school in Cairo continued to fly the faded tricolor. A sharp insight into the unusual thinking of the dark years comes from De Gaulle's 1943 speech in Algiers, marking the sixtieth anniversary of the Alliances Françaises. He called for bidirectional cultural relations and the intellectual permeability without which nations cannot live. France was great, he said, because it had left itself open to fresh ideas from elsewhere; without openness, decline sets in; art, science, and philosophy depend on international exchange; a nation's high values cannot survive in a climate of nationalism; French cultural influence, radiating outward to a grateful world, fed French growth.[16] In the light of De Gaulle's later nationalist strategy, it was a remarkably internationalist statement.

Universalism returned soon enough. Eight months after the liberation of Paris, a team of diplomats, educators, and charwomen reopened the Quai d'Orsay's trashed office of cultural relations; it would take a year to get things moving. By fall 1946 France was trembling from more than the cold; after five years of relentless and systematic German bloodletting, it faced financial oblivion. Yet it clung precariously to its empire. Once again, France played the education card.

A decade later cultural outreach was absorbing more than half the Quai's total budget. By 1949 fourteen new Cultural Counselors were in place in key embassies around the world, contrasting with the prewar practice of sending university-based directors to the institutes. Cultural treaties, a practice France had originated, proliferated. Before 1914, there were eleven, and by 1939 they had doubled; between 1945 and 1961, France added sixty more.

Even the French voluntary sector, stifled by the Popular Front, was growing back. Ministries like Education were active abroad, with arms-length Foreign Ministry guidance. Partially subsidized youth exchanges of pre-university and university students soared: two to three thousand French participants went to Germany each summer and the same number of Germans to France in an obvious effort at Franco-German rapprochement. A knowledgeable German cultural official in 1998 guessed that by 1990 as many as a million French and German young people had taken part in summer exchanges. He believed the "German Question," once the bane of France and Britain, had been erased by half a century of cultural preparation. German reunification, when it came, was easily accepted by France and England.

The French rebuilt education in their occupation zone in Germany. In the memory of the same German cultural official who grew up in the French Zone, France left a double image. On the one hand, anything that might help rebuild France, down to the lowliest cow, was subject to ruthless retributive expropriation; on the other, extraordinary French educational generosity, at the peak of which stood the newborn University of Mainz, adroitly designed a German university rather than an extension of the French system.[17]

At the hub in Paris, language was a continuing obsession. "Defending" and "illustrating" its language had shaped French cultural diplomacy since Du Bellay. In the early 1950s, recalled then-director Jacques de Bourbon Busset, France agonized over the dilemma: "Either concentrate on the projection [*rayonnement*] of French culture in all its forms, even at the expense of using the dominant language, English; or else focus on the growth of the French language throughout the world, at whatever cost, even at the expense of sacrificing certain possibilities of cultural projection." The decision went to French language, and investments in overseas French language teaching soared—no one could accuse the French of expecting early payoffs. In France's own schools, foreign-language teaching stagnated.

In France's postwar diplomatic priorities, culture was a tool of national power. French colonies and mandated territories, including Indochina, Africa, North Africa, Syria, and Lebanon, took first priority in cultural programs. The emerging nations of Latin America ranked high. The U.S. was taken for granted and neglected, after the ingenious low-cost building done in the 1920s and 1930s. As a US ally in the cold war, France agreed to restrain its cultural operations in the Soviet countries and China, and after the Suez crisis in 1956, operations in Egypt and Syria were reduced. But French investment in Italy remained high. By the end of the 1950s, the Third World, a major political target, was looking to France for intellectual leadership.

What Americans called "technical assistance" became, for France, either *assistance technique,* AID-type missions, or *coopération technique*—the name for its "Peace Corps" activities, voluntary action, usually in teaching and research, by new university graduates in lieu of military service. All such assistance was administered by the Quai's office of cultural relations and in the field by its Cultural Counselors, just as they managed all other French educational efforts in that country. The word "technical" was added to the Quai office's title, then the word "scientific" in 1969, to compose a clumsy new name: the Office of Cultural, Technical, and Scientific Relations (DGRCST).

In 1958, as France's Indochinese adventure began winding to its end, the Quai's worldwide cultural exports, beginning with two hundred in 1945, had soared to thirteen thousand. George Allen, director of USIA in the late 1950s, called on DGRCST-chief Roger Seydoux. Representing a country one-fourth the size of the U.S., Seydoux wore the hats both of State's cultural and AID offices, "and maybe mine too," noted USIA's Allen. "He has on his payroll 50,000 French teachers in various countries around the world, . . . 50 French teachers paid by the French Foreign Office in Chile alone." At the time, Allen's Chilean operation funded a few English teachers and a handful of Fulbright lecturers.

In all, even when crippled by war, France never abandoned its faith in cultural action abroad. Guided by an oligarchic administrative structure with staff from the peak of the academic pyramid and relatively unchecked by its legislature, France's postwar cultural policy showed a total national commitment to education and culture, run by an efficient centralized government that could sustain policies over time. Only history will judge what France's investments in these years produced; in design, they represented a seamless extension of the practices of 1919–40 and dated back to Francis I.

In the muddled populism of postwar Washington, only a few thoughtful men reflected deeply. Private America, on the other hand, with generous means but little coordination—and less help than promised in 1938 by Welles—had sprung into action. Postwar international private activities greatly surpassed those of the 1920s, after victory in the most destructive war in history and five years of wartime inaction. The coordinative mechanism that Welles and Duggan had put in place, under MacLeish's vision and leadership, might have allowed the U.S. to rival France, but the private effort ran on its own.

One indicator of prosperous international activity was a tremendous contribution to Europe's rebuilding of human structures. Merle Curti's compendious but admittedly partial listing of these efforts only hints at the scale of the activity;[18] Curti documents the unprecedented outflow of hundreds of organizations and thousands of individuals. Governmental generosity would soon join in, thanks to the Fulbright Program, the Marshall Plan, and German and Japanese reorientation; all these giant programs assumed public-private cooperation.

Given new US commitments, it was obvious that private power could not do it all. Only government working with the private world could act on the necessary scale; only government could watch the balance of investments at a national level and in a hundred or more foreign nations; yet only the private world of the universities could deliver the kind of high-quality product needed. Rockefeller, who had virtually invented public-private cooperation in cultural relations, kept his corporatist dream alive among his personal ambitions. Where Welles and Cherrington had reassured the non-governmental community that they intended nothing but facilitation, the Coordinator had done the opposite and paid full fare. In Rockefeller's vision the private world had nothing to fear from the potentially limitless means of the government. In this context, he helped government go activist, abandoning its helpmate role; in this sense, he made government leadership increasingly indispensable.

Old and new private programs flourished, both at the well-funded level of the Rockefeller and Carnegie domains and in smaller ad hoc arrangements. Taking the example of US and foreign students moving overseas, from high school through college and graduate levels, the nineteenth-century church-driven Student Volunteer Movement had dwindled but still survived; more important, it had spun off healthy alternatives for lay teachers and students abroad. The Experiment in International Living, born in the early 1930s, was expanding its work moving US undergraduates abroad; the ambulance drivers of two wars, as the American Field Service, had devised a global high-school exchange program which would set new standards in numbers, outreach, and quality. These were soon joined by other youth exchanges like the International Christian Youth Exchange, the Conference of Christians and Jews, International Farm Youth Exchange, the Quakers' Brethren Service Committee, the Grange, the 4-H Clubs, the Cleveland Program for Youth Leaders, Youth for Understanding, the Herald-Tribune Forum, the Catholic Welfare Conference, Kiwanis, Rotary International, and the Ann Arbor Council of Churches. Some of these were spun off from government, like the Cleveland Program, a child of German reorientation.

On the US university campuses, students could easily move abroad for part of their educational experience: the "junior year abroad," an expensive luxury for the few when it began at the University of Delaware in 1923, now became accessible to larger numbers, if not yet to the poor. Language training in the schools, even in the provincial U.S., was on the rise, in part thanks to military programs and the returning GIs. Most of the top colleges and universities, by the 1950s, listed an impressive range of language offerings; language education in primary and secondary schools continued growing through the 1950s. The Council on International Educational Exchange (CIEE) came into existence after the war, first to provide inexpensive sea transport via converted troop-ships, then to coordinate hundreds of university student-abroad programs. Transoceanic charter air travel was becoming affordable. Foreign universities, providing free tuition for their own students, could do no less for Americans; a few US colleges in response tried where possible to help out with scholarship aid and employment for foreign students. The overall activity was enormous and new support-organizations met the needs. The total number of foreign students in the U.S. began its steady climb to half a million at century's end.

Universities were internationalizing. The Army Special Training Program (ASTP) had trained linguists who were now in graduate study or teaching; they in turn launched undergraduate study programs abroad. The unprecedented GI Bill, which broadened university access for Americans, supported overseas study as well. By 1950, the return to the graduate schools of the first year's Fulbrights provoked a new burst of growth for overseas study; soon hundreds of campuses routinely sent American students abroad for part of their education. All these, as well as foreign students in the U.S., carried the virus of US democracy, and some Americans brought back ideas for alternative US lifestyles. American undergraduates and graduates were moving beyond the obvious countries like England, France, and Italy, where they totaled about five thousand students in each, to more distant settings in both the industrialized and developing world.

On the campuses, micro-programs were burgeoning, driven by energetic faculty and students. At the University of Washington, senior student G. Lewis Schmidt led a US delegation to Japan, the first step in a career leading to the top of USIA. At the University of Minnesota in 1947 students and faculty invented SPAN, the Student Project for Amity among Nations. Its first outbound group included future diplomats Bruce Laingen (to Sweden) and Jay Gildner (to Germany). Today more than four hundred SPAN alumni grace diplomacy, teaching and scholarship, banking, administration, medicine, science, public health, and international development; virtually all work in an international context and help fund SPAN's continuation.

Scholarship assistance to foreign students was growing in the U.S. The division's exhortations to the universities at a nationwide meeting in 1942 to expand foreign student numbers with IIE's help and foundation assistance led in 1948 to the creation of the National Association for Foreign Student Affairs (NAFSA). Campuses paid more attention to foreign students; professional foreign student advisors came into being, also providing counseling and advice for US students eager to go abroad. NAFSA worked at every step of the foreign student process, from monitoring and professionalizing admissions to student visas to health care and insurance. By the 1990s economists estimated that the U.S. absorbed into its vast university machinery more foreign students than all other nations put together, over half a million in residence at any given moment, representing an invisible export estimated at between $12 and $13 billion annually, the fourth largest US export in the service sector. The implications for foreign relations of this flood of the world's young people into America's universities were obvious to all but those who feared it. All this was happening in the single domain of US and foreign students, deftly supported by small sums from the federal government but primarily financed by the US educational industry itself.

In the foundation world, a mighty new private player exploded onto the international scene in 1950: the Ford Foundation. Founded in 1936, Ford had limited its activities to development in the Detroit area. With expanded funding, under the leadership of Chicago industrialist Paul Hoffman and his Yale classmate Robert M. Hutchins, former president of the University of Chicago, the Ford team set out to explore paths blazed by the Rockefeller Foundation. Attacking the problems of poverty, disease, ignorance, governance, and economic planning, the Ford Motor Company—which earned a sizable share of its revenue abroad—agreed to fund the world's wealthiest foundation, run by professionals insulated from the corporation. After a shaky start, Ford established a permanent international dimension under successor president Henry Heald.

One focus of the foundation was foreign regional and area studies in the US universities. An Office of International Training and Research (ITR), with generous budgets, was designed and headed by John Howard. Cooperating with other foundations, Ford's ITR helped build area-studies research and teaching into dozens of American universities, making grants not to individuals but to outstanding universities, which then re-disbursed the funds as they saw fit. Stressing the social sciences and economics, returned grantees were soon transmitting their experience to the next generations of students.[19]

Area-studies, growing quickly, became a new and uniquely American academic discipline. Robert McCaughey analyzed a one-year slice of this activity in 1966–67 and found investments of almost $60 million—$32 million from government and $25 million from the foundations, of which $21 million came from Ford alone. By 1981 Ford had spent about $5 billion, $2 billion of it in overseas work, three-quarters in developing countries. Ford's first two thousand US foreign-area fellows included historians (30 percent), anthropologists (12 percent), political scientists (12 percent), and economists (8 percent). The social-science stress was a departure from the humanistic traffic of the past, as well as from the open Fulbright process.[20] Ford opened offices abroad in cities like Caracas, Bogotá, Delhi, Beirut, and Cairo. Its agenda resembled a public administrator's checklist, stressing social and economic research, help to governments in economic and social planning, urban development, rationalization of small industries and crafts, population control, and training in public administration. Faint reactive rumblings in Congress about foundation power could already be heard in the 1940s and 1950s; populist Representative Wright Patman (D-Louisiana) would soon lead attacks on the foundations, but they would not hit home until 1969.

In this postwar internationalist flowering, hundreds of private organizations were at work, including the great research universities themselves, soon to become overseas agents for development via government contracts. US overseas research centers, born at the end of the nineteenth century in Athens, Rome, and Jerusalem, were joined by a dozen new research institutions in the ancient lands of the Near East and South Asia. Such outreach flowed two ways, feeding learning and experience at home and abroad.

Beyond the great private US institutions abroad, like the AUB and the AUC in Cairo, there were still heroic Americans at work on the front lines: Gordon Seagraves, the "Burma Surgeon," collected surgical instruments from the trash-baskets of Johns Hopkins and ran a fine hospital in Northern Burma; Sam Higginbottom set up his Agricultural Institute at Allahabad in India; Tom Dooley in Bangkok was developing Thai medicine; a second generation of the House family maintained the American Farm School in Salonika; Richard Soderberg worked in Afghanistan and John

Clark in Kashmir, to cull a few names from Curti. A trio of Harvard graduate students, guided by Austrian social scientist Clemens Heller, persuaded New York foundations to set up the Salzburg Seminar as an intellectual meeting place between East and West. Later Heller, on whom his Rockefeller friends bestowed Frederick II's name *stupor mundi*, would persuade the foundation to help France build a splendid center for international social science research and exchange in Paris, the Maison des Sciences de l'Homme. In short, government exchanges after 1940 could not have taken off without private help and could not operate without reference to what was being done. As usual public-private coordination in the field was closer than Washington rhetoricians remembered.

And yet the public sector was slowly taking the lead. The government's short-term foreign visitor program, for leaders (maximum 3 months in its first decade) and specialists (maximum 6 months), made growing demands on US voluntarism and was closing in on its permanent name, International Visitors (IV). In Germany the atypical reorientation program in the early 1950s brought an average of over two thousand short-term visitors to the U.S. per year, more than the rest of the world altogether. Local support associations for short-term visitors arose around the U.S. and they soon formed a national network, the Council for International Visitors (NCIV), which by the turn of the millennium was organizing local programs and hospitality, meanwhile generating the equivalent of more than $25 million in local support. The volunteer spirit, which Tocqueville had seen as the beating heart of American democracy, seemed ready to meet all needs—welcoming services at airports, study-tours to meet complex agendas, home hospitality, Thanksgiving dinners, volunteer drivers, tour guides, sports events and theater, and the like. As Welles had seen, Washington could do very little without the support of a countrywide citizen network. In the 1940s and 1950s government was grateful for the help, but later impatient activists in government would seek more control.

The foundations took vigorous part in the growth. When the Fulbright Program was finally funded by Congress late in 1948, two New York foundations responded to Laurence Duggan's plea to help IIE move Americans abroad a year early; when Ford noticed the English deficiency of its participants in Indonesia, it began a program to develop the science of English teaching for speakers of other languages, which soon was guiding teaching methods in USIS posts everywhere; as late as 1967–70 Ford helped USIS Tehran mount a program in legal research and education.

Reduced to lists or statistics, such activities conceal the complexity of their operations. Beneath each grantee experience lay unseen levels of organized expertise and effort. To take a simple example, among the dozens of sharply defined professional fields developed for the German and Japanese reorientation program, one lively theme was women's affairs. German and Japanese women were moving into professional life, as in other industrializing countries, but their progress was impeded by male attitudes and rigid legal, social, and economic structures—approximately what American women had encountered three or four decades earlier. Showing German and Japanese women another way, in democratic societies, was a priority. But Congress refused to allow State to hire a specialized staffer, so the division turned for help to the Women's Bureau of the US Department of Labor. The Bureau took on the task of designing and administering study-tours in the U.S. for foreign women leaders, but it could only do this because it had earlier mobilized the women of America. Supporting the Women's Bureau was an extensive network of women's organizations, among many others the Garment Workers' Union, the Association of University Women, the General Federation of Women's Clubs, the YWCA, the religious councils, Zonta International, Soroptimist, the Business and Professional Women, the League of Women Voters, and the Women's Trade Union League of America.

In short, the American private sector had again swung into action, more broadly and more professionally than ever before, and was proudly cooperating with government because growing world needs had been accepted as an American responsibility. Cooperative government funding and loose overall coordination kept things moving, especially Fulbright, after its beginnings in 1949 already working in dozens of countries.

Proliferating activity in devastated Europe and in the newly independent countries of the postcolonial era taught Americans a few obvious lessons. For example, clearly there was far more to be done than could be absorbed by the US private world—or the public sector, for that matter. It was obviously impossible to do everything and therefore agreed-upon criteria and priorities were needed. It was certainly easier to reeducate Germans than Japanese and easier to educate Japanese than many others; equally certain, reviving an old educational system was a lot easier than building one where none had been before.

The new trained area specialists, along with internationalist social scientists in the universities, read Malinowski and worried about the questions he raised. They insisted all the more that the work be done thoughtfully, slowly, and carefully, with preliminary research, detailed planning, and hard choices made beforehand. Without preliminary planning, the usual dangers of waste and overlap were complicated by the danger of counter-producing in delicate cross-cultural situations. On the less positive side, involved Americans were slowly becoming aware that foreign cultures were difficult to read, linguistically challenging, full of interlocked complexity, afflicted by what looked like corruption, and liable to react to stimuli in unpredictable ways. Real foreign experience was making internationalist Americans wary, less sure of themselves, more guarded in their expectations. Understanding that cultural intervention can provoke unpredictable change, impatient Americans were discovering caution.

From the developmental viewpoint, the foundations and government concluded that change, when it was already taking place, could be shaped and channeled; they believed they could and therefore should nudge for-eign systems toward different social, economic, and political outcomes. But some officials, perhaps wiser or merely less energetic, suspected that serious planning, adequate funding, continuity, and sensitive administra-tors were useless without a certain amount of luck. So-called scientific philanthropy, had shown the way to search out more sophisticated up-stream targets, but wise practitioners knew there was much more to be learned in heaven and earth than they had suspected.

Few Americans outside a handful of tight-fisted congressmen quar-reled with the growing funding role of government in the postwar period. Cultural offices remained open in US embassies; they found plenty to do, in the midst of the activity around them. The Marshall Plan's success tempted Washington to use the costly AID approach around the world. While Welles had called for private-public cooperation funded largely by the private world, Rockefeller had made government a principal funder; and the Marshall Plan mystique, forged in sophisticated European human economies, raised expectations and expenditures by government.

On the firing lines, a new class of internationalist Americans had begun to take shape, in the pioneering tradition of Morgan Shuster and Arthur Millspaugh in Haiti, the Philippines, and Iran. The foundations and the universities were dotted with returnees who had served in the division, OWI, OSS, or the two reorientations. With experience of devel-opment-oriented planning, they assumed that government involvement was indispensable and would inevitably bring progress, even if managed under less than optimal standards.

Part of Congress, however, remained unshakably skeptical, not so much about mighty AID or the CIA as about the cultural dimension of diplomacy. Except for certain beguiling programs like USIA's VOA, Con-gress squeezed federal funding and staff positions unrelentingly. The un-derstaffed division had to contract out its work to private organizations like IIE. If organizations did not exist, State and the foundations created them.

Inside government, the embattled few did yeoman work. For example, State's relations with the vast national foreign student and NAFSA com-munity, supported by the division, were managed as late as the 1970s by two tireless heroines, Marita Houlihan and Mary Ann Spreckelmeyer, who allocated their tiny budgets to the best possible targets by maintain-ing omniscient expertise about a thousand or more campuses. The under-funded IV support network similarly was energized and monitored over three or four decades by a handful of heroic government stalwarts, in-cluding Evelyn Barnes, Pauline Hopper, Mary Dennis, and Nan Bell.

Postwar philanthropy and the resurgence of voluntarism were remark-able in that the post–World War II period in government, as in 1919, was a time of anti-internationalist political backlash. The US elections of 1946 strengthened the nationalist tone in the Congress. There were early blunderbuss attacks on "pro-communists," and xenophobia was on the rise. Some hidden part of this was a nationalist attack on what Mrs. Luce called globaloney—her name for cultural internationalism. For the simple-minded in the politicians' world, cultural internationalism was easily confused with liberalism, which resembled socialism, which was of course a synonym for communism, and hence it could be easily used against political opponents. For those whose thinking ran this way, internationalism was a mild form of treason. As a result, internationalism's rise in the postwar private world was not paralleled in government, where serious officials argued in opposition to Fulbright and his friends that exchanges could only survive if concealed under meretricious and short-sighted rationales like propaganda and psy-war.

MacLeish had looked hard at questions of cultural internationalism, like those raised within government and those raised by Turner. Given time for a gradualist approach, and the freedom from congressional tugs-of-war that Roosevelt had provided, things might have turned out differently. American philanthropy and public-private cooperation might over time have learned to work together even better than they did. Instead, political process in the world's greatest democracy was already doing what Tocqueville warned it would—settling for less.

The work of Washington's cultural diplomats—once the only game in the nation's capital—was less exciting after the war. Fatigue was a product of underfunding. The clean gradualist definitions of 1938 no longer held; above all they made little sense to the action-oriented OWI veterans who surrounded the culturalists. Even inside the foreign-service community, approval was grudging: it was considered an act of high wit in the foreign service to call the USIS posts "useless" and to call cultural officers "culture-vultures." Diplomat Loy Henderson, in his memoirs, was not atypical: "Some of the old-timers of the State Department and Foreign Service . . . doubted the appropriateness of a division devoted to culture. . . . Cherrington and his two assistants . . . continued quietly to plant the seeds that germinated and developed into a giant organizational plant, the branches of which eventually extended into almost every corner of the globe." A sophisticated insider, Henderson, architect of the American buildup in Iran, blamed the postwar overexpansion of USIA, CIA, and AID on the maneuvering of three men with minuscule budgets who, in fact, did everything they could to keep things small, gradual, and facilitative.

The leadership of MacLeish might have made the difference. But his moment died with Roosevelt.

CHAPTER SIX

Early Field Staffing: The Point of Contact

> The way for us to make friends with South America is not to talk about ourselves, but about them. . . . All we can do is to induce in them as quickly as possible an image of our country as disinterested, in earnest, and mature.
>
> —Thornton Wilder, 1941

WHILE WASHINGTON TUSSLED, the field after 1942 went quietly about its business, improvising as it went. It is an appropriate time to pause, at the peak of possibility for the cultural diplomatic vision, to take a brief look at the early development of cultural officers and the services they provided in the field. Both officers and services grew out of circumstances, needs, local contexts, budgets, and available human resources. Soldiering on, the field staff had little time to worry about Washington's dithering over an understandable and compelling theory and structure to justify what they did.[1]

Field staffing was a late arrival. By Pearl Harbor the division was over forty months old. Its ICC component, among other cultural outputs, was providing technical assistance all over Latin America, administered mainly—except in Peru—by staff borrowed from other embassy duties. Designers of the field offices, for sufficient reasons, had chosen to bypass Congress and its hostility toward staff expansion, heeding Hull and postponing field staffing. Everyone knew that the real work of cultural diplomacy took place at "the point of contact," in the Fairbanks' phrase. But without funding how could the predictable surge in workload be carried? How could specialized expertise get the right people in the right places? How could the unique character of American intellect, education, and values be showcased as a function of US embassies?

In fairness, once they began performing cultural chores, embassies quickly understood the labor-intensivity of cultural diplomacy, which demands full-time energy, constant focus, persistent follow-through, and vibrant morale. And this had to take place every day of the year—even on Sundays—when airplanes had to be met or visitors entertained. Even veteran diplomats quickly realized that cultural diplomacy was not a job so much as a frame of mind, a focused commitment to a special point of view.

George Messersmith, Assistant Secretary for Administration, was a tight-ship diplomat whose role far exceeded his title. A famous one-man show, he wanted no outsiders in his embassies. He had come into State without a college degree and worked his way to the top via the Consular Corps. As a commercially oriented consular officer, he took a different turn when he was assigned to the consulate in Berlin in 1930; for four years, he wrote some of State's most penetrating analyses on the rise of Hitler and National Socialism. He held angry memories of the 1920s, when field representatives from the Departments of Commerce and Agriculture, over State's objections, disrupted the tight and collegial life in embassies he knew.[2] Opposing all specialized attachés and noting that the Axis used the title "attaché" for sinister purposes, his main point was human quality: diplomats already represented US culture at its best.[3]

Overlooking foreign precedents, Espinosa pointed out that specialized cultural officers, a general need for any US embassy, were first proposed early in the 1930s by Roger S. Greene, director of the Rockefeller-backed Union Medical College in Peking. Greene urged the US minister in China to recruit a special officer deeply familiar with China and its language. He saw a new class of intellectual modernizers, trained under the Boxer program, emerging and beginning to take over—especially in medicine. Back in New York as the Rockefeller Foundation's representative for the Far East, Greene kept up the pressure for special officer recruitment, making common cause with IIE's Stephen Duggan; after 1942 he commuted to Washington to help staff State's Far East division.[4] Shotwell's CIC also argued that cultural officers were indispensable in the field, recommending in 1935 that each embassy be assigned a special officer for intellectual cooperation, akin to a military attaché. Shotwell and Greene were especially concerned by mounting foreign restrictions on free intellectual pursuit and information flow. Following up on Buenos Aires in 1936, Samuel Guy Inman—still believing himself on track to head the cultural division when it was launched—weighed in as well, proposing "educational attachés" for all embassies who would "act as a source of information for exchange students and professors, aid literary and artistic exchange, provide for the interchange of books and reports . . . [and] prepare monographs on educational problems in both countries."[5]

These pleas from the most knowledgeable experts in the U.S. concurred with the thinking of the planners, but Hull believed it was a lost cause; the former Senator saw a Congress already mystified by the idea of cultural relations and opposed to adding staff. Even Messersmith changed his tune by February 1942, when he went to Mexico as ambassador and saw that cultural work required not only a full time officer but one with special university and linguistic credentials.

Rockefeller knew how to cut through most problems, although in doing so he often created a few of his own. Indifferent to tradition, disdainful of State, and unaware of his own limits, he wanted field agents and set out to get them, one way or another. With administrative ingenuity, insouciant anti-historicism, adjustable criteria of quality, deep pockets, and the cooperation of Elmer Davis and Colonel Donovan, he watched the embassies to the south begin to add cultural officers in 1942. To staff his private local committees as they developed, he seized on available part-time amateurs, mainly underemployed local businessmen. But for cultural officers he agreed with the division, as well as OWI and OSS, that university educators were required. Slashing away at red tape, he nicked an occasional tendon, e.g., causing pointless confusion by trying to conceal funding for the local committees from public scrutiny and keeping the very existence of the committees secret.

Every town of any size in Latin America had a Rockefeller committee, and most committees inherited or started up a BNC. In Mexico alone there were twenty BNCs; seventy others operated in Latin America, funded to some extent by low-tuition English-language teaching classes. The directors, usually Americans, had a lot to manage, beginning at the board level, where they dealt with under-informed board members from two language-cultures, mastered two different—and clashing—styles of administration, stroked a dozen or more board and staff egos, bridged the usual cross-cultural sensibilities, and kept passionate people calm. Directing a BNC involved shaping a daily program, managing a language school, handling complex financial accounting and strange local laws, and supervising a large work force.

In early 1942 the division, as well as the Coordinator, OWI, and OSS, were recruiting university intellectuals for the field, and area scholars moved into numerous embassies, in Latin America and elsewhere. A simple fact is worth underlining: A determined mindset on the part of four or five separate Washington agencies agreed that sophisticated field representation was indispensable. Whether this was skillful pressure by Welles and Duggan or whether it was simply obvious to all, the agencies agreed, perhaps without even spelling it out, that the work to be done was education.

The first cultural officers of the founding years, indeed of the first decade and a half, were American intellectuals by any definition. Most were university professors, usually country or area specialists. Some were local American educators like Giesecke in Peru or Joseph Piazza in Brazil, where he headed the American School; others were available scholars. Funded in almost random fashion by several different agencies, high-caliber cultural officers were in place all around the globe by the end of 1942.

In Latin America Argentina had two academics; Bolivia borrowed an anthropologist from US Indian Affairs; Brazil had Piazza; Chile had Berkeley historian Lawrence Kinnaird; Colombia had the polymath writer-editor Herschel Brickell; Costa Rica had Albert Gerberich of Dickinson College; Uruguay welcomed Duke professor of Romance languages John T. Reid, who went on to a distinguished career as a cultural diplomat specializing in the Far East and South Asia; Ecuador had San Francisco University professor of English Francis Colligan; El Salvador had a

US publishers' representative; Guatemala, a pre-Colombian archeologist; Haiti, a film writer; Mexico, a Rutgers professor of Spanish. Nicaragua had graduate student William Marvel, recruited in Mexico, then succeeded by Rodolfo Rivera of the ALA and the ACLS; Paraguay hired editor-publisher Morill Cody thereby initiating another fine USIA career; Peru finally gave the title to Giesecke and added his University of Pennsylvania friend, archeologist George Vaillant; Uruguay found a California state adminins- trator and former diplomat, then launched the foreign service career of Albert Franklin, professor of Romance languages at the University of Maryland; Venezuela borrowed the American director of the local BNC. Only the embassies in Honduras and the Dominican Republic fell back on young diplomats, in the latter case W. Tapley Bennett, at the beginning of his impressive career. More than administrators, these men—until 1946 there were no women—were hardy pioneers and creative improvis- ers. The job demanded that they be intellectual nerve centers and pump primers for enticing university scholars and students, intellectuals and educators into bilateral dialogue. Academics and intellectuals would dominate US cultural offices until the mid-1950s, then slowly fade away, recurring sporadically until 1974, when they were brushed away by a fiat of USIA personnel policy.[6]

Outside Latin America, the division could count on equally remark- able people hired by OSS or OWI: locally recruited Yale archeologist Frank E. Brown in Beirut, Sanskritist W. Norman Brown in Delhi, Persian scholar T. Cuyler Young in Tehran, Sinologist John K. Fairbank in Chung- king, Turkish sociologist Donald E. Webster in Ankara, Romance lan- guages scholar John Van Horne in Madrid, and others lost in time's mists. After World War II, cultural officers took up the reins in Belgium, En- gland, France, Italy, Portugal, and occupied Germany and Austria; the Netherlands welcomed the first woman CAO to a USIS post, Dutch resis- tance heroine Patricia Van Delden.

In 1946 Romance languages scholar Howard Lee Nostrand returned to the University of Washington after two years in Peru, where he succeeded Vaillant as Giesecke's colleague. His pamphlet of 1947 for the Hazen Foundation stands alone in the period as a conceptual snapshot of cul- tural field work in the 1940s.[7] Nostrand based his report on the far-reach- ing assumption that the U.S. conceives its "self-interest as interdependent with the well-being of other peoples, and not at their expense." The new IICA in Washington, he said, "has an unprecedented staff in the field, serviced by a complete battery of area divisions and technical divisions." He went on to underline ICC's work: It "supervises foreign projects of 45 government agencies." From 1938 forward, he wrote, Washington agreed that high-level intellectual expertise was indispensable in an embassy. The CAO's work was conceived in a university mode; they served univer- sities abroad and at home. Nostrand's long article confirms the records: for the moment at least, the battle in favor of cultural attachés had been won; the idea that they should be university educators was for the moment beyond question.

These outsiders were shaped by embassy cultures and country situations more than they changed the embassies. In Latin America there were two different models: one turned leadership over to Rockefeller's "private" coordinating committees, with the cultural officer as embassy liaison; the other centered on the cultural officer, "attached to" but not *of* the embassy. The incoming and outgoing flow of university educator exchangees kept the academic world involved. The cultural officers on loan from the universities, the division's heavily academic staff, and the high-level GAC with its academic subcommittees made for three strong layers of university insulation against short-range policy pressures or loss of quality.

Illusions came quickly, some imperceptibly, to light. On the receiving end, the bureaucrats of Washington and the field had unrealistic assumptions. They knew little about scholars, remembering only the tree-lined college campuses of 1920–40, where decent and caring faculty seemed to know everything and had endless time for their students. The bureaucrats thus expected academics to deploy the same caring magic overseas, day in and day out, through twelve-hour days, without summer vacations, speaking a foreign language much of the time, and without the comfortable support of an academic discipline, a library, tenure, and captive audiences of under-informed students. Why, they wondered, would a Romance languages scholar object to teaching American history and literature? Was it not enough that the scholar was an American, knew literature, and could bone up on the blank spaces? In fact, very few American universities in 1940–45 offered American literature—Princeton's first survey course was not offered until 1947. The modest Baudelaire scholar Jacob Canter, dragooned into teaching American literature in 1947 in Colombia, sighed: "At least I knew more than they did, which was zero."[8] For some the challenge was transforming: the late Leslie Fiedler, a Fulbright medievalist in Italy in the early 1950s never known for his modesty, had to be pressed into teaching American literature; accepting the chore, he underwent a life-change and turned the rest of his career over to critical studies of US literature.

A second set of illusions resided with the outsider attachés themselves, who expected in their role as cultural officer, at the very least, to be insulated from clerical tasks, as they had been in the universities. They soon learned that there was no one else to do the work. Canter literally begged embassy secretaries to type his reports. The academics had even deeper illusions: they thought of themselves as independent principals, not agent-servants of someone called a PAO. They tended to think, as the universities permitted them to believe, that they could avoid politics. But even the missionaries had learned that culture and education abroad were political questions, hence that the very presence of an American intellectual in the host country was politically charged. Further loss of innocence came when academics realized the government could not live up to the promises that exuberant recruiters had dangled before them. And so the academics enjoyed themselves, performed whatever daily miracles they could, and left when their tour was up, neglecting for the most part to write about the experience. Their embassy hosts, on the other hand, concealed their disappointment over their dear university professors who did not turn out to be the wizards they remembered.

The Washington designers, themselves activist academics, had assumed that people like themselves would somehow manage in the field and that local staff could be added when necessary. But field budgets were controled by the PAOs; hiring was not so easy as it seemed; and few foreign academics had Giesecke's flexibility, stature, or commitment, nor were they interested in working as an embassy "local," invariably treated in an embassy as a second-class citizen. Moreover, at the point of contact, additional staff was not always helpful. Local audiences wanted the real thing—an academic cultural officer's image could not be delegated any more than could Benjamin Franklin's.

A CAO career was early understood as a life-commitment akin to teaching, a kind of priesthood, as one CAO said; but unlike the universities, the embassies did not provide a system of support. Research into one more new country produced exhaustion instead of exhilaration. There were never enough hours for discovering the country's history and literature, or for meeting—and sustaining relationships with—all the interesting people. And there were never enough gifts to give. A cultural officer received frequent gifts, some of them touchingly humble; in return he had little to give but himself; some ended up giving more of themselves than they could afford. The great CAO John L. Brown, echoing MacLeish's "Ars Poetica," said it best: "A cultural officer should not Mean, but Be."[9]

The American virtue of impatience was another unsettling factor for academics used to tending young trees. Given a problem, Americans like to find solutions; USIS posts, full of media-men and advertisers, were eager to be "doing something"—a phrase that was the activist's indictment of traditional diplomacy and its alleged incompetence. "Doing something," for a CAO, meant distributing real and metaphoric gifts—grants, operating support to a BNC, an extra teacher for the language school, books, help in polishing a translation, a lunch invitation, a scholar-teacher for the local university, a performance for the presidential palace, a lecture in a school or college, and sometimes nothing more than a sympathetic ear and a little time or a handwritten note of congratulations or condolences. To their activist colleagues, some of these activities looked like slacking off. The barely manageable pandemonium of the CAO's life was captured in 1965 by a philosopher who had never worked in an embassy but had visited many: Charles Frankel, in his essay "The Man in the Middle," to which we shall return.[10]

A hyperactive agenda was implied in Hull's shopping list, but no one thought to add up the hours per week. Veteran cultural administrator and first deputy director of UNESCO, Walter Laves, in 1963 in a book he had begun with Charles Thomson before Thomson's sudden death in 1961, concluded that the job required omniscient giants with iron stomachs who never slept and who ignored their families. A CAO, he said, was routinely expected to have "a broad and rounded knowledge of the social, educational, scientific, and artistic life of the U.S., and of the leading public and private organizations in those areas, . . . to inform himself of similar activities and trends in the country where he was stationed, . . . to seek out and become acquainted with educational leaders, writers, journalists, musicians and painters, scientists, and other scholars." In short, he concluded, the CAO was "the human channel, or rather the human engineer who sought to make the two-way flow of cultural information and experience mutually helpful and useful."[11] And he also had to be dumb enough to accept the job, one might have added.

Language skills were assumed. In 1942 all the Latin American cultural officers were either Hispanists or had lived for years in the area. The GAC, commenting on language requirements, echoed Matteo Ricci and Alessandro Valignano in asserting that the CAO's language needs extended well beyond diplomatic fluency and basic literacy: "It may be assumed that they have a fluent command of the languages . . . but they should be willing to endeavor to learn to use the language with distinction, as well as with readiness."[12] The members of the GAC and their monolingual chairman knew the American CAO would be compared with impressive cultural colleagues from other embassies, including the dazzling French.

Each embassy culture was an unfamiliar world to outsiders, and those inside did not always make it easy. The field intellectuals were expected to get along with prickly ambassadors and pricklier ambassadorial wives; embassy colleagues uncomfortable with intellect, some of whom, including Messersmith, had not earned a BA; USIS colleagues competing for budget; occasionally high-quality but always underpaid national staff; clearance processes that meant no cultural officer could sign his own cabled messages (all were sent out under the ambassador's name); inadequate reimbursement for expenses and none for entertaining; hairsplitting rules of rank and privilege; inconsistent supervision; and conflicting mandates from Washington. Field intellectuals and their wives were jammed into a military-style pecking order and participated in a feast-or-famine schedule of demands driven by local circumstances, random visitors, and ambassadorial whim; meanwhile, they handled an alarming variety of field products flowing from half a dozen uncoordinated Washington offices and maintained relations with dozens of US private institutions. Other than that, the job was easy.

In 1942 cultural officers under the rules laid down by martinet Assistant Secretary Messersmith were second-class citizens like the local employees. They represented the universities, but the universities had nothing to say about assigning, reassigning, or dismissing them, nor about their daily labors. The costs of "representation," the foreign service word for entertainment at dinners, lunches, and receptions, were not re-imbursed—CAOs exhausted a pitiful entertainment account a month or two into the year, and after that, they could only invite a university rector or a poet to lunch if they paid for it themselves. Congress was primly penny-wise on this point; one legislator—who loved to visit embassies abroad where he demanded substantial alcoholic nourishment—famously called the entertainment account "booze money." Some CAOs managed to persuade their ambassadors to stage the larger-scale receptions they occasionally needed, some tapped into private funds through the BNCs, some repaid invitations by book-gifts, and all spent their own money—at least it was tax-deductible. In the 1970s one couple I knew, people of modest means, deducted over $10,000 annually in entertainment costs certified by embassy accountants. That so many did so and did so will-ingly, not only in 1942 but in 2002, suggests rare commitment to the "priesthood" that the CAOs formed; it also implies smiling persistence in the face of demeaning neglect.

There was no training for cultural work—before 1942 only Giesecke had ever done the job. And leadership was fragmented. In Latin America in 1943, the cultural officer dealt with at least four agencies in Washing-ton; if there were ICC experts on loan to the host-country's government, there were many more. And there was no end to sovereign private bodies, from IIE, ACLS, and ALA to the dozens of individual universities and professional associations on which their work depended—nor to the ex-pectations these bodies vested in "their" field agent.

Academic cultural officers coped with the problems of intellectuals everywhere, including inadequate time to keep abreast in their fields, few up-to-date professional or even general publications, lack of understand-ing from those around them, unavoidable trivia, agendas dictated by oth-ers, and brute fatigue. With their immediate bosses the PAOs, tensions were cloaked in civility but never far off; the burden was on the academic CAO to get along with his boss. Unlike scholars in the university world, CAOs dealt as well with the sly anti-intellectualism—perhaps non-intel-lectualism would be more accurate—of the embassy, flowing in part from the special character of 1940s Washington, a capital city without a major university dominated by a Congress of night-school lawyers. Truman had never gone beyond high school, and Messersmith dropped out after two years of teachers' college. Academic outsiders learned to reduce their focus to the narrower range of embassy concerns and dealt with the here-and-now of diplomacy.

The Ph.D., the badge of any academic, has its own history in US diplo-macy. Wilson Dizard, a USIA veteran of the 1940s and 1950s who later become a prolific writer on international communications, produced the first thorough insider's book on USIA in 1961—through the eyes of a PAO. His uneasiness with culture leaps out of sentences like this one:

"Usually cultural officers have doctorate degrees or other academic merit-badges which permit them initial access to the elite."[13] Aside from the slighting reference to "doctorate degrees" as "merit-badges," and the hint that access closed up after the "initial" stage, his overestimate of the number of Ph.D.s in USIA in 1961 says much. By 1961, in fact, Ph.D.s were no longer "usual" in USIA; the downward trend initiated in the mid-fifties continued until outside academics were no longer recruited by USIA after 1974. At USIA's end in 1999, there were few left, although new Ph.D.s began to filter back among other entrants in the 1980s. In 1961, speaking from personal experience, officers with doctorates who joined USIA or State were quietly advised not to mention it. At one level this reflected the reticence of patrician attitudes in men like Welles; at another, it reflected the discomfort of men like Dizard. Columbia University political scientist Wayne Wilcox, on loan as cultural officer in London, discovered in 1972 that USIA, unlike other government agencies, had a "declining educational profile." While the number of doctorates were rising in all government agencies, the numbers in USIA were falling.

In 1981 the situation took a peculiar twist: a flood of new political appointees descended on cultural affairs, some with unimpressive academic credentials, yet who *insisted* on being called "doctor." (In the research universities, it used to be said that the number of faculty calling themselves doctors was indirectly proportional to the university's quality.) From then until its end in 1999, under a director who was always called doctor, USIA bestowed the title primarily on political appointees.

Academics, by classic definitions, are expected to publish, documenting their continuous contribution to new learning. In the early stages of field service in USIS posts, some academics assumed they would continue to do so, but all too soon it was obvious that their jobs were totally consuming. Only the work itself provided a viable subject for research, but the outsiders were discouraged from writing about USIA by "rules" saying that Washington must approve all publications. Energetic scholars like Robin Winks, Cleanth Brooks, Carl Bode, or Wayne Wilcox in London and the driven intellectual-turned-career officer Ted Wertime in Tehran and Athens maintained records of scholarly publication; Wertime did it, he said, between midnight and 3 A.M. every night. Academic performance—and reputation—faded as scholars remained longer in foreign service. Summing up the depletion, Charles Blitzer, a Yale historian who directed the National Humanities Center and Washington's Woodrow Wilson Center in the 1970s, remarked that service with USIA "had a way of scrambling good brains."

In the field, the cultural officers had an unmatchable advantage: they approached foreign audiences under the banner of culture. Outside the Anglo-Saxon countries, the word "culture" opens many doors. In general, foreign audiences recognize any American diplomat who listens, asks informed questions, works hard, and gives an occasional gift. But the embassy title Cultural Attaché brings an immediate kind of fame which is best borne modestly.

Like Fulbright in the Senate, academic CAOs soon learned to adopt bland coloration, to dumb down vocabulary, and to pitch discourse to the middle level of their audiences. In the confusion about Tocqueville's fears about equality, American non-intellectualism has long been the unavoidable price paid by those who want to work in cultural diplomacy. To the foreign public, they are the designated extension abroad of US intellect; to US colleagues, intellect can pose various kinds of threat, real and imagined. John L. Brown, never called doctor—although his CAO son often is—stayed with cultural work for three decades before returning to his university. From his informational colleagues, this witty and fun-loving man of letters, a USIA legend, drew the standard slurs of non-intellectuals. He was called arrogant, lofty, disdainful, elitist, frivolous, unfocused, disorganized, administratively inept, negligent of priorities, and so on. An information colleague in Mexico boasted he had solved his problems with Brown by threating a punch in the nose—Brown remembered the episode as a moment to be gracefully overcome. Along the peculiar divide between information specialists and their cultural counterparts, both sides normally agreed to respect the other's professionalism, but this tacit agreement could fray, especially when the time came to carve up budgets. In general the cultural officers kept their end of the civil bargain better than the information officers, smiling through regular accusations of irrelevance to foreign policy, financial incompetence, inept administration, "pure-culturism," "culture for culture's sake," or in the inelegant words of one USIA officer, of living in the "artsy-f—sy" world.

Under such pressures, few of the early outside academics remained in the service for more than a single tour, and after 1953 USIA recruited fewer academics—its senior officials memorably falling back on the bland profundity that "Ph.D.s do not always work out." The decline from an all-academic cultural staff had begun in 1945, when many war-employed academics returned to their campuses just as legions of OWI staffers were swamping the division. Academic cultural officers persisted in several places of high cultural importance: Rome until 1958, London until 1976, Paris until 1972, and sporadically elsewhere. London continued longest as an academic post, for reasons obvious enough to make the point. In 1961 the Kennedy administration and Philip Coombs tried to reverse the antiacademic trend, bringing in prestigious outside cultural officers in posts like Delhi, Tokyo, Paris, Madrid, and Vienna. But USIA made sure these officers were kept away from power under the pretext of sparing them the dog-work. The cute sobriquet "Super-CAO" was coined during that period: it sanctified and isolated the exception. In the 1960s, through "lateral entry," outsider academics could be integrated into the service and a few academics like myself wandered in; but by 1974 lateral entry was abandoned as USIA director James Keogh explained laboriously to an irritated Senator Claiborne Pell: all officers were recruited, hired, and assigned as generalists. Even the political appointment process tended to overlook the campuses: in 1982 the London cultural office reached its nadir when the CAO position went to a political appointee, a dental hygienist who, it was explained, "had done PR" for an oil company.

With such disincentives for the scholar-CAO, it is the more remarkable that a few paragons and an occasional Protean were found and sometimes retained. Some stayed in touch with the university world, and a very few managed to rise to lead their information colleagues as PAOs. Recruiting more academic outsiders would have been a simple matter— dozens have told me they were eager for such an opportunity.

• • •

Fortunately we can look more closely at a few early cultural officers.[14] Cultural work is a remarkably human—and humane—kind of commitment. Cultural officers like to trade anecdotes over drinks. But few are comfortable telling their sorrows and glories in any public way, part of American *paideia*. The quality of these officers' work and their lives can only be recaptured dimly, even in their own memories. The five vignettes that follow convey only a small part of what it was like for early cultural diplomats in the decade beginning in 1942.

Jacob Canter was a Harvard Ph.D. humanist in Romance languages who went to Nicaragua in 1946. His experience, captured in 1988, told of his predictable expectations at home and abroad, the sharp drop in postwar funding, and the mismanagement of his talents through failure to recognize what he could do best. The memories of this modest and unassuming man did honor to his predecessors. He spoke admiringly of Herschel Brickell, William Marvel, later head of Education and World Affairs, and Rodolfo Rivera of ALA and ACLS.

After a dissertation on Baudelaire, Canter taught at Harvard, then at the Naval Academy. In Annapolis he came upon an advertisement for cultural officers in Latin America and soon found himself in Managua. There, dusty remains and a few beleaguered staffers bespoke the glory days before Central American field posts were cut—by 75 percent on the average—after World War II.

To his amazement, he was given the title Public Affairs Officer: "What on earth was a PAO? I had been told by my mentors that I would be the boss of both 'culture' and 'information'; they said the information part . . . would be handled mainly by local employees, so I could concentrate on 'culture.'" In this "morass," as he called it, the young, resilient Canter coped: "For a small country, the program was large, some of it based on vestiges of . . . the Coordinator." The national staff was more than adequate: besides himself, there were "an [American] Assistant Cultural Affairs Officer, an American secretary, a Nicaraguan secretary, and a collection of stalwart national employees for press, radio and movies."

He set to work to build "a scholarship program for Nicaraguan students, grants for teachers, and training grants in vocational education"; he organized a local selection committee and began interviewing candidates. "We had mountains of American books, some in Spanish translation for distribution to institutions and individuals. An excellent and much-used small library, set up by the ALA with funds from the Coordinator, housed our English-teaching program."

The information side of the house, in fact, did seem to handle itself, as he had been told it would—he noted that it was relatively simple work. Random circumstance dictated his schedule: "It meant spending one's nights, weekends and holidays responding to invitations—to school events, exhibitions, musical soirées dignified as concerts." He became a broadcaster: "Every Friday evening . . . I did a fifteen-minute radio talk on 'life and culture'—it may have reached some listeners, despite the honking of automobile horns through the studio's open windows." There were endless public appearances, "substantive talks . . . at the auditorium of the national capitol. . . . I managed a literary lecture in response to an invitation to honorary membership in the Nicaraguan Writers Association." He was supremely conscious that "in Nicaraguan eyes, I was there as a representative of American culture."

Canter was yanked away after only a year in Managua and given a bigger job in Colombia, succeeding the legendary Herschel Brickell, who was, as he admitted, "a hard act to follow, . . . a man of letters, a literary critic, the editor of the annual O. Henry short-story collection; they said in the Embassy that he carried his program in his head and on the back of an envelope, their way of saying he had no 'program.' Three years later his Colombian friends were still invoking his name." In Colombia too the program had been slashed. This time Canter, still bemused by his Managua title, bore a new title: Assistant PAO. But he still had to beg embassy secretaries to type his cables and letters. With Carlos Lopez Narvaez, director of Colombian secondary education and a major poet in a land of poets, he set about producing an anthology of American women poets in Spanish translation.

The embassy's unmanageable deluge of inquiries about study in the U.S. took too much time and a lot of ingenuity. After months of work, Canter managed to set up a student counseling service—several offspring of which survive in Colombia today. A scholarship program managed by IIE needed careful binational management in the pre-Fulbright years. (Latin America, with no US military surplus sales, came late to the Fulbright Program.) ICC exchangees came and went. He sent a few "Leaders" to the U.S. In Bogotá, the Athens of Latin America, Canter lectured publicly and called on the greats. He visited universities all over the country. He published articles on American and French literature. Poet Rafael Maya persuaded him to accept a professorship in American literature at the university, a post he held for two years, turning back his salary to the department to buy library books. In Colombia too he did a weekly radio broadcast. He was the perfect man in the right place.

"Then, in the midst of the radio series, of my teaching, of new funds, after being hailed as the only American ever to cross the threshold of El Automático [the select literary cafe]—in the midst of all that, I was sent to Caracas. . . . They said it was a short assignment. I would be back in Bogotá in about a month, they said."

"They" were either wrong or lying. He returned briefly, after three months, to tidy up before moving on to Havana. He had been dragged away from Colombia because the ambassador in Caracas had a brainstorm: a baseball festival built around a Chicago White Sox infielder, the Venezuelan Chico Carrasquel. But Canter, now completely hooked on his new career, concealed his feelings and soldiered on. In 1950 he moved to Cuba, then to Mexico, to Spain, and finally to a career in Washington, which he capped as Deputy Assistant Secretary of State for Educational and Cultural Affairs, the first—and the last—field officer ever to ascend to that position.

Looking back in 1988, he remembered a snide Stanford professor who said the work of the CAO was essentially that of a clerk. "He was at least half right. Why hire a Herschel Brickell to run a baseball project, to push papers, to enmesh himself in the myriad aspects of bureaucratic trivia? Yet we cultural torch-bearers did it all and Washington applauded our performance—as clerks. For good measure, it denominated us Assistant Public Affairs Officers, with no regard for the image and role of the fellow toiling, say, in the Athens of South America." Canter had encountered a deep trait of the American mindset: "It was as if the bureaucratic mores of the time required the hushing of the word, even the notion of culture." After retirement Canter taught at the Murrow Center of Tufts University. Back in Washington, he lived until just before his century's end.[15]

Albert Harkness. A snapshot from an earlier time shows another Harvard graduate student. In the midst of his Ph.D. research in Santiago de Chile, Harkness was recruited—on 7 December 1941. He had sailed with Samuel Eliot Morrison on the Harvard expedition tracing Columbus's voyages to the New World and was finishing his doctorate under Morrison. Harkness came from a long tradition of scholars and cultural internationalists: his family created the internationalist Harkness grants and the Commonwealth Foundation, pendant to the Rhodes; his great-grandfather founded the American School of Classical Studies in Athens.

On Pearl Harbor Day he was hailed from a trolley window by Rex Crawford, University of Pennsylvania sociologist then teaching at the University of Chile, courtesy of the Coordinator. In a matter of months, Crawford would be named the first US cultural attaché in Santiago before he moved east to Brazil. In Chile Harkness was funded by Rockefeller's local businessman's committee, probably from funds provided by the Coordinator; his job was to revive the newly reopened, privately funded Chilean–North American Cultural Institute, a CPI survivor sustained by

English teaching, one of the earliest BNCs in Latin America. The institute was fast asleep, used mainly for social occasions, with no permanent home. The local committee decided to make it the linchpin of the US cultural-information effort in Chile.

The institute's governing board included representatives of the National City Bank, the local American telephone company, the Rockefeller Foundation, and the head of the American girls' school, as well as a distinguished roster of Chileans. Roaming around Santiago with committee chair Joseph Dawson of City Bank, Harkness found a mansion in the "nitrate baroque" style, built by a nineteenth-century mining millionaire; he learned only later that it had most recently served as a flourishing brothel. On Pan-American Day, 14 April 1942, the new Chilean-American Cultural Institute was inaugurated. Harkness built the program: "We sponsored seminars, held art exhibits, maintained a library; but above all we taught English, . . . [our] main source of income. We started with eight students; when I left we had 2,000; and today I believe there are 5,000." Lawrence Kinnaird, Berkeley historian, succeeded Rex Crawford; his first efforts went into expanding academic exchanges.

After the war, back at Harvard, Harkness finished his doctorate and helped Morrison compile his history of US Naval operations. But he had caught the joy of cultural work abroad and soon returned to the profession, first in Costa Rica, then in Venezuela, where he coauthored with Pedro Grases a study of Manuel García de Sena, follower of Francisco Miranda and translator of both the US Constitution and Thomas Paine. Harkness then returned to Chile, seeing no contradiction in serving as PAO, the head of both information and culture. His career was launched. He followed Chile with assignments in Washington, Athens, Peru, Mexico, and Madrid. During the Kennedy years, he brought an academic CAO to Spain: retired and nearly blind Dean Leopold Arnauld of the Columbia School of Architecture.

Harkness considered himself first and always a cultural officer, even though he spent most of his career as PAO. For him, PAO meant not only heading the USIS mission but also shaping it as he pleased. His pervasive cultural focus reflected both his personality and his academic background, his intellectual experience, and his easy relationship with other scholars in various language cultures. He too ended his career teaching at Tufts, an ornament of US cultural diplomacy from the cradle days. He had no problem in being a PAO; he knew who he was and never doubted that the most valuable part of the work of a USIS post was cultural.[16]

T. Cuyler Young went to Iran in 1931 as a graduate Student Volunteer, a missionary-educator. Because his papers have not been published, I can only report on the man I knew. One item from our conversations remains particularly vivid: a torn and faded glimpse of wartime Iran. Iran missionaries like Young, Samuel Jordan, and Jane Doolittle, private administrators like Shuster and Milspaugh, and fervent scholars like Pope and his successors had done remarkable cultural and educational planting in Iran over the years. The scholarly Young joined OSS in 1942 as part of Langer's team, then was sent to Tehran as part of a worldwide network for gathering and analyzing information from open sources. Like Fairbank in Chungking, Young plowed his own furrow.

In his first experience in Iran, he had married a missionary-educator colleague also named Young, a biologist. After Langer's research and analysis, the Youngs joined the wartime embassy in Tehran. Young was easily the best Persian speaker, the best connected, and the best informed element in the embassy. It was as natural for OSS to smile on his cultural work as it was for them to smile on Fairbank in Chungking. Young's position gave him a title, an image he knew how to use, and a role in a world he understood. Because all events in Iran had deep historical roots, Young served as unofficial interpreter and educator to his embassy.

My memories of Young cluster around a single extended episode. By a happy accident, OWI had recruited an employee from India, where she had been following Gandhi's work. Nilla Cram Cook was the divorced wife of George Cram "Jig" Cook, founder of the historic Provincetown Playhouse, which had launched theater people like Eugene O'Neill, James Stewart, and Margaret Sullavan. Nilla Cook was a curious combination: dancer and theater person, linguist, Persian literary scholar, and woman of unusual philosophical curiosity, drive, and determination. She tried Young's patience but caught his attention.

The Russian tradition of ballet was a coveted art form in Iran. Mme Cornelli, a White Russian émigré, was imposing rigid classical Russian discipline on young Iranians, with mixed success. Cook set out in another direction, studying local dance movements, Iranian miniatures and paintings, sculpture, ceramics, music, literature, and mythology—anything that depicted the rhythmic movement of the human body. The Youngs agreed to help her persuade prominent families to allow their daughters to perform traditional Persian dance outside the confines of their high-walled homes. In an even bolder move, she asked the Youngs to help get parental permission for their daughters to dance publicly with young men. A small troupe was assembled, folk-ballets were put together in the method later made famous by Russian folk-choreographer Igor Moiseyev, and performances were staged around Iran, heralded by a notable evening performance at the residence before ambassador George Allen, who would soon take over State's cultural affairs. With the magic of costuming and lighting, the troupe made a resounding hit in Iran; and with the prestige of the embassy behind the enterprise, families and clerics kept their peace. Young then persuaded Iran's foreign ministry to fund and arrange a two-month tour to Turkey, which was successful enough to be extended by another six months, after which a reduced troupe carried on for another two years in Greece, Lebanon, and India. In Beirut they were greeted by PAO-CAO and Yale archeologist Frank E. Brown, recruited from his job in Damascus as Director of Antiquities for all of Syria.

The American-inspired dance troupe was a cultural mission of the Iranian government, an assertion of pride in the beauty and grace of their history, literature, and folk traditions, and a political gesture from Shiah Iran to other parts of the Muslim world. Ambassador Allen had no doubt this was worth the small USIS investment of Cook's salary and Young's time. With Iran at one remove from the Arab world to the east, the troupe was part of an early US effort to help link moderate nations of the area. Behind the troupe, all but invisible, stood Young and Cook, the American Diaghilev and Massine, proud of having brought some of the unsuspected beauty of Persia to the surface.

After World War II, Young shaped generations of Middle East students and scholars in Princeton's Department of Oriental Languages and Literature, later Near East Studies. His son and namesake became an important classical archeologist and helped unearth more of Persia's hidden treasure. A young tutor who accompanied the tour in Turkey went on to become the world's leading expert on Iranian foreign policy, spending a distinguished and devoted career at the University of Virginia. One of the troupe's lead dancers became his wife.[17]

Frank Oram tells a contrasting tale about Brazil in 1942–45.[18] Oram, a committed information officer with a new B.A. in economics, joined the office of the Coordinator then moved to Rio de Janeiro in the early 1940s. During the rest of his long career with USIA, he admired cultural toilers, but from a distance.

Strategic factors made South America, and Brazil in particular, vital to the US war effort. Among these factors were Forrestal's arrangement for building clandestine airstrips, and the Argentinian visas distributed to perhaps a thousand crew members of the scuttled German pocket-battleship Graf Spee, which enabled them to melt into the landscape. Rio had been chosen as the major outpost for Rockefeller's office, and the embassy had to accept. The independent committee grew fast, headed by Norwegian-American Barent Friele, a leader in the coffee business. Outposts under his committee's jurisdiction in this enormous country included two dozen BNCs. In 1941 Joseph Piazza, head of Rio's American School, was brought aboard as CAO, then in 1943 sociologist Rex Crawford crossed the mountains from Santiago and took over. Roy Nash, a social scientist from the US Bureau of Indian Affairs, went first to São Paolo, then to Porto Alegre, then back to Rio as CAO.

The star of the operation was Carleton Sprague Smith, New York polymath, professor of music at Columbia University, and head of the Music Division of the New York Public Library. Smith was a fine flautist, a gifted linguist, and an all-purpose Renaissance man. He had attended the division's Washington conference on music in 1939 and joined GAC's music subcommittee. For ACLS in 1940, he did a comprehensive survey of South American universities, and then became visiting professor at several Brazilian universities. In 1944–45 he served as CAO in both Rio and Sâo Paolo.

Political stress fell on São Paolo, where German immigration had flourished for decades. The USIS post there was headed by Arnold Tschudi, a General Motors representative. With few cars to sell, he moved to the Coordinator's payroll. Beneath him and his deputy Oram, there were five divisions: exchanges, radio, films, press, and libraries—including BNCs. The Brazilian staff numbered around thirty. In Rio Smith handled all exchanges and visited São Paolo regularly—his salary came from State. Oram remembered their first Leader Grantee, a novelist and writer from Porto Alegre, who returned to write a fine book on the U.S., critical but balanced.

After the war Oram stayed with information work, took part in the 1953 task forces designing the new USIA, rose to the top levels of USIA as Latin American area director, then went as PAO to Madrid. Retiring from USIA, he worked with the OAS in Washington.

In our discussions in 1998, he raised a serious question, perhaps not aware he was echoing Welles's famous 5-percent bargain and the thinking behind it: why did the government get involved in cultural relations at all? Most of what was done, he said, could have been done by grants to institutions like IIE for scholarships, ALA for libraries, and so forth. Much of what was done then and later was done by a kind of subterfuge, luring Congress into spending money that would allegedly be lost otherwise; even the Fulbright program and the PL 480 funds from the sale of surplus agricultural commodities could be described that way.

Given the skewing power of available money, Oram worried that government had done less than it might have. He remembered seeing, during his career, exorbitant funding and a context that discouraged clear thinking about priorities or quality. He admired Rockefeller and shared the view that traditional diplomats—inbred by the foreign service and its culture—were trained to negotiate and report but not to get things done. In his view, the Coordinator's office set the right priorities, provided funds, and stimulated private cooperation.

He greatly admired Carleton Sprague Smith. Asked to speculate on alternate structures in which Smith might have done more, while helping the government play a lesser role, Oram agreed that a small but collegial scholarly office separate from USIS, handling academic relations and exchanges, with Smith and a like-minded colleague in charge, might have done a better job. As a committed informationist and, overall, a Rockefeller unidirectionalist, Oram today displays the brand of dogged resilience, ingenuity, intelligence, and resourcefulness that marked the best of USIS's PAOs. And his admiration for CAO giants, including Smith and Crawford, is obvious. Like many of the early OWI people, and like CPI's Robert Murray in Mexico in 1919, he grew to think more in terms of long-range activities,[19] e.g., extending the network of USIS libraries around the world.

Charles Stevens was the first CAO in Mexico, 1942–44. Thanks to Kent Warren Smith's Ph.D. thesis on wartime Mexico,[20] we see that the specially recruited university figures did not always have an easy time. The Bostonian Stevens came out of the famous Latin School which had produced Benjamin Franklin. Born at the turn of the century, he interrupted his study at Dartmouth for service with the Navy in 1917, returned to graduate work in Spanish literature at Middlebury, studied in Madrid, taught languages, and earned a late Ph.D. at NYU in 1938. At Rutgers he seems to have been one of the indispensable figures who supported university language departments in the thirties and forties, available to teach any course but not expected to contribute to knowledge through scholarship.

Stevens was recruited with unusual speed: five weeks after Pearl Harbor he was in Mexico, the first American cultural figure there since Murray's CPI unit closed. His ambassador was the punctilious George Messersmith, still nervous about attachés of any kind yet keen on cultural relations. Messersmith, inheriting the embassy from the legendary Josephus Daniels, found alarming looseness, by his criteria; he instituted tight controls over all officers. Since Messersmith was reluctant to absorb outsiders into his embassy's priesthood, Stevens was placed under the supervision of the embassy's Second Secretary Edward Trueblood who, by complete chance, had come to Mexico fresh from pre-Vichy Paris via State's Division of Cultural Relations.

CPI had left frustration everywhere when its reading rooms in seven Mexican cities closed. Classes in English, bookkeeping, shorthand and French were cut off overnight, despite Murray's heroism. CPI's success in education-starved Mexico made its disappearance all the more deplorable, proving to skeptics that the U.S. was using Mexicans for its purposes.

Not surprisingly, Stevens found no guidelines, precedents, or job descriptions. Trueblood showed him around, protected him inside the embassy, carried on relations with Mexican officialdom, and moved the choking paperwork. He left Stevens free to travel all over Mexico, carrying out the three-part mission both men saw as theirs: first, field work, including recruiting candidates for exchange grants; second, developing friendly relations with Mexican cultural leaders; third, exemplifying American culture and intellect by lecturing and publishing on US education and history. Like Canter, he became an authority on the U.S. in under-informed Mexico, especially in the provinces.

Mexico was a nervous country with unresolved grievances against the gringos reaching back to the Mexican War. With his fine and literate Spanish, Stevens set out to let Mexico know he was there as a symbol of US culture and a man who cultivated interest in Mexico. He and Trueblood, in consultation with leading Mexicans, designed one-week trips to each of the provinces, touching base with prominent officials, universities, and schools. Week after exhausting week, braving the provincial hotels and restaurants and the usual maladies, he made contacts, scouted out promising students and potential exchangees, visited schools and universities, learned what kinds of American expertise were needed, and developed a sense of what was happening. The only limitation on Stevens's work was his own energy, of which he seemed to have a good supply: "There are all too few people in the world who have their hearts in their work and who have the zeal and the vigor of Stevens," wrote Messersmith's deputy in his annual review of Stevens's first year.

In Europeanized Mexico City, he knew the leaders. He managed projects, some of them launched by the Coordinator and his MIT humanist Robert Caldwell. The most visible of his projects was Rockefeller's new ALA-designed Franklin Library, directed by a Rockefeller-recruit, the librarian-giant Harry M. Lydenberg, former head of the New York Public Library and a founder of Columbia's world-famous School of Library Science. The parallel English-teaching cultural institute in Mexico City was developed by another giant, Michigan linguist Albert Marckwardt.

In 1943 the natural tensions in the institute's board boiled over. Stevens calmed the situation and strengthened its direction. Daniel F. Rubín de la Borbolla, prominent anthropologist and chair of Mexico's League-related CIC, took over the institute. Stevens and Marckwardt, both language-teachers, collaborated on a separate English-teaching program: its high-quality teaching materials set standards for the Latin American world and would soon set standards for USIS posts and BNCs everywhere.

Stevens did a hundred jobs. He brought a Smithsonian delegation together with the Mexican institute of anthropology. He supervised exchanges and took the heat when things went wrong. He fought off Naval Intelligence when its sleuths accused one of his potential grantees of being pro-German when in fact the candidate was involved in anti-Nazi propaganda. He managed a sizable book-distribution program funded by the Coordinator. He handled American scholar-visitors, like ACLS's Waldo Leland and Homer Rainey, president of the University of Texas. He attended any professional meeting in which Americans were involved. He spoke at dozens of formal ceremonies, often extemporaneously, and he lectured everywhere. He accompanied a group of Mexican intellectuals to Albuquerque to receive honorary degrees from the University of New Mexico. He attended art openings and book fairs. Sensitive to the implicit rules of gift-giving, he repaid obligations ingeniously with USIS-provided books and entertainment paid for out of pocket. Most days, he returned home too late for supper.

With no predecessor, he was inventing, improvising, seeding, and matching his own particular talents to the needs he felt in the Mexican pulse. With Trueblood at his side, he was foreshadowing what every cultural officer would discover in the decades to come—the natural demands, opportunities, and obligations that form the irreducible core of any CAO's daily routine.

Stevens's first two years were exemplary. Unfortunately they dramatize the collapse of his third. When Trueblood left, supervision fell to Press Attaché Guy Ray. Ray was busy with his own heady work, which involved assisting Hollywood in its attempt to upgrade the Mexican film industry. Ray, claiming to admire Stevens, seemed to have no understanding of the CAO's work. His own discomfort was obvious when he wrote that Stevens was "quite at ease in the rarefied intellectual atmosphere in which I am able to live only for a limited time."

Kent Smith's glimpse of Stevens's files was necessarily incomplete and leaves room for speculation. I suspect that, when Stevens lost his anchor in the embassy, he was suffering from the double-edged problem of any under-experienced cultural officer who knew a great deal about the country and who was inching toward exhaustion. His expertise and comfort with Mexican friends may have lured this well-meaning American into tackling problems over his head. In particular, he was given orders to combine the English institute, the Franklin Library, and the cultural institute into one location. Stevens may not have agreed that the three might function better as one; Kent Smith saw Messersmith's embassy seeking more control, by placing the three under a single *American* director. Surely Stevens objected that this would downgrade his prominent friend Rubín.

In a single week of stormy Latin passions, complaints about Stevens— including Marckwardt's—rained on the embassy. Stevens had already signed up for a second two-year stint and let Rutgers know he was surrendering his tenure; but overnight his world collapsed. In a week, two exemplary years were wiped away, and he was withdrawn from the program. Messersmith, away in Washington at the time, concurred; even Ray, whose failure had perhaps caused this sad loss, admitted it was wise. Stevens returned in defeat to Rutgers where he was allowed to pick up his tenure. When Smith interviewed him in the late 1950s, Stevens was directing the Rutgers Summer Language School.

After Steven's departure, things worsened, as the diplomats coped with the deep dilemma of a cultural stranger in their midst. Messersmith declined to replace Stevens, so the embassy went without a cultural attaché, but the work had to be done. Without consulting him, the embassy pressed ALA-hired Franklin Library director Harold Bentley to add the job of CAO to his other duties. Bentley could not decline, but he dragged his feet and did the minimum, arguing that he had come to Mexico to do a specific job for ALA, a job for which he was qualified. He argued that "attaching" him to the embassy would raise questions in the public mind about the independence of the library—which, ALA had warned, could easily be attacked as an embassy tool by the Mexican left. Bentley was not about to step into this vipers' nest. Finally, in 1946, the seasoned Morill Cody, a former editor-publisher, was brought to Mexico, after six years as CAO in Paraguay and Argentina. Life in the embassy returned to normal after three wasted years, but the issue of embassy control would persist.

In a final irony, Messersmith retired and accepted an offer from a business firm to remain in Mexico City. He soon became a board member of the Franklin Library, and in this role he became a fierce defender of the library's independence from the embassy.

• • •

These five vignettes of three early CAOs and an IO/PAO suggest how much there is to be learned about the remarkable improvisations of the early years when, as Hull admitted, no one knew what they were doing. All of these men acquitted themselves nobly, in the hectic years of wartime, making do with what was available, improvising when necessary, and getting the job done under difficult conditions.

Not every American could be expected to like this kind of work, but those who did tended to have a flair for it. We can see several of the useful American virtues for the practice of this art in these glimpses of men at work: optimism, gregariousness, pluralism, generosity, and energy. For those who fell into it, the CAO job brought out these qualities and transformed their lives. In some, it brought out the best. These men would all have understood what the late French cultural diplomat André Michel once said of cultural diplomacy: "C'est le plus beau des métiers"—it is the world's most beautiful craft.

CHAPTER SEVEN

Two Classic Cultural Products: Architecture and Libraries

Libraries? Nothing but a carrot and a stick. First you lure them in with the carrot, then you hit them over the head with the message.

—Thomas C. Sorensen, 1962

AFTER A LOOK AT SOME of the people who made cultural diplomacy what it was in the 1940s, it is useful to look at what they were achieving in the field, beginning with case studies of two cultural diplomatic products that extend back to the Greeks. The first, the "architecture of democracy," was the visible outreach of American culture in the twentieth century, with two thousand years of historical antecedents; paradoxically it owed nothing at all to the Division of Cultural Relations and its field staff. The other, overseas libraries, reach back to Alexandria and owed everything to the division. Both took shape early in the 1940s.

I take architecture as our first example in part because its advent in US cultural diplomacy emerged courtesy of some of the same men we have already met, particularly Nelson Rockefeller. In addition, Jane Loeffler's splendid book provides a useful background for the flowering of new embassy buildings abroad, the Architecture of Democracy as she calls it, a name which makes my point for including it in this narration.[1]

The movement toward exporting a new American architecture was not part of formal cultural diplomatic discussions in Washington or activities in the USIS posts, even though the timeframes for both coincided. Rather the new buildings were constructed with the self-generating outreach of American professionals, a rare example of private activity skillfully managed by faceless bureaucrats with Congress remaining at arm's length. US architectural outreach welled up almost by itself, in contrast to the case of Nazi Germany's internal redesign, which was led by Hitler himself and his architect Speer, or the earlier examples of the Romans, Greeks, and then the British;[2] in all these cases the imposition of architectural designs was an instrument of political power.

Ancient diplomacy even before the Greeks, as early as Bronze Age Amarna and probably earlier, assumed architecture as one of its prime tools, as did Augustus, Frederick II, Francis I, Louis XIV, and the British and French empires. That the American equivalent took place without

142

benefit of its formal cultural diplomats or even its political leadership is significant. The easy but surely incomplete explanation is that the architecture of US embassies was a spontaneous manifestation of US cultural expansion. However it happened, it is a reminder that a great deal was going on outside the tempestuous teapot of the cultural planners.

Official and private American architecture abroad, by a series of disconnected decisions and apparent coincidences typical of a minimalist governmental structure facing unexpected power, began to produce embassy buildings in 1948.[3] In retrospect, the embassies played a powerful role in shaping a certain kind of US image and presence abroad, while contributing in major ways to the expansion of US export of people, ideas, and materials. The new embassy buildings, designed by the finest American architects, projected the built forms of democracy. As Loeffler shows, their construction was aimed at goals parallel to those of cultural diplomacy, but the goals in this case—and perhaps in all cases because cultural impact is rarely predictable—were defined by independent forces. Unlike Augustinian Rome, the *rayonnement* of the Sun King, or the buildings of the British empire, American values embodied in extraordinary buildings in the world's capitals were not articulated by political decisions, even if for foreigners it was done by "the Americans."

The name Architecture of Democracy in fact came from Henry Luce, the prophet of the American Century, who until 1939 had worked closely with MacLeish. Luce was also a friend of Nelson Rockefeller and installed the offices of his publishing empire in Rockefeller Center. The rhetoric of the new architecture came not from political leadership, as it did in the Soviet Union, but from Luce, a baron of the political culture, backed by America's architectural profession, with a nudge from Rockefeller. But nothing could have happened had not two dogged administrators, buried in the boiler rooms of State, persisted. An accident of enlightened administration at a relatively low level of the federal bureaucracy made it possible, as two iron-willed State bureaucrats maneuvered to make sure that the architectural profession ran the show.

Loeffler does not mention Rockefeller or the Rockefeller connections of his alter ego, architect Wallace K. Harrison. In our context, it is hard not to see their hands somewhere behind the new embassies as plans began to emerge in 1948. In March 1953, sixteen years after the beginnings of formal cultural diplomacy, at the precise moment when Nelson Rockefeller's and Henry Luce's friend, Temple University president Robert Johnson, was settling in for a brief and unhappy stay as director of State's cultural and information division, Luce's *Architectural Forum* sounded a fanfare. After having proclaimed the American Century, Luce now pushed the architectural arm of his barony, blessed by internationalist Republicans, including Rockefeller, in the new Eisenhower administration to declare: "Whether consciously or not, the US Government has now made US architecture a vehicle of our cultural leadership."

The anonymous writer of this declaration knew the decision had been made invisibly, certainly not "consciously," certainly not by Eisenhower. In contrast to the firestorm touched off by Rockefeller and then William Benton in exporting modern painting, a little-known program had been quietly cooking since as early as 1945, its success proportional to its discretion.

Loeffler outlines the historical background of public buildings in the U.S., which were influenced by the neoclassical standards of Robert Mills after 1836. A student of Jefferson and Latrobe, Mills's vision of public building held firm until after the first war. In the overseas legations of the 19th century, there was no such guidance: all diplomatic premises were rented and no foreign buildings were built. Until 1924 American diplomats paid for their own lodgings and offices; missions were kept at the level of legations to keep costs low; US ministers worked and lived in leased space, defrayed by collecting consular fees. After the Rogers Act of 1924, a few key structures were built for diplomatic use in Europe, most significantly and memorably the dignified neoclassical embassy in Paris.

In 1936, the year of the Buenos Aires meetings, a State Department official named Frederick Larkin, better known as Fritz, moved over from Treasury to manage State's Foreign Buildings Office (FBO); it was part of the same shakeup that elevated Welles to Undersecretary and brought Messersmith from the field to handle administration. It is not clear when or why Larkin and his chief architect Leland King decided that foreign buildings like embassies should project the best in American design and thereby embody US cultural values. The year 1936 was a key moment for cultural outreach: the Good Neighbor Policy was in full spate, Hull had been impressed by the Buenos Aires conference, Sumner Welles was the Secretary's new deputy, and Welles's Latin American team under Laurence Duggan was hard at work shaping a cultural diplomatic function.

Nelson Rockefeller, in his corporatist-expansionist mode, was immersed in the building of Rockefeller Center and was similarly thinking about the projection of American culture. In Latin America in 1939, the young investment-minded millionaire decided to build the pathfinding Avila Hotel in Caracas with the help of his architect friend Wallace K. Harrison, an all-purpose man and founding force in New York's Museum of Modern Art (MoMA) who moved to Washington with Rockefeller in 1940. The Avila was both a financial and an artistic success. From the fall of 1940 forward Harrison and the Coordinator were proponents of all that was modern in art and architecture—yet there is no evidence other than supposition that either had anything to do with Larkin and King. Both returned to New York in 1946.

Larkin and King made their decision in 1948: they retained a firm to design two new embassies, for Rio de Janeiro and Havana. Given Harrison's experience in Venezuela, it might have been a coincidence that the firm was Harrison and Abramowitz. The firm was also in charge of the new UN buildings, which were built in New York thanks to a Rockefeller proposal. The main UN building looks strikingly like the Brazil and Havana embassies. By the time Eisenhower was elected, the process of selecting architects had been solidified: Larkin and King commissioned the best American firms to design embassy buildings and staff housing all over Europe, and no one in Congress objected. The State duo had worked a miraculous combination of enlightenment and stealth, and only Larkin's carefully cultivated friend Congressman John J. Rooney knew about it.

As plans for embassies became known, a few in Congress mumbled about the new buildings' failure to "fit in" and their "unrepresentative" quality. In the pre-Dulles era, internationalism was out of style; it had been attacked in 1943 by Luce's wife Clare as globaloney. Yet the *Forum* in 1953 celebrated the new architecture. Surely Rockefeller was stirring the pot.

Larkin, an independent bureaucrat, was an ingenious operator; his office was a private fief. He had no need to discuss things with Welles, with Luce's former senior editor MacLeish, with Cherrington, or even with Rockefeller and Harrison, although he must have known these men and what they were doing. Leland King, on the other hand, was an architect; he was a spiritual colleague of Harrison in that both were involved in the new American architecture. Larkin and King had read the moment, seized the initiative, and grasped a major cultural tool that could shape the image of the U.S. abroad as perhaps no other could. But they were discreet in a political system where know-nothingism can raise its head at any moment. Larkin wisely stayed in touch with the single member of Congress who controled the funds and who surely knew little about architecture.

In prewar Europe the U.S. had owned only a handful of embassies. In the rebuilding of postwar Europe, an extended embassy-building program was appropriate, having broad economic by-products beyond the buildings themselves and fitting easily into the process of stimulating the recovering construction industries in devastated areas. But the conceptual rationale for the program was cultural: to showcase the architectural synthesis achieved by and for the American Century.

The American synthesis of course included dozens of foreign-born and foreign-trained architects, in particular those schooled at the Bauhaus in Dessau. This muiltinational cast reinforced, for the internationalists, the comforting US assumption that America had inherited the mantle of cultural leaderhip from a failing Europe.

The style favored by Larkin, King, and their peer-review committees was dubbed, by both supporters and detractors, the International or Bauhaus Style. It was not ponderous but light, not closed and protective but open, airy, and welcoming, not dark and forbidding but transparent and shining in the night, not made of stone or brick but of newly available materials like steel and glass, not based on traditional forms but freely adapted to function and site. The phrase "International Style" was rejected by the architects themselves, who were simply developing new forms to meet new needs with newly available materials. For them, it was the American style.

Abroad, it was at first not seen as "American" but fell into the ready-made category of a Bauhaus offspring. But as more of the embassies opened up, their originality as well as their political meaning became clear—US embassies fly American flags. The next step lay just ahead. The style, identified with democracy, became known at first as the built form of the American Century, the embodiment of open government by and for the people. Not entirely coincidentally, the new style was also the precise opposite, in every respect, of Stalin's ponderous Soviet architecture and of Hitler's architects Troost and Speer before him. The symbolism of the American buildings was anything but imperial—yet they connoted a new kind of empire.

The process of getting embassies built was managed democratically by the architects and designers themselves through the ultimate democratic process of professional peer review—democracy's solution to the problem of excellence. This was not government at work, it was American thought and genius given full rein.

Almost as if to remedy an egregious oversight, Eisenhower's team fired Larkin in 1953. The victorious Republican coalition, after twenty years of frustrating opposition, set out to discredit the New Deal at all costs by, among other things, ridding itself of all incumbent jobholders. With Larkin gone, a good moment arose to attack the dominance of the Bauhaus style: Renaissance, Georgian, and Palladian models were proposed in its stead. The architectural profession, howling with laughter, prodded Luce to vigilance, and the Architecture of Democracy was proclaimed, part of the defense against the know-nothings.

Larkin left his successor a priceless gift: an external Architectural Advisory Committee (AAC). Making certain the AAC was accepted by a strong array of leaders in Congress, he went into comfortable retirement, a happy man. Like Fulbright, he had built peer review into the decision-making process so as to override the wild lurches of US political process, and he had written the peer-review clause so that it could not easily be revised. In the AAC chair, Italian-born Pietro Belluschi stood solidly behind Larkin's decisions. Peer panels continued to commission conspicuous modernist buildings. One new idea was added to the criteria of open, light, friendly, and inviting buildings; America's diplomatic buildings began to draw on design elements and materials from the host-country's visual traditions, "fitting in" while remaining very American. This fusion of thought produced Edward Durrell Stone's graceful embassy in New Delhi, such a success that it had to be opened to the visiting public on Sundays.

By the late 1950s the building program had tapped most of the important names in American architecture: Edward Larrabee Barnes, Marcel Breuer, Gordon Bunshaft, Walter Gropius, John Johansen, I. M. Pei, Paul

Rudolph, Eero Saarinen, Stone, and John Carl Warnecke. Some even managed to slip a building into traditionalist Washington.

For two decades the image of open democracy was projected by American architects and designers through buildings which literally jeered at the bunkers of the totalitarians. It was contagious: American architects were sought for design projects around the world, for the Australian capital of Canberra, for the parliament building in Bangladesh, for the renovated Louvre in Paris, for the National Gallery in London, for museums in Bilbao and Luxembourg, for a church in Rome, among dozens of examples. It all began with the Avila Hotel.

It ended in fear. The decline of the great architectural experiment grew out of national concerns about security, fed by bombings like those in Beirut, Oklahoma City, Kenya, Tanzania, and ultimately by the 2001 attack on the Twin Towers. New security criteria were imposed on buildings overseas and at home. Fearing public blame for potential disasters, leadership imposed a list of paralyzing regulations on embassy design. A powerful report by CIA Deputy Director Bobby Inman opened a new era of fortress embassies: buildings had to be separated from any street by acres of costly empty space, lower stories could have no windows, moats were advised, and so forth. In the fall of 2002, a new master plan shaped all future American building overseas. What had been open was now closed, what was light was heavy, what was welcoming and inviting was forbidding, what was handsome was now repellent, what was vibrant, confident, and creative was gone. As a Turkish friend said to *New York Times* reporter Tom Friedman about the new US consulate in Istanbul, "Birds don't fly there." The new fortresses, requiring at least ten acres of terrain, added new challenges for architects. Embassies were banished to urban peripheries and moved out of city centers; they devoured priceless real estate and drove up costs; they attracted the wrong kind of neighbors. Only in Ottawa, where there are arguably fewer terrorists, was David Childs allowed to produce his fine new embassy in the open style of the 1950s. Elsewhere, it was all over; an intelligence report had, in a single stroke, redefined America's global image, and the Architecture of Democracy had become the Architecture of Fear.

US participation in international trade fairs was an allied architectural and design challenge, less known to Americans. This program, however, was managed by the government, specifically USIA's design staff. The fairs, big and small, were regular events around the world. US participation had begun a century and a half earlier; by the 1950s it was an accepted matter of national pride, as well as sound business promotion. Architects and designers had learned to use trade fairs as trial runs for their most far-reaching ideas; in history, some fairs, in fact, left behind important monuments—the Eiffel Tower, major parks in Chicago, Saint Louis, Philadelphia, and New York.

After 1945 US participation in large and small trade fairs soared, drawing on high US creativity—particularly as competition with the USSR heightened. In 1958 a special office in USIA was set up to exploit an agreement between the U.S. and USSR to include fairs in its cultural pacts. Trade fairs were one of many important efforts to open the closed society of the USSR, memorable in the American mind as the banal setting for the famous Kitchen Debate between Nixon and Khrushchev. Staffing the Soviet fairs as guides were young American speakers of Russian, culled from the best Russian language programs in the U.S.—many of whom later found work in government agencies, including State and USIA.

The fair in Brussels in 1958 marked a decision by USIA and the Department of Commerce to set higher standards. A freewheeling team within USIA, built around dynamic Yale architect Jack Masey, was in charge. In 1956 Masey began work in Kabul, where he pulled off an architectural miracle in twelve weeks and introduced Buckminster Fuller to the world. Masey and Fuller reached a peak in Montreal in 1967, with the enormous iconic Fuller "bubble." In Osaka in 1970 Masey produced a football-field-size inflatable structure.[4] Smaller trade fairs tried out unusual and striking new designs, enclosing space in new ways; whatever the design, the point was always to display the new America's creative side with buildings, design, and even everyday objects—from the Sapporo fair's collection of a hundred hats worn by American professionals to exhibits of wooden duck decoys to the spectacular sixty-foot banner paintings hanging in Montreal by American artists like Robert Motherwell and Helen Frankenthaler. Pavilions and exhibits drew the usual small-arms fire from Congress, none of it lethal.

The golden years began to wind down in the 1980s. In England Prince Charles had begun his nagging campaign against "modern" architecture, and American conservatives led by Hilton Kramer were developing ponderous political theories to justify their yearning for the better old days. The Reagan administration, true to its hints that government should play no role in culture, made a radical decision, insisting that the private sector fund the lion's share of trade-fair participation. Decline set in instantly, painfully so in the case of the Seville fair of 1986, when private funding fell seriously short of what was needed. Some smaller trade fairs were spun off to US corporations: South Korea's Taegu in 1993, sponsored by Amway, brought out significant questions about relations between government and commerce, questions extending back to Rockefeller and to Creel before him.

The hope that private money would flood in to replace public funding turned out to be wishful thinking. Tied in knots by ambivalence, the Clinton administration ruled out an American presence at Expo 2000 in Hannover after prime space had been reserved, and the gaping hole in the fairgrounds spoke volumes about the new America. US participation in trade fairs, after the meddling of the 1980s, had fallen victim to the penny-wise 1990s.

In 1986, architectural critic Ben Forgey analyzed the Seville fair epi-sode.[5] He had seen it coming: after an impressive competition, "a fine design . . . got so whittled down by costs, cuts and other changes that the architect rightly refused to let his name be used in connection with the final product." In the end "the Seville pavilion was billed as a public-private partnership, but it ended simply as a public fiasco." In 1994 Con-gress, with no contrary leadership from USIA, all but dropped interna-tional exhibitions. "What had been mainly a public responsibility for more than a century, and then had been changed briefly to a joint public-private enterprise, was transformed almost entirely into a private obliga-tion," noted Forgey. The yawning space at Hannover announced to the world that America had quit the game.

The role of architecture and design in American cultural outreach has thus already had its beginning, middle, and end. The Architecture of De-mocracy was the first effort of its kind in the U.S., and it registered high success. Since then, government has all but given up its role in the over-seas projection of architecture and design. Unlike the successes of the Greeks, the Romans, and the British, America's successes were self-gener-ating expressions, coming from the architects themselves. Larkin's for-mula, like Masey's, was straightforward: delegate design to the best, then let them run it. Only occasionally did it cross either man's mind that they were extending or reinforcing the American Century. Their genius lay in their trust of the profession: excellence came spontaneously from the ar-chitects and designers under benign governmental directives. This had been Rockefeller's Avila style—an American path to public-private coop-eration, with instructions no more explicit than Diaghilev's instructions to Cocteau: "Astound us!"

Whether US architectural flair can continue to project creativity under the new siege conditions remains to be seen. Even if architectural flair persists in some ingenious way, it will project the new culture of fear and pay homage to the success of terrorism. One sensitive but saddened US architectural historian and planner put it this way: "The new fortress em-bassies are deplorable but perfectly expressive of our times and our impe-rial foreign policies."[6] Tom Friedman, faced with the new US Consulate in Istanbul, admitted its heavy design had saved it from the fate of the ravaged British Consulate, but noted that it "looks just like Fort Knox—without the charm." The earlier embassy was a welcoming historic old building in the heart of the city with its own library. The new embassy sits "on a bluff overlooking the Bosporus—surrounded by a tall wall, . . . like a maximum-security prison." Friedman imagines the plaque the Consulate might affix: "'Attention! You are now approaching a U.S. Con-sulate. Any sudden movement and you will be shot. All visitors wel-come.'"[7] With the fortress embassies and the end of trade-fair participation, America has unwittingly proclaimed its new values and new priorities. For US cultural outreach, this is the saddest loss of all.

• • •

US libraries abroad tell a different story. Unlike architecture, they are a direct product of formal US cultural diplomacy. Except for Carnegie's assistance to libraries in the British isles and scholarly libraries in various research institutes, the export of the American library began with Creel's reading-rooms in 1917. The half-century beginning in 1942 saw the U.S. quietly place open-access libraries in all the world's major cities as part of its formal diplomacy. During that period there were well over two hundred USIS installations at any random moment and close to five hundred if one counted the indirectly supported BNC libraries. Undertaken without an expression of national will, with fragile support from a divided Congress, with little thought to long-run costs, and again with a strong push from Rockefeller, the libraries were a unique American achievement, rivaled only by the British. In breadth of purpose, scope, and outreach, the USIS libraries had precedents, but in purpose and design, they are unique in world history.

At rare moments, empires, in fact, exported libraries to project knowledge and political power. The very idea of a library did not arise until humankind learned the political and economic power of storing knowledge in retrievable form and in communicating it over distance and time: Assyrian king Ashurbanipal in the seventh century B.C.E. learned cuneiform so that he could personally manage his collection, notes Lionel Casson in his delightful synthesis *Libraries in the Ancient World*.[8] With expanded literacy, private collections flourished in early Greece, none greater than Aristotle's; his pupil Alexander recentered Hellenism in Egypt's great seaport. There Alexander's Seleucid successor founded the Museum, a center for scholars like Euclid, and the great library, modeled on Aristotle's collection. Like Alexandria's lighthouse, the open-access library was a cultural beacon and a wonder of the ancient world.

Rome left Hellenistic culture comfortably in place: Antony, as a gift for Cleopatra, restored the library in Alexandria after a fire, looting Pergamum to do so. At home, libraries were focused on Rome's national purposes. Caesar designated the scholar Varro to build Rome's library. Under Trajan, separate Greek and Latin libraries were opened to citizen education; three centuries later there were twenty-eight branches in Rome.

After Rome's fall, Islam inherited from the vanquished Persians a reverence for books, exemplified by the Persian grand vizir Abdul Kassem Ismael, who never left home without his library—117,000 volumes carried by four hundred camels marching in alphabetical order. In Baghdad Haroun al-Rashid and his son Caliph al-Ma'mnun built the Bayt al-Hikmat, the House of Wisdom, in the ninth century, to focus Islam's intellect in their chosen capital. At the height of his power, the Persian Shah Abbas I in the early seventeenth century maintained a library for scholars and an attached workshop for the copying of and illumination of priceless volumes; at least two major branch libraries in Persia served the religious leadership in the city of Mashed and the more secular leadership in Ardabil as part of Shah Abbas's attempt to unify Persia.

In medieval Rome the tolerant fifteenth-century Pope Nicholas V planned his splendid new Vatican library and center for scholars, underlining Christianity's continuity with antiquity. A few decades later Francis I sent his ambassadors to Rome's and Venice's printshops, to fill the shelves of his Royal Library; Bonaparte nationalized the library and opened it to literate citizens as the Bibliothèque Nationale, complementing the world's first art museum in the Sun King's palace.

The American founders kept libraries near the center of their thinking, both as storehouses of knowledge and for the citizen-education they deemed indispensable to democracy. Franklin designed Philadelphia's public system on Trajan's model; John Adams wrote government support for libraries, learning, and education into the Massachusetts Constitution; Jefferson built the University of Virginia around his personal library and, with Adams, Madison, and Monroe, helped establish the Library of Congress; and John Quincy Adams expanded that Library into a scholarly treasure trove. The Constitution had left education to the states, but the founders assumed science and learning were at least in part a governmental responsibility. In the 1860s Justin Morill's Land-Grant Act paved the way for a new kind of university, in which theoretical and applied learning could work together. By then, it was an American commonplace to say that the library was the university's heart.

Citizen libraries flourished early in the new American republic. Joyce Appleby, in her survey of first-generation Americans,[9] notes the extensive American habit of reading: local libraries cropped up everywhere, often built on voluntary services and donated books. The "social libraries" of the eighteenth century were booming by 1850. Boston funded public libraries from tax revenues, and by the turn of the nineteenth century, more than half the American states had followed suit; New York City alone had sixty-five open-shelved branches.

Andrew Carnegie was the dynamo behind US library expansion. The immigrant Scot retained sad boyhood memories of a prohibitive $2 library reader's fee. He fathered a library support structure, the ALA, and he gave 56 million in turn-of-century dollars to support 1,350 libraries in small and large American communities. Of these, 138 in thirty-four US city-libraries had branches—New York City received 10 percent of his largesse. Nineteenth-century printing technology had made books affordable, but only for the wealthy; Carnegie made them accessible to all.

Library export began with Carnegie, driven by the idea of service to his impoverished birthplace. By 1902 with his surrogate ALA he was helping more than eight hundred citizen-education libraries in the British isles—but library exports beyond England lay beyond his imagination. The idea of equipping his British libraries with special collections of books about the U.S. only crossed the minds of his successors several decades later, the opening chapter in the growth of American studies abroad.

Europe had exported libraries for colonial systems aimed at schools. Foreign-sponsored research libraries graced historic cities like Rome, Athens, and Jerusalem. In the German case, Brazil benefited from the work of Humboldt's successors, laying the groundwork for future scientific relations. Outside the framework of empire, libraries as political exports began around 1900. Britain first, then France reached beyond their colonies. By 1918 the British were managing thirteen general libraries around Europe, and in 1919 a so-called Library of Information opened in New York. When the British Council went global in 1934, it built comprehensive general collections—in 1974 the Council library in Rome held fifty thousand volumes, as opposed to USIS holdings of somewhat less than three thousand. France's cultural diplomacy in the 1920s focused library exports on European countries freed from the Austro-Hungarian empire.

US missionary-educators sailed with private collections of their own books. The underfunded educators moved out from service-oriented colleges like Williams and Amherst—where Melvil Dewey had devised his user-friendly decimal retrieval system. They set up printing presses in their locales and published in the vernacular. Supported by a literate American civil society, animated by the notion of stewardship, and fed through church collection plates, the missionary-educators operated school libraries reaching out to the unfortunate of the world.

The Americans began formal governmental exports during the First World War, but CPI reading rooms were slashed in 1919; a few undernourished libraries survived in Latin American BNCs like the Peru–U.S. Society. In Paris the American Library, built by ALA in 1920 from a core of books left behind by CPI and US military education programs, amassed a sizable collection to serve the well-heeled American community; at one time it had branches in five provincial cities. In Rome Henry Nelson Gay's personal library became a center for American studies, and the "American" church of Santa Susanna opened a circulating library for English readers from donations. Other limited-access libraries were growing in teaching institutions like Yenching University in Peking and the American Colleges of Beirut, Istanbul, and Cairo, as well as in classical research centers abroad.

Welles's team in State began thinking about books in 1932. Latin Americans had always sought book exchanges, which had a prominent place on Hull's shopping list; Hull also mentioned the possibility of US libraries abroad, but with wafer-thin budgets, the division limited itself to arranging book exchanges. Alongside Welles and Duggan stood bookmen like Librarian of Congress MacLeish and Carl Milam, head of the ALA. Like the younger George Kennan and with the same generational approach, the designers used the metaphor of gardening when they spoke of libraries: changing minds was not a matter of engineering but must be done "in harmony with the rules of nature."[10] If the library was the heart of education, if cultural relations meant a gradual, organic educational process oriented to the long term, then books were indispensable.

Still, in their wildest dreams none of the founders before 1940 imagined that the U.S. would soon be exporting freestanding libraries and American librarians everywhere in the world. Again it was Nelson Rockefeller, financially unencumbered, free from most preconceptions, and careless of long-range consequences, who changed things. With access to talent, he and his imported dollar-a-year New Yorkers believed anything was possible. Libraries came more quickly to his mind than one might have imagined of the dyslexic corporatist. His own reading difficulties did not blind him to the uses of libraries; and he was wise enough to leave details—purposes, contents, numbers, locations, size of collections, time frames—to ALA. For the overseas world, Rockefeller was the new Carnegie and Milam was his guide.

Milam used a four-part rationale that involved giving educated English-reading Latin Americans access to general and specialized books; fostering foreign educational and cultural development; creating demonstration models and training centers exemplifying "American librarianship"; and selling American books. Beneath Milam's four points lay an implicit idea, better left unspoken: support for foreign policy and democracy would, just as Carnegie libraries had in the U.S., help educate a democratic citizenry of the world.

Three major libraries, with dozens of reading rooms, opened in Latin America, but alert PAOs saw two problems ahead: first, high costs could only rise with time; second, libraries—in OWI's world—were seen only as outlets for daily news and information and backup. But ALA had a totally different idea for library use. Instead of choosing one path over the other, the libraries were forced to do both. Thus the USIS libraries from the beginning served four masters: they were designed, staffed, and stocked by ALA and Milam, funded and protected by Rockefeller, managed by OWI and OSS, and coveted by the division. In short, they were the natural offspring of the strange American marriage of culture and propaganda.

From experience with the American Library in Paris, Milam knew that an overseas library implied a long-term commitment, specialized personnel, and ever-growing costs; but not surprisingly for a committed librarian he was convinced of the benefits. In Latin America Mexico City's flagship Benjamin Franklin Library, with a Rockefeller grant of $45,000, led the way. ALA recruited, and Rockefeller helped reimburse, its founding director Harry Lydenberg, who had just retired as head of the New York Public Library and was a founder of the Columbia Library School, a major training resource for US and foreign librarians. Rockefeller was working with publishers, prodding them to send out—free—hundreds of thousands of US books for libraries, schools, and individuals.

Milam wrote to OWI in July 1942 to propose a library for London. He said the British were ready; State, OWI, ALA, and the ACLS were aboard; and ALA's luster in England was high, after helping manage Carnegie grants and select books for half a century; Librarian of Congress Mac-Leish, traveling to London, would carry the message. "It should be a reference and circulating library and information center, *not a publicity and propaganda agency*" (Milam's emphasis). He wanted a small reference collection, books about all aspects of US life, a "choice collection" on US cultural achievements, current books about the war, and up-to-date US government documents, pamphlets, and periodicals. He wanted professional staffing, an open-ended commitment to new acquisitions and timely government documents, free loans, and extension services. In short, he wanted an honest library. His cost estimate for the first year was $75,000, then $50,000 per year thereafter. But Milam lost a vital battle in his quest for an honest library. He had urged that ALA or the Library of Congress sponsor the London library, specifically to minimize propaganda, but OWI insisted on taking it over instead, an early indication that OWI was eager to absorb cultural elements where possible.

ALA's Richard Heindel, a historian, went to London to set up the library. He took two large rooms in the London embassy and opened early in 1943 to immediate success. After the war Heindel returned to Washington to direct library services for State, leaving behind a library far too useful to close. The London library handled a thousand or more inquiries per month, keeping contact with eight hundred organizations and societies, 350 business firms, 175 corresponding British libraries, and school and university libraries all over the British Isles. By 1958 it contained 35,000 books, five hundred periodicals, government documents, and a collection of musical recordings and scores. For reasons of economy, the end came in 1967 when the library was turned over to the University of London where it still functions, invisible to all but a small world of specialists.

The London model spread to the industrialized world, replicated in particular by dozens of libraries in the German and Japanese occupations and in cobelligerent Austria and Italy. In 1949, to service Amerika Haus, Frankfurt's library—where users had access to 45,000 volumes—remained open twelve hours a day, seven days a week; it fed branches in twenty-nine cities in the US-occupied quarter of Germany.[11] In Japan a large central library in Tokyo fed smaller five-thousand-volume branches in twenty cities. Thanks to ample funding, the two occupations proved, to the satisfaction of the designers of the 1940s, that "American" libraries could be planted in any soil. Abroad they were seen as welcome examples of US generosity, without propaganda strings attached, part of the US commitment to education.

Developing societies called for a different design. Books were assumed to be indispensable to all growing societies, including those to which the communications revolution had come late or where politics or inadequate education interfered with learning—the Soviets were aware of the inevitable dangers, from their viewpoint, and prevented the opening of USIS libraries in the USSR and its satellites. In other developing countries, the US library model was a bold and far-reaching idea: exporting a library for citizen education meant transplanting a unique American institution. USIS libraries were expected to provide knowledge, research, and public information for building civil society, like the small town libraries fostered by Carnegie and staffed by Meredith Willson's "Marian the Librarian." Satisfying the propagandists' need to tell America's story, the small town library model told its own story: USIS libraries had American library furniture and lighting, Dewey decimal card catalogues, and ALA-recruited professional librarians.

After the war, with Rockefeller back in New York, the USIS-ALA libraries had spread to the world. But postwar funds were thinning, inflation was relentless, and Congress was increasingly puzzled. The extravagant German model, applied elsewhere, raised obvious questions of economy. From the other side, hard-line unidirectional cold warriors were raising the unanswerable complaint of the short-sighted: libraries offered no direct support to foreign policy because they reached no relevant political targets.

Other distant drums, those of witch hunters in Congress, were beating. By 1950 the libraries had caught the eye of Senator McCarthy. Arguing—with the Campaign of Truth—that the sole purpose of cultural diplomacy was to destroy the USSR, he began his no-holds-barred battle to purify the shelves of anything critical of the U.S. His minions Cohn and Schine scurried through Europe in search of books by "known communists," trampling on the openness and freedom which the libraries proclaimed. Foreign friends were dismayed: a sacred institution was under attack, with no one to defend it.

Despairing of educating Congress, the new USIA circled the wagons in defense. Discreetly cabled warnings reached field colleagues about writers like Howard Fast and Dashiell Hammett, but also about "Eleanor Roosevelt, Elmer Davis, Upton Sinclair, and Marshall Field," wrote Thomas Sorensen, an articulate and unabashed propagandist. He reported that a short-lived Eisenhower appointment "questioned the use of books by Thoreau . . . because his writings influenced foreigners who became Communists." In faraway Afghanistan, cultural officer David Nalle prepared for a visit from Senator William Knowland by putting his collection's single Sam Spade mystery by Dashiell Hammett into a desk drawer. Librarians became zealous weeders. One obedient soul was said to have collected the designated books and burned them—a point the Soviet propagandists did not miss.

The libraries were a minor campaign issue in 1952, with Eisenhower supporting them and their mission. But once in office the president declined to "get down in the gutter" with McCarthy. ALA, quietly elbowed from its earlier active role by USIA, was begged to enter the battle; it issued a firm statement and McCarthy retreated. By then the libraries had suffered the greatest setback in their first decade of life.

Under Eisenhower, information and most of cultural relations were moved out of State, along with the other so-called objects of culture, when USIA was founded in 1953. USIA's first director, radio executive Theodore Streibert, reduced the number of libraries to 158 in sixty-three countries. The McCarthy issues had been buried in shallow graves and the doughty library professionals soldiered on; ALA tried to keep a voice in matters but was increasingly accused of interference and finally left the fight. Book selection passed to USIA staff, which compiled monthly preselected lists, with both eyes on a Congress where another McCarthy might arise at any moment.

Costs were inexorably rising, and library defenders fought as best they could. In the field, some of the early OWI veterans emerged as committed book people. A rationale compatible with support to foreign policy was needed: the easiest road was to claim that libraries were vital to propaganda and supported foreign policy in that way. Having hinted at this, USIA leadership, caught in the circles of their own rhetoric, took this new justification one step further. Libraries had to focus, not scattershoot; political-elite targeting was the solution of choice. Memories of the Milam years were fading fast.

In the developing world the role of USIS libraries as demonstration-models and training-centers persisted, justified as part of telling America's story. Like the fresh new US embassies, libraries themselves showcased an aspect of US democracy. Their contents, access, user-friendly classification systems, furnishings, ample lighting, knowledgable and cheerful staff, open shelves, alternative or critical viewpoints, and free lending showed how a free citizenry gets its information. Working with Fulbrighters and occasionally with Peace Corps volunteers, libraries could get a lot done. In the 1960s in Iran, for example, the USIS library was a training center for Iranian interns. With Fulbright lecturers, librarians helped build and staff a Library School at Tehran University; Peace Corps brought occasional specialized librarians; American librarians helped found the ALA-equivalent Iran Library Association, helped design Tehran University's central library, and put early electronic documentation systems in place. In Iran, and around today's world, thousands of librarians learned their trade through USIS internships and Fulbright.

The USIS libraries made a strong political statement about America. Nobel laureate Wole Soyinka, haunting USIS libraries in Nigeria as a youth, learned that books are "objects of terror to those who seek to suppress the truth." Umberto Eco, like other young intellectuals all around the world, devoured every book in his USIS library in Milan. They were tasting something Americans take for granted: free access to a wealth of books, including those critical of their government.

In controled societies where they were permitted, USIS libraries had slow-acting influence. Even the democratic oligarchies of Europe tended to view their own libraries as restricted storehouses for the priesthood of knowledge, i.e., the privileged might read, under supervision, but no others. Closed societies went farther—the authorities noted who read what.

By 1955 libraries were central to the US presence around the world. In Germany libraries operated in twenty-nine cities. In India every single chair in a dozen libraries was filled during every open hour and borrowing was known literally to empty the shelves. Indirectly supported libraries were spun off to BNCs all over Latin America. As early as 1947, communist demonstrators were paying USIS libraries the high compliment of breaking their windows during demonstrations. What angered them was not so much the libraries' occasional propaganda, the price of USIA's insistence on "unmasking the Communist Conspiracy," but rather the freedom of inquiry they allowed users.

When USIA was created in 1953, "objects" of culture, including libraries, went to USIA and "people" of culture, or human exchanges, remained in State because Fulbright feared propaganda more than proximity to foreign policy. The absurd compromise ripped apart what belonged together. Field cultural officers oversaw both libraries and the people who read the books. Reporting to both State's educational and cultural division *and* USIA, they tried to make sense of all this.

Streibert's successor in 1956 was George V. Allen, a foreign service professional who had served as ambassador to four tough countries (Iran, India, Yugoslavia, and Greece), in which books were a compelling need. Allen's genuine passion for libraries flowed naturally from the hunger for books he had seen; he argued that, if all else had to be sacrificed, libraries should remain. He fed hope for library growth within USIA—and hope for reuniting the objects and the people of education and culture under a single roof. But after Allen, USIA leadership never again said with his conviction that books—because they were independent of government—spoke the most convincing truths of all.

Under the hard-nosed New Frontier and Ed Murrow, policies were shaped by unidirectionalist Thomas C. Sorensen, and USIA's vision was retuned. Cribbing from Madison Avenue, Sorensen based his approach on delivering messages to target groups. In Beirut in 1962 a young officer fresh from the university world heard the visiting Sorensen's droll attacks on USIA shibboleths: he ridiculed children's collections ("Do children vote here?"), overlooking the parents who brought the children and stayed to read; he assigned libraries a carrot-stick function to deliver the message. At the working level, few took him seriously; those who spoke out as a matter of principle found their careers stagnating.

USIA leadership boasted of its libraries when appropriate. Murrow's deputy Donald Wilson in January 1963 before a group of book publishers proudly listed 174 USIS-run libraries, another hundred assisted libraries in BNCs, total world holdings of 3 million books, and an annual book-outflow of 250,000. But at the working level, the gates were closing. A 1983 General Accounting Office (GAO) report chided USIA because, of the 426 libraries and reading rooms established before 1978, only 129 USIS-run and USIS-assisted libraries remained; of fifty-three professional librarians on USIA's roster in the 1950s, only eighteen were left.

In the developing world, the library could be the USIS jewel. USIS Ghana in 1962 decided to move the library to a new building on the other side of Accra. Librarian Emma Skinner cooked up the first "old-fashioned small-town American book parade," in which thousands of sign-carrying Ghanaian students bore eighteen thousand books three miles across the city, to the music of a marching band, with free Pepsi for all. "The circulation of books tripled in one month and stayed that way for two years," recalled Mark Lewis, then chief of USIS Accra.[12]

The concept of politically targetted libraries soon showed its darker side. Through the 1970s, USIA theorists pondered an idea from London: active outreach, sending bibliographies and content pages of periodicals to influential people and following up with books and articles. This was not enough. Manipulating the rhetoric of libraries to fit propaganda theory continued to produce prodigies of logic. The most ingenious was a thematic approach in the Far East, reported by visitors in the form of a flawless syllogism. Since each USIS post was required to define its goals as four or five program themes, it followed that USIS libraries should do the same. Since no post could undertake more than five themes, including the open-ended "American Studies," no library should need more than five sections. Since no thematic section could possibly require more than four hundred books—nor contain any fewer—it was argued, the collection by definition would contain precisely two thousand volumes. Since any library had to add new books, it followed that a new book could only be added if an earlier one were jettisoned—*quod erat demonstrandum*. The model found few imitators but its glib Washington-centered rigor provided an illusory focus and encouragement to those who believed libraries had no function except to "support foreign policy."

By the 1970s technology was beckoning. "Documentation Centers" began to spring up inside libraries with sophisticated information on foreign policy, priceless government documents, and early experiments with microfiche and Internet access. Books were fading—and the Internet was little help because few books were digitized. To feed serious students of American civilization, Encyclopedia Britannica was persuaded to produce an ultra-microfiche collection of nineteen thousand key books from titles prior to 1923 for which copyright had expired; the collection was to be augmented every few years as new titles came free. But the idea died when Britannica, with inadequate USIA subsidies, claimed inadequate sales and folded.

Late in the 1970s, microfiches and electronic systems began taking over. Rome in 1978 weeded its collection to the magic number of two thousand and transferred a thousand surplus books, furnishings, and staff to the private Center for American Studies; in the 1980s the "library" finally closed and its documentation service moved into the embassy compound behind tough security barriers, where information could be sought by telephone or by appointment. Paris closed its open-access library in 1979 and restricted access to its fine documentation services two years later. Doubtless the Internet opened new kinds of access, but the sophisticated new USIS systems could only be used by a few—even in the industrialized countries, they required "reservations-only" use. Scholars or journalists in the know could use the tools; others preferred not to be frisked by armed security guards. The general public concluded the USIS library had been closed.

In the U.S., which was decades ahead of the developing world technologically, the Internet was flourishing. Thinking in Washington terms, USIA in the 1990s cut back libraries even further, declaring boldly that the uncharted Information Highway would fill the gap. This rhetoric overlooked countries where computers were rare, phone lines shaky, electricity uncertain, and per capita income under $500.

After 1980, no USIA leader saw fit to defend the libraries. Library decline in fact delighted the White House–appointed USIA team in the 1980s, whose chief could not fathom why his agency had ever wasted a penny on a library. Decline also pleased the political appointees of the next decade as well, intent upon balancing the national budget at whatever cost. In 1985 a California member of Congress argued passionately against "giveaways" to Europe when his own hometown had no library—his city had overlooked Adams and Franklin's thoughts on funding citizen literacy by voluntarism and local taxes. Clinton's USIA pondered, conversed, wrung its hands, and looked concerned.

In 1995 a dutiful USIA library chief in Washington read out the party line to interviewer Mark Lewis: open-access USIS libraries in both industrialized and developing countries are too costly; Information Resource Centers (IRCs) meet today's needs; free lending limits access hence is abolished; appointment-only use guarantees focus on elites; and professional librarians are no longer needed. The spokesman neglected to list heightened security as a negative factor. Today Web sites for embassies abroad list the IRC as part of the embassy's press and information section; they serve to provide information on US foreign policy, economic and trade matters, domestic issues, and "society and culture," with "special focus on law and legislation and the regulatory process." In 2001 Berlin's Web site boasted that its audience was "government officials, the Parliament, political parties, journalists, researchers and others with professional-level interests in the U.S."; "researchers with serious interests" were encouraged to phone in their questions between 10 A.M. and 5 P.M. The site provides no advice on how to read an American poet.

Congress, faced with the "giveaway" canard in the 1990s, referred matters to the Chairman of the Senate Foreign Relations Committee, who forgot to answer. No USIA leader explained to the Congress the difference between domestic and foreign affairs priorities, or the role libraries played in the decline of the Soviet empire, or their capacity to nurture mind-change over time, or their function as cultural centers for interaction with Americans, or their role as backup and support to English-teaching programs, or their capacity to convey deep and convincing truths about the U.S.

In 1999 the surviving fragments of a demoralized USIA were absorbed back into State. In Africa and South Asia some recognizable libraries were still functioning because of irreducible demand. In a few USIS posts, die-hard PAOs managed things in a stealth mode; their IRCs looked suspiciously like the old libraries. The 160,000-volume American Studies Resource Center in India, after forty years of independent operation, was turned over to Osmania University in Hyderabad. Private and university American Studies collections still hung on; large collections dangled precariously in Rome, Brussels, and Berlin, where lavish funding had been available only so long as that showcase city highlighted the ugly Soviet alternative.

For nearly sixty years, the cultural diplomatic arm of the US government, in cooperation with the private world, built libraries in countries all over the world. It happened by a peculiar American miracle, overriding muddled ideas, contradictory purposes, wishful thinking, rising costs, anti-intellectualism, and the irresistible demands of propaganda. No one saw libraries as tools of empire—although one could argue they were tools for an empire of a certain kind. With dedicated leadership and professional staff, the libraries enabled people everywhere to read American books. They showcased a profound political message about access to information in a free society. They helped compensate for distorted journalism the world over. They trained local librarians. They provided a helpful and homey setting, which people still remember as their introduction to the wonder of America. Ironically they faded away at the moment of sudden birth all over the world of new nations parched for reliable information on the nature of democracy. The rise and decline of libraries went unnoticed by the US public, which was scarcely aware they were there in the first place.

The era of the USIS libraries has ended, yet we may look back on a moment in which Americans can take pride. For six decades, ingenious government-private cooperation, administered and served by three generations of dedicated men and women, made the most of the odd hand that history dealt. The libraries showed the world, as well as any other cultural tool, the habits of heart and mind that move the American nation. And they exercised another unmentioned function: the truth of books provided correctives, appropriate context, and broad perspective against which to view the rise and fall of unilateralist, ethnocentric, and nationalist zeal which have repeatedly infected US foreign policy in the last century. They helped keep US foreign policy honest.

CHAPTER EIGHT

Benton, Fulbright, Smith, and Mundt

> Apparently a lot of things have changed since the concept of the psychological warrior replaced that of the statesman and the propaganda trick replaced the simple truth.
>
> —Erik Sevareid (1953)

ROOSEVELT'S DEATH LEFT A CHASM. Whatever his virtues, Truman was no FDR. The cultural pioneers, with seven or more years of sophisticated thinking and experience behind them, now had to explain their unprecedented concoction to a man who was not interested, who had heard nothing about it in the Senate, who relied on a skeptical Acheson, and who, notwithstanding his wide reading, had no experience of universities or the educational model. Truman had learned about life in hardscrabble Missouri politics and the culture of Congress; he had never had to suffer under a college instructor brighter than he was. Yet he was a four-square internationalist, facing a mid-term election which he knew might move his Congress significantly away from that goal.

Against the vibrant trend to internationalize US intellectual life, electoral politics were moving toward nationalism. Cultural administrators had to deal not only with the usual congressional skepticism but with legislators driven by an ideological commitment to consider internationalism as globaloney and to delegitimize anything achieved by the New Deal—going so far as to aim cavalier accusations of high treason at its servants. The bureaucrats went defensive, hammering their rhetoric into new slogans and formulas, for all of which anticommunism was the ground bases.

MacLeish was caught in mid-stride by FDR's death. He and Acheson submitted their resignations the following day. Truman had no idea what MacLeish represented, nor did his Secretary of State designate Senator James Byrnes, ex-governor of South Carolina. Truman accepted both resignations—only to have Byrnes repair one error by frantically calling Acheson on Martha's Vineyard two days later, begging him to remain. No such call reached MacLeish, nor is there evidence Acheson lifted a hand to help. MacLeish lingered in the Divison of Cultural Relations until August; his replacement, William Benton, took over in September.[1]

Cofounder of the pathfinding ad agency Benton and Bowles, the new Assistant Secretary was "America's salesman." He was also, as it transpired, the first of the random accidents of politics and war that would divert cultural diplomacy from the designs of its founders. OWI veterans, outnumbering the culturalists ten to one, welcomed Benton as recognizably one of their own; so did admirers of his friend Rockefeller.

In October 1945 a survey team headed by OWI-veteran and *Washington Post* foreign correspondent Ferdinand Kuhn, surely with Benton's connivance, tackled the question of how to merge OWI, the Division of Cultural Relations, and the Coordinator's office, which had already been absorbed by MacLeish. Kuhn's group, well before the cold war came clear, arrived at the newsman's conclusion: culture, regularly relegated to the Sunday supplements or the "back of the book" by news editors, was a subset of information. Kuhn had seen USIS posts around the world where a mixed freight-and-passenger train of available activities was chugging along under informationist PAOs. Kuhn's report demeaned the greatest cultural talents the U.S. would ever send abroad—the Fairbanks, Morey, Donald Webster, Cuyler Young, and Frank Brown—by referring to them as "Contact Officers." He assumed that information and culture served a single unidirectional purpose, i.e., "telling the US story" with information the boss. Hull's 1938 agenda was ignored by Kuhn, for whom "exchanges" had one purpose: to move talkers out and listeners in.[2]

Benton was less short-sighted than Kuhn. He had left advertising to join his friend Robert Maynard Hutchins at the University of Chicago, as he told his friends, "to complete his education." Under Hutchins, his role at the university was ingenious: he helped transmit its learning to a larger public with methods he had developed in New York, especially in early commercial radio. Happy in Chicago, he did not seek the job in State and tried in fact to deflect the offer, knowing he was second choice—after his ex-partner Chester Bowles. Declaring he would stay no more than two years—a promise he kept—he took the job. He underestimated the assistant secretaryship, overestimated his own talents, and failed to anticipate the lure of power. After State he went into politics and ended his career in the Senate.

With limitless energy, Benton was convinced he could straighten anything out; he seemed to waste no time in thought, homework, or consultation. Soon he was soaring high, saying in a speech in Philadelphia: "The time has gone when we as a nation could afford to be indifferent to our scientific, educational and cultural exports." Thanks to cultural diplomacy, "the peoples of the world, all of whom want peace, will understand each other and be willing to tolerate differences because they understand them."[3] Typically he espoused all the right things, but no one before him had dared promise that peace would naturally follow understanding. He had made a salesman's overstatement.

Like his friend Rockefeller, Benton talked culture with fluid definitions shaped to the listener and the moment. Benton may have been the most remarkable adman of his time, but he was still an adman. For Cherrington, Thomson, MacLeish, and their committed followers, he was a cold shower.

In contrast to those in Europe, the postwar US information and cultural functions, carefully and purposefully separated in 1938 and again in 1945, were seen by Kuhn and Benton, and through them by Truman, as a single practice. Cherrington, from his base in the Rockies, made the independence of the cultural function his point of attack. In Europe only the Soviets and their satellites, geared for internal and external agitprop, used culture as a tool of propaganda. In the U.S. practitioners and politicians, in the interests of "getting it done" and with a profound faith in the flexibility of their version of "true" propaganda, were drifting ever closer to unidirectional information, on grounds that the Soviets did it.

No one bears more responsibility for failing to resist the drift toward unidirectional information than Benton. His failure was derived partly from background and personality, partly from his resistance to sticking with clear definitions, partly from the drive of a restless ego, and partly from the short time he allotted himself. The paradox of Benton is as fascinating as Rockefeller's, the difference being that Benton, after Yale and Chicago, had more reason to understand education from the inside, the history of the bureau in his charge, and the muddled contribution of Rockefeller himself, whom the adman had served for four years on a panel of three close advisors.

Benton was the son of an underpaid missionary-educator—the Benton School in Lebanon's B'hamdoun survived until the Second World War. He scraped his way through Yale on an inadequate scholarship and did well enough to be nominated for a Rhodes scholarship, which he declined on grounds of irrelevance to his planned career. In the world of advertising, he rose with lightning speed, partnering with Yale patrician Chester Bowles. A diplomat who knew both men wondered how the two could have worked together when neither ever stopped talking.

In 1936 Benton left advertising, as he had pledged to do when he achieved success, and took a lower-paying vice presidency under president Hutchins. Self-deprecation was a graceful cover for a wry truth. His assistant John Howe reported that Benton once asked him for a one-page memo on someone he had heard mentioned three times on the campus that very day—Thomas Aquinas.

At the university built by the senior Rockefeller, he filled a unique role as unofficial director of development. Hutchins said that Benton was less a man than a phenomenon and made no effort to contain him. More than a fund-raiser, Benton was a serious shaper of the young university, an architect of its relations with a broad, national public. His great gift to the university lay in persuading Hutchins to accept the benificent terms offered by Sears Roebuck for their faltering Encyclopedia Britannica, which he turned around and ran at a profit, ensuring a permanent "endowment" for the university. He put Chicago on the public map in other ways, e.g., by publishing Mortimer Adler's Great Books, with its Syntopticon, an index of all the ideas of humankind. He linked the university's economics faculty to the business world via Paul Hoffman, giving birth to the Chicago Roundtable broadcasts, then to the Council on Economic Development, illustrating and proclaiming the ideas of US corporatism. He had moved from hawking soap to selling the Great American University as the engine of US growth. Harold Lasswell, CPI veteran and student of Nazi psychopathology, had persuaded him that a great university had a special national mission: to offer "a program of preventive medicine that would help maintain America as a free society with equal opportunity for human dignity open to all." Carefully defined and translated into foreign affairs terms, this was an agenda for cultural diplomacy worthy of MacLeish; but Benton was neither a careful translator nor a diplomat. Still, his work in Chicago was highly visible and important; in 1945 he declined an invitation to preside over Columbia.

His links to Rockefeller reached back to 1936. Both were serious collectors of contemporary American art, although Benton admired the social realism of Reginald Marsh while Rockefeller preferred the abstractions favored by his beloved MoMA. Democrat Benton and Republican Rockefeller shared a fundamentally nationalist ethos in an international corporatist mode. Nelson Rockefeller and two of his brothers tried to persuade John D. Jr. to invest in Benton's proposal for educational filmmaking; turned down, Benton built Britannica's educational film division on his own. In 1942 Nelson invited him to join two other advisors, Henry Luce and MIT Dean Robert Caldwell, and Benton became the Coordinator's link to the advertising and communications industries.

The two were close. When Rockefeller left his Foxall Road house at the end of his Washington tour, he passed it on to Benton along with five servants and a chauffeur. (Benton later passed the house on to Secretary of State George Marshall.) Benton's children took over the Rockefeller children's places at the select Sidwell Friends School. In 1952, before the Fulbright-Hickenlooper Committee, Benton called Rockefeller "the pioneer of American peace-time propaganda."[4] From Benton, it was a compliment. For Cherrington, it was trouble.

Taking office, Benton had no glimmer of the potential in MacLeish's mandate. His biographer reported a poorly informed view that could only have come from Benton: "MacLeish had been in charge of some 1000 employees in the State Department library, the archives, the beginnings of the Cultural Relations Division, and a special section dealing with all the non-governmental organizations in contact with the Department." The thousand would be engulfed by "8500 OWI employees, 3500 people in Rockefeller's OIAA, and the OSS. Even without the OSS they represented more than half the employees of the whole State Department."[5]

Benton once again changed the office's name, this time to Public and Culture Affairs. Accepting State's public relations job and putting it first, he trapped himself in the exhausting work of public affairs. Benton, unlike MacLeish who planned to delegate it, tried to do it himself—and he paid a price, thanks to neophyte Secretary James Byrnes.

Benton firmly ruled out the word "propaganda," but he was, in fact, most often a soft-sell theorist, who forgot that advertising was a benign form of propaganda. The merger with propagandizing OWI presented problems, but Benton floated above them. Fresh from Chicago, he talked culture even better than Rockefeller. As he said, to promote "cultural relations between peoples . . . is the heart of political relations." While this was a fine statement, with time his definitions of culture and politics proved elastic. Working for Byrnes, the most demanding of Secretaries, he quickly learned the perils of State's public relations.

He had warned Hutchins of the dangers of government funding; he had also persuaded colleagues that the nation's intellectual treasure was a public trust and that sharing was a duty, with dividends guaranteed over time. In Washington he wanted to do nothing less for America. He drew his inspiration not from Welles or Cherrington, whose files he surely did not take the time to read, but from Rockefeller, the man he helped create. The cultural affairs function took second place in his priorities to State's public relations, to reorganization, and to launching UNESCO.

His first task, as he saw it, was to persuade Congress that a peacetime "information" program was essential to head off the mistake of 1919. In Congress a quiet group led by Fulbright was looking for another way to strengthen the tiny Division of Cultural Relations left by Welles, Duggan, and Cherrington. Instead of building outward from this core, Benton rode off to persuade Congress to save OWI.

He accepted a staff reduction of 75 percent for the three offices he agreed to merge; this meant the dismissal of at least nine thousand people. He looked for criteria for dismissal, or at least language, and came up with the word "loyalty." Suspicion had doubtless fallen on OWI staff recruited in the anti-fascist years of Soviet partnership, but not even McCarthy believed there were nine thousand disloyal people in OWI. Nonetheless Benton persuaded the famous anti-immigration racist Senator Pat McCarran to allow mass firing by devising a marvelously plastic criterion: "in the interest of the service." To smooth over the slaughter, he signed a special certificate of merit for each departing staffer. The best left along with the worst, but few complained.

Rejecting OSS was Benton's decision—even MacLeish had put it off for calmer times. The shrewd Donovan dragged Benton through an exhausting three-day briefing, at the end of which John Howe reported Benton's conclusion that OSS's "spy operations and 'black propaganda' wouldn't mix with the 'white propaganda' Benton was expected to conduct"[6]— Langer, Schlesinger, Adlai Stevenson, Bundy, MacLeish, and even Hutchins might have advised him differently. The OSS research and analysis function became the intelligence and research division of State; the rest of OSS, including foreign-broadcast monitoring, awaited the birth of the CIA in 1947.

Benton, a gifted but essentially lone operator, had no talent for seeking or listening to advice. In hindsight, he seems to have been in over his head, with too much on his plate, no knack for delegating jobs to good people, and few strengths other than his quick wit and bottomless energy. He had little experience of big bureaucracy and none of Congress. Even in his achievements, he ruffled feathers and made enemies, some permanent—including Acheson, Cherrington, and MacLeish.

The public relations job was torture. Secretary Byrnes, with no background in foreign affairs, made relentless, unrealistic demands; he could not understand why CBS and NBC did not routinely run full texts of speeches and statements that he said were important. Aware of Benton's access to the networks, he could not understood why Benton did not tell them what to show. But Benton endured; it was not the last time the demanding State public relations job would exhaust a leader of talent.

In February 1946 Byrnes's impatience flared: setting out on a long European trip, he told Benton he was on his own with Congress. "If he did not get their approval, the worldwide US information program would be out of business."[7] The persuasive Benton had failed to persuade even his own boss, and his irritation was mounting: "Unless I successfully did what [Byrnes] said I ought to do, I might just as well get out of Washington—or settle back into a postwar State Department version of Archie MacLeish's old job, plus UNESCO and the press department and a few trimmings."[8] A statement like this makes one wonder what kind of empire Benton had in mind.

The very existence of his office was in question. No legislative authorization existed for any of its activities except those of the old division; the rest was a collection of wartime leftovers. Like MacLeish, Benton knew he would have to educate Congress. Dousing State's daily public relations fires, he slowly began to cultivate congressmen one by one, pleading for the survival of information programs instead of expanding the division's existing mandate, helping the new Fulbright Act grow gradually, strengthening UNESCO, and shaping the pending Smith-Mundt legislation.

He was good with congressmen, who were beguiled by the millionaire business dynamo, but he had no time to befriend the well-over five hundred congressmen and fifteen hundred staff. Benton took credit for getting Fulbright's bill through Congress; in brand-name style, he insisted its fruits be known as the "Fulbright Program." He was equally proud of naming the Voice of America (VOA), which most credit to Robert Sherwood. In State, like Stettinius, he practiced name change; it would be seven years before names stabilized after Benton's tinkering: in the next four years the office passed through four directors and nearly a dozen name changes: CIAA, OIAA, IIIS, OICCA, CIG, IIE (divided into OII and OEX). These were all the same office.

Quick, articulate, and energetic, Benton was in the great hurry that induces intellectual laziness. He was a master of liberally bestowed buzzwords with spongy definitions. Culture was the "slow" medium, while mass communications and information were "fast." On Madison Avenue he was known for the soft sell, but his relentless style made his personal impact hard. In Ninkovich's analysis of Benton's view of soft and hard, culture and information, "the two approaches were not contradictory but rather complementary means along "a continuum for achieving . . . mutual understanding."[9] But information always came first. Despising propaganda, Benton admitted he meant only propaganda in the "evil or ulterior sense" and was proud to label Rockefeller a "great propagandist." Benton believed people should trust him because *his* kind of propaganda would work for America. He defined his style very loosely as "educational efforts of peoples speaking to peoples." Tossing aside the wisdom of the past, he believed he could out-talk any problem.

Benton was still managing the same five divisions grouped under MacLeish: for culture there were exchanges and libraries-centers; for information, radio, publications, and motion pictures. Rather than follow MacLeish and define "information" or even VOA as part of *education*, Benton looked for new slogans to cover old contradictions. Instead of defining two separate functions, he insisted on channeling his office and the remains of his gifted staff, from different worlds and continents, into a single mission; his favorite metaphor pointed out the need to scramble all eggs into one omelette. But this metaphor missed every point: it blurred ideas and definitions, it posited a single product from a single base in Washington, it misused talents and asked staff to do things they were not trained for—and did not always want to do.

With Congress, as in his lofty Philadelphia speech, Benton stressed the need for going over the heads of foreign governments to reach *the people*, i.e., the Creel-Wilson idea with an assist from Henry Wallace, supporting short-term foreign policy by manipulating foreign public opinion. At the same time he spoke, in Ralph Turner's terms, of foreign policy "in its long-range sense." He dwelt on facilitating and supplementing the private sector's work to "foster clearer reciprocal understanding."[10] Skipping about, avoiding hard questions from interlocutors or staff, he promised most things to all men. In Ninkovich's words, "Thus a great divide was traversed without fanfare or even the realization that it had been crossed."[11]

Benton had to be wary, above all, of Congress—which mistrusted both culture and propaganda. Instead of educating legislators, he catered to their ignorance; he felt free to refer to "the so-called cultural program." Congress raised its usual grab bag of objections: elitism, low-priority need, xenophobia, protectionism, budget-cutting, partisan anti–New Dealism, domestic tradeoffs, anti-liberalism, nationalism, and good old-fashioned know-nothingism. And an ominous new note was sounded— Representative Eugene Cox of Georgia, Benton's first newfound friend, was beginning to grumble about communists in State.

Congressional irritation exploded in late 1946 over a major exhibit of Benton's beloved modern painting, sent with MoMA help to Europe and

Latin America. Benton and the New York sophisticates had gotten ahead of the nation's elected representatives, indeed ahead of the president himself, who like Hitler, Stalin, and Khrushchev abhorred nonrepresentational art. The show was canceled in midcourse and the paintings sold at auction to lucky Washington bidders.

Benton's job was too much for *any* mortal, even himself. Bipartisanship in Congress was fading; any Democrat was fair game. Pork-barrel trading and budget-raiding were back in town. Benton pressed on, ignoring natural allies that Cherrington could have helped enlist in the institutions of education and culture and in the dozens of new private organizations like the American Field Service and the National Association of Foreign Student Advisors. True, he usually said the right thing, speaking passionately in defense of cultural work overseas and even in support of its separation from propaganda. He worked for the Fulbright Act of 1946, knowing it would strengthen diplomacy's educational component and add a few firm congressional friends. Where MacLeish would have led by educating and Cherrington by organizing constituencies, Benton, with remarkable gifts for both, focused on the underside of Congress.

The dangers in Benton's buoyant contradictions came clear in his role in birthing UNESCO.[12] Today in the U.S., where the intellectual sector uttered no audible complaint about US withdrawal from UNESCO in 1983–84, it is difficult to realize that Benton, a master at sniffing the wind, was a passionate believer in the UN cultural organization. Key to the thinking of the cultural founders, UNESCO was the multilateral supplement to what could be done bilaterally in cultural relations, hence a useful global corrective to perceptions of great power and, specifically, US interventionism. In May 1945 Fulbright had enlisted Robert Taft and Karl Mundt, key conservatives, to cosponsor a sense-of-Congress resolution calling for a postwar UNESCO-like organization; it passed by an overwhelming vote.

In 1946 Benton leaped into action, soliciting write-in support for UNESCO from American constituents. Thousands of NGOs and private organizations weighed in. The response led legislators to an unmanageable conclusion: a one-hundred-member US supervisory board created by Congress to represent everyone. The dysfunctional US commission was an early step in frustrating US participation in UNESCO, even with the redoubtable Milton Eisenhower as its executive director. In the 1920s and 1930s, Shotwell's informal CIC, along with Leo Rowe's CIC at the Pan-American Union, had helped US organizations link to the League's cultural activities, functioning as UNESCO later would. These two CICs, with the Council of Learned Societies and IIE, coordinated private American international cultural relations. Shotwell's lean CIC was the perfect model for a US National Commission. Benton missed the point.

If Welles, Fulbright, and MacLeish were UNESCO's fathers, Benton was their eager son-in-law. They had seen the need to coordinate international activities in education, science, and culture by a union of *sovereign* nations, with the U.S. working within that system. Some internationalists wanted a multilateral organization that marched to the American drummer; others wanted even less control and urged turning over coordination of *all* US efforts in culture and education to a single multilateral system. Fulbright held out for a balance of the two; the down-to-earth American pluralist knew the limits of his nation and its tendency to measure international agencies by narrow national criteria. He knew the difficulties of multinational administration and how little any one nation could do. He was uneasy with the urge to deploy US power in the postwar years and wary of the hegemonic thrust he saw it serving. And he respected the creative energies stored in the U.S., especially in its universities. He thus held out for a strong US bilateral and *binational* cultural outreach, designed to mesh with a multilateral agency.

Benton handpicked the US delegation for the founding conference in November 1946. Aware of MacLeish's unhappiness at being set aside, Benton astonished everyone by his statesmanlike insistence that MacLeish chair the delegation. But with the other hand, he took back the gift: incapable of delegating anything, he named himself as MacLeish's deputy, nullifying his bold gesture.

MacLeish-Benton's delegation was packed with stars.[13] Fulbright surely could have arranged to go, after his success in 1944, but he stayed behind to educate his fellow legislators. Arriving in Paris even at the end of the meetings, during which MacLeish had steered the delegation masterfully, Fulbright might have skirted the inevitable discomfiture of MacLeish, resulting from Benton's inability to resist running the show. MacLeish, a man of a few thoughtful words, eventually retreated into silence.

With UNESCO, as with the UN, the Soviets posed a problem, although they were abstaining from UNESCO in this early phase. It was already apparent that the world, even with a UN in place, was heading for bipolar conflict as soon as the Soviets joined the fray. And the Europeans, who treated culture as a serious proposition, were split: the gravely wounded Britain and France were dueling, and both were ambivalent about the U.S. Meanwhile the industrialized nations were busily overlooking the less-developed world, despite the US delegation's efforts to include the developing world in negotiations.

In Paris, MacLeish faded into the background after Benton arrived. Benton insisted on adding "communications," a word the world did not yet understand, to UNESCO's mandate, initiating years of confusion. The founding meetings went downhill from there, as seen by the delegation. Europeans had learned in the 1930s that culture and education were life-and-death issues, so the Americans in the delegation, for whom culture was a sideshow, were not prepared for the Old World's cultural hardball. Further, the Americans, trying to pull together the fractious US intellectuals represented on the elephantine one-hundred-person US National Commission, were divided, despite Milton Eisenhower's ingenuity.

Caught short by the lofty language and the gravity Europeans reserved for culture, the Americans were further concerned that links with Eastern Europe were shattering and that, outside Europe, there was a new kind of post-colonial chaos.

Three issues headed the US agenda: UNESCO's location, the siting of its biannual general conferences, and its first Director General. For location, the French delegation, with the great Socialist Léon Blum in the chair, graciously offered the world's most beautiful city, while the Americans held out for some "neutral" city. Paris won hands-down, albeit—at US insistence—for a "temporary" period of five years, which of course became permanent. For the location of biannual general conferences, Benton pressed hard: if Paris was to be the headquarters, then meetings should take place anywhere *but* Paris; on this he won reluctant agreement, but it was a hollow victory—as time went on, the meetings, on grounds of cost, drifted back to the City of Light.

The grand prize was the Director Generalship. Scientist John Maud of Britain, the great Americanophile Henri Bonnet, and Blum took informal charge. They had worked alongside MacLeish for two weeks. Now, as the educators had elected Fulbright to the chair in London in 1944, they called on MacLeish, a world-class intellectual and *mirabile dictu* a Francophone, knowing US participation would make or break UNESCO. To their surprise, MacLeish discouraged the idea, for reasons I am at a loss to explain. The three men turned instead to the most obvious Anglo-Saxon, Julian Huxley, noted British scientist.

At this point either Benton or the White House made a serious blunder: the Director General was to be *elected* by the member-nations, not *appointed* by the White House. The U.S. needed to *nominate* a compelling French-speaking American *candidate*, a man of towering intellectual stature who could save British face and win the day by being better qualified than Huxley—i.e., another MacLeish. Benton, instead of working through State, apparently cabled the White House directly, seeking guidance. The under-informed Truman saw this opportunity as the perfect parking place for FDR's Attorney General Francis Biddle.[14] With no understanding of the realities in Paris, the need for high excellence, and the necessity of gentle diplomacy to soothe America's bruised allies, the White House nominated Biddle, far less appropriate than Huxley.

The Americans decided the Huxley nomination posed a problem and said so. Loath to oppose Britain, they wanted an American—for the same reasons Maud, Bonnet, and Blum had advanced. Benton apparently leaked to the corridors that the U.S. opposed Huxley, alleging left-wing associations. Benton, who spoke no foreign language, consulted the suave Bonnet, asking whether it was essential that the Director General be fluent in French. Bonnet's advice was memorable. How ridiculous! Of course it was not essential, not even crucial . . . merely *indispensable!*

Having caused his own discomfiture, Benton made things even worse. Instead of good sportsmanship and pledges of full support to Huxley once elected, the American delegation imposed a two-year limit on the Director General's tenure, instead of the mandated six. Further, they demanded an American deputy director and recruited the wise and decent Walter H. C. Laves. Laves did what he could to mend fences, but Huxley took office cloaked in irony. Near-comic diplomatic ineptitude had guaranteed a minimalist solution: no one, either in Europe or in the U.S., was happy—with the possible exception of the French, who soon added the Director Generalship to their two geographical victories. France was delighted to add another beacon to project its cultural power.

MacLeish represented the U.S. on UNESCO's ten-person Executive Council for a year, but the damage was already done. UNESCO was off to a rocky start. Soon the USSR deployed its blunt obstructionism. With the U.S. tied in its own knots, more than three decades of frustration and neglect passed before the US Samson would shake the UNESCO temple by withdrawing. The US position on the Executive Council passed to high-caliber Americans like Milton Eisenhower, New York State commissioner of education George Stoddard, and Benton himself from 1963 to 1968.

When Eisenhower took over Kansas State University in 1947, he immediately set up a statewide UNESCO center on his campus.[15] At the University of Denver in the spring of 1949, Ben Cherrington with his assistant William C. Olson gave the first university course in the U.S. on "UNESCO and World Affairs" with a meticulous curriculum showing that Cherrington saw more future in multilateral than in bilateral cultural diplomacy. With Eisenhower's idea of statewide UNESCO organizations in mind, Cherrington created a Colorado council, chartered by the legislature.[16] In Washington, however, UNESCO was slipping off the nonpartisan track that Fulbright and MacLeish had envisioned. The organization's shaky start exemplifies the failure to understand the value of multilateralism based on respect. For the historian Ninkovich, UNESCO's birth embodies US unease with both domestic and international cultural questions.

Back in Washington, Benton soon resigned as promised, far too soon to have learned much. After his resignation, he got involved in Connecticut politics, taking for himself the Senate seat his friend Bowles had wanted. In State, the outstanding foreign service officer George V. Allen replaced Benton. He soon understood he was drowned in public affairs responsibilities. Meanwhile Truman had delegated vision in foreign affairs and global strategy to his gifted new Undersecretary of State Dean Acheson. Despite decades of friendship with MacLeish, Acheson's version of realism left little room for cultural diplomacy.

Benton's two-year tour turned the cultural question into a battleground for survival. Welles and MacLeish had envisioned an integrated American cultural diplomacy; with Benton, information took over and the cultural idea began its journey to the back of the bus. Meanwhile international politics had forced a cooler kind of war onto the American agenda; those like MacLeish and Fulbright who wanted actively to wage peace were being pushed aside. What should have been cultural diplomacy's time for recovery, recuperation, rethinking, and consolidation became instead a time for coping with irresistible new demands and fighting off the same old predators. The nation was gearing up for a new kind of war.

J. William Fulbright was a different kind of man from Benton. In his Rhodes quadrennium he had been uplifted and primed. When the list of heroes of American cultural diplomacy is drawn up, MacLeish will stand high; but "the Senator," as his admirers still call him, will lead all the rest. He and MacLeish met no later than the spring of 1944, when the Librarian joined Fulbright's delegation to London.[17] If Welles and Duggan had the idea of cultural diplomacy, Fulbright gave it permanence at a perilous moment by providing its principal funding resource, program activity, and basic ethos. Without the Fulbright Program, US cultural diplomacy would have evaporated by 1950; with it as its most important half, formal cultural diplomacy has survived relatively intact until our times.[18]

Fulbright's commitment to international cultural exchange sprouted at Oxford in 1924. From then until his death, six decades of consistent effort went into the fight for international understanding and the exchanges that would nourish it. In his eighties, Fulbright learned of an effort to establish a world prize for international understanding in his name. "Why?" he snorted. "I don't need a memorial—the *Program* is my memorial!"

His intellectual roots are a composite of influences. When a friend once asked him about them; he looked amused at the obvious answer: "One name—Woodrow Wilson." But there was more to it than Wilson. While we wait for the chroniclers of this extraordinary man's life to sort through the details, one can only list elements which helped internationalize this small-town boy and made him a worldwide symbol of cultural internationalism, an exemplar of the human values of educational exchange, one of three most-admired twentieth-century Americans abroad, and a model of the patient legislator who knew how to listen and get things done.

The family name was Americanized from the German Vollbrecht before their move from Missouri to Arkansas, the smallest of the southern states. Arkansas's isolated northwest corner was populated by Missourians seeking land they could live on without slaves; Fulbright remembered that the entire Fayetteville area, in his youth, had a black population of no more than fifty.

The Civil War shaped the Senator's approach to empires, cultural exchanges, and diplomacy. His South had been reduced to an economic colony of the North and so it remained for a good part of his lifetime. Seeing himself as a colonial subject helped him understand the postcolonial era through which half the world was living after 1945. His

Southern background may also explain his special gift for looking at the underside of a power relationship, his sympathy for the underdog, his understanding of colonialism and its aftereffects, his fear of giant national power unleashed on the weak, and his Jeffersonian faith in people's ability to make their own decisions. His Southern origins further shed light on his understanding of the idea of economic—and cultural— imperialism, an idea which the Marxians had appropriated and were broadcasting around the globe. For Fulbright, Marx had polarized and poisoned a human process which he saw going on around him everywhere in the world, a process about which he understood a great deal.

Growing up, he had everything. He was a top student, a triple-threat football star, a son of the first family of Fayetteville and an adoring mother, and financially comfortable. He accumulated business experience and a gimlet eye for budgets. His mother, a political power broker at city and state levels, taught him practical politics and intervened on occasion to advance his career. His internationalization began when he won, as he said, "on a fluke of regional distribution," a Rhodes scholarship, key to a great university and to one of America's most prestigious clubs, the Rhodes alumni.

Cecil Rhodes, the millionnaire who had ruthlessly "exploited" South Africa, committed a cultural diplomatic act of unforeseeable consequence in funding his famous scholarships. His way of disbursing his ill-gotten wealth was a plan for socializing foreign elites—in the U.S. and selected other countries—to the British vision of the world. Rhodes could not know that, for an empire in decline, Rhodes alumni would turn out to be a major intellectual lifeline to Great Britain.

Fulbright was only twenty when he arrived at Oxford. By luck, as a student interested in the study of the law, he was assigned to Pembroke College and to tutor Ronald B. McCallum, a twenty-seven-year-old Scot, himself an outsider from a historically proud, exploited, and resentful province. Unlike many of the Oxford dons who treated the rough-edged Americans with unnerving disdain, McCallum, who had spent the preceding year at Princeton's graduate school, in the shadow of Wilson, immediately engaged with Fulbright as a friend. Tutor (later Master of Pembroke) McCallum and Fulbright corresponded until McCallum's death in 1973; he was devoted to his Arkansas friend—Pembroke College today boasts a residential quad across the Thames named for Fulbright. The publication of the Fulbright-McCallum correspondence, long overdue, will illuminate this remarkable relationship and the influence of this "sophisticated but unrepentent Whig" on his American pupil.[19] McCallum, who helped international relations emerge as an academic discipline in England, taught Fulbright how to think about foreign affairs.

In his fourth Rhodes year, encouraged by Oxford to wander, he seized an unusual opportunity and apprenticed himself to foreign correspondent Michael Fodor, Hungarian engineer turned journalist and lifelong friend. Following him into innumerable interviews with major European figures, Fulbright learned how to relate unapologetically to the great men of his era.

Back in the U.S. in April 1929, Fulbright was caught short by the Great Depression. He took time to straighten out his family's businesses, then moved to Washington to work in the Justice Department while taking a law degree at the George Washington University. With his Philadelphian bride Betty Williams, he returned to Arkansas to teach law; he was soon named president of the state's university, then one of the youngest university presidents in US history. He made the relatively easy step to the House of Representatives in 1943 and to the Senate in 1944. Serving his constituents well, he focused from the start on foreign affairs and developed a national image of which Arkansans were proud.

Oxford and McCallum shaped his life with unusual credentials and training; he focused on foreign affairs. Foreign policy was a low-prestige specialty in Congress; Speaker Sam Rayburn was astonished when Fulbright asked for an assignment to the House Foreign Affairs Committee but nevertheless arranged it for the newcomer. In Washington he lived in a small apartment on Wyoming Avenue in the embassy-studded area called Kalorama, the name poet-diplomat Joel Barlow gave to his farmland. The Fulbrights left calling cards at all the foreign embassies, and the resultant invitations quickly defined an international social life.

At his maiden speech in the House, in US legislative tradition a momentous event to be carried off with panache, he was surrounded by the cream of the leadership of both parties; they heard a witty, biting, and thorough answer to the globaloney speech of his colleague Claire Booth Luce. His reputation as a compelling speaker spread, and he was invited to national forums like the Foreign Policy Association, the World Affairs Council, and the American Bar Association. Each speech grew from its predecessor; he was working out, by trial and error, the details of an American vision of postwar world order, revolving around a multinational organization like the League. Haunted by Wilson's failure, he believed the U.S. deserved a second chance. Meanwhile he dreamed of democratizing the Rhodes experience to include all Americans.

In Congress, he had entered a club more exclusive than the Rhodes alumni but he was unimpressed. In his first constituent newsletter, he noted that the intelligence of his colleagues seemed inversely proportional to the amount of time spent speaking on the floor. More discreetly, he wrote to his mother that he would grade most of his colleagues no higher than a B minus. Biographer Randall Woods explains: "Neither the House nor the Senate could claim to be a community of intellectuals. The typical member was a lawyer from a small city, a graduate of his or her state university with a B average, a participant in some sport, a stalwart on the debating team, and an active member of various fraternities, clubs, and political organizations."[20]

The House Foreign Affairs Committee was the fief of Sol Bloom of New York, a man with little time for serious thought and no time at all for young whippersnappers. Fulbright crossed Bloom in 1943, at a hearing considering Lend-Lease, by which large amounts of equipment and supplies were being sent to the British and others as interest-free loans, presumably to be repaid as war debt. As Fulbright knew, such debts were rarely repaid. The witness on that fateful day was Lend-Lease Administrator Edward R. Stettinius, later Secretary of State. Fulbright, in his quiet and gentlemanly style, asked whether any attention was being paid to the postwar period. Stettinius's aide Oscar Cox knew there was not, and on his advice, Stettinius ducked the question. Bloom was annoyed at the young congressman's intervention and warned Fulbright to behave.

Reading the exchange today, it is obvious that the Boxer Indemnities were on Fulbright's mind. He knew how John Hay had turned cruel reparations into scholarships—in fact, the British had done the same, a decade or so later, while Fulbright was at Oxford. The Southerner in him recognized that war debts and indemnities were not only crippling but humiliating. Why not then turn them to constructive use and mutual advantage? Instead of bestowing Lend-Lease without conditions, why not ease the terms of repayment and tie the loan to postwar cooperation—as Hoover had arranged with Belgium and Finland in 1918?

Fulbright pursued the matter with colleagues, asking parallel questions about establishing some kind of UN. Calling on Assistant Secretary Dean Acheson, he shared his deep agenda: "the settlement of world problems through collective security."[21] The hyperrealist Acheson was not impressed. Fulbright persisted, going over Acheson's head in a letter to Hull, who referred him to Welles. It was a true meeting of the minds: Welles had been looking for an interlocutor in Congress, seeking a way to stimulate postwar thinking, precisely what Fulbright wanted.

Encouraged, Fulbright presented his far-reaching 1943 House resolution, the so-called UN Resolution, committing the U.S. to foster and join a world organization after the war, committing Congress to do what Wilson had failed to persuade it to do a quarter of a century earlier. With Welles's letter of support in his pocket, Fulbright raised the question in Bloom's committee. The irritated chairman referred the question to State; Fulbright trumped him by placing Welles's letter into the record.

Reflecting his commitment not only to foreign affairs but also to its cultural dimensions, Fulbright made a risky choice, taking two weeks out of his Arkansas Senate campaign to chair the US delegation to the 1944 education meetings in London. Tennesseean Hull was delighted to name a fellow Southerner to the chair.[22] Once in London, Fulbright was nominated by Belgium to chair the meetings and elected unanimously. Out of this conference grew the first draft charter for a UN "Organization for Educational and Cultural Reconstruction."

In June, home from London meetings and five months away from the Senate, Fulbright reported to Roosevelt and caught the president's attention, with an assist from Harry Hopkins. With FDR's approval, he began lobbying colleagues for "the UN Resolution." It passed on 21 September 1944, its language reaching well beyond Roosevelt's more cautious support and calling for an organization with power beyond sanctions, not only military force to support decisions but the power "to control the productive capacity of instruments of aggressive warfare"— i.e., a UN with teeth. The Resolution passed by 360 votes to twenty-nine. The Senate, despite foreign relations chair Tom Connally's annoyance, soon followed suit with eighty-five votes to five. The bill was known thereafter as the Fulbright-Connally Resolution.[23] In the Congress less than eight months, he had managed a historic coup.

Fulbright and his codelegates from London were impatient to move. They urged funding for multilateral educational and cultural work focused on Russia and China. State supported the move, proclaiming a victory of "democratic cooperation"; but Roosevelt let it sit. Nelson Rockefeller might have helped break the log-jam—but no one seemed to have asked for his help.

Early in 1945 the young Arkansan acquired an ally in the Senate, Mr. Conservative himself, Republican Robert Taft of Ohio. In the upcoming Smith-Mundt debates of 1947–48, Taft would be a staunch supporter of educational exchanges. In early 1945 the two men stood together, along with missionary-son Karl Mundt of South Dakota, to cosponsor a resolution committing the postwar U.S. to "the establishment of an international office of education." The idea was not obvious to most of Washington, which knew little of the deeper agendas of education and culture; yet the Fulbright-Taft-Mundt Resolution passed handily, another victory without precedent. Fulbright was on the move.[24]

He had been appalled by his first glimpse of total war in London—the green England he had known had suffered no physical damage from the First World War, but now, in the shattered and depopulated London of 1944, war was never far from his mind. He saw old friends and added two new ones: former IIE staffer Ed Murrow, now the premier American radio war correspondent; and Winston Churchill, whose daughter-in-law Pamela Harriman, present at their first meeting, reminisced in 1993 that Fulbright's visit marked the first time she had ever seen her father-in-law listen to an American—presumably other than FDR or his American mother. The London visit strengthened Fulbright, both in his Atlantic commitment and in his appreciation of the uses of cultural diplomacy. He saw how serious the reconstruction of Europe and its educational systems would be. At the meetings, living examples of what enlightened nations might do together, he met decent, concerned Europeans eager to get started on the postwar agenda, and he recognized the common problems they faced.

Fulbright saw too that the U.S., if it did some things uniquely well, was a profoundly provincial nation, perhaps better advised to leave matters of extreme national sensitivity abroad to multilateral action. He certainly knew that a stable cultural diplomacy would be difficult to carry on with a populist Congress in charge. From the national vantage point to which his career had lifted him, he saw the flaw in the American understanding of collective action: it was a *conditional* merging of sovereignties. Multilateralism could only win widespread US support if its decisions were shaped, and seen to be shaped, to the service of US interests. On the other hand, he knew that collective security could only work among true equals who respected each other. Like Wilson, he was years, perhaps decades, ahead of American political thought. Fortunately Wilson's example had taught him the danger of being right at the wrong time.

In the Senate he paid a price for his perceived sins in the House; he was delayed in gaining entrance to the Foreign Relations Committee. While waiting, he worried about Yalta: Roosevelt had again bypassed Congress, in a high-handed process that might damage the peace. Fulbright's maiden speech in the Senate called for expanding Congress's role in foreign policy. He would become more and more convinced as his life unfolded that the Second World War and the rising cold war had shifted the balance of power over foreign policy away from Congress and into the executive branch; he wanted to make the Senate Foreign Relations Committee a countervailing force. At the same time, he never ceased pressing the idea of peaceful coexistence with the USSR, based not on US weakness but on America's overwhelming moral and physical strength and certain victory in time. For his inaugural Senate speech, he was again surrounded by applauding Palladins, including Republicans Vandenberg, Taft, and Saltonstall, accepting him into their club, expressing a commitment to bipartisanship, and marking him as a foreign affairs voice to be heeded. The speech was the beginning of his remarkable role in US foreign policy.

Roosevelt's death, in Fulbright's view, left a seriously under-informed man in charge. Fulbright and Truman knew each other only slightly. The Senator would have delightedly helped educate his Missouri neighbor, but Truman relied on Acheson, a man from a different world who had no room for Fulbright. Truman's unfortunate petty personal campaign against Fulbright grew out of a press flap in which Fulbright's thoughtful comparison of the US Congress to the British parliament was erroneously headlined by a careless journalist to say that the senator wanted the president to resign. Truman thereafter referred to Fulbright as "Halfbright." The Senator was deprived of access by this defeat; and over the years he came to believe that Truman and Acheson had strangled future relations with the USSR by cutting off conciliation, provoking confrontation, and settling into stalemate.

In October 1945 the titan Nicholas Murray Butler, after forty-three years as president and masterbuilder of Columbia University, announced his retirement. The trustees, having run through their first short list of four, sent out feelers to Fulbright. With Butler, Shotwell, Philip Jessup, Virginia Gildersleeve, with extended family members like Stephen Duggan, Inman, Cherrington, Murrow, and Studebaker, and with a record for teaching more living languages than any other US university, Columbia had stood for years at the peak of the cultural internationalist movement. The Rockefellers, Carnegie, and J.P. Morgan had helped Butler make Morningside Heights the Acropolis of New York, as they had helped make New York the intellectual and cultural capital of the nation. Fulbright was aware of what Butler had been able to achieve over decades as the quintessential internationalist; he was also aware that, although regularly mentioned as a presidential candidate, Butler had never been nominated. In the end, Fulbright declined, believing he could accomplish more from his base in the Senate.

The idea of an American Rhodes program had been in his mind since 1924, but he had no idea how to persuade Congress to fund it. He had not forgotten the discussion of Lend-Lease, but in 1945 he had not seen the connection between the two ideas. Four days after Roosevelt's death, Fulbright gave a national radio broadcast, touching on the exchange of students and professors and the translation of books, which he said were as important a contribution to peace as controling violence. He knew what Rhodes alumni were contributing to American life and British-US relations; he also knew that the Rhodes idea looked elitist in a populist democracy. His deepest fear was the lack of information about foreign affairs among ordinary Americans. At the end of his life, asked what he had intended by his exchange program, he anwered: "Aw hell, I just wanted to educate these goddam ignorant Americans!" There was little doubt about his goal; getting there was another matter.

As adaptive devices, in the subtle Washington games of non-intellect, he regularly twitted university-dwellers. Fulbright, an intellectual if there ever was one, delighted in teasing "the professors" on their narrow specializations and their naive view of Washington realities. As he aged, Fulbright's style became more Southern; he could show crackerbarrel amusement at the pretentions of intellectuals: "What does *he* know? He's just a professor." It was just window dressing: Fulbright was a citizen of the university world, a Rhodes scholar, a professor of law, and a university president who had declined the presidency of Columbia. To his committee hearings, he always invited academic figures, and his interrogations showed deep respect; field cultural officers were always warmly received in his office. He wore his intellect lightly, so as to preserve the common touch he needed if he were to function among his fund-controling colleagues and constituents. He knew from past debates that opposition could take irrational forms; he knew there were many times when reason would not carry the day. In his time he would hear the whole anti-exchange litany: xenophobic arguments about corrupting American youth, dilution of the US competitive advantage, giveaways, encouragement to communism, dangerous Wilsonian idealism, and so on.

The idea for his program was one of those accidents that strike the prepared mind. In September 1945 he ran into Oscar Cox, a former Stettinius aide, and they reminisced about the Lend-Lease hearings of 1943. Both knew there was surplus war equipment scattered around the world, valued at more than $100 million. Recalling the difficulties of debt repayment after the First World War and recognizing that forced conversion of foreign currrencies into dollars would strain fragile recovering economies, the two men hatched an idea that was brilliant in its simplicity: funds generated overseas by the sale of military surpluses would remain in that country of origin as a permanent endowment for bilateral exchanges, to be administered binationally, Boxer-style. This time, unlike the Boxer moment and the Rhodes idea, it would not involve one country but the entire world: swords were to be turned into plowshares.

On 27 September Fulbright submitted an amendment to the Surplus Properties Act, specifying that military surpluses should be sold and the proceeds put toward promoting "international good will through the exchange of students in the fields of education, culture and science." He argued it would cost nothing, and no one noticed what he had done. The bill was delivered without fanfare to the Committee on the Military. The next year was spent in shrewd, quiet, behind-the-scenes politicking, often in the form of conniving with a few key supporters to make things happen when opponents were away from the floor of the Senate. On 1 August 1946, the Senate passed the final version, which was quickly signed into law by Harry Truman as PL 584, watched by Fulbright and a beaming Benton—who took credit for rounding up votes.

Fulbright's program had come to birth—in theory. Like the creation of the Division of Cultural Relations, the details wherein lay God or the Devil remained to be worked out. Hanging over the idea's head was the fact that, within a few years, available military surpluses would disappear. Fulbright had settled for the possible and opened a door, but the institution remained to be built. Without a permanent congressional authorization, without programs lodged in a secure agency with a strong political base and a stable budget over time, the idea would dissipate in a few years. His legislation was a flimsy starting point; he had done no more than drag a reluctant Senate onto the public record. Now he needed bipartisan support—and the help of the American intellectual world.

Delegating leadership to others, he drew back from the center. Searching for allies and supplemental legislation, he found two cosponsors, both Republicans but from different worlds: Senator H. Alexander Smith of New Jersey and Representative Karl Mundt of South Dakota. Smith was a lawyer, a cautious patrician, and a cultural internationalist, a New Jersey Republican political figure who had been Herbert Hoover's wartime deputy for relief in Belgium, Finland, and postwar Europe, hence highly aware of the binational Boxer-style agreements with Belgium and Finland. He had also served as vice president of Princeton for development under president Harold Willis Dodds. Regular mail reached him from his friend in Rome, Princeton professor of art history and CAO Rufus Morey.

Mundt, born to China missionaries, came instead from a modest background and was divided in his mind. On the one hand, he was a keen supporter of exchanges and international education, highly aware of the Boxer precedent from his years in China; he had stood with Fulbright on the UNESCO Resolution. On the other, the "loss" of China so dismayed him that he made the long and emotional leap to conclude that communists had infected US foreign policy. While working for the Smith-Mundt Act of 1948, he took over the chair of HUAC, the House Un-American Activities Committee; his mean-spirited comments on Laurence Duggan's death came from the less attractive side of the man.

Master salesman Benton, taking up the cudgels, had focused on the OWI function and its continuation. Smith-Mundt thus reflected two distinct ideas: Fulbright's cultural exchanges and Benton's information. So long as he was in charge, Benton wanted to scramble all wartime functions into a single global, information-dominated omelette. While the salesman knew culture and information were distinct functions, he also thought he knew what would sell in Congress, hence the expedient omelette. In his hurry to leave his job, he believed he could not get the legislators' attention back to the long-range, slow-paced concept of the old division; Fulbright's naturally patient approach was not an option. Benton's tactics instead drew on the unilateral informationists, "telling America's story," while alluding to the threat of war. His betrayal of principle, as Ben Cherrington saw it, would dismay the culturalist constituency.

As GAC chair, Cherrington clashed with Benton from the first day—a friend once said he had never known the generous Cherrington to hate a man, with this single exception. Yet, for better or for worse, the Division's founding director had to admit that Benton's war talk had caught the congressional conscience. Perhaps Benton believed that, with Fulbright aboard, cultural diplomacy in time would find its own way; his friend Milton Eisenhower believed so. But Benton, intent on leaving, only had time to sell unilateral informationism. Cherrington was right to worry.

Discussion of Smith-Mundt began in the House Foreign Affairs Committee in 1946 and dragged on for two years. Laves and Thomson later wrote: "Few laws have been longer considered or more carefully examined. . . . It was in process of approval for two years. It was twice rewritten in committee, twice debated and approved on the House floor, and twice favorably reported by the Senate Foreign Relations Committee. The need for it was assessed by a joint Congressional committee on a two-month trip to Europe. Some fifty members of the Congress proposed more than one hundred amendments."[25] The so-called fact finding could not conceal the opposing tensions in the bill. Congressional visits to Europe were, as usual, manipulated: congressmen were programmed by the embassy and USIS posts, hence briefed by the PAO. Part of the PAO's business was to know what Congress wanted to hear and to make sure what legislators heard. The "junkets," orchestrated by Benton, skewed congressional attention even further to the informationists.

Smith and Mundt, each for his reasons, understood that information was *not* education. Yet, with omelette chef Benton talking their ears off, it did not occur to either to insist on two separate agencies. Perhaps they believed, as Milton Eisenhower argued, that administrative questions were best left to executive decision. More likely, they knew what they could get through an inattentive Congress. This time, it was impossible to replicate Fulbright's earlier stealth tactics—the bill was too prominent; trade-offs helped forge a single piece of legislation, one which stabilized cultural relations, but at the cost of wrapping the idea in a hard-hitting anti-Soviet information campaign. Again and again in the bill, education and information are defined as separate entities; but no one pointed out the contradictions or attempted to define the relationship between the two.

High bedlam prevailed on the semantics of culture. Mundt himself later said he had never "heard such a disorganized collection of misinformation circulated about any one piece of legislation."[26] Opponents threw up any idea, right or left, to the point or not, that came to mind: the weak US economy, communists in State, the program's uselessness, the futility of "selling America" because "things which are self-evident require no proof," xenophobia, the danger of importing "communists and agitators," the "overcrowded" US universities, a plot for government control over universities, damage to US competitiveness, scandalous "giveaways," and—paradoxically—a favorite theme of the Soviets, "cultural imperialism."[27] Benton's two annual budget knockdowns with Congress had reined him in: for fiscal year 1947 his bureau had been given a paltry $25 million, and in 1948 the House attempted to cut his budget to zero before Senate action forced a bitter compromise of $16 million.

Even the super-salesman could not talk his way around the yo-yo effect of such budget swings. With little dialogue between the two sides, the issues soon drifted downward to low common denominators. The myth that culture and information were a single function, fed by expedient field practitioners, slipped past sketchy historical memories. Informationists remembered that since 1917 they ran a subordinate cultural branch—"It had always been so"; therefore culture and information needed a single field chief, a single office in Washington, and a single mandate.

Busy congressmen thought they were voting for anti-Soviet propaganda. Even Fulbright, in desperation, found himself using the rhetoric of war. Asked years later whether he had not himself fed the illusion that his program was a vital weapon in the cold war, Fulbright admitted to expediency: "I'd say *anything*, so long as they gave us the money."

When the bill was introduced, Benton stage-managed bipartisan endorsements from giants like Marshall, Harriman, Dwight Eisenhower, John Foster Dulles, and three veterans associations. Following Benton's guidance, all supported the unilateral information approach—only General Marshall argued *against* propaganda in favor of building *trust*. The question of separate administration never arose.

Instead focus fell on a side issue: truth in propaganda. Benton agreed with Marshall on trust but quickly slid from trust to "true" propaganda, pleading for virtues like playing the news straight, "telling America's story," holding a "mirror" up to America rather than a selective "showcase," providing a "full and fair picture" of America. Foreign students, noted Benton, see the good and the bad about America and sort it out for themselves. There was no harm in unidirectional exchanges, he argued in circular fashion, so long as foreigners learned and Americans "told the story." The best of the new supporters were liberal internationalist propagandists, children of Rockefeller and Benton. In their high-minded moments, they insisted that US propaganda be true.

Benton's mirror-showcase paradox beguiled legislators who were already inclined to see the VOA as the only question. The mirror theorists, Rockefeller informationists, culturalists, and scholars believed a mirror held up to America, reflecting reality, would advance the US cause because the cause on balance was good; the mirror might even on occasion be adjusted to highlight certain aspects of US policy, but its primary job was to be a mirror. The showcasers on the other hand were hard-line marketeers who wanted to display selected aspects of America at their best, under skillful lighting and before compelling backdrops; they wanted the showcases to be visited only by the right people, if possible with a persuasive guide at hand. Benton usually argued for the mirror, but the agency Smith-Mundt created would soon be run by showcasers.

Cherrington, from Denver, launched strong but quixotic counterattacks, aimed at the wrong targets: obviously information must be true, yet the function of cultural relations was not to convey information but to let exchangees find their own truths. He pleaded for separate functions, in theory and practice, at home and in the field. Congress however was trapped in Benton's vision and by VOA glamor—radio was still king. The legislators were looking for an affordable way to fight global communism at a level below warfare.

All but the most perceptive liberal internationalists were diverted by Benton's energetic bypass and his arabesques on the showcase-mirror paradox. No one dealt with the deeper question: whether cultural-educational and information-propaganda programs should or could live together comfortably without diminishing each other. From his Denver mountainside, Cherrington's letters flowed. A few pro-separation witnesses, primarily university figures—many of them long-standing division associates—argued in compelling terms for the integrity of intellectual relations. Smith tried to apply what he was hearing from his university friends, but these were complex arguments, inappropriate for the Senate floor. In the end, the debate generated intense heat but no light. Unilateral informationism framed all questions, and pre–cold war language carried the day.

The universities' concerns come clear in correspondence between Princeton President Harold Dodds and Cherrington. In November 1947,

Dodds asked whether government should be doing these things at all. Cherrington, at his wise best, said service in State taught one to "understand the great difficulty of insulating the educational program from extraneous activities." He suggested the question be given longer-range consideration later on by a public-private national council. Dodds, swayed by Cherrington's experience, admitted he could not, in fact, think of "a better agency than State for a home base."[28] A month later Dodds's friend Smith supported separation.

In October a tougher letter had reached Cherrington from Milton Eisenhower. Eisenhower, director of the one-hundred-member US national commission for UNESCO, had put Cherrington on his executive committee, along with MacLeish and his deputy at the Library of Congress, future UNESCO chief Luther Evans. Eisenhower invited Cherrington to draft the commission's position paper on separating cultural affairs from information. He took the occasion to lecture Cherrington in favor of Benton, who "has fought the battles for us in the State Department. He has made everyone, from the President to the chore boy, understand that what we are doing is important." He chided Cherrington for calling Benton a propagandist—it is a "fighting or derogatory word," he admitted. "You and Bill Benton seem determined to misunderstand one another. . . . I think you are wrong about most of the things Bill has tried to do." He went on to redefine information in Benton's—and OWI's—terms: "Propaganda has as its purpose the indoctrination of men's minds. Information has only the purpose of spreading truth or factual information. Hence the distinction between the two types of work he has handled is not as sharp, I think, as you indicate." In the end, he pleaded for expediency: "The fight [for separation] at the moment might jeopardize the substantive legislation which is needed. . . . Bill would get the legislation through . . . then straighten out the other issue administratively. . . . The two activities would have to be in the same department to accomplish what you have in mind." Eisenhower was begging Cherrington not to divide the supporters by insisting on the principle of separation.

Indeed, had Milton Eisenhower headed the agency administering the double-barreled product of Smith-Mundt, things might have been different. But Benton did, and not for long. Cherrington knew him well; he also knew where the OWI veterans were sitting. From a former deputy to Elmer Davis, Eisenhower's analysis was predictable. From the coordinator of US participation in UNESCO, from a great future university president, it was less impressive—nor did it sway Cherrington.

Cherrington wrote back to say the issue had been resolved: Mundt "has come to the decision that his bill should . . . require the divorcement of information activities from the educational, scientific and cultural activities in the Department of State." Lulled by the illusion that separation had been decided, he took the time to dissect Eisenhower's peculiar definition of propaganda: "I am persuaded that [your] distinction is only accepted by citizens in the sending country and not by all of them. Those on the receiving end don't draw such fine distinctions when the program is unilateral. To them it is national propaganda." It was Cherrington at his most wise.

Two points colored this discussion for the next half century: first, the totally unrealistic idea that, left to themselves, bureaucrats would sort it out administratively and come to the right conclusion, regardless of background and numbers; second, the distinction, understood by few, between Benton's white-washed version of propaganda and Cherrington's vision of cultural relations as a straightforward extension of the American university ethos abroad.

For those seeking a middle ground, where culture and propaganda might work in constructive parallel, Eisenhower waved away the problem. By administrative legerdemain, he killed the idea of separation, a puzzling move in view of the American academic community's widespread endorsement of separation. In the end, one of the bicephalic PL 402's heads would speak to half of the contradiction, one to the other half, with no communication between the two. In classic labor-relations parlance, the language had gone to one side, the decision to the other.

It was a pyrrhic victory. Smith-Mundt was a recipe for continuing tensions. Referring more than once to deepening "mutual understanding" over time, its aggressive context swamped its plea for dialogue. One telling sign: with memories of Creel still alive, PL 402 prohibited propaganda *inside* the U.S. Fear of propaganda was alive and well, when it affected Americans.

Doubtless Smith-Mundt was all anyone could have hoped to get from the "good-for-nothing, do-nothing" Congress against which Truman campaigned in 1948. Certainly Fulbright believed he was lucky to get as much as he did. Even the weary Cherrington saw hope. In Rome Smith's friend, scholar-CAO Rufus Morey, outside of the policy mainstream, rejoiced in finally having dollars to move his exchanges both ways. Those who wanted to get on with it at all costs were pleased: the bill certified congressional support for an ongoing effort abroad; it authorized programs, with practices to be worked out over the years. But closer readers saw that it also provided a mandate for muddled thinking and self-interested leadership, neither of which was in short supply in Washington; it said nothing about the caliber of field staffing. And solving things administratively was exactly what the informationists wanted—the reins of power were firmly in their hands.

The culturalists, worn down by the ever-present threat of losing the entire game and by the never-ending waves of OWI veterans, beat a silent retreat. They could only beg the informationist administrators to exercise wisdom, while quietly building their strength for the moment when another window of opportunity might open.

In Smith-Mundt's final form, information came first: the US Information and Educational Exchange Act of 27 January 1948, Public Law 402, dodged every deep issue, bowed to both sides, and codified what the government had been doing. The marriage of cultural and informational diplomacy had been institutionalized. Ahead lay five decades of triumph and failure, costly and unheeded studies, fruitless inquiries, and destructive reorganization.

And yet the bill missed no opportunity to stipulate that the two functions should be managed separately. It called for *both* unilateral informational activities and bilateral cultural relations programs. It protected a major safeguard of education by preserving the Fulbright legislation and its supervisory Board of Foreign Scholarships (BFS). It created, in fact, *two* new advisory commissions, one for information and one for education and culture, in addition to the BFS. Another irony would shortly come clear: PL 402 assumed that technical assistance, still lodged in State and ICC, would continue to be part of the educational exchange program; in fact, within a few months, technical assistance or "training" would be sliced away and turned over to another agency.

The Smith-Mundt jumble, prefaced by fiery pre–cold war language, created an *information* service which contained an educational exchange program. Practical circumstances, budgets, and time soon made cultural exchange a "medium" of the information function. Over the years both unidirectional propagandists and cultural internationalists would claim—correctly—that Smith-Mundt supported *their* claims. The BFS in 1948, while designing the Fulbright Program, assumed that field cultural officers for the most part were reputable academics. But Smith-Mundt counter-assumed that information and culture in the field would be directed by one officer, an OWI-style PAO. As information officers continued their steady takeover of the public affairs offices, committed CAOs who wanted to stay with work they knew and loved faced a choice: either quit cultural work, or take what they were given, be grateful for it, and cope with a context they could not change. For two decades and more, those who stayed with the fight were dedicated but critical, occasionally rebellious, and rarely happy.

Both Smith and Mundt, as legislators, underwent an education on cultural relations during the debate; both found reason to defend their new faith with the large constituency they knew was there. Mundt argued to his audience that it was foolish to economize on peace; both he and Smith reminded colleagues that business and commerce followed educational exchanges. Mundt told audiences that the U.S. was perceived abroad as an imperialist power and that only exchanges and human examples could set the record straight; both reminisced about their travels abroad and about investments in long-term human growth. In Congress the pot continued to simmer. A decade later Fulbright put the problem in a broader context: "The over-riding question before us is whether this nation is prepared to accept the permanent and inescapable responsibilities of having become a major power. . . . Our national purpose is a process to be advanced. . . . That process is the defense and expansion of our democratic values, the furtherance of which rests ultimately on the wisdom, the maturity of judgment, and the moral fiber of a society of free individuals." Smith-Mundt was a mere skirmish; the war had not ended.

The division trudged ahead with a vague concept, inadequate leadership, too few staff, and absurdly small budgets. It could not fend off predators when serious slicing-away began. In the larger picture great new opportunities lay before the U.S., the predictable products of intelligently deployed global power. The American Century was waiting to be articulated and defined, its corresponding responsibilities recognized and accepted, its work sanctified by American intellect. A man of MacLeish's caliber might have launched an ongoing discussion of how this could be managed over time, how the best minds in America could be attracted to Washington and the embassies, and how to forge a broad consensus on what the U.S. should be doing abroad. But nothing of the kind happened: normalcy had returned to the nation's capital and the postwar era was under way.

CHAPTER NINE

Products and People:
English, Books, and Two Visionaries

> Our situation today evokes comparison with that of Europe in the 7th
> and 8th centuries, after a period not unlike that which we have recently
> been through. . . . For all humanists, the responsibility is plain, the
> mission clear: to keep the light of humanistic learning burning through-
> out the world until these times can turn from materialistic delusions to
> enlightened common sense.
>
> —Charles Rufus Morey, 1946

FROM WASHINGTON MURK TO FIELD CLARITY, we turn again to products and
people: two more field products and two early and farsighted CAOs.

The most consistent USIS field program from 1917 until today has
been English-language teaching (ELT). Among the human arts, none
matters to diplomacy more than language. The teaching of language to
foreign speakers has occupied a place at the center of cultural diplomacy
through history. In the US case this practice extends back to Franklin's
advice to the future Citizen Genêt and to the missionary-educators. For
Americans ELT has always been a superb example of an activity carried
on for relatively disinterested long-range purposes, even when spinning
off shorter-range by-products. In contrast, the French saw their language
as a requirement for political expansion, then survival; they tried to ele-
vate French to a world movement. The British first found it useful to teach
English for utilitarian reasons of empire, then developed a taste for its
value as cultural communication. The Americans, on the other hand,
from the missionary-educators forward, taught English for communication and public utility. After 1945 English was for the developing world
a road to participation in modernity; public and private Americans did
their best to meet the huge market demand as a matter of convenience
and general internationalist educational vision. Like the missionary-
educators, laboring heroically in the vernacular, USIS posts in 1917–18
and over time taught English as a tool for learning, a means of dialogue,
a key for entry to the middle class, and a door to global access.

Americans early learned a useful fact: ELT could fund itself. Even when
CPI was slashed in 1919, various BNCs in Latin America managed to
survive by teaching English. Depending on satisfied, paying customers,

the US approach tended to be educationally clean, eschewing political "freight"—US teachers abroad, including those who worked for USIS, succeeded in warding off attempts to freight the teaching process with political messages.[1]

Doubtless some saw English as a door to Western and even *American* thought—a language is in fact a system of thought and it is difficult to project democracy or self-government when the host-language culture has no words for such ideas. Indoctrination however was not the point: the three dozen or more USIA English teachers I have known and worked with overseas during the last four decades kept politics out of their teaching, even when they recognized that one of the benefits of English was to open up study of the US experience. For the enthusiasts of the American Century, an English-speaking world was indispensable; US universalists, even the best, did not always see the ethnocentricity buried in the idea. Purist teachers of English may have carried messages unknown to themselves. But they tried to keep politics out of the classrooms.

ELT happened, not as a projection of US power but as a convenient way for the world to communicate, and only incidentally as a means of carrying on USIS and BNC work. In colonies like Greater India, the British had learned that a continent speaking over four hundred languages needed a lingua franca. After 1918 English was the only real candidate for a world language, with French a scarcely plausible alternative. As time moved forward, no one needed to persuade anyone that English helped individuals and nations modernize and forge global links.

During the Second World War and between the wars in Latin America, where BNCs survived, ELT earned its keep. By asking for tuition, kept as low as possible, ELT could cover costs while maintaining quality. When budgets were throttled back after World War II, centers expanded their teaching and plowed profits into continued existence. With costs covered, USIS posts and their Washington masters graduated from direct funding to managing schools and providing teaching materials; next came training for foreign English teachers, through in-country seminars and US study.

The linguist Albert Marckwardt went to Mexico City in 1942, where he generated linguistic theory and indispensable teaching materials from his experience; his first CAO-colleague was Rutgers Spanish-language teacher Charles Stevens. Marckwardt's team in Mexico produced nine volumes of teaching materials, which circulated all over Latin America, a process replicated for different language-areas around the world. Even within single countries, materials were shaped to different regions—in 1960s Nigeria, Jeffrey Binda produced textbooks for two dozen Nigerian dialects. Other USIS posts were doing similar pioneering, customizing texts to the local language-culture.

In the U.S., Marckwardt's insights fed an emerging scholarly discipline, the teaching of English as a second language (TESL) centered first at Georgetown University's School of Languages and Linguistics.[2] In the

1950s the Ford Foundation discovered the value of ELT in Indonesia and invested in theory and teaching methodology there and elsewhere, often in cooperation with the British Council. With little fanfare, USIA's direct-hire Americans and academic linguists compiled a remarkable record, carrying on the activities of the early missionary-educators, many of whom had fed into the American school of synchronic linguistics.

Teacher training for local school systems was provided everywhere by USIS and Fulbright, through summer seminars for teachers and in-service training. In Porto Alegre an early annual seminar trained sixty Brazilian public-school teachers and raised ELT quality in the schools of southern Brazil. With Washington help, USIS posts recruited "directors of courses," who ran ELT programs everywhere on ungenerous contracts. For in-service training, foreign ministries of education lent their teachers and maintained salaries, with USIS contributing space, materials, and instructors.

Language is a major—perhaps *the* major—component of culture. US teaching materials and textbooks went to extremes to maintain honest pedagogy, but they could not avoid cultural content.[3] USIS teachers, over time, proved a feisty lot, in fact resisting hard-edged USIA pushes for "freight" and avoiding indoctrination. Their example sent far more important messages than their textbooks. More than one teacher has told me he or she would have resigned had it been otherwise. In contrast, the French assumed that learning French meant learning France; even the understated British illustrated their textbooks with quaint country lanes and sunny English villages. European textbooks, in fact, too often failed to resist digs at industrialization, mass culture, crime, or other aspects of what was becoming known as "Americanization."

In BNCs it was easy to find space for an ELT school. In other cases, ELT was the base on which new BNCs were built: the post rented space, brought in a US teacher on a bare-bones contract, provided textbooks and a small library, then cut the center loose when it achieved financial viability. Occasionally, as Frankel's imaginary CAO discovered, the BNC's management raised problems. But the market for English was elastic; available classrooms and hours were easily filled and expansion was limited only by USIS administrative energies and available teachers, some recruited from locally resident Americans. Raw figures on student numbers were reported to Washington, to feed congressional curiosity.

A few vignettes may help convey the flavor of this activity. The first example is Gloria Kreisher, a third-generation Polish American from Phoenix, who arrived in Brazil in 1949 after teaching in primary schools in the US Southwest—where Spanish was part of the school curriculum.[4] In Porto Alegre as teacher, then as Director of Courses, she found that half her student body were university students supplementing the university's thin offerings, and half were working professionals—doctors, lawyers, engineers, etc., who saw the need for English in the postwar world.

She traveled to every major city in that southern state of Brazil, visiting teachers, schools, universities, and branch education offices. Moving to Mexico as Director of Courses, she succeeded the academic Harold B. Allen, on loan to replace Marckwardt; Kreisher was one of the first USIS-experienced officers to replace the borrowed university linguists. With branch posts all over Mexico and the fine Franklin Library as pasture for her flock, Kreisher's team in Mexico was teaching four to five thousand registered students at any given time. The Ministry of Education was delighted with her continuing help in supplementing student learning and improving teacher skills. After Mexico she went all over the world, including tours in Iron Curtain Poland and in Italy.

Asked in 1999 of what she was most proud, Kreisher pointed without hesitation to the integrity of the textbooks. Admitting that unplanned insights into US culture crept into all ELT by definition, she was proud to have declined during her career to use any teaching materials that contained indoctrination or propaganda. She was disappointed that British and French texts, with their sophisticated anti-American undercurrents in the style of the European cultural left, did not meet the same criteria. For her, freight was self-defeating.

A second vignette catches Susan Fitzgerald in 1960s Beirut, where she was the full-time USIS English-teaching officer.[5] A tall Bostonian out of Bryn Mawr with fluent Spanish and German, she went to the Peru BNC in 1949. After Peru came Turkey; five years in Turkey led to six in Beirut.

There she ran a small teaching center across the street from the American University, supplementing the AUB's offerings. In addition she supervised a network of fourteen smaller USIS-founded centers throughout tiny Lebanon. She taught English at the military academy and its outlying stations; she ran one-week residential seminars for teacher-training several times a year; she worked with individual teachers and interns; and she provided consultative services to USIS posts throughout the Near East. Alongside the outstanding AUB staff and their tailored teaching, she helped produce remarkable materials, written by the gifted US-British team of Richard Yorkey and Neil Bratton. At the Beirut center, she imposed minimal fees, token sums to engage student responsibility. USIS paid the rent for the center, but all other classes took place in borrowed space. Her teachers, like those everywhere, were recruited and trained locally.

Lebanon, still run by the French-trained Maronite elite, had a population of 1.5 million at the time. Fitzgerald was responsible for fifteen hundred students a year. With no national decision to make it so, she was helping Lebanon become a trilingual English-French-Arabic country and implicitly helping to resist the slide toward isolationist Arab nationalism.

Two other ELT case studies touch situations more than people; both lay bare the deeper politics of English. The first comes from Sri Lanka, a former British colony where the educated class that took over the country after the Second World War spoke English as a lingua franca. This kept the Tamil-speaking minority and Sinhala-speaking majority at relative peace. When Oxford graduate and nationalist Prime Minister S. W. R. D. Bandaranaike in 1958 threw out English as the "medium of communication," making Sinhalese the official language, he ignited a bonfire. Sinhala was the language of a 70-percent majority, but it was spoken by no other language group in the world. The industrious Tamils, only about 12 percent of the population, were employed at higher levels of the national administrative service and business sector, thanks to schools like the American missionary Jaffna College. After 1958 Tamils were slowly disenfranchised. Imported illiterate Tamil tea-plantation laborers from South India added volatility to the mass and Tamil nationalism began its trek to armed insurgency. By the 1970s, civil strife in the island was catastrophic.

For a short period in the 1980s, the Sri Lankan government reversed itself: universal English training was seen as a way to reduce the problem. The English-speaking countries and UNESCO were invited to organize a cooperative and multinational approach to reinstating English as the second language of the island-nation—and as the common language of administration and the professions. Seven different foreign elements took part: on the US side, USIA, AID, and the Peace Corps took on three-sevenths of a coordinated multinational, hence nonpolitical, effort, with the British, the Canadians, the Australians, and UNESCO each taking a share. The well-designed project was making steady progress when it was ended by a change of governments; the island fell back into turmoil.

A second case study hints at the tenacity of ELT, once launched.[6] In Tehran in 1966 USIS Iran had an enormous ELT operation, begun in the 1920s at the Iran America Society (IAS), founded by mythic American educators like Arthur Upham Pope and Samuel Jordan. In the 1960s two American contract teachers were in residence, sent by Washington; they taught, trained teachers, supervised classes, and managed the school in space provided by the IAS. USIS reported annually that 100,000 Iranians were studying in Tehran and in IAS branches in five provincial cities.

The Iranian case was impressive. Extensive teaching in the schools was provided by dozens of Peace Corps volunteers; the Iranian military was taught by US-trained instructors, products of IAS. American missionary schools were still operating in the 1960s, teaching in English. Pahlavi University in Shiraz, built by AID, set out to teach all classes in English. The salaried USIS ELT officers, led by professionals like Robert Murphy, Edward Bernier, and Dennis Shaw, supervised and trained local American residents. With Iranian teacher-administrator Ali Zangi in charge, IAS adapted USIA materials to its uses and produced its own with the help of another local legend, Gertrude Nye Dorry, a USIA English teacher who had married an Iranian and stayed on to train the Iranian military and Peace Corps teachers; Dorry was helped by long-term resident Terence O'Donnell, an under-recognized American writer. Her IAS teaching materials were self-operative: with minimal training and light supervision, most educated Americans could handle a class as native informants.

Profits kept the IAS solvent. IAS filled all its available classrooms and constantly sought more space, with tuition rates held a shade below British fees; a quiet system of scholarships helped those who could not meet the fees. The Fulbright commission routinely sent near-miss Iranian candidates to IAS on scholarships to improve their chances for the following year. Embassy families pitched in as teachers and staffed English conversation groups at the IAS youth center near Tehran University. Some teachers offered special classes, taking ELT into Iranian government offices like the Plan Organization; others undertook one-on-one teaching with prominent personalities. The French-speaking Dean of the university's Law Faculty, aware that Iranian law's Swiss-French-Islamic base distanced it from the Anglo-Saxon common-law system that ruled commerce, shipping, and constitutional thought, asked the CAO to set up classes for a small group of younger faculty to facilitate application for Fulbright grants; new arrival Lois Roth took on the job. The Dean himself, a proud Francophone, attended regularly.

In a highly class-structured society, the IAS classrooms were a cross section of urban Iran; secondary and university students, housewives, taxi drivers, servants, shopkeepers, professionals, students headed to the U.S., and anyone else who wanted to learn all sat side by side and engaged in laborious conversations about the weather, the time, and travel itineraries. It was a remarkable bit of democracy in action, unique in that authoritarian state with its traditional class divisions.

US competition with the British finally struck Washington and London as wasteful. Until 1961 USIS and the British had competed worldwide. The problem of working together was tackled at the top by Assistant Secretary Philip Coombs. State's cultural office (CU) and the British Council began annual talks, the first of which in Cambridge was attended by a representative from the Ford Foundation and a wary observer from the Quai d'Orsay, keeping tabs on the wily Anglo-Saxons.

British-US cooperation had three goals. The first was political: since ELT associated with a single nation was linked with propaganda, the British and the Americans, and later the Canadians, the Australians, and the UN, pledged to work together. Second, both nations agreed to modify the heavily academic approach of the British, which contrasted with the more practical American stress on daily usage and life situations. The British slowly moved away from teaching the English of Shakespeare to emphasize usage—conversation first, then reading, and finally writing. Third, both sides agreed to minimize the perception of competition and the idea that the two nations spoke different languages. London and Washington helped Marckwardt and Randolph Quirk of the University of London circulate their engaging pamphlet *A Common Language*, which reduced the snob appeal of Oxbridge English speakers—although weaker students continued to blame American pronunciation for their failures. In 1967 USIS Tehran and the British formed an ELT coordinating committee, meeting four times a year to discuss problems, progress and joint programs. With an occasional helpful visitor from the U.S. or London, this well-coordinated effort reduced frictions and maximized help to Iran's progress.

After the hostage crisis and the Ayatollah's revolution in 1978, the Iranian program proved remarkably durable. IAS was taken over by the new regime; an Iranian Language Institute was established on its base and in its buildings. Today the institute is said to teach English and other languages to 300,000 Iranians in seventeen centers around the country, more than tripling the peak output of the IAS years. There are no ways to evaluate quality, textbooks or "freight." One suspects, as other Muslim countries have done, that they are exploring ways of teaching "Islamic English."[7]

In Washington the old division, now called CU, kept government agencies together on the subject of English teaching until 1977. The skillful Jane Alden, a CU veteran, was advised by Marckwardt; she moved from the British-American talks to coordination of the entire federal government and guided, almost invisibly, the work of USIA, AID, the Peace Corps, and the Department of Defense, all of which had extensive ELT programs abroad. At a given moment, she estimated that well over 300,000 people were learning English under some kind of US government auspices, in well over fifty countries. With her intelligent and unthreatening style, Alden kept ELT flowing, a rare example of US intra-government, public-private, and multinational micro-coordination. Few outside the specialist ELT world knew of Alden or the work she was doing.

Overall the US effort in ELT, from the start, followed paths opened up by the missionary-educators; it was quiet, practical, inexpensive, extensive, and largely self-funding, a superb example of a cooperative multisectoral national approach to an educational problem. CU and USIA, for once, worked well together, with USIS posts playing the coordinating role. Purposes were never in doubt: the US was not trying to Americanize but to help nations link with others, modernize, and gain access to the world's knowledge. The partisans of "freight" were never a serious threat; they knew that English, well taught, was its own message.

As USIA reoriented itself to closer support of foreign policy in the late 1970s, direct ELT took lower priority and began to fade. Some of the fine ELT specialists went into foreign service, first as CAOs, then as PAOs; others served as Regional English Language Officers (RELOs), watching over a dozen or more countries and working with ministries to improve ELT. Peace Corps too was moving out of English teaching—except in newly liberated Eastern Europe—just as USIA's interest was dropping off. Doubtless the world's primary and secondary ELT had improved, but no one could argue that the need had disappeared. Before its absorption into State in 1999, USIA had jettisoned most of its direct support to ELT: thirteen RELOs tried to cover two hundred countries. USIA had jettisoned one of its most impressive achievements.

From 1917 until about 1990 direct ELT was a central part of American cultural projection. Today Congress seems to believe it can no longer afford such "luxuries," despite the astonishingly low costs. Some argue that TV and the Internet make ELT redundant. Until the 1980s USIA and State believed that an intelligent approach to helping the world learn English reached well beyond narrow diplomatic purposes: it was a factor of national growth abroad, of sophistication in international relations, and of deep cultural communication. Each US teacher, learning in the process deep lessons about other cultures, projected a little of the national style. When decline set in, each closure lowered the water level in the reservoirs of goodwill.

•   •   •

Books were another focus of USIS programs as early as 1917. It was natural for CPI to ship and distribute large numbers of US books, provided free or at low cost, with tax deductibility to cooperating US publishers; CPI also assisted and published translations of American works. Allied to English teaching, they provided the pasture in which ELT students grazed. Welles and Duggan heard pleas for books from Latin America; Rockefeller deemed books essential; for USIA director George Allen in the late 1950s, books carried the most credible truths of all.

State in 1938 had no funding for books, but Rockefeller revived CPI practice in 1942 and went miles farther. He pressured US publishers to make large quantities of books available for distribution and library building, initiating a steady flow to the South. He reopened the USIS reading rooms and built three major US libraries. He fostered translations and helped field officers midwife others—for example, Canter helped with an anthology of US women poets. Rockefeller further changed national reading habits in the southern hemisphere with his support to the expansion of the *Reader's Digest* and the *LIFE*-clone periodical *En Guardia*.

After World War II USIS posts did not question the assumption that books were a central part of the agenda. In Europe postwar readers had a lot of catching up to do, and the Americans, like the French and the British, tried to assist in some cases at a lower level. In Rome, while the French were distributing the books Italy had missed under Fascism, the Americans under future *Time-LIFE* director James Linen were printing a monthly news bulletin and pamphlets on US farming or schools. Translations initiated by Italian publishers were done at questionable levels of quality, except when USIS provided help. In Paris a series of translations from American literature and criticism was launched, with USIS subsidy, in a collection called *Vents d'Ouest*, West Winds. By the time of its demise two decades later, the series had produced fifty volumes in a handsome and memorable format. John L. Brown, in Paris in the 1940s as press officer for the Marshall Plan, wrote his famous *Panorama de la littérature américaine*, a critical anthology which became a French best seller and remained in print for decades. In Rome a quartet of young Italian intel-

"contract" in the Middle East is itself a translation problem. Whatever the word meant in Arabic or Persian, it did not have the same connotation for an American. It turned out that some publishers had no intention of carrying out their work, and wise book officers learned to insist on seeing a full edition, stacked in one place, which they examined below the top layers and down into the center—where they sometimes found bound volumes of blank paper. Another Middle Eastern publisher negotiated a generous price for printing, generous enough that, instead distributing the books to bookstores for sale, he could afford to pulp them and still show a profit.

Like ELT teaching materials, books were among the "objects" assigned by Smith-Mundt to USIA's care. The book program was carried out, against all odds, for half a century, placing millions of American books in foreign hands. That it has fallen off in the last decades, and that it has tended to be restricted to books seen as bearing political messages, will come as no surprise in the context of our story as it unfolds.

• • •

For people, we are privileged to be able to look back at the most imaginative of the early cultural officers, two men from the period 1942–50 who left unusually rich records: Harvard's John K. Fairbank in China between 1942 and 1947 and Princeton's Charles Rufus Morey in Rome, 1945–50. Both returned to their universities, but unlike others, they left behind extensive thoughts about cultural diplomacy. Together, they provide insights into what might have been.

Fairbank was a historian of Western interaction with China, having studied the nineteenth-century British-run Customs Service for China; both he and his wife Wilma wrote perceptively about their dozen years in cultural diplomacy.[11] In his learning years in Peking a decade before the war, Fairbank had lived in a high-powered community of American missionary-educators and philanthropists; with them, he watched the two cultures interact. With the coming of war, he spent a year with OSS and Langer, fifteen months as CAO in Chungking, twenty months in Washington, then nine more months in Chungking as PAO with OWI, returning to Harvard only in July 1946. Wilma first worked on China for ACLS, served on the division's China desk, then was CAO in Chungking and Nanking from 1945 until April 1947. Collating his "fifty-year memoir" and her meshing history of the early China program, we can watch as they literally invented formal US cultural diplomacy in China.

Fairbank had moved from Sioux City High to Exeter to Harvard to Oxford. Courtesy of Cecil Rhodes, he reached Oxford the year Fulbright left. He was an economic historian, studying China's treaty ports and customs offices, focusing on the work of British administrator Robert Hart and his multinational team. In 1932 his Rhodes grant permitted residence in Peking. There he married Wilma Cannon.

An extraordinary group of American educators and scholars greeted them in Peking, some of them only fifteen years away from trashing at the hands of McCarthy and friends. W. B. Pettus directed the College of Chinese Studies; Guy Thelin taught agronomy; Andrew Tod Roy ran the Nanking YMCA; missionary John D. Hayes was an educator; future ambassador J. Leighton Stuart presided over Yenching University; art historian Lawrence Sickman collected treasures for Kansas City's Nelson Gallery; Robert Gailey, resident since 1908, was a YMCA retiree; anthropologist-journalist and later MIT professor Harold Isaacs was studying, as were scholar Owen Lattimore and his wife Helen Holgate, daughter of a former president of Northwestern University; missionary-educator and publisher John C. Ferguson helped oversee the Palace Museum; Carl Whiting Bishop of Washington's Freer Gallery was buying Chinese art; and Roger Greene and staff ran the Peking Union Medical College (PUMC), the Rockefeller-supported center dedicated to training a generation of Chinese physicians and introducing Western medicine to China.

PUMC was especially pleased to welcome Wilma, daughter of noted physiologist W. B. Cannon, and the couple's intellectual life was launched. It centered on the Yale- and Harvard-linked Yenching University, later absorbed into Peking University, and the parallel Tsing Hua University, set up in 1908 to prepare students for US study under the Boxer program. Fairbank's early Chinese associates, primarily scholars and heads of research centers, already knew English. Many were returned Boxer alumni—there would be two thousand in the program before it was throttled off in 1949. Hu Shih, whom Fairbank called China's "modern Voltaire," reflected the impact of John Dewey, who visited China during the Sun Yat Sen period (1919–21); he remembered Dewey's visit as "the high point of American liberalism in China."

In 1932 Chinese liberals of the center were being savaged from right and left. As a student of Tocqueville, Fairbank would in due time become a sensitive political analyst, but for the moment he was busy prowling the Customs Archives. Around him swirled a life-and-death struggle between the two Leninist parties which had split the Sun Yat Sen revolution: the Kuomintang (KMT) and the Communists (CCP). In Tientsin, the Deputy Commissioner of Customs, American Everitt Groff-Smith— whose son would become a US cultural diplomat—opened the archives to Fairbank. The half-Chinese Ida Pruitt, teaching social work at PUMC, was a mine of information and language.

When Rhodes support ran out, the Fairbanks patched together enough earning power to stay on. Wilma sold her paintings, high-quality relief rubbings, and carpet designs; John got partial funding from Harvard and from ACLS's Mortimer Graves to help support Chinese studies in the U.S. In 1935–36 he finished his Oxford Ph.D., published his thesis, and began his Harvard career.

Three months before Pearl Harbor, he joined Langer in Washington. He lived a surprisingly free life, since neither he nor Langer saw the need for espionage or covert sources; everything necessary could in fact be learned by reading Chinese and Japanese sources. For example, an elaborate British report about Japanese plans to construct a tunnel from Japan to Korea came through the US Navy's intelligence; Fairbank brushed the report aside, quietly noting that the distance to be covered was 122 miles. At the Library of Congress, he worked alongside MacLeish's Far East director Arthur Hummel Sr. to help build the Library's collection. He helped White House advisor Lauchlin Currie. Stanley Hornbeck, older by two decades, was a Rhodes and Harvard colleague in Chinese studies who handled the China desk at State; he ignored Fairbank. Fairbank paid as little attention to him, but he tried to work through Hornbeck's deputy Alger Hiss, intelligent and sympathetic, although fiercely loyal to Hornbeck. Fairbank's impressive friend John Paton Davies was also in State; at the Pentagon, among others, was Dean Rusk, a young Army captain working in Far Eastern affairs.

Government was recruiting China hands, e.g., in-and-outer Doak Barnett, born to a YMCA family in Shanghai in 1921. Barnett, after Marine Corps duty, completed an M.A. at Yale, wrote for the *China Daily News*, headed USIS Hong Kong, spent three years with the American Universities Field Staff consortium, directed foreign area studies for State's Foreign Service Institute, and finally took up academic careers at Columbia and Johns Hopkins. With Graves at ACLS, Wilma worked on cataloguing Chinese experts in the cultural division under senior China hand Willys Peck, fresh off the repatriation ship *Gripsholm*. Peck persuaded Roger Greene to serve as consultant, commuting from Massachusetts. Greene had retired as the Rockefeller Foundation's Far East representative and as board member of the Boxer-funded China Foundation. Ruth Guy, PUMC pediatrician, handled Chinese exchanges for the division. By early 1942 the well-staffed China cultural desk was given its first job: sorting out and funding seventeen hundred Chinese students stranded in the U.S.

Shipping to Chungking was nearly impossible, but space-available transport on military flights could move priority items. Although the British managed to send books, the Division decided to miniaturize, sending scholarly materials on microfilm to Chinese universities; only after war's end could books begin to flow. Chinese educators and artists visited the U.S. Welles's ICC sent out various US government experts, notably China-experienced irrigation-engineer Walter Lowdermilk of the Department of Agriculture, who left plans for twenty-two pilot irrigation projects behind him—all later implemented by Mao's government. Hornbeck recommended, against the advice of his entire staff, that the division fund the KMT social club in Chungking. Fairbank's protest made no difference.

OSS's China staff produced report after report, which were left unread—as Fairbank noticed during his visits to Currie's office in the White House. In 1942 the Japanese took Singapore and moved on Burma; Stilwell's mission to China was still in preparation. Beyond Japan's reach in

China, the KMT and the CCP were dueling for supremacy. Fairbank was disappointed that Washington had invested overwhelmingly in the KMT. OSS decided to send two officers to collect printed materials in Chungking; when they failed, Fairbank volunteered.

Reaching China was a saga. The planes could only fly short hops; space-available travel meant waiting for days in outlandish places. Pan-American's no-longer-secret airstrips in Latin America and Africa were nearing completion. Fairbank's five-week itinerary tells the story: Washington-Miami-Trinidad-Belèm-Recife-Ascension Island-Accra-Lagos-Kano-Maiduguri-Khartoum-Cairo-Basra-Karachi-New Delhi-Allahabad-Assam, and over the Hump to Kunming on the Yunnan plateau, where he found US-educated Tsing Hua University friends starving in exile. From Kunming he began sending letters destined for Currie but routed by necessity through Hornbeck. Knowing Hornbeck would not pass them on, he tried using Hiss as a bypass, but Hiss loyally shared them with Hornbeck and Fairbank's reports stopped there; he turned to Wilma for discreet help.

In his first letter he argued that the major issues were predominantly cultural, not political or economic. The war was a combat between old and new, "a cultural struggle, in which values are being created and the future created accordingly." US-educated Chinese, "who think and speak and teach as we would, constitute a tangible American interest in China." Washington was not prepared for this viewpoint; there, cultural questions were "an unimportant sideshow. On the contrary, I am coming to the conclusion that the main issue here is cultural." Arms given to the Chinese have not always been used against the Japanese; the right ideas matter as much as the weapons. "American ideals . . . cannot be defeated here and the war really won at the same time; . . . an idea-program for China has been delayed and frustrated by lack of imagination in the proper places in Washington."[12]

No American before him had spoken of the cultural dimension of diplomacy in such political terms. The logic was disturbing, not only to Hornbeck but to the cultural division. Hornbeck tolerated cultural programs and exchanges only when they served political purposes, but Cherrington's early division staffers were reluctant to admit politics into their work. If the problems in China were in fact cultural, then the division had to confront them as a central part of long-range foreign policy, precisely as argued by Ralph Turner. Duggan and Cherrington at their most incisive, dealing primarily with industrializing countries of European origin and culture, were baffled by China. A cultural attack on deep political cultural issues was an idea Turner understood.

Fairbank's life in Chungking was tense: "The rocky peninsula between the Yangtze and Chialing rivers had only a few new streets strung along the hillsides on which modern traffic can go. Everything seemed to be under a quarter inch of mud." When the ever-present clouds and rain broke, the Japanese bombed. The embassy's outstanding but exhausted staff welcomed the newcomer to the pandemonium. Fairbank, without directions or boss, had been sent by OSS to collect print materials. Sizing up the situation, he voluntarily assigned himself two additional jobs: act as agent for the Library of Congress and serve as the cultural division's man in China. Fairbank, as cultural attaché, was self-appointed.

As CAO he knew about gifts but understood he had little more to give than himself. His borrowed office in USIS, headed by China journalist friend Mac Fisher, whose job was to produce leaflets to drop on the Japanese and to handle the daily US news output for Free China, had excellent communications; but Fairbank insisted on reporting directly to Ambassador Clarence Gauss. Beyond himself, Fairbank gave Chinese scholars extensive American university publications on microfilm—his small jerry-rigged prototype microfilm reader became a model for local replication. This allowed him to fly the banner of reciprocity, "reviving the flow of printed matter in both directions between China and the U.S." Gauss and his deputy John Carter Vincent were delighted to find an informed and helpful colleague—dashing and colorful heros like Claire Chennault and Stilwell had a reputation for ignoring the embassy.

Document collection simplified when a Tsing Hua friend was named national librarian, but Fairbank soon faced technical print problems: fluctuating current, poor paper, humidity, and inferior ink. By the end of 1943, microfilms were flowing between Washington and Chungking; OSS was receiving a regular twenty-two-page subject index to its Chinese publications; and Washington was receiving seventy-five periodicals monthly, plus occasional reports from Fairbank.

His employer was still OSS, struggling in the Far East to centralize intelligence despite military foot-dragging—US military commanders had long relied on the Navy, and MacArthur wanted nothing to do with OSS. A larger-than-life figure with the improbable nickname of "Mary" Miles, actually Milton Miles, Commander USN, presented Fairbank with a letter from Colonel Donovan assigning Fairbank to Miles's staff. Fairbank quietly explained his three-cornered job, asked Miles and his people to stay out of his way, and offered to resign if Miles preferred. In retreat, Miles asked a single favor of Fairbank: that he not deal with Gen. Wang P'eng-sheng. Wang was the major rival of Miles's principal contact Tai Li, head of secret service for Chiang Kai Shek, the most feared man in China. Wang was also one of Fairbank's major sources. Accepting Miles's request, he opened a new file under the name Gen. P. S. Wang, commenting: "Miles was fighting to defeat Japan by all means. My small office in Chungking was on a different track. Like many civilian China hands, I was concerned about China's future and the American role in it."

In touch with the best of China's US-educated modernizers, Fairbank traveled everywhere. He visited missionaries and schools and lectured to US troops. Foreseeing civil war after the Japanese defeat, he found high disaffection with the KMT among Chinese intellectuals; he doubted the KMT could crush the communists and argued for staying in touch with both sides. He wrote regularly to Hiss-Hornbeck, with no expectations.

In December 1942 he wrote: "China is a battleground where we should seek to make our values prevail, insofar as they are suitable to Chinese life. But the Cultural Relations program so far has dealt with means instead of ends. . . . We cannot leave the American way of life to sell itself; the result will be the propagation of Main Street all over the world. . . . We must seek contact at a level above that of Life Magazine." Unlike the KMT social club, the Sino-Russian Cultural Institute "has art exhibits which attract hundreds of people. It has a public tea-house and makes a conscious effort to present the best that Russia has to offer in the arts and in ideas and literature."

In Washington Wilma circulated his letters and built up silent support, but matters in China had gone too far to change. Deeply critical of the communists but unable to visit them in faraway Yenan, Fairbank watched hopeful young Chinese intellectuals turn from the KMT to the CCP; he was more convinced than ever that the KMT was losing ground.

In December 1943 he left Chungking to fly home—this time only a three-week trip—with Colonel Donovan himself. Switching from OSS to OWI, he spent 1944 in Washington under Elmer Davis, a Rhodes colleague, and a polished trio of New Yorkers: Ed Barrett of *Newseek*, T. L. Barnard of the J. Walter Thompson advertising agency, and James Linen of *LIFE*. By early 1945 the war's impetus had passed to the Allies. In May Wilma left MacLeish's staff for the journey to Chungking, where she was to formalize the embassy cultural section that her husband had built, i.e., as part of USIS. Fairbank returned in October to serve as PAO. Now his well-funded USIS sheltered its poor cousin cultural office, as OWI had sheltered him before; but he was the same Fairbank, and now he was in charge.

His postwar ambassador was Pat Hurley. Hurley, against the advice of State and embassy advisors, decided to eliminate any doubt and throw total US support to the KMT. Even the most ingenious cultural or informational diplomacy cannot make up for bad policy, and Fairbank spent his last year "building up an American information program in a gradually worsening situation."

The 1946 mediation visit of Gen. George Marshall—who in exasperation pronounced "a plague on both their houses"—was a moment of truce. The Fairbank team seized the occasion to urge making contact with the younger generation of communists and got full embassy approval. As Fairbank recorded it, to "carry out General Marshall's policy of evenhandedness in China's civil conflict, [Wilma] secured his agreement to invite the CCP's North China Associated University at Kalgan . . . to send four academics for a year in the U.S." The couple journeyed to Kalgan to set up the exchange, but "in the end the four CCP nominees were refused Nationalist passports, and a few years later, when the McCarthy era got under way, we all quietly forgot the episode."

In 1946 USIS China was slashed back, like posts throughout the world. The Fairbank couple had "hoped that USIS could somehow help to stem the disintegration but we really had no chance."[13] Fairbank left China in July 1946 and would not return for twenty-six years. Wilma stayed on for another nine months to integrate the division's programs with OWI's successor and to launch the Fulbright Program. Confused in the Chinese mind with the Boxer Foundation and hampered on the US side by fear of the decaying situation, the Fulbright idea moved slowly. Fifteen months later it became the world's first Fulbright agreement, signed in Nanjing on 10 November 1947 by Ambassador J. Leighton Stuart. The attending cultural attaché was not Wilma, who had left in April, but her successor, anthropologist George Harris with his wife Elaine. Beginning with a flourish, the Fulbright Program closed abruptly under Mao in 1949. The U.S. disappeared from the Chinese mainland for more than three decades, and a century or more of extensive and positive American private and public presence was shelved.

Scholar-diplomats like Rufus Morey and Howard Lee Nostrand reported the same sentiments from other posts. Ninkovich notes, "as the war drew to a close, the OWI began to think in terms of long-range activities."[14] Fairbank, seized with the problem, left an important afterword on the diplomacy of cultures. Published four decades later, it suggested how an experienced cultural diplomat might have designed a realistic approach to a country outside the European orbit, through enlightened "information," as defined by MacLeish. The point was simple: provide relevant information in sufficient depth to meet local needs. Boiled down from a series of staff circulars written in 1946, Fairbank's final definition of the USIS role in China read like this (italics are his):

1. *Information, not propaganda.*
2. *Action as well as understanding.* We want to present evidences of American experience in facing and overcoming modern problems in such a way as to stimulate the Chinese people to face and overcome their own problems.
3. *Modernization, not Americanization.* What we have found good for us will not necessarily be good for China. The Chinese problem may be formulated as one of combining science and democracy and applying them to the life of the masses in the context of the Chinese cultural tradition.
4. *Realism, not salesmanship.* Present a thorough, complete and truthful picture of the American scene without attempting to play down . . . the difficulties, problems or failures.

Fairbank saw no contradiction in stepping from culture to information—information was part of education for him, not a euphemism for propaganda but a synonym for knowledge. It meant using every means to circulate all kinds of knowledge. Shaping or spinning the truth was not only useless, it was criminal—it was already hard enough to know what truth was. Fairbank returned to Harvard after China and ended his sturdy career there, living into his nineties. To my knowledge, he was never consulted about cultural affairs by the government he had served so well.

• • •

From culturally remote China, we turn to Italy, prime source of Western civilization but more distant from the U.S. than it first seems. After the war, the most visible American cultural element in any country, other than the cinema, was the USIS cultural office itself. Libraries, cultural centers, book programs, and pre-Fulbright exchange programs were all cumulative long-range projects, which took time to show their effects, but they allowed people to be on the ground in daily contact with their audiences. CAOs manned the vital "point of contact." Of these, none shone more brightly than Charles Rufus Morey in Rome.

The following portrait sketches a major scholar's five years as cultural attaché in Rome in 1945–50.[15] Morey (1877–1955), the second chairman of Princeton's Department of Art and Archeology, was the first of five academic outsiders in sequence to serve as CAO in Rome; all five were distinguished university figures, mainly from classical studies. Morey created a CAO tradition in Italy, but it survived him by only eight years.

Princeton's connections to the division were close. Morey was a close friend of Harold Dodds, Princeton's president and member of the division's first Smith-Mundt advisory commission; Morey was also an ex-colleague of Senator Smith. He knew MacLeish, who was in charge of the division when Morey was recruited; early in World War II, MacLeish had organized art historians and museum directors, including Morey, to alert FDR of the need to guide the US military in saving Europe's art treasures from further war damage and returning art looted by the Nazis.

For Rome, Morey needed no briefing. His office was in a showcase architectural setting that he knew well: the vast Palazzo Margherita, built for the first Savoy queen after Italy's unification as a flamboyant symbol of the Piedmontese monarchy. Today the building has acquired a different meaning, symbolizing the postwar American pro-consul. Italy was not an enemy but was defined as a "cobelligerent," not precisely occupied by the Allies yet tutored by them.

Mr. Morey, as his students call him to this day, graced the American university era in which no one held a Ph.D. because few US universities granted the degree—in contrast, every Italian university graduate was called *dottore*. Morey arrived a month before V-E Day, at the age of sixty-eight. He had just retired from an illustrious thirty-nine-year Princeton career as a shaping national figure in the creation of art history and museum administration as academic disciplines.

Rome had been liberated at the end of August 1944, and Italy was slowly rebuilding its physical and human structures. Morey was no stranger to the troubled Italian parliamentary monarchy, only seventy-five years into its experiment with "democracy, Italian-style."[16] Early ministers from the peak of the American educated class had graced chancery and embassy first in Florence, then in Rome. In 1945 the capital city had been tainted by two decades of Fascist rule.

In the euphoria of liberation, educated Italians' attitudes toward the U.S. were as ambivalent as CPI had found them in 1917. The first US official to call on the Minister of Education under the new Badoglio government in Bari was T. V. Smith, a distinguished American educator; he began the meeting with a rhetorical flourish on the Roman and Italian tradition, expanding on the US intention to help restore and rebuild that greatness. Startled, the Minister asked the interpreter to repeat his translation and, satisfied that the American had been translated correctly, asked his interpreter, with a jerk of the head: "Chi, *loro*?" (Who, *them*?).

The positive and well-intentioned side of the US presence showed at many levels: the masses remembered the distribution of cigarettes, food, and smiles; a smaller audience knew of the erudite and heroic American-led effort to return Italy's stolen art treasures and reopen its libraries. Reminding Italians of the US commitment were fifty thousand well-tended American graves in military cemeteries scattered about the peninsula.

The negative slant, on the Italian side, was part historic and cultural and part political, both right and left. From the right, Badoglio's haughty Minister symbolized the European elitist education, Italy's classical Roman lineage, its role as the bastion of Catholicism, and the cultural elements of its embarrassing collaboration with Mussolini. Traditionalists saw Americans as brash, irresponsible, immature, undereducated gumchewers and deplored the casual destruction, as they saw it, of treasures like Monte Cassino. Further right were those who still believed in Mussolini, coaxed by Hitler into hatred for decadent British and American "liberalism." On the left a strong Communist Party was in the lead, basing its reputation on its role in the anti-Fascist resistance and bearing the usual litany of Marxist-Leninist slogans. More moderate parties on the left tried to keep the balance: Garibaldian "republicans," "socialists," "liberals," "social democrats," and moderate "Christian democrats" of all stripes. None of these parties coincided in ideological terms with American political thought, even when they recognized progressive elements in the blurred synthesis of New Deal "liberalism."

The U.S. went at its work warily; Italy, after all, had allied itself with Hitler. Support for Mussolini in the Italian-American community and in US banking circles in the early days had been firm. America's rigid postwar anticommunism meant loose alliances with right-wing forces and a corresponding failure to sort out the rainbow of left thought, ranging from anticommunist socialists to the Anglophile Millean liberals and Garibaldian republicans who had helped defeat Fascism as much as the communists. Meanwhile, establishment America still shared Woodrow Wilson's ambivalent view of southern Europe.

Italy had been cut off from much of Europe and was starved for cultural news. Writers like Cesare Pavese discovered American writing in the twenties and thirties through clandestine channels; he and others translated it as a concealed contribution to the defeat of Fascism. Younger figures like Umberto Eco were soon reading every book in the new USIS libraries. American military propaganda operations and USIS Rome, under future *Time-LIFE* chief James Linen, missed this vital point, approaching the educated classes briskly and efficiently through the methods of the media. In March 1945 USIS Rome launched the biweekly magazine *Nuovo Mondo* (New World) under two editors soon to become famous for their own work: novelist Giorgio Bassani and editor Arrigo Benedetti. A content analysis of its eight-month run showed that the only articles that could remotely be called "cultural" were those focused on the "blessings of democracy." During this same period the London-based *Il Mese* (The Month) published lengthy reviews of plays by Sartre, Camus, and Anouilh. The French had only to stock bookstores and libraries with the works which educated Italians—for whom French was still the second language—had missed.

Morey, born three decades before Fairbank, came from a hardworking but modest family in small-town Michigan. His M.A. in classical studies at the University of Michigan (1900) came from a classic Land-Grant institution; he never bothered to obtain a doctorate. A three-year fellowship took him to Rome for residence at the American School of Classical Studies, not yet incorporated into the American Academy. There he polished his mastery of the Latin classical literature, which would support his scholarship and lead to his appointment as a curator at the Vatican Museum. At Princeton he built his new department to national prominence, commuting to New York to help latecomers Columbia and NYU develop their own departments.

In Rome as CAO, Morey and his wife, making the transition from war to peace, lived modestly at the American Academy, where he was appointed Acting Director for a period during his service as CAO—a unique moment in US cultural diplomatic history. Martha Lou Stohlman, an embassy staffer who in 1946 married Morey's student and colleague Frederick Stohlman in Rome, was one of several embassy secretaries who lived at the Academy as well. She remembered that "ten or twelve of us ate together every evening. . . . To one ignorant of his achievements, [Morey] was not awesome as a person. He was quiet, friendly, modest, responsive, often amused and amusing, and as willing to listen to clerks as to ambassadors."

In his modest style Morey brought outsized attributes to USIS Rome: a fine command of Italian, scholarship and extensive publications, administrative vision and skill, collegial relationships with prominent people all over Italy and Europe, and a generous and engaging personality.

His gift to scholarship was the colossal Index of Early Christian Art, a cooperative project with hundreds of collaborators begun in 1917 and continuing into our era, covering in photographic and iconographic detail every piece of Christian art up to the fifteenth century. Another scholarly gift was more diplomatic in nature: for an important archeological excavation in Syrian Antioch and its suburb Daphne, Morey in the 1920s persuaded the French government to work with three American universities. His reach in the U.S. was equally long, especially in the world of museum professionals. Alfred Barr, founder and first director of New York's MoMA, was devoted to his teacher; the great Columbia art historian Meyer Schapiro said he learned research methodology with Morey, who helped found the Columbia Art Department. At Princeton, his vision of a laboratory-library, derived from Pope Nicholas V's Vatican Library, provided the idea around which Princeton's Firestone Library was built in 1947–48. He helped found the Institute for Advanced Study in Princeton and the Institute of Fine Arts in New York, both providing shelter for some of IIE's refugee scholars.

In the embassy he was a mere attaché—but he gave such titles no importance. Leaving Princeton at the peak of his scholarly reputation, he had donned a new hat. Rensselaer Lee, his successor as Princeton chair, described his activities in a eulogy published after Morey's death: "He stuck to a few main activities. . . . He worked hard to establish and maintain American libraries in Italy as a sound means of increasing knowledge of Americans among Italians. He was instrumental in helping Italian universities to replenish their staffs after the overthrow of Fascism. He was tremendously interested in the cultural exchange of persons, and it was largely through his efforts that the Fulbright Act became valid in Italy. . . . In working for the cause of international understanding, he was also rendering notable service to scholarship. . . . He became the first president of the newly created Union of Archeological and Historical Institutes which was created to receive and take charge of the contents of the German libraries when they should be returned to Italy."

His office was in the graceful Villino, a level above the Savoy Queen Margherita's palace, where she had exercised her own cultural diplomacy, receiving the visits of the Bologna poet and fierce liberal antimonarchist Giosuè Carducci, ultimately reconciling him to Piedmontese rule. The Moreys' apartment in the imposing compound of the Villa Aurelia, the Academy's architectural jewel high on the Janiculum overlooking Rome, was modest. Morey was no better funded for entertaining than other CAOs, wrote his staff assistant Isabella Panzini, who like most Italians called him *professore*: "He did not give special dinners or parties frequently. He preferred to receive high-level people at his home." At the office this septuagenarian routinely worked ten- or twelve-hour days, receiving streams of visitors and letters. Panzini: "The Cultural Office was literally besieged by all kinds of people and requests, from those wanting to visit the U.S. to those who wanted US help. . . . So many hopes, ambitions, proposals, some of them highly valid, others a bit daft. . . . Professor Morey instructed me, in the spirit of great humanity, to receive everyone with equal courtesy, with no ranking as to lesser or greater importance. . . . No letter went without a personal answer." Cipriana Scelba, Morey's choice to manage the new Fulbright Commission and later its first Italian director, cherished those ebullient years spent with her adoptive grandfather: "The Morey period makes me wistful for those heroic, enthusiastic, innocent and cheerful times when every day brought a new discovery."

Morey's cultural vision focused—as did US policy—on reconstructing Italy, *pace* Badoglio's Minister. While the Marshall Plan was rebuilding bridges and railroads, he worked at restoring Italy's cultural heritage, beginning with the great research libraries of Rome through his creation, the Union of Institutes. He helped rescue Nelson Gay's Library of American Studies from years of Fascist misuse. Without "the pursuit of truth to which libraries minister," he believed Italy could not regain her place among the great nations of the world; he further believed that the pursuit of truth about the U.S. had special relevance to the needs of emerging and modernizing Italy, and that reliable, accessible information, as defined by Fairbank and MacLeish, led to understanding. He served foreign policy by doing what he did best.

He had the courage and the wisdom to cut corners. Early in his tour, the diamond jubilee of New York's Metropolitan Museum provided a chance to show Americans that Italy was again a trusted friend. Overlooking staggering transportation and insurance costs, he persuaded the Vatican to lend the earliest known piece of intact Christian sculpture, the *Good Shepherd*, and he convinced the Italian government to add the Michelangelo *tondo* of Madonna, Child, and St. John from Florence. To pull off this minor miracle, he convinced the US Navy to ship the works aboard the USS *Missouri* and to transfer them to and from dockside with a variety of weapons carriers with motorcycle escorts. Because costs were unthinkable, he persuaded the Italians to waive insurance—twenty-five years would pass before Congress would indemnify priceless art objects loaned for American exhibits. When Stohlman warned him of the disaster of damage or loss, Morey asked with a broad smile: "Would insurance money really make any difference?"

A memo dated June 1949 recounted a typical two-week jaunt through the universities and research institutes of the North, covering thirteen cities and forty-one institutions, exploring possibilities for the newly launched Fulbright Program, while a colleague covered Tuscany. Finished with the North, the two joined to canvass the less-developed South, Sicily, and Sardinia. Their tour was eclectic: the Zoological Institute of Turin, the hydrobiological station at Pallanza, the Conservatory of Music in Venice, and the University of Turin's proposed station for studying cosmic rays at Cervinia. Morey reported "surprise and disappointment" among the Italian scholars about the one-way nature of Fulbright exchange possibilities—before Smith-Mundt, the Fulbright Program could send Americans to Italy but not take Italians to the U.S. He wrote a letter of complaint to Princeton president Harold Dodds, member of the division's advisory committee: "Our program of educational exchange as it exists at present is decidedly a one-sided affair." To compensate, he helped IIE find private support for Italians in the U.S. And, as he said, he "soaked the rich" whenever he could to raise private support funding.

His collegial relations within USIS and with the embassy are veiled in discretion. Panzini: "With regard to [USIS] Italy, publications, films, etc., in the beginning Dr. Morey did not have much to say about it because all that was the responsibility of the USIS Director. . . . At that time, intellectuals, scholars and artists were not considered 'Leaders' by USIS. . . . Most propaganda was aimed at union leaders and political VIPs. Only later was a broader Leader Program set up, to include high-level Italians in all fields."

Martha Lou Stohlman reported an incident in which he dared to bypass the embassy: at dinner one night, "he looked like a chastened but not very repentant schoolboy when he told of Ambassador Kirk's calling him down for not clearing a visit to the Quirinale to enlist the Queen's help." She noted that Morey was "certainly much esteemed but I suppose there must have been friction on occasion. As for the Communist threat, he did not seem too concerned and let USIS officials worry about it."

Rensselaer Lee, Morey's successor chairman at Princeton, recalled entering Morey's Rome office for the first time, probably in the early summer of 1948. Without looking up from the paper he was writing, Morey motioned Lee to a chair and said: "Damn! If that ambassador would just put on his hat and go down to see [Foreign Minister] Sforza, we'd have a Fulbright Program in this country!" Cipriana Scelba, who would spend forty proud years with the Fulbright Commission, was hired by Morey in June 1948 after service in the Italian Resistance and work as a secretary for OSS. Her new job was to "assist with the negotiations for the signature of the Fulbright Agreement," she writes; "After the signing of that Agreement on December 18, 1948, Dr. Morey asked me to organize the secretariat of the new binational commission—a secretariat consisting of myself!" Taking office in July 1949, she was in time to greet the first contingent of American students in October—the commission today claims over ten thousand Italian and American alumni.

From Italy Morey lobbied Washington for the Fulbright and Smith-Mundt legislation. In Italy he was the undisputed father of the Fulbright Program, but in Washington his voice was fainter. Panzini wrote, he "spoke to me about what later became the Fulbright Program. He thought of it because of the Boxer Indemnities"; he was delighted when Fulbright did the job. Against all odds, Morey—with IIE help—got Italy's first US contingent in place in the fall of 1949. For Smith-Mundt, Scelba said, "he worked hard on his former Princeton colleague Senator Smith and on

Senator Mundt to push through the Act." Letters in the Fulbright Archives in Fayetteville, Arkansas, reveal dialogue with the pathfinder BFS.

These Archives also contain his remarkable "squawk" of January 1949 to Harold Dodds, member of the first advisory commission on educational and cultural affairs. First, he throws Dodds an orchid for his "stiff stand for an education that will issue in something other than 'chewing-gum culture,' as our Communist friends over here are fond of calling American materialism." Then he got to work: Dodds was "the only member [of the Advisory Commission] that I know well enough to bother with the following squawk."

> There has never been, since I have been connected with the State Department, . . . a Cultural Program in Italy. Exchange of students, scholars, teachers and professors has been impossible (except for the little we could do on private contributions) owing to no appropriation under the Smith-Mundt bill, and the absence until a week ago of a Fulbright Agreement. . . . We cannot hope under existing regulations to get any grants before the academic year 1949–50, nor for any but advanced students and scholars and [then only for] a year's duration.

He wanted immediate authority to cut red tape for a group of handpicked Italian scholars, who were ready to go; he wanted a softer BFS stand on the nine-month minimum for foreign stay; he wanted the Dante Alighieri Society removed from the Attorney General's list of subversive organizations, to underline binationalism; and he pleaded for a less academic view of the Fulbright Program, e.g. opening it to high school students.

> A CULTURAL PROGRAM FOR ITALY: There is none at present. My office simply functions as an adjunct of the Information Service, aiding Italian-American contact and exchanges in scholarship, helping Americans over here with research and study, doing what we can . . . to promote Italian-American cultural cooperation on a private basis, etc. etc. The effort to help Italian reconstruction has placed the emphasis, in our "Projecting America," on the material side, with the result that, whereas two years ago Italians were beginning to get over the notion that this is all there is to American civilization, their overt and covert criticism is more deprecatory now than before.

The crux of the matter:

> The point is that to understand a people, you have to know its philosophy, literature and art, not only its capacity for industrial production, its technology and its science, since the genius of a people finds intelligible expression in the former and is often misunderstood in terms of the latter. The British and French conduct their

programs on this principle, and on one other, particularly applicable to Italy: . . . [they] know something that seems not to be understood in Washington, namely that in Latin countries, and particularly Italy, the masses take their cue politically and socially from the intellectuals.

Last came his proposal for an American Institute in Italy, modeled on the French institutes, with subcenters in university cities, drawing on a revolving faculty of US Fulbright professors in American history, literature, and society, teaching courses bearing university credit but open as well to the large English-speaking public. He wanted a nucleus around which to group "our presently sporadic activities of exhibitions, films and occasional lectures, to make in ensemble a coherent program that would 'project' a quite different United States from that which now furnishes material for Communist (and non-Communist) gibes."

Concluding, he broadened his case: "This is no individual squawk: nearly every Public Affairs Officer or Cultural Officer in Europe will say pretty much the same thing. . . . It is idle, in the present circumstances, to talk of Educational Exchange as a means of cultural understanding. Migration of students and scholars will have sporadic effect in this direction but no impact."[17]

His dream of a US open university in Italy was far from implausible, but it fit no private or government agency priorities or models and was not replicable in most other countries. The Fulbright oversight board (BFS) struggled with the idea, tempted by Morey's eminence, but in the end BFS turned the idea down because there could be no guarantee of such high-caliber leadership in USIS posts over time. In Italy a lesser structure was put in place with its own disappointing history.

Morey and his wife returned to Princeton in 1950. His performance encouraged Washington to recruit four scholar-successors from the academic world, but the idea of an academic CAO finally gave way in 1958 to that of a USIA veteran. Scelba's memories of a visit to the Moreys in 1952 suggested that Morey continued to follow the life of cultural diplomacy and of Italy in some detail. He died in 1955, honored by friends, students, and scholars the world over.

For the wise and easy-going Morey, the frustrations must have seemed the sadder in that he had switched at the end of his career from scholar to Academy director to diplomat without missing a beat, remaining precisely who he was. Fairbank at the beginning of his career had a similarly clear sense of self, a generous vision of humankind, and an unambiguous sense of the American role in that vision. The idea ran throughout a celebratory speech Morey delivered at the Princeton bicentennial celebrations in 1946. He compared the postwar role of the U.S. to seventh- and eighth-century Europe, after the barbarian incursions. America's task was like that of the Benedictines in preserving humanistic learning "until these times can turn from materialistic delusions to enlightened common sense." Art historians, he argued, had a special role: "They speak the language of art, the only international language the world has ever known." They are "humanists at large."

Morey, with his idea of a free-form, Fulbright-fed American multicity open university in Italy, reminds us what American cultural diplomacy might have been. In the spring of 1945, under MacLeish, everything was in place to build a powerful and effective agency for cultural diplomacy, with posts in every world capital. The recruitment of the right kind of people, over time, if Morey was any example, was not the problem; cultural diplomacy then, and still, amounts to getting the right people into the field, then backing them so they can do their best work. For Morey, as for Fairbank, human quality alone determined what happened. Each insisted on shaping his own job in the context of the country he served. Fairbank worked with OSS, then took over USIS China and turned it toward culture; Morey ignored bureaucracy and plowed, as he always had, the straight furrow of the humanist at large.

CHAPTER TEN

Postwar Losses and Fulbright's Gift

> That community is already in the process of dissolution, where each
> man begins to eye his neighbor as a possible enemy, where nonconfor-
> mity takes the place of evidence, where orthodoxy chokes freedom of
> dissent. . . . Those who begin coercive elimination of dissent, soon
> find themselves exterminating dissenters. Compulsory unification of
> opinion.
>
> —Learned Hand, cited by Edward R. Murrow, 1952

BY 1948 THE GREATEST of US wars had been won, the UN and UNESCO had
come into existence at US insistence, the Marshall Plan was rebuilding
prosperity in Europe, Germany would soon be transformed by the Allies,
Japan by the U.S. alone, and the nineteenth-century colonial system was
being dismantled around the world. New nations proliferated, communication technologies were shrinking the world, healthy US economic
growth was underwriting European recovery, and global assaults on
problems in public health and agriculture were making encouraging
headway. Everything seemed possible.[1]

A reluctant leader, the U.S. had no mechanism for planning its role in
the world and had to rely on the genius of a few individuals. A handful of
congressional figures, a few diplomats, New York financiers, and scattered
university experts stood ready to help think things through; but planning,
or looking ahead—a private-sector specialty—was confused with the New
Deal and mistrusted by the nation's elected representatives; only the
thought of Stalin managed to focus—and to some degree unify—the US
mind. The result was a reactive posture, recalling Hitler's boast that fear
of totalitarianism provokes imitation.

Truman's White House, overwhelmed by the day-to-day, spent little
time on the longer range. Acheson's brand of realism easily prevailed;
few could criticize his brilliance constructively. The UN, it was soon clear,
was no panacea, nor was UNESCO. And the unchecked attacks of McCarthy, demoralizing the bureaucracy, made a Republican victory in 1952
seem more plausible. Defensive interventionism looked like a reasonable
stance in international affairs and the great bipartisan and multilateral
hopes unleashed by wartime alliances dispelled. Absent a national emergency, the legislature fell back on its usual horsetrading.

For cultural diplomacy, MacLeish's variant on Cherrington's view, relying less on universities, held that the cultural dimension of international

relations mattered as much as politics and economics, stipulating that cultural diplomacy worked best when free of immediate policy considerations. The long-range vision was alive as well in Fulbright's mind and, of course, in the universities. The startling success of educational transformation in Germany and Japan, conceptualized by MacLeish, would soon create other illusions, thanks to its relative ease. Few noticed that German-Japanese reorientation was, in fact, an unprecedented triumph of *cultural* diplomacy, and only a handful of the unheeded wise saw a promising model for what might be achieved more generally in the world.

In State, while the self-styled realists moved their chess pieces, overworked foot soldiers in its forgotten cultural division went about their daily business of exchanging Americans and foreigners. The death of Laurence Duggan in 1948 stunned staffers, who remembered his leadership with affection and awe; for veterans of the division, it signaled a loss of innocence. Despite Fulbright's unflagging efforts to cover the division's work with the mantle of bipartisanship, it was seen as a New Deal product. Nationalist zealots took advantage of hindsight to taint it, congressional budgeteers continued to keep it cruelly understaffed, and everyone overlooked its potential for helping manage postwar change. The future was in the hands of the Wise Men, "realists" of a certain kind, led by the dazzling Acheson.[2] Few wondered which reality the realists served, or why their followers felt themselves compelled to caricature Wilson as a blind idealist.

In a macho and nonintellectual world, it was easy to overlook the softer power projected by cultural diplomacy—it would take half a century for neo-realists like Huntington and Nye to remind Americans that culture too mattered. In 1948 few saw that the great issues were cultural—e.g., the breakup of colonial empires spawning dozens of new countries without identities, the dark behavior of the culture-haunted Soviet Union, the tensions between a modernizing Israel and a traditionalist Arab political culture, or the religious orientation of the partition lines in Greater India and Ireland. Nor did many understand the idea of political culture or cultures in conflict—the very language for this kind of analysis was still rudimentary. Those who shared MacLeish's idea that everything began with education lived in university bunkers, far from the eyes of the mighty.

The undeclared war with the USSR overrode thinking about an independent cultural diplomacy. Cultural gradualism, as conceived by the founders, fell victim to the machinery of a dynamic and very American style of propaganda derived from Creel and Rockefeller. The unspoken ethnocentric assumptions of US exceptionalism prevailed. Provincial Americans knew their truth was truer than others' truths and expected a mesmerized world to hang on every US word; the informationists had no second thoughts about gearing everything to "telling America's story." In the division a standard witticism depicted the unidirectionalists' definition of dialogue as a warm, sincere invitation to "sit down together for a talk—about *me*."

Truman had skipped the university but was well read in history; he and his Yale-Harvard friend Acheson, in a friendship overriding their opposite backgrounds, pondered Thucydides. Acheson's friend MacLeish might have helped draw a truer line between hard and soft power, but after Acheson's non-support, MacLeish had retreated to Harvard.

Unrecognized cultural tensions, clear in retrospect, encumbered foreign policy. The bluntly applied US anticolonial ideal, for example, colored relations with two key allies; the colonial system, for all its faults, was at least a system, and suddenly it was being dismantled with reckless haste, unleashing conflict in former colonies all over the world. Another flaw was the US political culture's one-sided vision of multilateralism as service to US interests. In the UN the well-intentioned but flawed American idea of multilateralism followed its collision course with the Soviet Union, in the UN structure for world governance the U.S. put forth in San Francisco.

Unprecedented success in "reeducating" the US quadrant of Germany and all of Japan swelled cultural confidence in American power overseas. England and France, with centuries of imperial history behind them, handled Germany in more affordable, sustainable ways, but the Americans went first-class; the impact was impressive, and Washington toyed with the illusion that the U.S. could remake any part of the world in no time at all. US universalism, spurred by impatience and fed by unprecedented prosperity, was proving more aggressive and tenacious than France's.

The long-fought battle in State between the educational and informational approach maintained its fitful truce. But Ralph Turner's strictures on short-range policy purposes were fading. MacLeish's idea of redefining information as a tool of education had been folded into Benton's omelette. The self-confident informationists and psychological warriors moved straight ahead.

While Fulbright had given cultural diplomats the greatest gift ever, familiar bureaucratic predators were chipping away at the Welles-Duggan design; they began gnawing at the tiny division in 1942, when new agencies recognized the utility of cultural tools. As Welles's iron insistence on State's coordinating role for foreign cultural activities weakened, other agencies paid the division the high compliment of pilfering its functions. MacLeish had set out to expand State's capacity to meet all agencies' needs, but the starved division could not fend off its children's wealthy suitors.

Serious loss began soon after Smith-Mundt. Between the end of the war and 1953, the aggregate cultural dimension of both private and public American diplomacy rose steadily. But the formal outflow from Washington, which had been the responsibility of one divison of State and its ICC, was being managed by five separate agencies by 1954, and others lay in wait. Carving off pieces, predator agencies pledged coordination but quickly forgot. The first loss came in 1948 when "technical assistance," the ICC training function, was wrenched away from education and was assigned to the Marshall Plan. Soon after, part of the division's responsibility for dealing with the world's intellectuals slipped unnoticed to the newly-minted CIA. By 1954 the new USIA and the Department of Education would take their own slices.

First came the Marshall Plan, or Point Four, or Mutual Assistance, or AID.[3] Education had included training, before 1948. Welles's leadership of ICC had been firm; the question of calling it training and separating it from education never arose. But Welles's successors lost control. "Technical assistance," the defining phrase, meant short-term training in the U.S. for foreign technicians learning new skills, with supporting visits by American experts abroad—two-way movement for one-way knowledge-transfer. ICC's fine work, under Cherrington's ingenious prodding, had extended beyond government staff on loan; the universities were already involved. But Congress persistently throttled back the division's budget and staff; patience, vigilance, and energies were flagging.

AID's takeover of training was to some extent a relief; a partner had offered to share the division's burdens—State, in principle, was still expected to "coordinate." But no one knew how to coordinate training, the mainstay of Paul Hoffman's giant Marshall Plan. While the midget division retained "education," the loss of training meant its visible output had shrunk by a third. Tortured definitions of "training" and "education" were devised to keep budgets clean. Where the cultural planners, in league with Rockefeller, had built the field posts into adult education centers, with libraries, ELT, book programs, academic and nonacademic exchanges, lectures, and arts presentations for foreign audiences, the division by 1950 was primarily defining its work as education as carried out by the Fulbright Program.

AID's vision, methods, and processes were born in Latin America and reshaped in Germany and Japan—industrialized countries with educated populations, where US economists could deal with counterpart economists. In Europe, for example, the sophisticated economic concept of productivity was the program's guiding principle.[4] In the intermediate and more dynamic developing countries, Rockefeller's more familiar practices were the model. The problem in the undeveloped world was very different from that in Europe; to attack it, AID looked to business-government cooperation. In Latin America Rockefeller's *servicio*, adapted from the joint ventures of American business, was a form of guided binationalism. The *servicio* would circle the globe under different names—in Africa it was called a joint fund—but each had the same idea: local teams working on projects directed by US expertise. Until the 1950s Rockefeller dreamed of US "cultural" outreach, extending his model to a worldwide development effort, imagining himself at its head. His preelection booklet *Partners in Progress* laid out this agenda in 1948—Truman was among many who neglected to read it.

One Rockefeller enthusiast did: Ben Hardy was a mid-level bureaucrat at State; circumventing his bosses, he got a draft of the ex-Coordinator's idea for a global development agency into the hands of White House speechwriters, just in time for Truman's inaugural address in January 1948. The speechwriters added a paragraph as a fourth point for foreign policy and Point Four was born. When Truman appointed Averell Harriman to head Point Four, Rockefeller was bitterly disappointed and settled for the chair of its advisory commission. Despite his loyal soldiering, he realized that things had changed: Truman no longer needed a token Republican by his side; and worse, Acheson was only one of many senior officials who mistrusted him.

With Point Four in action, the division's training function was gone. The coordinating role in technical assistance passed to State's regional bureaus, which now budgeted and administered training grantees directly. Point Four soon built its own bureaucracy, a hardy survivor; in the field, the work began. Still, confusion remained. The first active field program of Fulbright exchanges, in 1948–49 in Burma, found early US and Burmese exchangees working in sectors designated by development-minded embassy economic officers: two Burmese nurses from Gordon Seagraves's up-country hospital went to the U.S., and a US university-level economist-educator joined the agricultural-extension specialist Oscar Hunerwadel and his wife Helen, models for the famous "Ugly American." After 1948 Fulbright Burma, under BFS guidance, would redefine itself as a university-to-university program, leaving the practical side to AID. BFS soon hammered the new definitions into Fulbright policy, leaving university subjects like applied science, engineering, public administration, medicine, and public health to AID. The attention of a cold war–dominated Congress, where those of a populist mindset were already detecting "elitism," drifted away from Fulbright exchanges. Without coordination, education and training were soon operating in two distinct vacuums in Washington.

The AID function soon outgrew narrow definitions. After capital transfers and infrastructure building, technical assistance—renamed human resource development or capacity building—was AID's basic component, especially in the preindustrial world where the first need was for human skills. In Africa, for example, AID trained human cadres for gradual modernization. An AID officer who served in Ethiopia between 1952 and 1957, based on a broad definition of education as the transfer of knowledge from one person to another by any means, estimated that 90 to 95 percent of the mission's work went into some kind of learning or technology transfer. Every American expert who worked in the country had one or more "counterparts" who learned by working alongside the expert—on-the-job education, in the British colonial tradition. The same AID officer, serving later in Nigeria, found more capital transfer and infrastructure building but estimated that two-thirds of the budget still went into "education." Another AID veteran cautiously estimated that over the decades about 50 percent of foreign-assistance funding world-wide went into some form of education or training. In contrast to the division, the scale was immense: the Ethiopian AID program cost around $30 million per year in 1952–57, more than the entire budget of the division. If one-half of US foreign-aid funding since 1948 went to "educa-tion," at a conservative estimate, it would amount to well over $50 *billion* by the turn of the century, roughly $1 billion per year. In contrast, the *total* Fulbright Program in the same fifty-year period added up to slightly over $1 billion, perhaps 2 percent of AID funding. The U.S., with the approval of Congress, was spending a great deal of money for "educa-tion," but AID's "training" traveled a separate path. The outside world, accustomed to the French version of education as a single function man-aged by embassy cultural officers, learned once more that "the Ameri-cans" did things differently.[5]

As usual the collegial flexibility of good and decent people in the field provided a kind of coordination. In my own experience of a dozen years in three developing countries, coordination between USIS and AID at the working level was sometimes minimal and occasionally vigorous, but constant. In two exceptional cases, the total US cultural and educational effort grew into a single function. First, in India in the mid-1960s, under the insistence of ambassador Chester Bowles, USIS, AID, the office of the science attaché, the Peace Corps, and in informal parallel, the Ford Foundation made sure that US educational investments flowed together. Then, in late-1960s Iran, a determined CAO drew on the Bowles model to persuade AID, Peace Corps, and the science attaché to meet regularly on education questions along with younger interested political and eco-nomic officers; a parallel binational embassy subcommittee on ELT met regularly with the British Council. Contrasting with the gigantic India program, educational programs in Iran by 1967 were small and results were easier to see. When AID in Iran followed Ford in closing down (1968), two skilled AID-funded Iranian staffers were reassigned to the USIS cultural office, where they managed residual AID programs: the new Pahlavi University in Shiraz, grants to Iranian students at the American University of Beirut, training for Afghan technicians brought to Iran for third-country experience, relations with the AID-trained Plan Organiza-tion and the office of personnel management, follow-up on AID return-ees, and continuation of an important AID project in local government, "training" young district governors. When a new PAO arrived, immovably persuaded that AID programs had no place in a USIS program, these faint efforts faded away. The local government project for district governors survived as a binationally funded IV project for seven years before a suc-cessor PAO ended it.

The Indian and Iranian cases underline what Fairbank discovered in Chungking: that Americans, working at the point of contact, will usually do the right thing, Washington rhetoric to the contrary. The history of US cultural diplomacy from 1948 onward is a story of good people muddling through in a bad structure; once in the field, they worked together.

Then came the Central Intelligence Agency. The second slice off the cultural diplomatic loaf went to the new agency, created in 1947, which deserves a chapter of its own. Again State's loss was flattering to the idea of cultural diplomacy; the new CIA would undertake activities to combat the USSR that were clearly foreshadowed in Hull's letter.[6] Unlike the mushrooming AID function, the CIA's slice turned out badly.

The carefree Rockefeller had dabbled in intelligence in Latin America to Welles's dismay. In the weightier mind of Colonel Donovan, the OSS team—including Langer's researchers—served the idea that culture and intelligence might work together. When the CIA came into being as part of Truman's effort to gear up for undeclared war with the USSR, the first US peacetime intelligence organization outside the military saw the need to work with intellectuals around the world.

MacLeish had been ready to absorb OSS but ran out of time; Benton was persuaded by Donovan to reject any part of OSS, which he was led to see as a purveyor of "black propaganda." Mutating from OSS to OSO, then to SSU in the War Department, then to CIG, the OSS finally became CIA through the National Security Act of July 1947, midwifed by Truman advisor Clark Clifford. The agency's initial mandate focused on research and analysis, intelligence and counterintelligence. Men like Fairbank in China and Young in Iran, in tune with Langer's division at home, had showed that high-caliber US intellectuals could do research and analysis; some carried on sound cultural work at the same time. When these broad-gauged men returned to their campuses after the war, they left Washington behind. Those who stayed were mainly specialists in closed societies like the USSR and China.

Benton's rejection of OSS was shortsighted. The division, in fact, needed precisely the kind of research and long-range thinking that Langer had created; what finally became USIA in 1953 would have benefitted from global area-sensitive research, and the VOA could have used the "ears" of FBIS. Instead USIA's office of "research" narrowed in scope; country and regional studies, evaluation and self-study gave way to public-opinion sampling, staffed by academics whose university credentials had expired.

The Czech coup and the Berlin blockade, among the events of 1948–49, had clarified Soviet intentions beyond any doubt. National Security Council memo 10/2 added covert activities to CIA's mandate in response to what it called the USSR's "vicious covert" propaganda activities. The new responsibilites of CIA's Deputy Director for Plans included culture and intellect.

Writers on the CIA, too often obsessed with espionage in general and hampered by difficult access to documents, have produced a sizable, imaginative, and occasionally fictional literature about the agency, little of which concerns our story. But CIA's cultural dimension—especially its support to American and European intellectuals and to cultural and educational organizations designed to counter Soviet infiltration of European cultural life—is central to our story. Its keystone was the Congress for Cultural Freedom (CCF). The theoretical door through which the new CIA undertook cultural diplomacy was political action, through covert cooperation with private-sector organizations.

By 1949 it was obvious that the USSR had no intention of playing by the gentlemanly rules of the West—the West's fine points were meaningless in a society with no private sector. If the individual was a cog of State machinery, so was the scholar; foreign scholars were indistinguishable in Stalin's mind from spies. The scrupulous West had no open response to such paranoia and went undercover.

Clive Rose's diligent compendium of the Soviet cultural program network listed well over a hundred organizations openly serving Soviet foreign policy across the globe, with total cost in 1979 dollars estimated at $75 million (cost estimates differ wildly on such matters, still shrouded in secrecy and distorted by dubious ruble equivalences). In comparison, it is chastening to realize that costs for an estimated aggregate of similar American-supported institutions working abroad, including both public and private entities like the foundations, added up to a great deal more. The late Cord Meyer, in charge of CIA's "cultural" work for many years, explained in his guarded memoir that a Western countermovement was developed to meet each lance in the Soviet charge. Much more beyond his jurisdiction was mobilized by the rhetoric of the moment and by private energies.

The Soviets in Europe exploited post-Fascist and post-Nazi fears, working through local communist parties (CPs) whose appeal was based on their legendary wartime resistance. The Soviets systematically bored into existing European organizations, targetting labor unions, youth movements, student groups, associations of intellectuals, artists, jurists and writers, and sports organizations—the complete list awaits further opening of the Soviet archives. Financial assistance flowed through the CPs, for example, to youth groups organized in country chapters under the World Federation of Democratic Youth (WFDY) or the International Union of Students (IUS). Attractive meetings in world capitals, with spectacles and shows, drew young people from everywhere, including the West. Dozens of "fronts" akin to WFDY and IUS, some concocted and others infiltrated, were financed and run from Moscow.

In the West the Soviet cultural offensive came clear in the Italian elections and the Prague coup of 1948. The West's response was military— e.g., the Berlin airlift and the Korean War. It was agreed as well that nonmilitary countermeasures were needed. The CIA offered to do the job; with concealed budgets, it could dodge congressional scrutiny. The dilemma was sharp: no one believed that Congress would authorize open outreach to the noncommunist left (NCL) in Europe, so it was slipped under the table. Thanks to Congress, State was powerless, leaving the CIA to take up its cultural role out of necessity and deceiving Congress in the process.

US and foreign nongovernmental organizations (NGOs), were enlisted in the covert effort; others were created with ample budgets. Foreign labor unions, with important educational components, were put into contact with the US labor movement. The Free Trade Union Committee was formed to relate to the AFL-CIO. Each of these NGOs was a micro-battlefield of intellectual issues.

The National Student Association (NSA) is a case in point. Founded at the University of Wisconsin in 1947, after a Soviet-sponsored conference in Prague had attracted numerous US student groups and revealed the extent of Soviet infiltration, NSA split into two schools of thought, reminiscent of the division of Murrow's student association in the 1930s. One worked for the narrowly defined welfare of university students in the U.S. and abroad, while the other saw itself as the only available counterpoise to Soviet student activities. Covert CIA funds began to flow. An NSA vice president, then a graduate student at Harvard working in Paris, handled international relations in the French capital. The budding political theorist took over responsibility for a variety of activities, including a program to develop foreign student leadership by bringing selected figures to the U.S. for study tours. Eschewing embassy relationships, he juggled his scholarly research with recruitment of student leaders and activities for the program, which took up perhaps a third of his time, as he remembers it today. In the U.S., campus foreign student advisors, unaware of the funding source, made sure his candidates were given good programs. One US program officer, the late Cassandra Pyle, was perhaps not unusual in guessing where the money came from, but she went along with the game. Even today the history of NSA is incomplete, awaiting the memoirs of its participants and the research that will explain how its operations were carried out.[7]

Until 1961 the CIA placed a small number of selected personnel undercover in USIS offices, in some cases in cultural offices. The *Washington Post* in August 1998 reported the death of Harry Lunn, a world-scale collector of photographs, noting that earlier in life "he became a major player at the National Student Association, rising to the directorship of the Foundation for Youth and Student Affairs—which quietly collapsed after a 1967 piece in *Ramparts* magazine disclosed its links to the Central Intelligence Agency." Lunn, said the *Post*, "had served at the Pentagon and at the US Embassy in Paris," but he "was no longer much use as an intelligence officer." Lunn, concealed as an ACAO in Paris, is the only man I ever met who freely admitted that he had served undercover in a USIS cultural office.

Lunn's Foundation for Youth and Student Affairs added a "leadership" dimension to the work of the unwitting NAFSA. Lunn's group worked with prominent NAFSA figures like Pyle, who was rising to prominence in the US world of international education. Looking back, those managing programs saw that remarkable things were accomplished. The finest foreign student leaders, for example, were helped to discover the U.S. through well-designed programs while the designers were kept in ignorance of deeper purposes. They benefitted from the honest and open style of US hospitality, even if dishonesty was later disclosed.

In 1961 new USIA director Ed Murrow—with bruises to show from his clashes with both the Soviets and the FBI—emphatically ended the practice of USIA cover for CIA officers. From then until USIA's death in 1999, its leadership boasted that USIA sheltered no CIA agents, though it admitted that a few might have slipped in earlier. Yet even Murrow, at the behest of his advisor Thomas Sorensen, hired two recent CIA "retirees"—as staffers were told. Reflecting his discomfort, Murrow refused assignment for one to the geographic region for which he was uniquely equipped by native language gifts, on grounds that he had earlier worked there for "the other agency."

At the intellectual peak of CIA cultural activities stood the Congress for Cultural Freedom, a dazzling collection of leading world intellectuals from the NCL.[8] Peter Coleman saw the CCF as the key to the "mind of postwar Europe," as did Volker Berghahn's protagonist Shepard Stone. To carry off this idea, the CIA recruited Rockefeller protégé Tom Braden, who worked first for the Committee for a United Europe, which was later turned over to Cord Meyer. In 1950s Berlin, Melvin Lasky, editor of the USIS-sponsored monthly *Der Monat*, and Michael Josselson, working out of the USIS cultural office in Berlin, organized the Wroclaw Cultural Conference for Peace, with leading intellectuals, including British historian A. J. P. Taylor and Cherrington's friend and GAC colleague Bryn Hovde, a key player in the cultural internationalist movement and president of the New School in New York.

Emerging from Wroclaw, CCF flourished. It published high-caliber monthly journals all over Europe, spearheaded by Lasky's matchless *Encounter*. The idea in 1949, noted Arthur Schlesinger, was to focus the European left on resisting Soviet incursions. The NCL concept was understood by government advisors at the highest levels, men like Kennan and Bohlen in the U.S. and Isaiah Berlin in England. For Secretaries of State Byrnes and Marshall, neither known for his dedication to the left, the NCL idea was "a quiet revolution" in that it permitted relations with intellect, noted Schlesinger, himself a veteran of both MacLeish's OFF and OSS.

Cord Meyer worked with leaders of the most prominent organizations in the U.S. and Europe. His memoir dodged budget estimates, but it is clear the work was generously funded—in 1966 the budget for CCF alone topped $2 million.[9] Universities like mighty Harvard, through the mediating role of Professor William Y. Elliott, joined the game. Rockefeller biographer Cary Reich says that one of Elliott's graduate students, a German immigrant named Kissinger, was involved in editing a short-lived periodical in the early 1950s called *Confluence*, a Cambridge look-alike of *Encounter*. Longer lasting was the famous Kissinger Seminar, held every summer at Harvard through the mid-1970s; it gathered highly selected younger intellectuals from around the world. Cultural offices, including my own, proudly submitted candidates for the coveted program; but we had no clue as to the seminar's funding source.

In 1966, when McGeorge Bundy left the White House to take over the presidency of the Ford Foundation, top Ford staff remember his concern at his first staff meeting about the precarious covert arrangement between the CIA and the voluntary associations; he feared it was about to explode and was looking for alternatives. He was right about the explosion, but it was too late for preemptive action. Charles Frankel, directing State's Bureau of Educational and Cultural Affairs (CU), was part of the team inside government dealing with the *Ramparts* revelations in February 1967;[10] Frankel insisted that the problem of NSA funding was an educational issue and that former Carnegie chief John Gardner, then Secretary of Health, Education, and Welfare, be part of the decision. According to Frankel, Gardner raised the obvious questions: "Why did the program continue for so long? . . . Couldn't the people in charge recognize that it was bound to come out in the open?" The problem remained: "What to do next?" A three-man committee was named, consisting of the Undersecretary of State, CIA Director Allen Dulles, and Gardner. Frankel witnessed a dramatic example of the peril of mixing intelligence and culture; the disaster resulted from scattering responsibility for educational and cultural relations around Washington. For Frankel, it showed the vital need for cultural diplomacy, capable of far more than it had ever been allowed to undertake. Admitting the impossibility of funding such activity on a year-to-year basis, given the control of random congressional tyrants, he insisted in 1967 that ways be found "to support the activity of private nonprofit groups in foreign affairs while giving them maximum freedom and keeping the bureaucracy out of the act." To Frankel, the ironies were overwhelming: "Congress has been willing to grant such autonomy when the government works through the CIA but not . . . through agencies working aboveboard." In Stockholm Frankel met Swedish Prime Minister Olof Pälme, a graduate of Kenyon College widely accused of being anti-American. Pälme confessed that his deep disillusionment with the America he had loved as a youth came from his innocent entrapment in the CIA-backed World Assembly of Youth. Similarly, the Italian writer Ignazio Silone found his life ripped to shreds by the CCF revelations. Braden moved on to a better job.

Called upon in 1968 to rescue as much of the situation as he could, Frankel refused to allow his office to become "the CIA orphan asylum." He knew that CIA's funding had consumed many times CU's entire budget. He proposed a new agency to carry on political-cultural activities in the open. Fifteen years later the National Endowment for Democracy (NED) came to life, originally intended to carry on overtly some of the good CIA work that had been terminated; in the intervening years the idea had been transformed by Washington skeptics so that the NED of 1983 bore no resemblance to Frankel's original proposal.

Coleman suggests that the CIA's blind funding of NGOs was often carried on as a game of wink-and-nod, with many more people knowing precisely what was going on than were later willing to admit it—including the the board members of the Fairfield Foundation, created as a covert channel to the CCF. Coleman and Cary Reich mention prominent people who may have been involved, but at the working level, few knew—or admitted—they were being misled. Coleman concludes that CCF allowed "idealistic, courageous and far-sighted men and women [to fight] in this war of ideas . . . against Stalinism and its successors. It was, as we know, a necessary war, fought when much of the world was quite unaware of the fact that it was taking place."[11] The CIA effort was well funded and brilliantly staffed. Congressional budgeteer John J. Rooney, who knew about CIA's adventures in cultural diplomacy, welcomed the CIA project, but when Allen Dulles urged him to transfer responsibility to State, Rooney refused.

The *Ramparts* articles destroyed the covert structure. The CIA had been caught with no exit plan—Evan Thomas hints that CIA's cast-iron mind-set believed the "good times" could continue forever.[12] In the outside world, after covert interventions in Iran, Guatemala, the Dominican Republic, and Cuba came to world attention, the acronym CIA took on a darker coloration as a household name for concealed interventionism and a symbol of all that had gone wrong with America since it donned its hegemonic mantle—for America's enemies, it was the perfect target, an off-the-shelf US devil.

Were there alternatives? Open funding for American and European voluntary associations overseas, offered publicly in the 1950s, while possible, would have been less effective, but surely longer-lasting and less lethal. In 1949–50 the public mood was alert. Honest and decent people joined the government or worked alongside it because they believed Soviet tanks were poised to roll across Western Europe.[13]

Imagined alternatives only point up the dilemma. Could the U.S. have built close cooperation between State and a bipartisan congressional committee like Fulbright's, under strong leadership and the protection of a public-private body like the BFS? Could organizations have been started up, and then have covert support phased out—as was done with a prominent CIA-initiated US university European extension program that survives today on its own? Could a freestanding public-private educational and cultural "foundation" of impeccable integrity, under an ongoing board and national intellectual leaders, have managed better? Could contributions have been funneled through a prestigious American outside body like the British Grants Commission?

None of these options was realistic in 1948–49. American philanthropy, whose goals had always been educational and developmental, was not ready to accept an open-ended commitment to political warfare at such high cost. Even if Congress had been told convincingly that an active overseas arm was needed, it would not have agreed to fund it year after year at spiraling cost and would have been as skeptical about other organizations. The imaginary scenarios reflect an unresolved dilemma of US world leadership, one that haunted Fulbright: how does one persuade Congress to support a permanent nonpartisan mechanism that provides open support for a diplomacy of political action in education and culture yet remains compatible with the values of the US polity and its universities?

The Welles-Duggan vision of cultural diplomacy had offered one expandable approach, but Congress was never enthusiastic about it; and its capricious funding of State's cultural relations since 1938 has proved the point: there was probably no real alternative to covert funding. The CIA did what was necessary, but its clandestine style meant the U.S. did precisely what MacLeish feared: borrowed the tactics of the totalitarians.

Historians, as the decades pass, may perhaps some day be able to measure more precisely the damage done by CIA's failed cultural diplomacy to the fabric of national and international cultural discourse, as well as to US political thought and civic conciousness. While Americans have notoriously short memories, the rest of the world remembers all too well and no longer trusts the U.S. The failed CIA cultural effort blotted the US image, discredited a century and a half of private American philanthropic generosity, tainted decades of formal government cultural relations programs—including the least guilty of all, the Fulbright Program—and poisoned relations between government and the American intellectual world. I have come to believe that an American counteroffensive was needed but that it might have been mounted more wisely, with an eye on a more distant horizon, accepting the risk of lesser impact.

Some small part of the damage to cultural diplomacy itself can perhaps be measured by the fact that cultural officers came under growing foreign suspicion after 1970, and US private institutions were less trustworthy—today, field representatives of the National Endowment for Democracy, created to do openly what the CIA did under cover, report deep suspicion of their work. Institutionally, the impact on the division was more clear. CIA in the 1940s took away a second chunk of the cultural mission outlined by Hull; the CIA's flamboyant and well-funded role in the front lines of the war of ideas took further political wind out of State's sails and reduced its relevance. While Turner, MacLeish, and Fulbright knew that all international cultural action was political, they believed it could be done in culturally acceptable ways, and hence be permissible politics in a longer time frame. MacLeish's team—or Rufus Morey— would have managed the CCF openly, less lavishly and built for a longer run, with broad coordination and university cooperation. In that case would the USSR have imploded any later? If the CCF were still in place, might it not be useful in dealing with some of the tough intellectual questions of today? There are no answers to such speculative questions.

•   •   •

While the postwar realignment of cultural functions raged, Fulbright's exchange program was forging its identity. Over the years it would grimly retain its integrity, its transparent binationalism, and its structural protections at home and abroad. The character of its founder kept the program above the fray, even after he left the Senate in 1975. It is time in our story, after examining the CIA's failed experiment in engaging world intellect, to look at the early progress of this remarkable American monument which *did* survive.[14]

The Fulbright Program, still the core of formal American cultural diplomacy, moved from concept to operations in 1947–50. The shaping body was the Board of Foreign Scholarships (BFS), an ongoing team looking closely at policy. The early years reveal the Senator's intentions, the dangers he foresaw, and the remarkable consensus he built. The BFS was to be a powerful oversight board, strong enough to fend off party politics—its title revealed its scholarly ethos. It would take time, plus trial and error, to form the program's identity, but the BFS in first few years made Fulbright what for the most part it remains today.

The discussion of the program's policy, with the senator himself at the center until his death, was slightly delayed—Fulbright had completely forgotten to provide for a supervisory body in his initial legislation and it took subsequent action to bring BFS to life. In slipping his original bill past potentially hostile colleagues, Fulbright had evoked the Boxer model, adroitly introducing a letter from Herbert Hoover about the binational Belgian-American experience and his efforts in 1923 and again in 1938 to turn all foreign debt into exchanges. With Hoover in support, Republicans Taft, Smith, and Mundt joined Fulbright to make the idea bipartisan.

BFS was not conceived as an advisory body but as an executive board, in the manner of Cherrington's GAC. BFS faced sizable policy questions from its first day on the job. Outsiders to academic practice and to the competing pressures that make up foreign policy find it difficult to see why the Fulbright Program needed serious "policy" decisions; they reflect the program's location at the poorly defined intersection where universities meet government. BFS had thus to juggle two opposing visions of foreign policy, the internationalist and the nationalist views. Embodying the fundamental bargain struck by Welles and Duggan in 1938, BFS enlisted university cooperation on an unwritten proviso: that program decisions—mainly selection and placement—would remain recognizably with the universities. Watching over this interchange, BFS was designed to patrol the political frontiers.

Fulbright, his friends, and BFS were aware of enemies lurking around

Washington; the Senator pressed BFS to defend university autonomy, anticipating short-term policy pressures and domestic political interference. At home and abroad, his first priority was protection against propaganda, or lying by his simple definition, a total contradiction of what he had in mind.

The ten-member BFS was unique in being nonpartisan. The board was to be appointed by and report to the president as head of state, not head of party, at the recommendation of the division. Since BFS was to represent US education, it would be heavily academic; and it would elect its own chair. Given this extraordinary independence, BFS quickly decided to make all selections itself and to oversee all "foreign scholarships," by whatever government agency.

The high level of the initial appointments to BFS helped etch these concepts into stone. Of the ten, nine top-level educators spanned the geography of US universities, representing different types, different state systems, and different disciplines; the division's carefully balanced proposal was endorsed by the White House, with Fulbright's concurrence. The tenth member, the only non-educator, came from an even higher level: war hero Gen. Omar Bradley was a mandated representative of the Veterans Administration, which through the GI Bill held a large stake in postwar US higher education. BFS's educator-members represented three university administrators, the presidents of all-female Vassar and predominantly black Fisk, and the graduate dean of Washington's Catholic University; three university professors from different regions of the country and from different disciplines (history, physics, and English); two educational administrators from government, New York State's Commissioner of Education and John Studebaker, US Commissioner; and IIE's new chief, division architect Laurence Duggan.

Underlining its importance, BFS was given generous staff and budget to permit in-depth field visits by all members. With clerical support, two top cultural staffers moved to BFS from key jobs in the division: the executive director was Rockefeller-import Kenneth Holland, and his deputy was Francis Colligan, professor of English at San Francisco State, first cultural officer in Ecuador, now chief of the division's Office of Exchanges.

BFS held its first meeting in October 1947, then met five times in 1948 and six in 1949. It immediately established five regional subcommittees corresponding to State's geographical areas; another subcommittee took on technical matters like stipends and selections; outside selection committees, staffed by academics, were established for the various intellectual disciplines. Soon, as many as three hundred people from American higher education, reimbursed only for expenses, were making the program work. But Fulbright, before its Smith-Mundt supplement, was still a one-way process, limited to outgoing Americans funded from military sales.

For the university calendar, October 1947 was already late. The selection process would be long and State's small staff could not handle it.

Duggan offered IIE's services; BFS agreed and the scupulous ex-diplomat quickly resigned to avoid conflict of interest. He knew that getting university-related grantees moving abroad under normal circumstances required at least a year, in which case grantees would not be in place until the fall of 1950. BFS asked Carnegie and Rockefeller to help crash fund the first year's selections by IIE. With heroic measures, IIE got US grantees on ships to Europe in October 1949.

After Duggan's death, BFS executive director Kenneth Holland took over IIE. Under his direction, IIE began its growth; its demonstrated capacities would soon earn it the right to administer German and Japanese reorientation exchanges. IIE, a new kind of governmental client, depended on government but it was by no means, as Ninkovich suggests, its "ward."

The earliest Fulbright country programs were a handful of exchanges with China and Burma. Then came the massive first wave of exchanges in Europe: 270 graduate students sailed for France on a single ship in October 1949 and as many went to Italy. At France's provincial University of Dijon, for example, five US graduate students arrived in late October with untranslated credentials and no warning, leaving the startled university to cope with this latest wave of "invaders," as one administrator teased.

That first year, the new binational Fulbright Commissions abroad felt their way. In France, for example, monthly stipends were overgenerous—Fulbrighters in Dijon were better paid than the university rector. No one but BFS worried about disproportionate numbers in single countries, appropriate research facilities, inadequate welcomes, foreign universities' overtaxed absorptive capacity, or unrealistic US expectations. In an era of high excitement and possibility, something of the lavish Rockefeller mode washed over Welles's cautious gradualism.

Participant-historian Walter Johnson recalled the key BFS idea: manage the program closely, rather than reign over it at a distance. BFS decisions followed this concept: binational administration in the field, a focus on university-to-university relationships, independence from politics, high academic quality, merit selection through peer review, open competititon, public-private cooperation, reciprocity, focus on individuals not institutions, and skepticism about questions of "loyalty." It was a spelling-out of American university values.

Peer review was the indispensable core. University faculty selected university graduates, teachers, and researchers, just as Fritz Larkin's architects chose their peers to build the new embassies. Though less than perfect, peer review was the best solution to the public-private interface; minimizing political meddling, it could solve the problem of excellence in any democracy by passing tough decisions on to the professions. The process made its own political statement at home and abroad; it was the democratic instrument of merit, as opposed to the nepotism of the preindustrial countries or the state-dictated choices of the totalitarians.

Some resisted peer review in principle, not only populists who accused it of elitism or informationists who wanted to use intellectuals as weapons, but others: economy-oriented observers who found it time-consuming, nationalist zealots who argued for tighter political selection criteria, and those rejected by the process, who called it cronyism. For BFS, peer review was a given; it would not come under serious attack until the 1980s, when it was accused of bias by a self-proclaimed "conservative" coalition of ideologues, alleging that peer review perpetuated the so-called Liberal Conspiracy. In 1948 there was no such question, and BFS set peer review at the heart of Fulbright process.

Three early policy decisions suggest the problems the pioneers faced. For ELT, BFS worried that the overwhelming demand for English worldwide would absorb the entire program and decided Fulbright should invest only in teacher training, opening a program category called "linguistics" for teachers of language-learning methodology. For science, BFS concluded it was wise to resist the equally overwhelming demand for American technology and decided that Fulbright would resist applied science and deal primarily with basic science; besides, many rich funding opportunities for applied science were already in play. In its decision to deal only with university graduates, BFS believed that the first college degree would sort out the best and limit applicants to a manageable number; as demand increased and fewer grants became available, BFS raised the requirement to a year or more of graduate study.

The Senator originally had his Rhodes experience in mind; he first imagined an American Rhodes program geared to new graduates. But, yielding to BFS urging, he agreed to open Fulbright to the entire range of university activity. An immediate consequence, which nagged at the Senator all his life, was the need to fund accompanying families.

BFS wanted total oversight. It explicitly deplored the loss of training and technical education to AID; the board believed that "no field of education or scholarship was specifically excluded or included," wrote Johnson and Colligan in 1963. In Fulbright's mind BFS was designed, as its name suggests, to supervise *all* government academic exchanges—i.e., "foreign scholarships." AID made peace with BFS by leaving "education" to Fulbright. But BFS lost control of training.

BFS readily included intellectual institutions other than universities—museums, libraries, research institutions, as well as labor education and social work training programs, art schools, and music conservatories. Burma's first Americans included nurses and an agricultural extension agent. BFS oversight over Office of Education teacher exchanges faded with the years, more so when the Office of Education became part of the mighty Department of Health, Education, and Welfare (HEW).

Selecting and placing American students and scholars was labor-intensive, beyond the reach of the division. BFS, therefore, contracted out the work to well-staffed external bodies, like IIE and the Council for International Exchange of Scholars (CIES), with their own university-based boards and peer-review panels. The selection process was thorough. For

US predoctoral graduates, IIE collected candidate dossiers, already processed by campus committees, and then ran them through discipline-oriented US selection committees; finally the overseas commissions made the selections. Only after the commissions approved candidates did BFS make selections final and inform the grantees.

CIES was a different kind of organization handling postdoctoral research and university faculty placement. With no obvious organization in place, a group of associations led by the ACLS set up CIES, which has since handled all postdoctoral research and teaching, US and foreign;[15] during the Clinton years CIES merged with IIE.

With firm foundations in place, the program was launched, but the long range was uncertain. Continued funding was a serious problem, especially with funds from military sales in foreign currencies as the only source; such funds were available only in a few countries—specifically, not in Latin America. Foreign currencies, when available, could cover transportation and maintenance of US grantees in foreign countries, but there was no funding for maintenance of foreign grantees in the U.S. Only after 1948 would Smith-Mundt make dollars available for two-way flow. The US universities stretched to provide extra scholarship support for foreign students when possible, with Fulbright covering travel costs; IIE and CIES sharpened their skills at finding funded university placements for foreign students.

In the field, the Boxer and Belgian models were the prototype. Building on the model of the China Foundation, BFS decided that every participating country had to sign a formal agreement with the U.S. to establish a foundation or commission—the word depended on local laws and language. Members of the commissions were to be comparable in rank to the prestigious BFS members. Henry Kellermann, participant-historian of the early German cultural program, said it simply: the commissions were intended to "facilitate the translation of American interests and their passage into the national 'language'"; and in the U.S., they served to "interpret to Americans . . . the needs, interests, and opportunities characteristic of their countries, . . . each with its own culture, educational system, and economic and social preoccupations."[16]

The size and balance of overseas commissions were initially problematic. The China Foundation had twice as many Chinese citizens as Americans—ten to five. For the new commission in China, BFS called instead for a majority of two Americans, reasoning that funding would come uniquely from the U.S. and that financial control in China might be a problem—BFS was keeping a wary eye on Congress and wanted a model in which Americans could control tax-dollar contributions. The shift from Chinese to US control delayed the Chinese Fulbright Agreement by a year, to Wilma Fairbank's disappointment. In Europe the ever-alert French were quick to point out that the idea of a US majority contradicted the idea of binationalism. Wise friends like Henri Bonnet convinced the embassy that a fifty-fifty arrangement would better reflect US traditions—

while soothing the left's concerns about cultural imperialism. BFS saw Bonnet's wisdom and adopted a new worldwide policy for balanced membership. A single hedge was put in place: all agreements named the US ambassador as Honorary Chairman, entitled to vote in the event of a tie. In one sense, it was a purely ceremonial gesture, rarely invoked—I know of only one occasion on which the ambassador intervened to try to remove a US board member for reasons peculiar to the politics of the moment and that effort failed. The honorary chairmanship was a cautious step back from pure binationalism, justified by fear of a skittish Congress.

In fact, two less de facto obvious hedges were also in place in the start-up decade: both chair and executive director of the early commissions were to be Americans, both reputable US academic figures. Even so, the US chairman of the binational commission was not all-powerful, by any means; on the foreign side of the commission, the chair faced high-level colleagues—university rectors and deans, top foreign ministry and education officials. A CAO of Morey's caliber reassured both the US universities and the foreign side of the board.

The executive directors of commissions were also Americans. After asking Cipriana Scelba to set up the commission, Morey hired a US academic as director, Richard Downar, later director of the commission in Cairo and later still a mainstay of the ACLS. Still, a strong American executive of the commission would not tell a commission what to do, any more than a US CAO could. The two Americans could only sway its decisions, assuming they agreed, by being better informed and more involved. Over time wise chairmen tended, when resistance arose, to defer, to anticipate problems, and generally to move the program gently forward in noncontroversial directions. Men like Morey, as early CAOs, established a tradition of civility and respect. In this way, the commissions carried on business in a spirit of cooperation, trust, and good humor. Indeed the American chair and executive were often more imbued with honest binational spirit than some of the foreign commissioners, for whom binationalism was a bizarre idea.

With time, each commission took on its own life, depending on the country, the nature of US relations, the people named to the board, the staff, the CAOs, the executive directors, the history and size of the program, and the university culture with which the commission worked. The first executive directors were young American academics like Rome's Downar, Brussels's Gene Horsfall, or London's Alan Pifer, later head of Carnegie. At first most CAOs were US academics; even after 1955, when academic CAOs began to give way to USIA generalists, academically qualified USIA officers like Canter and Harkness replaced them.

As the first decade passed, binationalism moved forward. First, at the end of the 1950s, US commission executives began giving way to foreign directors. After 1961 foreign nations began contributing to commission budgets, in some cases more than half—foreign government funding accounts today for about 30 percent of Fulbright costs. After unmeasurable in-kind contributions from abroad in staffing panels and in recruitment, foreign cash contributions were a significant step, deepening binationalism. With joint financing, chairmanships in many countries began to rotate between the U.S. and the host nation. Binationalism was both a passionate concern and a growing source of revenue for the American cultural diplomats, until at least 1980.

History offers no precedent for systematic and voluntary contributions from receiving countries to a foreign cultural program; in this sense the Fulbright Program is a unique historical achievement, making binationalism into a cogent and bountiful reality. But binationalism had its enemies. For one thing, it lessened US control and was viewed as a mixed blessing by USIA's unidirectional informationists. A second irritant to the unidirectionalists was growing: cooperation between commissions. In close-knit regions like industrialized Europe, independent American and foreign commission directors began meeting annually to discuss problems and plan joint activities, without the PAOs.

Fulbright's relationship to foreign policy continued to preoccupy BFS; the boundaries between commission and embassy demanded vigilant patroling. Extended field visits by BFS members helped monitor the process. Pressures were managed, barriers strengthened, and boundaries kept clear. But with the steady decline in the academic credentials of the CAOs and with shrinking BFS travel budgets, the lines began to blur. By the time Fulbright left the Senate in 1975, turnover in commission directors, often under pressure from USIS, was rising. Strong academic CAOS in the commission chairs had defended Fulbright's independence—in US interest, as they saw it. When USIS generalists took over the jobs, commission independence was challenged.

BFS insisted that Fulbright country programs flow from treaty-like binational agreements. The CAOs negotiated and renegotiated these arrangements, often in nations whose laws and lack of experience with the US idea of philanthropy complicated things. Still, by 1950, following China (which closed in two years) and Burma, agreements had been signed with fifteen industrialized and developing nations with military surpluses: Australia, Belgium-Luxembourg, Egypt, France, Greece, Iran, Italy, the Netherlands, New Zealand, Norway, the Philippines, and Turkey. Coming aboard in the 1950s were Austria, Ceylon–Sri Lanka, Denmark, Finland, India, Iraq, Korea, Pakistan, South Africa, Thailand, and Sweden. In Germany and Japan, reorientation exchange programs converted to the Fulbright mode as soon as feasible.

In Latin America, cultural diplomacy began without military surpluses; the full power of Fulbright's idea only blossomed after Smith-Mundt provided dollars and especially when funds from sales of surplus agricultural commodities were made available in the later 1950s under PL 480. Latin America took off with Argentina, Brazil, Chile, Colombia,

Ecuador, Paraguay, Peru, and Uruguay. The boom in new Fulbright agreements would peak in 1963, then slam to a halt for seventeen years.

The problems of the Fulbright Program can be traced in the contrast between Fulbright and Smith-Mundt legislation, designed to be complementary yet vastly different. First, the two pieces of legislation approached advisory bodies in opposite ways. With the nonpartisan BFS already in place, Smith-Mundt added a second commission to oversee cultural affairs—and another for information. The new cultural commmission, successor to Cherrington's GAC—which had preceded BFS by nine years—was instructed to avoid crossing the BFS path. With the newer body looking at cultural diplomacy in general while leaving academic exchanges to BFS, the tiny cultural division had to handle *two* advisory commissions from 1948 until 1977.

In September 1948 the new Advisory Commission on Educational Exchange held its first meeting, superseding the flexible, informal, and unlegislated GAC. Its five appointed members were even more distinguished than the BFS members. In the chair was Vanderbilt University president Harvie Branscomb; then came Princeton president Harold Dodds, MIT president Karl Compton, the Director of Education for the Garment Workers' Union, and Dean Martin McGuire of the Catholic University Graduate School—a deliberate link to BFS. At the first meeting, Branscomb knew the moment was weighty; he drew from the cultural side of Smith-Mundt's schizophrenic language, noting the US "stake in the preservation of a world order in which countries can live at peace." In the style of Stephen Duggan, he continued: "Educational and cultural exchange—not cultural penetration—rests then on a simple and familiar principle. Neighbors who are to cooperate need to become acquainted. In the modern world all nations are neighbors. . . . Exchange is the natural expression of the democratic principles on which and for which we stand."

Second, Fulbright and Smith-Mundt, signed a year apart, differed deeply on partisanship. While BFS was totally nonpartisan, the five-member Smith-Mundt commission was to be appointed by party affiliation—with no more than three members from either party. The chair was to be appointed by the president, not elected by the commission; and in this capacity the president by definition was acting not as head of state but as head of his party.

A third difference lay in the legislation's attitude toward security and loyalty. Fulbright legislation said nothing about loyalty or FBI name checks, as the university world expected. In contrast, Smith-Mundt's Title X calls for FBI investigation of all US participants and surveillance of any "doubtful" foreign grantees once in the U.S. The BFS, designed to be a shield against US political interference, had no choice but to grapple with loyalty questions at home and abroad—Smith-Mundt forced the issue.

These major differences flowed from the rapid shift in congressional climate in the 1940s. Senator Fulbright, relying on bipartisan support, could create a nonpartisan program; a single mind had drafted the law and carried it through, with little discussion and with a great deal of friendly support from both sides of the aisle. His language reflected straightforward cultural internationalism, even if the act could only be funded because he avoided debate and convinced key congressmen that it would cost nothing. Fulbright's act was as close to a genuinely nonpartisan bill as could emerge from the Congress of those years. Smith-Mundt, on the other hand, anticipated and literally invited the hammer-and-tongs trade-offs of US political process. The legislation passed during a witch-hunting climate, in which innocent words and behavior turned sinister; the moment called forth self-protective proclamations of patriotism. The horse-trading of US consensus democracy, suspended for a brief moment by Roosevelt's leadership, by the depression, by the war, by brilliant New Deal outside appointments, and by Fulbright's guile, was back in town. With zealots like McCarthy making sure that every word a man ever uttered could haunt him, even the brave held their tongues, took shelter behind foggy verbiage, and practiced spin-control.

The Congress of 1946–47 had accepted—surely with little understanding—Fulbright's Rhodes-inspired idea of honest academic exchanges generating two-way understanding. But a year later Smith-Mundt politicized the advisory commission and subjected all grantees to FBI scrutiny.

BFS turned to academic loyalty. The State Department was reluctantly compelled to require security clearance for all US Fulbright participants. The FBI and State worked out a time-consuming procedure: the FBI declared a given candidate "appropriate" and shared the files of those it deemed "inappropriate"; State then acted, in conjunction with BFS, with wide latitude for wisdom. By September 1949 BFS boldly insisted that selections were *its* responsibility, but there was a snag in their assertion: BFS members were not legally authorized to review FBI files. Ingeniously, because State needed it, BFS members were sworn in as formal consultants to State and were thus given FBI access, allowing BFS to begin its struggle with the cumbersome problem.[17] In the Senate, Fulbright defended BFS; McCarthy in 1953 spent an hour in a hearing badgering his Senate colleague about whether he *personally* had carried out name checks for Americans. Fulbright won the exchange by a cool display of dignity and unspoken disdain; McCarthy never again crossed his path.

BFS files contain few records of security practices, for obvious reasons. The memories of veterans indicate that the screening process, in fact, turned up very little: FBI files were random and unconvincing, and few names were rejected. But there were occasional problems, note Johnson and Colligan. One veteran remembered the case of poet Sylvia Plath, questioned because she had been in a mental institution—BFS ruled her suitable. In another case, the BFS agreed it would be unwise to send a serious alcoholic abroad. The memories of division old-timers are merciful; most remember few "unsuitables" or politically motivated turndowns.

Questions of loyalty arose with more bite when it came to division staff. Omelette chef Benton had used loyalty and "the good of the service" as a criterion for winnowing out thousands of OWI employees. A division veteran recalled two cases, outstanding colleagues accused of disloyalty: one could afford a lawyer, easily won her case, and remained on staff; the other could not afford counsel and, with a trade-unionist brother, thought it wiser to resign.[18]

For foreign applicants, US security checks, against all odds, were handled with wisdom. The problem was delicate—Rockefeller and the FBI had run roughshod over seventeen hundred alleged Nazis in Latin America. Since foreign grantees needed visas, the decision lay with the embassy. But embassies, notwithstanding foreign paranoia, kept scant files on foreign populations; they relied on the host-country police for both data and evaluations. In friendly countries, with civilized police forces, this was handled in as reasonable a way as the questionable idea permitted; but in controled societies like the USSR, where the police were part of the problem, the embassies had to make decisions in the dark. In both cases, the embarrassing process was concealed from foreign grantees. For the most part, criteria were broad and permissive—an embassy refusal to issue a visa, after all, could raise prickly diplomatic problems, as it did in the case of Chilean poet and Nobel laureate Pablo Neruda or Italian socialist politician Pietro Nenni. With the transparent Fulbright Program, the problem raised more risks: all selections were carried out in the open, so that by the time a visa was requested, dozens of selection-committee members knew the ranking of candidates. Decent Americans acting with wisdom did their best to keep the process humane.

Other policy questions concerned BFS. One was solved on the spot: when BFS learned that USIA had asked all American Fulbrighters to write weekly reports on the political climate of their areas, it quashed the order. Other problems were solved by individual wisdom: Fulbrighter Robin Winks reported his rebuff in the 1950s to a USIS CAO in Malaysia who asked to review his lecture notes for a course on British imperialism—with assigned readings from Karl Marx. Informed of Winks's refusal, the ambassador indignantly came down not on Winks but on the CAO; over a gracious dinner he apologized to Winks for the clumsiness. Similarly, senior Fulbright scholar in American studies Richard Pells in 1983 felt himself unable—for reasons of common courtesy—to decline the inappropriate request by John Loeb, politically appointed ambassador to Denmark, to visit his class at Copenhagen University; Loeb attended and no harm was done, other than the casual breech of sacred academic and Fulbright protocol.[19]

BFS faced a nagging question, largely imaginary, about government efforts to recruit talented grantees. US students or senior scholars returning from sensitive areas of the world were occasionally invited by government officials to "debrief"; there was no requirement to comply, but those who did might on occasion have been offered employment, some of it covert. In the land of free choice, it is difficult to rule out recruitment and the BFS wisely did not try to interfere. Those in the universities however who asserted that grant selection was governed by potential future employment, for Americans or foreigners, have yet to prove their case.

Illustrating the range of BFS policy making is the episode of Morey's imaginative proposal of an American Council in Rome, an early "open university," staffed by a continuing flow of Fulbright lecturers. BFS framed the question in global terms—not as a limited Italian project, but as an idea which might be replicated elsewhere. Could BFS "recognize" the "university" in Italy as a legitimate institution of higher learning, worthy of welcoming students and scholars like any reputable Italian university, without granting the same privilege to USIS in other countries? BFS members, and other close observers like Morey's friends Harold Dodds and Senator Smith, trusted Morey and his idea. But there was no guarantee Morey would be there to oversee it. Could BFS allow other posts to create mini-universities wherever they liked, under whatever CAO? The BFS thus declined the idea; Morey's dream for Italy was diluted into a program for American studies with a center in Rome and another in Bologna, which would be taken over in 1956 by Johns Hopkins University president Milton Eisenhower to found a branch of its School of Advanced International Studies. Might the BFS have acted differently if convinced that the unassailable academic quality of CAOs worldwide would remain a strong line of defense against embassy pressures over time? In fact, among the defenses of Fulbright integrity, the weakest was the declining quality of cultural staff in the field.

By 1949 the hopes engendered by Cherrington and MacLeish for a single cultural diplomatic program to help the U.S. relate to the world had faded; two large pieces of the whole had already been sliced off by other agencies and more lay ahead. International politics had spawned a new wartime mentality, and nationalism was on the march. With undeclared war dominating the American agenda, men like Fulbright, who had long reached for peaceful alternatives, slipped into the background. In Congress he had brought resilience, power, and academic integrity to cultural diplomacy through a unique American program of worldwide exchanges couched in binational terms; but the country's elected representatives had other preoccupations. The presidentially appointed BFS had smoothed Fulbright's pathway into the twenty-first century and put concentric defensive walls in place. But events in Washington were moving steadily in other directions. The stage was being set for the rebirth of psy-war and propaganda in the soon-to-be-born US Information Agency.

CHAPTER ELEVEN

Reorienting Enemies,
Campaigning for Truth

[German reorientation] brought . . . a growing recognition that people could be changed only with their consent, that democratic attitudes could be inculcated only by democratic methods: advice and persuasion, encouragement of indigenous effort rather than reform by fiat, collaboration rather than imposition.

—Walter H. C. Laves, 1963

USIA WOULD BE CREATED in a spirit of nationalist renewal, as a separate agency for nonmilitary psychological warfare. That it included both cultural diplomacy and informational elements, the children of both Welles's division and OWI, flowed from Smith-Mundt. More important, a victory for John Foster Dulles, it was a permanent defeat for the culturalists. In cultural diplomatic thought, ever since the Smith-Mundt debates, confusion and contradiction had been on the loose. After 1953 an independent cultural diplomacy was a dying idea in government.

While Washington adjusted to a nationalist lurch, the rest of the nation was busily redoubling internationalist commitments.[1] By 1950 a new second-generation wave of internationalization was beginning to wash across US campuses, changing higher education forever. In general, US educational participation rates were rising impressively. By 1945 a greater percentage of Americans were completing high school than in any other country in history, even if European educators—misled by US education's focus on shaping citizens rather than producing elites—saw the U.S. lowering academic standards. More Americans were going on to college, then to graduate school, than ever before; US post-secondary enrollment already led the world. And the new US university students were greatly curious about other cultures.

War had sharpened demand for an internationalized curriculum; the way had been carefully paved by the giants of the 1920s and 1930s—Butler, Gildersleeve, the senior Duggan, Shotwell, Cherrington, Merriam, and dozens of others. Where the U.S. had once drawn its intellectual substance from Europe, now Europe began to suspect it might need American educational connections. Foreign students on US campuses were no longer an exception, and US student travel for overseas study was becoming commonplace.[2] Breaking away from European traditions, the classic disciplinary frameworks were expanding, softening, combining, and developing new social sciences like sociology and anthropology, subsets like economic or social history, special education for business and for social work, and the various hyphenated hybrids of science. In the social sciences multidisciplinary approaches were assumed by Americans; these were especially important in the proliferation of regional and area studies, often sheltered in schools of public administration, whereas earlier area scholars had come from historical linguistics and classical literature. A new field called International Relations, long the subject of experiment in the U.S. and England, was taking hold. The graduate curriculum still aimed at the few, as did its internationalist programs. Georgetown's School of Foreign Service and Syracuse's Maxwell School were designed to prepare a few students for government and foreign service. In all, the postwar universities were challenging US provincialism, expanding the range and reach of international studies, bringing more foreign students to campuses, and sending more Americans abroad.

Three crucial government actions had accelerated and nurtured this change: the Army's Special Training Program (ASTP) and the GI Bill were unintended internationalizers and brought new social classes to the universities; Fulbright's exchanges, on the other hand, deliberately aimed to internationalize, under the banner of "mutual understanding." The flagship Fulbright Program, designed precisely to "educate these goddam ignorant Americans," aimed at generating understanding on both sides of the oceans. The Arkansan Rhodes alumnus helped democratize access, globalize outreach, widen disciplinary focus, and boost foreign language study. With the supervisory BFS, he made certain that his exchange program reached all segments of society and touched all elements of learning.

In science little help was needed. International scientific development was all but self-sustaining, thanks to earlier investments by Carnegie and Rockefeller and a century of European study by Americans. Four decades of foundation investment had put the U.S. at the center of world research, with some help from Europe's totalitarians, who unwittingly catapulted their finest scholars into America's universities. Americans had believed since Franklin that science and the search for free inquiry lifted all boats. Postwar America changed from a net importer to a heavy exporter of new scientific knowledge, thanks to intellectual refugees and heavy private-public funding. The lament of the Brain Drain was new; it would wax and wane over the next fifty years, be exploited by foreign politicians, and finally fade away as it became obvious that, over time, the best brains went where they were best used, with enough returning home in the longer run to meet local needs. At the end of the century Americans still produced twice the rest of the world's total output of published scientific papers, even if their predominance was shrinking.

A few foreign nations, realizing that their universities had fallen behind, unapologetically used US exchanges for systematic regeneration, as the U.S. had done with Europe after the Civil War. Postwar Norway, for example, upgraded its universities by the planned use of US exchanges—sending its best students and scientists for long and short periods and importing key American academics when useful. But overall foreign student flows to the U.S. responded less to national planning than to market flows.

Students began pouring into the great US research universities after 1945 so that by the turn of the millennium well over half a million were in place. The US post-secondary foreign-student population, the world's highest, earned for the U.S. In 2002 the annual invisible export advantage was estimated at $12–13 billion, beyond its unmeasurable contribution to US foreign relations.

All this could not have happened so swiftly if the private-sector decisions of 1919 and the US government decisions of 1938–46 had not prepared the ground for augmented flows of students; it was done largely by exhortation but also by support to professional foreign student advisors through the universities and voluntary associations, study abroad, the pump-priming Fulbright Program, overseas English teaching, USIS libraries, and student counseling in the embassies. Welles's guess that State would do no more than 5 percent of the work turned out, in the case of foreign students, to be not far off the mark. Direct funding of foreign students, Fulbright's pump-priming function, would gradually drop below 1 percent of the total. In education, America in 1919 had accepted the challenge of world leadership, and the private world responded more broadly than Stephen Duggan could have imagined. As for Congress, it seemed ready—in its tight-fisted style—to help train the human components of internationalization; it seemed easier once constituents were convinced of the Soviet threat.

Despite the focused private and public internationalist proliferation, the disarray in Washington had splintered the idea of a single coherent US government educational and cultural foreign policy. No one had ever been totally in charge, even Roosevelt and his surrogate Welles in wartime; but by 1950 there was a great deal more going on. Some on the private side reveled in the absence of leadership, fearing government control more than waste, duplication, or over-investment. On the eve of the creation of USIA in 1953, national responsibility for the government's educational outreach abroad was scattered in five active government agencies and a dozen other Washington bodies, none of which spoke in any depth to the others. USIA would boast that it "supported foreign policy"; State's cultural programs said so as well, though less loudly; the military and its massive International Military Education and Training (IMET) preferred not to mention it; CIA concealed it; AID called it training; and the USOE said it was strengthening US education, while admitting in private that it was difficult to wash only one hand. In the field, energetic embassy cultural offices monitored activity and nudged diplomatic colleagues into cooperation. But after 1948 and in the field after 1956, with no more Moreys in sight, the State Department and its CAOs slowly lost coordinative oversight.

The first major postwar miracle, as the Germans call it, was underway by 1950[3] as Germany and Japan, two enemy nations, were "reoriented." So were less clearcut countries like Austria, Italy, and Korea. The Allies had faced the common dilemma of any victor: what to do with the vanquished. The US response was unprecedented in world history: not only to rebuild infrastructure but to recast a foreign political culture. Few noted that remaking two giant enemy nations was a triumph of cultural diplomacy.

It began with MacLeish, asked to chair a State-War-Navy Coordinating Committee (SWNCC) on postwar Germany in May 1945. His memo 269/5, reaffirmed and expanded a year later, put education first. MacLeish's task force delegated to the American Council on Education the task of designing international educational reconstruction. ACE formed its Committee on the Occupied Areas (COA), to link government, military, and the world of education for the purpose of handling German and Japanese reorientation; under ACE supervision, crash programs were launched for both countries.

No one, except elements of the military, seriously questioned the premises of the MacLeish memo and its core idea that education was the primary vehicle. The inventive reorienters merged the values and the methods of the American universities with the Latin American practices put in place by Rockefeller. The historical practices of empires were eschewed as precisely the wrong approach—instead, the Allies set out to avoid both imperial errors and the mistakes of Versailles. Comparative evaluations of the American approach, as opposed to the British, French—and Soviet—practices, have yet to appear.

The main lines of the story are laid out in the indispensable work of participant-chronicler Henry Kellermann. His history of the early US cultural program with West Germany shows how the U.S., outspending the elite-focused British and French, earned the cooperation of the vanquished by rolling out the full range of available cultural and educational resources.[4] In Germany, the funding was virtually limitless and the body of "students" was willing—Germany and Japan were both eager to rejoin the civilized world. To the field went dozens of talented Americans, well intentioned but totally inexperienced—in fairness, no experience could have prepared people for this work.

The process moved past the anger of its early military phase—"non-fraternization" and "de-nazification" were the understandable keynotes in the early days. A second cooperative phase followed quickly, its farsighted educational vision articulated by MacLeish, implemented by Gen. Lucius Clay, and led by Indiana University president Herman B Wells. Wise planning, with abundant funding, minimized inevitable mistakes. German readiness to change made the work easier and so did the nation's technical sophistication, built-in discipline, and extensive support funding. In the Soviet zone, by contrast, a new totalitarian system was being imposed on the base of the old.

Aspects of US wartime behavior had already impressed the European "enemies": the prisoner-of-war camps; the rescue and restitution of looted art-objects; the voluntary relief programs; and the military's extensive radio network. The POW camps are a forgotten chapter for Americans, but in Germany and Italy one still finds major figures who first encountered the U.S. as wartime prisoners.[5] Except for hard-core Nazis who tyrannized fellow inmates, German POWs found the US military permissive, education-minded, and "democratic"; they were given learning opportunities and allowed free interchange with their captors, as well as with surrounding communities.

Italianist political historian Norman Kogan recalled duty in a camp in New Jersey, where Italian prisoners volunteered to run the kitchens and raised everyone's morale. In return, they were permitted to utilize neighboring educational facilities. Kogan shepherded small groups of Italians to nearby Italo-American communities and homes. In rural Oklahoma, political scientist Inis Claude recalled the camp's system of technical education—e.g., a former butcher retrained in paramedical surgical and laboratory skills. In Claude's camp, security was relaxed. Assigned to night guard duty, he recalled being issued a useless pistol, which he hid in a ditch until morning. When two prisoners later escaped, the camp commander reacted calmly: "Let them run, there's no place for them to go—they'll be back for dinner," as indeed they were. The citizen military understood that democracy is best learned by living among democrats; the POW camps, within obvious constraints, showed how democracy worked. To the East, less fortunate Europeans never forgot their contrasting treatment by the Soviets.

A second reminder of US generosity toward the vanquished—and the heritage of humankind—was the farseeing US handling of art treasures. Key participant Craig Hugh Smyth has told this story of high professionalism and altruism, reflecting university-government cooperation at its best.[6] The question was forcefully raised in Washington in 1942 by the Fogg Museum's George Stout, who remembered Harvard's Arthur Kingsley Porter, the only foreigner appointed in 1915 to the French commission assessing damage to art and architecture behind German lines. By January 1943 ACLS went into action, convening a committee headed by Columbia's William Dinsmoor, president of the Archeological Institute, with Francis Henry Taylor of New York's Metropolitan Museum, David Finley of the National Gallery, Paul Sachs of Harvard, and Rufus Morey, soon to be CAO Rome. In response, FDR created the American Commission for the Protection and Salvage of Artistic and Historic Monuments in War Areas, with Supreme Court Justice Owen Roberts as its sponsor. With Dinsmoor as chair, the commission added Librarian of Congress

MacLeish and ex–New York governor Herbert Lehmann, Director of Foreign Relief and Rehabilitation.

The military established its Monuments, Fine Arts, and Archives Service (MFA&A) to limit war damage and to return looted objects. The Canadians and British quickly followed suit. The USSR abstained. MFA&A officers joined the Italian campaign in 1943 and were successful in minimizing damage to Italy's artistic heritage. MFA&A was in place for D-Day; and when the fighting ceased, the enormous task of recuperating, transporting, sorting, storing, cleaning, and protecting thousands of the world's greatest art treasures began.

Then came restitution. In 1945, on MFA&A advice, Truman ordered unilateral restitution in the US zone; the French and British quickly followed suit. The Soviets continued to resist, having already expropriated the Schliemann treasures of Troy for Moscow. Cluttered with legal problems but facilitated by the military's capacity to protect and transport the objects, the process began in August with the return to Ghent of its famous altar piece. By now Stout had moved on to Japan where, with Langdon Warner, he would set the same process in motion.

A third factor impressed postwar Germany: the flood of generous American relief workers, another facet of America at its best.[7] Relief groups like the Quakers could be found all over Germany, for example, operating youth canteens to help feed the starving nation, again with military help. Parallel insights into US life came from the American military style—happy-go-lucky GIs, contrasting with the grim conquerors of the past and the ruthless pillage of the Soviets. The smiling Americans and their gifts projected the face of democracy and its unimaginable prosperity.

A fourth element was the Armed Forces Radio Service (AFRS), which later added television services. Designed primarily for the welfare of US troops, its broadcasts were easily picked up in host countries. For every American listener to AFRS, there were an estimated twenty foreigners. By the mid-1960s AFRS had two hundred radio and thirty-eight TV transmitters around the world, far exceeding the reach of VOA—with no coordination between the two. The fare was standard US media programming, without commercials. What these broadcasts said to foreigners and what they did for the image of American culture, for better and for worse, remains to be explored. Certainly they cast an informative light on how American democracy functioned.

Even with these preconditioning factors and the clear guidelines of SWNCC 269/5, it took time to move from reeducation to enlightened reorientation. In Japan General MacArthur's terse instructions caught the flavor of the first phase of both occupations: "First, destroy the military power. Punish war criminals. Build the structure of representative government. Modernize the constitution. Hold free elections. Enfranchise the women. Free the political prisoners. Liberate the farmers. Encourage a free economy. Abolish police oppression. Develop a free and responsible press. Liberalize education. Decentralize political power. Separate church from state." It was a victor's agenda, expressed in the simple language of the soldier—a list of imperative verbs plus object.

The first GIs in Japan and Germany, especially those who had seen the death camps, had reason to go about their business grimly; Nuremberg justice and "anti-fraternization" were harsh. But Lucius Clay, listening carefully to Wells and his educational advisors, remembered growing up in Georgia and learning that democracy could not be imposed. That simple truth led back through MacLeish, Cherrington, and the division's values to the missionary-educators: it dictated a binational work style and respect for partners; it provoked cooperation, it taught by example; it relied on the private world; and it strengthened existing institutions— universities, schools, and civic administrative structures.[8]

While the Allied military was struggling to provide food, fuel, and medical supplies to a starving and shattered Europe, Clay moved smoothly from reeducation to reorientation. In August 1946 an eleven-person ACE mission spent a month in Germany. Aware of heavily authoritarian German traditions of education, the committee recommended large-scale two-way exchanges. The military's Education and Religious Affairs Branch—a revealing name—doubled in size, if not in budget. Sensitive to haste and oversaturation, the committee urged expanded private efforts. Germany hungrily absorbed US energies. At its first meeting in 1948, the cultural division's new Smith-Mundt-created Advisory Commission assigned Germany first priority.

Military government (OMGUS) faced giant problems, like the killing winter of 1946–47. Clay also worried about the reaction in the U.S. to exchange visitors from Germany after the brutish war. To rebuild a functioning Germany, Clay's instincts placed economics and politics before education, but the ACE team soon softened his view and a compromise was forged. Clay and Wells saw each other as kindred leaders; Kellermann concluded that in Germany education on the US agenda ranked with and was "pre-requisite to political and economic rehabilitation."[9]

Wells began as Educational and Cultural Advisor in November 1947. When Clay received a group of professors from Humboldt University in the Soviet sector, Wells convinced him, without Washington approval, to turn over military space and counterpart funds to create the Free University of Berlin. Clay, he said, "brushed aside all doubts, said it could be done, and asked me to put the machinery in motion."[10]

Early budgets were not generous. Clay, a master at dealing with Congress from his days as head of the Corps of Engineers, awaited the right moment to approach the legislators for funding. Meanwhile Wells was earning the respect of traditionalist Germans; he found a ready student as well in Clay: "The education program was raised from branch to division level. Its scope was enlarged to include the fields of community activities, women's activities, youth, health and welfare," notes Kellermann.[11] With Wells by his side, the farsighted Clay was ready to tackle Congress.

Germany had been deprived of contact with the liberal democracies for years, so Wells made reciprocity a keystone of all exchanges, first sending Germans to the U.S. then bringing Americans to Germany. From 1947 to 1948, exchanges quadrupled to 354, including 214 German students, then soared from there. In the U.S. ACE and IIE set to work, guided by State's cultural division. Clay's fears that German visitors would be received badly in the U.S. proved groundless.

The exchange program was massive, bigger in Germany alone than the total of all other US cultural programs worldwide. In its first phase Clay and Wells surrounded themselves with superb people like James Pollock, president of the American Political Science Association; Joseph Dodge, New York banker; William Draper, of Dillon, Read; Edward Litchfield, later president of the University of Pittsburgh; and Carl Friedrich, Harvard political scientist.

The Americans had modest goals; no one expected permanent change to come overnight, even if the preconditions in Germany were uniquely favorable. Genuine learning is not instruction, it is a long-range two-way process, requiring continuity over decades. Democratic theory can be explained in a single lecture, but the practice of democracy—especially when grafted onto nondemocratic political cultures—takes longer. Clay and his military administrators understood that the *process* of education was as important as the product. Years later Walter Laves wondered how much measurable success was achieved in teaching democracy in Germany; but he rested his defense on the certainty that "something was done in democratizing *teaching*."[12] Clay was wise enough to know that democracy could not simply be pumped into a country like oil; some American advisors went further, confessing that they themselves were not entirely certain how US democracy actually worked, beyond the reductionist formulae of the high-school textbooks. German audiences were struck by the openness of the discussion.

Clay saw the need for a new German cultural identity, and he understood the value of symbols in cultural communication. His handling of German's art treasures shows him at his best. Pledging his personal responsibility, Clay had rescued the Kaiser Friedrich collection from its salt mines; but the collection's home had passed to the Soviet sector. Fearing Soviet confiscation, he decided to send the paintings to the U.S. In two years at the National Gallery, the paintings underwent serious curatorial work. Then Clay learned that there were moves afoot in Congress, apparently fomented by gallery director David Finley and naively sponsored by a new Senator named Fulbright, to expropriate the paintings as German reparations—precisely what Clay had feared from the Soviets. A flight to Washington permitted conferences with leaders of Congress and others. A stern memo of 4 April 1948 argued the case: the paintings were German property, the U.S. had established "sufficient museum capacity" in Wiesbaden and Munich to receive them, their return had been pledged by OMGUS and Clay himself, and a triumphal return had already been announced; on the other hand, expropriation would be a monstrous blow to German faith in America. Clay noted dramatically, "The effect of such action on American reputation and prestige would be devastating indeed and would place us in the same position as the Red Army and other vandal hordes who have overrun Europe throughout the centuries."

Clay's intervention won the day. The paintings were displayed to the public at the National Gallery in September 1948 in the first US block-buster show ever, then moved on to tour thirteen US cities, raising $2 million for German children's relief. At their spectacular homecoming in Munich, it was obvious to all that the paintings were in far better shape than before the war. In 1950 the paintings returned to Berlin, as the core of the Prussian State Collection. Clay knew what he had done. His biographer believes the episode "marked the beginning of a new era in German-American relations." In Clay's words, "perhaps never in the history of the world has a conquering army sought so little for its own and worked so faithfully to preserve the treasures of others."[13]

The cultural and educational program in that small quarter of Germany occupied by Americans exploited and expanded Rockefeller's work in Latin America. The educational idea was broadly defined to include both short-term and long-term experiences. Two-month leader-grantees came from education, religion, and information activities—press, radio, and films—from civic, welfare, and youth organizations, and from professional associations. They included key figures and persons of promise early in their careers. Budgets went far beyond Rockefeller's, as befitted the awe-inspiring goal authorized by the circumstances—nothing less than transforming the mind and political culture of Germany. Over two thousand German visitors traveled to the U.S. in both 1952 and in 1953, more than State's total cultural intake at that time and more than would come from the entire world in 1980.

There was predictable traditionalist German resistance. Reform of education, or education for citizenship, was not popular among German educators; they complained about the low caliber of the American advisors. Such disparities were the price of the American redefinition of intellect and scholarship that had begun with the land-grant universities, like Wells's own Indiana. The design aimed well beyond elites; it was a general approach to the entire country, at all social levels, in all sectors of knowledge. By contrast, France and Britain adopted a more elite-focused—and less costly—approach, noted Kellermann; they cultivated "the more sophisticated elements in German society and . . . flattered them by sending outstanding members of their own intellectual elite to Germany." The Americans instead "exhibited for a while a curious indifference towards catering to the taste of the intelligentsia."[14] In fact, it was neither in the nature of the US military, Congress, or the Missouri-born president of the U.S., nor probably of the American republic, to promote the guided change of Germany through its traditional elites, especially when the very concept of "elites" had been tainted by Nazi ideology. Americans like Wells, from the Midwest's Land-Grant institutions, were committed to representative democracy, which for them began with democratic education. For the American reorienters, elites were not born but created, through meritorious performance in democratic educational institutions. Traditionalist opposition faded under the American wave. Outstanding educators like Alonzo Grace, Connnecticut state commissioner, succeeded Wells and exchanges remained a policy priority. With the loosening of US military control, German participation and funding increased.

In Washington, State's cultural division was managing the programs, with funding from the War Department. Returning to Indiana, Herman Wells chaired COA; with ACE and IIE, he mobilized the universities. Prominent Americans began visiting Germany, including artists like young conductor Leonard Bernstein, harpsichordist Ralph Kirkpatrick, and writer Thornton Wilder.

In May 1949 OMGUS became HICOG—the High Commission for Occupied Germany—in a step toward German statehood. Civilian "Wise Man" John J. McCloy of Dillon, Reed succeeded Clay. Education and culture were moved into the Committee for Public Affairs, directed by New Orleans newspaper publisher Ralph Nicholson, soon replaced by Humboldt Ph.D. Shepard Stone.[15] Reorientation moved ahead; but education and culture had become part of public affairs (PA).

Wells and his successors in the U.S. pressed to maintain educational assistance and to keep the focus on democratization, arguing that the US presence must persist "for some time to come." State's cultural office agreed, noting that the U.S. "cannot afford to spend billions on economic reconstruction without a valiant effort in the field of education and cultural relations." They knew that the task was the "hardest and longest of all our responsibilities."

The German program was massive—it drew nearly half the HICOG budget. It was targetted—to individuals, groups, and institutions that might make a difference. It was stratified—reaching into every geographic and social area of Germany. It was innovative—designed to help solve specific educational and societal problems as they arose and to anticipate others. It was participatory and increasingly binational. And it was interzonal—working when appropriate with the British and the French.

On the information side journalist Stone—later of the Ford Foundation and the Aspen Institute—rebuilt and in some cases invented parts of the German media. The Public Affairs staff in 1950 comprised almost twelve hundred persons, of which 503—about 40 percent—were Americans; by 1951 it had grown by an order of seven, to over 8,500, but with only 567 Americans—down to 7 percent of the total.

In structure PA's branches imitated the USIS posts in Latin America, with a PAO in charge and two branches for information and cultural affairs. There were 181 Resident Officers scattered around the country; twenty-nine Amerika Häuser were set up in the cities, overseen by Patricia Van Delden, American-born heroine of the Dutch resistance and the first woman to exercise leadership in a major USIS post. The scale of the operation can be visualized in the example of the Frankfurt library, modeled after Mexico's Franklin. Where USIS libraries in the 1990s, if they existed at all, contained perhaps two thousand volumes, the library of the Frankfurt Amerika Haus in 1950, central repository for all of Germany, contained 45,000. The collection was open to the public from 9 A.M. to 10 P.M. seven days a week, staffed by forty-five full-time librarians. Hans Tuch, veteran of USIS Frankfort in these heroic years, remembered that it had "absolutely nothing to do with the cold war"; "we were providing education where it was needed, where it was wanted. It was the greatest job I ever had."[16]

Reorientation, in the American style, was both reciprocal and binational; the formal German Fulbright Agreement took over academic programs in 1952 and marked a vital step toward normal relations. State's cultural office similarly pressed for Fulbright agreements in Austria—where academic exchanges converted to Fulbright in 1950, five years before the peace treaty—and in Japan, where Fulbright was born in 1951. Laves reported "a progressive replacement of military by civilian administration, the enlistment of private American agencies, . . . and a growing recognition that people could be changed only with their consent, that democratic attitudes could be inculcated only by democratic methods, [by] advice and persuasion, encouragement of indigenous effort, . . . collaboration rather than imposition."[17] These attitudes would endure.

The punctilious Kellermann, our mentor for this unusual experiment in guided socio-political change via the methods of educational and cultural diplomacy, saw reorientation fitting into the division's tenets: reciprocity without coercion, relevance in educational exchanges, change coming from the Germans themselves, binational decision-making. Nothing was more political than the goals of German reorientation, but cultural relations remained focused on the long run; even its short-run programs were conceived as education, not indoctrination. US educational efforts, insulated from daily policy, helped bring Germany back into the community of nations.

German reorientation was a unique historic triumph of cultural diplomacy, but it was not described in those terms; the dogged cultural bureaucrats who did the work knew what they had done, but they got few rewards. Nor did the kind of programs they believed in flourish elsewhere as a result of success in West Germany. The managers stayed behind the scenes, fearing that publicity would nullify the effect. Certainly the American program could have been carried on at lower cost, but then perhaps less might have been achieved; there were advantages in the built-in surplus capacity. In the field, in Washington and New York, a group of public and private servants were learning how to process thousands of high-quality exchangees and administrators were learning new skills, earning the self-confidence that success can generate. In time, field staff carried their optimism and their values back to Washington, to the universities, to the foundations, and ultimately back out to other field posts.

• • •

Japan was more than a different culture, it was another world, one for which unfortunately we have no Kellermann as guide. The US occupiers followed the same line laid out by MacLeish.[18] Education was still central, but beyond that the differences at the receiving end were gigantic. Four powers ruled Germany, but the U.S. alone ruled postwar Japan. German war prisoners had been well treated, but the U.S. in the Pacific "took no prisoners." The German occupation lasted ten years; Japan's, only seven. Germany's governing bureaucracy was decimated; Japan's, relatively intact. The purging of German militarist cadres was harsh but less thorough than the cleansing in Japan. Germany's war damage was massive; in Japan, outside the special cases of Tokyo, Hiroshima, and Nagasaki, it was slight. Germany could produce its own food, given time; Japan had never been able to feed its population. Germany was industrialized; Japan semi-industrialized. Germany was a largely flat and compact country with easy intercommunication; Japan was a chain of rugged mountains and islands. German culture was essentially Christian and European, its language closely related to English; Japan's culture, religion, and language were totally alien to Americans. The German population, highly schooled in technical skills, knew English; Germany was part of Western history and had nourished the U.S. through immigration and education. Japan, in contrast, despite Morse and Fenollosa, knew no English. In its government, fifteen years of pre-Nazi Weimar and the examples of various nearby nations had given Germany a taste of democracy; but in Japan there was little beyond the memory of a few missionary-trained liberals and their students; militarism had frustrated any efforts by the Meiji dynasty to produce a more democratic society. Large-scale German immigration to the U.S. had been easily and usefully absorbed, but the fewer Japanese immigrants to the U.S. had been kept out of the American mainstream and interned in camps during the war. Many Americans knew or were able to learn German, but only the rare American knew Japanese.

Yet in both cases, the overriding US goal was the same: to safeguard against future impediments to peace. In both, the American authorities, consciously or not, assumed that this meant implanting "democracy"; for Americans the word was a synonym for stability and peace. Americans assumed that all peoples, naturally and inexorably, strive toward freedom and democracy and thus that removing the barriers that impede its growth would open democracy's doors. Three corollaries, whether true or false, were unquestioned articles of American faith: that democracy depends on a constitution; that democracy, once achieved, will persist; and that democracies do not wage war on other democracies.[19]

MacArthur wisely borrowed Clay staffers Dodge and Draper for his team. Agreeing that change had to come from the Japanese, he stressed adaptation of US practices rather than imitation. Because the cultural gap in this case was wider, MacArthur had no time to let the generations roll by. His impatience turned out to be a disguised blessing—the seven-year occupation amounted to a total coordinated push and was more cleanly ended than efforts in Germany. MacArthur had an advantage: he could be more efficient than Clay, who shared responsibility with three other nations. But he also shared the then-common American prejudice that Japan was underdeveloped and its people were "like children"; he had little insight into its centuries-old civilization.

MacArthur left the Emperor in place as his principal bargaining chip. The Americans thus could deal with an obedient and highly disciplined political culture, eager to fall into line. About constitutionalism, MacArthur had virtually religious convictions: "Modernize the constitution," he ordered.

Participant-witness to the constitutional process was Beate Sirota. She grew up in Japan, the daughter of a Kiev-born pianist who began teaching in Japan in the 1920s. She was recruited in New York and sent to Tokyo by the US Army after the war as part of its research office. On 4 February 1946 she relates, the office was informed that they had precisely eight days to draft Japan's new constitution. The Japanese draft submitted to MacArthur had fallen far short of expectations, skirting major issues like freedom, democracy, and women's rights. MacArthur wanted an acceptable draft constitution in place in time for approval by the Japanese before the elections on 10 April; he would take care of approval. Since the work had be done in total secrecy, there could be no help from Japanese lawyers or scholars. While he could impose the document, he preferred it be acceptable to Japan.

Day and night, the team, a random collection of thirty lawyers and constitutional amateurs, hammered out a text. Sirota was assigned women's affairs, the sixth of MacArthur's fourteen priorities. With no Japanese help permitted, the team bent over backward to anticipate Japanese reactions. In the group, pragmatists countered idealists. The idealists defined the "underlying spirit" of the ninety-two-article, twenty-page draft, so that, "in the end, benevolence rather than vengeance emerged as the dominant principle";[20] but the pragmatists were there to make sure it would work.

With little to go on but the outdated Meiji constitution, the debate came alive for Sirota in one exchange. One side argued that the team had to "effect a social revolution, . . . to force through a reversal of social patterns by means of the constitution." But the pragmatists carried the day: "You cannot impose a new mode of social thought on a country by law." It was MacLeish's principle revisited.

The team met its deadline, MacArthur delivered the counter-draft, and three weeks of tough negotiation with the Japanese followed. On 6 March the revised draft, with few changes, was published as the work of the Japanese government. After the April elections it was promulgated on 3 November 1946 and still stands.

In Europe similar constitutional debates, under similar conditions, were taking place. In Germany a complicated document emerged; in Italy a well-intentioned jumble came into force, hobbled by fear of a Fascist revival. In the Soviet bloc, in contrast, Moscow-dictated constitutional "parodies," as Hungary's Deputy Minister of Justice called them in 1988, were put in place.[21] For Stalin, constitutions were simply a means of consolidating Soviet power; for the Americans in Tokyo, the constitution was a way of supporting the healthy social, political, and economic growth of democracy in an alien culture.

Postwar Japanese education, for the American victors, was a major target, seen as an indispensable part of building democracy; education was to move democracy forward "by developing independent thought, respect for the individual and for the rights of others, and international friendship with tolerance for people of all races and religions," wrote Walter Laves. The occupiers helped build into Japanese practice the idea of equal educational opportunity, decentralized control through local school boards, and academic freedom—all embodied in the new constitution and in the Japanese education law of 1947. Curriculum was rewritten and access to secondary education enlarged. A decade later Laves wondered whether the changes might have been more successful had they "been linked to traditions that antedated . . . militant nationalism." He noted that "American influence on Japanese education had been strong in the 1870s and again after the first World War and in the 1930s." Laves knew how well Townsend Harris and Fenollosa and Lafcadio Hearn had done their work; with more time, under different circumstances, their legacy might have provided a basis for a new Japanese liberalism, organically related to Japan's past.[22] But few Americans could have known this, and there was no time to mull things over. Yet educational reform in Japan was a second triumph for an impatient US cultural diplomacy.

By 1949 Japan was judged ready for exchanges. From then until 1952, when a Fulbright commission took over the academic side, two thousand Japanese studied in the U.S. on funds provided by the military's Government and Relief in Occupied Areas (GARIOA); over six hundred traveled each year. Well below German levels—because it was a smaller country with inadequate English—Japanese exchanges were still massive. In 1952–53, nine hundred studied in the U.S. without US help; by 1953, fifteen hundred leaders had made the visit, while smaller numbers of Americans had gone to Japan. In the U.S. voluntary associations like the Asia and Japan Societies, with Rockefeller and other foundation backing, were helping project Japanese culture more broadly in America.

USIS Japan mushroomed during the occupation. Twenty-three USIS information centers, reflections of the German Amerika Häuser, were scattered around Japan; twenty textbook and curriculum centers were set up to support educational and curricular change; dozens of books and articles were translated, plays were produced, and American music was played. A handful of private American musicians headed by Philadelphian violinist Broadus Earle took first chairs in the Tokyo Symphony and brought that fine orchestra into being. Professor Deming's lessons on industrial management, brilliantly adapted, gradually lifted Japanese industry to world leadership. Meanwhile the Americans, with no radio station, newspapers, or magazines of their own, preferred to pass ideas on through the receptive Japanese media.

Neither the German nor Japanese cultural and educational makeover was perfect, nor did anyone expect perfection—enlightened or not, they were still military occupations. The staff consisted of well-intentioned professionals, recruited from America's citizen-military and from its private world; they worked in the dark, without precedents, language, guidelines, or specific skills. In fact, the U.S. had few Japanese or Asian area-specialists—Japanese studies in US universities lay thirty years in the future. Had the U.S. been able to enlist battalions of sensitive American Asian—or German—area scholars, things might have turned out differently, yet perhaps not better.

A second participant-witness was Carl Bartz, a young English teacher in Korea pressed into USIS press service in Tokyo in 1952.[23] At the end of his life he looked back on USIS and its cultural focus. He worked with the legendary Dr. Kenneth Bunce, USIS planning officer and scholar-teacher in the Japanese Ministry of Education during the 1930s. Bunce headed the occupation's Religious and Cultural Resources, mirroring the title of Herman Wells's German office. Another of Bartz's colleagues was Glenn Shaw, pioneer translator of Japanese literature. Patricia Van Delden, fresh from building the Amerika Häuser in Germany, was in charge of shifting Japan's new USIS libraries from US-military to Japanese standards.

Bartz began with book translations. In two years he subsidized seventy or more translations of US books, distributed a monthly Japanese review of American books, published a quarterly based on reprints from US learned journals chosen by a distinguished Japanese board, and handled purchasing for twenty USIS libraries. USIS published a business magazine in Japanese, under the editorship of future Harvard dean Henry Rosovsky and James Abegglen, expert on Japanese industry. For Bartz, USIS had a "far more cultural than informational slant simply because that was what was needed. We all understood that. We agreed that [largely anti-American] Japanese academics and intellectuals . . . could be reached over time through the printed word." Bartz, an educator like Bunce, kept educational values at the core of his work. Decent individuals like Bartz and their programs mediated between American policies and the Japanese and German publics. Below the level of policy and design, sensitive people like Bunce tempered the cold logic of the situation.

In Japan one individual who stood out in the second wave is our third witness. The late Leon Picon spent eight years in Japan in the 1950s. Picon, from a family prominent on New York's Yiddish stage, was a scholar of early Semitic and Near Eastern languages; his studies interrupted by the war, he had ended up on a team breaking Japanese shipping codes in Washington. Proficient in both classical and modern Japanese, he was assigned to USIS Tokyo in the mid-1950s, where he has been memorialized by the biographers of William Faulkner as the sly shepherd who kept the alcoholic writer out of trouble.[24]

One evening, observing a kite-flying contest outside his home, Picon was approached by a neighbor. The stranger invited him to his home to meet a few friends. Picon accepted and an extraordinary friendship began, based on biweekly meetings stretching over six years. Dozens of Japanese, to whom he was never introduced, came to the evening seminars. As the years moved on, he began to recognize the faces of prominent political figures. The purpose of the gatherings, unspoken so as to serve its end, turned out to be a continuing seminar on US political practice. The Japanese wanted to bring their questions to an ordinary Japanese-speaking American, not to a constitutional specialist or a lawyer or a philosopher, in the hope of learning how things actually worked in the U.S. They understood of course that Picon was no ordinary American—for one thing, he knew Japanese to an unusual degree—but in compensation they knew his vision was not distorted by specialized expertise and attendant arrogance; his decency and honesty were obvious to anyone who knew him. Focusing on questions like how the party system works, the six-year seminar stimulated Picon to brush up his own education. At the end of his life, he estimated that one hundred or more high-level Japanese political figures may have interrogated him in considerable depth. USIS wisely extended his tour from four to eight years.

A visiting American, who had served in naval intelligence in the Pacific during World War II, was impressed by Picon's impact on Japan and his grasp of the culture; this man was Charles Frankel, Columbia University philosopher touring the world in 1963 to gather information for his Brookings report on the US cultural attachés. Frankel later confessed that Picon, more than any other USIS officer he met, shaped his views of cultural diplomacy. Picon later served as Frankel's special assistant when he headed State's Bureau of Educational and Cultural Affairs. At the end of his life, Picon was certain he had never done anything more important than his eight years in Japan, despite a tour in Ankara that left with him a deep love for the Turkish people.

Admittedly there are few Leon Picons in our world—he was an ordinary but deeply intellectual American and that was what the Japanese saw in him. We may assume that dozens of other ordinary Americans, all in their way, whether publicly or privately, contributed both to the vigorous rebirth of Japan and more generally to the understanding of US democracy around the globe. But none was Leon Picon.

When it was all over, the heady successes in Japan and Germany, as well as the abundant occupation style, carried over into US cultural diplomacy everywhere and shaped what happened during the next half-century. USIA would owe much of its postwar field vision and many of its top-ranked officers to these two country experiences. In educating their former enemies with lavish resources, USIS officers in "public affairs" were shaping their sense of how a mix of cultural and informational diplomacy might be practiced in the years to come.

At the same time the two occupations left illusions. Veterans of Germany and Japan assumed, for example, that there had to be binational centers, exchanges, libraries, book programs, and ELT, both in the capital and in lesser cities, in every country, and this as a matter of course. Despite the heavy educational focus at the outset, both occupations placed cultural affairs under the informationist USIS. Questions of appropriateness, sustainability, comparability with other nations' diplomatic style, or cost-effectiveness were not always considered. The PAOs emerging from Germany and Japan had little patience with Welles's and Cherrington's "stimulation, facilitation, and coordination," or with limiting USIS to helping the private world. They had seen what *could* be done, given money and American flair, and they had felt the thrill of action.

The contradictions buried in these models have been noted by many but were rarely accommodated in USIA's in-house rhetoric. It was easy for a media-minded operation to think in terms of "the story": "getting out the story" fed the natural tendency to inflict the idiosyncratic US viewpoint on every foreign context. In Germany and Japan it was believed that *any* energetic educated American could do the job, as had been proved by well-intentioned Americans with modest language and an equally modest command of history and culture; it was easier for such good souls to tell a story they knew to their eager German and Japanese, in a necessarily simplified version, than to understand the deeper contexts into which their stories were flowing. A companion assumption held that America's story was all one needed to know; story-telling staffers believed the best program themes were those that flowed from US experience, with host-country interests a distant second. They repeated the US story to an endless supply of new listeners, a practice that brought early burnout in more cases than we care to remember. The story-telling style tended to underestimate the sophistication of audiences—hence patronize them, while it overestimated audience interest.

Another carryover was the compelling need to spend available money, for fear of "losing" it—i.e., seeing it returned to the US Treasury. The fear of "lost" funding could lead to spending more than was necessary. When abundant, money could become a handy substitute for forethought and substance.

In USIS field planning, there was a hidden assumption that officers' skills at politicial analysis were reliable—the Country Plan concept demanded that short-time resident Americans, with minimal language facility, could analyze a society in depth, choose the right subjects for dialogue with Americans from another planet, plan out a year's activities, and corral sufficient expertise to stay, like Jacob Canter, ahead of the less-informed. But the Germans and Japanese were not Nicaraguan students, even if the decades of forced intellectual isolation from which both societies were emerging made them initially hungry for information.

The aptitude of audiences too was misjudged. Both Germans and Japanese had the same reasons for wanting to please the Americans, while improving their English. The occupied countries were sophisticated products of centuries of civilization; they knew enough to search behind the reductionist USIS messages and slogans. Audiences elsewhere were not always so compliant or so easily beguiled.

At a deeper level an occupation-reinforced attitude came from attitudes toward change and innovation, both high American ideals. In Germany and Japan in the 1950s, where the single idea was to turn lethal political cultures into safe friendships, there was bilateral agreement on the need for sharp change. But older cultures like Italy and Austria and France felt no such need. The ahistoric Americans inclined to consider past practice the enemy; modernization was therefore the key and new was better. For every foreign individual who was impressed by this American logic, others were appalled—but too polite to say so. American activism could easily edge over into propaganda. With time, the confusion would become more obvious.

•   •   •

Back in Washington, postwar politics was beginning to encroach on foreign affairs. Stepping back a few years, new levels of tension were reached in 1949, thanks to the Czech coup, the Berlin blockade, and the search for the so-called traitors who "lost" China; the Korean War was just ahead, and the cold war had been all but declared. Truman's National Security Council, reacting to these events, called for an expanded, hard-hitting propaganda program; and soon the need for "truth" abroad would call forth its own campaign, a formal declaration of verbal cold war and a peacetime remake of CPI-OWI. It would be called the Campaign of Truth.

Greek and Turkish AID was under way, as a first act of the Truman Doctrine and the Marshall Plan, with "educational" elements, e.g., help to various American schools, including Pierce College for women in Athens, the American Farm School in Salonika, and Robert College in Istanbul. In response, Soviet propaganda and counterpropaganda were accelerating. The moment seemed to call for defensive measures.

While the BFS was forging the principles and processes of the long-range Fulbright Program and while practical educators were building a new Germany and Japan, Washington was preoccupied with other matters. The hawkish preamble to Smith-Mundt in 1948 prefigured the new undeclared war. To meet the challenge, the Creel-Rockefeller-OWI blend of "information" and "psy-war" took charge, dragging cultural relations behind it. Information was considered the only valid policy weapon for the cold war; the "realists" paid little attention to suggestions that culture be allowed to carry its own messages or that education could reshape national attitudes over time and perhaps even bring down the USSR.

Those culturalist-educators who favored a separate government agency for their work had high respect for the nationalist informationists and their skills, but they were baffled by the insistence on subordinating cultural relations to propaganda. The culturalists knew an information campaign was necessary, and they respected the fine professionals who could carry it on. The informationists, in contrast, assumed the culturalists were part of their team; they were impatient with the "culture vultures" and obdurate about keeping the two functions together, under their direction. They claimed to need the cultural programs and demanded they be part of their tool kit. As a high-level USIA officer once said, in an irritated outburst of honesty, "Face it, the cultural program has always been the cover under which the information programs have operated." Hans Tuch put it more diplomatically when he said that the task of "public diplomacy," a later euphemism for USIA's work, was to balance long-range US cultural interests against the short-range demands of foreign policy; the trick, he said, was to get the mix right. But even sophisticated officers like the German-born Tuch fretted over the slow pace of academic exchanges, the tedium involved in honest respect for binationalism and reciprocity, and the need for accountability to the US and foreign intellectual worlds.

War in Korea broke out in June 1950. That same year OWI-veteran Edward Barrett replaced George Allen as head of the twelve-year old division, and immediately launched his Campaign of Truth. Barrett was the fifth director in five years—after MacLeish, Benton, Allen, and Allen's deputy Howland Sargeant. Barrett, editor of *Newsweek*, had his plans ready with Korea at the focal point. A nationalist liberal, Barrett's memoirs of this period would bear the Creelish title *Truth is Our Weapon*, reflecting the times far more than his impressive talents—he would soon become a distinguished dean of Columbia's school of journalism.[25] But in the late 1940s, all eyes were fixed on the new cold war. Thanks to this Benton-derived campaign, Truman succeeded in pressing a hostile partisan Congress into a supplemental budget, tripling previous allocations. He also succeeded in triggering an array of belligerent Soviet reactions.

The Campaign of Truth had four goals: create a healthy international community and unite it behind US leadership; present the U.S. fairly and counter lies; stress America's peaceful intentions as well as its preparedness for war; and reduce Soviet influence. Culture or education did not appear in Barrett's program. His confrontational tactics may have impressed Congress, but they hardened the Soviet position. Over the heads of men like Fulbright, who believed the undeclared war was a step backward, the Campaign slammed doors shut. The USSR narrowed communications, stepped up jamming of VOA, closed USIS posts in Eastern Europe, and banned the magazine *Amerika*, produced for the Soviet bloc since the mid-1940s as part of an exchange of publications.

When Barrett left Washington a year later, he issued a list of claims about the impact of his trebled funding: expansion of VOA, recruitment of top media talent, opening of new USIS posts (for a total of 133), publishing in foreign languages of 2 million copies of 277 books and documents, increasing the audience for USIS films to 400 million per year, and making his voice felt at the top levels of US policy. He mentioned no increases in Fulbright, in other exchanges, or in cultural tools like libraries. No one in Congress, at least publicly, accused him of spin.

Information had boldly taken over culture's kingdom. Congress had been encouraged to expect victory in a new kind of war, measured in hours of VOA broadcasting, new USIS posts, and polled insights into the US image abroad. Stressing the short-term results that propaganda can plausibly promise but rarely prove, Barrett forged ahead. The Pentagon, also at war, proposed an even stronger information service and sought a voice in its operations, but Barrett had his own empire in mind and declined.

Inside State, where Barrett's division was still lodged, the informationists champed at the bit. To ward off internal dissension, Truman did what master politicians do: he created an interdepartmental committee, with Barrett in the chair. Then he added a higher-level group at the Undersecretary level, the Psychological Strategy Board (PSB). Barrett's group slipped under the PSB and took the name of Psychological Operations Coordinating Committee. This kept everyone busy and changed nothing.

Barrett too tinkered with structure. As frustrated as his predecessors by his consuming public relations responsibilities for State, and with less access to policymakers than he claimed, Barrett decided to merge the division's two unequal halves—culture and information—into the International Information Admininstration (IIA), directly under the Secretary. It was the same office.

When Barrett left for Columbia University, he was succeeded by the sixth director since 1945, a man of a new stripe: Wilson Compton was an academic economist and a university president; he was also a Republican, probably chosen by Truman in the hope of assuaging McCarthy. President of Washington State University, Compton was the first university president to hold the job. He was the least famous of three Compton brothers: Arthur, Benton's and Rockefeller's physicist friend at the University of Chicago, was president of Washington University in St. Louis; Karl, another physicist, headed MIT and had served on the first Smith-Mundt cultural advisory commission.

McCarthy was not interested in being assuaged. IIA was a convenient target, and with no supporting constituency it was defenseless. The un-provable assertions of the Campaign of Truth were a gift to the Wisconsinian, offering a set of bulleted criteria against which to measure the work of IIA. To defend the discreet and even invisible part of IIA's work meant articulating complex truths, but McCarthy's gift for simplistic sloganeering threw Compton off his stride and made him look evasive. McCarthy, reelected in 1952, was at the peak of his power. He chaired the Senate's Permanent Committee on Investigations of the Committee on Government Operations.

With McCarthy clearly on the warpath, it was the wrong moment for Compton to set IIA reform in motion, especially an IIA embedded in a resistant State Department, without the support of Acheson, who by now was openly professing his scorn for world opinion. Acheson cut Compton loose, and he drifted toward disaster. The instrument of his downfall was the deplorable book-selection controversy, triggered by McCarthy and his henchmen.

In the logic of McCarthy, Barrett's criteria set IIA's agenda. The all-out campaign flaunted a single goal: winning the "war" against the Soviets. With that goal in mind, McCarthy argued that libraries had to show US superiority to the USSR. How then, he asked, could IIA afford to stock books critical of the U.S.? McCarthy and his team exploited this apparent contradiction, holding up the slogans of Barrett's Campaign against the realities of the flexible, multipurpose activities of USIS posts around the world. Compton responded in-house with a sensible memo defining the library's role, but a McCarthy spy in IIA passed it to the Senate. It was all over for Compton, who was allowed to resign. The book-selection question would fester until Compton's successor called the ALA to the rescue, but McCarthy had already moved on to more fertile fields.

A totally coordinated and independent cultural relations program was no longer possible. International power politics and reawakened US nationalism had brought undeclared war onto the American agenda. FDR's surrogates, Welles and MacLeish, had looked beyond war to the structuring of a permanent peace; when the nation returned to war, diplomacy had to fall in line. The very idea of cultural internationalism was made to seem a naive dream, almost treason. To the self-styled "tough-minded" and "hard-nosed," the internationalism of the last fifteen years smelled like vaguely un-American globaloney. Cultural diplomacy, precisely at the time it was grinding out the daily victories that reoriented Germany and Japan, slipped lower on the agenda. Its subtle, long-range and interconnected work baffled even its stout defenders, who could not find the language to spell out internationalism's value in the sound-bites that comprised Washington discourse.

In 1952 candidate Dwight Eisenhower allowed himself to be involved in the issues of informational and cultural diplomacy, even if he was of two minds on the subject. During his campaign that fall, he regularly reflected the patrician strand of his party's thinking, praising what he called "people-to-people" work; at other times, he was a keen partisan of psychological warfare. Where Truman had spent his life in ward-heeling politics, Eisenhower had risen to the top of the professional military discipline, with heavy political and international responsibilities; he had served around the world, in places ranging from the Philippines to Europe, where he managed two of history's great international military coalitions. As president of Columbia University and admiring brother of university president Milton, he was no stranger to education; moreover, the US military that shaped him had itself a persistent record of substantial investments in education and reeducation, rising to the victories of German and Japanese reorientation. Eisenhower knew and respected hard psychological warfare of the black variety, but he knew its softer versions as well—he had abiding faith in the potential of US voluntarism. His high-ground view of politics contrasted with Truman's Kansas City hardball. Those struggling to maintain a decent cultural and educational element in American diplomacy saw promise in Eisenhower.

During the campaign, while his foreign policy advisor John Foster Dulles kept quiet, Eisenhower said he intended to make IIA an effective instrument of foreign policy, implying that it was not already so. In January 1953, before his inauguration, he again promised to improve "all activities related to international information, linking such programs to national security." With his encouragement in some cases and pressed by potential political change in all cases, a surprising number of study-groups undertook to review the IIA question. Concurrent with the copious Fulbright-Hickenlooper Senate hearings, six other studies of IIA were underway in 1952–53, led by Robert L. Johnson, W. H. Jackson, Mark May, Tracy Voorhees, Wilbur Schramm, and Nelson Rockefeller (a second cluster of surveys would appear at the end of the 1950s, with the waning of Dulles's influence). Lois Roth, in an ingenious historiographic study first done in 1981, analyzed these surveys and other reports on foreign affairs between 1952 and 1977, some sixty-five of them; she found that most dealt in some way with "the IIA question."[26]

The Fulbright-Hickenlooper hearings in 1952–53 were by far the most important of these studies; they are the most thorough congressional study ever of cultural diplomacy, and the least read. The hearings began in October 1952 and lasted seven months, producing over two thousand pages of testimony.[27] Fulbright himself was chief probe, even after the chair passed to Iowan Bourke Hickenlooper when the Republicans took over the Senate in January 1953.

In these hearings the debate on cultural relations was a constant as Fulbright attempted to counterbalance congressional fascination with the Campaign of Truth. Fulbright, one of few Senate colleagues McCarthy feared, faced the culture question frontally; he linked his investigation to ex-Senator William Benton's Resolution 74, all that remained of his overambitious "Marshall Plan of Ideas." Benton had called in fiery words for an American riposte to Soviet propaganda because "the first weapon of aggression by the Kremlin is propaganda designed to subvert, to confuse and to divide the free world, and to inflame the Russian and satellite peoples with hatred for our free institutions." By the time the thorough hearings ended, the creation of USIA was only two months away.

Fulbright-Hickenlooper's exhaustive survey was comparable in depth and scope—but not in confusion—to the chaotic 1948 Smith-Mundt debates. For more than half a year, the committee heard from three directors of IIA and a hundred other witnesses. When Hickenlooper took the chair, the persistent civility of the process and the tranquil continuity of the hearings exemplified the bipartisanship Fulbright had fostered. Behind him stood a strong nonpartisan Foreign Relations Committee staff of public-policy scholars, directed by Francis Wilcox and Carl Marcy.

Fulbright was fair to both sides: two-thirds of the witnesses came from the information side of the ledger. He wanted a thorough discussion of US *information* programs overseas; but his approach drew on the MacLeish school rather than Benton's or Barrett's. Senator Benton's Resolution 74, stressing propaganda and counterpropaganda, had deflected attention from the cultural question. In response, Fulbright sought a way to keep cultural and educational diplomacy alive in the new wartime climate.

From the viewpoint of cultural relations, a selective reading of these hearings provides God's plenty, both in truths and ironies. Here is a delegate from the Department of Agriculture, casually describing his department's vast range of educational programs around the world but admitting he has never heard of Smith-Mundt. Here is Fulbright, whimsically asking why not bring European communists to America to learn the truth? Later, he courteously scrutinizes the little-known but massive and costly military education program IMET, underscoring the comparative modesty of State's work. Still later, he delivers a ringing plea for careful coordination of overseas exchanges. Here is IIA's Donald Cook, a division stalwart, noting that twenty government agencies do overseas exchange activities, with no coordination between them; he defends the cost-effectiveness of contracting IIA's work out to fifty-one separate citizen-staffed organizations; he praises BFS's refusal to require political reporting or propaganda support from US Fulbright students and scholars abroad; he reports growing US and foreign contributions to the program; and he warns that US universities, overtaxing their finances, cannot provide more support for foreign visitors.

Here is IIA psy-warrior Reed Harris, soon to meet martyrdom under McCarthy, evading Fulbright's sly question about why education was left out of IIA's new Compton-initiated title—too long, says Harris, and besides, "in the broad sense information *does* include education. Education is a form of passing information to other minds." Fulbright lets the obfuscation pass and presses Harris, who admits awareness of Compton's strong opinion that exchanges and libraries are IIA's single most important activities. Here is Mark May, Yale professor of communications and chair of IIA's Smith-Mundt Advisory Commission for Information, recommending that IIA leave State and become a single agency, containing both functions, with cabinet status for its director.

Publisher Dan Lacy, later of McGraw-Hill, describes the rich and interlocking activities of USIS book programs and libraries, help for indigenous libraries abroad, and cooperation abroad with private publishing programs. Flora Luddington, librarian of Mount Holyoke and chair of ALA's international committee, reviews her years as USIS librarian in Bombay, her inspections of the German and Japanese programs, and her study-visits to forty-five other USIS libraries; Hickenlooper is delighted to discover that science and technology, "a-political" topics, are the libraries' most sought-after holdings.

Here is Senator Smith, dwelling on the high relevance of his days with Hoover's binational Belgian and Finnish Relief in World War I. Earl McGrath, US Commissioner of Education, details USOE's near-century of work in overseas education, pleads for interagency coordination of all US education abroad, and urges more attention to secondary education in the Fulbright Program. Here is ex-IIA director Wilson Compton, two weeks after his traumatic resignation, loyally defending IIA and its informational mindset, but insisting that wars begin in the minds of men; that Americans are decent people unused to lies, deceit, and propaganda; that America's promise rests on its moral foundations; that short-range policy focus interferes with long-range effect; and that America's voice is and has always been trade, commerce, and travel; hence that it is more important to restore and support that "voice" than to set up government mouthpieces. Compton is skeptical about VOA, a heresy to the informationists and a concealed cause of his defeat; he suggests beaming VOA solely to the USSR, replacing it elsewhere by assistance to local radio stations.

Here is Benton's friend George Probst, University of Chicago historian and Chicago Round Table director, preaching another heresy: that educational radio is a better model for VOA than propaganda, or as he says, than Goebbels. Fulbright returns, to grill Eric Johnson of the Motion Picture Association. Hollywood films project a nation of useless millionaires, he says; Johnson denies anything is wrong and insists that in any case nothing can be changed—Fulbright is appalled and caught without a response. A phalanx of publishers echoes Dan Lacy in defending libraries and books.

Here is the wise Martin McGuire, Dean of Catholic University and member of GAC, then both BFS and the Smith-Mundt Advisory Commission on Culture; he proclaims the classic Cherringtonian vision, noting its reinforcement by his visits to USIS posts in two dozen countries; he says Fulbright Commissions are sturdy barriers against propaganda; he deplores merging information and culture—it may strengthen information but it will certainly damage education; he wants IIA to remain in State, if only for reasons of prestige; he mentions the promise of a growing network of Fulbright alumni (at that time the alumni could not have numbered more than ten thousand worldwide, contrasting with well over 300,000 today).

Here is Fulbright's law school classmate, the subtle propagandist Lloyd Free, public opinion expert and PAO Rome, who has been called home to Washington to "help" Compton's successor think through IIA's future and perhaps to smooth things with Fulbright. Here is Kenneth Holland, Rockefeller import, IIA veteran, former executive director of the BFS, and now Laurence Duggan's successor at IIE; he pleads for private exchanges supported by the government, as opposed to government exchanges supported by the private sector; he sees exchanges as the most potent weapons the U.S. has in the war of ideas; the impact of exchanges depends on quality, not quantity; he deems binationalism enlightened and indispensable.

Here is Rhode Island's octogenarian Senator Green asking distractedly whether the U.S. gets "credit" for funding exchanges; Fulbright impatiently reminds him that "credit" is a by-product, not a purpose. Here once more is Fulbright, outlining a gradualist funding strategy for the program: "A little progress, very gradual and slight, each year during the last four years . . . [The goal is to] keep it alive so we can improve it in the future." He conducts a rich extended dialogue with his friend Ed Murrow on news and government journalism; Murrow admits that a journalist must be free to criticize the U.S. but agrees he cannot do so if employed by VOA. Fulbright concludes, and Murrow cannot disagree, that VOA, by definition, can never be anything but a "propaganda" organization.

Here is the ever-patient Fulbright goaded to belligerence by IIA hardliner Joseph Phillips, Compton's tough psy-warrior deputy for information; Phillips asserts that separation of information and culture is irrelevant because foreign audiences do not know the difference; Fulbright overlooks the arguable falsehood and notes bitingly that *Washington* knows, and hence that Washington bears responsibility for murky guidelines and contradictory definitions. Fulbright notes the independence of the British Council, to which Phillips glibly responds that it works under "policy" control, without defining what kind of policy or what kind of control. Fulbright finally snaps when Phillips refers to exchanges as an important "instrument" of IIA then graciously allows him to withdraw the offending word. Phillips insouciantly sees no harm in USIS attempts to use US and foreign students for propaganda and reporting purposes; Fulbright manifests polite outrage.

Here is Edward Barrett, father of the Campaign of Truth, now Columbia's dean of journalism; he boasts of his wartime work with Eisenhower on psychological operations. Fulbright draws Barrett into supporting IIA's new policy on book selection for libraries; he gets Barrett to agree that all the recent red hunting has never turned up a disloyal IIA employee. Here too is Benton, boasting of his work with Nelson Rockefeller, "pioneer of American peacetime propaganda."

Throughout these remarkable hearings, Fulbright plays the shrewd moderator-interrogator. His sharpest questions focus on the wisdom of separating IIA from State, which he seems to believe is on the way: is it a good idea, will it work? Again and again he feeds witnesses easy questions, then leads them to pointed conclusions. In the end his agenda is clear: if IIA stays in State, he wants to insulate information from cultural relations; if it is removed, he wants *all* cultural elements to remain behind in State. For him, VOA and educational exchanges have nothing in common. On security he ridicules McCarthy's allegations. Interrogating cultural veterans of the cradle-years like Cook, Francis Colligan, and Russ Riley, he patiently draws out well-known information in the interests of educating his Senate colleagues.

In short, he puts the Eisenhower team on warning that taking IIA out of State is a decision of the highest importance, which must not be allowed to damage the cultural operation—Fulbright had few fears about the encroachments of foreign policy, but he never ceased hating the lies of propaganda. It is a shot across Eisenhower's bow; if a new agency were to come into existence, Fulbright is saying, it would take culture out of State over his dead body.

Of the six other studies, that of Mark May, Yale communications expert and chair of IIA's Advisory Commission for Information, was the most straightforward. May recommended separating IIA, both culture and information, from State and giving the agency cabinet status. Wilbur Schramm, Dean of Communications at the University of Illinois, writing for a group of academics and publishers, dwelt on communications process and information programs. Nelson Rockefeller, appointed by Eisenhower to chair a powerful new three-man Committee on Government Reorganization, turned his committee's attention first of all to the IIA question and recommended leaving IIA where it was—only later to recommend separation. Tracy Voorhees, wartime aide to Stimson and Robert Patterson in the War Department and member of Robert L. Johnson's Rockefeller-funded Temple University task forces abridging Hoover's giant study on government reorganization, argued for separation but ducked the culture-information issue. At the same time, Voorhees warned of dangerously unclear program objectives; he had done trouble-shooting surveys for Robert Johnson, including a survey of VOA with the help of Theodore Streibert, soon to be USIA's founding director, and he later helped Streibert design the new independent agency.

There is no doubt that the culture-information dilemma in 1952 was on a lot of minds, but there was no consensus on the issue because all thinking, rather than focusing on function or ideas, dwelt on the technical questions of reorganization. When function was considered at all, the argument became murky—separation of information from culture was totally unacceptable to the informationists, who made a point of muddying the waters. The major issue instead was the need for "truth" in propaganda—the time-honored Benton diversion. At higher levels it was convenient to dismiss the culture-information dilemma as an administrative problem—Milton Eisenhower's idea (he was one of the Rockefeller committee's two members); the president's brother must have known that, between 1948 and 1952, "administrative decisions" had already inflicted continual and persistent damage on the cultural diplomatic function.

While the hearings were proceeding, the McCarthy buck passed to Eisenhower's desk, but the new president turned it back—he had no intention of "getting down into the gutter," as he memorably said. With Compton gone, Eisenhower responded to this teapot-size tempest by appointing a second university president, Robert L. Johnson of Temple University, to IIA. USIA was coming closer by the day.

CHAPTER TWELVE

The Birth of USIA

Americans are the world's worst propagandists. Perhaps during the next ten years we shall come to admit this fact and stop trying.

—George V. Allen, 1963

USIA is a propaganda agency. Don't ever forget it.

—Richard E. Neustadt, 1964

ONE OF EISENHOWER'S FIRST ACTIONS was to fill the gap left by Wilson Compton's departure. In his campaign he had pledged to "do something" about IIA, but it was not so easy—the flinty Dulles ran foreign affairs. Eisenhower understood propaganda, or the "P programs," as he called them; to him they meant the psychological warfare he had known. To his credit, he also had genuine affection for what he called "people-to-people." He was too wise not to see a contradiction but too shrewd to let it show.[1]

Nelson Rockefeller also saw both functions but saw no harm in jumbling them. In 1952 he stepped back into a ring he had never really left. Asserting Eisenhower's support, he had funded Hoover's 1948 commission on governmental reorganization, with Acheson as Hoover's deputy for foreign affairs. He then funded Temple University president Robert L. Johnson in his effort to abridge the mammoth Hoover document, convening nineteen different task forces to do so. Eisenhower referred to both efforts during his campaign. Friends watching Rockefeller position himself closer to Eisenhower concluded he intended to succeed him.

After the election, on 30 November, the president-elect appointed Rockefeller to chair a unique three-man Special Committee on Government Organization and assigned two wise men to help him—OWI-veteran Milton Eisenhower and Arthur Fleming, presidents of Penn State and Ohio Wesleyan respectively. Rockefeller headed the committee until December 1958, just before he was sworn in as governor of New York.

Johnson was a long-standing friend of the president, managing Temple in Philadelphia while Eisenhower reigned over Columbia. Like Dulles, Hoover and Acheson saw information and cultural relations as a redundant burden on State and recommended removing such "operational responsibilities." Instead, they thought that a "general manager" should run IIA, under an Assistant Secretary of State. Johnson's shorter version of the Hoover report suggested that information and the VOA, apparently without education and culture, might become a "government corporation." Both studies were significant in insisting that State persist in exchanges; both called for high professionalism. Perhaps Acheson had learned something from MacLeish after all.

In this context, it was the more significant that Eisenhower chose his friend Johnson as IIA director, its second university-president head in succession. The Johnson appointment indicated that Eisenhower was aware of the educational dimension of IIA's function; perhaps he intended to reinforce IIA's links to the university world. At Columbia he had learned that managing a great university required unusual human skills and vision, and a university president like his much-admired brother, used to presiding over dozens of dueling fiefs, might just be the right man to straighten out the IIA mess. The soldier and the educator in Eisenhower came together on this point: both saw less costly paths to international peace than warfare and the arms race. For this crucial decision, Eisenhower's new friend Rockefeller, long a disciple of a separate but intact IIA and Johnson's sponsor, doubtless had the president's ear.

Johnson had begun managing Temple in 1941. He was a Republican businessman who had helped Henry Luce found *Time* in the 1920s and a public-service-oriented millionaire by forty; he had headed Pennsylvania Relief during the Depression.[2] Two different Johnsons appeared before the Fulbright-Hickenlooper committee in April 1953 at a three-day interval: the first masterfully analyzed culture and propaganda in MacLeish's terms; the second three days later, after his handlers had reoriented him, sounded like the perfect informationist.

He must have known he was stepping into a swamp because he hesitated long before accepting the job. The thoughtful administrator in him insisted warily on delaying his takeover of IIA, giving himself a three-month pause to do a serious study of the agency before carrying out Dulles's orders to remove IIA from State. Dulles and Eisenhower pledged not even to allow his name to be rumored. On this condition, Johnson accepted.

Obviously Johnson knew the issues. He understood both sides of IIA's work and saw the pros and cons of mixing culture and propaganda. He was wise enough to see difficulties ahead; a study period was a shrewd idea. He seems as well to have foreseen the cut-and-slash tactics of the opposition and perhaps to have suspected that the experience of managing a university, where the stakes were lower, would help little in dealing with the nonnegotiable terms, practiced contradictions, alternate pleading, leaks to Congress, and self-interest of the informationists. He was surely unprepared for their refusal to see that the independence of cultural diplomacy would enrich their own work. IIA was not a university; it was more like an advertising agency into which had been tucked a small, low-quality, and nearly invisible junior college, funded by a single cranky and mercurial client and dominated by a dozen warring division chiefs, operating in every country in the world, in scores of languages, with a powerful but paranoid broadcasting division. Engaging with IIA staff, he found an odd collection of people reaching back in some cases as far as 1938 but more preponderantly to 1942. Among the informationists and the culturalists, some were superb, some were time-serving mediocrities, some were dangerous zealots, and some were lethal McCarthy spies unembarrassed by deceit.

The astonishing betrayal came not from staff but from Dulles himself. Whether by oversight, a shift in tactics, or sheer duplicity, Johnson's appointment was announced on the same day that Compton learned of his removal. In hindsight, Johnson's downfall was sealed on that day in March; trapped, he saw no choice but to soldier on. Meanwhile the enemy forces inside IIA had been warned to gear up for battle.

In Congress IIA's work was overseen by a dozen distracted friends of psy-ops, a few implacable and confrontational propagandists, and a handful of friends of Fulbright and education. IIA's cultural element had two prestigious advisory boards, both inclined to help but as powerless as most advisory bodies; a third body, the BFS, was linked to Fulbright and hence more independent but limited to university exchanges. There was impatience with the IIA question everywhere, up to the top of the White House. Johnson, like Benton and Allen, had no time for study or reflection; unlike Benton however he knew the dangers of impatience.

Another betrayal came from Hoover. Calling on his friend, Johnson was stunned by the ex-president's general rancor and blunt nationalism. Johnson's special assistant, Martin Merson, present at the meeting, reported Hoover as saying that IIA was "full of OWI hangers-on," "Communists," "left-wingers," and "incompetents"; IIA, he said, "ought to be liquidated." In Merson's eyes, Hoover reflected the views of "the right-wing Republicans who controled most of the key Congressional committees" and were bent on eradicating all memory of the New Deal.[3] Hoover's animus, mirroring McCarthy's, put a damper on Johnson's enthusiasm.

It was demoralizing news. IIA had been treated noncommittally by Hoover and Acheson, for whom it posed an unresolved problem of a conceptual and managerial nature—although Acheson too was bothered by the idea of cultural relations inside IIA. Johnson, rather than resign, persisted in the study-group approach, even as IIA director. He put prestigious teams to work, hoping to buy time, provoke thought, cut through prejudice, and get the right things done. But he gave the opposition time to organize. From the first day, he was buffeted by contradictory advice and threats. He was also deluged by people expecting jobs; most important of these was Scott McLeod; he believed he had no choice but to appoint the McCarthy staffer as IIA's director of security, a move he would bitterly regret.

Where he had leeway, he looked for high-quality people. He supported fine inherited colleagues like the stalwart Russ Riley and ex-Dean William C. Johnstone, who had run exchanges in IIA for four years and was principal backup for German reeducation. And he was able to add three fine outsiders: Washington insider Tracy Voorhees, President-emeritus Robert Clothier of Rutgers University, and Merson, a Republican Philadelphian from the Dixie Cup company who had managed the Hoover abridgement. Voorhees, with Harvard president James Conant, MIT's Vannevar Bush, and Ed Murrow, was a founder of the Committee on the Present Danger, an anti-Soviet group urging engagement with the USSR. Johnson had Clothier in mind to head education and culture. Johnson himself, juggling the hot potato he had been handed, found solace in Dulles's thought, from his recent book *War and Peace* (1950), that "we have spent little on the war of ideas in which we are deeply engaged. . . . We are just beginning to wake up to the need." Johnson took words seriously.

From Compton, he inherited a bureaucratic tar baby. The Budget Bureau had imposed a substantial cut in IIA funding and personnel. Johnson saw no choice but to implement a disheartening decision. Polling top officers, he decided to maintain Compton's even-handed resolution to spread the cut across all elements of IIA, including VOA. This was a fatal mistake; he had underestimated VOA's might.

The educator Johnson appeared before the Fulbright-Hickenlooper committee on 22 April, speaking the language of Cherrington. For eight months, via the Temple rewrite, he had been studying both of IIA's functions, "the US international information and educational exchange program." He believed "the moral leadership of the U.S. . . . can be the big difference between world war and world peace." Like Eisenhower, he believed that, "as a nation, everything we say, everything we do, and everything we fail to say or do will have its impact in other lands." Government should "supplement what America is already doing abroad," reach across artificial barriers to touch other peoples, and "invite them to appraise and to balance so that understanding may replace suspicion." "Our reassurance to the rest of the world takes many forms. . . . [It is] a small segment of the great flow of American ideas which reach other peoples." IIA's job is to "mobilize our total energies, public and private, and direct them toward a common purpose." He proudly announced Clothier as his overseer for education and culture and underlined the high importance of cultural diplomacy by citing a conversation with James B. Conant, former president of Harvard, US High Commissioner in Germany, and soon-to-be first postwar US ambassador there. Conant had told him that, given a choice, he would have preferred running IIA's education program in Germany—Herman Wells's job—to being High Commissioner. On radio and motion pictures, the Johnson of 22 April wanted audiences to see both as truth; foreigners are like Americans, they "do not like propaganda." Looking ahead, he says that, even if the Krem-

lin were to collapse, America would require educational diplomacy because a world revolution was in train. His far-reaching thoughts echoed
MacLeish in positing an independent cultural diplomacy as a factor adding substance to the informational mix. This businessman-educator understood foreign audiences and the need for engagement through patience
and process. To the IIA problem, he brought an open mind used to dealing with ideas.

On 25 April, another Johnson took the stand. He had been worked
over by top staff and Fulbright-friend Lloyd Free, brought home from
Rome to help guide Johnson's thinking; and he had had a discouraging
private discussion with Fulbright—surprisingly negative, for two men
who had everything except party in common. The new Johnson toed the
line of the total informationist.

Within IIA, the recalcitrants saw culture not as potential but as trouble.
Their fight to destroy Johnson was waged at the borderline of viciousness.
One story is a troubling mystery. William C. Johnstone was a Denver
graduate and Cherrington associate, a Stanford Ph.D. in South Asian politics. Dean first of the George Washington University, then of its School
of Government, he took leave in 1946 to go to New Delhi as PAO; after
two years with USIS he returned to take over IIA's Office of Educational
Exchange when Frank Colligan moved to the BFS. For the next four years
Johnstone managed all IIA exchanges, including the foundations of German reorientation.

Johnstone was a university man all the way, a man whose language
Johnson—and Compton before him—spoke well. Compton had made a
bold and creative decision, switching Johnstone to the information side
of the IIA house, as deputy administrator for Field Programs. There, beyond overseeing the USIS posts, he supervised all Washington information programs, including VOA. He was in this job when Johnson took
office. For Compton, Johnstone had also headed the task force dealing
with the Budget Bureau's cuts. Both men underestimated the fears among
IIA's informationists and in VOA—during Johnstone's four steady years
with exchanges, the counterpart position in information had been held
by five different incumbents. The IIA budget-review team came to a unanimous conclusion: the post–Campaign of Truth information program
"suffered from too-rapid expansion and lack of an adequate, centralized
mechanism of policy and management control." It seemed an even-
handed solution; Robert Johnson decided to carry it forward.

Without warning, Johnstone resigned on 5 May, alleging a sudden desire to rejoin academic life—at a very odd time in the academic calendar.
An overlong explanatory letter to Johnson dwelt in detail on his impressive anticommunist credentials, as though someone had questioned
them. In the background, McLeod had just taken over IIA security, bent
on pinpointing "weakness"—which for him meant communist sympathies (in his years with USIA he never proved a single staffer to be disloyal). Johnstone, a sophisticated and experienced South Asianist, was

precisely the kind of intellectual McCarthy's men relished as targets, more vulnerable than Fairbank or Owen Lattimore because he had committed himself to government service. No charges were brought against him, so one can only guess that his resignation was forced by some form of blackmail, McLeod's everyday tool; at the same moment, Cohn and Schine, equally short of proof, were hounding American staff out of their jobs at UNESCO and running roughshod over USIS libraries in Europe.

On 13 May a VOA officer known to colleagues as a McCarthy source testified before Fulbright-Hickenlooper. He reported Johnstone's departure with unabashed glee: VOA's budget cuts were the "plan of a man who decided that the so-called free world should not be broadcast to by the Voice of America, that it should be wiped out. . . . That man resigned last Friday evening, Dr. William B. [sic] Johnstone . . . but we are stuck, the U.S. is stuck, with the loss of 201 relays, loss of prestige and friends."[4] It was a slanderous misrepresentation, announced with unmistakable animus. Johnstone wrote a denial and Johnson corroborated it, saying he had backed the committee's unanimous decision for generalized cuts with total personal conviction. Merson reports literal tears from Johnson on learning that "an unnamed colleague" had resigned after McLeod questioned a minor element of personal history unrelated to politics. Future historians may learn if anyone other than Johnstone was close enough to Johnson to evoke tears, but it seems unlikely. Johnstone spent the rest of a productive professional career teaching at the Johns Hopkins School of Advanced International Studies, a permanent loss to cultural diplomacy.

This example of the deadly crossfire of the McCarthy era hints at the climate inside IIA, which only worsened. Johnson's health was bending under the pressure. He escaped the book-selection maze by calling back the ALA, which, in the interests of IIA "control," had since 1946 been gradually pushed aside; ALA's stern statement on the matter halted McCarthy, who in any case was moving on to other targets. In July, after his hundred days, the dispirited Johnson returned to Temple, leaving his deputy Howland Sargeant in charge. Two university presidents in succession had tried to make sense of IIA; together the two had lasted less than a year. To make matters worse, Johnson, believing he had nothing to lose, wrote a parting-shot letter to McCarthy; the vindictive Senator took it out on IIA with a 20-percent budget cut. Appointing Johnson was a bold decision for Eisenhower; he had chosen a fine man. But he forgot to stand behind him.

IIA was a tricephalic office, without a mission statement, housing the contradictory functions of cultural and informational diplomacy and disproportionately influenced by a radio division straddling the fence between news and propaganda. With no time for serious study, Johnson was compelled to do what university presidents and even businessmen rarely have to do: improvise. Merson's acidic book about his service with Johnson warned that State and IIA "would be a battleground in the fight between two irreconcilable wings of the Republican Party, . . . a plain back-alley fight for political power and control." But more was involved than party politics. The issue of IIA's two functions had gone untouched. From the cultural relations viewpoint, intertwining questions were snarling the work. Johnson, trying to reconcile culture and information, learned there was no such thing as a middle path in Washington. Johnson's resignation forced Eisenhower to act, and the president responded with apparent vigor by appointing another committee.

Meanwhile, good people were keeping the cultural idea alive. The various studies of IIA in 1952–53, triggered by imminent political change, agreed in one way or another that the U.S. needed a continuing presence abroad in both information and education.[5] The unanswerable question with which Johnson had grappled was how to house both in the same Washington agency. Compton and Johnson went the route of defining separate functions—no one had yet been able to spell out a single mission covering both sides. Meanwhile, the McCarthy shadow lay over IIA as over no other government agency.

Smoothing Hoover's sharper edges, Rockefeller-Johnson's abridgement had defined the IIA question. Rockefeller's new committee on government organization, in fact, placed the issue first on its agenda; he had always wanted to loosen the links of cultural affairs to short-term policy and to keep the functions in State. The juxtaposition of AID's dilemma with IIA's reawakened the Rockefeller dream of globalizing his wartime achievements. He wanted the hypothetical new "information" agency to contain *all* informational, educational, and cultural programs then handled by IIA, AID, and State, including those in the occupied areas—in effect melding IIA and even AID into one. And he wanted them inside State, to expand his Latin American work to the world. But Rockefeller had missed a point: the AID and IIA functions, in his absence from Washington, had acquired separate lives; and as usual he ignored the fact that IIA contained two separate ideas.

Rockefeller's two strong-minded committee colleagues disagreed, and on 7 April, to the delight of Dulles, they recommended separation of both IIA and AID from State. The committee recognized that the new IIA would be an experiment. Its functions would depend on "the skill and wisdom of its operations" as much as on foreign policy. Milton Eisenhower's long-held faith in the wisdom of administrators had once more won the day and Rockefeller's hopes of reviving 1942–45 died.

And Rockefeller had again missed out on managing worldwide economic assistance. Instead Eisenhower assigned him to the new Department of Health, Education, and Welfare, as Undersecretary to founding-Secretary Oveta Culp Hobby. After loyal soldiering in that job—where he would help absorb another slice of IIA's work—he would move into the White House as advisor to Eisenhower for psychological warfare, developing far-reaching ideas like the Open Skies proposal and Atoms for

Peace. Still, IIA-USIA remained his favorite hobby; he was behind the scenes more than can be documented.[6]

Eisenhower's committee on IIA was deliberating. Commissioned in March less to make sense out of the earlier reports than to recommend a means of carrying on psychological warfare, the biased group was chaired by cold warrior William H. Jackson; he hoped to end months of White House exasperation. With the much-beloved public relations professional Abbott Washburn as staff director, the committee's psy-war membership—with only one university representative—set to work. Like Jackson, New York lawyer and former deputy director of CIA, most members were wedded to psychological warfare. Two businessmen, an advertising agency head, the Deputy Secretary of Defense and head of the Psychological Strategy Board, cold war super-hawk C. D. Jackson of *Time-LIFE*, and Gordon Gray, a university president with a public administration background—all were mesmerized by the tough-talking psy-warriors.

When Fulbright questioned Robert Johnson in April, neither admitted to having any idea what Jackson's or Rockefeller's committees were thinking—and neither chairman was invited to testify. On 6 May Undersecretary of State Gen. Bedell Smith asked acting IIA director Howland Sargeant about separation from State. Sargeant said that separation would reduce State's responsibilities for operations and keep information and cultural relations, exchanges, libraries and books, together.

Jackson's committee records show no concern for cultural relations—the two Jacksons considered themselves the country's top psychological warriors so that was what they discussed. Committee staffer Townsend Hoopes, remembering the work of the committee vividly, recalls it as having been directed only to set up the US approach to psy-war; he had no recollection that culture and education were ever discussed.[7] Lois Roth wrote of the committee's conclusions in 1981 that "of 59 recommendations, only one dealt with educational and cultural programs. The relationship between educational-cultural and information programs was dodged." The question of field staffing was left once more, Milton Eisenhower–style, to the administrators. The constituency that had fought for separation of functions in the time of Smith-Mundt had been overrun by the cold war. Jackson, like Rockefeller, wanted things together and pressed for a plausible, binding, and final recommendation to keep IIA in State.

The hard noses of the Jackson committee were not hard enough for the flinty Dulles. Despite his committee's consensus to keep IIA in State, Jackson caved under Dulles's protest and, with equally passionate conviction, recommended the opposite, a deep bow to Eisenhower's need to keep peace in his house. By 16 May the question reached the desk of Eisenhower's chief of staff Sherman Adams, who called the principals together. Merson, representing Johnson, believed the question was still open; at the meeting he learned it was not. His protest was outvoted

11-1. For reasons of "expediency," as Adams put it, IIA would be split from State, taking libraries, books, centers, and ELT with it. Only exchanges would remain in State, in deference to Fulbright.

In Merson's telling, he and Johnson had grown wiser: "Johnson and I knew [exchange] was one of the five principal media our agency used . . . all over the world. *It was the best.* [Merson's stress] . . . the hard core of our program."[8] But the discussion was over, and no one was happy. Dulles had managed to push only two-thirds of IIA out of State and exchanges would linger there until 1977; Fulbright was furious at the dismembering of education and the rise of propaganda; Rockefeller's dream empire went dark; Eisenhower's people-to-people programs were in limbo; IIA had lost its exchange component; and culture had lost its field people. It was the bureaucrat's nightmare; all parties settled for much less than half.

Reorganization Plan 8 went to Congress on 1 June. A two-thirds vote was needed in Congress for approval, but no vote was taken. After sixty days, USIA came into being—by default—on 1 August. It was a soggy and unconvincing beginning. In USIA, as the years passed, the doubts, the hedges, and the swivels of Jackson were overgrown by myths, and Jackson's report became the sacred founding covenant for the new USIA.

Fulbright, fearing propaganda's contamination, had hobbled the new agency. Its loyalists accused him of sabotage and raised him to the top of their enemy list. From the culturalist viewpoint, he was a hero: he had kept exchanges in State, while losing books, libraries, centers, ELT, and American studies, in the third major slicing away of functions since 1945 for the old division staff. Fulbright's fight for bipartisanship was a faraway memory—his friend Robert Taft, defeated in a hard fight for the presidential nomination, was winding up his career.

Fulbright's rear-guard action had far-reaching consequences. From birth USIA was a totally different entity from IIA—the strong academic counterpoise of culture had been removed, and open domination of the new agency by cold warriors met even less resistance. For educational and cultural affairs, Fulbright's principled intransigence would delay the inevitable full merger for twenty-five years, embittering an already-angry debate. USIA's new loyalists never relented in plotting to absorb exchanges. As usual, the CAOs hunkered down somewhere in the middle.

When USIA blinked to life in August 1953, the cold war, now the driving power in the land, had a weakened cultural diplomatic capability. Yet over the next four decades culture would prove a major factor—some believe *the* major factor—in undoing Soviet totalitarianism, as it had democratized Germany and Japan. Now the sloop of cultural diplomacy was bobbing along in USIA's wake. The splitting of IIA was guided more by expediency and trade-offs than logic. Instead of the usual rhetoric about fast media versus slow, the formal division of IIA in 1953 separated USIA's "objects"—books and libraries, cultural centers, ELT, and exhibits—from State's "people"—exchanges, plus the overseas American schools and relations with the already-troubled UNESCO. In the field the PAO's power over staff was reinforced and the academic CAOs continued to fade. A decade later participant-observer Philip Coombs commented: "The rationale for this strange division was that State would handle 'cultural relations' while USIA handled 'cultural information'—regarded by some at the time as a distinction without a difference which might have amused medieval metaphysicians."[9]

Partisans of cultural diplomacy have long pondered the wisdom of Fulbright's intervention. Might USIA have evolved differently had IIA been transferred whole? If USIA had contained the balancing effect of exchanges, if it had had the constant injection of substance in its message from scholars and intellectuals, if it had been watched closely by Fulbright and his friends in Congress, by BFS and the cultural advisory commission, and by the universities and foundations, might it have turned out differently? With an internal brake on propaganda, might USIA in fact have been less free to move toward unidirectional information? Might the cultural officers have kept their loyalties intact and built their presence within USIA?

Fulbright himself had no answers to such speculation. But certainly the relentless tightening of information's control over culture made it seem that the game was already over for the culturalists. USIA, without exchanges, was free to do as its leadership wished. Its directors, supported by a strong media-based advisory commission, were exempt from concern about the traditions and values—and even the legislation—that had been generated by cultural relations since 1938. CAOs played a minor role in USIA's direction, and then only if they agreed to speak the language of PAOs. Considering how badly USIA turned out forty-five years later, when it was forcibly merged back into State, almost anything might have been preferable to the kind of autonomy which it was given. In hindsight, however, the independence of cultural diplomacy had ended.

For better or worse, USIA came to life by congressional inaction. Like any agency, once in place it staked out its piece of the high ground and began shoring up its defenses. Despite omens and counter-indications, despite the unhappiness of many who cared deeply, despite the wisdom of thoughtful reports and observers, the US Information Agency had arrived; its name and its ethos descended directly from Creel and his euphemism with an assist from Rockefeller. The new agency was clouded by fears from its past, from internal and external wars, from buried contradictions, and from its close call with the Wisconsin senator. In the climate of fear appeals by the culturalists, however reasonable, appeared threatening. USIA was born as a hybrid, an intellectual paradox to those who worried about intellect. It perched between nationalist and internationalist views of foreign policy, between psychological warfare and cultural relations, between telling the story and honest dialogue, with a nod to the former in all three cases. These compromises were Benton's—scrambled eggs, with information as chef. Only the cold war, only Dulles's insistence on removing IIA from State could have brought such a strange beast to birth. Insiders called it the Toonerville Trolley, or a Rube Goldberg contraption, in honor of famous cartoons of the period.

For the psy-warriors, this latter-day version of Creel's CPI, OWI, and the Campaign of Truth offered a nonmilitary home for information programs, free of State's alleged morass. The propagandists had been given the chance to prove their worth in dealing with the Soviets in the odd no-war-no-peace stand-off between nations. To carry out US aims, a psy-war agency was obviously needed, but no one explained convincingly why it had to include and dominate cultural diplomacy.

Inside their propaganda home, the culturalist CAOs found some small advantages: a cultural office in all US embassies, however circumscribed, was now assumed; the central part of culture—the Fulbright Program— had kept its independence and integrity; and the field CAOs, in the splintered remains of IIA, still had a countervailing *amicus curiae* in Fulbright. Some saw a chance at last to get on with it, to settle down to work, after years of turmoil, by cultivating their PAO friends and awaiting better times.

Eisenhower appointed Theodore C. Streibert as USIA director. He was the first broadcasting executive to head the information function since Elmer Davis and a sharp change from the two university presidents. A friend of VOA, he had directed radio station WOR in New York and chaired Mutual Broadcasting. He was a Rockefeller man who had served as a radio consultant for German reorientation and worked with Tracy Voorhees on the VOA question in Johnson's rewrite of Hoover. As deputy, he wisely chose Abbott Washburn, executive director of the Jackson report. C. D. Jackson landed in the White House as advisor for psychological warfare.

Streibert took over responsibility for press, radio, films, books, periodicals, ELT, American studies, libraries, and cultural centers— everything but exchanges. Field staff were also under his control. Working with what remained after McCarthy's attacks and Fulbright's "meddling" as they saw it, Streibert and Washburn drew up task forces from the officer corps to design the new structure. The new arrangement they assembled would remain in place for decades.

USIA, with the usual administrative component, was divided principally into area offices—five geographical offices with country desks—and the "media"—divisions for press, film and television, VOA, and Information Centers Service, cultural programs seeded by Rockefeller, strengthened by two reorientations, and transferred from State. An office of policy was charged with making sure programs reflected foreign policy; beginning a long tradition, this office was headed by the agency's top professional, under the politically appointed director and his deputy.

The field posts remained as they had been, off and on, since 1917; the IIA task forces could not change what was set in stone. Participant Lawrence Norrie recalled clearly that the idea of two separate offices in the field for information and for culture was rejected only for practical reasons. No one believed USIA could provide sufficiently high-caliber personnel to hold two seats on the ambassador's team. The single commanding PAO was only a temporary measure. If Norrie remembered correctly, the structure like many temporary measures in Washington, soon became permanent. Norrie also remembered that the famous Wireless File, an in-house press service out of Washington, was fully expected to phase out when American international wire services like the Associated Press acquired their full strength.[10] This too never happened.

Streibert, from all reports, was a tough, aggressive, and often cruel man, but wise enough to let the gentlemanly Minnesotan Washburn run things below decks. They presided over an agency with morale that had long scraped the bottom yet which held responsibility for 217 USIS posts in seventy-six countries. Streibert and Washburn gave USIA and USIS the organizational shape they would keep until the end in 1999.

By 22 October, after years of silence, a mission statement for USIA was put in place, the first attempt ever to tease words into covering the mix of IIA's functions, as they had now sifted into USIA. The statement, flowing from a unidirectionalist and informationist mindset, was a far cry from what Johnson might have written. The new agency was to "submit evidence to peoples of other nations by means of communications techniques that the objectives and policies of the U.S. are in harmony with and will advance their legitimate aspirations for freedom, progress and peace." Four measures were specified to reach this goal: explain US government policies to others, show how US policies "harmonized" with other nations' aspirations, counter hostile propaganda, and "delineate" aspects of US life and culture that helped understand US policy. The loose syntax, probably deliberate, left one to guess at whether this meant delineating *all* aspects of US life, which would obviously help others understand, or only those that specifically illuminated policy—the mirror versus the showcase.

For the CAOs, the statement ducked every issue. It omitted the words "education" and "culture"; it did not mention the broad-gauged functions of cultural and educational relations spelled out in 1938; it said nothing about helping the private sector do its work, nothing about mutual understanding, nothing about helping Americans understand others, nothing about binationalism, multinational organizations, clashing political cultures, facilitation and coordination, or linking US universities to others. While the language did not explicitly stop cultural relations from moving forward, it provided no help and no direction. Education and culture were assigned no priority, nor was any sense of the long history of culture and education in US diplomacy reflected in the document. If CAOs were to be judged by the new mandate's criteria, then they might as well look for other work. USIA's rhetoric tied it tightly to government foreign policy, not to foreign relations; it made no distinction between short and long range; and it overlooked the distinction between immediate realities and those which could be changed by educational nurture over time. There were other questions—e.g., which national aspirations were "legitimate" and which not. But all this was forgotten in the general rejoicing over USIA's long overdue mission statement. Loyalists hastened to commit the text to memory.

Streibert and Washburn had been spared concern about the implicit values in exchanges by Fulbright's own action. USIA thus could gently tighten its control over the field and its work, including the cultural offices, with little resistance. True, State "approved" all cultural officer assignments, and allocations to field posts from State helped fund a few national positions in cultural offices, but in fact USIA held all the cards.

Streibert, in an early letter to his new agency, gave vent to heavy-handed exuberance. In Bentonian terms he eschewed the "propagandistic tone"; only "true propaganda" would be tolerated. He soared high, prescribing a USIA laundry list based on US values that should be extended to the world: individual and national freedom, the right to own property, the right to a decent standard of living, the common humanity of mankind, the vision of a peaceful world with nations compromising their differences and cooperating with the UN. To this naiveté, he added another American value: belief in a deity. Thomas Sorensen, a partisan Kennedy democrat and a dedicated propagandist and psychological warrior, quoted one critic to the effect that "the administration was 'trying to turn all foreigners into Republican Episcopalians'" (1964). He reported that a political-appointee, under the title Chief of Religious Information, proclaimed publicly that USIA would win over millions of "card-carrying Christians" abroad; mercifully the man soon resigned.[11]

The slapdash and carefree nationalism of the new agency opened the door wide to such ideological tinkering. Over the years USIA would struggle heroically to keep nationalists and internationalists, Hawks and Doves, the unidirectional storytellers and the substantive dialoguers all on the same team. The three-dimensional tug-of-war followed a zig-zag course over the next decades, as the agency reacted to micro-shifts of foreign policy, instead of keeping them at arm's length as the BBC and the British Council did; meanwhile, the cultural services followed Fulbright in seeing exchanges as the stratocruiser flying high above storms. USIA insisted on braving all storms head-on.

•   •   •

After 1953 three separate cultures emerged from this muddle: the USIA culture in Washington, the culture of the leftover IIA in State, now called CU—for the first two letters of culture—and the USIS field culture.

THE USIA CULTURE

It was jealous, self-absorbed, and assertive. Like any institution, it molded its officers and their values. Morale, for USIA loyalists, would strengthen, but the agency would never lose its deep defensiveness about perceived threats to its survival, whether from Congress, from State, from American intellectuals, or from within its own ranks. The former IIA cultural tools moved to USIA in 1953 survived and even did well within the rhetoric of USIA and the strict limits imposed by the budgetary choices of informationist PAOs. These "objects" of culture waxed and waned, as we have seen in the case of the libraries. Only over a long period of time would it become clear that USIA's cultural budgets were suspiciously flat, even when other elements were rising. The USIA culture behaved like that of any other agency, pressing ever onward for higher budgets but allocating it to selective purposes. Cultural and educational programs had been on a relatively steady gradualist course, following Fulbright's instincts; USIA leaders were much less constrained and found it natural to seek ever-increased funding. USIA's budgets covered a mosaic of sharply different country situations—and the dreams aroused by the lavish German-Japanese models inflated the vision. USIA field posts described their proposed work in a Country Plan, useful to Washington in building a coherent USIA budget request.

Within USIA the CAOs faced a dilemma: the path to promotion in the agency was laid out in USIA terms and few CAOs moved into the upper reaches. Those who preferred cultural work accepted second-class status. To keep the CAOs in the family, the more perceptive USIA leaders asserted that the cultural dimension was the jewel in USIA's crown or that the cultural dimension overseas enhanced USIS's impact abroad or that they lent Fred Astaire's class to Ginger Rogers's sex. Blunter PAOs argued that culture was the only umbrella under which USIS could carry on psychological warfare. And hard-core informationists said it was a take-it-or-leave-it situation, that CAOs faced a Faustian bargain because propaganda was all that Congress would ever understand. The loyalists professed sorrow but shrugged their shoulders when cultural officers declined to take on informational responsibilities. Officers who held out for cultural careers stagnated. In Washington assignments, CAOs were counseled to avoid working for CU. Those who feared that their beloved cultural relations might already have been sold irretrievably down the river practiced biting their tongues. A few resigned; some published caustic articles in out-of-the-way journals. Most did not rock the boat.

For the USIA culture, the 1950s were years of consolidation. Book-selection stabilized, thanks to ALA; but once McCarthy disappeared, a defensive book-selection process tightly managed by USIA went into operation and ALA again faded away. In Congress USIA as a psy-war agency was understood, where State's education and culture were not. Know-nothings like Rooney pilloried the cultural side—where impact and effect could only be proved over time—while welcoming the no less unprovable assertions of the informationists.

Fulbright avoided attacking USIA. Defending exchanges, ducking book and library questions, he still worried about propaganda; for him, VOA was a questionable, provocative, and interventionist relic of warfare for another era. If the educational world did not attack USIA, they did not go out of their way to defend it; USIA's friends likewise did little for CU and education. It was less a feud than a mutual indifference. For USIA, interagency coordination was a thing of the past. Even USIA forgot about CU, and the other expanding agencies—AID, the new HEW, and CIA—pursued their educational work overseas as they pleased.

The USIA culture was well defended. The private supporters of cultural relations had only a dim view of what was happening. Abroad, academic travelers visited the USIS posts and saw that overseas culture and education were subsumed in USIA's supposedly higher mission, but their CAO friends tried not to stir the pot. As for foreign observers, they saw little difference—USIS was already an old story in which they were already losing interest. BFS members nervous about PAO rule could do little about it—the day had passed when a single letter from Morey in Rome could activate both Senate and the advisory commission.

USIA officers were instructed to present the best agency face possible for public consumption, at the risk of budget cuts. The academic world reserved judgment; even though USIA seemed an odd compromise, perhaps it could be changed in time. Legislators wearied of the question. In the Senate Fulbright could not move things forward. At the top, Eisenhower was shielded by his advisors from the tensions in the ranks.

A factor at work was rising costs. Some cultural programs—libraries in particular—were more expensive than others. Waving the banner of economy was persuasive to a Congress acutely aware of costs but only vaguely of benefits. Open-access libraries were repeatedly held up to McCarthy's question: how did they contribute to foreign policy? In State, with libraries no longer a CU responsibility, no one leapt to their defense.

THE CU CULTURE

This was another matter entirely.[12] State lay a few blocks to the southwest of USIA; there the IIA remnant, now called the Office of Educational and Cultural Affairs (CU), was another world. CU had a long history and a longer prehistory, outlined in books on cultural diplomacy, beginning with *The Cultural Approach* in 1947. Over the years information and psychological warfare had been more turbulent than the cultural diplomatic function, which forged quietly ahead and only went public with the book-selection issue. Growing gradually and steadily, as Fulbright wished, culture flowed smoothly, but it was ever the lesser of the old IIA's two functions.

Lodged under State's public affairs, IIA did not warrant a politically appointed leader and was managed by stalwart veterans like Russ Riley and Hal Howland. Without a political head, the office was at the mercy of State's personnel and budget offices; it would only move toward bureau status with its own Assistant Secretary in 1957.

CU, like the founding division, was never large. Starting in 1938 with a staff of eight, its cultural staff never passed three hundred, while USIA in 1961 had twelve thousand employees, counting national employees in the field. CU's Old Guard retained a spirit of dogged hopefulness, but committed cultural officers like Jacob Canter knew that trouble was inbuilt. The understaffed and overspecialized CU offices kept more and more to their knitting.

CU in the 1950s consisted of US-oriented program specialists, directed by toughened veterans. They had to rely on the CAOs as their eyes, ears, and hands in the field. The CAOs in turn counted on CU for expertise on US developments. Into this covey of specialists, "hedgehogs" as Charles Frankel affectionately called them, trickled a flow of foreign service officers, most from USIA. In 1971, with one foreign service officer for four domestic employees; the foreign service ran CU. It had already acquired a reputation, with some justification said Coombs, as a graveyard for once-promising diplomats and burnt-out cases from both USIA and State. The USIA officers who cared enough to insist on serving in CU found this context disheartening.

No one in CU below the director was assigned to the big picture, which was left to a small office of policy and plans; the hedgehogs were too busy to worry about breadth. The issues tackled by Turner and MacLeish eluded the harried second-generation veterans. CU could not bring vision to bear in "coordinating" giants like CIA, AID, the new HEW, and the military. Being small had advantages, in principle and in practice, but it also produced small and defensive thinking. In 1953 the hardy few who kept Cherrington's faith had watched the hopes of the early postwar period grow dim. CU was a minor office buried under the Assistant Secretary for Public Affairs, and John J. Rooney used CU as the favorite setting for his annual death-of-a-thousand-cuts show.

The advisory commission was no GAC—it was advisory and had little impact on the CU culture. About eighteen months after USIA was created, the advisory commissions for both CU and USIA, in an unprecedented joint action, responded to a specific complaint and set up a CU-USIA task force on which Canter represented USIA.[13] The team reported friction at four points, all of which involved education and universities: the "University Participation Program," American studies, ELT, and overseas seminars. The university participation question sprang from a case in Greece in which USIS Athens had brokered and funded a relationship between Athens College and Hamilton College. USIA jumped at the idea of similar affiliations worldwide, but the CAO in Athens neglected to inform CU and the BFS; meanwhile USIA had already offered the idea as a global model. The 1955 task force survey, with barely disguised irony, reported USIA's discovery that CU's cultural diplomacy actually supported *USIA's* purposes: "Recognizing that certain of its information objectives could best be achieved through cultural means, USIA [in mid-1954] began to expand and give new emphasis to cultural activities. . . . [USIA planned] to appoint 'cultural representatives' and to request funds for the development of American Studies in nine European countries." Another surprise: of the basic factors responsible for confusion, "chief among them was the fact that USIA has the only overseas staff, including the Cultural Affairs Officer." *Mirabile dictu*!

The 1955 report, a blip on a large screen, recommended that the task force become an ongoing watchdog committee for CU-USIA relations; this idea was disregarded. Instead, a new position was set aside in USIA's Office of Policy, where a high-level officer—Canter was the first—would spend his time monitoring CU-USIA communications. It was the highest post a committed culturalist could hold in USIA.

The predominantly academic BFS also offered full support, but it could help only at the margins. Overseeing Fulbright exchanges and representing the university world, it solved academic exchange problems, formulated policy, managed the government-university interface, and in principle spoke directly to Eisenhower through its annual report. BFS professional staff was still strong, including an executive director, a deputy, and two program officers, plus clerical help, with ample funding for travel; BFS members regularly visited thirty-odd formal commissions and two dozen other country posts involved in academic exchanges. But BFS knew the real question—field staffing—was off limits. BFS and the CU advisory commission could not change the illogical division of responsibilities; CU, in the end, was alone, with only the Senator as its champion.

CU's structure reflected its functions. Until 1963 it was a set of offices each dedicated to a single program category: academic exchanges, short-term foreign visitors, American schools abroad, relations with US voluntary institutions, performing arts, and foreign students. The foreign student office, for example, kept track of nearly two thousand US universities, their foreign-student advisors, and their professional association, NAFSA; hedgehog Marita Houlihan knew every inch of the territory and every advisor's first name. Most CU officers communicated directly with field posts, with the six area divisions of State and of USIA, and with dozens of universities and intermediate organizations like IIE; each office competed for its share of the CU budget. For the collegial private agencies, it was a good structure: IIE dealt with one small team for all US and foreign predoctoral students.

Germany and Japan taught the staff how to process large numbers of qualified grantees through spin-off. Since Congress limited CU staff, much of its work had to be contracted out to specialized private agencies like IIE and CIES. The spun-off agencies ran well, tailored to CU needs; they kept the US educational and cultural sector involved and soon were generating their own activities. Duggan and Welles were right: most of CU's work was being done by the private world, even if on government funding.

Inside CU, staff maintained expertise over an array of US developments in international education and culture, covering the entire country and the multilateral organizations, private and public. They shaped their foreign-bound products across cultures in a hundred or more countries, working with an experienced and talented cadre of experienced CAOs at the point of contact. Thus CU's internal culture was two-layered: a thick US-expert culture and a thinner outward-looking culture, with foreign service officers managing both.

CU's problem lay with its field agents. CAOs, required to serve in Washington every decade or so, found that USIA jobs available to them were at low levels—in American studies, ELT, BNCs, books, or libraries— whereas IOs served in the prestigious geographical area offices, in positions with "policy implications," as was said. Even in CU there was room for only a few USIA officers at a time, but at least they held appropriate rank. As a result mistrust reigned between domestic and foreign-oriented staff. CU domestic staff could rarely travel abroad.

To help bridge this gap in the 1950s and 1960s, a three-layered process called "familiarization" was put in place. First, newly recruited USIA officers, in training before departure, spent two of their eight weeks in CU. Second, CAOs on home-leave were expected to spend one of two weeks of "consultation" in Washington with CU colleagues. Third, CAOs were reimbursed for US travel to consult with relevant program agencies, foundations, and corporations, mainly in New York. But all too soon entropy took over and the system decayed. Tight budgets were blamed, but there was more: hard-pressed CU staff could not always spare the time for long chats with field officers, and few were good teachers in any case. Field officers, after the heady experience of foreign service, saw the hedgehogs as obstructionist.

One example covering twelve years of one man's experience may suggest the difficulties. In 1961 a recruit from the university world reported to USIA for training. The new CAO would have had every reason to consider CU his home base; USIA's training office, a graveyard of its own, neglected to mention CU to him. Eager to get the officer into the field, the two-week CU visit was overlooked in favor of a useful area studies seminar at the Foreign Service Institute. When USIA suddenly had second thoughts, the recruit was yanked out of the seminar two days early and sent to CU for a two-day visit.

CU was unprepared. He was led by a secretary to a small windowless room with counters along three walls holding the eleven-volume how-to-do-it Manual of Administration, an unreadable reference available in all USIS posts. He was instructed to "read the Manual" and left to himself. Breaking ranks, the recruit arranged meetings with available CU officers, two of whom were openly hostile. His days in CU were pointless. Only after two years of field work did he see that CU was his real home.

On his first home leave, the CAO reported eagerly to CU for his week of consultation. Greeted again by impatient CU staff, he persisted and managed to learn something about the office. Seven years later, with an outstanding record as cultural officer in three posts and a mid-career university fellowship behind him, he came due for his first Washington assignment. Ignoring portentous USIA advice, he insisted on serving in CU. Despite CU reluctance, he persisted and served for two years, overcoming CU's basic hostility toward USIA field officers. His experience was not uncommon; in general, CU-USIA relations were barely polite and tended to worsen.

In the 1960s, as USIA tightened control over the CAOs, the three-layered familiarization program was slashed repeatedly: USIA home-leave consultations were shortened to one week, then to three days, with no time specified for CU. CU training for new USIA entrants was reduced to a single day, then to a two-hour seminar. Consultations with colleagues in the cooperating agencies and in the private world were done on the officer's time and money. USIA officers ignored CU and CU returned the compliment. Natural civility and collegiality prevailed in the field but in Washington, tensions—the end product of historical ignorance—ran high.

Interagency coordination, the old ICC idea, was an empty formula by 1953. In the field, government agencies, including the Library of Congress, the Smithsonian, the Department of Labor, the National Science Foundation, and a variety of research-oriented government agencies like the National Institutes of Health, managed their intellectual and research relationships, touching base as needed with the CAO. By 1960 overseas educational activities were carried on by a dozen powerful agencies on their own, keeping the CAO informed, if he or she cared. After Welles, no ICC was in charge.

THE FIELD CULTURE

It was a bureaucratic culture in itself, altogether a happier situation. As we have seen with Fairbank and Morey, collegiality in the field was high. But tensions lay just below the surface because cultural affairs was rarely a diplomatic priority, definitions were unclear, and funding was skewed. The "cultural types" handled CU programs; and at the field end of the program funnel, available officers used what they were sent, spent what they were given, and when necessary did without funding. The standard structure for all field posts, whatever the country context, was fixed: a triangle with a PAO at the peak, commanding both IO and CAO. Fulbright was still arguing for two separate field units, an information service and an educational-cultural office. Task-force discussions in 1953 "postponed" the idea and the question never arose again. In truth, a separate cultural field structure would have added 60 percent or more to the field administrative budget, even if in the longer run there would have been important savings.

American intellectual travelers collected their favorite howlers about the USIS staff they met—like the CAO who confused Claude Lévi-Strauss with the manufacturer of blue jeans, or the CAO who had never heard of Lionel Trilling, or the branch PAO who wondered why a visiting string quartet needed music stands—were they "still on sheet music"? But the humor stayed under cover.

The field culture was commanded by PAOs, some of whom were very good. The PAO, perhaps with a deputy and an administrative officer depending on the post's size, managed a branch for information headed by the IO and one for cultural and educational affairs headed by the CAO. If there were branch posts, they were headed by a branch PAO and perhaps a deputy. The country PAO was supposed to make information and culture flow together, representing USIS on the embassy's Country Team and dealing with USIA in Washington. Only in the 1980s did a few brave USIA officers admit openly that the PAO position was a costly vestige, serving no function that the IO and CAO could not have handled directly. But instead of phasing out the PAO, USIA slowly strengthened the position. In 1977, when CU was absorbed into USIA, CAO independence was further reduced. By 1980 CAO field positions and local staff were dropping away and by 2000 the number of one-person USIS posts had skyrocketed.

The unwritten 1953 compact between the new USIA and the fifteen-year-old CU was a bargain for USIA. USIA-designated officers administered CU's programs in the field, and CU reimbursed USIA for a percentage of their salary costs and for some local salaries. For example, in a large European post like Italy, as late as the 1970s, CU was still reimbursing USIA for one full-time American salary, split between two officers, and for two local employees, while contributing to the costs of the Fulbright Commission. The shared-cost agreements between USIA and State, which also covered space, communications, transportation, and a variety of other charges, were the subject of increasingly acrimonious and ever-mysterious annual negotiations in Washington.

Beneath the calm surface lurked the demons. CAOs, like Stevens in Mexico, reported to USIA officers who might or might not understand what they were doing. CAO field assignments were approved by CU in theory, but in fact it was an ongoing horse-trade—CU knew that turning down one candidate might guarantee worse. Funds for housing, entertainment, and other expenses were doled out by the PAO, who had priority on the post's automobiles, furnishings, and services. Annual personnel reports, the building blocks of promotion, were written by the PAO and reviewed in Washington by compliant USIA desks—advice from CU was sought but used only when it fit USIA purposes. CU criticism could not by itself harm a USIA officer, but CU knew its praise could damn one. Power bureaucrat Thomas Sorensen, ranked third in USIA in 1962, told a new recruit who had impressed CU director Philip Coombs, "we know the Assistant Secretary for CU thinks highly of you, but we have decided not to hold it against you."

Career profiles of cultural officers and academic qualifications declined steadily after 1953. In 1942 most cultural officers had graduate degrees, university teaching experience, and perhaps a tenured faculty position, but attracting talents like Fairbank, Harkness, Brickell, Carlton, Sprague Smith, Canter, and Morey was only the first step; to keep them in service, USIA had to offer satisfying work, freedom from as many pointless frustrations as possible, respectful and understanding supervision, assignments appropriate to their expertise, encouragement to continued growth, motivated younger colleagues as assistants they could train, promotion when appropriate to greater responsibilities, reimbursement for expenses, and salaries commensurate with those of their IO colleagues. University educators were not used to having bosses, but they knew how to work with colleagues; independent scholars expected comparable independence in USIA. They wanted a voice in their assignments; they wanted to use the languages they knew in countries they understood; they wanted time to prepare in depth for new country assignments; they wanted to continue their research and publications. Most would have been attracted by a rough life-career plan, foreseeing five or six postings abroad, and two or three assignments in Washington; they wanted some kind of goal within the service. But these reasonable aspirations were impractical, their careers were governed by expediency, they were treated like clerks, directed by informationists who, at their best, had little understanding of their talents, and called to serve whims like Venezuela's baseball project.

The ambitious CAOs, required periodically to work in Washington, aspired no higher than to serve as one of the deputies to the politically appointed Assistant Secretary for education and culture in State—although only Jacob Canter, with diplomat Arthur Hummel, ever achieved this. Few committed cultural officers aspired to be PAOs or even ambassadors. Like Canter, they believed themselves unqualified for that work and saw no reason to learn it; many thought they already had better jobs. All PAOs on the other hand wanted embassies of their own. In my quarter-century with USIA, ten or twelve colleagues became ambassadors—to countries no larger than Nigeria.

After 1974 academics or holders of doctorates were no longer recruited by USIA except by accident, and none were trained specifically for a CAO specialty. With most committed cultural specialists gone, all new entrants were classified as generalists, available for assignment in any slot. With age, fatigue, and burnout, and with the option of early retirement, the cultural corps declined in quality; the CAOs' role as intermediaries between the intellectuals and the universities of two or more cultures drifted toward irrelevance. It was the last phase in the decline of CAO independence and quality, the sadder in that American universities, after the war, had leaped forward in international sophistication and were producing fine young talents with good language skills, ideally suited for facilitating intellectual flows abroad.

In short, after the creation of USIA, CAOs—primarily field-oriented officers—were quoted or misquoted, tasked or ignored, praised or damned, promoted or left to stagnate, transferred or retained—all at the iron whim of the PAO and like-minded superiors. True, many noble USIA PAOs—men and women like Albert Harkness, William King, William Weld, Barbara White, Jay Gildner, Robert Amerson, Marilyn Johnson, and William Weathersby—did everything in their power to make life fruitful for the career CAOs and the prestigious outsiders who occasionally graced their posts. In my experience, these broad-gauged USIA figures handled CAOs as colleagues, not subordinates. Their CAOs were grateful. Yet even under outstanding leadership, it was clear to most that they were being handled.

Three administrative cultures existed then, separate but unequal. People moved between them and managed to get along, but only if they accepted USIA's right to run things. The CU-USIA arrangement was a precious gift to USIA, but a disaster for CU and the idea of an independent cultural diplomacy. Dedicated cultural officers knew that the arrangement compelled obedience and loyalty to a set of values not theirs. The system worked, but just barely; certainly it produced less than it might have. As a matter of principle, it was an administrative and a personal nightmare.

• • •

In Washington the slicing away of cultural functions had not ended. After USIA took the largest slice of all, Health, Education, and Welfare (HEW) got to work and set up its own overseas educational programs. AID had already defined training as different from education; now HEW took charge of the American side of education, choosing grantees for their capacity to enrich American learning; they went abroad to learn and were instructed not to teach. HEW's international component, built under Undersecretary Nelson Rockefeller, soared when Sputnik convinced the U.S. to strengthen education in certain fields. The National Defense and Education Act of 1958 (NDEA), motivated by Soviet success in launching a basketball-sized satellite, responded to the shocked US discovery that a supposedly backward rival could master the applied science of rocketry. Congress, uncharacteristically, reached for educational solutions; its first draft of NDEA proposed better science and math education in the secondary schools, only later adding foreign language and area studies. State, with a few additional personnel and existing field staff, could have handled the area-studies component of NDEA via the Fulbright Program, but Congress assigned responsibility to HEW. CU was helpless amidst the giants.

HEW was the sixth government agency, counting IMET, to enter cultural diplomacy. From 1937–48 US Commissioner of Education John Studebaker had worked closely with State; a member of the GAC until 1948, he accepted the wisdom of Welles's argument that all foreign activities should flow through State. In 1947 Studebaker and each successive US Commissioner was named *ex officio* to BFS but the job after Studebaker was delegated downward. The system apparently recognized that coordination was essential. But the mighty HEW increasingly ignored this point, perhaps because NDEA funding for language and area studies was larger than CU's entire budget. State was left with "mutual understanding," looking less and less meaningful to a Congress hungry for action. In the field, grantees from yet another agency took up CAO time.

In New York the Ford Foundation, with its ITR, was building US area-studies programs in parallel, also without coordination—Ford did not worry about duplication or competition from HEW and NDEA. No one thought about excess investment or uneven distribution; no one worried about how the nation allocated its resources.[14] In fact, duplication, even in the private sector, was rife, overtraining in some fields was obvious, and other needs were going unmet, as McCaughey has noted.[15]

Soviet propagandists were delighted to find the Americans linking education with "defense," just as they relished a US propaganda agency's control over cultural affairs. CAOs in the 1960s were surprised to find their names listed in scurrilous Soviet publications unmasking CIA agents. Foreign skepticism about the integrity of American overseas educational activity, fed by these Soviet publications, grew steadily. Only the binational Fulbright Program (and its Soviet extension IREX) was protected from mistrust, and that only in part. US intellectuals and the universities were no happier about the hawkish cast of NDEA than with the implemental culture of AID, which by the mid-1950s was issuing gigantic contracts to American universities for vast educational projects abroad in the developing world, including unstable countries like Vietnam. The universities, like the CAOs in the field, adjusted to realities, learned to get what they could, used what they could get, and did as much as they could with it. Even Fulbright admitted that he would use any argument for his program's funding.

To meet government's capacity to issue massive contracts and grants, professional fund-raisers and grant-writers moved into the universities and foreign area studies blossomed. In 1987, Richard Lambert, a University of Pennsylvania South Asianist who grew with the NDEA programs, added up the numbers. In the 1940s there were no more than fourteen language and area programs on US campuses; by the end of the 1960s there were over three hundred. The awarding of doctorates rose from one hundred to nearly one thousand annually by 1970. In the universities of 1940 there were perhaps four hundred area specialists; by the 1980s there were over eighteen thousand—Harvard's Archibald Carey Coolidge was a distant memory.[16] Only the voluntary educational associations around Washington's Dupont Circle, like the ACE, had any sense of the whole picture and its costs. Meanwhile, with real money flying about, the small change handed out by CU dropped below the universities' range of vision.

As humans do, and as Americans do particularly well, USIA, CU, and its staffs pulled together, especially in the field. The collegial style overrode problems from day to day. Everyone wanted the system to work—the universities took what they could, the cultural officers had little choice, and the PAOs had every reason to keep the CAOs happy in their place. Field officers remained cheerful, overrode the negatives, and faced daily needs and opportunities. "Relations with CU," the USIA leadership would dutifully report, "have never been better." CU leadership—with gritted teeth—would say the same of USIA.

CHAPTER THIRTEEN

George Allen in the Middle

If the functions of USIA were properly conceived and executed, members of Congress would no more think of calling on that agency to "throw the book at Castro" than it would of calling on the Associated Press, or the New York Public Library, or the Rockefeller Foundation to do so.

—George V. Allen, 1963

The real mission of USIS is to be the embassy's outreach to the cultural and intellectual elite of that country, and the mode for doing it is not the same as for conveying substantive information.

—Wayne A. Wilcox, 1973

EISENHOWER WAS THAT RAREST OF LEADERS, one who learned on the job. But in the case of cultural diplomacy, his learning curve was slow. After letting Dulles remove IIA from State, he moved gradually toward his own view, too late to make a difference.

In 1957 a new Undersecretary of State was named: internationalist Christian Herter, an experienced diplomat who had been with Wilson at Versailles. A man of Wellesean stamp, he grew stronger as Dulles's health declined and then was appointed to replace him. To lead CU and cultural diplomacy, he invited his friend Robert Thayer, gave the office its own bureau status, and provided political leadership and access to the top.

Thayer's energetic behavior was a signal. He immediately reopened the culture-propaganda debate. In the Senate, Fulbright took note and, with Hubert Humphrey and Lyndon Johnson on his team, ordered another outside study, this time by the Brookings Institution. Meanwhile, the Senator set his staff to drafting the legislation that would become the Fulbright-Hays Act of 1961, spelling out the results of his long meditation on better ways to run the peculiar railroad of cultural relations. At the same moment, CU's advisory commission weighed in, and the New York foundations rejoined the battle. Three ideas were still alive: creating a better-funded and better-protected cultural diplomatic function, building an expanded US university presence in diplomacy, and providing stronger cultural representation in the field.[1]

Streibert returned to New York in November 1956 and, to no one's surprise, joined the Rockefeller Brothers Fund. Arthur Larsen, ex-Dean of the University of Pittsburgh Law School, lasted eleven months as USIA director—his executioner was Lyndon Johnson, retaliating for Larsen's sharply partisan campaign speeches written for Eisenhower. Expelling the director took little of Johnson's time. The larger-than-life Texan, close to Fulbright, agreed—with little sense of the long-range implications—that US education had a responsibility to the world.

At USIA Washburn remained as deputy and chief operating officer, carrying over to serve Larsen's replacement, veteran diplomat George V. Allen. Allen, an experienced foreign service officer, had commanded four difficult embassies and had followed Benton in IIA. His thoughtful and well-informed vision of field needs made culture a central factor in USIA's work. In Benton's terms, he was a mirror theorist; he wanted to project America by soft-sell honey rather than persuasive vinegar, even with the greedy Soviet bear.

Before his death Washburn still spoke of Allen's reign as USIA's golden years.[2] Allen was a contemporary of Laurence Duggan at State who had risen rapidly; in 1947 he was the first to understand the crippling nature of the public affairs side of the job. By 1957 he had served in Iran, Yugoslavia, India, and Greece, then as Assistant Secretary for Near East and South Asia. From this background, he drew his unique sense of field needs, communications, the crucial nature of credibility, USIA's global reach, its difficulties relating to State, and congressional hostility. His wise professionalism lifted staff spirits. When he retired in December 1960, the *Washington Post* noted: "If he was unable to recoup the deficiencies of national policy, he at least restored the dignity of USIA, improved its relations with Capitol Hill and provided a needed sense of direction." Significantly, the *Post* after only four years of USIA's life believed the new agency's dignity needed restoring.

This North Carolinian, via Duke and Harvard, came to USIA at fifty-two as a seasoned Middle East hand. Abroad, he had admired the impact of the "slow media"—USIA's name for cultural affairs. He took a unique interest in libraries, but he knew about exchanges, ELT, book translations, and BNCs. He often said that if he had to start from zero in any country, he would first open a library. More than anyone, he understood the misbegotten USIA-CU split.

Allen's productive years at USIA followed the death of Stalin, the end of the Korean War, and Khrushchev's so-called Soviet peace offensive with its intimations of détente. As the U.S. continued opening outward, "peaceful co-existence" seemed a realistic possibility. After Eisenhower's 1955 summit meeting with Khrushchev and Bulganin, negotiations on cultural relations began; by January 1958 the first US-USSR exchange agreement was in effect.

With USIA on a relatively stable track, Allen could focus on the longer range. But CU was in trouble. Allen's relations with Herter and Thayer were exemplary—he was one of State's own and respected the dogged CU team. But CU was depressed; John J. Rooney's tyranny was in its early phase. In 1951 the budget had sagged to $16 million, then slumped by 1955 to less than $10 million, in constant dollars. CU's total grantees for the world fell under five thousand per year, compared with three thousand for Germany alone in 1953. And CU's slowly accumulating responsibilities were diluting the quality of its attention. In 1957 there were ninety-seven participating countries, doubling demand since the 1940s, diluting funding for all. Ingenious use of foreign currencies helped, with new PL 480 funds from sales of agricultural surplus making available generous funding in countries like India, where the giant USIS post spent all available money. Slow budget growth for CU did not begin until 1959.

In May 1959 Herter moved into Dulles's chair. He came from a first family of Massachusetts, where he had served as governor. Educated in his beloved France and at Harvard before the First World War, he had been posted to Berlin and Washington, then to the Versailles Conference. He assisted Secretary of Commerce Hoover and knew his pre-Fulbright thinking; he graced the board of Johns Hopkins University during Milton Eisenhower's presidency; and he learned binationalism on the board of the Belgian-American Educational Foundation. The New England patrician, as Secretary of State, contrasted sharply with the obdurate Dulles; and he was a genuine fan of CU-USIA.

A few blocks away, George Allen, himself no ordinary foreign service officer, was reassessing culture and propaganda. An unabashed liberal internationalist serving a Republican president, he was the classic public servant, what the 1924 Rogers Act was designed to produce. By his side, Abbott Washburn was the ideal political deputy and a sensitive manager. To help the public understand USIA, Allen made dozens of speeches, salted with pointed personal stories, reminiscences, and wisdom. His unusual grasp of history set a context for understanding the growth of US cultural diplomacy, which he had by then followed closely for twenty-five years. Through his speeches and writings, we may glimpse his thought at three different moments: his first encounter with the division (1947–49), his three years as head of USIA (1956–60), and his early retirement (1963).[3]

As head of IIA in the 1940s, Allen was a learner; but he was afflicted with crushing public affairs responsibilities. A secure realist, he understood the uses of soft power; by experience, he was a practical culturalist. Invited to join his friend Duggan at an IIE conference on foreign students at the University of Michigan in May 1948, he rejoiced in meeting his new partner, the National Association of Foreign Student Affairs. For IIA, he said, private education was the *senior* partner of government (author's stress). What worked best was government funding stimulating private exchanges and private agencies executing government programs. Government can only *facilitate* exchanges because the government depends on educators for "experience and counsel." His agenda was that of Welles: partnership, stimulation, facilitation.

In September 1948 Allen reached out more broadly, addressing the new Smith-Mundt cultural advisory commission. He lamented the decades-long US delay in moving into cultural relations and added that education is a slow medium, producing no miracles; he said budgets alone cannot immediately settle the world's problems. "Negotiated settlements, to be lasting, must be based on understandings between peoples who are thoroughly grounded, through education, in the basic principles of democracy." Education is and must remain autonomous. "The task we face is to keep alive and promote the principles of academic freedom which we Americans cherish so dearly." He denounced the US seekers of subversion: "The totalitarian mind is not confined to Eastern Europe. We must combat . . . misguided individuals of any totalitarian stripe, either at home or abroad. . . . The play is for the mind of man. . . . The winner leads the world into a new realm of intellectual freedom, the dignity of man, and worldwide understanding and peace."

For Benton, UNESCO had been central. Allen's approach to the organization, although positive, was more critical. In September 1949, heading the US delegation to the UNESCO General Conference in Paris chaired by Director General Julian Huxley and his deputy Walter Laves, Allen defined UNESCO's task in three parts: "to develop international understanding among the diverse peoples of the world, . . . to mobilize the will to peace, . . . to tear down barriers to communication so people can know each other directly." UNESCO must become "a dynamic force for peace." Two months later in Beirut to ratify UNESCO's convention for the exchange of audio-visual educational materials, Allen dwelt on Lebanon's history and its great American University. Speaking near the AUB campus, he added praise for French and British educational contributions to the area. Gently chiding UNESCO for a slow start, for vague language, and for unclear project descriptions, he warned about loose financial controls. He urged expanding UNESCO's audience: "Intellectual cooperation must not be confined to cooperation among intellectuals. We must bring UNESCO to the masses and the masses to UNESCO." He decried the jingoes who believed America had all the answers; he struck at the geopolitical "realists" who, in thinking about the UN, "appear genuinely to believe that . . . the question of whether different peoples understand each other or cooperate will not matter . . . since peace will be maintained by force." He stressed innovation: "Freedom to try new methods is one of the essential characteristics of democracy itself. . . . We are prepared, under democracy, to tolerate every idea except intolerance. . . . The free flow of ideas is our only salvation and UNESCO was created to bring this about." His speech was vintage MacLeish.

Nine years later, as head of USIA, he wore a different hat, managing an agency he surely knew had compounded the CU dilemma. Ever a committed State Department officer, he had continued to grow. In November 1957, off the record, he told USIA staff of his commitment to cultural relations; he spoke of openness to ideas and change: "We need to concentrate on activities that prove effective, but we also need the con-stant fertilization of new ideas." Promoting democracy was the point. "To encourage democratic processes throughout the world, we should give the peoples of the world, as openly and frankly as we can, explana-tions of what we are doing, so that they can, in the democratic process, make up their minds about us." For him, cultural tools lay at the center: "There is a long-range need for such things as our overseas information libraries, to give one example, which would continue whether the Com-munist conspiracy existed or not."

Seven months later, again quietly with USIA staff, Allen tackled propa-ganda as an idea Americans naturally mistrust. Providing information and explaining the U.S. is not "propaganda," he argued; Americans must accept USIA as a "proper arm in the conduct of the foreign relations of the U.S."At the same time, USIA cannot contribute to policy if it has nothing substantive to contribute; USIA's substance resides in the quality of its officers.

In January 1958 Allen spoke to public administrators about interna-tional interdependence. In September, writing to a member of USIA's advisory commission on information, he urged focusing "on long-range operations wherever possible." Information had limits. Drawing on a USIS field report of French and Soviet successes in North Africa, he said, "It is possible, in this day and age, to manipulate public opinion, . . . to create loves and hates [or] needs where there are none. But that is not enough: it is difficult to tamper with fundamental beliefs." One must work from what is already there; that side will succeed "whose aims come closer to the natural aspirations of the people."

A month later at Wagner College he tackled education with "The Best Road to Freedom." He said, "The work of the USIA itself is education. Our goal is understanding, . . . and understanding always infers a certain amount of education. . . . If I had to maintain just one USIA activity and no more, my choice would be our libraries." In early 1959, before a House committee, he pondered American values: "Our national interests coincide with the interests of a large proportion of mankind: the desire for liberty, peace and progress." In June 1959, at Huron College in Karl Mundt's South Dakota, he promised that USIA would not "try to picture the U.S. as having achieved perfection," but "Congress made it clear that those of us who engaged in this field should [project] a sense of what we Americans know we are—a strong and alert democratic nation dedicated to man's best capabilities." He identified "the heart" of USIS operations as its 251 cultural centers and BNCs around the world, each with its li-brary. Interagency coordination? If fifteen other US government agencies do exchanges, he thought, the more the better. "True" propaganda leads to understanding; "honest and straightforward presentation of facts is the best basis for international understanding."

Speaking to teacher-educators, Allen warned of the dangers inherent in the idea of reaching people over the heads of their governments, citing

Franklin in Paris and the nefarious Citizen Genêt in the infant American republic. Speaking of libraries he said, "The U.S. has inherited most of its institutions from our ancestors in Europe or elsewhere, but one thing we have invented ourselves is the public library." Information has limits: boasting offends and broadcasting details of a negotiation ruins outcomes. Emphatically, USIA's business is *not* to "sell" America.

Before a tough-minded audience of high-ranking officers of all three armed services at the National War College, he chose to focus on US cultural programs. With a rich command of history, he spoke of private programs with China, the Boxer Indemnities, the Iranian indemnity, Belgian and Finnish war relief, Rockefeller's work in Latin America, and the origins of the Fulbright Program. He dwelt in detail on foreign students, arguing for more exchanges with the USSR. Standing firm against Soviet expansionism, he said the U.S. must convince the Russians that Americans "are democratic people who want to be friendly and to achieve a decent, peaceful world."

To a group of top-level US university administrators in November 1959, Allen said the East-West conflict mattered less than the search for "an international organization strong enough to maintain law and order." Warning of rising expectations, he calmly accepted the fact of growing US hegemony but wondered "whether we deserve the position of leadership which history, consciously or unconsciously, absent-mindedly or not, has thrust upon the U.S."

Before another high-level audience of educators at the American Council on Education, with Robert Thayer and AID director Leonard Saccio on the platform, he tackled interagency coordination, speaking to the university and foundation audience on "A Foreign Policy for Higher Education."[4] At a time when copious university contracts for educational development were flowing, he compared himself with humor and modesty to his French counterpart Roger Seydoux, who headed the French equivalent of USIA, which included both the equivalent of CU *and* AID. In Washington, by contrast, no one was in charge of foreign cultural relations. Allen wanted to do "ten times more than we are doing," but noncoordination made it tough. He teased CU's Thayer, "coordinator of educational exchange activities," for his "initiative and enthusiasm to go ahead and call meetings and get groups together without worrying about whether he was authorized to do so by some executive order." He thanked God "that we have people with enough initiative to go ahead and do it." Many believe, he said, that culture and propaganda "should be handled by two separate agencies"; but to underline how much was being done as things stood, he put together an aggregate picture of CU and USIA programs and cultural activities. Addressing public affairs, Allen outlined efforts *in* public and *with* publics: USIS's librarian in London spent most of her time handling reference questions from the British Parliament; Professor Myers, back from Germany at Washington and Lee

College, recruited a dozen Americans to teach American literature in West Germany.

On US education, he sounded like Fulbright. For him foreign policy coincided with USIA's purpose: not to *sell* the U.S. but to build international understanding. At the same time, he could not justify "education for education's sake." Education alone does not defeat Communism— Kerala for example is India's most literate state yet also its most communist. In a colonialist analogy, he said the British were still beloved in India because they introduced free institutions like British law and education and built bridges between two extremely diverse civilizations. British India "took time; it took work. But it was done and can be done again. . . . Our task, in foreign educational activity, is to build international understanding."

Thayer and Herter were pressing a slow shift in Eisenhower's foreign policy in his second term, and Allen, in every word he uttered in public, seems to have been on their team. With Rockefeller in the White House pressing for Open Skies and Atoms for Peace, Thayer and Herter, with Allen's cooperation, turned the administration to "waging peace"—there could have been no more Fulbrightian motto.

Our third glimpse of Allen's thought comes later, at a single moment in 1963. The director had left USIA in 1960 and thereafter maintained the discreet silence of a professional.[5] Marking the agency's tenth anniversary in August 1963, Allen felt compelled to break his silence with a full page of probing criticism of USIA in the *New York Herald Tribune*. America's attempt to tell the world about its aims and aspirations, he wrote, "is today and always has been, in my view, basically unsound"; credibility was all that mattered, he added. He attacked USIA and VOA for their self-proclaimed vigor, exemplified by their recent massive radio campaign "throwing the book" at Castro's Cuba during the Missile Crisis. Allen argued that the energetic campaign had solidified rather than weakened Castro, while damaging US credibility with obvious propaganda. He pressed for extended English-only broadcasting, BBC-style, noting that the military radio-television system already girdled the globe. While BBC served its former empire's need for information, VOA dealt solely in propaganda. USIA's serious handicap was Congress, which assumed it was a propaganda agency; on the contrary, USIA was—or should have been— the government analog of "the Associated Press, or the New York Public Library, or the Rockefeller Foundation." Any other view distorts the agency's purpose: "The trouble with USIA . . . is its tendency to satisfy American demands, not to win friends and influence people abroad." In any case, propaganda was the wrong road. "Americans are the world's worst propagandists," so it would be wise to "stop trying." In closing, he turned to libraries, the "most valuable activity of USIA in my opinion, chiefly because the books and materials they contain were obviously not written or published for the particular country in which the libraries are situated."[6]

Allen's deepening thought and conviction over sixteen years remained remarkably consistent. Perhaps not a man for *all* seasons, he covered most of them. He did what two USIA predecessors had failed to do: articulate a convincing and humane vision of USIA and defend an honest cultural diplomacy in its own terms. His thought covered his experience of CU and the needs he had seen abroad.

Robert Thayer, Allen's CU counterpart, was also part of a burst of new thinking. By the time he arrived, Dulles's "rollback" was shifting to "waging peace"; détente was in the air. By 1958 an exchanges agreement had been signed with the USSR. CU had been elevated to bureau status and had shed its public affairs responsibilities. As Herter's special assistant, Thayer was a suave and cultivated Francophone, like Herter a patrician obsessed with public service. After St. Mark's School, Amherst, and Harvard Law, he had run housing and antidiscrimination for New York City, served with ambassador Amory Houghton in Paris in 1951–54, returned to Washington in 1954 to direct Western European affairs for Eisenhower's Operations Coordinating Board, then moved as ambassador to Romania in 1955. Piloting the demoralized CU in the Rooney years, Thayer cultivated the mercurial congressman; budgets inched upward, while he watched for new opportunities. Thayer's bold gradualism was the only reasonable path, in his mind.

A few blocks away at USIA, entrenched hardliners and unidirectionalists feared CU's openness to change. For the culturalists in USIA, the nagging questions papered over in 1953 had in fact never been solved, merely concealed. Allen's leadership, Washburn's wise deputizing, and Thayer's strong presence in CU helped counterbalance the hard-line propagandists.

In the White House Rockefeller's committee on government organization was now chaired by Arthur Fleming with Milton Eisenhower and Gordon Gray; it took up the USIA-CU cudgels again. Fleming opened the USIA question—one must assume with Herter's and Allen's approval. Envisaging a Republican victory in 1960, Thayer tried to enlist the vice president, but Richard Nixon's mind was otherwise occupied.

In March 1958 Fleming's committee was hard at work. Thayer—certainly with Herter's approval—wrote to Allen to suggest they "annul" Reorganization Plan 8 and return to pre-1953 IIA. The courteous and collegial Thayer must have known from Allen that the iron was warm. As head of USIA, Allen had to demur; but in answering questions from the Budget Bureau in July he left room to maneuver. He said he opposed USIA's return to State, but he supported the idea of putting the two cultural halves back together; he was ready, he said, to follow orders, if it were decided to move USIA into State. This was not the passionate defense of USIA independence that the zealot Streibert might have composed; Allen's civil response left the door ajar.

Congressmen led by Fulbright were pushing in the same direction. A draft bill to bring USIA back, proposed by State, was in final draft by early August 1958. Fleming's committee published its conclusions at the outset of 1959. With Dulles gone, it reversed the 1953 position and argued that both USIA and AID, now the International Cooperation Agency (ICA), should return to State to help shape and execute overall policy-planning for the longer range. Congressional drafters sped up their work. But the standpatters in USIA, articulating the classic anti-State diatribes, were circling the wagons.

The stage was set for as serious a debate as Washington can usually abide on a complex question of low visibility. Herter and Thayer sought the advice of J. L. Morrill, chair of CU's advisory commission and president of the University of Minnesota. Morrill found funding for a quick survey. His report, oriented to university relationships, urged State to return to active coordination of *all* educational activities for the government—including AID's technical assistance. With Herter and Allen in apparent agreement, Eisenhower's in-principle approval was easily obtained. An interagency committee at the Undersecretary level—modeled on Welles's ICC and headed by Herter's Undersecretary of State Douglas Dillon—raised the discussion a notch.

In USIA Allen tried to persuade his team that return to State would not harm but strengthen the agency. The deck was stacked—Allen could not even convince Washburn, who wanted nothing to do with State. The USIA director was warned of new burdens on the CAOs, but he knew the CAOs were already quietly coordinating with other US agencies in the field and dismissed the idea. In Congress Fulbright's draft legislation posited an International Cultural and Information Adminintration under a Deputy Undersecretary of State—the third level in State. USIA loyalists, with time to organize, pilloried the unfortunate acronym ICIA.

The tar baby USIA-CU question was intact. The two agencies' missions—contradictory, as even Eisenhower admitted—nagged at all serious observers. Distant murmurs came from the universities. Fulbright charged Brookings foreign policy expert Field Haviland with looking into the question. Haviland boldly recommended a totally new Department of Foreign Affairs, headed by a "Super-Secretary" of State, paralleled in the cabinet by a high-level super-coordinator of domestic affairs. The new State Department would have three divisions: one Assistant Secretary would head politics, another economics, and a third of equal rank would head information and culture, with autonomy for each branch. Of cultural relations, Haviland said that "longer-term, less controversial, and ultimately more decisive influence may be gained through these channels." He came down strongly for independence for cultural relations.

In 1959 Thayer and Morrill, with Allen, convened a small but broad-gauged conference on the role of American universities in overseas development. Washington officials met with eight university presidents and three foundation heads, including future Secretary of State Dean Rusk, then head of the Rockefeller Foundation. The outcome: Morrill, Thayer, and conferees asked the Ford Foundation to carry out a major national study of the university role abroad—a question at the core of the CU mandate. Midwifed by Ford's John Howard, the report became *The Universities and World Affairs*, the most comprehensive of the outside surveys of the late 1950s, speaking for an even broader sector of the American intellectual world than had been convened in May 1938, at the birth of the State's new division. Howard, founder-director of Ford's ITR, enlisted staffers, including Waldemar Nielsen, Phillips Talbot of the Universities Field Staff consortium, and security expert Adam Yarmolinsky; he enlisted his Scarsdale friends Rusk and John Gardner of Carnegie, plus CU advisory commission founding-chair Harvie Branscomb, president of Vanderbilt University; University of Wisconsin president Robin Flemming, CU advisory commission chair; UCLA president Franklin Murphy; and two CEOs, from Owens-Corning and General Electric. A more blue-chip representation of the American university and business world had not looked at cultural diplomatic questions since 1938.

Morrill sought "a considered view of the important role of the university in world affairs" because the U.S. was "awakening to the fact that world affairs are not the concern of the diplomat and soldier alone." Abroad, there was a new "upsurge of demands for independence and economic development among hundreds of millions who have known little of either."[7]

In response to this remarkable document, USIA loyalists shored up defenses. They argued that universities were AID's work and persuaded USIA to ignore this rich opportunity for its own growth. USIA's CAOs, who knew that the US universities were the core of their efforts abroad even when funding came from other agencies, tried to persuade their agency that this was an opportunity for USIA greatness.

Six of Morrill's twelve recommendations aimed at universities and colleges: (1) include world affairs in the undergraduate curriculum; (2) maximize international competence in graduate and professional schools; (3) strengthen training of students for international careers; (4) improve conditions for foreign students; (5) establish overseas linkages and assistance; (6) plan the growth of global studies. Four others targetted the federal government: (1) upgrade US education in world affairs; (2) build education into foreign assistance; (3) strengthen cooperating overseas-oriented institutions; (4) guarantee funding over longer time periods. A final pair of recommendations aimed at state governments: recognize the economic importance of global trade and invest in international education. Other suggestions dotted the report and urged more active contributions from the foundations; help in internationalizing education from business; and persuasive support for government-private cooperation from US educational leadership. Morrill also proposed a private organization to coordinate and lead because deeper staff expertise in world affairs was needed. In all, the report recalled Cordell Hull's letter.

Updating the ideas of 1938, *The Universities and World Affairs* was a strong volley from the private-sector court after years of silence. But its style was indirect, subtle, and allusive, an effort to avoid offending any agency; it was not written in the kind of language that could stir Congress to change its mind. The foundations were pressing for more and better-coordinated university involvement as a cultural diplomatic function. The universities, at last, had taken a stand on government organization and leadership. The Department of State was praised for Thayer's upgrading of cultural relations; perhaps USOE might follow suit, and the president might ask all relevant cabinet officers to consider education and world affairs a special subject for intra-cabinet coordination directed by a presidential assistant.

Morrill and Howard, in their report, reflected the activist view of cultural diplomacy. They believed a single overseas educational or cultural point of contact in each country was a dire need. Only an embassy cultural or educational officer could play that role; only a person of stature, fully supported by the universities, could do it well. Morrill insisted that America's overriding obligation abroad was high-caliber field staff; if USIA and State could provide it, this was their work—if not, AID should seize the opportunity.

Morrill's tact was wasted on the belligerent USIA loyalists. Only five years old, USIA had already become a tough status quo agency, run by people who liked things precisely the way they were and lacked the imagination to see that Morrill offered their agency an enormous opportunity. USIA loyalists were confident of their friends in Congress. Opposed to the interests of cultural diplomacy and the multitasked CU, still struggling to keep its head above water while handling an oversized agenda, the thriving USIA was already an unbeatable single-interest lobby. When it came to the long-range interests of USIA, the shortsighted missed the point.

The Morrill report, the most far-reaching private study in the cluster appearing in the late 1950s, was written gracefully by hard-headed men. It proposed an ambitious yet highly practical national agenda. It conveyed a serious request from the universities for a single government voice to meet the growing needs of the American universities, helping them deal with the rest of the world. The Ford Foundation, which had invested heavily in university area studies and in mobilizing university help abroad for foreign education, set the tone. Its leadership wanted the nation to tap into this investment and extend the quality of national outreach. With his report, Morrill gave birth to a new NGO, Education and World Affairs, directed by the same William Marvel who had served as CAO in Nicaragua in 1944. But nothing else happened.

Other statements on cultural diplomacy appeared in 1959–60, anticipating the election. The CU advisory commission, now headed by Franklin Murphy, former dean of medicine at the University of Kansas and now Chancellor of UCLA, delegated its inquiry to Walter Laves, back at

Indiana University. Laves's *Towards a National Effort in International Educational and Cultural Affairs* opened Morrill's wide-angle focus a bit wider. At the Carnegie Endowment, John Gardner added *The College and University in International Affairs*. ACE published its own conference under the title *Toward a Foreign Policy for Higher Education*. IIE chief and former Division of Cultural Relations staffer Kenneth Holland wrote the *Report to the President of the U.S.* In Ford's Education Division, young human-resource economist Philip Coombs filed an internal report on educational relations, urging that USIA's cultural functions return to State. All agreed on one point: the necessity of a central US government mechanism to provide coherent planning and coordination for the international challenges of *education*, especially higher education. An unusual concentration of intellectual power had found national consensus on this key issue. But USIA was not listening.

In the Senate, Fulbright's drafters, after Haviland's 1960 Brookings report, were polishing a major restatement of the original Fulbright and Smith-Mundt legislation. For this purpose, Fulbright's committee invited a group of notables, including Rusk, Holland, Amherst College president Calvin Plimpton, Ford's "Champ" Ward, and others, to Washington to meet with Thayer and Allen. In corners of Congress, interest in education abroad was popping up. New York City Representative Adam Clayton Powell warned about the new Lumumba Friendship University in Moscow and proposed twelve thousand four-year US scholarships for Asia, Africa, and Latin America—a proposal that would have cost at least $10 million a year at the time, half the CU budget, and that would have quadrupled the numbers of students flowing in. On the revolution of rising expectations, Powell said, either the U.S. "can make it a constructive transformation or we can ignore it"—he did not spell out the consequences of ignoring it. His bill went nowhere, and in time Lumumba proved less of a threat than imagined when the Soviets failed to persuade Africans of the joys of living in frigid, racist, monolingual Moscow. In fact, the university was a deep compliment to the U.S., a quixotic Soviet effort to compete with the waves of foreign students flowing naturally toward America.

Douglas Dillon's Undersecretaries committee was finally ready. It sent a firm report recommending reintegration of USIA into State to the White House. Washburn, present when Dillon presented his conclusions, said that USIA independence was only "saved"—to Dillon's frustration—by the persuasive intervention of Elmer Staats of the Budget Bureau, reinforcing Washburn's own gentle persuasion. Staats, soon to be Comptroller General of the U.S., was a trusted friend of Eisenhower, who heeded his words, missed the moment, and turned aside the Undersecretaries' consensus. USIA, attracting an odd assortment of friends, was proving a hardy survivor.

The matter continued to nag at Eisenhower. In December 1959, ten months before the elections, he appointed the most prestigious committee ever to tackle this question: the Special Commission on Information Activities Abroad. The title suggested bias, but in fact it was a powerful and relatively balanced team: he named Thayer's friend New York industrialist Mansfield Sprague as chair. Under him were Herter, Allen, CIA director Allen Dulles, Dillon, Eisenhower advisor and Rockefeller successor Gordon Gray, and prominent government officials and businessmen, including C. D. Jackson as a link to 1953. The committee's purpose: to revisit the Jackson report.

Time was short, and Sprague's committee was unwieldy. Eisenhower seemed ready to deal with the USIA issue; he had put it in the best hands he could. Sprague's report was one of the most comprehensive ever; in fact, it resolved the USIA-CU question, albeit in the direction of hardnosed realism. Herter, Allen, Dillon, and Allen Dulles all signed it (Dillon and Dulles would soon join Kennedy's bipartisan team). Its conclusions: (1) USIA, notwithstanding six names and four reorganizations since the war, had improved its capacity to "integrate psychological factors into policy"; (2) Soviet effectiveness and the growing importance of public opinion had raised the stakes, and continued growth was in order—meaning more US funding, better training, a clearer role for information, and closer coordination;[8] (3) The time had come to stop the ceaseless rehashing of the USIA-CU question; (4) USIA and CU functions needed to have their best possible growth.

The report also endorsed an expanded USIA, a broader CU mandate and budget, and the long-sought independent foundation for overseas education. While Lois Roth cited Sprague's "reservations about 'wholesale mobilization of private American international activities,'" Sprague proposed an expanded role for private foundations and the establishment of a quasi-independent Foundation for International Educational Development, calling for "facilitating visits to the U.S. by leaders of the political left by revising cumbersome visa procedures" and urging that "a single government facility work with universities to coordinate long-range policy." Sprague vested this function in State's Bureau of Educational and Cultural Affairs.[9]

Participant Waldemar Nielsen of the Ford Foundation reported an annex to Sprague—which like the report itself has never been made public. Nielsen said the committee recommended a separate agency for cultural affairs, uniting USIA's cultural elements and CU. But the 1960 elections ended that discussion. Sprague's report reached Eisenhower's desk on 23 December, a Christmas gift for a very lame duck.

Almost everyone had come to see that neither side of the equation was well served by Jackson's odd arrangement, bulldozed by Dulles and sandbagged by Fulbright. But the defenses of an embattled USIA had hardened. In the end, decent and informed men watched the complex issues shrivel into the simple question of USIA's independence from State—only the invisible Sprague annex raised the question of an independent public-private cultural agency. In only six years, the "Rube Goldberg" division of functions between USIA and CU spawned by Jackson had become dogma.

Eisenhower later admitted that he had missed his chance. In 1965, at Lyndon Johnson's suggestion, USIA director-designate Leonard Marks spent a day with the ex-president at Gettysburg. Eisenhower said during their meeting that information-culture was "one of the big mistakes I made, . . . I didn't realize the value." Further, he said, the USIA budget should be 2 percent of the military budget, i.e., an astonishing $1 billion in 1965. (By that standard, today's budget for "Public Diplomacy" would exceed $20 billion.) When Marks told Eisenhower he would not know how to spend $1 billion, the former president smiled indulgently and said, "You'd learn very quickly."[10]

The studies in 1958–61 sprang in part from Thayer's energy, as he looked at potential US political change, détente, and the expanding role of American higher education across the globe; but they also reflected an unsolved problem on everyone's mind. Even so, the committee efforts ultimately amounted to a waste of time. Notwithstanding these mighty statements, America's politicians, like USIA's tough psy-warriors, considered education irrelevant to foreign policy. Even the skills and convictions of George Allen never changed the minds of die-hard entrenched legislators and USIA staff. After 1960 USIA owned the debate and answered all inquiry with the question, was it good for USIA? The attacks of the late 1950s reminded USIA to target its enemies, some of whom were inside the agency. Outside USIA, the search for diplomatic alternatives was flagging. In 1960 only a few hardy cultural internationalists were still dedicated to changing the basic structure of American diplomacy, and fewer die-hard culturalists kept up the fight for reform. As a veteran of the foundation world recalled that year there was "loss of heart" everywhere.[11]

The excitement of the Thayer-Allen period gave way to a different excitement, that of the vigorous Kennedy years. Morrill's spin-off Education and World Affairs, during its short life, became a rallying point for university-oriented CAOs. The universities and the foundations did not ask for much: merely high-level leadership in Washington and a single prestigious and well-staffed point in the field around which to focus a unified approach to educational relations abroad. USIA could easily have made peace with this idea, if the agency had seen it as a rich possibility instead of a threat. But it was too late. After November 1960 everything stopped to await the next act.

• • •

While Washington dithered, fieldwork went on. The life of a CAO is a well-kept secret of American life. We have seen a few examples from the 1940s. By the 1950s, while Washington fretted about structure, the profession was into its second decade of experience, growing and changing by the day. The cultural officers had created a *métier*, which each new officer learned from scratch, sometimes without the help of his supervisors. With no historical memory and little help from their employing agency, the CAOs were nonetheless turning culture and education into a new professional dimension of American diplomacy.

It worked, sometimes better than seemed possible, by ingenious improvisation. In the field a cultural officer's life was exciting and exhausting. Charles Frankel was the first to observe CAOs at work systematically. He interviewed some three hundred USIS officers and CAOs in thirteen countries and Washington in 1963–64. In his resultant book on US cultural relations, he tried, in a chapter called "The Man in the Middle," to capture two days in the life of an imaginary CAO. Any veteran of the cultural ranks in the years between 1950 and 1980 knows that he made more sense out of the work's inherent chaos than most could, amidst the trivia, diversions, and glories faced.[12] They also know that he understated rather than exaggerated the totally absorbing CAO duties.

Day one sets the tone. Frankel's imaginary CAO "in a smallish developing country in the southern part of the world," which he names Evolutia, neighbor of Progressia, begins his day with correspondence, most from CU or USIA. A college glee club for Evolutia? Staff must look into travel itineraries, performances, housing, and opportunities for personal interaction. But the British Council has just brought the Old Vic and the Russians staged a traveling company of the Bolshoi, so the CAO prefers another option, a major symphonic orchestra scheduled for Progressia. The CAO suspects, in any case, he will probably get both. His PAO wants program suggestions for a parliamentary group planning to visit the U.S. on their government's funds. Three fully funded US university placements are open for postdoctoral Fulbright researchers from Evolutia. And a new post librarian is finally on her way. There is also less good news: a US historian scheduled to keynote a seminar in American studies at the university has canceled.

There are other letters, e.g., from a student from another country looking for an opportunity for US study. His preparation and English are poor, and the CAO's exchanges are restricted to Evolutia, but he has consulted a friend in a small Pacific Coast college who wants more information about the prospective student. Also, a leader in the US people-to-people program writes to say she is planning to visit her town's "sister city."

He interrupts his correspondence to dash to the nearby Fulbright House for the quarterly commission meeting. As chairman, he knows the agenda and has prepped all members. The board reviews the panel of Evolutian candidates for the next academic year. The problem: inadequate English among applicants. He has set up special classes for university candidates in the fall at the USIS library (the BNC's ELT has declined; the BNC is reorganizing its board on which he sits, but over which he has little control, even though the BNC was built on embassy-provided land). He asks a Fulbright board member, Dean of Arts and Sciences at the university, to look into the progress of a talented student they have been watching—will his English be good enough next year?

He is late for a meeting of the embassy's International Visitor (IV) committee, which is chaired by the ambassador—luckily the ambassador is also late. The political officer, the labor officer, the economics officer, the head of AID, the PAO, and the Consul General in Evolutia's largest provincial city each has one or more candidates in mind for a handful of grants. The CAO has his own list; he makes his cultural pitch by reporting that last year's grantee, the national librarian, is restructuring the library, drawing on the ALA and other US organizations, meanwhile raving to friends and colleagues about the homey American citizen-education libraries. The CAO proposes to ignite similar reform via the director of the National Art Museum. The swing grant goes instead to the joint political-labor nominee, a union leader said to be close to the new president.

After the meeting, the CAO stays behind with the ambassador, PAO, and AID director to discuss a problem in Progressia. An American secondary school there, a missionary survival, receives partial support from CU. The CAO wants to send Evolutians there, but CU cannot fund study in Progressia. The ambassador suggests a Washington friend who might be able to help; the AID chief agrees to handle it. The CAO uses the meeting to raise two other questions. First, the Minister of Education wants his ministry included in the process of selecting IV grantees. The CAO has strongly discouraged this, explaining that for IV grants, US selection practices are irrevocably unilateral; he reminds everyone to hold strongly to this position. Second, the Ministry of Culture has asked the U.S. to help an Evolutian folk dance troupe tour the U.S. The CAO notes that the 1961 Fulbright-Hays legislation permits such "reverse-flow" but no US funding has been allocated; the ambassador will try to get a US corporation to help.

From the embassy, the CAO drives his own car to the airport to greet Evolutia's leading dancer, after a privately sponsored tour of the U.S. He has arranged a lunch with friends in her honor, paying for it out of his own pocket because his entertainment allowance was exhausted in the first month of the program year.

Back in the office, he spends half an hour with a national employee, victim of a budget reduction, who must be told of his dismissal. He winds up the day's correspondence and sets to work on an overdue report to CU on the reactions of exchange returnees—fodder for the unpredictable budget questions of Congress. A young Evolutian grantee-designate interrupts. He has learned that the US university he had thought to be top-class is an agricultural college. The CAO spends an hour explaining that the "ag college" is in fact a first-rate university, perhaps especially pertinent for this young man from the countryside. They talk about his career goals.

The PAO calls to ask for a look at the CAO's proposed remarks for the summer music festival in the mountains, where a concert of music by American composers is scheduled for the next evening. The CAO, who always improvises his talks from notes, sends a copy of his sketchy talking points. The ambassador's wife calls in search of the right book—in Evolutian—to give the president's daughter to read on her way to the U.S. By luck, he has just received a prepublication copy of the perfect book, a translation his office funded two years earlier; he sends it off with a hand-written note explaining what it is. He spends an hour with a US visitor doing a study of educational and cultural diplomacy, then turns back to his report on returnees.

At 6:15 P.M. he is late for an informal student discussion of Faulkner he has agreed to lead, at a young faculty member's house. Faulkner is of course a pretext; the discussion moves to race relations in the U.S., social-ism in Evolutia, the underdevelopment of Progressia, and the future of jazz—it breaks up just before midnight. Dinner is a dry sandwich and tepid orange soda.

This single day of Frankel's two-day vignette, written in 1965, is evoca-tive for experienced CAOs of that era, though perhaps on the light side. Frankel, pondering the CAO's life, conclude that the "assignment calls for an unusual combination of qualities. . . . The ideal or 'Compleat' CAO would be a protean character, among other things a gregarious intellec-tual, a warm cross-cultural communicator, a tough negotiator, an admin-instrator of a large staff and program who spends a lot of time out of the office, a dutiful bureaucrat dealing with colleagues and their spouses, professors, students, musicians, poets, athletes, and American VIPs." In short, "a man of parts with the tastes of an aristrocrat, the patience of a saint, and the constitution of a shotputter; . . . [with] a beautiful and charming wife who loves his job as much as he does, speaks the language of the country as well as he, and has inherited a comfortable sum of money."

In the real world, there were few of Frankel's Proteans. But, he implies, there were dozens of CAO's in the field who could do much more with better support and less trivia. More important, there were dozens of fine candidates, quasi-Proteans all, waiting eagerly in US universities for a crack at the job.

Frankel's CAO hero in fact makes it look easier than it was. Those cultural officers who insisted on doing the most they could soon learned which colleagues to count on, how to settle for less, how to work twice as hard as others, how to let others take credit for their work, how to make sense out of contradictory orders, how to explain repeatedly but ever patiently why something matters, how to find compelling reasons for what should be obvious, how to suffer ignorance with a smile, and how to work twelve hours a day.

Frankel's CAO was able to ignore Washington chaos. For Philip Coombs, writing in 1963 after a disastrous tour as CU chief, the chaos was impossible to overlook. As he saw it, the CAOs were expected to "serve as part-time 'field agents' for State, with two Washington bosses, yet on the USIA payroll and promotion ladder and under the jurisdiction . . . of the Public Affairs officer . . . . [They] lived apart in Washington but together in the field. It seemed a sure-fire formula for perennial discord, and so indeed it has proved to be." What kept it alive was its excitement. The joys of cultural field work were such that the contradictions rarely showed—everyone was too busy.

The people cultural officers administered, like Fulbright exchangees, were funded by CU. As one CAO put it, "We labored for USIA in the morning, but in the afternoons and far into the evenings we worked for CU—mostly we worked for the U.S." Frankel's colleague Wayne Wilcox, Columbia political scientist who served two years in London, put it differently: CAO success happened not *because* of USIA but in *spite* of it.

In USIA's world various factors made the CAO's mandate hard to pigeonhole. For example, tight-ship administrators could not understand the open-ended nature of the CAO's work, in which it is always easy to attend one more art opening, one more reception, one more ceremony, and thus to make one more new friend for America. Nor could they see the complexity of a field like foreign students, which requires a lifetime to master; or the depth of the exchange process—since exchanges, properly done, are labor-intensive educational acts, each episode of which involves a human life going through dramatic and life-shaping change. Time is the inelastic factor for the CAO. Accumulating and nurturing foreign friends uses up time, and maintaining too many friends takes more time than humans have. The CAO's problem: to achieve quality without spending more time than there is in twenty-four-hour days.

The Fulbright process was the major case in point for CAO time management. Fulbright exchanges draw half the CU budget; they should therefore involve at least a third of any CAO's time. Managed correctly, the program is a demanding business; but many let their responsibilities slide or trusted their commission executive director to help carry their loads. This process, fully understood, dramatized the CAO's dilemma: done well it was consuming; done casually it could be wasteful. Yet, despite the problem of time management, Fulbright's process, almost as much as its products, manifested three major values in action: binationalism, merit systems and peer review, and the centrality of education.

Every cultural officer handles the Fulbright Program differently; each country is a different challenge, and each CAO sees a different part of the Fulbright elephant. The following depiction of the Fulbright process reflects the experience of a CAO (1961–85) who first encountered the program in 1949 as a new-B.A. graduate student and who since then has been in greater or lesser contact with different parts of it, its programs, and its alumni in three dozen countries and the U.S.

Until 1980, with exceptions, the CAO chaired the board of the Fulbright Commission or Foundation; after 1970 PAOs began preempting this job. Around 1963 chairmanships began to rotate between the US

CAO and the host country. Executive directors were Americans until around 1960, when foreign directors began to appear.

Commissions included from eight to fourteen prominent persons, evenly divided between both countries. On the US side, the commission-members were the best available Americans from the embassy, education, and business; on the host-country side, the representatives were promi- nent university educators and government officials. Chairing such a board meant managing it and required the educator's patience; working in a foreign language made it harder. Commission cultures vary from country to country, but few follow US board practices or Roberts's Rules of Order.

CAO relations with board members, to be productive, had to be regu- lar and substantive. I made a practice of holding an extended meeting with individual foreign board members, usually over lunch, alone or in pairs, at least once before each meeting. Board members were included in dinners and receptions at home and at the embassy, especially when relevant visitors—BFS members, CU staff, prominent academics, or con- gressional staff—came to town. CAOs who skimped, ignored the com- mission, or tried to rubber-stamp it to his or her will paid a price, if only in the barely visible coin of lowered quality and unspoken friction.

Selection of foreign grantees is the most consuming job, and it goes on all year. Recruitment is done on host-country campuses by advertise- ment, circulars, and word of mouth. There may be hundreds of candi- dates or none at all, as in the first year for Fulbright in France when French students literally had to be cajoled into US study. Academic com- mittees in the disciplines screen the first cut. Then a commission subcom- mittee reviews the entire panel, determines priorities among different fields, and allocates available funding to a balanced panel, so that not all candidates in a given year are, say, chemists.

In the U.S. selection and recruitment of Americans similarly goes on outside of government: IIE recruits and selects American predoctoral stu- dents and CIES recruits and selects postdoctoral candidates, both using academic committees. Most campuses have a committee to rank its stu- dents in priority order. IIE and CIES send ranked US panels to each coun- try for placement by commission staff and boardmembers. Foreigner pre- and postdoctoral candidates go to IIE and CIES for placement in US insti- tutions. As in all education, the trick is to match each human element with an appropriate academic situation. IIE seeks additional scholarship and fellowship funding. Once the Americans are placed in foreign univer- sities, the CAO visits them and their host departments; in the U.S. IIE and CIES supervise foreign placements, when budget permits.

Orientation is hard to time. Foreign grantees leave at different inter- vals, and predeparture briefing can consist of a single discussion with the CAO or commission staff, plus discussions in the U.S. with IIE and CIES and on the campuses where Fulbright alumni in the local communities help. For Americans, post-arrival orientation happens more regularly be- cause they arrive in host countries around the same time and the commissions take over. Since 1980, extra orientations for foreign students and researchers have sometimes taken place in Washington.

There is little or no post-return follow-up in the U.S. Abroad, follow-up takes various forms. A wise Fulbright commission stays in touch with its alumni and involves them in its work. Informed and involved returnees can help smooth the path for others. Formal alumni activities may be occasionally appropriate, especially in countries like Italy and France, where alumni lists have climbed beyond nine thousand, and in Germany and Japan, where they have gone far higher. A CAO gets to know foreign alumni working, by definition, in fields relevant to US intellectual relations. Some countries have well-organized Fulbright alumni associations—in Japan, alumni raise impressive funding for the program. A US Fulbright Association has tried valiantly to locate the seventy to eighty thousand US alumni but, as of this writing, has less than half that number in its database in part because of US mobility and in part because of the inexcusable destruction of government files.

Americans abroad need more help than one might imagine, including reminders to stay out of local politics. "Research" is not always easy, especially in developing countries where it may be equated with espionage or subversion; required government permits for research are not unusual; and many countries limit access to important libraries and archives. To improve the endless research-permit process in Iran in the 1960s, a CAO once documented the time it took to get a research permit for a single young American scholar: 104 days of combined work by the grantee, commission, and CAO, plus countless letters, visits, phone calls, and casual conversations at receptions. The result: the US ambassador brought the CAO's day-by-day record to the attention of the Shah and the delay dropped immediately—by about 40 percent.

Commissions do more than give grants. They are clearinghouses for all university relations between two countries; they provide indispensable student counseling for thousands of foreign students seeking entry into American colleges and universities on their own; they may administer grants from private US sources; and they follow up with alumni in the U.S. and in the host-country.

The major board function is planning. A Fulbright program can be a precise tool for better relations between the U.S. and the host country or a hit-or-miss collection of grants in random fields. Broad and indicative planning was key. Every educational exchange is and ought to be an investment in long-range growth, every grant has to be designed to put the right student from the right field into the right learning situation. Deciding what will be fruitful means careful analysis of national interests on both sides. The board must think ahead and follow intellectual developments in both countries. In addition the board may want to rectify bilateral educational imbalances, note new fields of interest, and all the while counter unwise pressures from individuals, ministries, politicians, and even the US embassy.

By 1970 PAOs began to assert their influence over the Fulbright Program, heretofore the unquestioned domain of the CAO. The redoubtable Leon Picon, after two decades in Japanese affairs and as specal assistant to Frankel, was the first CAO I knew to be openly kept from chairing the commission; arriving in Ankara in 1968, he was so informed by his PAO. That day, he said, he knew that the covenants protecting the integrity of US cultural relations had crumbled. I was not kept from chairing a Fulbright Commission until 1979.

Fulbright is roughly a third of a CAO's work, but the other two-thirds are harder to pin down; I knew no good CAOs who worked less than sixty hours per week, closely intertwining their lives and their work. A host of embassy chores end up on the CAO's desk. In Paris the PAO quipped that the embassy needed a special American officer to attend art openings. US and foreign visitors make constant demands in proportion to the attractiveness of the host country. Foreign visitors cannot be turned away, but they usually want little more than information. US visitors also must be received. Some bring treasure—an enhanced budget, a priceless contact, a brilliant lecture, a valuable parallel private-sector activity, access to a network of colleagues, or simply a marvelous new friend; others can waste time. In the developing world, visitors' planes arrive at and depart from outlandish airports at all hours of the night on all days of the week, Saturdays and Sundays included. No cultural officer in a developing country, at least until the 1980s, sent a visitor alone to an airport; and if the plane was late they sat in grim departure lounges with the visitor until the plane left the ground.

CAO Sterlyn Steele once said ruefully that, all things considered, cultural officers were neither Jacob Canter's "clerks" nor Rockefeller's "office boys," but "glorified travel agents." Travel agents, for sure—exchanging people means travel. But there is real glory too. Exchangees and visitors are often remarkable people, by definition, and the peculiar circumstances of their visits may break down barriers; CAOs find vast rewards in friendships made with such travelers. On a flight back to Tehran from Shiraz in Iran, Lois Roth encountered Luther Terry, former Surgeon General of the U.S., who had just visited the US-created Nemazee Hospital there. She invited him to her home in Tehran the next day, then called together the cream of Iranian medical educators, administrators, and practitioners to meet with him; after lunch and five hours of dialogue, she improvised dinner for a dozen deans and university presidents to maintain the momentum of the improvised seminar on the interconnected public policy fields of contemporary medical education, medical research, public health, and medical administration.

Year by year, from country to country, cultural officers all over the world built personal networks, not only of people they met in their countries of assignment but also those from earlier posts, from UN agencies, and from foreign embassies. Washington had no idea of such friendships, which visitors sometimes preferred go unreported. A CAO's network grew, ripened, and carried on through an officer's career, as happened when CAO Dino Caterini stayed close all his life to a young man he befriended in Milan in the 1950s—Umberto Eco. CAO colleagues were often told by prominent figures, "When you need me again, either in this country or elsewhere, let me know and I'll work out the details." Or perhaps they would say, "I am overflying your country next November and would love to stop over with you for a day or two." CAO homes needed guest bedrooms and a good cook.

It was assumed that CAOs knew their country better than most, in the tradition of Fairbank and Cuyler Young, even if after 1955 CAOs were no longer selected for their area expertise. After 1960 USIA was never willing, as a matter of policy, to invest in area-studies recruits. In fact, the officer himself was left to acquire some degree of area expertise, with limited help in language. A CAO's knowledge of a country most often began in the country, after reading low-common-denominator and telegraphic Washington briefing papers and perhaps a book or two.

Learning a country takes skill and patience; the focus naturally, but not always, falls on what is going on between the U.S. and the host nation, especially in education, intellect, and culture, as well as between the host nation and other countries. The best CAOs begin learning in Washington, then carry on the process after arrival with an extended series of calls on embassy colleagues, government officials, multilateral organization officers, and foreign embassy cultural offices. By asking naive questions and pursuing answers, they learn from those with whom they will be dealing. The vital initial calling routine can be tedious. In my first assignment abroad, I was appalled as I traveled around Beirut with my chief, a tired CAO from the pre-USIA days. For him, calls were a necessary chore: he needed to show my face to the world so that I could take the crushing weight off his shoulders. His calling routine was a study in the deployment of clichés, doubtless influenced by the grandiloquent Arab style; he invariably rose to a climax, with the same portentous conclusion: "Yes, it is true, Beirut more and more is becoming a cultural crossroads." Contemplating the depths of this remark, we would rise solemnly and bid our host farewell. In time I came to see that I was learning more than I thought, but at the moment it seemed like a tour of dozens of shabby offices to the music of endless clichés.

Planning the cultural program, until the early 1970s, was left to the cultural officers; they inherited and carried forward their own cultural Country Plan, prepared for CU under educational criteria. CU's plan, a more demanding document than USIA's, was a useful learning opportunity—our annual plan for Iran ran over sixty pages. In Sri Lanka and Iran, we also did a monthly report for the PAO, who regularly passed it on to Washington, where we later learned it was discarded. A decade later I learned to my dismay that even the demanding CU plan was rarely read by CU desk officers, yet I remember the exercise as useful.

• • •

Any general insights into CAO work can only be understood through specific cases. Like scholar-visionaries Fairbank and Morey, many scholars took time from their universities to serve as CAOs. Until 1976 London was staffed uniquely from the intellectual world—it was USIA's admission that high-level academic cultural officers were indispensable. A brief visit with two London academics—Carl Bode and Cleanth Brooks—may help understand how it all fit together.[13]

University of Maryland Professor Carl Bode, first president of the American Studies Association, was CAO in London in 1957–59 and later lectured in Yugoslavia, Hungary, East Germany, and France. In 1988 he reminisced about a time when the U.S. "was emerging as the premier power on the globe," after Carnegie, Ford, and Rockefeller had invested in deeper university study of the U.S.—we called it "American Studies." As CAO, he ran Fulbright and was in charge of the program, with vigorous help from his deputy.

The morning after his arrival, Bode was "deposited on the train for Nottingham to attend the annual conference of the fledgling British Association for American Studies . . . [meaning] any American subject." There the British welcome was "cautious but moderately receptive"; key players were there, he would later learn. Bode admired the career-commitment of the British Americanists, "although no tenured posts . . . were open to them." Beyond a few British books on America, reaching back in some cases a century or more, the libraries were weak; little scholarship on the U.S. was being done. Bode set out to help. Fortunately the USIS library was still outstanding, seminal, and heavily used. Book distribution of publisher overstocks of US books to institutions everywhere was directed by the cultural office. A fellow of the Royal Academy of Literature, Bode lectured widely, published poetry and prose in British journals, expanded British awareness of the American poets, published two collections of his essays, and persuaded three universities to open permanent positions or "chairs" in American subjects.

In more general terms, "there was work to do, but certainly not of the hard-sell sort." There were no political pressures at the embassy: "I was a longtime Democrat and shared platforms when invited not only with academics but with non-academic extremists ranging from Communist Party members to members of the Civil War Roundtable, who came to meetings dressed in Confederate gray and had opinions to match."

He was skeptical about his impact. Much of his time went to daily duties, like helping Americans understand contemporary England. "Every now and then I found myself waking up at 4 in the morning with the awful suspicion that I was doing more harm than good. But then I would remind myself that I was doing my best. In the great game of Ultimate Consequences, we are all amateurs." Bode was grateful that his ambassador, John Hay "Jock" Whitney, supported his efforts to "enlarge

British acquaintance with the best in American culture" and that the PAO, Fairbank's Chungking friend Brad Connors, did not interfere, sparing him from "inconvenience, though he viewed some of my projects with more enthusiasm than he viewed others."

Bode was only a few years beyond the witch hunters but they were not forgotten: "Some of the career people at State and USIA still bore the scars of the McCarthy investigations. . . . With a job to return to, I was able to help a bit in restoring a sense of proportion. One of Britain's leading playwrights [Christopher Fry] applied for permission to enter the U.S. . . . He had had a turbulent, left-leaning youth. But keeping him out would have raised the scorn of intellectuals on both sides of the ocean; I persuaded my colleagues that he could do us no harm." Again, chairing his maiden meeting of the Fulbright commission, he was shocked when an embassy colleague proposed that "all Fulbright Fellows should be adept in American Studies"; fortunately "the other members listened thoughtfully, then voted the motion down."

Bode kept an eye on USIA after his return; lecturing abroad, he knew what was happening in Europe. "Since I left London, the resources of USIA and State have been scattered over the rest of the globe." He concluded of the 1950s, "In my biased view it was a Golden Age. By the mid-60s that age was over. Budgets shrank." Another sign of the end was pressure to close the London library. His irony is obvious: "After all, why not? In Washington's eyes, the Atlantic was narrow enough and Great Britain would by necessity remain our best ally." In his tour, he managed to fight off the closing. He remained an understanding friend to fellow cultural diplomats until his death.

Yale's Cleanth Brooks adds another dimension to insight into CAO work in London. In 1964 the reknowned critic and professor of English began his two-year stay in London. His first deputy, the elegant Francis Mason—who went on to a distinguished career outside USIA—eased him into the governmental office. In 1965 Mason was succeeded by another committed cultural officer, Fulbright alumnus, Ph.D. in American studies, and South Asianist Martin C. Carroll. Brooks's deputies freed him to move around the country.

In 1988 this Rhodes alumnus looked back "from the outside, from the viewpoint of the American university world, and indeed to some extent from the standpoint of a British citizen." He was philosophical: "My considered opinion today: the less a cultural officer is associated with the propagation of American political opinion and American foreign policy decisions, the better he can serve his country. I am not so naive as to think that he can cut his ties with the country and culture that he represents, nor would it be desirable if he could. . . . But he is more effective in his job if the British, and particularly Britain's university people, accept him as another university professor." Such status "gives him an authority and a credibility on those occasions when he does speak to the subject of American attitudes and politics." He concludes: "If we are to have cultural officers at all, they should be first and foremost cultured officers, representing the best in American cultural values. . . . If culture is the great common denominator of the separate nations, . . . the CAO will be more effective if he is regarded primarily as a member of that great republic."

Brooks knew England and lectured widely. "Today it is hard to realize but in the two years I was abroad I gave over 130 lectures. . . . [The British] asked me to talk about American writers or other aspects of American literature." He chaired the Fulbright Commission, with the fine executive director John Hetherington managing the work: "This was a serious group, . . . with a very powerful British representation that included two or three heads of British universities and Sir John Wolfenden, the Chairman of the Grants Committee and later Director of the British Museum." Brooks sat on other boards like the Ditchley Foundation and served as host and orientation speaker for the private Rhodes, Marshall, Guggenheim, and Fulbright scholars. He watched over teacher-to-teacher exchanges, spoke in lieu of the ambassador, helped British researchers, received every visitor he could, took friends to lunch, helped the Cleveland Orchestra and the New York City Ballet come to London, tried without success to reduce barriers to the importation of US books, lectured around Europe and the Near East, cheered up his CAO colleagues, and enjoyed sharing administrative burdens: "for a CAO, even a so-called 'easy' post is not easy if he takes his work at all seriously."

He was finally forced by Washington to close the five-thousand-volume USIS library (reduced from fifteen thousand), with its extraordinary outreach and reference service. For him, it was a bitter decision; with Martin Carroll, he was able to place the books at the University of London, whose Vice Chancellor, the American-born Noel Annan, was a member of the Fulbright board. Once lodged there, the library sank slowly from view.

In 1988 Brooks wrote: "I reluctantly come to the conclusion that it might be well to sever connections between the CAO's work and USIA." His alternative: "We ought to be able to find some national instition which could nominate and present potential cultural officers to our government for its approval." The goal: "to remove any suspicion that American culture is being used as a means for promoting special political goals. American culture, presented for its own sake and in its own terms, might turn out to be the best American asset of all." Brooks returned to Yale and died in New Haven in 1994, at the age of eighty-seven.

A persistent reader will by now begin to suspect that the CAO had a wonderful job, full of joys, discoveries, and just as many sorrows. No day passed without learning. Devoted cultural officers made a preposterous and ramshackle system work; in the field, colleagues by and large helped each other. Looking back, the CAO's work seems a miracle of everyday practice and of friendship. Most of the outsiders left USIA, but a few stayed, took the guff, put up with inappropriate assignments, handled the trivia with grace, suffered inadequate, meddlesome, and sometimes foolish colleagues, and worked their way around poor direction because they believed they were doing something useful, something they understood. They loved the work enough to do it right. Yet we must not be misled; these generous-minded Americans did their best under administrative conditions that could scarcely have been worse.

CHAPTER FOURTEEN

New Frontiers for Old: Murrow and Coombs

> We as a nation are not allergic to change and have no desire to sanctify the status quo.
>
> —Edward R. Murrow (1961)

KENNEDY WAS ELECTED on a platform of renewal, in a glow of rhetoric, pledging to "get the country moving again"—as though it had stopped—and making opulent promises in the shiny language of American political campaigns. His narrow victory over Nixon reassured few yet triggered widespread internationalist enthusiasm.

JFK's style was more convincing than Nixon's, in part because of new electoral determinants: television and the so-called debates. Managed by CBS's Frank Stanton, the new medium drew predictable accusations of bias from supporters of the untelegenic Californian. Kennedy was aware of his narrow margin of victory and made bipartisan appointments, including Eisenhower's Undersecretary of State Douglas Dillon as Secretary of Treasury. The new president also pressed Stanton to accept the leadership of USIA.

In the presidential transition process, the discussion of cultural diplomacy revived—in minds who had no time for the findings of Sprague and Morrill. A status quo USIA was stoutly defended by realist advisor George Ball, but Fulbright's law school friend and communications expert, Lloyd Free, and his colleague W. Phillips Davison at Columbia, both sophisticated unidirectional informationists, urged higher status for USIA and its director, and recommended that USIA absorb CU—but with a radically new kind of agency in mind. Their proposed titles for the new agency catches the drift: either US International Exchange Agency or US Cultural Exchange Agency.

To tend the two vineyards on opposite slopes—cultural and informational diplomacy—Kennedy managed to recruit two remarkable New Yorkers: CBS's Edward R. Murrow for USIA and Ford Foundation's Philip H. Coombs for CU, both recommended by Undersecretary of State Chester Bowles. The two acquaintances, Coombs remembers, pledged in New York not to let their subordinates divide them; but, in fact, Coombs seems to have occupied little place in Murrow's field of vision once he reached USIA. In the three Murrow biographies so far in print, neither Coombs nor his key book is mentioned.[1]

Murrow's rich life before CBS began in 1930 when he was elected, as a college senior, to the presidency of NSFA. The election happened at Stanford University, at a conference for which, by chance, George Creel was the keynoter. According to Murrow's NSFA colleague Deirdre Mason, Creel said that day, "We fooled your parents last time with all the non-sense about German soldiers bayoneting Belgian babies. It wasn't true. Don't let it happen again."[2]

Notwithstanding three biographers, we have only begun to pin down the Murrow myth. After his riveting wartime broadcasts from London, he emerged as America's most trusted, courageous, and FBI-tracked radio-television journalist. Arthur Schlesinger wrote to him in 1961 that he already *was* the Voice of America before Kennedy made it official. Murrow knew the new president wanted the image as much as the man.

Murrow moved to New York for NSFA in 1932; his energetic manage-ment of its foreign affairs outreach caught the eye of IIE-founder Stephen Duggan, who invited Murrow to bring NSFA into IIE and made him his deputy, delegating to him the Emergency Committee in Aid of Displaced Scholars. With Albert Einstein, Murrow's committee relocated nearly three hundred of Europe's finest refugee minds in American universi-ties—"the most satisfying thing I ever did in my life," Murrow remem-bered.[3] His early efforts at IIE to develop student exchanges with the USSR, frustrated by Stalin's bureaucrats, provided early entries into a thick FBI file. Duggan, meanwhile, encouraged Murrow to grow; his lifelong dream, even in his later years, was to preside over a liberal arts college.

Murrow thus spent the early 1930s as deputy, disciple, and adopted son to America's premier international educationist and brother to Dug-gan's sons Laurence and Stephen Jr., living by the Duggan credo: "Educa-tion is the only certain road to the attainment of world peace."[4] Murrow's experiments with radio began as an educational activity, first at NSFA, then at IIE; soon he was producing the charismatic Duggan's weekly radio broadcast, *The University of the Air*. As war closed in, Murrow moved to CBS as director of "talks," its public education component.

He had began accumulating an impressive collection of friends, with Duggan and Einstein expanding its range. He was learning to deal eye-to-eye with world figures like Toynbee, Gandhi, Churchill, Jacques Maritain, Felix Frankfurter, Norman Thomas, Eleanor Roosevelt, Harold Laski, Edouard Benes, Jan Masaryk, Rabindranath Tagore, Paul Tillich, Martin Buber, Herbert Marcuse, and Henry Morgenthau. His links to the Colum-bia University internationalists, particularly James T. Shotwell, were close; he and Shotwell wrote a book they called *Channels of International Cooperation*, in praise of the League of Nations. Harold Laski dedicated his *Reflections for the Revolution of Our Time* to Murrow, a fact overlooked by all but Senator McCarthy and J. Edgar Hoover.[5] He was known throughout the world, and much honored, as an early fighter against German and Italian totalitarianism; his frustrating experience with the Soviets destroyed any illusions about Stalin's Russia. At the end of his life, he held dozens of broadcasting medals and honors, fourteen honorary degrees, the British OBE, officer status in the French Legion of Honor, and Belgium's Order of Leopold.

In his years of stardom, the internationalist Murrow continued to think of himself as an educator, but he had been mugged by the Nazis. Instead of college teaching, Murrow was exploring new forms of education via the media, treading paths at which his friend MacLeish had hinted. His own life-shaping education, as a speech major under an unforgettable college teacher, was the prologue to his status as a respected world-scale American intellectual, in that special sense of the word that meant admission to the close company of other intellectuals. Home on furlough from London at the end of 1941, a few years removed from IIE, the thirty-three-year-old Murrow was given a testimonial dinner by CBS's creator William Paley; seated between Paley and MacLeish, he heard speaker MacLeish say that Murrow had destroyed "the superstition of distance and time, . . . the ignorant superstition that violence and lies and murder on another continent are not violence and lies and murder here, . . . that what we cannot see and hear and touch can have no meaning for us." The poet-statesman in his speech dwelt on Murrow's impact: "You laid the dead of London at our doors and we knew the dead were our dead—were all men's dead." He alluded to Murrow's enemies: "There were some in this country who did not want the people of America to hear the things you had to say, there were some who did not wish to remember that the freedom of speech of which this country is so proud is freedom to hear."[6]

Murrow's commitment to cultural diplomacy thus began twenty-two years before USIA was born. His survey of Latin America for IIE and his connections with Laurence Duggan put him in touch with the heroes of cultural diplomacy—Welles, Cherrington, Kelchner, Pattee, Thomson, and Turner. He met Fulbright in London during the then-congressman's 1944 mission to the meetings of exiled ministers of education; the two men sustained dialogue over the next decades, exemplified by a probing exchange on propaganda during the Fulbright-Hickenlooper hearings in 1953. In parallel with Fulbright, he fought McCarthy; his national TV program was the turning point for the Wisconsin legislator. In 1947, as a board member of IIE, he helped recruit Laurence Duggan to succeed his father. Upon Duggan's death, it was in response to Murrow, preparing his radio report on the death of his adoptive brother, that Sumner Welles called Duggan the most patriotic public servant he had known.

Murrow thus seemed a superb and natural successor to George V. Allen in 1961; but the choice was not so simple. Murrow's mistrust of the Kennedys was no secret. In London he had been critical of Joseph Sr.; he was disappointed in John Kennedy's Senate voting record and, after a television interview with the president, saw no reason to revise his judgment; he was even warier of Robert, who seemed to him to have served too long as counsel to the McCarthy committee. Apparently the Kennedys reciprocated the mistrust. Donald Wilson says that, when Murrow spoke at a banquet in 1955, Robert Kennedy walked out. Murrow knew that he was not Kennedy's first choice for USIA. Besides, as the most assiduous of his biographers wrote, perhaps reflecting Murrow's own opinion, "the job itself was no great plum—taking charge of propaganda for a country that didn't believe in propaganda, at least by government." Murrow also knew that the agency "was suspected by the left for its identity with ideological cold warfare and by the right as an alleged nest of egghead-liberal pinkos."[7]

Only four years away from his wasting death from the smoker's disease, he was "flying on one wing," as McGeorge Bundy put it. This national icon thus took a job he knew others had declined, at a considerable cut in salary, far away from his New York base; his acceptance was born of conviction. To serve the president, he began with loyalty, but this lessened the contribution he uniquely might have made to his country in blending two conflicting mindsets he surely understood. On the one hand, Kennedy, egged on by his brother Robert, wanted to dynamize foreign outreach, put new energy into AID, and create the Peace Corps. All this had educational implcations but relied on an unacknowledged urge to expand US hegemony, in unspecified ways. On the other hand, Murrow had grown up in the world of Duggan, Welles, Cherrington, Shotwell and MacLeish, proponents of dialogue between cultures.

Murrow's personal synthesis in 1961, as reported by Kendrick, was lopsided: he wanted to accept the job of "psychological warfare, political not military battles, though not excluding the happy possibility of dialogue."[8] To Fulbright's committee, he made two key culturalist distinctions: he wanted to make US policy "intelligible and wherever possible palatable"; but he insisted that the US example mattered far more than its money or its words.

For both cultural relations and propaganda, the nomination of Murrow—like that of Coombs—bordered on the radical. It epitomized the Kennedy contradiction; clash was inevitable. Few noticed—or cared—that the forces eroding cultural diplomacy had continually gained strength. The thin Jackson-imposed CU-USIA consensus of the 1950s was fraying; underlying problems surfaced continually. Coombs saw the dilemma clearly but there is no indication Kennedy did. Murrow could not have believed all was well.

He must have known, for example, the ideas of his predecessor George Allen. If he did not, the files and voluble staff left over from Allen's era were there to remind him that the two men had shared ideas for decades—Allen too was a Duggan friend. Murrow must have known that a BBC poll in 1961 had made Allen's very point: "What Communist audiences wanted most was straight news [which] they did not get from their own governments. After that came cultural affairs, science and technology, and Western music. What Communist listeners definitely did not want was anything ideological. They were as suspicious of counterdogma as of dogma." Murrow himself had reminded the Fulbright-Hickenlooper committee in 1953 to "remember that dissent, division and criticism are rare commodities in many countries we address."[9] Nothing would have been more natural for him, in the light of his years with IIE, than to follow the Allen-Thayer path, perhaps leaning on the Sprague report. But new frontiers demand radical change, new people and new approaches at the expense of the old. Murrow was sucked into the excitement of the administration and White House power; his deputies encouraged him to press forward, reminding him of his own brave slogan: "difficulty is not an excuse history has ever accepted." Unfortunately he read less recent history than he might have.

Therein lay the Murrow mystery. Instead of strengthening USIA's educational content and substance, building on what had already been achieved to create a far greater agency than before, Murrow presided over an aggressive and unidirectional reduction of USIA, sabotaging its own educational component and rejecting the rich potential of Coombs's partnership.

The idea guiding him was packaged in the confrontational concept of "counterinsurgency," put forth by the younger Kennedy and pressed inside USIA by Murrow's two chosen advisors. The point: to gear up an activist US counterattack against communist-supported insurgents in developing countries. The rise of left regimes around the world, pursuing Leninist simplifications of Marxian thought and riding the wave of nationalism set off by postcolonialism, threatened world security; the tactics USIA adopted were the hard-sell showcase theory. The U.S. was said to have fallen seriously behind the USSR in various strategic fields, like missiles, so activist countermeasures were needed; activism displaced Allen's soft sell, which assumed inevitable US victory over a flawed opponent.

The Dulles-Eisenhower ring of defensive anti-Soviet alliances encircling the USSR was in place. Moderating the roll-back theory, which had, in fact, rolled back little, the Kennedy team sought to take the fight against communism everywhere, from the high ground of the noncommunist center-left. In the alliances Dulles set up, the U.S. would now feel free to pressure even its annointed friends, even authoritarians and an occasional totalitarian, for overall political and social progress. Eisenhower's alliances and the new counterinsurgency were induced to flow together, as in the case of the administration's inherited stance on Cuba and Vietnam.

Appointing Murrow was not simple. He was first recommended to Kennedy by Fairbank's friend, old China-hand journalist Theodore White, not as USIA chief but as the perfect ambassador to England, a job that had already gone to David Bruce. For USIA, Kennedy wanted Frank Stanton and perhaps another candidate. When Stanton declined, Chester Bowles, deputy to Rusk at State, suggested Murrow. Discussing the position with Kennedy, Murrow insisted memorably that he would not take the job unless assured that he could be "in on the takeoffs as well as the crash landings"—a straightforward request for a role in policy formation. He accepted Kennedy's promise of a USIA seat on the National Security Council, unaware that Kennedy would pay the NSC less attention than Eisenhower had. Even in accepting the job, the wary Murrow insisted that Kennedy put his pledge in writing; a JFK letter drafted by the USIA transition team said Murrow was to be Kennedy's "principal advisor on psychological factors dealing with foreign affairs"—language that caught the psy-war view. The letter went on to say Murrow would participate in the development of foreign policies, "as appropriate."[10] The letter omitted many details—and Murrow knew less than he should have about the kind of pledges he needed; his advisors forgot to tell him that presidential promises—witness Dulles-Eisenhower's pledge of a three-month delay for Robert L. Johnson—are not always kept.

With Murrow aboard, Kennedy hoped to polish the image of his administration with the moderate liberals and intellectuals, while strengthening USIA, an agency about which he knew little. Murrow was the most famous name appointed by JFK; as much as the excitement of Kennedy's campaign, the president's appeal to the "best and brightest," and his frank liberal internationalism, Murrow's name helped attract a wave of Americans young and old to offer their services to government and USIA. Few knew what kind of agency they were joining, but all admired Murrow and believed in Kennedy. Murrow himself seems to have been uncharacteristically beguiled by the Kennedy rhetoric; in its frequent metaphors of war, a little of the London adrenalin may have flowed.

While in USIA, Murrow accepted, as he said, the "administration's view of the job"—psychological warfare. But was this indeed the administration's view of USIA or the transition team's view? Sperber concluded that Murrow was "taken in hand" by his deputy Don Wilson, former Washington bureau chief for *Time*, who himself admitted he was "imposed" on the director; Wilson too was nervous about managing "a government warren of 12,000."[11] And was the total reversal of Allen's USIA priorities a Murrow or a Wilson idea? For Allen, engagement through dialogue and trust had come first, with psychological warfare to follow when and where needed; now the policy that emerged was confrontation everywhere. As Wilson later wrote, "Murrow, in general, abandoned his earlier commitment to cultural diplomacy and presided over a more unidirectional USIA. . . . I'm not sure why it happened, but it did."[12] The artificial dramatization of difference fostered by the campaign resulted in a broad-based activism, a commitment to psy-warfare, an extension of USIA's reach, most visibly in Africa, and a further downgrading of cultural affairs.

The solution to the mystery probably can be found in the third member of the Murrow team, Thomas C. Sorensen. To Sorensen we owe the most readable book ever written on USIA, an engaging and revealing statement by an unabashed propagandist psy-warrior and a passionate admirer of Bernays.[13] In 1961 he was a thirty-four-year-old USIA officer, with ten USIA years behind him, holding a desk job in the office of Near East and South Asian Affairs. It is axiomatic that an officer's foreign postings shape his or her vision of State and USIA. Sorensen had carried out four tense and dramatic assignments in the strife-ridden eastern Mediterranean: Beirut, where he learned Arabic; Cairo and Suez, as the IO handling the British-French invasion of 1956; Beirut again in 1958, where as IO he managed the public face of the US landings; and Baghdad, working with the Baghdad Pact countries and thus deeply aware of the violent deposition of Nouri Es Said in 1958 and the brutal rise to power of Abdel Karim Kassem, harbinger of Saddam Hussein. In such frontline hotspots, the articulate, combative, and politics-obsessed Sorensen had no room for Allen's soft sell. Allen, at higher levels, had served in equally tough assignments and knew the needs of USIA from a global viewpoint. Next to the North Carolina gentleman, Sorensen was a truculent Midwestern confrontationalist who relished street fights. He had no patience for engagement or for building long-range credibility by indirection, by "demonstrating" and "presenting" what the U.S. was about. He demanded "persuasion," in his style, the quicker the better. In the old Benton paradox, Sorensen wanted not only a showcase but, standing beside it, a gifted and tireless linguist, policy wonk, and champion debater, making sure everyone saw exactly what he wanted them to see.

One bit of bait Murrow accepted, as a first-priority task, was USIA's heretofore hollow claim to a direct role in foreign policy formation. Murrow focused on relations with the White House, located only one block to the east; USIA's "advisory role" became a consuming goal. To carry it out, he set aside his longstanding mistrust of the Kennedys. Few cultural diplomats knew about the educational values he had learned at the feet of Stephen Duggan and the ideas he had defended since 1930; they knew only his open-minded broadcast record. As for VOA, in faraway southwest Washington, Henry A. Loomis and his colleagues watched Murrow warily. Loomis decided to persuade Congress to issue a charter protecting VOA's efforts to be "intelligible and where possible palatable"; Murrow's advisors insisted on adding a call to give as accurate a picture of US policy "as can most persuasively be presented." Missing the point, Murrow agreed with his advisors; Congress, on the other hand, rejected the change.

Propaganda or even "persuasion," in Sorensen's hard-edged sense, had never been Murrow's style—if anything it was the opposite. His powerful advocacy flowed from a natural instinct for telling it straight. Murrow had heard Creel admit to lying; his extended comments to the Fulbright-Hickenlooper inquiry played on the mirror-not-showcase theme, urging openness in a world where "dissent, division and criticism" are too often stifled, he said in 1961.

Overnight, Murrow found himself too busy to do much thinking out-side the box his two advisors tightly defined. Overlooking CU's Siamese-twin connection to USIA, Murrow waded knee-deep into a different swamp. Without his intervention, USIA and CU were soon engaged in an undeclared guerilla war which Murrow gave no evidence of under-standing. In contrast to Coombs's pertinent expertise, governmental ex-perience, and detailed preparation for his work in CU, Murrow came to his job as a world-class professional media journalist, ignorant of both government and USIA. He found a USIA staff in need of renewal; they were "somewhat tattered legions," mused Wilson four decades later.

It is hard to explain his ignorance about CU, the creation of his adop-tive brother Larry Duggan. His self-assurance had always concealed self-doubt; his biographers say this lent an attractive open-minded quality to his television work. But Washington and the moment demanded light-ning-quick decisions from this thoughtful man. In the hands of his strong-minded and self-assured deputies, he focused on foreign policy; Sorensen, the more downward-looking of his two deputies, managed the housekeeping details, where devils dwelt.

He was indeed flying on one wing; his wasting disease would soon carry him away. Various New York colleagues offered to come to Wash-ington with him, but in Washington he learned that there would be room for few and that the effort of bringing even one aboard drained energies needed elsewhere. Without trusted friends, he made his most far-reaching managerial decision and accepted the two transition aides suggested by the White House, who were already in place on a temporary basis. *Time* bureau-chief Don Wilson was a fine choice, but bringing Sorensen from a middle-level desk to the third position in USIA set off alarm bells in the shabby corridors. Cynical veterans assumed he would serve as a link to his brother Ted, a key JFK advisor. Both he and Wilson were "capable, ambitious young men in their mid-thirties, going places, whose connec-tions to the White House and the Kennedy circle far outstripped Mur-row's. And whose recommendations had already helped shape the direction of Kennedy's USIA."[14]

Murrow's decision to appoint Sorensen was fateful, and he may have regretted it. After his tenure at USIA, Murrow laughingly deflected a com-pliment on his ability to spot talent by admitting to "one spectacularly bad appointment," and added, "when I blow one, I blow it *real* good!"[15] It is unclear whom he had in mind.

At lower levels, Murrow made perceptive appointments to shake up the USIA timeservers: CBS writers William Hobson and Alexander Ken-drick and correspondent colleague Mike Fodor, a Fulbright friend since 1930, for VOA; *Time-LIFE* staffer and future historian David McCullough to produce a glossy magazine for the Arab world; Mildred Marcy as wom-en's affairs officer; Africanist musicologist Leo Sarkisian to VOA Africa; black American Horace Dawson to the officer corps; and McCarthy-victim Reed Harris, as a symbolic apology for the witch-hunting years.

USIA-insider Barbara White was sent to Chile as the first woman PAO in a major USIS post. William Handley, sent to Mali, became USIA's first ambassador.

Murrow, "coming in cold and given the President's instructions, was therefore working within the framework of an approach outlined by his own deputy, now in charge of Policy and Research [and] responsible for effecting the new, close policy-product relationship."[16] Sorensen wrote of the Murrow-Wilson-Sorensen "Troika," as it was predictably called, that Murrow "ran the agency and we never forgot it, but he liked to discuss all major problems and decisions with Wilson and me, and he preferred to have us direct the staff work that formed the basis for his decisions."[17] But bureaucrats knew better: those who run staff direct policy.

Was Murrow subtly boxed in by his own enthusiastic appointees? One sad story suggests so. A distinguished potential replacement for Murrow, Richard Heffner, was interviewed over lunch by the Troika in 1963. Heffner recalled that "they treated [Murrow] with contempt—made it so clear that *they* were in charge. Cut him off when he spoke, talked across him, talked directly to me as though he weren't there." Leaving the lunch, Murrow spoke glowingly to Heffner of the excitement he had found in his USIA years.[18] After leaving Washington, Murrow, with his friend Bill Paley, left a different impression: ill-concealed disappointment.

In August 1963 George Allen broke his self-imposed silence to offer judgment on the new USIA. In the *New York Herald Tribune* he went for the heart: instead of building credibility, he wrote, USIA had let itself be pushed by the Kennedy moment into the kind of propaganda that destroyed American believability. The agency's tactics, he said, had probably helped Castro. Commenting on Wilson-Sorensen's boasts (Murrow was undergoing his first pneumectomy at the time) of having "thrown the book" at Cuba in the Missile Crisis, Allen pointed out what actually happened: "All sections of USIA promptly undertook emergency measures. A mobile transmitter was installed in record time at Key West. Regular VOA broadcasts were rescheduled to provide time for the additional programs beamed towards Cuba." All this, he said, missed the point of the agency's mission: USIA should no more "throw the book at Castro" than the New York Public Library should.

Sorensen, before entering the investment world, went to some lengths, if not by name, to refute Allen in his 1965 book. Two opposite visions of USIA were at play: Allen took a predominantly cultural approach to engagement, with implicit and important policy-support capabilities; Sorensen's predominantly hard-sell policy-support capability was confrontationist and reduced culture to a minor tool. Allen, a seasoned Near East hand, a thirty-year veteran of the foreign service who had served three presidents in four countries and led IIA in the 1940s, issued no answer to the pugnacious younger man. It was an internal USIA discussion of the basic issue which plagued the agency and led back to Mac-

Leish's 1943 shoot-out with OWI. Sorensen's positions, with minor variants, would dominate USIA thinking until its end in 1999.

Allen had moved USIA closer to Thayer's CU and perhaps intended to go even further. but Murrow, too busy to read prestigious reports like Morrill's and Sprague's, turned USIA to shorter-range purposes. The Allen style was replaced by "a more broadly political short-term approach . . . conveying broad understanding of American life [but] subordinated to giving specific understanding of and favorable responses to American foreign policy initiatives," notes USIA apologist Robert Elder.[19] Sorensen's deputy, foreign service officer Burnett Anderson, was not uncritical; he described Murrow as "totally subservient" to the White House.[20] Others, German-reorientation veteran Hans Tuch among them, blamed Sorensen, giving Murrow credit for limiting damage—without Murrow, Tuch said, the pendulum would have swung even further toward unidirectional activism.

Within the limits of his flagging energies, Murrow learned. As détente came closer, Murrow helped Kennedy, for example, with the far-seeing 1963 American University speech dealing with hegemony and spelling out the US idea of peace. By the time Murrow left USIA, the world had begun to change. The partial test-ban treaty, the end of Soviet jamming of VOA, a new USIA stress on common US-USSR interests—all this was on the horizon. Perhaps Murrow had begun to remember what he had known all along: that the U.S. had an important long-term educational contribution to make to the world, beyond the politics of the moment. Just before leaving, he reminded USIA staff that there was another war for the U.S. out there, the fight against "ignorance and fear, suspicion and prejudice"—his words sounded like his friend MacLeish.[21]

Inside USIA, Murrow lifted morale with his star quality. Wilson was proud to quote Murrow in a speech on America's long-range goals: "This victory will see no ticker-tape parades. . . . It will be a victory which will take years, perhaps decades, . . . not a victory of the U.S. over the Soviet Union, . . . of capitalism over socialism. It will be a victory of revolutions realized . . . without violence, . . . of men and nations . . . standing for their individuality as nations, . . . of hope over despair, of accomplishment over frustration, of action over apathy, . . . of freedom in the world as men have the right to know it and demand it."[22] Murrow and Wilson knew something that Sorensen would never admit: that USIA had to be more than a collection of "mere publicists," however gifted. Murrow's farewell stressed substance. "Mere publicists," without substance, he said pointedly, would doom USIA's efforts "to but slight effect."

Murrow's contribution to USIA's national image was transformative; but for cultural diplomacy, it was a serious setback, a moment missed. He was one of few who, like Allen and Thayer, might have made a structural contribution to bringing together the two conflicting functions of USIA in a way that enhanced each. Joining both facets of his own life— education and public information—he might have created a greater

USIA. Even so, his achievements were noteworthy: opening new posts in Africa, boosting Spanish and Portuguese broadcasting to Latin America for the Alliance for Progress, increasing the number of books translated and distributed. He was the first USIA director—and perhaps the last—to have some small input into foreign policy; in Sorensen's admission, Murrow's influence was "less than decisive but more than peripheral." He graced the NSC and occasional cabinet meetings, although like Adlai Stevenson he was disappointed at his distance from the center. He pressed for the racial balancing of USIA staff and initiated the upward movement of women. He brought in outside talent and reinstated a legendary McCarthy victim. He boosted USIA morale and made the agency better known to Congress; as a *Washington Post* headline on his departure noted, "His Luster Rubbed Off on USIA."

Yet what the Troika in fact built in USIA, and publicized to the White House and Congress, was a hard-hitting policy-support machine, eager to "throw the book" at major problems. Sorensen, in the powerful office of policy and plans—the highest-ranking career job in the agency—was seen by career colleagues, except for the outspoken few like Tuch, with the tolerant cynicism reserved for the US style of appointive politics. Hospitalized during the Cuban decisions, Murrow never came to terms with the contradictions Allen underlined in 1963. He rejected the use of USIA for CIA cover yet tolerated Sorensen's love affair with intelligence and allowed him to assign two CIA friends to high-level USIA duty.

Under Sorensen, the Bernays-derived Madison Avenue rhetoric of target audiences and messages to be delivered became USIA's operational logic, embodied in field planning and reporting. With minor embellishments, this plan remained in place until 1999. In 1963 the USIS chief in Saigon, the most counterinsurgent of posts, seeing no alternative to the Diem regime, was given explicit permission by Washington to weed out books from the USIS library as ordered by the Diem government; the CAO at the same moment "allowed the regime to pick the students for American scholarships."[23]

No one decision of Murrow's was determinant in itself, but each blocked alternative opportunities; and, cumulatively, they made a huge difference. The journalist in Murrow never found the strength to review the unilateralist "tell the story" thinking of his advisors. Lifting USIA morale and boosting recruitment, he allowed Sorensen free rein for the rest.

Murrow resigned immediately afer the Kennedy assassination, but Lyndon Johnson wanted him in place, if only as a symbol. Murrow knew that LBJ "saw things differently. A man without the 'style' attributed to Kennedy, he expected a style could be created by manipulation of the instruments of image-making. Instead of basing propaganda on policy, his inclination would be to substitute propaganda for policy."[24] Finally Johnson let him go, recalling the fine black journalist Carl Rowan from his embassy in Helsinki.

Murrow died two years later, wasted by the chainsmoker's disease.

Today, a neglected bronze plaque in the tiny triangular park bearing his name, opposite the former USIA building at the corner of 18th Street and Pennsylvania Avenue, celebrates Murrow, saying that he "demonstrated what America at its best could be." At its *best? Could* be? Murrow had dedicated his life to avoiding such weasel words, trying to show what America *was*. As Schlesinger said, he was already the Voice of America.

• • •

The other New Yorker on Kennedy's cultural diplomatic team was Philip Coombs. Coombs, although in perfect health, left even earlier than Murrow, to the joy of Sorensen—who bragged to anyone interested about "getting rid of Philsy." Coombs had found himself the enemy in an undeclared bureaucratic war, a war that Coombs himself, in his reticent telling, was too decent to describe.[25]

Coombs was a deep-dyed educational internationalist of another hue, little known in his quiet but powerful position as the Ford Foundation's Director of Education. He was a human-resources economist from the same industrial-relations movement that produced CBS's Frank Stanton; he had taught at Amherst and Williams and served with Governor Chester Bowles in Connecticut. There and at Ford he had developed his unique expertise in the practical economics of education. As executive and prime mover of the Paley commission, he produced a ground-breaking report assessing US national needs for the world's resources over the long range. At Ford, he had worked overseas, consulting on education in Turkey and India; and he had reported on CU. In a few years he would create and direct UNESCO's Institute of International Educational Planning in Paris, which over time reshaped educational planning and budgeting in every nation in the world.

His mentor Bowles, with his friend Benton, had compiled a notable career in advertising, had served memorably as ambassador to India in the early 1950s, then settled for the Connecticut governorship when Benton went to the Senate; Coombs was part of Bowles's team. Kennedy named Bowles undersecretary of state, moving Republican Douglas Dillon to the Treasury. By temperament and experience, Bowles was fascinated with the developing countries. Now he was deputy to Dean Rusk, Far Eastern hand, former president of Rockefeller and central participant in the discussions organized by Thayer, Fulbright, and Ford on the future of cultural diplomacy. In State Rusk, Bowles, and Coombs knew the cultural issues in detail.

In contrast to Coombs's preparation in depth, Sorensen had only the dimmest view of what CU—for him, one of USIA's "media"—might conceivably bring to foreign relations; he had seen USIA at work in four crisis posts, where dramatic events had marginalized the long-range reach of USIS's cultural relations. He might have reflected on the meaning of the

American University of Beirut he saw from the window of his office in the Beirut embassy, but he was too busy arguing politics with Arab friends.

At the top of USIA, he adopted a pseudo-systems approach to USIA, using glib Bernaysian logic to call for getting out the US "message," and "targetting" it to specific foreign "audiences" analyzed by sectors. His USIA dealt only with "influentials" and opinion-molders. In this paradigm, CU's exchanges were mere tools for message-delivery. He was slashing the "irrelevancies" Allen had brought to USIA. Murrow's CBS colleague Alexander Kendrick, now in VOA, reflected Murrow's parody of the theory: "His Public Affairs Officers abroad, part of the Country Teams, had to reach Target Audiences (including Opinion Leaders and Mass Audiences) with Psychological Objectives, as outlined in Program Memoranda, while keeping their activities within the PPBS, or Planning, Programming, Budgeting System."[26]

Coombs instead was a genuine systems analyst who knew education; he was a driving intellectual with an informing discipline—human resource economics—at his core. While he had never run a large organization, he had worked in state government. He was a conceptualizer who worked down from ideas toward budgets and programs. He had studied the recent history of cultural diplomacy, and he had unique expertise on the costs and benefits of higher education and universities, with stress on the high relevance of universities for developing countries. At the end of the 1950s, Coombs, at Ford with Rusk, Gardner, and others, had joined John Howard and Robert Thayer to design a rearrangement of USIA, CU, HEW, and AID, so as to maximize the contribution of US higher education to foreign relations. The foundation and university world, with their latter-day missionary-educator instincts, had based their work on university research; the foundations had been building area studies on US campuses for a decade, even before HEW joined the game. Coombs knew the private and public reports of the late Eisenhower years and had participated in some.

Anyone who has watched a US political transition knows that theoretical writing is most often ignored. An impatient man, Coombs was understandably reluctant to take the CU job. He finally yielded to Bowles and Rusk; with such powerful friends, men who knew him well, he cannot be blamed for thinking his skills were wanted and his vision valued.

Shortly after taking the position, Coombs made a significant decision: interagency coordination became the central point of his attack. He believed in fact that he had been asked to pull it all together, and perhaps he had. His 1964 book tells of the obstacles to occupying the high ground that he was convinced Kennedy had assigned to him. Coombs did not realize that Kennedy was reading from a script he only half understood.

One omen of the difficulty of coordination was the founding of the Peace Corps on 1 March 1961, which brought inside government the nineteenth-century missionaries' student-teacher movement.[27] It is significant that Coombs was not consulted about this key spin-off of the cultural diplomatic function; the idea of linking the Corps and its educational work with other Washington agencies was specifically excluded in order to insulate it from government. Corps designer Sargent Shriver was a strong-minded ego who wanted no interference. The episode might have warned Coombs that coordination was problematic.

Coombs's second point of attack—field staffing—was even more perilous. The CAOs lay somewhere near the top of his agenda. If a coordinated approach in the field was the necessary foundation for anything done in Washington, he needed strong and qualified people abroad. Expert in human resources, he knew that the quality of cultural diplomacy—complex programs of intellectual interchange—began and ended with its people. On the way to Delhi, he met a young cultural officer fresh from the university world; from India he cabled back instructions to "find ten more like him."

Coombs's views appealed to the intellectuals Kennedy was wooing. A burst of White House appointments of prominent American minds to embassies could only have happened with his concurrence. With luminary ambassadorial appointments like John Kenneth Galbraith in Delhi, Edwin O. Reischauer in Tokyo, and John Badeau in Cairo, a handful of academic CAOs were sent to USIS posts: to Delhi went Bowles's and Coombs's close friend Robert R. R. Brooks, another labor economist and Coombs's former colleague at Williams; to Tokyo went Reischauer's friend Charles Burton Fahs, Harvard colleague and veteran of Japanese reorientation; to Brazil went Columbia Dean of Architecture Leopold Arnaud; in Paris, Lawrence Wylie, Harvard sociologist of French life, took the job. Galbraith, in one of his famously irreverent cables, asked USIA for a PAO combining the virtues of Robert Frost and Carl Sandburg; he settled for the gentlemanly Mississippian William Weathersby, and both were pleased to accept fellow economist Brooks as his CAO.

Coombs set out to improve the quality and morale of the career cultural corps, not realizing that he was poking a stiletto at USIA's heart. One of his early innovations: regional CAO conferences around the world—in each of State's six geographical areas there would be one each year. Joining the field CAOs at these meetings were representatives of the CU area office, BFS, the CU advisory commission, IIE or CIES, a high-level USIA officer, and Coombs himself. Such professional interchange among cultural officers deepened communications, shared techniques, lifted spirits, built esprit de corps, strengthened professionalism, displayed CAO strengths and weaknesses, and cemented collegiality.[28]

USIA was decidedly not amused. Sorensen already saw CAOs as the enemy within; behind their courtesy, he saw CAO discontent. The CAO conferences in his eyes were gripe sessions—the cultural officers were "ganging up on us," said one PAO although the informationists still outnumbered the committed cultural officers by at least six to one. Few USIA loyalists understood or admitted that the small body of cultural officers had anything to complain about any more than they saw the potential contribution the CAOs might make to strengthening USIA. The combat-ive Sorensen set himself the task of following right behind Coombs and his CAO conferences, "to put out the fires he lighted."

USIA cultural veteran Carl Bartz recalled in a memoir the Bangkok CAO conference of January 1962, held over the protests of USIA's area director. From Bartz's vantage point in the field, Murrow may have reigned but Sorensen "ruled over and tyrannized the field." The Bangkok meeting laid bare the deep tensions in Washington and the "divisions which could make the role of the CAO almost unbearable." The Bangkok CAOs did nothing except explore common problems; but Bartz reported high PAO nervousness about the "volatile mix of CAOs, who they knew would compare notes and pool discontents." By coincidence, Bartz was present nine years later, again in Bangkok, when PAO John Hedges opened a conference of PAOs and CAOs with a vulgar analogy: the CAOs "served the same purpose as a massage parlor: they softened target audi-ences for the serious business, the media policy message"[29]—pure Sore-nsen five years after his departure.

Under pressure from a hostile USIA, the CAO conferences soon van-ished. Within five years, assistant cultural officers were being renamed "program officers," reminiscent of the postwar Kuhn report that called CAOs "contact men." By 1973 a PAO could say, without embarrassment, to a group of cultural officers in Washington, "A Cultural Attaché? I hope I never have one in any post *I* run." By the mid-1990s more USIS posts were without CAOs than with them. Coombs, in fact, did set fires, but he intended them as campfires; USIA's defensive reaction to Coombs drove the CAOs underground. Those who could not afford to leave their jobs fell silent; the game was rigged.

In Washington Coombs was hard at work. The new Fulbright-Hays Act of 1961, which Coombs helped see through to passage, strengthened his position, but only in principle. The broader authority bestowed by the new legislation reflected Fulbright's eternal vigilance. Senate staff had been crafting language since 1958, when Fulbright met with Thayer, Allen, Gardner, Rusk, and Kenneth Holland of IIE, to update, restate, combine into one, and thereby supersede both the Smith-Mundt and Fulbright Acts. Congressman Wayne Hays agreed to cosponsor the bill, although Fulbright was no friend—Fulbright's staff chief Carl Marcy, an Oregon cultural internationalist and Columbia Ph.D., got the two ene-mies together on paper and moved the bill to the Senate floor where it easily passed both houses, in pointed contrast to the two-year fight for Smith-Mundt thirteen years earlier. In his book Coombs took little credit for shepherding the act through the administration, yet his role was cru-cial; any initiative coming from Congress requires executive approval and Coombs handled the back-breaking job of finding it. It was a marvelous opportunity for Coombs to make friends and lay the groundwork for future cooperation. But wary agencies, with friends in Congress, were not charmed by Coombs's relentless drive. The idea of coordination was a red flag; under his direction, it looked like empire-building. His friend Rusk in State supported the legislation but without enthusiasm; AID said it did not care; the USOE supported it, eager to carve out chunks for its own use; and USIA was aggressively unhappy. USIA loyalists, trapped in the siege mentality of their embattled history, wrote Coombs (1964), feared "that USIA might be stripped of its cultural programs and cultural affairs officers." In a USIA struggling for survival, whether the threat was real, negotiable, or fantasy, Coombs's vision was declared a *casus belli*.

He managed to get consensus on Fulbright-Hays, with minor changes, and reported the administration's approval to Congress. During the process, the shrewd yet naive would-be coordinator of education abroad admitted in 1963 that he learned something: "Plainly the Kennedy administration had inherited in this field an accumulation of long-standing bureaucratic rivalries and anxieties." That was putting it mildly!

The Fulbright-Hays Act was a milestone. It sprang from the ideas of the late 1950s and the recognition of the need for change. It marked certain growth in the Senate since 1948, most of it attributable to the leadership of Fulbright and his powerful committee's brilliant staff. Cold war rhetoric was missing in the new bill, which had four goals; first, "to increase mutual understanding between the people of the U.S. and the people of other countries" (people, not elites); second, to strengthen the ties which unite the U.S. to other nations (interdependence); third, to promote international cooperation for advancement in education and culture (multilateral organizations—UNESCO, OECD, or the OAS); and fourth, to aim for international relations that are "friendly, sympathetic and peaceful." No mention of foreign policy or the cold war occurred in the text, in contrast to the heated language of Smith-Mundt and the daily claims of USIA.

The means attached to the second goal—interdependence—indicate that part of that idea was to help the U.S. understand other cultures. This notion, whose history extended back at least as far as the Buenos Aires Conference of 1936, was written into Fulbright-Hays at the very moment the Peace Corps was coming into being, with its openly proclaimed "third goal" of educating Americans; it came only half a decade after Ford and HEW began deepening foreign-area expertise in US education. The idea seemed unexceptionable, but it was in fact revolutionary; it clashed directly with USIA's tell-the-story viewpoint. In due time interdependence would be named the "Second Mandate" and feed USIA irritation, justified by the agency's fear that Fulbright-Hays would arouse congressional fears about propagandizing Americans, once a real vestige of Creel but long submerged in more important concerns. Area studies of course were not propaganda. Congressional leadership rejoiced in Fulbright-Hays, and the bill passed both houses by wide margins. But assassins lay in wait. Both predatory agencies and budgetary gatekeepers were honing their knives.

Fulbright-Hays gathered up all informational and educational-cultural programs into one package and opened new possibilities. Representative Hays noted, "This law is intended to give all the possible authority needed to develop this field adequately. If you don't find what you need, ask your lawyers to look harder." It even authorized "reverse-flow," the funding of US visits by foreign performing artists. Theory was fine, but Fulbright and Hays did not hold the purse-strings, and many of the expanded cultural programs authorized by Fulbright-Hays would never be funded. Worse, Fulbright-Hays ignored the idea of a focused cultural diplomacy, field staffing, and substance within US overseas communications. Drafted in a period of potential reorganization and consolidation, the bill reflects the thinking of 1958–60 and the Morrill report; it contains the seeds of a new look. But its potential for shaping a single coordinated US effort in overseas education and culture was killed by Congress in one day's work when staffers and agency representatives carved it up, gerrymander fashion, dividing responsibility for its functions among four uncoordinated agencies—State, USIA, AID, and HEW. Although tidier and less bicephalic than the old combination of Fulbright and Smith-Mundt, it turned out in fact to mean little change for cultural diplomacy.

One significant, hopeful, and highly visible change was accepted: the bill doubled the size of the Smith-Mundt advisory commission on cultural relations. In May 1962 Kennedy gave Coombs a boost, approving the appointment of ten superb members, doubtless chosen by Coombs's team, to the new CU advisory commission and naming John Gardner, head of Carnegie and key participant in the 1958 discussions, to its chair. The commission was partly depoliticized; only its chair was to be appointed by the president, with other members chosen without regard to party from clearly specified sectors of US intellectual and academic society, as recommended by State. Its new membership reached far beyond the campuses: Roy Larsen, a *Time-LIFE* figure, was vice chair; there were two academics—economist Walter Adams of Michigan State, and veteran BFS-member historian Walter Johnson of Chicago; three university presidents—Luther Foster of Tuskegee, Father Theodore Hesburgh of Notre Dame, and Franklin Murphy of UCLA; a journalist-publisher, James Fleming; and the outstanding black principal of New York's New Lincoln School, Mabel Smythe. Committed to excellence, the commission was a collection of fine minds, chaired by a national educational titan.

Pressed by Fulbright, Congress assigned the new commission to study "the activities of a reasonably representative cross section of past recipients of aid"—building on Morrill's report. Drawing on member strengths, the group labored hard for over a year. Appearing in April 1963, *A Beacon of Hope* picked up Louis XIV's metaphor of radiating light.

Beacon set a comprehensive context for CU. It dealt with all CU's products and achievements, including performing arts and American studies.[30] A nonuniversity research organization had done scrupulous quantitative work, although more interested in IV than Fulbright. It surveyed 2,700 former short-term "leader" grantees from the period 1949–60 and cross-checked twelve hundred non-grantee colleagues in twenty countries. Ambassadors were asked to report on operations as they saw them, producing answers from 130 officers in twenty-six countries. Six commission members traveled to three continents. A large selection of US helpers and program observers were queried at all levels; officials in Washington were interviewed; university foreign student advisors were canvassed; office-chiefs in CU were surveyed; past research was reviewed; and members contributed personal views and experience. Overworked toilers in the field made the time to talk openly with the commissioners. *Beacon* gave cultural diplomats a voice, and it provided new reasons for optimism.

In 1961 the administration's frontiers had expanded but were seriously out of kilter when it came to cultural diplomacy. On Murrow's side, funding soared; on CU's, it sagged. USIA was opening new posts all over Africa, while Coombs was staggering through two ill-prepared congressional hearings under the relentless Rooney bullwhip. Moral support came from every direction, with no effect on funding. The Thayer years had already declared international support to education to be a US responsibility, lest we see "our civilization destroyed." Representative Powell's call for more foreign study in the U.S. was on the record. Hubert Humphrey's Education for Peace resolution in May 1961 called for help to other nations, so that they might "establish, improve, and develop their educational systems." There was support scattered all around Washington, New York, and the universities; but like Tantalus, Coombs was not able to drink.

In CU he had moved boldly forward. He put in place a highly useful annual field-planning document, which was time-consuming but sound; it assumed that field activities could be defined by the gap between US and foreign educational institutions. This was a new approach to thinking about cultural work, geared to long-range embassy objectives for each country. It asked cultural offices to specify what they needed to help bridge educational gaps. USIA exulted in the plan as further evidence of irrelevance and time wasting. In the field, CAOs now had to work on two distinct plans; and while some were pleased with an exercise that forced useful reflection and brought coherence, the PAOs were displeased by this use of "their" staff's time. The CU plan gave education and cultural affairs a concept around which to build a program: everything was keyed to the state of development of the receiving country and the US capacity to mesh with it. Properly done, CU's plan had another advantage: it linked the work of CU, USIA, AID, and the Peace Corps—as well as foreign and multilateral efforts—in a single concept. Where USIA's plan was a list of themes and targets borrowed from a struggling advertising agency, CU's would have been at home in a university.

In the language of educational planning, the CAO was asked to depict the total educational context in that country, i.e., what was being done by US public and private programs, foreign embassies, multilateral organizations, and the host country itself. It asked then how US resources might contribute to overall educational growth, bringing that country closer to the U.S. USIA asked what USIS posts wanted to do; CU asked posts to look at what was already being done and find ways to help. The CU plan assumed that growth in education, over time, would link the U.S. to ongoing processes of change and develop contact between professionals; but USIA wanted only to "reach" influentials. CU wanted to join the host country to the U.S. in educational partnership; USIA wanted only to explain present policy to selected targets. Speaking as one CAO only, I saw the CU plan as the theoretical basis for all my work in the 1960s, while the USIA plan provided nothing.

Coombs cannot be blamed for believing in 1961 that "the time was ripe and the need was great for welding the government's scattered educational and cultural activities into a stronger and more coherent effect," as he wrote later.[31] Nor can he be faulted for believing there was a consensus within the government and in the Senate about what should be done. By extending manpower economics to foreign policy, he had spelled out a clear and non-hegemonic idea for harnassing American educational power to build a stronger world order. Cultural diplomacy since MacLeish, indeed in world history, had never seen so potentially productive an idea, including but reaching well past the "mutual understanding" of Roosevelt, Welles, Cherrington, and Fulbright. Coombs sought to revive the moment in 1945 when US education abroad was one and when even "technical assistance" or training fell to State's cultural division. And it provided in effect an activist—yet binationalist—foreign-policy rationale for the soft power of cultural programs.

In 1964 Coombs looked back and evaluated the intellectual ferment he saw in the job: "The common theme was that the diverse educational and cultural activities were a vitally important aspect of US foreign policy and should be accorded higher priority, greater support, and stronger leadership." Coombs's theory today seems sensible, practical, and promising. But being right in Washington can be dangerous to the health. It can be especially dangerous when the point is made in the rigorous language of the economists, and lethal if it seems to threaten other agencies. USIA's guerilla warfare flowed from the latter danger.

With Rooney unchecked, CU budgets continued their slump. Suddenly, after less than two years and without warning, Coombs was invited to resign by Bowles's successor, Undersecretary George Ball. No reason was given. To his intellectual biographer Randolph Wieck and others, Coombs has expressed continuing puzzlement over his removal. Wieck, in retrospect, saw warning signs: Coombs had little sense of the enormity of what had to be overcome, nor of the daunting obstacles and the skill-ful bureaucrats who lay in ambush at every turning, nor did he under-stand the everyday, routine agonies of the snail-paced Washington political and administrative process; nor did he have any inkling of the size of the institutional and individual egos he was ruffling. In his words, the assignment was "to clarify, unify, and strengthen . . . the educational component of US foreign policy."[32] Three simple verbs, but each threat-ened dozens of bureaucrats who liked things as they were.

There were other factors. Coombs's style, whether despite or because of his intellectual sophistication, could sound aggressive. Statesmanship, noted Adlai Stevenson, is the capacity for endlessly reiterating the obvi-ous; Coombs had little of that skill. Having spoken clearly, he was reluc-tant to repeat himself and impatient with those who did not understand. He was subtle, conceptual, original, disciplined, learned, and allusive, a sophisticated, cutting-edge economist who had lived in the high-oxygen world of the campuses and the foundations. But even in Connecticut he had been sheltered by Bowles, an imaginative public giant; in Washing-ton instead, he encountered the irreducible dilemmas of the American version of democracy. The paths of cultural diplomacy were already strewn, after twenty-five years, with valuable ideas and with genuine and would-be men of greatness.

For example, in Beirut in the fall of 1961, he met with a dozen top staff of the American University and its president, a wise, solid, kindly, and likable AID veteran. Coombs warned the AUB team that all future funding, including AID's, would require serious and costly self-study. To those in the room, whether intended or not, his language sounded threat-ening. Afterward, the president reassured himself by phoning friends in Washington that Coombs did not speak for AID and ignored the visit. The same conversation one-on-one, over drinks, as a friendly hint from a Dutch uncle, might have been useful. In public, the blunt presentation embarrassed all present; and it raised the level of alert for AID. Coombs's core idea, in the history of the issues we have defined, was to bring the government's role in overseas education and training back together, bridging the gap between CU, AID, and HEW—precisely what Morrill had recommended. But his manner gave AID reason to join USIA in the enemy camp.

Coombs's ideas rested on another familiar but poisoned assumption, at least in USIA: that cultural relations required distance from propa-ganda. USIA-loyalists were aware of this view—he was not shy about broadcasting his ideas. Where mighty AID's war on Coombs amounted to little more than ignoring him, the threat to the nervous USIA-CU rela-tionship was too important for a still-fragile USIA to overlook. Quiet preemptive action was set in motion.

The impatience of Coombs, even inside CU, did not always make good sense to his colleagues. With assistants like Joseph Slater from Ford, he worked to build a new CU for the 1962 appropriation request; he wanted to foster better relations between government and the private educational world, to stimulate more cooperation and coordination within the government, to raise awareness in the US embassies about the idea of human-resource development as a key to gradual sociopolitical and economic change, and to earn the right to US leadership in multilateral educational organizations like UNESCO. His two implicit goals were to: show US education's flag abroad, where possible waved with the Kennedy sparkle, and to enlist foreign support for a global attack on the problems of ignorance.

To move forward, he needed a CU as well staffed as his earlier Ford base; so he imported Ford staff, with little sensitivity to the downside. The newcomers turned the quiet, diligent, uninspired, but productive CU into a "beehive," as Coombs said with pride. Unfortunately the bees were angry. The so-called Slater Exercises, a dozen study groups, enlisted some five hundred prominent Americans and used great chunks of staff time. The teams considered five sectors: technology in educational and cultural development, publishing abroad, human resources, international medical education, and geographical area studies. Wonderful as a constituency-building tool over time, the exercises moved too quickly, took too much manpower, and promised too much. They were a confusing way to impose a challenging new mission on an overburdened and underbudgeted bureaucracy.

Wieck judged the exercises "prodigious, yet creative."[33] He studied one task force, devoted to technology, which had fifteen private members, five government staff, and 142 international consultants, scholars and academics, administrators, and publishers, including the presidents of Encyclopedia Britannica and Houghton-Mifflin. They worked intensely for ninety days, in the days before Xerox, fax, or e-mail. The sixty-five-page report produced twelve recommendations on the long-range nature of both education and training, the need for immediate action, and the need to mobilize the private educational world. It boiled down into a familiar idea: a semi-public foundation, "to conduct and administer educational assistance."

Slater's five brigades came to far-reaching and freshly stated conclusions. For the politics of overseas development, they saw two paths: either force-feed, at the expense of individual freedoms, or grow gradually, which would take decades at least. Rejecting Soviet quick-fix tactics, Slater's team defined a third path: maintain freedoms while generating rapid growth. It was a challenging idea, culturally complex and ingenious, compatible with a full-scale coordinated government-private effort. But it was preposterous to expect to implement it from the uncertain CU base.

In all, three hundred recommendations flowed from Slater's work, ranked at four levels of priority. *Pace* Wieck, less sympathetic Washingtonians, and even some of CU's faithful few, saw the exercises as one of the great time-wasters of history. None of the Slater Exercises reached field officers. CU denizens, starved by Congress and swamped with managing too many ongoing programs, saw the excitement as a false dawn. Deep experience augmented skepticism; in this case, they faced new reports popping up every day, each requiring immediate response. To long-suffering CU staff, the human-resource economist and the high-powered social scientists were opaque and arrogant, their deadlines terrifying; CU people wrote memos but had time to read little beyond their in-boxes. The imported Ford culture instead was rooted in the American universities; its self-confidence taxed staff patience. Bureaucrats, even when clothed in apparent mediocrity, have their own brand of wisdom.

With Congress, Coombs, like Benton in late 1945, had to start from the bottom. Benton was a great salesman and marvelously skilled in suffering fools; Coombs had neither gift. In his book, he is too polite to mention the ignorance he faced on key congressional committees—or too short-sighted to understand that his discussants may have had bigger problems on their minds. He thus came across to many as domineering. Coming from a world where clear ideas carry the day, he had little feel for Washington, where success is at best the art of the scarcely possible. He managed to irritate provincial congressmen, CU, and loyalist USIA staff. Even abroad, the new science of manpower economics played poorly in bilateral and multilateral relations; in the Old World, economics in the universities was still a subset of philosophy and history.

Slater and Coombs seemed strangely unaware of two facts of Washington life: ideas carry no weight by themselves but succeed only on their backers' prestige and their support in Congress; and no one reads long reports. If Coombs had been running things from a firm power base, with adequate budgets and at a slower pace, the Slater ideas would have held high value, but he skipped that step. He never saw his first need: to run a functioning CU, he had to acquire and stabilize his power over time.

His haste is inexplicable; perhaps he wanted to make up for two decades of wasted time in CU's history. Oddly, for a man of such intelligence, he had little sense of the political facts, the bureaucratic mountains, and the legislative roadblocks. The records of his underprepared congressional hearings show brutality from the quicksilver Rooney and even impatience from the normally friendly and civilized Fulbright. Looking back, in 1964, he declared that Washington had taught him two facts of life: that the bureaucratic system was cumbersome, crippling, and resistant to change in any short time frame; and that the budget process was by itself a full-time job. These truths came clear too late to help.

At USIA ideas mattered as little as anywhere, once the agency mounted its ad hominem attack on Coombs. Only eight years past its tumultuous birth, USIA was more fragile than it liked to admit, and its defenders were the more passionate. From the propagandists' viewpoint, Coombs was rocking USIA's boat, generating chaos, upsetting priorities, and trying to "steal the CAOs"—it was rank treason. The informationists saw only a devious plot to take over USIA's cultural functions. In administrative practice, the question might have been negotiated; an agreement between Murrow and Coombs might have enriched USIA for decades to come. But Coombs was far ahead of his own colleagues, and in USIA the issues he was clarifying were blurred by the ill-concealed disdain of Murrow's advisors. Meanwhile Murrow spent his days courting the White House. As usual, it was said in USIA that relations with CU were never better. No one dared admit they had never been worse.

Coombs's dream, years ahead of its time, blew up into a thousand pieces. He left office a bewildered man. Moving to Paris, he built one of UNESCO's finest affiliates, still rendering signal service to educational systems and planning the world over. But his failure in CU left deep traces and discouraged the faithful. Even the private world was dismayed. A leading foundation figure of the period said years later: "We were eager then to follow sound leadership from government. But there was none."

Murrow, with a different dream, would die sadly in 1965, two days after his fifty-seventh birthday. For cultural diplomacy, the burst of Kennedy talent, the bright hopes, and the efforts of two extraordinary men— all this produced little more than disruption, discouragement, the alienation of private support, and continued erosion of the cultural diplomatic function. Even the new John Gardner–chaired advisory commission slid rapidly downhill. Only six years would elapse before the commission, under the chairmanship of University of Colorado president Joseph Royall Smiley, would entitle its annual report *Is Anybody Listening?*

Coombs resigned on 20 April 1962, at the request of Chester Bowles's granite-nosed successor George Ball, one week before the publication of *A Beacon of Hope*. Based on his fourteen months in Washington, Coombs wrote a unique book, the best general book before Frankel about foreign policy and cultural relations. Only nine discreet and allusive pages cover the specifics of a Washington experience that must have left a bitter taste; *The Fourth Dimension of Foreign Policy* was the first book to analyze American cultural and educational power as a factor in foreign relations. It appeared under the prestigious imprimatur of New York's Council on Foreign Relations; it was funded by Carnegie and prefaced by Fulbright. A panel of experts reviewed the draft, including many whose names recur in our story: three had occupied high office in the German reorientation; another was Carleton Sprague Smith, the jewel in USIS Brazil's diadem in the 1940s. The book thus spoke not only for Coombs and to some extent for Ford but also for a significant and experienced slice of the foreign affairs and the educational establishment, which clearly continued to care deeply about cultural diplomacy.

Slim and clear, Coombs's book is the first overall general public-policy book on cultural diplomacy, even if based on human resource economics, to open up thinking about foreign cultural relations. Between the lines, it is a personal statement, a sad account of the defeat of a talented participant, a record of one more link in a lengthening chain of losses for cultural diplomacy. Coombs did achieve one thing that eluded even Thayer. He was the first Assistant Secretary of State for Educational and Cultural Affairs to bear that title, which has survived until today. For Coombs there was little joy in it. Wieck saw Coombs as a symbol of the failed dream of Kennedy's New Frontier. But whose dream was it?

CHAPTER FIFTEEN

Battle's Rescue and the Birth of the Peace Corps

What returned Peace Corps Volunteers have learned is that the meeting of idealism and reality, of principle and pragmatism, need not always result in an uneasy compromise but rather in a more precise and exact perception of the country and the world.

—Loret Miller Ruppé, 1983

AT THE MOMENT WHEN PHILIP COOMBS was retreating to his home in Connecticut, few noticed in the excitement of the Kennedy transition that a dramatic new agency had sliced away another piece of cultural diplomacy from the original vision spelled out by Cordell Hull. The Peace Corps had come to life at the precise moment when Coombs came to Washington; by the time he left, it was a fact of US foreign outreach.

Before looking at this innovation, we must close off the story of Coombs and his dream. There is no better way than a look at Lucius D. Battle's brief moment as his successor. In April 1962 the gifted foreign service officer "Luke" Battle inherited a demoralized CU.[1] In a short but restorative tour, his classical and gradualist administrative style suggests that settling modestly for the possible was the only feasible path, given irreducible obstacles. Yet Battle's style, in the end, curtailed even more of the 1938 dream, not to mention the fresher dreams of 1961. In a beleaguered bureau of State, at the edge of despair, questions that once seemed critical vanished in the battle for survival. Battle's quiet tenure helps understand the mistakes of his predecessor because he had the patience to build for the very long run, even knowing his tenure would be short—and with no idea what lay beyond. But his victory was another step in the relentless fading of the designers' vision. Repairing the damage he found, Battle managed a miracle and perhaps saved formal cultural diplomacy from oblivion. But the costs were high.

Battle was a gentlemanly foreign service veteran from Florida, handpicked by Acheson as special assistant in the last years of the Truman era. He had left State in disgust during the McCarthy years and took refuge in directing the restoration of colonial Williamsburg. He returned to State shortly before Coombs arrived. Battle was the consummate quiet, intelligent, effective administrator, perhaps the only kind who can succeed in

Washington's political climate over time. He saw no alternative to strengthening what was in place and adding to it at the margins.

He returned at Kennedy's request, accepting a difficult job as head of State's Secretariat, the nerve center through which all communications in and out of State flow. Barely into his new job, he was astonished to be invited to move down one floor to take over the bruised CU. A deeply cultured man, he had a rich sense of the importance of cultural affairs—and, as one of the lucky buyers of a painting auctioned off after the call-back of Benton's 1947 traveling exhibit from Czechoslovakia, he knew some of what he was up against. He resisted the invitation to a job leading nowhere but accepted when CU's peril was made clear.

Assessing the damage, his first act was to close down the poisoned performing arts program in order to stifle the furor raised by the acidulous Dorothy Kilgallen's reports on the tour of the hapless variety troupe led by comedian Joey Adams.[2] The shutdown provided a needed cooling-off period.

Next he set about cultivating Congress with weekly visits. He knew, as well as Coombs's key CU staff did, that brilliant ideas in Washington lose out to the chain of action, which is no wiser than its least-informed link. In his earlier work with State, he had been reluctant to deal directly with Congress or to spend time persuading distracted legislators to focus on foreign affairs; he had little experience of the congressional culture and worried he could not do the job well. Instead, he discovered in CU that he was very good at it and confessed later that he actually enjoyed it. Doubtless Congress was only too ready to welcome Coombs's replacement, but for Battle things went well from the start.

He nurtured his connections with the White House staff as well, knowing that the most fervent wishes of a strong president are only smoke unless he is willing to devote time, staff, prestige, and perhaps trade-offs to carrying them out; he needed the support of White House staff and, in a pinch, of the president himself. Inside CU, as in any government bureau, he cultivated his staffers respectfully—he knew nothing was possible without the support of subordinates, even apparent incompetents. Staff support, in Battle's view, was not an entitlement but a privilege to be earned. He knew that nothing gets done without allies, so leadership means being ahead of one's followers—yet close enough for them to see the wink of an eye.

Above all, he understood the cardinal rule of administrative leadership, adapted from Steven Muller's law of university presidents: if a bureau-chief gets the funding, then nothing else he does will matter; if on the other hand he does not get the funding, then nothing else he does will matter. Battle put budget first. He was a practical bureaucrat with no temptation to the visionary; he willingly settled for small incremental progress, day by day. He worked upward from what was certain, with the help of a bureaucracy whose rules, values, and experience he respected;

Coombs instead had begun with a superb idea and worked downward, into the murk of a bureaucracy he secretly deplored.

Inside CU, to boost morale and feed Congress's sense of what mattered, Battle reorganized, but he did not resort to cosmetic acronyms, like Stettinius and Benton. The key to his new structure was geography in parallel to the dominant geographical bureaus of State, USIA and AID. A geographic structure for CU, he reasoned, would attract stronger foreign service officers into the bureau; he was already scouting the ranks for candidates. His overarching goal was to impress State and Congress with CU's relevance to foreign policy. Ralph Turner's distinction between policy of the short and long range had long ago been lost in the archives, but Battle's practical instincts were sound. Relying on his own sense of the lines between CU and the rest of State, he left no guidelines for less sensitive successors.

The decision to go geographic had downsides. For one thing, it complicated the work of the academic support agencies. IIE complained that, to deal with the American student program, their staff now had to deal with six CU area offices instead of one student office. A more basic difference, on the classic question of proximity to foreign policy, was that he moved CU one step closer to policy than before; others would exploit the opening. The geographical structure's advantage of paralleling other foreign affairs agencies was thus purchased at the cost of looking—and being—more political, in a shorter time frame, than Turner would have wanted. Linking cultural relations more closely to the State and USIA focus on policy, his CU stepped outside its classic fortress of academic integrity—or so history would suggest.

Battle attracted impressive personnel, including officers like his special assistant Nicholas Veliotes, later ambassador to Egypt. Battle was able as well to ease out a few of the softer CU apples. Deferring most international travel, he mended domestic fences. He devised adroit ways of increasing the surplus foreign currencies going into the program, augmenting CU's budget by 20 percent. Against Fulbright's advice, he came to an agreement with the Devil himself, Congressman Rooney, agreeing to keep to a low annual budget target of around $50 million, in return for funding stability. Soon CU budgets began to rise as Rooney's random attacks turned to more diverting targets.

Foreign student questions had overflowed painfully into public consciousness, as a by-product of the administration's newfound stress on Africa. Battle managed to calm tensions by forming unassailable external committees, and he buffered tough decisions that might attract congressional lightning. For performing arts, after cooling things down, he quietly revived their export, using a peer-review system with subcommittees for dance, music, and theater. Soon performers were again moving abroad. He sent artist-in-residence John Ferren to Beirut for a year. For the University of Hawaii's East-West Center, which was dear to Vice President Lyndon Johnson, he appointed a committee to plan and manage

CU support. He built friendships and constituencies. When a prominent Washington hostess complained of his abrupt cutoff of performances, he went to tea the same afternoon with the racy performing arts file under his arm, entertained her with snippets of misbehavior, and made a stalwart friend. Erasing any hint of predatory intentions, he befriended Washington agencies like HEW's USOE; he reassured AID's managers; and he soothed the angrier elements in USIA, who were all too delighted by Coombs's departure. The word "coordinate" disappeared from Battle's vocabulary.

In the circumstances, he was a very gradual gradualist. His first priority was survival. Even when survival seemed assured, his style was evolutionist. He saw no choice but to establish and settle for what CU had, then to build patiently. He had no personal ambitions in CU except to leave things better than he had found them; he knew he was an interim CU director, sent in to put out fires. When Lyndon Johnson moved into the presidency, Battle was assigned to Egypt as ambassador in 1965. He had done a remarkable and indispensable job in CU.

To take his place, Johnson assigned a talented younger man with no apparent qualifications other than his quick mind and proximity to the president, his young Texan assistant Harry McPherson. Johnson had no intention of jettisoning a favorite staffer; McPherson's immediate priority was to find a successor. In a version of temporary duty, Washington's TDY, the indispensable McPherson was daily called back to the White House and deprived of the chance to get to know CU, its issues, and its people. Recently he admitted he was little help to CU, accepting its leadership knowing he would not stay; with obvious irony, he admitted that the post was attractive in part because it would fatten his CV. Still, McPherson had the president's ear, and there were no other candidates in sight. In fact, both men had their minds on the difficult transition following the Kennedy assassination.

CU morale and output had mounted along with Battle's budget increases, but the pleasant, smiling, and likable McPherson, for the CU staff, was an absentee—"a Cheshire cat," said one staffer. Fundamental CU contradictions awaited resolution. Yet CU's good soldiers were getting on with it as usual; and in the field, as ever, the CAOs trudged dutifully ahead.

•   •   •

Battle's tenure marked a peaceful era for CU and in cultural diplomacy. It is thus a good moment in our narrative to examine some random aspects of the bureau's work, as they had developed since the 1940s: the Fulbright Program, now in existence for almost two decades; CU's unusual advisory and oversight bodies; and the Peace Corps, a new player in the fields of cultural diplomacy. To these items, sketches of two more early CAOs, Paul Child and John L. Brown, will flesh out this portrait of the 1960s.

The bright spot in Battle's and CU's world was the Fulbright Program, on the threshold of its third decade.[3] We have examined the process this complex interuniversity exchange had called into being, but Fulbright was a living, growing program, and by 1961 changes were taking place—changes not foreseen by Coombs. For Fulbright Battle's tenure was a time of consolidation and stabilization.

Fulbright was the core of all cultural programs, consuming about half of the CU budget. Fulbright's first two decades were the one continually bright note in cultural diplomatic development. Even Battle's rehabilitation, a period of relative but optimistic penury, did not slow the steady progress of Fulbright exchanges, whose patron in the Senate kept careful guard. Within the program, patterns were beginning to emerge, twenty-five years after the founding of the Division of Cultural Relations and ten after the birth of USIA. By the time of Battle's departure, Fulbright was moving steadily and independently under its own BFS-trimmed sails, at the center of CU and the CAOs' work.

By 1950 Smith-Mundt dollars were permitting Fulbright commissions to move grantees in both directions, bringing the first foreign students and academics to the U.S. By 1960 forty binational agreements had been signed and there seemed to be no reason for the gradual expansion not to continue. Commissions were in place around the world, even if some had proved premature and closed early. Doctrinal turmoil in Washington left the core of the Fulbright Program intact because of its careful layers of insulation from day-to-day politics, put in place by the founders and carved into stone by the BFS. Fulbright reached around the globe; by 1960 its US and foreign alumni numbered over fifty thousand, from dozens of countries, representing every aspect of university activity, a broad variety of academic disciplines, and a dozen professions.

Progress however was about to grind to a halt. Coombs, in pressing forward the Fulbright-Hays legislation, had launched new agreements; between 1961 and 1964 ten new commissions, each requiring a binational agreement, were in place; first in Portugal, then in Nepal, Ethiopia, Cyprus, Ghana, Malaysia, Afghanistan, Tunisia, Liberia, and Yugoslavia, in that order. Coincident with Coombs's departure however, Fulbright growth stalled until the end of the 1970s. Since CU had every interest in expanding the program and Congress was supportive, only a stealth move by USIA leadership can explain the sudden checking of momentum. No one knew at the time, nor could one have foreseen, that after Yugoslavia no countries would join the Fulbright family for eighteen years. In its first two decades, Fulbright built fifty commissions abroad, losing three or four; in its second two decades, only one commission was added. As a participant, I can only suggest that the stunting of Fulbright growth is not explained by the documents; one can only speculate that PAOs impatient with commission independence and post-Sorensen USIA directives supporting foreign policy put on the brakes. Whatever the cause, it was the first successful slowing of Fulbright's progress.

In the U.S. CU's links to the universities kept Fulbright stable, with the Senator's help; so did BFS, with a sound staff, extensive travel budgets, and two strong private-sector selection agencies, IIE and CIES, each managing a network of peer-review university-based selection committees. Abroad, powerful binational commissions, comprising the host-country's most prestigious educators, protected the integrity of selections and placements. In the field, notwithstanding the loss of the academic CAOs, strong foreign executive directors, sometimes fiercer defenders than the academic CAOs, were replacing the stalwarts who had trained them.

CAO Carl Bartz, in his notes on the early 1950s, told how Fulbright in Burma separated itself from developmental goals too late to prevent its downfall. In Rangoon, where the first US and foreign Fulbright grantees had been handled, the Fulbright commission had grown, managing about 150 grants per year, part of a substantial overall US educational presence. Bartz's PAO, Arthur Hummel, education-minded son of Fairbank's ex-missionary friend and director of the Library of Congress's Far East Collection, was on his side; Hummel would later backstop McPherson as deputy in CU, then act as Assistant Secretary, before moving to Taiwan as ambassador. In 1988 Bartz remembered the cultural program in Burma: Rangoon's USIS library was the best in the area, directed by locally hired Zelma Graham, a respected ex-missionary in Burma since 1937. The Ford and Asia Foundations were mounting sizable operations. New "chairs" in American studies, Fulbright funded, were in place in the Burmese universities. The turning point, noted Bartz, was discerned by Fulbright student Joseph Lelyveld, later foreign editor for the *New York Times*; Lelyveld warned him that the U.S., with its heavily developmental agenda, was pushing political modernization too hard, underlining the wisdom of Fulbright's indirect and organic gradualism. In April 1962 the military government headed by the xenophobic Ne Win slammed the door on the Western presence and Burma entered a long period of isolation; the Fulbright commission was closed, and the binational agreement was abrogated. Burma's intellectual class scattered, and the new nation began its rapid descent toward the lowest ranks of the underdeveloped.[4]

For Fulbright in Japan and Germany after 1950, the transition from defeated nation to ally moved quickly. Converting reorientation's exchanges to a Fulbright Program was a step toward normalization. The occupations' ad hoc systems of academic exchanges were reshaped, under the guidelines of Fulbright binational agreements and commissions. In Germany, the German membership of the first Fulbright Commission was handpicked by Chancellor Konrad Adenauer, who named his special assistant, future prime minister Walter Hallstein, to head the German half of the board.[5] Both Germany and Japan would soon be putting more funds into Fulbright than the U.S.

Early Fulbright programs, disproportionately large because of available funds, leveled out with time as more countries participated, military funds dried up, counterpart funds from food sales waned, and finally as foreign governments tried to make up the difference. In most countries, Fulbright grew despite rising political tensions—precisely as Fulbright had envisioned. Newly independent former colonies, with deep problems of identity, were beginning to rattle the stable structures left by the imperial past. Hovering over all else was the threat of the US-USSR confrontation. In the 1950s, Americans were encouraged to build and stock bomb shelters in their backyards to protect against atomic attack, and schoolchildren practiced huddling beneath their desks. Fulbright's program however was planned so as to fly high above all this. And, because the Senator had kept McCarthy at bay, US politics had little effect on the program—a tribute to the survival of bipartisanship however weakened.

In 1953 Eisenhower, with the presidency of Columbia University behind him, a ringing popular mandate, and a solid congressional majority, took over. Fulbright, vice chair of the Senate Foreign Relations Committee, gave way gracefully to Iowa's Bourke Hickenlooper and stayed close to him. Republicans like Taft, Smith, and Mundt were enlisting others to the cause, in defense of the national treasure they had put in place. In 1963 Fulbright exchanges were growing healthily and there were few clouds in the Fulbright sky.

• • •

CU's two advisory bodies, however, were running into problems. They were an element of the protections that Congress, in bursts of wisdom, put in place around cultural diplomacy in 1947–48. The story of the CU advisory commission and BFS begins with clear intentions, restated more than once, and suggests the importance that elements in Congress gave to cultural dipomacy. But it is also a tale of entropy, neglect, waning bipartisanship, and an inattentive outside world. Viewed from 1938 until 2002, the story of the advisory bodies trends steadily downward.[6]

In the period leading up to 1938, outside advice to formal cultural diplomacy was deemed indispensable; experience and information were vital, and close communications and clear channels to and from the universities and the US intellectual world were the base on which everything was to stand.

In government, oversight commissions can be genuine collaborators or window dressing. US advisory bodies are normally appointed by the president and are politically, geographically, and ethnically representative—whatever else they may do, they are designed for political communications. It is thus significant that in the case of cultural relations, the first advisory commission for cultural diplomacy was absolutely different. The division's GAC, devised as soon as Cherrington was in place as director, was Cherrington's creation; it was the wide bridge he needed to the American intellectual world. The founders, and in Congress Fulbright at least, saw GAC as the government's two-way conduit to the private educational sector, not as a voting constituency but as the primary actors in cultural diplomacy. Welles's 5-percent bargain held that the government was little more than a helpmate.

In 1938 GAC members were appointed by FDR as proposed by the division. Its initial membership was four plus Cherrington, named chair by his colleagues. All were frontline participant-designers: IIE's Stephen Duggan, Columbia's Shotwell (usually represented by Waldo Leland of ACLS), Carl Milam of ALA, and John Studebaker of the USOE. Expertise, experience, access to the active participating bodies of cultural diplomacy, like the universities or the libraries, and constituent representation were the *only* criteria. Party affiliation, ethnicity, or geographic balance were not considered—although New York or Washington residence may have been a requirement, for budgetary and transportation reasons. The chair was left to GAC's choice, as was the size of the commission—GAC was free to add members and soon did.

This unusual ad hoc Washington body, highly informed, professional, and detached from politics, took an executive rather than advisory stance. GAC met every month, with most division staff in attendance—eight to ten people, at the beginning. Subcommittees—wholly composed of professionals—extended GAC's reach into the intellectual world. The subcommittees worked out exchange policies and other questions raised by the Buenos Aires Convention of 1936. "Hundreds of persons met periodically as active members of these committees," noted Espinosa.[7] Over these subcommittees, GAC was the governing body.

In February 1940 GAC expanded six months before corporatist Rockefeller came to Washington. Cherrington knew he would soon return to Denver and wanted GAC to become "more widely representative," including representation of businesses active in Latin America. He then retained the GAC chair, flying in monthly from Denver. Adding expertise as needed, GAC behaved like a highly active board of trustees, shaping policy in a direct way, implementing and overseeing its implicit bargain with the educators. Meetings were still attended by the entire division staff, now numbering twenty to thirty. The mainstays were ACLS's Leland and second-wave appointee George N. Shuster, president of Hunter College in New York. One activist new member was Vice President Henry A. Wallace, representing FDR. GAC continued under Cherrington until 1948, when it was superseded by Smith-Mundt's five-man advisory commission, marking the end of the Cherrington era.

With GAC in place, Fulbright was lured into forgetting about legislating outside oversight in his initial bill, but in 1948 he saw the mistake and established the Board of Foreign Scholarships. The generalist intent of BFS was lodged in its name; it was to supervise *all* government scholarships of any kind. Fulbright was strong enough, both in his convictions and in his position in the Senate, to create a nonpolitical body and to expect it to resist the challenges he already saw ahead, with the help of his colleague McCarthy. The BFS was the tiny division's second advisory commission—surely the division was the only Washington agency of its size—no more than three hundred employees—ever to have more than one. Like GAC, BFS in its role went far beyond mere advice; it too bridged the gap between State and the universities. By choice, it was a strong executive decision-making body. The legislation called for ten members, appointed by the president at the recommendation of the division. All but one of the first members came from the educational world; all appointments were made without regard to party affiliation; and BFS elected its own chair.

As we have seen, the first BFS, with its precisely balanced membership, made a strong educational statement. It included the presidents of Vassar and Fisk, and the dean of Catholic University's graduate school; three scholars—Ernest Lawrence in physics from California, Walter Johnson in history from Chicago, and Helen White in English from Wisconsin; two directors of education—for USOE and New York State; and architect Laurence Duggan. The nonacademic was Gen. Omar Bradley, representing the Veterans Administration. The nine educators represented one traditionally black university, one Catholic university, one women's university, two land-grant universities—and no Ivy League university. Two members were women. There were representatives of the basic disciplines and a military leader. Geographically, members hailed from California, the Midwest, and the South, as well as the predictable Northeast.

BFS, an oversight board with policy and executive responsibilities, soon waded into the thicket of decision making. The board insisted, for example, on exercising final selection rights over all grantees, confronting the jarring question of security clearances. The Fulbright Act had called for a nonpolitical program, but the Smith-Mundt legislation demanded security clearances for all grantees, US and foreign. Security would soon be BFS's thorniest problem.

To supervise an exchange program that would operate in most countries of the world, BFS members and staff were given travel budgets. Assigned to its first staff were two of the division's best. With two additional program officers and supporting clerical staff, BFS could send members and staff around the the world. The high-caliber staffing and generous budget underlined BFS's importance as the Senator's eyes and ears, while assuring smooth government relations with the academic community. BFS members were appointed by the president from lists provided by the division. The balance of early appointments suggests that the White House did not interfere.

Smith-Mundt in 1948 opened a third chapter in the story of cultural diplomacy's extraordinary reliance on outside advisory commissions. The legislation replaced GAC with a trimmer commission and added another commission, for information. PL 402's bifurcated thinking was manifest. Rather than scramble the issues and put them before one oversight body, Congress carefully mandated one commission for each side of the information-culture divide. The three thousand-person division, with the OWI contingent absorbed and renamed IIA, now had *three* advisory bodies, a never-to-be-equalled Washington record.

The two Smith-Mundt commissions, unlike the BFS or GAC, were politicized in the classic American mode. In a sharp turn away from bipartisanship, this decision reflected the cold war, the sharp debate over the legislation, and the partisan swings of Congress in 1946 and 1948. Each of the new commissions was to have five members, with no more than three from either political party; the chairs were to be appointed by the president. Congress was on the record: it understood perfectly well the separate natures of the informational and cultural functions.

The Smith-Mundt debate took a major step away from bipartisanship, so it was even more crucial that appointees to its five-person commissions came from the peaks of professionalism. The first appointees, as proposed by IIA, set the highest standard. Even respecting party affiliations, the caliber of the first cultural commission outstripped BFS. The founders' intentions were intact, and the universities were reassured that matters were still firmly in academic hands. The cultural advisory commission was chaired by the president of Vanderbilt University and included the presidents of Princeton and MIT, the graduate dean of Catholic University (also by design a member of the BFS), and the director of education for the Ladies' Garment Workers' Union—a political gesture to a different sector of education. All five were educators, four came from major universities, three were university presidents. In the politics of representation, the commission had a southerner, a Catholic, and a labor educator; in the politics of institutions, there were four research universities; one northern, one mid-Atlantic, one southern, and one Catholic; and there was also a powerful union representing women.

Five years later came the next shift in the evolution of advisory commissions overseeing cultural diplomacy. With the creation of USIA in 1953, the information commission moved into the new agency, while the CU commission and BFS remained in State. Prominent chairmen included J. L. Morrill, president of the University of Minnesota, and Franklin Murphy, chancellor of UCLA.

In 1961 more substantial changes were put in place. The Fulbright-Hays Act left the BFS untouched, but, while retaining the right to name the chair for the president, it doubled the size of the CU advisory commission, depoliticized membership, and mandated high professional representation, with specific sectors designated by law. The Fulbright-Hays Act went to unusual lengths to stipulate what was intended and what fields were to be represented. The new CU advisory body was an expanded ten-member infra-political rotating board, with "distinguished representatives of cultural, educational, student advisory and war veterans groups, . . . public and private nonprofit educational institutions"; it included *ex officio* representatives of USOE and the Veterans Administration. Kennedy set a high standard by appointing John Gardner, head of Carnegie and future Secretary of HEW, to the chair.

The new CU commissioners, impressive as ever, were less university-dominated than the Smith-Mundt commission and reached beyond the educational world. In addition to Gardner and an executive from *Time-LIFE*, we find three university presidents (UCLA, Notre Dame, and Tuskegee), two professors (history and economics) from Chicago and Michigan State, the publisher of a Fort Wayne newspaper, and the head of New York's famous experimental New Lincoln High School. A historically black and a Catholic university were not new, nor was the failure to include the Ivy League. But a voice for secondary education was a novelty. And the surprise was the addition of two journalist-publishers to the CU commission.

The next shift came in 1968. A departing Lyndon Johnson, in a moment of inattention or revenge against his former Arkansan friend, wiped away two decades of careful planning. Deeply offended by Fulbright's desertion over the issue of Vietnam, Johnson managed to sabotage the Senator's crown jewel by ignoring tradition; BFS appointments during his administration's last days were said to have resulted from a sign-up list posted on the White House bulletin board. He appointed three White House friends, for the first time taking the choice of BFS members out of the hands of CU professionals. Partisan Republicans would take note that elective politics and cronyism now ruled; in 1968 they would act on that premise. In 1968 as well, the CU advisory commission, which had gone from the bright hopes of its first year into despair under Rooney's defeat of Frankel, called its annual report *Is Anybody Listening?* The erosion of advisory commissions, and their relevance, had quickened; looking ahead of our chronology, it had not yet ended.

In 1978 Carter's reorganizers, wedding CU and USIA, would neglect to consult a Congress that no longer included the senator from Arkansas; the White House task force lumped both advisory commissions into a single seven-member commission, balanced as to party and with a presidentially appointed chair, i.e., fully politicized. A sluggish appointment process under Carter meant that the commission's chairman sat alone for a year; during this period, he decided on his own to rename the commission the Advisory Commission on Public Diplomacy: he believed the alternatives were too clumsy. The belated first round of appointees to the new commission included two academic representatives out of seven members. Under its new name, the commission would include no other academic representation of stature. In 1999, when USIA merged back into State, State's planners threw the advisory commission away, considering it a redundancy. Thanks to the protests of commission members past and present, Congress granted it an extension and the Advisory Commission for Public Diplomacy continues, as of this writing.

This brief history of the various public advisory bodies related to American cultural diplomacy since 1938 follows three interwoven threads: politicization, de-professionalization, and the submersion of education and culture under the undefined "Public Diplomacy." Working their way through the system over time, these three trends illustrate the inexorable erosion of formal cultural diplomacy in the US government.

• • •

Another new player darted onto the Washington scene in 1961: Sargent Shriver's Peace Corps. Fulbright's initial dream of sending substantial numbers of newly graduated Americans abroad, with long-range benefits for the nation, had yielded to BFS's wise insistence on a broader range of university participation. In 1961, reviving the missionaries' Student Volunteer Movement, the idea of youth export came back to life, a new wrinkle on an old idea. Fulbright was irritated enough to criticize its unidirectional style, its failure to include leadership among its criteria, and some of its pretentious early pledges; but he moderated his comments in deference to his friend Hubert Humphrey.[8] To underline his commitment to youth activism, Shriver's Peace Corps opened a path for cultural outreach to the young. The Corps picked up a time-honored dimension of US cultural diplomacy.

It was done without consultation with either CU or USIA. Declining at first to coordinate or cooperate with other agencies, in order to stress its independence and its insulation from policy, the Corps had its birth in a Washington too sure of itself, too vigorous in its mindset and too counterinsurgency-oriented to be swayed by other views. From the CU angle, the Peace Corps was a familiar story; another government agency had sliced its own piece off the loaf of cultural relations. Insisting on the right to follow its own self-defined rules, the Corps ignored the bureau that had been tilling the same fields for twenty-three years. Corps field volunteers went abroad under instructions to avoid contact with the embassy—no one remembered Welles's insistence that all foreign educational activities must pass through State.

The Corps, a unilateral Kennedy White House action, was born in a campaign speech in October 1960 at the University of Michigan, where Kennedy proposed that young Americans live and work in developing countries. He urged young people to "contribute part of your life to your country." Kennedy and Humphrey seemed unaware that they were merely secularizing the Student Volunteer Movement, which had sent fifteen thousand young graduates to teach in mission schools since the early nineteenth century and had brought back thousands of foreign students as well. For example, in 1923 Jane Doolittle's hometown raised $3,000 to send her to Tehran; she remained there for the rest of her life and became a legend in women's education.

Other nations did similar things, on a smaller scale and with less fanfare—first of all Britain's Volunteer Overseas Service. Broader in concept was the French effort, which offered "technical cooperation" positions abroad to young university graduates exempting them from compulsory military service; this program was less oriented to teaching than to training counterparts. Maintaining the idea of national service while alleviating pressure on the military to absorb more conscripts than it needed, as well as reducing intellectual unemployment, France aimed technical cooperation primarily at social and human science research, but the focus was flexible and implemental. By the early 1980s France stretched "cooperation" to cover a hundred or more young scientists scattered across the U.S. in major universities and cities and reporting to eight Science Attachés in the French diplomatic mission around the country. Each *coopérant*, placed in a university as a nondegree student, was a link between US and French science. Skeptics saw the system as an elegant form of scientific espionage and worried that the U.S. was giving away its secrets, but calmer heads argued that there were few secrets in science, that floods of new knowledge were generated daily, that science was already publishing more "secrets" than could be absorbed, and that the French youth program would in the long run link the French and the American scientific worlds as closely as they had been in the time of Franklin.

The Peace Corps, compared to the French and British programs, set out in a flamboyantly different direction. While it offered no exemption from US military service, it was used by some volunteers to avoid service in Vietnam. It offered no access to foreign technology or research interests but aimed instead at a small number of the least-developed nations. And it offered no opportunity to continue graduate education through directed research. At the outset, half of its volunteers were untrained, even as classroom English teachers, the predominant work of the Corps. Other untrained volunteers worked in the open-ended field of "community development."

Overriding sharp US and foreign political change, the Corps managed to adapt, survive politics, and flourish over time by the familiar Washington stratagem of offering many things to all people. Perhaps the most important shift away from the Corps's initial premises came when Peace Corps teams flooded into semi-industrialized Eastern Europe after the Soviet implosion. The Corps, bypassing its own nonpolitical mindset, sent teams to the former Bloc and the Newly Independent States of the former USSR for purposes like ELT, in the absence of more generous and more professional US help. At the turn of the new century, the inevitable happened: Russia declared Corps volunteers underqualified and cut back the program.

The Corps's founding rhetoric was inflated. It was soon obvious that volunteers needed minimal medical assistance, modest but decent housing, and additional supplies in countries where the per capita income was under $400 per year. Initial Corps rhetoric ignored the basic building block of all development: counterparts who would work alongside the volunteers and carry on their work after they left, perhaps later studying in the U.S.; Corps precepts for accepting host countries were swiveled when deemed advisable. For example, the Corps passed up the opportunity to work in the Arab countries by refusing to pledge it would send no Jewish volunteers; and it worked in "developed" countries in Eastern Europe.

Over time, the Corps's touchiness about proximity to US foreign policy waned. The initial strong language was perhaps useful to lessen suspicions of espionage and affect a purist stance at the time of Kennedy's counterinsurgency activism: volunteers were instructed to provide only *passive* anti-Soviet propaganda, displaying by example the generous and youthful side of America and avoiding discussion of any third country. Minimizing US diplomatic contacts was one thing, but shunning the embassies and the Fulbright Program was another; the unnatural behavior only augmented skepticism about Washington's noble pronouncements. The Corps learned for itself that assertions of purity were no defense against accusations of spying.

By the end of the 1960s the Corps's strictures softened, at least with regard to embassy cultural offices. Volunteers in fact had every reason to relate to cultural work, especially in ELT, where years of effort had built a substantial repository of teaching materials, trained teachers, and library resources. Wise Corps field administrators kept in touch with cultural colleagues involved in education; volunteers were encouraged to nominate host-country nationals to Fulbright for US study.

In Iran, for example, the Corps' ELT advisor was the same Gertrude Nye Dorry who advised USIS and IAS English teachers and sat with the British-American coordinating committee. The Corps director joined the embassy's informal committee on education. Individual volunteers worked with the IAS in theater, music, and mounting exhibits. The Corps director's wife starred in productions of musical comedies. One volunteer, a fine pianist doing music education for the blind, played recitals and accompanied the IAS chorus; the Corps's deputy director, a fine classical and jazz bassist, saw value in helping Tehran's music conservatory train Western musicians and recruited US instrumentalist-teachers to teach at the conservatory. The musicians and teachers also played in Iran's symphonic and opera orchestras and for IAS musicals like *Guys and Dolls*, *The Fantasticks*, and *The Music Man*; in their spare time, three of them—including the fine percussionist Phil Shutzman—built the IAS jazz group.

In 1961 the rhetoric of the Corps, at the Washington end, was high-flown: to help other nations meet their needs for trained manpower, to create better understanding of the U.S., and to promote a better understanding of other peoples by Americans. This third point was daring in a city where Congress too often proclaimed that foreigners had nothing to teach Americans. The Corps was unidirectional, sending Americans abroad but receiving no foreign counterparts—a US experiment in "reverse-flow" in the late 1960s was a failure. Still, from the beginning and, with no apology, US learning was its "Third Mission," and Corps alumni, over time, have agreed that US learning was the primary benefit of their service.

Had it been launched in 1938, the Corps would have been part of State's Division of Cultural Relations. But by 1961 AID had taken over training, CIA was wooing intellectuals, HEW had begun developing American university area studies, and USIA had all but rejected CU's commitment to US learning. The Corps took up one more chunk of the fragmented US cultural diplomatic outreach that neglect had made available.

The idea of the Third Mission, in the world of CU and USIA, was a bothersome issue, thanks to fears of Representative Rooney. In 1972 CU chief John Richardson stepped up to the dilemma. Noting that each of CU's six area offices gave implicit prominence to US learning in their budget preparation, he decided to make the point explicit in CU's overall statement. Office of Management and Budget specialists handling CU were surprised enough to ask if Richardson really wanted it, given historic congressional hostility, but Richardson persisted. The "second mandate," as it was disparagingly called in USIA, became a key issue in the brief life of the new USICA when USIA and CU briefly merged in 1977–81, but it was soon dropped by another nationalist-unidirectionalist administration. And yet the idea of US learning would not go away; it could not, for the simple reason that it was built into every act of educational exchanges, which by definition were bidirectional. In an agency which after 1980 was increasingly unidirectional in its rhetoric and dominated by propaganda, psy-war, and close support of foreign policy, the idea gradually disappeared. But the hard fact remained: those who go abroad to teach always learn.

In 1983 the thoughtful Corps director Loret Miller Ruppé summarized its activities. Half the volunteers were in ELT; the remaining fifteen hundred were technical assistants in agriculture, rural development, and fisheries; 165 worked in energy and appropriate technology, e.g., devising efficient stoves, better charcoal production, solar food-drying, and biomass conversion; two hundred other assistants planned and supervised construction of small dams, spillways, irrigation canals, and water systems in rural areas; one thousand worked in health education and community health; and two hundred helped village sanitation. More than 15 percent of Corps alumni by 1983 had gone into government, well above the national average for university graduates; they were working in foreign affairs agencies, including AID, USIA, State, and probably CIA. There were alumni in Congress. Half the staff of the Experiment in International Living in Vermont in the 1990s were returnees from the Corps. Twenty alumni were serving the Chase Manhattan Bank, including seven of ten officers in the African division. In 1980 27 percent of Corps alumni were working in education and 60 percent had decided upon return to go on in higher education. In language-learning alone, Ruppé noted, the Corps "has become one of the nation's most imaginative language-learning institutions." CU-USIA had no means to compile a comparable breakdown of its alumni's activities.[9]

Veterans of the Corps, products of an intensely emotional experience, banded together to create a Development Education Program, with Corps support, to share their experience more widely with American communities. By the mid-1980s, over 100,000 Corps alumni—roughly five thousand per year—had returned to America, changed forever. Unhampered by prescriptions against lobbying—which dogged USIA because of language in the Smith-Mundt Act—the Corps had openly supported its alumni organization; in contrast, USIA-CU's sporadic help to the Fulbright alumni worldwide has been occasional, constrained, and begrudging.

In the spring of 1999 Congress voted to forward-fund the Corps—meaning allocate funding for several years at a time—for four years. It was a first in the history of overseas cultural outreach. Congress also decided to double volunteers in five years to reach ten thousand annually. The late Michael Kelly, editor of the *National Journal* at the time, wrote of this decision words that could have been Cherrington's about the paradox of indirect support to foreign policy. The Corps, he wrote, "attracts idealists and free spirits, and it does not tell them that they are to advance American foreign policy. But they are, and they do, because they think they are not so doing." He added that "a volunteer is an arm of American foreign policy precisely inasmuch as [he] is not an arm of American foreign policy. . . . A creation of government that actually understands and exploits human nature! What an idea."[10]

•   •   •

Looking at field CAOs in the period 1945–65, two transitional cultural officers have left traces: Paul Child and John L. Brown. Both began in the high professionalism of the 1940s and managed to keep their cultural faith over time, each in his own way. While Washington was braiding its usual circlets of words, field staffing was changing rapidly from the early days of imported academics. Child and Brown, mavericks from the start, endured longer than most, then retired to other lives.

PAUL CHILD

Child devoted his life to the visual arts and for a brief moment found a niche in cultural diplomacy. Thanks to a biography of his famous wife, Julia, detailed information is available about the sixteen years the Childs gave to cultural diplomacy.[11] Born just after the century, Child finished Boston Latin School, entered Columbia University, then left to learn on his own. In Paris in the 1920s, he worked in stained-glass; he then shipped aboard freighters, made film sets and more stained glass in Hollywood, taught art and French at a Connecticut prep school, and did portait photography. In 1943 he joined OSS's Visual Presentations staff. In OSS he found lifelong friends, theater, film, and architectural greats, including Garson Kanin, Ruth Gordon, Budd Schulberg, John Ford, and Eero Saarinen.

Sent to Ceylon, Child joined Mountbatten's headquarters in the hills of Kandy, where he designed, built, and maintained the central situation room. He later became deeply aware of the US educational impact on the foreign national staff—when Ceylon gained independence in 1948, OSS alumni moved into political leadership positions; at an OSS reunion in Thailand in 1991, sixteen Thai "alumni" of OSS gathered, all MIT graduates occupying key posts in the country, including the presidency of Bangkok University. In 1944 Child moved to China where, in Kunming and Chungking, he again designed war rooms, this time for his friend Gen. Albert Wedemeyer. With his future wife and colleague the ebullient Julia, he was part of the Chinese world depicted by John K. Fairbank. Like most of his American colleagues, he was impatient with US subservience to the KMT, with Chiang and Tai Li, and with OSS operative "Mary" Miles. Association with long-time US observers of China like journalist Theodore H. White would cloud his security file.

In postwar Washington, the Childs moved among gifted friends—Paul Nitze, sculptor Jo Davidson, Archibald MacLeish, Yale art historian George Kubler, Preston Sturges, Burgess Meredith, Walter Lippmann, Julian Huxley, and OSS colleagues of note, some of whom, including Richard Bissell, would shape the new CIA. In the Benton bloodletting of March 1947, IIA let him go; quickly rehired, Child joined USIS Paris as Exhibits Officer, alongside the stellar Americans gathered to execute the Marshall Plan—Averell Harriman, Paul Hoffman, Charles Bohlen, David Bruce, and younger men like Harlan Cleveland, Arthur Hartman, Richard Bissell, E. A. Bayne, and John L. Brown.

With Julia, Child lived first at the Hôtel du Pont Royal, a center of French intellectual life near the publishing house of Gallimard and the base for Princeton professor and translator Maurice Coindreau, feeding the "Age of the American Novel" with his translations of Hemingway, Dos Passos, Faulkner, Steinbeck, and Caldwell. Child himself, without knowing it, was fostering another kind of revolution in that Julia was becoming a passionate Francophile and culinary diplomat.

For his visual arts staff, he hired the daughter of the great French art historian Henri Focillon, who was then teaching at Yale. Hélène Baltrusaitis, herself a member of France's visual arts elite, became the Childs's French teacher, general guide to France and its culture, and closest friend over the years. Meanwhile she earned mythic fame in the embassy cultural office. Child was in charge of photography and exhibits for USIS; with a small staff and a vast photo archive, his bread-and-butter job lay in creating small photo-exhibits as needed. For example his staff changed the two show windows flanking the USIS entrance weekly, at 41 rue du Faubourg St. Honoré, now the ambassador's residence.

Child knew he was living history and missed no chance to exploit the richness of Paris and Franco-American relations. He was taking photo-graphs and painting—fine detailed cityscapes and Parisian rooftops. The USIS chief was diplomat William Tyler, who was totally bilingual in French and an architect of US-French postwar relations. Child's art linked him to the best, including photographers Man Ray and Henri Cartier-Bresson, composer-teacher Nadia Boulanger, New York's Modern Museum photo-chief Edward Steichen—who bought Child's photos—Jackson Pollock, and dozens of others. With Darthea Speyer and Hélène Baltrusaitis, pathbreaking shows of US photography and painting went up, including firsts like Frank Lloyd Wright or Mme Baltrusaitis's famous show from Sylvia Beach's collection on the American writers of the 1920s.

Then the Childs were reassigned to Marseille. As branch PAO, he covered the southern coast of France, working from the same Consulate where Hiram Bingham IV helped Varian Fry save thousands of European refugees in the Vichy years. Routine courtesy calls, the beginning of any cultural officer's tour, brought him into contact with universities, city and government officials, and newspapers. He had a cultural center with a library; he arranged exhibits of American artists and lectures by visitors and friends; he handled exchanges, press and information, radio and motion pictures, helping a photo festival in Arles and the film festival in Cannes. The French staff adored the Childs, as did the Marseillais; they lived on the Old Port in the leave apartment of a Swedish diplomat, while Julia explored the foods of Provence. On a nearby hillside Le Corbusier had just completed his much-acclaimed apartment-house, the Radiant City—one more manifestation of Louis XIV's sun metaphor.

McCarthy surrogates Cohn and Schine were on the prowl. ACAO Larry Morris arrived in his Paris office to find "two young men with their feet up on his desk." To get them out, he agreed to their demand for a full staff meeting on Easter Sunday afternoon—a special family holiday in France. The irritated staff assembled, awaited the duo for an hour and a half, learned that they had overslept after a long night of partying, and went home. Meanwhile, the two sleuths found a copy of Theodore White's *Thunder Out of China*. They "burned it and reported the purge to the *New York Times*," notes Julia's biographer. The Childs, having donated several books on China to USIS libraries, fretted; but neither of them imagined the trouble was serious. Julia had begun to cook in earnest; in Marseille, their dinners were the marvel of the diplomatic community.

In the spring of 1954, Streibert's new broom at USIA swept clean. USIA required its officers to leave any country where they had lived for more than five years, regardless of their language ability or cultural proficiency; it was a move designed to keep peace among field staff by sharing the "good" assignments, but making France a reward for service in Africa was a blow to substance and cultural depth. The Childs were sent to Bonn, a sleepy provincial town chosen as capital of West Germany because it was home to Konrad Adenauer. Neither Child knew a word of German.

Paul, in charge of exhibits for all of West Germany, had scarcely arrived when he was recalled by security chief Scott McLeod, McCarthy's legacy. In Washington he sat idle for six months, while the degrading security investigation dragged on. With his background in China, there were easy allegations to be made, but none stuck; it was an enormous waste of money and time, like dozens of other cases McLeod pursued, and it ended any serious contribution Child might have made to the German program.

The torture had a silver lining. At the MoMA in New York, Child saw Steichen's remarkable show "The Family of Man" and pressed USIA to send it to Germany. In 1955 the monumental exhibit opened in Berlin—thirty thousand visitors saw it in September, before it moved to Frankfurt and Munich, and from there it covered the world. In fifteen copies, "Family" showed in every single country in the world and sold over 3 million of its catalogues.

In Bonn Child helped negotiate US participation in the Brussels World's Fair of 1958 and planned exhibits on police work, physical therapy, social work, and peaceful atomic power, as well as painting and architecture. On his own time, he showed his photographs at a gallery in Cologne. Finally promoted, he was still earning less than $10,000 a year. His annual "efficiency reports" reflected his supervisors' philosophical-political values and worked against him; reviewers complained that "his interests [were] primarily cultural" or that he showed impatience with administration. His reticence, a high quality in Europe, was seen as "self-effacement"—a negative in dynamo-driven USIA; he was said to lack ambition. In 1959 he was recalled to Washington to head USIA's Exhibit Division—meaning he organized photo and poster shows.

Then came Oslo, unsolicited and unattractive. The Childs were tempted to resign; they had bought the Josiah Royce house in Cambridge and rejoined old Cambridge friends from other times, including the composer Randall Thompson, the J. K. Galbraiths, the Arthur Schlesingers, and the Fairbanks. Now they were off again. In Oslo Child, in a handsome, controversial embassy building designed by his friend Eero Saarinen, worked evenings and weekends—with a USIS staff of four, everyone had to meet planes. He ran the cultural program—directing Fulbright and the library; mounting exhibits; working with Oslo University's famous Sigmund Skard, father of American studies in Europe; entertaining visitors, including Pearl Buck, Buckminster Fuller, and anyone in the arts or education; and organizing a performance by the New York Philharmonic under Leonard Bernstein. The Childs invited American Fulbrights to the embassy cafeteria for Thanksgiving dinner. As he did everywhere, Paul promoted America by example, especially in contrast to the USSR—our "running competition with the Russians," he called it. There were trips for Fulbright interviews, for a librarians' conference in Bergen, for English teachers in Leangkollen, and for friends everywhere. The couple kept busy.

Though happy and surrounded by appreciative colleagues, their enthusiasm was flagging. The rewards were few, the salary absurd, and the future dull. As Child approached his sixties, he saw that persistent non-promotion was a condition of his employment, and he could not forget the cruel stupidity he had seen during his brush with McLeod. In December 1960, after retirement, this gifted, versatile, and much-loved man wrote: "I do a great many things well, but the coercive structure of foreign service needs and regulations makes no place for them." His pension after sixteen years of service came to about $3,000 per year—that same year a thirty-year-old first-year assistant professor at Columbia was paid more than double that amount.

The Childs' principal service to cultural diplomacy was yet to come in the form of Julia's career as "The French Chef" on public television—she consistently refused network offers to go commercial. She never failed to say she could not have done it without Paul as manager, visual advisor, set designer, and stage director. Whether USIA recognized their talents or knew how to use them, Paul and Julia Child were cultural diplomats to the core. They represent one of USIA's most egregious misuses of talent; like many such—but not all—they were fortunate in finding a better platform when they left.

JOHN L. BROWN

Brown is another USIA myth.[12] Remaining with USIA through the 1970s, Brown was the only one of the original outsiders, besides Canter, to make a full career in cultural work. After Hamilton College, Brown had studied in Paris in the 1930s at the elite Ecole des Chartes, France's highly selective school for archivists and epigraphers. A Latinist, he earned a French doctorate on the Renaissance French philosopher and economist Jean Bodin. In 1942 he joined OWI in New York, moved to London in 1943, and then to newly liberated Paris.

For four years after the war, he worked with publisher Houghton-Mifflin and as Paris correspondent for the Sunday edition of the *New York Times*. Then, at the invitation of his friend ambassador David Bruce, he joined the Marshall Plan as director of information. His critical anthology the *Panorama of American Literature* in 1954, written in French, earned a top literary award in France and stayed in print for decades, introducing generations of French readers to American literature. Joining the new USIA, he served as CAO in Rome, Brussels, Paris, and Mexico City before retiring in 1969 to Catholic University in Washington as professor of comparative literature, where he remained until his death in 2003. Brown was the last of the pre-1950 cultural officers to leave USIA.

In 1988, relating fragments of his story in the playful style of the classic man of letters, he waxed wise. On job descriptions: "The Cultural Attaché is, in himself or herself, a rather curious and complicated figure whose qualifications have never been satisfactorily defined, whose job description is the despair of orderly personnel people, and whose real accomplishments can rarely be measured." On status: "I deplore the lack of status of the Cultural Attaché in the official hierarchy, but simultaneously I point out even greater dangers if he should become too respectable. I am mad enough to insist that the CAO be both generalist and specialist." On identity: "When people asked me, 'What do you do, Mr. Brown?' I wanted to explain to them that my real purpose in life, if you wanted to get down to it, was *being* and not *doing*."

He was bearish on bureaucracy but respected the daily grind: "Much of the time, I am afraid, I was doing nonsense things, engaged in those absurd rituals of telephoning, conferring, meeting, lunching, cocktailing, exchanging memoranda, keeping pointless appointments, raising my glass, talking, talking, talking." On the CAO's work: "In an embassy, when a problem refuses to fit neatly into the political, economic, agricultural, military or administrative piegeon-holes, it is normally sent on to the Cultural Attaché."

On the word "culture": "Of course the word *culture*, which seems now so rarefied and abstract, is itself thoroughly concrete and earthy in its origins. The Greeks . . . did not have a word for it. For them . . . culture was just a normal function, . . . you had 'culture' rather as you had a good stomach. . . . They did use the word *ethos*, which would correspond roughly to the way our anthropologists now use the word Culture. But they had no word to express what we would call a 'cultured man,' or 'humanistic culture.' The great Roman Cicero was among the first to speak of *cultura animi*, the 'nurture of the mind.'"

On US impatience: "Americans, being of a pragmatic turn of mind, tend not to realize how important simply being there can be, even if you do not do or learn anything 'useful.' 'Wasting time' pays off . . . and it often pays off with bigger returns than constantly 'saving time' for some other purpose. Our supervisors do not always understand this. . . . A successful cultural operation simply cannot be carried out in an office from 9 to 5. Cultural work . . . means getting personally involved with people; and the culture of the country . . . usually relies on lengthy ceremonies."

Weaving through his hilarious examples, funding is a constant refrain: "The elements of grace like housing—these atmospheres cost money. Culture has always cost money. . . . One cannot help but be embarrassed by the shoddiness and lack of style of much that we Americans do, from official receptions . . . to the xeroxed invitations we often have to send out to invite guests to our cultural affairs."

Cultural diplomacy may be indispensable to human discourse, but is it "useful"? "Was it worth doing? Cesare Pavese, in his haunting diary, asked himself shortly before his death: 'What is the real reason we want to be big, to be creative? . . . To carry on our daily toil with the conviction that whatever we do is worth doing, is something unique—for the day, not for eternity.'"

To do something worth doing, not for eternity but for the day—the modesty of *paideia* lay beneath the burnished surface of Brown's seamless career as writer, poet, critic, teacher, and cultural diplomat. USIA, it must be said, accorded him the privilege of being himself for three decades, but he had to earn the privilege anew each day. Delighting thousands of foreign friends, he drove some US colleagues to despair; his information counterpart in Mexico boasted that he kept Brown in place by occasionally threatening a punch in the nose.

Brown was *sui generis*. He was himself, graceful and learned, ironic and perpetually amused. He exemplified Charles Frankel's "compleat cultural attaché." At his memorial, a young African poet, an adoptee, spoke with emotion of Brown's mentoring and teaching. Even in the last days of his life, he never stopped serving his country.

CHAPTER SIXTEEN

The Arts of Vision

> If we can come to attach to [the arts] a respect and a significance compa-
> rable to what is given it abroad, we will have come a great step on the
> way to the improvement of our international situation generally. . . . If
> we do that, it will not be in our external relations nor in what we mean
> to other people that our gain will be the greatest. . . . Our most impor-
> tant gain will be the gain for our own sakes, the gain in what we mean
> to ourselves—and in what, I suspect, life means to all of us.
>
> —George F. Kennan, 1956

THE "ARTS" AT THEIR HIGH POINT never consumed more than a sliver of formal US budgets for cultural diplomacy, yet none of cultural diplomacy's
products is more appealing to thoughtful Americans. Indeed the glamorous visual and performing arts, in the minds of many enthusiasts of cultural diplomacy, are the only point. These observers are thinking of a
small part of the whole, what we might call arts diplomacy, and forgetting the context and staffing needed to mount displays of fine and performing arts abroad. It is a good moment to break our chronology again
for a look at the arts in diplomacy.[1]

Americans certainly did not invent the idea of art in diplomacy. The
arts have played a central role in diplomatic relations since the dawn of
civilization, when the exchange of formal gifts, the daily bread of proto-
historic diplomacy, involved precious man-made objects of beauty, the
stamping of official coins, and the architecture of empire. Amarna's
gilded statues in the thirteenth-century B.C.E., the earliest detailed example
on record, imply a sophisticated practice going back centuries before. As
groups developed strength and linked to others, spectacles, theater, and
games were commonly exchanged. The world's wandering poets and
bards, like Homer or the troubadours who flocked to the court of Frederick II, carried myth and message around their world. By the time of Francis I, exchanging art in Europe was a standard diplomatic technique,
highly developed by the Italian city-states. In China Ricci found perspective portraits of the Virgin to be one of his most useful tools.[2]

The arts have always had the advantage of transcending language barriers. One can admire Phidias without Greek, Van Gogh without Dutch
or French, Richter or the Bolshoi without Russian, or Bartok without
Hungarian. The arts also have a corresponding, if sometimes useful, disadvantage: imprecision. What is seen by the receiving audience is rarely

specific and not always what the sender wishes, even when it is a strong message in itself.

In the US case, informal fine arts outreach came early in contemporary world history, in the form of exported artists. The first artist to go abroad was Pennsylvania-born Benjamin West (1760); he went to study in Britain and stayed on to become famous, a founder of the Royal Academy, and in 1792 successor to Sir Joshua Reynolds as president. West was teacher-guide to the first generation of formal American painters. For a century or more Americans like West, if they were recognized abroad, were praised not for their Americanness but because they had mastered European painting. By the end of the century, John Singer Sargent, James Whistler, and Mary Cassatt, early cosmopolitans, made their own mark on the history of art, but it was European art.

The American artists went to London, Paris, and Berlin to learn; in Paris they studied painting at the Académie Julien, and in Giverny they sat at the feet of Claude Monet; in Rome, they studied the painters and sculptors of history, with the help of the American Academy (1896). The Academy in Rome, heavily supported by J. Pierpont Morgan, helped make the riches of Rome available to US painters, sculptors, architects, landscapers, and later composers, as the French had done with the help of Poussin, then with the Sun King's Académie. Training in painting, architecture, and sculpture were European monopolies; Beaux Arts in Paris long credentialized American architects.

While the artists were learning, so were the scholars. In the research centers of Rome, Athens, Berlin, and Jerusalem, they studied European scholars as well as artists, just as West had learned from painter Anton Raphael Mengs and from scholar Johann Joachim Winckelmann. From the middle of the nineteenth century on, US archeologists were also at work, especially in the Holy Land as reported by the first book of John Lloyd Stephens; his two later books on Latin America (1841, 1843) launched American scholar-archeology in the southern hemisphere, spelling out fresh new practices and implicit protests against European expropriation. His successors Ephraim George Squier and Hiram Bingham III stressed the rescue of national art heritages from negligence and foreign pillage; these early Americans spelled out a protective hemispheric style, based on new practices of documentation, pioneered by Napoleon's scholars, and including expanded use of photography, so that treasures could be left in place. Edward Morse and Ernest Fenollosa went to Japan to teach and then to save Japan's artistic treasures from misguided administrators and Western dealers. Bernard Berenson used different methods to a similar end, helping Italy save its art by simply drawing attention to its value. Arthur Upham Pope dedicated his life to making known and preserving the arts of Persian civilization. Three decades after Pope, at nearby Dura-Europa in Iraq, Yale's Frank Brown impressed his Arab colleagues with his energy and probity, enough so that he was appointed director of antiquities for Syria when the French were distracted by the beginnings of World War II. In 1915 Arthur Kingsley Porter had served France behind German lines; his student Kenneth Conant helped rebuild Cluny in southern Burgundy. Harvard's George Stout and a group of art historians organized the rescue of art in Italy and Germany during and after the Second World War; and Langdon Warner led the same effort in Japan. These Americans, and dozens of less famous names, reached out to help others preserve, record, interpret, repair, and restore artistic treasures, part of their "duty to mankind," as Fenollosa said.

Studio art was not taught in the early US universities, and art history was an unknown discipline before Charles Eliot Norton at Harvard and William Cowper Prime at Princeton (1882) began teaching art and archeology, even if—as Norton's son remarked—his father's teaching reduced art to a means of shedding the light of example on human ethics. Art history in the next generation became a respected discipline in US universities. What Prime began at Princeton, for example, was carried on by Allan Marquand and Charles Rufus Morey, then transformed and deepened in the 1930s by a wave of European refugee scholars like Erwin Panofsky, Richard Krautheimer and Richard Ettinghausen.

Before 1945 America's artistic production and its practicing artists were treated with courteous condescension in Europe. Few critics or connoisseurs considered American visual art worth taking seriously, until the totalitarians gave the U.S. a great gift—dozens of refugee scholars and artist-teachers like Marcel Duchamps, Hans Hoffman, Max Ernst, Josef Albers, and Gyorgy Kepes, who helped both Americans and Europeans recognize that Americans had been producing a characteristic national art for a century without knowing it. Art historian Hubert Landais, director of French museums in the 1950s, visited the U.S. during his tenure on a USIS Leader Grant; he discovered American art, as he said, hidden away in the storerooms of a dozen US museums.[3] By 1940 New York's Whitney Museum and the militantly internationalist Museum of Modern Art (MoMA), a favorite of Abby Aldrich Rockefeller and her son Nelson, proclaimed the existence of an American art worthy of hanging alongside the great modern Europeans.

In France, the monarchy had supported artists and built the royal collection since Francis I. Successor governments all over Europe, whatever their political stripe, carried on the work, through continued state patronage. And they democratized art—Bonaparte turned the Louvre into France's national art museum, accessible to all. In the era of kings paintings were kept safe for the elite and exchanged as diplomatic gifts, often with special messages encoded. Yet it occurred to few nation-states to send their art abroad in any systematic and purposeful way. If anything, the opposite: nation-states indulged in gentle piratic importation, building prestigious national collections for their capital cities.

The idea of US government support to artists occurred to none of the Founding Fathers. Artists were workers like any other and had to earn their way in a tough market. The great individual collections of the late nineteenth century, rich in the Old Masters of Europe, were passed on to museums specially built to display them; American public collections and museums were a natural consequence of prosperity and the drive to emulate Europe. The ethic of stewardship drove the wealthy, pressing them to give away their riches for the common good; it was the US version of Bonaparte's Louvre.

The New Deal marked the first federal effort to support artists, aimed less at enhancing national glory than at reducing unemployment. FDR's Works Progress Administration supported painters and sculptors, musicians, writers, photographers, folklorists, and theater professionals; it also carried out other enterprises in art, including the Farm Security photos and the Index of American Design—a massive catalog of folk and commercial art. The New Deal expanded the national park system and developed its historical underpinnings; the cheap labor provided by the Civilian Conservation Corps turned the unemployed to protecting and showcasing the national landscape.

In Europe exporting individual collections of art, as a national policy, had been practiced between monarchs since the Renaissance. It is thus the more surprising that modern European diplomacy did not at first pursue this practice. In the U.S. the export of visual art showed up earlier in formal diplomacy. Once again, the idea and drive came from Nelson Rockefeller. Listening to Latin America, Sumner Welles and his team had heard pleas for art exchanges for years; Hull's famous list included artists among individuals to be exchanged. But it took the innovative Oil Prince to send the first collection of American painting abroad under government auspices in 1942.[4] From then until the turn of the millennium, however precarious and haphazard the funding, the visual arts were a persistent component of US cultural outreach, in a random and underfunded way, yet even so more than in the diplomacy of other nations.

Rockefeller had studied modern art at Dartmouth: He discovered the vibrant painters of Latin America in the 1930s—they were a bit too vibrant, as it turned out in the famous case of Diego Rivera's murals for Rockefeller Center. Beneath Rockefeller's natural exuberance lay an ill-formed but compelling idea that would be articulated and proclaimed a decade later by Henry Luce: the American Century. Rockefeller seemed to have had no deeper motive in art export than displaying to the world the quality of his country's artistic production. The government-sponsored tour of American painting in 1942 was mounted by MoMA, hence completely modernist. Rockefeller's work with art went further: In his private Latin American travels, he found ways to support archeology; as Coordinator he sent a ballet troupe to the south; he helped solo musicians perform; and he sent sculptor Jo Davidson to do portraits of ten Latin American heads of state. He had already showcased US architecture abroad with Wallace Harrison's Avila Hotel in Venezuela.

Rockefeller's deep pockets overturned the gradualist thinking of the founders of cultural diplomacy. After 1942 formal US cultural relations, albeit with troublesome interruptions, found it natural to export both artists and their art. Other nations would soon follow suit. In time, with the rise of the great museums and the growing dialogue between them, the idea of the "museum without walls," Malraux's "musée imaginaire," came to reality through the multi-museum international "blockbuster" shows, which could be said to have begun in 1946 when Washington's National Gallery sent the Kaiser Wilhelm collection around the U.S. before its triumphal return to Germany. For half a century, until cut off in 1994, formal support to US art exhibits abroad waxed and waned, even though persistently judged essential by the embassies.

There were conflicting opinions in the diplomatic community. For those in favor, art exhibits projected truths about the U.S. beyond language, truths that came nearer than other means to revealing the national style, spirit, and soul. For other friends, they merely showed the flag. But opponents, including hard-line informationists, thought them a costly frivolity. In Congress, enemies were numerous and even friends wanted a say in the selection of works to be shown. With a few spectacular exceptions, the legislature allowed the process of art exports to continue over half a century, saving its anger for the grants of the National Endowment for the Arts (NEA).

The Rockefeller style, which left a permanent hornet's nest in Congress, posed long-range questions. Congress, populist and predominantly nationalist, was already skeptical about fine arts diplomacy in general, but specifically legislatures worried about the exclusively contemporary stamp which Rockefeller's instincts put on early exports. Opposition began to gather strength after the war's end and FDR's death; Benton's show, including a scattering of figurative painting, was called back in mid-tour and sold at auction. Members of Congress, with an occasional exception like Senator Clark's personal founding donations to Washington's Corcoran Gallery, had never spent much time in art galleries; they spent even less time trying to understand contemporary art. A Senator named Truman, himself a sometime painter, was especially unhappy about the modernist bias of the 1942 and 1947 shows; Fulbright was no fan either. In 1945 modern art in Washington was easy to lampoon—and easy to associate with the left. Like Hitler and Stalin, Washington's moguls knew what they liked and liked what they knew—landscapes, social realism, and historical drama.

By 1950 a few new American embassies showcased US architecture and its democratic values, thanks to Fritz Larkin's keeping selections away from congressional meddling. A more thoughtful Rockefeller might have seen the point: if his 1942 show had been selected by a broad-based jury of art experts beyond reproach, if it had included a broader range of artistic expression, and if Congress had been consulted appropriately, the opposition might have been less fierce. But Rockefeller, in his usual hurry, turned matters over to MoMA and affronted both the political right and know-nothings in both parties. Rockefeller's approach to modern art, in fact, had a surprising avant-garde cast: the stalwart Republican, after all, was responsible for choosing Mexican communist Rivera for Rockefeller Center and left-of-center Jo Davidson to sculpt portraits-busts of Latin leaders. The story of American art export is a story of clumsy handling, usually blamed on legislative ignorance, with the result that diplomatic export of art and the National Endowment for the Arts, another of Rockefeller's enthusiasms, are plagued by ideological tempests to this day.

In 1946 Benton, Rockefeller's close friend, advisor, fellow collector, but defender of the more acceptable social expressionism of Reginald Marsh and the Ashcan School, ran into his share of trouble when he sent out a traveling show of new American painting. J. L. Davidson, with the help of USIS London's founding librarian Richard Heindel, who was now in State in charge of libraries, organized a balanced show called "Advancing American Art." Still, *Newsweek* noted the show's slant to "the experimental and creative side." Republicans in the new Congress gleefully seized a chance to embarrass Truman—whose sympathies lay fully with the attackers. Truman joined in the fun, as Khrushchev would later with his comments comparing modern paintings to the products of a paintbrush tied to a donkey's tail. After the show opened in Paris, where the critical reception was surprisingly warm considering the ambivalence of the hosts in the self-styled art capital of the world, the show moved on to rave reviews in Czechoslovakia. There, mounting pressure from Congress convinced Secretary of State Marshall to recall the show.

US work with visual art had dimensions beyond the reach of Congress, as in the enlightened rescue work done by the US military in Italy, Germany, and Japan. The world art community was astonished by this effort, demonstrating US efficiency, professionalism, objectivity, and generosity as teams collected and restored art, then restituted looted objects to their owners. The contrast with Soviet expropriations of art as a form of reparations was noted. At a giant opening of the returned Kaiser Wilhelm collection in Munich, Gen. Lucius Clay and his team spotlighted the moment with a celebration; he knew then, he wrote, that the U.S. had turned the corner in reorienting Germany.[5]

To assure a flow of art abroad despite congressional ambivalence, ingenuity at home and in the field was high. In 1950 IIA painter-administrator Robert Sivard began experimenting with shows of graphic art—less costly hence less controversial than painting—for Europe. But it was a stopgap game of hide-and-seek—the government's formal art exports were limited to what Congress might not notice. Inside USIA, professionalism was growing through the selective hiring of art-world professionals; in the field energetic officers like Paul Child were performing small miracles of ingenuity. USIA's art director David Scott, a museum professional, persuaded noted critic Adelyn Breeskin to join his staff, but while USIA's art team set out energetically, it was soon pushing its limits. Low-key exhibits slid past Congress unnoticed, but success meant bad news. The 1964 Venice Bienale brought far too much publicity for the comfort of those terrorized by John J. Rooney.

McCarthy-victim Reed Harris, reinstated by Murrow in 1961, tossed the hot potato back to the professionals. In 1965 a formal agreement was signed between USIA and the Smithsonian Institution to set up an office in the National Collection of Fine Arts, called the International Arts Program (IAP). IAP's job was to provide the expertise and the authority that USIA lacked in organizing exhibits for world use. IAP was headed by USIA-veteran Lois Bingham, aided by alter ego Peg Cogswell, who had been lured away from New York's American Federation of the Arts (AFA).

Sivard, with Bingham and Cogswell, managed the fine arts branch of USIA, training new officers like the young Edward McBride. Sivard, heading USIA's Exhibits, was a painter of delightful faux-naïf portraits of Paris shops, into which he inserted well-known Americans—he created a portrait of USIA director George Allen peering from a Parisian kiosk that displayed USIA's publications. By buying several strikes of a print from an artist, Sivard was able at low cost to send out dozens of exhibits of framed graphics to posts around the world with the help of the AFA. Field demand was high because CAOs had public wall space to fill—most BNCs had small art galleries; even tiny embassies like Oslo carved out display space in or near the embassy. The Amerika Häuser in high-priority Germany, as usual, got more than their share. No one in Congress paid much attention.

Cogswell today refers to the era of the 1960s as the "glory years."[6] Dozens of small shows were sent abroad, and US participation in various biennials was turned over to outside peer review. A major IAP show of American impressionists, designed for East Europe, opened at the Petit Palais in Paris before moving on to Romania. In 1968 McBride took charge of visual and performing arts for the embassy in Paris. He began with a major show of Stuart Davis at the cultural center on the Rue du Dragon. In East Europe Cogswell remembers shows like one diverted to Czechoslovakia in the late 1960s, spun off from the cultural agreement with Romania. Borrowing East European shows for West European posts was a regular accident of ingenious administrators—even if the shows designed for the East were often decoded critically in the West as obvious weapons in the cold war. East-West tensions meant no big shows of painting went to the Soviet Union, although expensive performing arts groups put on regular events there. Washington ingenuity took other forms: USIA's trade-fair dynamo Jack Masey used US participation in commercial fairs around the globe to display American art, design, and architecture; in the giant Buckminster Fuller "bubble" for the Montreal World's Fair of 1967, he used soaring interior spaces to hang sixty-foot banner-paintings by Motherwell and Frankenthaler.

Ingenuity in Washington and the field meant enlisting the private world. In 1963 a major show of one hundred contemporary paintings, curated by Dore Ashton and funded by the Johnson Wax Company, circulated widely through the Far East with USIA help; complete slide collections of the paintings were sent to all posts, where they found use as lecture materials and for window display. In Sri Lanka and Iran, for example, untrained but articulate CAOs based popular lectures on the slides; timed projections of the collection were used as background for other art shows. In Iran an extensive collection of art slides was built around the Johnson slides, permitting illustrated lectures by cultural officers around the country on various aspects of American painting.

In some cities the visual arts mattered more than in others. In Paris and Rome competition was keen and audiences hungry and sophisticated; an important visual arts presence was a necessity. In Rome the French Academy, directed in the 1970s by the painter Balthus, hung an imposing annual show of a French artist who had worked in Italy. In my four years in Italy (1974–78), only the US bicentennial in 1976 made it possible for the cultural office to present a major show, a magnificent anthological survey curated by Anne Vandeventer but designed for Yugoslavia, with painting from the eighteenth century until the present. Roman crowds jammed the show during its run, but Italian intellectuals, accustomed to the scholarly shows of the French, expressed greater or lesser disappointment according to their ideological commitment. Italy's leading scholar-critic, from a Marxist base, caricatured the show's message: "Look, guys, we have *art!*"

With little support coming from Washington, the many cultural centers or USIS offices still somehow managed to put on shows. Quality was obviously mixed, as well-intentioned USIA officers made decisions beyond their competence, sometimes in response to local pressures. On the other hand, remarkable moments were recorded. In Paris, for example, where small shows could be piggybacked on other events, Frances Switt in 1979, directing the cultural center on the Rue du Dragon, returned from home leave with an entire show of Jackson Pollock works on paper and a photo show by Hans Namath of Pollock at work in East Hampton under her arm; the fine small shows coincided with two larger Pollock shows: one at the museum of modern art and another at a major private gallery. Pollock's widow Lee Krasner graced the openings. Soon afterward, Switt assembled another remarkable show, in parallel with a private showing of the work of Rafael Soyer. Her companion show traced Soyer's friendship with the Yiddish writer Isaac Bashevis Singer. The show, with supporting printed materials, later moved on to Tel Aviv.

Outside USIA a realistic conclusion had been reached by the art world as early as 1950: if anything serious was to be done, continuously and over time, the private world would have to do it. The USIS posts, even with professional expertise, could do little more than make sure work was well displayed. In MoMA an office under Porter McCray and Waldo Rasmussen opened in 1952, funded by the Rockefeller brothers; it was then adopted by MoMA's International Council, a group of wealthy donors—to whom George Kennan in 1956 made his telling remarks about art's capacity to convey what "life means to all of us." McCray traveled widely to survey the scene; he then began assembling small, thematic, and multinational traveling shows mixing Americans and foreign artists, designed to educate the world about contemporary art. He helped extend the reach of US art by providing USIS libraries with a continual supply of catalogs of important US art exhibits. New York Times art critic Michael Kimmelman, in the New York Review of Books (27 May 2004), cited a confidential memo from McCray in 1956 to MoMA director René d'Harnoncourt, urging more MoMA involvement because the new three-year-old USIA's orientation made it clear that USIA-sponsored exhibitions would become "increasingly conservative," meaning less open to the avant garde. The full story of McCray's energetic International Council still awaits telling. His shows mixed wartime US guests like Lionel Feininger, Max Ernst, Marcel Duchamps, Enrico Donati, Arshile Gorky, Hans Hoffman, Josef Albers, Max Weber, and Willem De Kooning with American artists; the mix proclaimed that America had assimilated Europe's best and become a new world art center. It was the visual arts face of the American Century.

In the field, ingenuity made the difference. Once a USIS post or BNC set aside space and equipped a gallery, its walls could not remain empty for long. With no dependable stream of exhibits from the U.S., the cultural offices used their wits, their networks, and locally available art to cover the yawning walls. Some built small permanent collections of American or local art. The story of art in rapidly developing Iran stretched back to the 1920s and Arthur Upham Pope. In the 1950s IAS had created the first art gallery in the history of Iran; Iranian groups were quick to follow suit. In the 1960s Barbara Spring began devising important shows of Iranian art, past and present, reasoning that US appreciation and understanding of Iran's art demonstrated deep intellectual interest in Iran. Tiny foundations like that of Abby Grey helped Spring and the cultural office by training foreign artists and educators and bringing small exhibits from Iran to the U.S. The cultural office with the help of Pan Am pulled together an Iranian contribution to a show of contemporary Near Eastern art at the American University of Beirut in 1970. In Iran in the late 1960s regular shows of prominent young Iranians were mounted at the IAS, in return for a single work by each artist for the IAS permanent collection, on continuous display. IAS-director Lois Roth in 1968 traveled to London to beg the loan of print collections for a series of shows from commercial galleries. In 1969 she hired resident US painter Douglas James Johnson as IAS's visual director, and for three years he and his team put together a series of shows of American and Persian art, past and present. For American works, they produced shows without Washington assistance of work by Robert Kitaj, Larry Rivers, and others; the small shows sent out by USIA, such as a Smithsonian show of small sculpture in 1970, were magnified by display techniques and sensitive didactic support. Meanwhile popular Iranian art—including its nineteenth-century itinerant history painters or the giant handpainted film posters common to Tehran—were honored by IAS shows, revealing US awareness of native talent and beauty that most Iranians overlooked. In 1971 the hit of the year was a show of architectural detail from Shiraz, with entire walls, panels and ceilings brought to Tehran, brilliantly mounted and lighted. Such initiative by officers overseas was not mentioned in the budget or the Country Plan, nor did it show up in reports to Washington or in officer fitness reports. Instead, USIA year after year questioned the principle of showing non-American art. No one paid any attention.

Even in tiny countries, ingenuity could produce moments. In Sri Lanka in 1965, the embassy, with no gallery of its own, was invited to participate in an "international art show" but had nothing to show. Polling Americans in the embassy and the local community, the cultural office was able to lift enough art off the walls of homes and offices to fill a corner space with a dozen paintings, drawings, and prints by reputable American artists—creating the most interesting collection in the show. In Rome in the 1970s, USIS hired Douglas James Johnson to purchase work from US artists resident in Italy; he produced an inexpensive show on paper, called "19 Americans." Circulating around the smaller cities of Italy, it registered unexpected success. Other works were added, and it grew to "23 Americans." The next phase was planned to exemplify one trend or another within the collection, e.g., minimalism. But, in one of the many reverses of direction so common to the USIS world, a newly arrived PAO decided to cut off all Rome-produced exhibits for provincial cities. The works already purchased, most of which had grown considerably in value, ended up on USIS office walls, where most remain today.

In adroit ways, USIS posts—often without Washington's knowledge—managed everywhere to mount art exhibits, by hook or crook, supplemented by an occasional USIA show of graphics, posters, photographs, or art books. Resident US artists, most of them in Europe, provided some of the rest. In the developing world, if there was art professionalism on the foreign or American staff, posts borrowed the European shows or else worked with resident US artists. A USIA-funded office in Vienna, set up to assemble small exhibits for Eastern Europe, quietly circulated its shows elsewhere after Eastern Europe had been served. In Paris, a similar office borrowed and devised exhibits of art and crafts, as well as lecturers, performers and book translations, for posts in Francophone Africa.

The admirable but slapdash methods of the field officers raised obvious questions among the professionals of the art world; I fielded a painful inquiry myself from the elegant Porter McCary. But the CAOs knew that anything was better than empty walls. In Washington the ongoing threat of congressional backlash persisted, and after 1970 budget decline in Washington was felt in the field. For the visual arts, despite occasional victories, the trend was steadily down.

In 1978 USIA absorbed CU. For the first time since 1953, fine and performing arts were handled by the same office, even if the office was not part of cultural affairs in USIA. Instead of new energies, decline soon set in. A baffled USIA, with McBride in charge, finally reached for the peer-review principle in the fine arts, coming to an agreement to use the selection-panels of the NEA. Peer review might have been the right answer in principle, but forty years earlier. Now budgets were pitiful, and no reimbursement was offered to NEA to cover the costs of its panels. NEA soon lost interest and folded the selection process into other panels unattuned to overseas needs. In the Senate, Helms was sharpening his knives for the NEA.

International exhibits like the Venice and Saõ Paolo biennial shows posed a problem. MoMA and McCray had assembled peer-review committees, absent a formal government mechanism. In 1954 MoMA bought the derelict US pavilion in Venice's Bienale Gardens for $20,000; within three months, with the help of Venice-resident Peggy Guggenheim, the freshly painted building contained an exciting show of Willem De Kooning. Ambassador Clare Booth Luce in Rome, no admirer of Peggy Guggenheim, resisted her staff's entreaties to attend the opening until the very last moment. In Washington the brilliant University of Chicago art historian Joshua Taylor had taken over the IAP in the 1970s. With decreasing support from Smithsonian and USIA and with political dissonance from the art world over the Vietnam War, he had to beg for continued support. He and director Thomas Messer of the Guggenheim Museum formed an International Exhibitions Committee, which achieved neither the distinction of the IAP nor its budgets. Venice needs were met by the private art world.

The most universal of MoMA's ventures, widely exploited by USIA, was the photo exhibit "The Family of Man." Photography director Edward Steichen had long sought to put together a show for MoMA that would dramatize the horrors of war by dwelling on peaceful humans at work and play. The great Luxembourg-American photographer and his MoMA colleagues sorted through thousands of photographs, assembled them, and mounted them in an installation designed by young architect Paul Rudolph. The show took New York by storm. Paul Child, on leave from Bonn, was in Washington answering demoralizing security questions; in Steichen's show he saw the perfect USIS vehicle and convinced USIA to send it abroad.[7] Responding in style, USIA ordered fifteen copies of the historic photo-essay with their own mounting structures; a handsome catalogue was reprinted and translated into dozens of foreign languages. The show attracted literally millions of visitors. The catalogue, still in print, has sold over 3 million copies. Steichen, traveling with his brother-in-law, poet Carl Sandburg, attended openings in Europe and

Tokyo. In Moscow, the show initiated a series of high-impact US-USSR visual exchanges generated by the agreements of 1958. "Family" lasted for years and reached every single USIS post. When it broke up, its photo panels found their way onto the walls of USIS libraries and offices, where many hang today. A reconstituted version of this epoch-making exhibit stands in the castle of Clervaux, near Steichen's birthplace in Luxembourg.[8]

"Family" helped turn world attention to the art of photography, but USIA never found or commissioned an equivalent successor show. Rare small shows of American photographers like Paul Strand or Harry Callahan had invariably high impact—yet photography as art was never seen by USIA as an attractive export. In Paris Virginia Zabriskie decided to do it herself and set up her own gallery, teaching the rules of dealership in fine contemporary and vintage photographs to French gallerists.

Field ingenuity was all there was, both a blessing and a curse. For one thing, it left the impression that visual arts in Washington could be improvised without budgets; for another, continuity depended on individual energies and tastes—shows in one era could rarely be sustained in another. Resident US artists in each country—and even Sunday painters in the embassy family—were tempting but presented more problems than opportunities. In cities like Rome and Paris, dozens of serious American artists and sculptors—some of them former Fulbrights—were given shows, but choosing one of these artists was a dangerous political act for the cultural officer. Wise CAOs set up local peer-review committees and guarded the names of participants to protect them. Still, the empty walls of USIS cultural centers often tempted managers to hang the available. Only one cultural office, to my knowledge, built high permanent professional standards into its national staff: Paul Child hired Hélène Baltrusaitis, who spent her entire career in the cultural office as art advisor to the embassy. USIS Paris arts officer Darthea Speyer, working in the 1950s with resident Americans of high caliber, like Ellsworth Kelly, Sam Francis, Joan Mitchell, and Shirley Jaffe, put on major shows of museum quality, then sent them to provincial cities. The USIS cultural office helped introduce postwar US art to France. Speyer, sister of the curator of modern art at the Chicago Art Institute, finally tired of swimming upstream against USIS indifference and founded her own gallery in Paris. At the USIS center on the Rue du Dragon, various directors like Don Foresta, John Frankenstein, and Frances Switt kept things lively until USIA declared it superfluous in 1980.

Meanwhile, USIA had come to a fatal decision: to end the recruitment of officers with special skills and talents and to discourage any kind of officer specialization. All USIA officers after 1974 were hired, trained, and assigned as generalists. The end of substantive professionalism lowered standards—it was no longer possible to train a McBride or tolerate a Lois Roth or a Frances Switt. USIA and its field posts were poorly equipped to ride the wave of growing private art exchange around the world—a growth for which USIS posts had primed the pump.

Films presented other difficulties. For decades, the American film industry declined cooperation with USIS posts, overlooking their potential for building the reputation—and the sales—of American films. The industry seemed to believe that even select USIS showings could only damage local commercial distribution. Technical problems also arose: USIS posts had only 16 mm projection equipment, and video projector technology lay well in the future. Beneath these problems lay a conundrum: the US film industry saw films as products, and thus expected commerce to pay the bills for this most costly of the arts; they saw filmmaking as a business, requiring business methods. European nations and their students in the Third World, however, saw films differently, as a natural extension of the art of the theater and, therefore, as worthy of government subsidy as theater or music or books.

In the U.S. the idea of public-private cooperation in film had suffered a crushing blow immediately after the war when MoMA lent copies of its unique collection of classic films to a major national European film library to help reconstitute its world-famous collection. MoMA then learned that the films it lent were turning up in pirated copies on the commercial market—the library had lost control of the copying process. The episode confirmed the worst film industry fears and private-public cooperation stalled for forty years. Only in the late 1960s could USIA persuade Hollywood, through the Motion Picture Association of America (MPAA), to let field posts arrange special showings for selected audiences. For this purpose, a collection of twenty-two classic American films in 16 mm was made available to USIS posts in 1969. Posts welcomed them, after decades of famine, and set up showings with supporting lectures and exhibits. The success prodded a second collection into existence. As the film industry began to see the advantages of such cooperation, US distributors abroad cooperated more and more willingly. In Rome, by 1995, the distributors had helped the embassy equip a fine projection theater at the ambassador's residence; they provided prerelease feature films for special invitational showings, a regular event on the ambassador's personal cultural calendar.

USIA in 1969–70 assembled a package of experimental cinema, assembling three two-hour programs of art films, accompanied in the field by filmmaker Tom Palazzolo; he presented the films, interpreted them, and during off-hours taught film techniques to interested filmmakers and students. In Iran another film hit was the IAS showing of the annual prize TV commercials, which became teaching instruments for local film technicians. The thriving Iranian film industry of today may owe part of its origins to USIS.

Video art was a special case. In Paris, Don Foresta, director of the Dragon Center in the early 1970s, showcased video artists like Nam Jun Paik and developed his own reputation; like Speyer, he resigned from

USIA to stay on in Paris, teaching and producing audio-visual and video materials.

CU had given away the fine arts to USIA in 1953 as "objects"—except for the tight frameworks established by bilateral agreements with the Soviet countries. In the fall of 1962, CU revived Rockefeller's idea of an artist in residence upon Dean Rusk's question that reminded Battle of a memo from Beirut requesting not paintings but a painter. New York and East Hampton artist John Ferren, a Francophone who had worked in Paris in the 1930s, where among other things he had helped Picasso stretch the canvas for *Guernica*, moved to Beirut for a year's residence. With his artist-wife Rae, Ferren's presence in Beirut meant a literal transformation of the visual world for the local artists.

His case illustrates various dilemmas. To explain his absence to US friends, he quoted the purpose his embassy handler and project-designer had written him: he was to be "an artist, in the deepest sense of the word." Once he tired of hearing insinuations about espionage from Lebanese and Syrian friends, he explained that he had a *bourse*, a scholarship, which quieted them. The intellectuals and artists of French-mandated Lebanon and Syria had been in thrall to the French since the First World War, when the French embassy helped a Postimpressionist painter-educator named Georges Cyr set up residence in Beirut. Cyr's students inaugurated contemporary painting in Lebanon and Syria; with minimal French assistance, they dominated the field. An occasional exhibit of recent French painting convinced Beirut's intellectuals that Paris was still the center of the art world. At the American University superb arts educators like John Carswell and Arthur and Fay Frick were quietly suggesting to their students other ways of looking at art, but progress was slow.

Ferren's stay broke down the French-only vision in the Middle East and established a balance, opening eyes to what was happening in the U.S. Ferren's impact on painting in the eastern Mediterranean has not yet been assessed, but *Newsweek* noted at the time that he ignited the art worlds of Beirut and Damascus. Franco-Lebanese poet-playwright Georges Schehadé captured the attitude of the French-trained intelligentsia: "We knew about Boeings, but Ferren took our breath away." Ferren's year in Beirut was capped by a major retrospective show, including his new Beirut work, in the spring of 1964.

From Ferren's viewpoint, his time in Beirut was a personal transformation, and he dreamed about returning to the Middle East until the end of his life. Beirut reshaped and revitalized his work, bringing sparkling Mediterranean light and colors and a new broad-brushed simplicity. Sophisticated, intelligent, and charming in three languages, he was assumed by everyone in Beirut, despite his *bourse* story, to be a spy—though no one was clear about what he might have been reporting. It was the only plausible explanation for his stay, in a country where education and culture were still mired in colonial history and European manipulation, in the midst of the Arab nationalist pressures sponsored by Egypt.[9] Even this enlightened act of US cultural diplomacy did not make sense to the skeptics, accustomed to years of propaganda.

When the U.S. began building splendid embassies to exemplify the "architecture of democracy," progenitors Larkin and King could do nothing about décor and furnishings. The forgotten element was art in embassies. The government was powerless to adorn the new buildings with anything but stodgy bureaucratic furniture. Ambassadors, in the early years chosen predominantly from the wealthy, sometimes brought their own art and donations occasionally reached embassies, but these were unreliable accidents.

Even donations were not easy. In the early 1950s, a prominent French businessman donated a dozen Cézannes to the ambassador's residence in Paris. This was in the McCarthy years, and one of the pieces was automatically declined—a painting of nude male bathers. Six of the original bequest were sent to Washington, where they disappeared from public view. An alert art historian in 1974 stumbled across a photo in which two of them flanked an archway in the family area of the Nixon White House. A decade later, after years of irresponsible curatorship at home and abroad, all such donations and USIA holdings of art were catalogued and inventoried by professionals, but the Cézannes still remain hidden from the public.

Walter Annenberg brought part of his collection to London in the early 1970s. In Caracas Ambassador William Luers, later president of the Metropolitan Museum and then of the UN Association, found Venezuelans difficult to reach until he and his wife managed to assemble a fine collection of US painting for their residence. To Paris in the 1990s the late Pamela Harriman brought part of the Harriman collection for display in a residence from which, two decades earlier, Mrs. Thomas Watson had removed layers of the grey paint first applied by the occupying Germans. Mrs. Watson, with donations from an ad hoc group called the "Friends of 41 Faubourg St. Honoré," restored the mansion to its full grandeur and soon the residence, a former Rothschild residence and a Third Empire building, attracted various collections of highly visible long-term loans, beginning with those Mrs. Watson arranged. The high point of this informal "American Museum in Paris" came when ambassador Arthur Hartman and his wife Donna managed to borrow some 130 works, ranging from folk art to contemporary painting; they kept company with the three remaining Cézannes and two Bouguereaus. With a sleek catalogue kept alive by successors after the Hartmans left, the "museum" continued to play its role—so well that special arrangements were necessary to handle visitor demand. In Moscow the Hartmans continued. With donated funds, they managed a brilliant restoration of Spasso House, filling its public spaces with US art and a newly gifted Steinway—which enabled Vladimir Horowitz to make his triumphant return to Russia. Such episodes of individual ambassadorial energy and ingenuity in the great European capitals were of small help in the long range and none in the global picture. Where France and Great Britain dipped routinely into their vast national treasuries of decorative and fine arts, the U.S. could only decorate public spaces abroad through hard-earned loans.

The private world saw the problem. MoMA moved in 1952, followed in 1959 by the Stanley Woodward Foundation and in 1960 by Mrs. L. Corrin Strong, who had borrowed paintings from friends when her husband served as ambassador to Norway. Loans by individuals and a network of private foundations and museums were facilitated by modest government help for shipping, insurance, and hanging costs. For example, MoMA's International Council, during its first decade, placed forty-one collections on embassy walls, a quarter of what was needed. A unique collection of Rothkos hung in Edward Stone's graceful embassy in Delhi so successfully that the embassy had to set up weekend visiting hours. Efforts picked up speed in 1963, when Kennedy's State Department created the Art in Embassies Program (AIEP), directed by diplomatic spouse Mrs. Llewelyn Thompson and Nancy Kefauver. AIEP had little funding but remarkable volunteer spirit. All this was made necessary by the congressional refusal to fund art for embassy walls.

In the purist confines of the art world, some scoffed at the semi-professionalism of the patchwork embassy collections, depending on what could ingeniously be pried out of galleries, the unpredictable taste of ambassadorial couples, and available space. One art-sensitive ambassador, receiving a fine collection, found a superb abstract painting far too tall for the low-ceilinged rooms of the residence, so he turned it on its side and delighted in watching sophisticated visitors who did not notice.

A tale of three politically appointed ambassadors in a single art-conscious European capital illustrates the peril and potential of the peculiar slapdash American means of embellishing its embassies. The first delegated the choice to his wife, a motherly woman who loved to paint circlets of flowers around guests' placemarkers. The collection she chose was strong on bucolic realism, cows, flowers, and—for her husband who loved railroads—freight trains. The successor ambassador also turned matters over to his wife, a dynamic, sophisticated, and totally modernist woman who talked the best galleries in New York into lending priceless canvases by famous contemporary painters. The giant works, overflowing the moldings on the residence's nineteenth-century walls, made a startling and very different statement. The third ambassadorial resident was an Ohioan who chose eleven Ohio landscapes from the Dayton Art Institute. From such transitions, observant visitors learned a great deal about the U.S.—for better and for worse.

State's ceremonial rooms were furnished and decorated by similarly ingenious public-private begging and wheedling. Decades of persistence by Clement Conger brought the public rooms slowly to life in the ingenious American way—early American furniture and paintings were teased out of owners in exchange for a moment of fame and a tax deduction.

Conger's success took years of cultivation, persuasion, and focused energy. Upon his departure, professionals were impressed when his skilled deputy Gail Serfaty was named to succeed him.

The layman can only guess at the time and work all this highly inefficient American activism involves. AIEP Director Gwen Berlin minimized the toil in a recent pamphlet: the value of art hanging in America's embassies at any given moment is estimated to exceed $70 million. There are no estimates of the costs of planning, insuring, and installing collections.

AIEP with its private-support group, the Friends of Art and Preservation in Embassies (FAPE), began commissioning large works on paper in 1989. It began with a six-foot print by Frank Stella, in an edition large enough to be sent to every US embassy—141 copies. In 1984, the same year that USIA cut off fine arts, FAPE made the project an annual event, with a formal presentation at the White House; between 1995 and 2002, Roy Lichtenstein, Robert Rauschenberg, Ellsworth Kelly, Chuck Close (with his portrait of the late Roy Lichtenstein), Jasper Johns, James Rosenquist, and Elizabeth Murray produced prints for the embassies worldwide. The commissioning of art by government had no precedent in America except for FDR's WPA. Still, it was only a modest step toward solving the embassy problem and doing what the UK and France do as a matter of routine with a few curators.

AIEP-FAPE had no connection to USIA-CU's formal role in arts diplomacy. The 1977 merger of USIA and CU, badly managed, failed to recreate a complete cultural office. The two arts functions—called Arts America—were put into USIA's Office of "Programs" (P), along with publications, press services, films, and photo shows. Arts America never had a chance to prove itself, even under its first chief Edward McBride. McBride remembers maddening years in Arts America and P in the late 1970s. As one of his staffers put it, "P is after us every day for long-winded explanations, rationalizations, justifications; but ECA [cultural affairs] never has to ask—they *get* it!" McBride, with the Smithsonian group, now renamed SITES and with less funding than before, tried a few bold but low-visibility visual arts ventures. In 1977 SITES sent a major show of American poster art to major cities in Europe. But this was small change, considering USIA's 160-odd art-famished posts. Hopes for a budget rise evaporated as the Carter team focused on the Iran hostages.

By the 1980s USIA had other things on its mind, and the dogged defenders of the arts were wearying of the endless uphill trudge. Mary Gawronski, veteran CAO turned PAO, worked in Arts America in the early 1980s; she loyally defends its activities: "It was pitifully underfunded," she admits, "but it continued to do small circulating shows. . . . We had a tiny but very nice American quilt show in France, . . . great in the provinces [and] circulated to several countries." Staff helped find things "for special events, e.g., a show for the first US exhibit in recent memory in the Old Town Hall in Prague in 1989, before the Wall came down." Quilts for France were fine, but this was one of only half a dozen visual arts presentations for the entire world. Gawronski, later CAO Paris, points to the growth of direct museum-to-museum contacts in France, which had been stimulated and brokered by USIS cultural offices and staffers like Hélène Baltrusaitis in the 1950s. Exchanges, thanks to the generosity of US and foreign museums, were adequate for France, she insists. But outside Paris, it was quilts; and outside Europe there was nothing at all. The new USIA, after absorbing CU, had higher priorities.

People at home and in the field tried harder. One CU victory in 1976 had rich consequences: the US indemnity law. Costs of international art exhibits had long been prohibitive, and insurance was a major component, overlooked by Morey in 1946. John Richardson's assistant Peter Solmssen, later head of Philadelphia's University of the Arts, persuaded Congress, with the help of Representative Sidney Yates, to consider indemnifying loss or damage to works of art loaned by or to the U.S. A few effective legislators, in a Congress otherwise disinclined to help, managed to pass the legislation.

Another victory of sorts occurred in the 1980s when the new USIA, with CU absorbed into it, acquired a function that Cherrington would have relished: Congress tossed the agency the responsibility for a complicated law, implementing a global convention to help nations repatriate art illicitly acquired by other states. With a powerful examining committee representing museum experts, scholars, and dealers, it was a natural CU function. USIA only reluctantly assigned staff and opened an office in the Bureau of Education and Cultural Affairs (ECA), hiring gifted staffer Maria Pappageorge; she masterfully accumulated expertise on the movement of art treasures around the world and assembled a supporting network of US archeologists and art historians.

Given internal lack of focus and competing priorities, McBride in Arts America had searched for useful cooperative projects. Discussions with the Federal Council on the Arts and Humanities led to the Fund for US Artists at International Festivals and Exhibitions. To build an annual budget of over $1 million, USIA contributed $300,000, matched by equal contributions from the Pew Trusts, the Rockefeller Foundation, and NEA. To fend off political interference and reduce staff needs, administration and peer panels were handled by the private IIE. The fund, after years of accidental and wasteful ingenuity, finally guaranteed a consistent and coordinated US presence at important international arts events, at minimal cost. When Arts America was closed in 1994, the fund continued at its usual low level of visibility.

About the same time in State, an alert administrative chief convinced State to provide a special fund so that embassies could contribute small sums to archeological projects in their countries. In 2001 the former CU, now State's ECA, persuaded Congress to provide $1 million per year for the Ambassador's Fund for Cultural Preservation, permitting US embassies to do what Nelson Rockefeller had casually done in 1936—write checks to assist archeological research and preservation. Grants ranging from $10,000 to $40,000 allow embassies to "show another side of America—one that recognizes the contributions of cultures in other countries that enrich us all," noted ECA director Patricia Harrison.

These mini-triumphs reversed neither amateurism nor the downward trend of funding. After 1980 visual arts in the increasingly policy-dominated USIA were marginalized, and in 1994 the office fell victim to the Clinton budgeteers. USIA director Duffey found no words to explain, within his agency's narrow view of what it did, why art was indispensable; his team apparently did not *get* it.

The small steps backwards and forwards underline the miles yet to cover, merely to return to what the U.S. had been doing, even sporadically, in the half-century beginning in 1942. Such pale successes, for the most part linked to private energies, may help understand the intellectual vacuum in which cultural diplomats have labored for more than half a century. While Europeans regularly accuse the U.S. of conspiring to usurp leadership in the world of art, by some sort of sinister and covert private-public manipulation, the volumes on this dark plot invariably overlook the realities. First, the vigorous, energetic, and innovative art coming out of the U.S. might just have met, on the weary Continent and elsewhere, an eager audience. Second, USIA and State, in their eternal one-legged waltz with Congress, were too divided to conspire. In all, US cultural diplomats, after six decades of visual arts improvisations merely to keep their heads above water, find the conspiracy theories amusing.

For half a century in fact, gifted and dedicated Americans toiled at hard labor to fill the yawning gaps left by legislative shortsightedness. They could not build on the bases laid by US by predecessors like Fenollosa, Bingham, and Pope. Unavoidable foreign policy imperatives, e.g., US participation in the Venice Bienale, produced in parallel a sad set of subterfuges.

Since 1942 America's diplomatic presence in the visual arts has been managed at a minimal level by quiet brokerage, field officers' ingenuity, and hundreds of persistent citizens, working together on their own time against all odds. Without some stable means of doing what European nations do routinely—through their national art treasuries, their systems of coordinated museums, and their permanent circulating collections—the U.S. is doomed to sell itself short in the eyes of other nations. Without support from Congress, without focused professionalism in Washington and in the field, and without a clear role for the arts as one of the enduring values of a decent cultural diplomacy, US cultural diplomacy will have to agree to leave the field of arts diplomacy to others, relying on the erratic market movements of inter-museum interchange, the random migration of artistic talent, the whim of private and corporate donors, and the taste of exhausted cultural diplomats, formal and informal.

In the proud American amateur tradition, one can take some pride in what has, in spite of everything, been accomplished. But, in the present state of maturation of the American republic, the U.S. has reached a point where the nation might do well to face issues like the projection of its arts abroad. Beginning in 1942 a few wise men might have looked ahead, persuaded Congress that an enlightened, low-cost art export policy was essential, and begun to assemble the expertise and perhaps the flexible loan collections necessary to display the extraordinary output of the American nation and the American visual imagination to a world eager to understand. And this might have made a difference.

CHAPTER SEVENTEEN

The Ordeal of Charles Frankel

> A sensible government, when it begins to touch the life of the mind, has
> to exercise the good judgment to erect safeguards against its probable
> bad judgment.
>
> —Charles Frankel, 1969

THE "YEARS OF LIGHTNING," as USIA called its film on the Kennedy presidency, came to an end in November 1963. Those who had thought there could be a difference in American politics slipped back to their routines. Lyndon Johnson, when he finally agreed to let the declining Murrow resign, called the fine newsman Carl Rowan back to USIA from his embassy in Finland. In CU Battle was performing his feats of gentle gradualism and budgets were inching upward.

Inside and outside government, Coombs's defeat left a sour taste. The educational and foundation worlds were losing hope in CU. The bureau's activities, especially the Fulbright Program, were useful for faculty and students, but for vision—and for institutional advantage—the universities looked elsewhere. Even Fulbright's prestige dwindled as other giants emerged and budgets tightened. Senior faculty stipends now covered only part of their salaries, with no allowance for the travel of dependents, leaving the best to stay home or scout around for second grants. Universities no longer rewarded faculty when they took a year off, whatever the purpose, and younger faculty hesitated to leave the rigid tenure track.

In Washington Coombs had poisoned the word "coordination." In the field, dedicated CAOs labored to help foreign universities build de facto coordination with colleagues representing agencies like AID, HEW, the science attaché's office, the Peace Corps, and even the military, but such efforts rarely earned PAO praise. In Delhi larger-than-life ambassador Chester Bowles in the mid-1960s imposed in-embassy coordination; elsewhere, coordination was the product of a persuasive cultural officer who could make it seem useful—and cost-free. In the uphill struggle among American cultural officers to work toward a single focus for US educational interests, countervailing inertia was strong; many had thrown up their hands, setting out to "cultivate their distractions," in the words of one of the disillusioned.

The Fulbright Program sailed slowly forward, but growth was barely visible. With inflation, budget growth was wiped out and CU staff morale, even with Battle in charge, was not high. No new Fulbright agreements were negotiated in almost two decades after 1963.

In HEW there was good news: Johnson had convinced Carnegie-chief John Gardner, founding chair of CU's new Fulbright-Hays advisory commission in 1962, to serve as Secretary. Under Johnson education seemed at first to thrive. Yet there would be no protest from the universities in response to his three last-minute choices for BFS in 1968. Was anyone in fact listening?

Apparently the modest Hazen Foundation was. Director Paul Braistead clung doggedly to the idea of a decent cultural diplomacy. In response to Gardner's first CU commission report *A Beacon of Hope*, Braistead persuaded Brookings to join him in mounting one more study, this time of overseas exchanges. In 1963 the two bodies called on Field Haviland, author of the farseeing 1958 report for Fulbright's committee, and Haviland recommended Charles Frankel, professor of philosophy at Columbia University. Frankel was the right man for a serious and thought-provoking book. Looking only at the two compelling and indispensable books he gave us, it is clear that the choice was right. Frankel agreed to commit three years of his life to cultural diplomacy; the time would stretch to five years and would give the world the most articulate analysis that any nation had yet seen.[1]

A New Yorker to the core, Frankel was a child prodigy, had moved from Brooklyn to New York's elite Townsend Harris school for boys, then finished Columbia at nineteen. After four years with naval intelligence in the Pacific, he returned to Nicholas Murray Butler's great internationalist university on Morningside Heights to pursue philosophy, studying with John Dewey and Irwin Edman. He specialized in eighteenth-century European political thought, but his study of the public philosophers of the Enlightenment was only a springboard, as philosophy had been for his mentors, to public policy. His books on the issues of higher education, on "the case for modern man," and on "the democratic prospect" are those remembered today. Abroad, he held Fulbright professorships in Paris and Dublin, traveling widely with his engaging wife Helen.

The cosmopolitan Frankel, in response to Hazen and Brookings, insisted on a sound foundation for his study—a two-year traveling survey of field posts. He set off to visit fifteen countries, ostensibly to interview foreign educators, but in fact quietly talking to CAOs like Leon Picon in Japan. As the Council on Foreign Relations had done for Coombs, Brookings provided Frankel with an advisory panel of forty members, including many met in the course of our tale: Luke Battle, Edward Barrett, Paul Braistead, Frederick Burckhardt of ACLS—former chief of German reorientation—Jacob Canter, Don Cook, John Gardner, Harvard historian and BFS chair Oscar Handlin, Reed Harris, Walter Johnson, Ford's Francis Keppel, William Marvel, caretaker CU chief Harry McPherson, the father of German reorientation Herman B Wells, USIA's Don Wilson, and four other USIA officers, none of them notably committed to cultural work.

After *Beacon of Hope*, the all-out effort by the first Fulbright-Hays advisory commission, Frankel believed that depth was needed of the kind that could only be provided by a full-length book. A message to a wider public was in fact overdue. It was time for a look from a different angle, for an attempt to put cultural diplomacy into understandable language.[2]

Frankel's focus was the subject of early discussion. Brookings president Robert Calkins, in his preface to Frankel's book, was clear that this was to be a "more thorough analysis" than *Beacon* of the overseas aspect of US government exchange programs, "the most broadly based survey yet made of the program both overseas and in the U.S. of State Department grants." *Beacon* had spelled out recommendations for action by a US president, practical conclusions covering all the issues and a few more, but for all its originality it was a government pamphlet produced by a committee.

Frankel himself went in a different direction as he moved through one CAO office after another. With time, he became interested in following one of *Beacon*'s unexplored hints: studying the cultural officers and their status, a decade after USIA's creation. Braistead, Haviland, and Frankel doubtless knew that this point alone had poisoned Coombs's relations with USIA. Although his comprehensive book brushed past the quality of field staffing, Coombs had made various moves affecting the CAOs while in office; his were moderate ideas that were not seen that way by Sorensen's USIA. Frankel wanted to seize the nettle. He convinced his sponsors that a book built around a portrait of the CAOs might allow a broad range of readers to see the dilemma of cultural diplomacy through the practitioner's eyes, and he believed this viewpoint would illuminate the issue better than any other.

The result was a conceptually clear, historically grounded, and memorably written insight into cultural diplomacy, as seen from the field. An important harbinger appeared in *Foreign Affairs*; his article "The Scribblers and Foreign Policy" posed the larger questions revolving around intellect and government and warned Washingtonians who read it what was coming. The article and the book were rallying points for concerned American intellectuals and the CAOs themselves. In other countries his book was recognized as the best on the subject; Frankel was consulted regularly and at length, e.g., by Sweden when it redesigned the Swedish Institute a few years later.

Frankel's original purpose, as defined by Calkins's preface, called for a list of recommendations, which turned out to be considerably more moderate than the suggestions of *Beacon*. Frankel in his own introduction wrote: "My main purpose has been to clarify principles. I have hoped to write a handbook that might be a useful guide to those who wish to think systematically about educational and cultural affairs."[3] A handbook on cultural affairs might indeed have served to reframe the discussion, given time, especially under bipartisan Battle-style leadership. But in its final pages, Frankel obeyed his mandate, exceeded his introductory remarks, and turned the handbook into a manifesto. Ending with policy advice, it guaranteed that it would be read from back to front.

Appearing in December 1965, the book, in its prescriptions, called for less than *Beacon* had, but its adroit wording and trenchant thinking had more bite. The five USIA advisors assigned to his advisory team, especially Wilson, must have known the book would be seen by USIA as another Coombs-like attempt to steal its CAOs, but apparently none of them warned Frankel or managed to get the attention of a man not known for modesty. Thus, instead of shaping discussion as promised, the book, in the siege mentality of USIA, seemed to throw down the gauntlet. For every cultural toiler in USIA's vineyards that it inspired, it offended three of his or her bosses.

Perhaps Frankel forgot that a book can be ignored everywhere except in the academic course for which it is assigned reading. But it never occurred to him that he might be saddled with the responsibility of putting it into operation. Frankel's book, left to itself, might have focused the eyes of the intellectuals on the USIA target while they awaited the right moment to take action. Instead, the White House put Frankel on the spot, before the book appeared, by naming him to head CU. In effect the handbook-manifesto became a battle plan.

Feelers about the job had reached him in July 1965, after his draft had circulated to all advisors, including McPherson. He saw immediately that, as the author of the book he had written, the CU job was a disastrous idea. Frankel said as much, however tempting the possibility of putting ideas into action may have seemed. McPherson, full-time at the White House while dabbling in CU, supported the idea of Frankel from the start—he may, in fact, have suggested it, although he says he does not remember doing so.[4] Meanwhile Johnson seized on the idea, seeing it as a carrot for his then-beloved friend Fulbright. Fulbright had read Frankel's draft, was struck by the sharp analysis, and agreed that Frankel was the right man for the job; he too underestimated the opposition, as he overestimated the durability of Johnson's support.

Frankel maintained a dismissive stance. Confident in his own abilities, he was too intelligent not to know that his book would instantly poison the well for its author by revealing any strategy he might forge. Fulbright, rolling out his gentle southern manner, pressed him. Frankel objected, saying he needed the job "like I need a hole in the head." Fulbright reminded him that after twenty years in the Senate he knew about such holes. Others pushed Frankel to accept: Carnegie chief John Gardner—surely knowing he would soon move to Washington himself—encouraged him. So did John Kenneth Galbraith, in his inimitable way: "You'll find [State] is the kind of organization which, though it does big things badly, does small things badly too."[5] At one point Frankel was relieved to learn that Johnson had turned down the idea. But Fulbright had the bit in his mouth; he had found his man. With "flint in his voice . . . [Fulbright] told me that this was no time to back out. I said I didn't want a position that the President had any hesitation about giving me. He replied that the issue had grown larger than my personal feelings." Fulbright said the time had come to "straighten the whole area out, and I was not to complicate the matter by withdrawing my name."[6]

Fulbright had decided on a shoot-out, and Frankel ultimately yielded to the Senator's flint. In late September 1965, two months before the book appeared, he took over CU. Frankel was doomed, if only because of USIA's predictable reaction to *The Neglected Aspect of Foreign Affairs*. He had been warned during his Senate hearings when Fulbright's bipartisan friend Bourke Hickenlooper asked about Frankel's membership in the American Council of Civil Liberties, "a left-wing version of the John Birch society," as he said. Johnson himself must have known that, to help Frankel, he would have to do battle at the very least with USIA. McPherson, the only Brookings advisor who could have known Frankel was in line for the job, knew the book challenged USIA. The book was a time bomb set for December 1965.

Washington wisdom saw Frankel as a bone Johnson threw to Fulbright. In hindsight, it seemed a quixotic idea. When feelers reached Frankel in July, Johnson already knew his Arkansas friend was restive over Southeast Asian policy—the first Fulbright speech gathered in his *Arrogance of Power* (1966) was made a month earlier in June. Johnson wanted to bring Fulbright back to his side, but he must have known that the Senator was not a man to be bought off on a question as important as Vietnam; Johnson, who believed that all men had their price, must have believed his choice of Frankel might muffle the Arkansan critic.

After Johnson's landslide reelection in 1964, there was every reason to believe that he and his team, as he often said, were committed to "education," even if his colleagues suspected "education" was not a word they wanted to define. Frankel, like Coombs before him, can be forgiven for assuming that the Johnson team wanted him, perhaps precisely *because* of what he had written. Doubtless he was over-impressed by the predictive ability of the political tacticians who advised him—including Fulbright. Collectively they underestimated the opposition; and they overestimated Johnson's power—and willingness—to impose a new vision on USIA and its adamant congressional supporters; they also underestimated LBJ's vindictive reaction to Fulbright's stance on Vietnam.

Frankel had thousands of friends in the university world, some in power, but few in political life. His supporters were intellectuals and Washington imports—Gardner and Francis Keppel, both now in HEW, among others. He knew he could count on the New York internationalist and educational establishment. But in Washington, where politics was the only ideology, he had to depend on Fulbright and a few stalwart congressmen like Indiana's John Brademas. This base was not enough; even Fulbright needed the support of his Texan friend because in the shadows waited the irrepressible John J. Rooney, still smarting from the

Coombs episode. Unwisely, Frankel, who had grown up in Rooney's Brooklyn district, chose not to worry.

The first months of the Johnson era, like the beginning of the Kennedy moment, nurtured their share of illusions, which radiated in part from lustrous Johnson appointments—the former heads of Carnegie and Rockefeller (Gardner and the retained Rusk); Ford Foundation staff, including Keppel and Harold Howe; White House intellectual advisor Douglas Cater and later John Roche; and other luminaries of the educational and foundation world. The BFS, in the first Johnson years, retained its totally academic core under the chairmanship of historian John Hope Franklin; political scientist James Roach, a Texan friend of the president, would soon succeed Franklin, and a newer member was awaiting his turn—Princeton Soviet historian James Billington, who would later move from the chair of BFS to the Woodrow Wilson Center and then to the Library of Congress. In Congress, higher education–oriented legislators and Johnson friends—like Fulbright, Humphrey, and John Brademas—were in place. And the man in the White House was a famous Fulbright friend, dedicated to "education."

McPherson tired quickly of the superfluous CU burden. He had no real interest in CU himself—he confessed later that he acceded to his chief's insistence without knowing what was at stake. During his frequent absences, CU was managed by China mission son Arthur Hummel—Calkins's preface to Frankel singled out both McPherson and Hummel for special thanks. McPherson remembers that Frankel had heavy support, certainly by Fulbright, and he remembers liking Frankel and his ideas. But McPherson was caught up in the usual frenzy of a White House transition and could not have been thinking clearly about matters as minor as CU. And certainly, since the idea of war with USIA was unthinkable, it could not have occurred to McPherson that Frankel's name might trigger one.

Frankel's second book, a marvelous postmortem written after leaving CU, fills in the details. In the amusing, humane, and saddening *High on Foggy Bottom* (1968), he told parts of the story the earlier book omitted. Now a classic in public administration literature, this is the book of a witty, urbane, and incisive humanist political philosopher about moving from his campus to the inside of the US government. For those interested in cultural diplomacy, it is an indispensable afterthought to Frankel's more analytic 1965 study.

Frankel took office in September 1965 with one year of Johnson's mandate already spent. Aware of trouble ahead but confident in his abilities, Frankel later confessed that USIA had every reason, from its well-defended but circumscribed viewpoint, to fear his agenda. In Washington few enough books are read, and when they are, they are read selectively. For Frankel's book, no reader in a position of power began on page one.

Frankel, surprisingly, had not seen the dangers of working, like

Coombs but unlike Battle, from the top down, from vision to implementation. Although very different men, both were visionary administrators. Of the two, Frankel seemed more practical because he relied on a broad and humane vision, rather than human-resource economics. His book, in its clarity, also made it all look simple. To reassure CU staff, for example, he used calm and adroitly reasoned language, not political theory. But the clarity, once his strategic plan went public, made ambushes simpler to plan.

USIA was worried and defensive. Frankel had done the unthinkable: he had dared to speak for thousands of prominent American intellectuals and academics and a good number of USIA insiders, who over three decades had gently but persistently challenged USIA dominion over both propaganda and cultural affairs. That his analysis sounded reasonable and that it had widespread support in the intellectual world sharpened the agency's responses.

Three months after taking office, Frankel began to see what he was up against. He was invited to a small White House conference on international cooperation, with high-caliber participants. The conference issued a thin report, prepared by the National Citizens Council's special subcommittee on "culture and intellectual exchange"—Frankel and McPherson were both listed as consultants and LBJ's assistant for intellectual relations Douglas Cater watched over the process. The report called for elevating cultural relations within State to Undersecretary level—at the time an Undersecretary would have outranked the head of USIA. It recommended CAO independence and suggested raising the level of those who administer cultural programs, both in Washington and abroad; and it argued that American cultural programs abroad must operate "independently of those government agency desks whose chief, or readily identifiable functions are political in nature"—Ralph Turner would have defined the word "political." USIA manned the defenses; its chiefs had seen the agenda.

In the book, Frankel's method was straightforward: he had projected himself imaginatively into the shoes of his imaginary "compleat" cultural attaché, in a brilliant central chapter evoking two days in his life. Then he imagined himself as CAO in a city like Paris and decided how he wanted the job organized. His imaginary composite CAO, reflecting dozens of CAO interviews, is the book's core. From it, he examines the administrative setting in which the CAO works, his or her relations with other embassy officers, and relations with other US educational efforts in that country. Next, he looks at the public and private sectors in the U.S. and abroad, and at the foreign audiences for US education and its products.

He saw four disarmingly simple—even obvious—purposes in cultural and educational diplomacy, each the domain of a separate US agency: (1) to promote good will and understanding was the business of CU and Fulbright; (2) to advance US foreign policy was the concern of USIA (in

High he added a small refinement, recognizing CU's political role with intellectuals: "Students and professors, writers and artists, scientists and intellectuals, are important social groups, and important politically"); (3) to assist the development of other nations was the business of AID; and (4) to facilitate scholarly and intellectual interchange was a matter for private American intellectuals and universities. In sum, he saw education and intellectual exchange as a single public-private process, which Washington caprice had chopped up and assigned to a gaggle of competing agencies, the most central of which had propaganda as its primary mission.

To serve these four ends, he saw five means: (1) linking US and foreign educational systems; (2) improving the international communications context; (3) shaping and extending international intellectual discourse; (4) contributing to educational development; and (5) furthering cultural diplomacy as an end in itself. The five pursuits, however separate, demanded a single coordinated focus. His goals may have been obvious, but significantly his analysis bore no resemblance whatsoever to USIA's self-defined mandate.

An irreducible factor was the endless variety of foreign audiences. In two hundred countries and many more language-cultures, he warned, there were tough national sovereignties, many with internal sub-sovereignties. His taxonomy was standard, based on levels of development—especially as measured by national educational systems. Its three time-honored categories distinguish the industrialized countries, the developing world, and controled societies like the USSR. US efforts had to to be sensitive to all of these broad contexts and sub-contexts, while tuning outreach to each setting.

At the same time, bilateral efforts had to mesh with multilateral programs. UNESCO, a body parallel to CU, did multilaterally what bilateral relations could not do. US thinking had to define where cultural bilateralism ended and UNESCO began.

Frankel's recommendations, under the inoffensive title "Principles and Practices," harken back to his introductory intentions: "It is only reasonable to measure generalities against specifics, . . . [and to] indicate, with regard to certain central questions, some of the practical implications of the genteel principles I have put forward." His concrete proposals hung on three abstract needs: raising US cultural relations policy to a level consonant with its high significance for US foreign relations; changing the way US educational and cultural policy was formulated and implemented abroad; and shaping a more cooperative and binding relationship between government and education. In short, his field interviews in the early 1960s had led him to a pure distillate of Cherrington and MacLeish, with a nod to George Allen and the Morrill report.

The cultural officer in the field, he concluded, was the best possible focus for analyzing and understanding cultural diplomacy. The implication therefore was that the CAO had to be a person of high intellectual caliber. But such people need appropriate working conditions. He thus suggested ranking the CAO as a coordinate to the PAO, heading an independent cultural branch with its own staff. This was a stab at USIA's heart, in effect downgrading the PAO to a senior IO. Frankel believed the CAO needed independent and direct access to the ambassador, relative autonomy including budget, the backup of dedicated staff, and maximal freedom to follow, with the CAO's unusual access and personal talents, all paths of interest.

Regarding programs, he wanted libraries and book programs returned to CU, to be managed in Washington as they are managed—by the CAO—in the field. He wanted to house the embassy cultural operation separately from press and media offices, so as to make the separation clear in the eyes of foreign publics. He wanted the cultural program to have its own budget. He wanted to split the short-term IV program in two: a small part for the targetted political-action needs of the embassy and the rest for a cultural and educational program under the total control of the CAO. He was most concerned about human quality. Embassy cultural offices needed American and foreign staff of sufficient caliber to maintain a high level of dialogue; CAOs needed help in moving around the foreign geographical and human landscape, with daily office management in safe hands. For personnel evaluations, the CAO had to be judged by peers, under long-range criteria reflecting the nature of the work. The CAO had to serve on all embassy committees relevant to his or her work, e.g., for AID educational programs, USOE's NDEA grants, Peace Corps, and National Science Foundation projects. High-level academic figures should be recruited, as in the past, for short-term or longer-term CAO assignments around the world.

These suggestions were explosive enough, but Frankel had a surprise in store, reaching back twenty-five years to USOE's John Studebaker, the idea of educational attachés based in HEW. Surely he did not intend the idea as a main point but as a by-product—it does not appear in his book. The idea probably arose after the book was finished, almost by accident, in the summer of 1965, during a long discussion with Studebaker's latter-day successor, the newly appointed Francis Keppel. In August, with his book already in press, Frankel received an unrelated letter from Keppel, asking for new ideas that USOE might propose to Congress. In an off-the-cuff response, Frankel suggested that HEW might take the lead in solving the cultural diplomatic dilemma. He saw rich internationalist possibilities in HEW; in principle, the idea of a network of embassy education officers seemed appropriate. He also saw Keppel as a potential ally.

The idea might have stayed in the letter to Keppel, but as USIA negativism became obvious to him, it grew in Frankel's mind, moving from his fallback position to the front lines. Faced with the intransigent USIA, the USOE alternative became more attractive. USOE, already evolving into a separate Department of Education, might in fact be a more appropriate home for educational and cultural programs. This fateful decision over-looked the wisdom of Sumner Welles; Frankel had only meant to specu-late in a letter to a friend, not submit a proposal, a blandishment, or a threat. But USIA's response quickly drove him into a corner and made USOE seem the better alternative, given the educational framework in which Frankel viewed the CU question.

None of this was new. Anent the CAO, Frankel had collected the wis-dom of the last three decades, in the U.S. and abroad; he had then re-stated it in clear and simple terms, framed it in a coherent intellectual context, and supported it with his normally eloquent wit and telling prose. Little of this meant much to USIA leadership; they had heard it before, were disinclined to rethink matters, and were too busy at first to see the potential for USIA in Frankel's thinking. As it had done since 1953, USIA circled its wagons against another attempt to destroy the agency. In fact, this could have been a a golden opportunity to strengthen USIA, if the obdurate agency had not asserted its commitment to the status quo. Frankel elevated his remarks to Keppel to a pilot proposal for a small, select group of education officers assigned to foreign embassies. Perhaps he reasoned that adding a professional educator to field outposts was a less perilous tactic than "stealing" the CAOs; in time he believed it might achieve the same thing.

All this was in Frankel's mind in December when Lyndon Johnson made a remarkable speech at the Smithsonian, reading almost without change a draft Frankel had casually dictated in the presence of two awes-truck CU colleagues. Johnson proposed an International Education Act (IEA), based on the ideas of the Morrill report. With IEA, HEW would be able to build links between American and foreign universities by direct grants; to administer these, major embassies would need an "education officer" and specialized staff. In time, these would begin to "make inter-national education central in foreign policy." Once the universities were in charge, it "would help to take educational and cultural relations out of the State Department or the Information Agency . . . and end the sub-ordination of international education to public relations."

One wonders what LBJ thought he was reading at the Smithsonian. Close observers were beginning to suspect that "education" for him re-flected little more than his rugged childhood and career as a public school teacher. To Johnson himself, education seemed to mean schools for the educationally deprived, including those abroad. Frankel's draft instead laid out a broad agenda, internationalist and even universalist; it extended the motto of the University of Wisconsin to claim that the responsibilities of American education did not end at its shores, that American education served the world.

Encouraged by Gardner, Johnson named a task force to "recommend a broad and long-range plan of worldwide educational endeavor." Most of 1966 was spent focusing on that task force and pressing for IEA. The task force's final report called for a separate agency for educational diplomacy, located outside USIA and State, with its own budget, and field posts staffed by significant American intellectuals, the whole supported by education-sensitive administrators. With no field tradition behind it, HEW would have to play this new role slowly at the outset—sending twenty or thirty pilot education officers abroad, with staff backup and budget, to selected embassies. CU meanwhile had to be strengthened, said the task force, by its director's promotion to Undersecretary of State. In the embassies the education officer would be a coordinate, not a subordinate of the USIS chief. By now, Frankel was hurdling USIA intransigence, intent on taking the fight over the agency's head. The tentative quality of Johnson's backing was also beginning to show.

For USIA, the new direction of the attack was sinister: leadership saw the blue-ribbon international education task force as a rigged means of carving up USIA. Even Frankel's admirers worried. Within the task force, to defend the unconditional USIA refusal, a velvet-gloved hatchet-wielder was delegated; Burnett Anderson, USIA's top policy officer and successor to Sorensen, would soon become famous for his sardonic proposal that, if there were to be an embassy education officer, then there should also be a fine arts officer (not an entirely bad idea for USIS posts like Paris, which Anderson would shortly head). In Anderson's view, fine arts and education were and should be no more than fingers on the PAO's hand. The other members of the task force wanted an agent of their own, a field officer who could "take over the educational exchange programs entirely." Anderson insisted that this decision, like that of a jury, required a unanimous decision—in which case his USIA dissent amounted to a veto.[7]

Frankel, in drafting the final version of the task force report, was sufficiently cowed by Anderson's stony position to shave down the education officer's role to no more than planning and coordination, in an attempt to placate USIA. His supporters on the task force begged him to stay the course, but Frankel opted for the softer approach. To no one's surprise—except perhaps Frankel's—USIA was not at all assuaged; Anderson maintained his dissent. Task force member John Hope Franklin, two-term chair of the BFS, finally reached the stage of exasperation. In his ringing baritone, he said: "If USIA continues to dissent from this decision, then I shall have to dissent from USIA's dissent." Anderson did not budge.

Feelings ran high. At a dinner, Frankel's wife Helen was cornered by an unnamed USIA official who explained to the bright university woman, who had lived abroad and circled the world, that "foreign languages are overrated, and that Americans have no need to speak any language but English, even those Americans in foreign service." After the encounter, Frankel asked her what she had answered: "Nothing. I thought you already had enough philosophical disagreements."[8]

During this dialogue of the deaf, the IEA seemed to be moving forward in Congress. Johnson in February 1966 had called for the legislation, including field education officers reporting to the ambassador. IEA sailed handsomely through both House and Senate, with sizable majorities. Congressmen like Greek-American John Brademas were urging Frankel to think bigger and ask for more. From the viewpoint of ideas, things were going well.

The darker question was funding. The Office of Management and Budget, with perhaps little understanding of the isues, was not friendly to IEA. And both congressional appropriations committees—especially Rooney's—were uninterested by what they dismissed as "new initiatives." Hardcore USIA loyalists, on whom Frankel had given up, lobbied their best. Rooney bided his time. Frankel, meanwhile, focused on building HEW's Center for Educational Cooperation. In *High* he reported a "heated meeting" with USIA at the White House, raising all the old issues—"each agreement that we make seems to come unbuttoned," he lamented.

Two years later Frankel, in his postmortem, was less guarded in expressing his opinion of USIA. As an example, he recalled the joint Japanese-American cultural conference (CULCON). Frankel, who knew Japan well from his years in naval intelligence, reported that one USIA officer blatantly patronized the Japanese, a habit Frankel had earlier seen in USIS-sponsored academics who lectured in Japan, "as though it were necessary to introduce the members of this sophisticated culture to elementary truths." From other countries and from UNESCO, support for the ideas of the IEA was streaming in. But USIA had manned the trenches and truth was as usual the first casualty.

Brademas, studying IEA in the House, called various witnesses, including USIA's new director Leonard Marks, high-powered communications lawyer and friend of the Johnson family. Marks was careful to speak favorably of the idea without showing enthusiasm. He admitted that it would enhance American competence in foreign area studies—and that this would be useful to USIA in upgrading its staff (USIA in fact only recruited products of the area-studies programs in the case of Eastern Europe). He praised his friend Frankel and his stalwart support of the education officer idea, but he claimed to Brademas that USIA's BNCs and libraries, teaching English and holding seminars, were already "small universities"—e.g., serving some 23,000 "students" in Peru. The subtext: USIA was already doing all this, IEA will only waste time.

Frankel, grasping at a straw—and still overestimating LBJ's power—made a profound mistake. He urged Johnson to invite Rooney for a session of "jawboning." The former prosecuting attorney, armed to the teeth, was only too delighted by the invitation. He caught Johnson off-guard by hitting him where it hurt most, said Frankel: "The Congressman angrily told the President about the opponents of the war to whom we were giving grants."[9] Ill-prepared for Rooney's passionate convolutions, Johnson ended the discussion—and might that day have lost interest in IEA. LBJ was not the first to find no carrot to tempt Rooney—embassy officers for decades had entertained him graciously abroad, meeting his heavy need for liquid refreshment while overlooking his contempt for "booze allowances."

Meanwhile, Frankel was trying to keep Secretary Rusk abreast of the state of play. But Rusk had other concerns, notably in Southeast Asia. Each Frankel visit was harder to arrange and shorter in length. Perhaps Rusk had concluded that Frankel's cause was no more of a winner than Coombs's earlier effort. In mid-May of 1966, the war between Frankel and USIA reached *Time* magazine, which gave it two pages and aggravated all tensions.

Ramparts's revelations about CIA support of international cultural associations triggered a serious diversion. Kennedy advisor McGeorge Bundy, leaving the White House to take over the Ford Foundation in 1966, warned his New York colleagues at their first meeting that the CIA activities were certain to come unstuck soon and wondered if Ford could do anything about it, but it was already too late.[10] Within a year, dozens of important organizations were orphaned, reputations damaged, and lives destroyed. Frankel considered the blow-up a matter of grave concern. CU, as he saw it, would have been the logical place for the organizations to find refuge, but Congress was not interested in raising CU budgets—and CIA's ample funding had raised private-sector expectations. Frankel proposed that Gardner chair a three-man committee on the question, to include CIA. He proposed that CU do openly what CIA had concealed, the idea that would in time lead to the creation of the NED. In the final analysis, rescue of the "CIA orphans," as they were called, was partial; some slipped into CU, where they would be miserably underfunded, but most simply faded away.

Rooney never granted a penny to IEA, and the widely supported act was never funded. Frankel's strategy fell apart. Once again, the discussion of cultural diplomacy went underground. In October 1967, two months before Frankel returned to Columbia, another conference gathered in Colonial Williamsburg to rehash the same issue. The World Conference on the Crisis in Education, chaired by Cornell President James Perkins, took one more crack at the old questions, in the Coombs-Frankel vein. Its report, one more ringing message from the academic community, passed unnoticed.

At the end the defeated Frankel could do no more than "slow down the retreat from the purposes expressed in the Smithsonian Address." If he had focused on the purposes of Fulbright-Hays and worked Battle-style from what existed, he might have headed off the worst budgetary decline in CU history, but that was not Frankel's style. Instead, knowing he was right, he bet the store. Even his friends found it hard to go all the way with him.

The dream ended when simmering tensions between LBJ and Fulbright finally blew up. It began with the Foreign Relations Committee's examination of the US response to the Dominican uprising; by mid-September 1965 Fulbright knew that his committee had been badly misled on the Gulf of Tonkin episode. The gap between the two old friends quickly became a chasm over the Vietnam issue, tragically for both. Fulbright's best-selling *Arrogance of Power*, a collection of his speeches from the preceding year, came out in December 1966, putting an end to a long and close friendship. A year later, in an all-too-familiar administrative style driven perhaps by malice, Johnson took revenge on his former friend with a final burst of inappropriate appointments to Fulbright's watchdog BFS. The move touched off a steady growth in the number of political appointments in government, which would continue into the next millennium.

The split finished Frankel. After two losing budget tussles with Rooney and with dwindling access to Rusk, Frankel resigned in December 1967. He had spent almost five years on cultural diplomacy but only twenty-six months in office—short of a thousand days. The press story of his resignation, crowded to page four by other events, said Frankel laid the blame for his departure on the government's growing preoccupation with Vietnam. The cold war had in fact made it harder to find consensus on softer questions; Vietnam on top of the Soviet threat doubtless made it impossible for Frankel to get his point across. Perhaps Vietnam was not the sole cause of Frankel's defeat, but it was as good an explanation as any.

His friends and admirers, even those in the White House, like Douglas Cater, were dismayed. He had been unable to move the mountain he had so clearly described—he had forgotten that it was in fact a real mountain, which wiser men might have circumvented or tunneled under. McPherson, deeply involved in the episode, reduced it in what he remembered to an administrative question: cultural diplomacy needed an administrative structure for it to work in the field, where USIA held unshakable dominion, and it was unlikely that any other machinery could be developed, at that time and in those circumstances.

To replace Frankel, the Johnson team, by now obsessed with Rooney, came up with an idea they thought ingenious that was in fact demeaning and, as it turned out, counterproductive. They named a fine man to the job on grounds that he was a close friend of Rooney: Edward Re, a customs judge and legal educator from New York. A decade later Re would find his fifteen minutes of fame when he succeeded in having Richard Serra's gigantic "Tilted Arc" removed from the plaza in front of his office building. Rooney friend or not, Re absorbed a further heavy cut in the CU budget. His deputy, Jacob Canter, testified before Rooney and reminded him how far Re had stretched, making heavy internal cuts and sacrificing 109 positions, a quarter of his total complement. Rooney, still fuming over Frankel, was not impressed. Re returned to his customs court after Nixon's election in 1968, with Canter acting as a six-month caretaker during the interregnum. In an admittedly imperfect search, I have found no records marking Re's passage through CU. In the mid-1970s, when I met him by chance in Rome, he had only vague memories of CU. His friend Rooney, over a three-year period, had slashed the bureau's 1968 budget by 36 percent, from $50 million to $32 million in 1970. Without funding, ideas in CU, even those as well supported as IEA, were empty words.

Frankel's defeat notwithstanding, it is obvious three decades later that in his two books on cultural diplomacy he had given the world the most complete vision it had ever seen of what cultural diplomacy might be, especially in its American version. The books meant his legacy was deep-etched and far-reaching. It is equally obvious that in Washington he learned that books can do more harm than good. Where other nations may claim him as a prophet, Frankel's broad-gauged ideas and vision were not honored in the capital of his own country. His ideas failed not because they were bad—clearly they were not—but because they were Frankel's.

High ponders his failure. Looking back, he made a few changes in his original vision. One was to restate the three ways the US government could nurture educational and cultural affairs abroad, beginning from the particular integrity of USIA, AID, and Fulbright-CU. But, he said, while AID and CU stuck to their business, USIA dabbled in the work of the others. Propaganda, he believed, had far outlived its time—as an idea, it was "crass and naive." Advancing the arts and sciences and promoting international understanding served the national interest as much as support to short-term policy. The US intellectual community "plays the major role in cultural exchanges, and few of its members are going to go along willingly with a public-relations counselor's view of their function."

He had no more patience for USIA. Coming well after the battle was lost, his words were hard, even if written in sorrow. Looking back, it is clear that USIA leadership could never understand or admit that Frankel in 1965 had laid out a way to *help* the agency grow to meet the challenges of the next decades. As the agency had rejected Morrill and Coombs, now it had trashed Frankel's ideas. USIA seemed intent on remaining precisely what it was—even if it had been what it was for only fifteen years.

To AID's agenda, he was kinder in his criticisms. AID sought instruments for producing trained manpower and promoting economic progress; in a word, it wanted to educate. But the AID educational stance, relentlessly utilitarian, missed a major point about political cultures: there were habits of mind, attitudes, and values lurking beneath life choices; economic development has profound roots in ideas, not only in the receiving countries but in the donor's world. Frankel spelled out what Huntington would articulate three decades later: in an era of cultural clash, "culture matters."[11]

Anticipating Nye's "soft power" and picking up the threads of Turner's work, Frankel made it clear that culture is not a frill but a vital dimension of diplomacy. The AID and USIA viewpoints, properly defined, were—or should be—interlocking parts of a larger idea. But both agencies had their eyes glued to their own past.

Frankel's third way, CU's or Fulbright's "mutual understanding," puzzled a Congress impatient with the fuzzy overtones of the shopworn phrase. He believed that legislators wanted to foster understanding, but they had no notion how to do it, thanks to the confused rhetoric issuing from USIA's and CU's past. Frankel's vision of cultural diplomacy sought "the rectification of imbalances of intellectual power" and "the control of cultural aggression"; he wanted to build institutions with "an international stake, so that the edge is taken off international hostilities and the reasons for keeping peace are multiplied." This was a great deal of thinking to assign to busy legislators, intent on promoting understanding but concerned first with reelection.

Synthesizing AID's development role and USIA's information work into one, he placed them under a higher rubric: cultural relations between nations. His premise: understanding must underlie all stable international relationships. If this was true, then understanding needed programs to promote and activate it and to support institutions embodying it over time. Understanding required education, in every sense of the loaded word.

Reflecting his experience in Washington, Frankel listed six chores CU could not avoid: (1) running a "large educational foundation, working through an elaborate system of committees and commissions in the U.S. and abroad"; (2) helping develop national policy in a major area of foreign relations; (3) advising on the international implications of domestic educational policy, in matters related to the arts, sciences, humanities, and communications; (4) serving as diplomat, negotiator, and principal government representative in all international educational relations; (5) coordinating and providing leadership for the activities of fifteen or more federal agencies touching on international educational or cultural relations; and (6) sitting on relevant government boards and coordinating councils—at least twelve in Washington by his count, for institutions including the National Endowments, the Smithsonian, and the Kennedy Center—while conveying the government viewpoint to a variety of other committees and task forces. On this last point, Frankel cautiously estimated the annual number of such meetings—some of them several days in length—at seventy, or 1.4 per week.

These chores can all be found in Hull's letter to Cherrington and in the words of MacLeish, Thayer, Allen, and Coombs. Thoughtful observers had seen for years that certain unavoidable problems in intellectual relations flowed naturally and irresistibly to the Department of State, both from inside the U.S. and from a world of very different societies and cultures. Once in State, the problems went straight to CU, but CU was not staffed or budgeted to handle them, either in Washington or in the field, in part because of congressional insistence on starvation budgets. The cultural problems flowing into State were anything but trivial; they reflected vital functions of the kind governments must handle, especially in an increasingly interdependent world. In all, Frankel saw that few nations had matched US insouciance about the need for a central government office for cultural problems.

High is Frankel's testament. His practical recommendations sound familiar because for thirty years before him wise men and women had been reiterating them: augment CU power and budget, strengthen its coordination over other government agencies, put first-class cultural officers into the field, insulate cultural work from propaganda and narrow interpretations of short-range foreign policy, and—a perennial call—set up a semiautonomous "foundation" for educational and cultural affairs, akin to the Smithsonian.

Yet in retrospect, wiser CAOs were puzzled by Frankel's aggressive pursuit of a brilliant vision with sizable potential for mischief. Even his idea of high-powered outsider CAOs, multiplied to cover the world, raised problems. His imaginary CAO looked to his staff for clerical backup more than for wisdom. A race of superb academic CAOs would have turned their assistants into clerks. Educator Frankel had an answer: he promised younger officers they would be groomed for a career, serving under the lustrous outsiders, then begin as CAO in a small or middle-size post followed by a retooling stay at a university. Yet even Frankel privately admitted that few USIA career officers he had known were worthy of occupying the cultural office in Paris or London; he reserved those positions by definition for someone like himself—a certified, practicing once-and-future American intellectual. Some CAOs would have been proud to serve under Frankel and to learn from him, but none believed they could function at his level.

For USIA loyalists, Frankel's failure was a vast relief. But committed CAOs who admired him, those who were trying precisely in Battle's gradualist style to broaden USIA's mission in the very directions Frankel indicated, saw an unwitting but real betrayal. To one of these dogged gradualists, he inscribed a copy of *High*, for one who "stays with the good fight." But those who stayed with the fight, trying to help USIA grow from within and over time, found that Frankel's incomparable agenda and sparkling postmortem, in the last analysis, made their lives more difficult.

High is a profound meditation on the problem of sound government in a democracy, on excellence in a populist country, on the intellectual's role in the nonintellectualism of American political process. But ultimately Frankel had to face Harold Dodds's old questions to Cherrington: should government even *try* to do such things? Why not delegate them to an intermediate sector specially created for the purpose? Unfortunately, by 1970, the universities and foundations, themselves damaged by *Ramparts*, were victims of a silent attack on that same intermediate sector. The intellectual institutions were branded by ideologues as a vast "liberal" conspiracy. The Tax Reform Act of 1969, triggered by Ford Foundation grants to outgoing Johnson friends, curbed the foundations' earlier freedom. The universities' proximity to government was darkening the very idea of an intermediate sector.

Frankel's defeat was LBJ's and Fulbright's and McPherson's as well; it was as total as it could have been. CU budgets were nearly halved and his ideas were pilloried—in USIA it would be almost impossible to raise a "Frankel" question, or any question at all, for years. Frankel's name was anathema and the remotest connection to the man bore a price. After Frankel, no White House paid any attention to the dilemmas of cultural and informational diplomacy. Six years passed before the next serious attempt to divide cultural relations from short-term policy would well up, this time from inside USIA. While these new ideas looked like Frankel's, the tactics were shrewder. Yet even so they failed.

Frankel had attacked USIA at its heart, and the paranoid agency had risen to heroic countermeasures. Despite Frankel's close collegial relations with the CU staff, who knew they had encountered greatness, and despite his dedication of *High* "to my colleagues in CU," the cultural loyalists had turned skeptical; Frankel's failure proved them right.

Frankel left the good fight to his friends, returned to Columbia, wrote his postmortem and an allusive parable about the Vietnam years in the form of a novel; he then founded and directed the North Carolina Center for the Humanities, while chairing the Committee for the Future of the University. In 1979 he and his wife Helen were murdered by intruders in their bedroom in Bedford Hills, New York.

CHAPTER EIGHTEEN

The Arts of Performance

I look forward to an America which will reward achievements in the arts as we reward achievement in business and statecraft, . . . to an America which will steadily raise the standards of artistic accomplishment and which will steadily enlarge cultural opportunities for all of our citizens, . . . and to an America which commands respect throughout the world not only for its strength but for its civilization.

—John F. Kennedy, 1963

He's the *real* ambassador.

—Dave Brubeck, 1980

BRUBECK'S MUSICAL COMEDY *The Real Ambassador*, written for Louis Armstrong and Carmen McRae, was never produced. The slight story line concerned a jazz giant traveling abroad for the Department of State. The title song made the point: traditional US diplomacy meant little compared to Armstrong's impact.

Like the architecture of new embassies, the creation of libraries, the opening of US cultural centers, and the export of visual art, American performing artists, after particularly active informal beginnings, were ready by 1942 to play a role in formal US diplomatic relations. Early discussions with Latin America, embodied in Hull's shopping list, had only hinted at performers; moreover the high-culture cast of the discussion did not encourage the idea of drawing on the US popular culture. Again it was Nelson Rockefeller who set things in motion.

The prehistorical background of performing arts was richer than that of the visual arts. While painting and sculpture in America grew slowly out of a European matrix toward an independent, national, non-European style, the new nation's characteristic performing arts, reflecting its rich popular culture, emerged more quickly and were soon appreciated by Europeans. Meanwhile the great American performers in classical European music, theater, and dance, working within the European tradition, only began to attain world stature after the Second World War.

Long before then, popular performers had begun attracting the notice of the Old World. By the 1870s American performers were appearing in Europe, via private and commercial channels. A brief review can only hint at the extent of the private activity that led to the emergence of the U.S. as the world's capital of the popular arts.

A forgotten dancing banjo player named Joel Walker Sweeney, who later formed a song and dance group known as Old Joe's Minstrels, performed solo by royal command for Queen Victoria in 1843 and amused her mightily. A more prominent episode of private outreach took place in 1872 when Fisk College's Jubilee Singers brought the negro spiritual to European ears. The high art of the Fisk composers, conductors, and singers made the choir a popular cultural event at levels up to royalty. When the group performed before Queen Victoria and Prime Minister Gladstone, the U.S. was still dependent on Europe for culture, but the Fisk Singers caught the Old World's attention and announced that something new was happening in America. After a year's respite the Fisk group returned to Europe for a full year, earning $50,000 for their university in the era's dollars on their return in May 1875. The impact of the black artists, who offered performing music never heard before, fed Europe's enduring curiosity about Black America.[1] In these same years the American minstrel show with its ugly racist stereotypes found imitators and widespread audiences in Britain. It was perhaps the first foreign imitation of a completely American art form.

In the nineteenth century, the greatest American commercial performing and sports event by far was Buffalo Bill's Wild West Show, traveling widely through Europe and beyond. The show was unreplicable and left little trace in the arts of Europe, but from a management viewpoint it showed both sides that a large and complicated transatlantic event could finance itself and benefit both sides. Other American performers were sailing to Europe well before the First World War, e.g., "exotic" dancers like Loïe Fuller and her veils, immortalized by Toulouse-Lautrec. Fuller paved the way for the performances of Isadora Duncan, the creator of modern dance, who lived and worked abroad after 1904. Isadora, unschooled in the steel discipline of classical ballet, traveled her own path and invented new forms of dance expression, feeding the growth of a national American style in dance.[2] For opera Mary Garden, Scottish immigrant to America trained in France, was an isolated case.

In New York the imported phenomenon of the international Yiddish theater brought its own stimulus; it showed the feasibility of international performance and contributed to the growth of US performing arts and its infrastructures. The actors performed, in a common language, in the major cities of northern Europe; they added New York and Chicago to their itineraries when the audiences were large enough, around the beginning of the century. It was theater beyond national boundaries, using a common language, and with the less extensive Italian popular theater in the U.S. it reached immigrant populations. Ethnic theater served as a training ground for various American theatrical and musical talents, both in performance and in arts management.

The military played its role as well. General Pershing, called Black Jack because of his admiration for black American soldiers, launched an epoch-making American musical export, via the unique marching bands of black musicians which in 1917–18 played all over France. They introduced the polyrhythms of jazz to astonished European ears. Tyler Stovall has traced the story of the black regimental marching bands that captivated France, especially the 369th infantry's Harlem Hellcats, under James Reese Europe, with Noble Sissel as drum major.[3] Pershing was sufficiently impressed by French military bands during World War I to ask the French to set up a school for American band musicians—it is still not clear why the land of John Philip Sousa made such a request. The school, founded in Chaumont to the southeast of Paris, survived the war and grew into a Franco-American arts education center, relocated in Francis I's vast palace in Fontainebleau. Under the direction of the legendary Nadia Boulanger, it trained artists, architects, and musicians, conductors and some of the finest American composers, including Aaron Copland and Leonard Bernstein.

America's black culture, through its musicians, had found special welcome in Europe forty years before Pershing. After the Fisk Singers came Will Marion Cook, black violinist befriended by the Czech composer Antonin Dvorak when he was setting up a New York music conservatory in 1892–94. In Europe Cook's remarkable jazz orchestra was praised by major musicians, including conductor Ernest Ansermet, who proclaimed after a concert that he had heard the future. After World War I, Sidney Bechet and Josephine Baker were the most visible stars of a group of black American musicians and performers who took up residence in France, responding to the demand for the exciting new music and its dance movements. Composers Ravel, Poulenc, Milhaud, and Stravinsky in France, and Weill and Hindemith in Germany, listened closely.

European composers were also exploring the U.S. Frederick Delius, more than a decade before Dvorak, lived in Florida. Before Dvorak's "New World" symphony and his "American" string quartet, Delius drew on American themes and evoked US sites, e.g., *Florida* in 1886, *Appalachia* in 1902, and in 1903 *Seadrift*, an orchestral and choral setting of poems by Walt Whitman. To learn the classical musical tradition, American musicians and composers went to Europe before the Civil War—primarily to Leipzig; after 1920 they went to Fontainebleau and the Rome Academy. American classical musicians began performing abroad in the 1920s.

The impact of the Fisk Singers meant the biggest names at first were black performers. A Fisk product, the classical tenor Roland Hayes began performing in Europe after the First World War, mixing German lieder and spirituals. Marian Anderson captivated Europe and the basso, and actor Paul Robeson, after his London debut as Othello in 1930, earned world fame—for his politics as well as his art.

Pianist-composer George Gershwin, with his New York–fed blend of black and Yiddish sounds, was an icon of American popular music in

Europe; a memorable visit to Paris brought him into touch with an admiring Maurice Ravel, who declined Gershwin's request to study with
him because he preferred first-rate Gershwin to second-rate Ravel. Gershwin's *Porgy and Bess* toured Europe in triumph in the 1950s under State
Department auspices.

Opera, the highest-prestige art of all, remained a European monopoly
well into the 1960s. World stars flowed through New York's Metropolitan
Opera and only slowly did American-born singers perform there. All told,
American performances of opera, and classical music in general, were a
matter of imports. But symphonies and opera houses were slowly hiring
US artists. And the new private conservatories like Curtis, Eastman, and
Juilliard and the great university music schools like Indiana and Kansas
were transplanting European training. Exceptional American singers like
Rosa Ponselle, Gladys Swarthout, and Risë Stevens had followed the path
laid out by Geraldine Farrar, a mainstay at the Metropolitan in the years
1906–22, and performed regularly at the Met in the 1930s. Leonard Warren, Richard Tucker, and Jan Peerce emerged in the 1930s. Tenor Edward
Johnson had to change his birth name to Eduardo di Giovanni for his
career on stage before he reverted to his birth name and became the Metropolitan's general manager.

American classical music, in an organic and gradual process, was a
European import, made accessible to Americans by ingenious public education. After the pioneering work of conductor Leopold Damrosch at the
turn of the century, followed by his sons Frank and Walter, Dvorak and
his benevolent grocer-patroness Jeannette Thurber launched their New
York conservatory. After the First World War, Leipzig-trained Frank
Swarthout built the great music school at the University of Kansas. Conductors like Leopold Stokowski began building the great American orchestras, starting in Philadelphia at the turn of the century, built around
key imports from Europe. For the training of audiences, Walter Damrosch's radio broadcasts in the 1930s educated a nation, and households
tuned in by the millions to the weekly corporate-funded Metropolitan
Opera broadcasts, with the engaging didactic trimmings of Milton Cross.
Audiences were enriched, in the great urban centers, by the influx of Europe's refugees in the 1930s.

The New Deal's attack on the Great Depression made drastic measures
seem appropriate. The federal government intervened in the arts for the
first time in US history with Roosevelt's Works Progress Administration,
which helped musicians survive by subsidizing affordable lessons for
millions and supporting small local orchestras. The depravities of Stalin,
Mussolini, Hitler, and European war injected a stream of great artists into
US music and helped internationalize America's arts. These musical
giants prepared the way for their students. Composers like Schönberg,
Hindemith, Bartok, Stravinsky, and Rachmaninov; conductors like Sto-
kowsi, Toscanini, Koussevitzky, Monteux, and Bruno Walter; performers

like Horowitz, Menuhin, Hoffman, Heifetz, Stern, Milstein, and Rubin-stein—these artists not only taught but set performance standards and helped build paying audiences. In dance similar importation was at work in the case of George Balanchine. In theater and film imports from Germany included Bertholt Brecht, Erwin Piscator, and Max Reinhardt. In literature Thomas Mann was one of several German refugee writers. From France came film-artists René Clair and Jean Renoir, Claudette Colbert and Charles Boyer. In the dynamic US context, America's arts soared, thanks in part to this European influx. With the end of the World War II, two-way flow was reopened and renewed connections with Europe went with the process.

Sports warrant a chapter of their own—they have long been categorized by US bureaucracy among the arts, part of the performing arts office (Cultural Presentations) which stayed in CU until 1977, when it moved into USIA. Like that of the performing arts, the prehistory of sports diplomacy is long. As early as 1888 an all-star baseball team traveled around the world, demonstrating the new national pastime; the initial tour is memorialized in a photo of the uniformed players draped over various parts of Egypt's Sphinx. Volleyball, invented at Springfield College, was a contagious pastime that quickly became the single most popular global sport. Basketball, another Springfield creation, took longer; with the help of US soldiers in the Second World War and finally television, it now covers the world. Baseball and softball have spread less widely, but are prominent in Japan. At Oxford the Americans took up rowing and out-rowed their British friends; Fulbright, at Oxford, starred in another exported US sport, lacrosse. Sports are part of America's universal image, and now the flow has reversed. Americans are playing soccer and rugby and racing bicycles, and Japanese players grace major league baseball.

Sports were not part of the cultural officer's tools until well after the Second World War. Stories of visiting sports teams are traded over drinks by CAOs; one can find dozens of less foolish sports stories in the files than Jacob Canter's story about the White Sox's Chico Carrasquel in Venezuela in 1948. For example, the great Olympic middle-distance runner Mal Whitfield traveled to Africa for USIA in the 1950s and liked the work so much that he spent the rest of a forty-year career there, developing world-class athletes in the sub-Sahara.

American athlete-performers had early excelled in the Olympic Games, begun in Athens in 1908 to articulate the cultural internationalist vision of the Swiss Baron de Coubertin, who saw sports competition and the ethical values embodied in "sportsmanship" as paths to a more peaceful world. In time US participation in the games would take on high diplomatic significance and turn competitive, beginning in 1936 in Nazi Berlin and then, with the cold war, becoming a major cultural jousting field for the U.S., the USSR, and later China.

Films, already noted as a visual art (and assigned to USIA with other "objects" in 1953), were performances. Certainly the greatest cultural impact America had abroad came through this new art form, which developed more quickly in the U.S. than in Europe. Viewed in the U.S. as a popular art, American cinema grew with the help of European imports. The universal icon "Charlot," Chaplin's sad clown—itself a recycled import from the London music halls—swept the globe. American films were soon delighting the world, while their distributors developed dominant commercial channels that would provoke laments about imperial Hollywood and, more recently, globalization.

In all, the private American outflow, especially in popular culture, was sizable. US commercial channels abroad, carrying films and popular music, developed fast and became massively successful. The long history of American performers abroad, like that of US educators, prepared the ground for the government to step in; viable commercial performance channels already existed in Latin America in 1942 when Rockefeller first offered government assistance. When the US government found itself ready to use performances for cultural diplomatic purposes, much of the foundation had already been laid.

The step from the outreach of individual performers through commercial channels to formal and intentional cultural diplomacy is long. Exported performances were part of formal diplomacy long before the Greeks and Romans systematized the exchange, as early humans tried to reach, to touch, to please, and to impress foreign audiences with dance, music, spectacles, theater, and games. But after the fall of Rome, the use of performances by nation-states was rare outside the framework of empire. The great change came a millennium or more later, under the pressures of war, when France decided in 1915 to help its performers move around the world and plead the French cause, with pianist Alfred Cortot in charge.

A dilemma lay buried in the US performing arts: while America was powerful in its popular arts, it was weaker in the classical disciplines— and formal cultural diplomacy has traditionally tended to deal with high culture. At first US cultural diplomats worked on the assumption that the popular arts would flourish on their own; Hollywood certainly needed no help nor did Tin Pan Alley. Since popular art was flowing on its own, the cultural diplomats tended to try to fill gaps, stressing US strides in high culture. Allied to this problem was another: the image left by American popular cultural products like Hollywood's was not always felicitous; sometimes it prompted a strategy of remediation.

US government help began to flow with Rockefeller's commission to Lincoln Kirstein in 1942 of the first officially sponsored overseas performing arts event in US history, the American Ballet Caravan. To choreograph the dancers he was able to hire, Kirstein engaged a young Russian émigré named George Balanchine. For this tour, Balanchine created what would become the New York City Ballet's classic opener *Concerto Barocco*, set to Bach, and the recently revived *Ballet Imperial,* set to Tchaikovsky's second piano concerto.

For performing arts, the Caravan did little more than break the ice, but it was a giant initial step. The US export of performances, until the Eisenhower years, remained random and occasional, and it quickly became obvious, after the Caravan tour, that government alone could not afford to move but only facilitate and supplement performers abroad. Rockefeller's office helped US artists who were already planning a foreign tour to extend their reach. To await the growth of natural commercial channels would have taken decades, even after Rockefeller had primed the pump with a fully funded dance troupe.

Caravan was an expensive precedent, even if the company's budget was only $4,000 per week. The obvious alternative—direct government subsidy, while helping commercial channels grow—was more tempting, but it could not be done everywhere. Where US performances were important but channels inadequate—in the Soviet countries, or in developing countries where there were no theaters or pianos—it was clear that nothing could happen without government help. The USSR would never have seen *Porgy and Bess* or Balanchine's New York City Ballet without US government subsidy. In the performing arts, only government and corporate largesse could start making things happen; if commercial channels failed to grow, the well soon ran dry.

American cultural diplomats began to see three options: funding performances at high cost (full cost); adding small grants to what was being planned (topping off); or letting things develop on their own, standing ready to help with communications or an embassy party (buying in). As with the visual arts, ingenuity and flexibility were indispensable. In all, given congressional disinterest, it is remarkable that since 1942 a great deal of performing arts activity has taken place; the mid-1950s through the early-1970s could be considered the golden years.

As we have seen, Charles Frankel's imaginary CAO, invented in 1965, was knee-deep in peformances, receiving on the same day news of a visit by a college glee club and a major American orchestra and keenly aware of competition from British and Soviet colleagues. When Frankel carried out his field survey in 1963–64, he had no way of knowing he was traveling in a period of boom. In those years it was relatively standard practice for all USIS posts to handle two performing events a year, one large and one small. Major posts facilitated other events, by topping off or buying in. Then, after 1978, when responsibility for performances passed to USIA, fine and performing arts steadily declined, without explanation or apology; finally in 1994 both functions were cut from the USIA budget.

Significantly, Rockefeller began with dance, which already by 1940 reflected a new and deeply American approach to a classic form; US dance was popular culture's contribution to a high art. At a cost of $100,000, Kirstein's Caravan spent 28 weeks in wartime Latin America— Rockefeller's Dartmouth friend Kirstein would shortly move to German occupation duty helping recuperate looted art treaures, before renewing his long and magical association with Balanchine.

In parallel with the fully funded Caravan, State's Division of Cultural Relations persuaded private performers like college glee clubs that they could travel to Latin America cheaply, stay in US homes abroad, and generate thousands of friends. The Coordinator and the division also sent artists—American writers, composers, and a sculptor, classified as performers because they read from their work, lectured, or practiced their art. Writers Waldo Frank and Thornton Wilder—following the success of his Latin America–based novel *The Bridge of San Luis Rey*—had particular impact. Composers conducted performances of their works and occasionally produced compositions honoring their hosts, like Aaron Copland's "El Salón Mexico"—precisely what Copland's friend Darius Milhaud had done in Brazil, as cultural attaché at the French embassy during the First World War.

By 1950 government help in exporting performances was an assumption, however shaky the funding. In the German occupation, the US military sponsored its own orchestra in Berlin, part of Radio in the American Sector (RIAS) and surviving today as Berlin's second orchestra. The German occupation was enriched by solo performers like the young Leonard Bernstein, harpsichordist Ralph Kirkpatrick, and Jascha Heifetz. The Fulbright Program in the 1950s would direct a flow of young Americans into the German opera houses, whereas in proud Italy US singers could study but were kept from performing by union regulations. In Europe and in Latin America, performing arts rested on a slim but firm commercial base; as the years passed, government help steadily reduced to buy-ins and top-offs. Outside Europe and Latin America, where commercial channels had not yet been dredged, little was possible without full funding.

Eisenhower, surely prodded by his friend Rockefeller, took a leap forward; his faith in what he called "people-to-people" included performing artists. Rockefeller's friend USIA director Ted Streibert took credit for persuading Eisenhower to give USIA a special fund for "exhibits," derived of course from Congress. This fund, Streibert boasted, "was the start of sending philharmonic orchestras and other performing artists overseas." The burst of activity and the ample funding, after years of cautious experimentation, took hold and survived until 1994, through vertiginous ups and steeper downs. In 1954 the budget for "Cultural Presentations" climbed to a high point of $3 million but never again reached that level, certainly not in constant dollars.

Under CU director Robert Thayer, a more systematic overseas flow was initiated for music and theater. Thayer introduced peer selection, as a protective means of distancing government from selections, and the American National Theatre Association (ANTA) took over the job. Thayer's CU sent out Helen Hayes in Wilder's *The Skin of Our Teeth* and *Porgy and Bess*, assisting commercial channels. Both took Europe by storm, while *Porgy* opened new avenues for musical theater. Elsewhere, things were happening as well. For example, in Amman, the desert capital of Jordan, those who saw it will never forget the costly engineering miracle of "Holiday on Ice" in 1960, which involved US ice-skaters performing on an artifical rink in the Roman amphitheatre of Philadelphia. In short, the Eisenhower years, with relatively stable funding flows, managed to make performing arts a staple item of formal US cultural diplomacy. For two more decades, as support steadily eroded, performances survived as part of standard USIA-CU fare for the simple reason that everyone wanted them.

During the 1960s, even when Kennedy and Coombs were unable to keep CU budgets at reasonable levels, US performing arts in the field still flowed. To expand the numbers, CU tried low-cost university groups and proved that low-budget foreign barnstorming was a marvelous educational experience for young performers. During my experience in three posts in the Near East and South Asia in 1961-71, there was a continual flow of performers, all appropriate—or made appropriate by the cultural offices—to the milieu in which they were presented. Looking back, I realize that in my cultural offices we spent a good percentage of available time acting as impresario, local troupe manager, press agent, and gofer, on top of our other duties.

At the risk of relying on a single viewpoint, let me summarize the performances in my three posts in the 1960s.[4] Arriving in Lebanon in August 1961 as apprentice to veteran CAO Russ Linch, I learned the post was assured of two performing events per year, one large and one small, perhaps with additional individual performers and others through commercial channels—which in Beirut primarily meant the American University. CU pressed the CAOs and USIS to help performers reach wider and younger audiences, by means including teaching and coaching situations with young counterparts, but also recital-demonstrations. In my first year, Beirut received the Eastman Symphony, the fine student and faculty conservatory orchestra from Rochester, New York, conducted by composer Howard Hanson and his deputy Frederick Fennell. The second year brought a young ballet company that had yet to make its mark in New York, headed by Robert Joffrey. A string quartet, a youthful outgrowth of the Aspen Festival, and an individual performer or two filled out our program. American artists occasionally appeared at the summertime Baalbek Festival, although the competitition from the French was hard to match. Pianist Eugene Istomin appeared commercially for a single performance at the American University and the cultural office bought in.

In those years the thirst for the arts of vision and performance was unquenchable in countries with Western aspirations like Lebanon. But there was a huge problem in bringing arts to such countries: outside the campus of the American University, there was no local professional help available for staging, and no reliable impresario who could rent the hall, clean it, hang posters, sell tickets, and manage the appearances. The cultural office was thus obliged to publicize, present, and stage events with inadequate help, hoping to train professional presenters for future needs. Our choice was simple: either educate impresarios and their staffs, do the work ourselves, or decline performances. Looking ahead, we assumed that educating professionals would allow them, some day, to take over and support a commercially viable and self-sustaining flow. The American University's fine concert hall permitted a modest program of recitals, but the audience centered on the AUB community. Other nations brought their performers to Paris-oriented Beirut: the British brought an occasional Shakespeare play and Emlyn Williams did Charles Dickens; the French occasionally brought a play or a pianist, and more for the Baalbek Festival; the Germans brought a steady stream of chamber musicians, a high-culture effort to remind audiences of the gentler side of Germany's contribution to world history; Italy brought the great cellist Enrico Mainardi.

Locally, there was a lot going on in the performing arts, under improbable conditions. British conductor David Wooldridge had taken over the small Beirut Conservatory chamber orchestra, assembled by some miracle in that fragmented community. The orchestra survived on sheer will power—the White Russian cellist who directed the Beirut Conservatory had to live with Lebanon's system of allocating jobs according to religious communities and would periodically ask me, sadly but with a wry smile, if I could help him find a Shiah Muslim bassoonist. When Wooldridge wanted to perform American music, we borrowed orchestral scores from the USIS libraries in Frankfurt or London. Beyond such help, he relied on his wits, for example composing lyric impressionist pieces of his own evoking local sites. Wooldridge pushed the cultural office, in cooperation with the resident American community, to organize the first children's concerts in Lebanon or the Arab world (so far as I know), including the first performance in Arabic of Prokofief's *Peter and the Wolf*.

One memorable moment illustrated the life of music in Beirut at that time. For a performance in the AUB hall of the Beethoven violin concerto with the British violinist Aldo Parikian, Wooldridge was busy rescoring the French horn parts for trombones and the bassoon parts for tenor saxophone when he learned that the US Sixth Fleet was to pay a visit to Beirut harbor. At his request, the CAO cabled the fleet and helped him borrow two French hornists from the flagship band. Private rehearsals helped the two ordinary seamen perform well beyond their experience. At Wooldridge's insistence, despite the chilly November weather, they wore their sparkling summer white uniforms. At his request, they stood during their long slow-movement dialogue with the solo violin. Parikian brought the two young US Navy musicians to their feet again and again for bows after the performance.

The large foreign community in peacetime Lebanon pitched in. Theater in French-educated Beirut was a national craving, and the private community worked hard to feed it; but the gap between the US-educated and the dominant French-educated majority was wide. USIS staff joined the Anglo-American resident group in mounting three plays per year on the AUB stage, using Anglophone residents and students, American and Lebanese, from the AUB, the French, and the Lebanese universities. The American Repertory Theatre (ART) performed American plays at a decent level of quality, to full houses. Meanwhile members of ART were helping the young French troupe across town. In June 1963 ART gave the first Beirut performance of *The Voyage*, translated by the assistant CAO from the French of the Lebanese playwright Georges Schehadé, a major figure in French theater. For US plays, CU negotiated performance rights, while USIS staff—with tacit permission from the PAO, unreported to Washington—quietly helped with printing and publicity, handled audio effects and music using VOA equipment, and played onstage roles. Lebanese theater, meanwhile, was picking up its own steam—summer performances of *Hamlet* in Arabic were mounted in the ruins of Byblos. Lebanese apprentices from the Anglo-US team performed elsewhere, in French and in Arabic—the group, especially the young AUB students, was a "seedbed of talent," noted Schehadé, who had never before strayed off the Beirut-Paris axis.

USIS brokered, topped off, and entertained American performers, like those recruited for the Baalbek Festival. US choreographer-director Bert Stimmel, working in Cairo under USIS auspices, was invited to Lebanon by the festival, met the staff, and spent years shuttling between Beirut and Cairo, in the tradition of Nilla Cram Cook, building a traveling troupe performing traditional Lebanese dance and music. Various visitors, private and government-sponsored, like Howard Hansen, Istomin, and conductor James De Priest, were welcomed, assisted, and brought into contact with appropriate musician-counterparts. All this was going on in 1961–63 in Beirut, a city of half a million in a country of a million and a half.

Moving to tiny Sri Lanka, population 11 million, in the summer of 1963 for a three-year tour at a time of strained relations with the U.S., I learned on arrival that we were scheduled to have five performances by Duke Ellington and his orchestra in just ten weeks and that nothing had been done. The only large hall in Colombo held no more than seven hundred; so instead we rented the city's race track, set up a rickety galvanized-iron, rain-proof shell in the infield looking up into the stands, and played four concerts to over three thousand listeners each night. Predictably for October, torrential cloudbursts enlivened the performances, with the musicians safe and dry under their shed and the audience sheltered in the stands. Ellington's sound was filtered through ten yards of sheet rain—for years we were teased about the Duke's Water Music.

Additionally, we staged two recitals each—on available pianos—by Ann Schein and Lucy Ishkhanian, and tours by the University of Kansas Brass Ensemble, the University of Illinois Jazz Ensemble, the Cornell Glee Club, and a variety show from Brigham Young University. The university groups were especially attractive, since we were able to put them in touch with Sri Lankan young people around the country and because they showed a healthier side of American youth than normally made the news.

In Colombo, embassy staff played in the local orchestra, sang in the chorus, and performed onstage. Sri Lanka, in the tradition of the British colonies, had its theater group run by the British. Bert Stimmel came to Sri Lanka from Cairo, after we saw a good homegrown British production of *The King and I*, to stage *Kiss Me, Kate*—a future cabinet minister played a role.

In Iran in 1966–71 help continued to come from Washington. The Los Angeles Symphony was a gift for the Shah's coronation in 1967, and we staged a good number of university performing groups: the Georgia State College Brass Ensemble, the Gettysburg College Choir, the Manhattan School Percussion Ensemble, the Milliken University jazz orchestra, and the Amherst College Glee Club. Working with the Tehran Philharmonic Society or simply with the IAS, we helped bring the Dorian Quintet, the New York Dance Quartet, soprano Louise Parker, and pianists James Tocco, Joseph Bloch, Agustin Anievas, and Ruth Slenczynska. With the Shiraz Festival and Iranian TV, we helped the Juilliard Quartet, the Staples Singers, Max Roach and Abby Lincoln, Artur Rubinstein, and Eugene Istomin.

At the IAS, a gifted Anglo-American-French-Iranian theater troupe dotted with past and future professionals began in 1963 with Wilder's *Our Town*; by 1967 they were doing three or four productions per year in the three IAS theaters—an indoor theater, an outdoor amphitheater, and an experimental warehouse stage. Annually there was a musical comedy, two comedies or dramas, and smaller experimental one-act plays in the warehouse theater. IAS also sheltered a choral group; a US international school production of Shakespeare's *Midsummer Night's Dream* was held at the warehouse-theater. Iranian groups were encouraged and assisted by stagecrafter semi-professionals in adapting the theaters for their productions.

The crowd-pleaser was a jazz ensemble pulled together from resident Americans and a Teagarden-inspired British trombonist, playing in styles ranging from Dixieland to the Cool, mixing in Iranian and other foreign folk tunes; the group performed monthly, outdoors when weather permitted, to large audiences of over a thousand.

In Sri Lanka and Iran, CU—which sent most of the performers—knew our cultural offices were ready for any challenge. In 1965, when events in Indonesia caused cancellation of a Far Eastern tour of the University of Illinois jazz group, we offered to fill the gap in their schedule by staging them in Sri Lanka; we sent them to various provincial cities, while carrying out our previous comitment to stage the Cornell Glee Club in Colombo. The CAO at the time of this double visit was flat on his back with a case of dengue fever.

Sports in the 1960s, in my three posts, were constant. There were resident basketball coaches for Lebanon and Iran, demonstration basketball teams for Lebanon (the Philips Oilers), Sri Lanka (Springfield College), and Iran (University of Kentucky), plus US soccer teams for Lebanon and Iran. Most of these played against inadequate national teams, hence spent more time teaching and, in the case of basketball, imparting the crucial skills of refereeing.

A superb example of the attractive possibilities of university groups took place in Sri Lanka in 1965 with eleven performances by the Kansas University Brass Ensemble, directed by the energetic thirty-two-year-old barnstormer Kenneth Bloomquist. Kansas was given a contract at bare subsistence rates for an extended tour of South Asia. Bloomquist, an amateur carpenter, spent a month in his garage, building special carrying crates for the instruments, to save money and space and to make sure they fit into the cargo doors of available aircraft. The young Kansans played an opening concert in Colombo, then traveled all over the island before returning for a repeat in Colombo, totaling twelve concerts in eleven cities. They played at nightfall in galvanized-iron sheds improvised on village greens throughout the island. Audiences ran over a thousand wherever they appeared, for a total audience of at least fifteen thousand. In the tropical rain forest of Sri Lanka, they were lucky that only one performance was interrupted by driving rain, in the hilltown of Ratnapura, where the deluge was heavy enough to cause a power failure. With the help of the local police, the group moved into the Town Hall and played to a packed house by the light of dozens of candles reflecting from the gleaming brass instruments. Ann Bloomquist, a lyric soprano, performed Gershwin, Sri Lanka's national anthem, and the Star Spangled Banner. It was her first trip abroad; in Sri Lanka she began her collection of world folk music, especially children's songs, which led to a successful publishing and teaching career of her own.

While no one will ever know what the Sri Lankans who attended these concerts heard, saw, or learned, what the Kansans learned is known. One stalwart of the Kansas group, Bill Lane, today is principal horn for the Los Angeles Philharmonic; trumpeter Roy Gunther heads the music department at the George Washington University; Clarence Ayala recently retired from the top of Hawaii's state education system; and the rest are top-flight musicians in various cities, with several teaching in universities. Meanwhile the Bloomquists moved on to Michigan State, their lives forever transformed. First they tried to join USIA to do cultural work fulltime, but USIA's lack of enthusiasm convinced them to stick to private diplomacy and they began organizing tours around the world. Over three decades, they led two dozen group tours abroad, covering fifty countries; more than fifteen hundred young American musicians traveled and performed with them; and hundreds of thousands of foreign audiences and students heard them and worked with them in coaching sessions. Ann published her collections of folk songs and choral arrangments for world distribution. "The experience taught us, by its example, the worth of all people, and the value of the arts in promoting peace and understanding," wrote Bloomquist.[5] Although we know little about the Sri Lankan reaction, none of the original Kansans was the same after the visit to South Asia. The paltry cost of the first Kansas tour produced life-changing impacts on more lives than one can count.

Most visiting performers taught, coached, and befriended people wherever we sent them. The dancers taught class; the musicians gave master-classes; the performers listened to younger performers; Ellington and four sidemen visited Radio Ceylon, at an improbable early morning hour, where they recorded and interacted with Sri Lankan musicians. In Beirut Ellington recorded two programs for the city's radio jazz program, initiated in 1962 by the cultural office and the local VOA chief, who sent the tapes for follow-up in Colombo. In Sri Lanka the Illinois jazz group's percussionist outdueled two Sri Lankan drummers; athletes coached and taught refereeing; and young people mixed with young people. It was a practice, at least in posts I know, that US musical groups would play or sing the national anthem and perform local music. The cultural office did everything possible to move performers out of the capital cities. We helped them leave behind something of human value.

What did all this mean? Cynics look back and call it trivial, in light of the collapse of civilized behavior in the Near East since 1970, but others recognize that, in the 1960s, there was still hope that the thin veneer of the East-West synthesis might be strong enough some day to survive the turmoil that was surging up underneath. Looking only at Beirut, star performers like Ellington, Joffrey, Istomin, and Hansen had special historical meaning simply because they came to Lebanon. The country's long Western tradition reached back to Hellenism and the Crusades; and it had been colonized in cultural terms by France's Jesuits in the seventeenth century. In the first twenty years of the postwar period, it was an island of Westernizing intellect, tolerance, prosperity, and moderation in a sea of nationalisms. By 1961 the "events"—as the US Marines' brief 1958 intervention was called—were still fresh in memory, but clearly there were greater dangers ahead. The cultural office knew, from Fulbright teachers and UN friends, that the *madrassahs* flourishing in the Palestinian refugee camps were relentlessly teaching the hatred of Israel and little more. In this turmoil, the educated classes of Lebanon and their students at the country's universities sought to shape a viable and sensitive two-way synthesis with the West, respectful of both sides of the equation, that might endure over time. And the West in turn was seeking to support and reassure them, to say that they were not forgotten, that the enduring links were still there, and that the potential for future cooperation was rich.

US performances, surely a minor tool in the struggle for civilization in the Near East, were highly visible; they seemed to us to play a central role. They provided glimpses of an attractive internationalist alternative to destructive regional nationalism. In a Near East dominated by brutish politics and suppressed violence, USIS cultural officers in the 1960s knew, without writing it into their telegraphic Country Plans, that the arts reached beyond the banality and brutality of daily life, conveyed the joys and beauties of a peaceful world, provided insights into the US national character and identity, stimulated thoughts about Lebanon's own identity, and even brought moments of Aristotelian catharsis. American performers in the 1960s, as we watched them at work in distant outposts, added a helpful US presence in that turbulent area; US performers helped us remind audiences that there was more to life than technical and economic progress—Schehadé's Boeings—and a great deal more than oil-generated revenue.

There were also the deeper habits, those of the mind and the heart. The arts offered glimpses into what humankind valued, and they exposed audiences to the sounds and sights of democracy. Through it all, perhaps especially in the case of the younger performers, ran a subtle message of freedom, the kind that jazz projected in Eastern Europe with special impact. It was a refreshing antidote to the crushing boredom and grinding futility of the never-ending political discussions that served as the national pastime, along with backgammon, in the Near East.

In Beirut we had an unspoken subtheme: we tried to remind the Lebanese that our beloved colleagues, the French, though not always seeming to be America's best friends, made common cause with the U.S. when the chips were down. We wanted to show Lebanon that the two nations stood together, despite their quibbles, on basic values. The joint French-American theater project to produce Schehadé's *Voyage* in Beirut went further, reminding our friends that the two nations working together made a very good team.

• • •

Since records of other places are distant and ill-recorded, I have focused on my own experience in the Near East and South Asia. But similar things were happening everywhere. As we have seen, USIS Mexico during the war helped Hollywood upgrade the Mexican film industry; performances fostered by the US occupations in Germany and Japan and behind the Iron Curtain reminded these nations that countries did not live by bread alone; and Tom Palazzolo's visit to Tehran may have contributed to the exciting Iranian film industry of the last decades. It is easy to overlook the sound US intentions behind early cultural efforts in Vietnam. In 1955 USIS Saigon cooperated with the Vietnamese government in making the first Vietnamese films—a weekly newsreel, plus two AID "how-to" films and one political film every month. Meanwhile, USIS officers Fred Rein and John Campbell managed a traveling drama troupe presenting folk theater through the southern part of the country, from the back of a van. In 1964 Sri Lankan theater discovered the translatability of Tennessee Williams, relocating his plays in a historical Sri Lanka. In 1976 in Abidjan, visiting cultural officer Philip Benson directed a production, in

French, with local actors in national costumes, of Eugene O'Neill's *Ah, Wilderness*, reset for the Ivory Coast.[6] These are only a few amidst the dozens of stories CAOs tell each other.

Back in Washington, things were less joyful in CU's office of "Cultural Presentations" as performances were named. With all the success—and the obvious value—of these efforts by individual officers around the world, decline of funding was relentless. For Congress, performing arts were never as controversial as the visual arts, but there were invariable problems. Negative press attention to the Adams variety show in 1962, multiple postponements of the USSR visit of *Hello, Dolly!*, a legendary jazz musician sent home for alleged drug use—these were minor events, magnified by the prominence of the performers. On the other hand, especially with student groups, it helped that a congressman occasionally noticed university groups traveling from his or her home district.

Philip Coombs in 1961, in pushing through the new Fulbright-Hays legislation, had opened a long-sought possibility no one had believed possible: helping foreign governments send performers to the U.S.—the so-called reverse flow. But it was a lost cause; predictably Congress never approved funding for the idea. Ironically, the first reverse-flow event in US history that colleague CAOs can remember took place in December 2003 when the State Department invited the National Symphony of Baghdad to perform in Washington, for reasons which must be obvious. The event, an embarassing piece of propaganda, was a mixed success. While those present were moved, in the presence of the presidential couple, to see the Iraqi players sitting amidst the players of Washington's National Symphony, with cellist Yo-Yo Ma playing in the cello section, *Washington Post* critic Tim Page quietly caught the ironies that others missed: as he said, State "flew 60 musicians the 6,200 miles from Baghdad to play for less than an hour, . . . rarely have so many traveled so far to do so little." With high praise for the traditional Iraqi instrumentalists who performed on the program, Page noted the lavish follow-up: an American foundation had completed a drive to furnish the entire Baghdad orchestra with new instruments; another group contributed scores for five hundred works. The Secretary of State made the stunning claim that the event denoted "the historic re-entry of Iraqi culture on the world scene." Cordell Hull, had he been there, might have echoed Golda Meir in asking what took America so long.[7] It will come as no surprise to know that there has been no reverse flow event since then, even from Iraq.

In 1962 John J. Rooney caught up with CU, and Coombs paid the price. Exploiting the newly opened possibilities of the Fulbright-Hays legislation, he had inherited a CU budget for performing arts of $2.5 million, and in 1962 previously scheduled US performers dating to Thayer's years went to 306 cities in ninety-two countries. But Coombs's deputy Max Isenbergh took the heat for a far-reaching disaster launched by Thayer. A variety troupe headed by stand-up comedian Joey Adams was traveling around Southeast Asia when national columnist Dorothy Kilgallen, animated by irrepressible nastiness and fed by a source from inside the troupe, wrote a series of biting columns regarding the performances.[8] To Congressman Rooney, the stores were raw meat and the resultant cuts were vicious, impacting heavily on the total CU budget. Battle, replacing Coombs, suspended all performances and moved ahead cautiously, building unassailable peer-review panels, stressing inexpensive and congressionally popular university groups—which many CAOs outside Europe preferred in any case.

When USIA absorbed CU, three different and conflicting arguments were buried in the general downgrading of performances. One line of thought, left over from the German and Japanese occupations, insisted that the U.S. had to go first class or not at all, an absurd idea outside Europe and not a good idea even in Europe where commercial channels claimed the first-class performers. A second line of thought came out of the informationist hard-liners who decried performing arts because, by definition, they were mass-oriented products that could not deliver targetted policy messages. And a third group of USIA insiders, bent on tighter control of field activities, had begun to notice that cultural officers spent a great deal of time on performances, time taken away from the priorities PAOs wanted to set. The third group was not wrong; I would estimate that 20 percent of my total energies in the decade of the 1960s went into performances, but in assessing this cost, critics as usual overlooked the value of the product.

Overall, it was a losing battle. By the mid-1970s CU-funded performances were tapering off. CU's performance budget had dropped from $2.5 million to $500,000 by 1970 and only rose to $1 million when Congress was reminded that East European treaty commitments *required* performances. This opened a tiny door, allowing performing groups designed for the USSR on occasion to be routed through other countries, although rarely to places outside Europe. Rome, during the bicentennial year of 1976, received a visit from the Los Angeles Symphony, returning from Poland, and a major show of painting on its way to Yugoslavia. European countries outside the Bloc occasionally shared Moscow's rich fare, including Washington Arena Stage productions of *Our Town* and *Inherit the Wind*, Jessica Tandy and Hume Cronyn in *The Gin Game*, Mahalia Jackson, Louis Armstrong, Duke Ellington, the dance companies of Merce Cunningham, Paul Taylor and Alvin Ailey, the Los Angeles Symphony, and the New York City Ballet. But for the world outside Europe there was next to nothing.

In fact, the era of performances was already over, killed by Rooney; an equally difficult successor from North Carolina would not be inclined to revive it. By 1975, even European posts expected no performers, other than what they could buy into or scrape up locally—a full-time national employee in Paris did just that. Where the commercial flow was healthy, the embassy and USIS sometimes helped out, gave a reception, invited local leaders to performances, or suggested possible didactic spin-off appearances. The cultural offices had no choice but to develop the classic top-off and buy-in techniques, but many—encouraged by their PAOs—decided the effort was not worth the candle and forgot about performances. Minimal in Europe, in the developing world performances were all but history.

In the early 1980s, USIA's Near East office watched the Middle East drift away from Western cultural values, as governments were wrested from the hands of the educated. USIA's best young Arabists pondered ways to reach the new leadership, in the hope of maintaining some kind of contact with semiliterate audiences. Various popular arts, including break-dancing, were explored. The McLain Family Band performed its country music in the Arabian peninsula and Saudi Arabia, although the Saudis insisted that female band members perform behind screens. Since high culture was not feasible in the area, the search focused on popular and street culture, to what end was not entirely clear.[9]

In particular, USIA values overlooked the value of performances after the Soviet implosion, and CAOs were actively discouraged from supporting performers. Even in Europe, top-off depended on the whim of ambassadors. In the early 1990s the book industry of a key European nation brought twenty top American writers and poets to the capital for its annual book fair, at considerable expense. The organizers asked the embassy for nothing more than one of its glittering receptions at the showcase residence, to which the ambassador had loaned several paintings from a magnificent family collection. The CAO's pleas were turned away for weeks; finally the ambassador agreed to put on a small reception, with a restricted guest list and minimal food. One of the visiting US writers commented that it was the stingiest reception she had ever attended. Such things are better not done than done badly.

If in Europe there was too little, in the developing countries there was nothing at all. The growth of commercial channels under gentle USIS tutelage had slowly ground to a halt and the structures quickly decayed. With less commercial traffic, the image of America as a seedbed of art went dark. After the merger of CU and USIA in 1977, USIS posts had to get along with videos, photo shows, and news releases.

The Reagan team in 1981 pledged to get government off everyone's back. In a concealed drive to eliminate all federal funding for the arts and humanities, the new Congress allowed both National Endowments to languish, and USIA leadership dropped Arts America to the bottom of its priorities. By 1984 the U.S. had turned its back on UNESCO. But soon the new team unwittingly proved the opposite of what was intended. After 1985, it was obvious to any honest observer that the private sector could not take on the job of helping American visual and performing arts reach abroad at the proper level to all the diplomatic outposts in the world. A disheartened private sector abandoned hope of enlightened government cooperation.

In fact, the needs of 150 countries around the world were too complex to be met by private energies without some kind of central coordination and a network of motivated field staff. Since performances abroad had few domestic constituents, no voice was raised in Congress. By 1992 the Clinton team, obsessed with balancing the budget, harped on costs and ignored benefits.

Yet odd things happened as the whims of the powerful ricocheted here and there. Shortly after Wick took charge of USIA in 1981, his piano teacher, from a Pennsylvania college, wandered into the new USIA-CU, now called the E Bureau. On orders from the top, bypassing the Arts America office, he was put on a generous salary and given an office. He devised the pretentious name "Artistic Ambassadors" and, ignoring the agreements for peer review, established his own peer panel. The panel was impressive; it selected young unknown pianists. The field was only too eager to stage any performer. The program's didactic stress focused on music conservatories—in the tradition of CAOs in the period 1955-75. Untried new talents were especially useful outside the prestigious concert halls of Europe. From pianists, he moved to other solo instruments and was preparing to try small ensembles. His most original and unprecedented achievement was to commission original scores by important American composers so that each performer could present the world premiere of a new piece.

The Artistic Ambassadors idea was *sui generis*—it succeeded in a vacuum, but it was unreplicable. Indeed, had it continued to grow to cover the world, it would have reconstituted CU's Office of Cultural Presentations, at a higher cost in staff and budget. Before then, it would have come to the attention of Congress, no longer concealed as a salary, expenses, office space, and travel funds. The experiment showed that USIS posts were hungry for performers and that young performers would play for little or no reward other than experience—just as we had learned from the university groups of the 1960s. At the same time, it proved that performances on a global scale raised serious problems in Washington. For global coverage, fullhearted and enlightened government facilitation were indispensable adjuncts to private energies.

The 1980s proved that private funding alone could not do the job. In the 1990s Clinton's USIA faced a choice: either fund the arts more or less adequately, or drop them entirely. With no interest in Congress, under an administration obsessed with budgets, USIA arts funding dwindled until 1994, when Arts America was finally put out of its misery. There was no press announcement of the decision, and no mourning for what had been lost. In fact, no one in America noticed that an era had ended.

Late in the Clinton years, a glamorous and star-studded conference at the White House asserted that "the arts" in diplomacy were a very good thing indeed, apparently without knowing that the current administration had itself caused the arts cut-off. Conferees agreed on the importance of global art exchange, although porous definitions of key terms meant that few knew what they were agreeing to. While the enthusiasm was pleasant, it was too late for change. Rebuilding will be more than a matter of budgets. It will require experienced field staffs, willing local sponsors, and relaxed security restrictions. It will take years of stability and growth merely to return to where we were in the 1960s.

America, as John F. Kennedy proclaims from the inscription etched in the marble walls of his eponymous Center for the Performing Arts in Washington, continues to look forward expectantly. But Americans who know politics see little chance of change. As for foreign audiences, Potomac gridlock is an irrelevant mystery; they see only the absence of a one-time staple—US fine and performing artists—as further proof that America has forgotten them.

CHAPTER NINETEEN

Intellect, Government, and Fulbright Drift

> [Mutual understanding] has to do with the rectification of imbalances of intellectual power; with the removal of hindrances to communication and negotiation; with the control of cultural aggression, witting or unwitting; with the creation of institutions and enterprises in which there is an international stake, so that the edge is taken off international hostilities and the reasons for keeping peace are multiplied.
>
> —Charles Frankel, 1967

FRANKEL'S DEFEAT TURNED UP A DEEP PROBLEM underlying his two tumultuous years in Washington. It taught anyone who cared to listen that the rules of scholarship or the values of the university campus did not apply in American government. The university intellectual has long been uncomfortable in and with the general culture of foreign service, and Frankel's story, before the Vietnam era drove intellect and government even farther apart, shows why. Superb intellectuals had dotted the foreign service since it came into existence in 1924, but they had to cope with the fundamental context of nonintellect that prevailed, driven by real-time deadlines, among other factors. For cultural diplomats, by definition members of a select club called the foreign service once they have committed their careers to it, reconciling intellect and government was no minor issue. It was, perhaps, the only issue.

The Frankel experiment was more than a loss for cultural diplomacy, it was a defeat for intellect in government. For cultural diplomats, the issue lay at the heart of American ambivalence about cultural diplomacy, both before and since its institutionalization in 1938. The American republic, in its political life, is unusual among great nations in its mistrust of intellect and intellectuals, reflecting wariness by the general public. The world's great nations since Greece recruited their best intellects for government and especially for diplomacy. Nations always sent abroad their best educated, most learned, cultured, and creative citizens. But US political process has never been comfortable with this idea, which arose most vividly in the days of FDR's Brain Trust. The administrations of Wilson, then Roosevelt and Kennedy, showed the limits of government's ability to absorb certified intellectuals. American political discourse is less anti-intellectual than non-intellectual: American politics does not oppose intellect, it merely ignores it.

Discomfort with intellect explained the ferocity of Rooney's attacks on his fellow Brooklynite, after he had torn the economist Coombs to pieces. For cultural diplomacy, the discomfort was not new; it had been the unspoken subtext of clashes, some civil and some not, between Hull and Welles, Cherrington and Benton, Fairbank and "Mary" Miles, Welles and Rockefeller, MacLeish and Truman, Morey and Ambassador Kirk, Fulbright and McCarthy, and Coombs and Sorensen. The young Fulbright, arriving in the House, said he would grade his congressional colleagues no higher than a B−.[1] In Congress he adopted the folksy cracker-barrel campaign-style he used in the Ozarks, to get along with his colleagues.

Frankel, of course, had not been elected, hence was fair game for Rooney. Certainly he was more of a threat than Coombs. He was a philosopher of public life who, except for his years with naval intelligence, had lived totally in the university world. His article in *Foreign Affairs* preceding his first book wryly called intellectuals "scribblers," a deprecatory eighteenth-century epithet. He opened the question of the "scribblers" because he wanted an answer as to their place in government. Unfortunately, he got one.

Frankel, in fact, was like Coombs and hundreds of other politically appointed intellectuals in one respect: he knew little about the realities of Washington life, and he knew less than he should have about the history of American cultural diplomacy—in fact, few Americans were expert on either. Scholar-CAOs like Rufus Morey, had Frankel known him, were perfect models of his "compleat" cultural attaché. Building a decent cultural diplomatic presence in his beloved Italy, Morey tried to make it possible for other Moreys to serve in countries appropriate to their expertise. Morey himself stayed in service for five years and urged longer in-country service for all CAOs. Frankel agreed. He believed his country deserved the privilege of sending an Irwin Edman or a Jacques Barzun or a John Dewey as a philosopher-diplomat to occupy an office in US embassies around the world, and he knew that many such people would rejoice in the opportunity. Frankel's idea of a CAO was distilled from interviews with field staff, but it was also shaped by the world of intellect he knew from the inside, a world of teacher-scholars, defined by their teaching and research and judged only by colleagues and peers. The values of his world were not understood by the country or by its elected representatives in Washington.[2]

A greater percentage of Americans study past the post-secondary level than do citizens of any country in the world, but few cross the desk to teach or earn gradual access to collegial relationships with their teachers in graduate school. Even educated Americans have little understanding of the criteria and the values of intellect, of the life of the mind, of the community of scholars, of lives spent searching for new truth. This is a world captured by Frankel's colleague Jacques Barzun's *House of Intellect*, or by the collection of ACLS's annual Haskins Lectures, under the collective title "A Lifetime of Learning." Some graduates, having suffered at the hands of faculty—as Voltaire and Diderot suffered at the hands of their Jesuit masters—will never be comfortable among them, any more than the White House staffer in the Clinton transition who vetoed a prominent professor of law for an appropriate position because he had once given him a C.

At the center of Frankel's thinking was the academic intellectual, especially as defined by the tradition of the great American research universities.[3] His models were the men and women he knew at Columbia. In that sense, he aimed too high; perhaps his child prodigy self-assurance did not always help his cause. But he posed the issue clearly: intellect is uncomfortable in US public life.

In the eighteenth century Jefferson, Franklin, and Paine, intellectuals by any definition, traded on their identity as "scientists" in a world where science meant knowledge, where knowledge was power, and where intellect was international. Another century passed before US universities began to become research institutions, in the sense that they created new knowledge. Until well after the Civil War, US colleges merely transmitted existing knowledge. Production of new knowledge through graduate scholarship, science, and research began then and flourished only after the First World War. Humboldt graduate Daniel Coit Gilman first founded Yale's Sheffield School for science, then struggled to transform Berkeley, and finally opened the first US research-based university in 1876, The Johns Hopkins University. Three decades later Carnegie, with the help of Gilman's friend and fellow Humboldt graduate Andrew White, began to push American science to reach beyond its shores; the senior Rockefeller and his advisor Frederick Gates reached high in founding the University of Chicago. US scholarship, by the end of World War I, had begun to lift the level of American cultural and intellectual contact with the world. Except for Justin Morrill's enlightened post–Civil War land-grant college legislation and the funding it ensured at the state level, US political life and its legislators had little to do with this growth.

Intellectuals had conducted informal cultural diplomacy for America since Franklin went to Paris; for a century, well into the 1930s, the U.S. relied on the private world of intellect to foster relations abroad. The early American diplomats themselves came from the small world of college graduates, and it was to be expected that the cultural officers of the 1940s would be university-based. State's division of cultural relations, Rockefeller's office, OSS, OWI, the BFS, the Smith-Mundt advisory commission, the German and Japanese reorientations—all were heavily staffed by imposing academic figures.

For the CAO-intellectuals, this began to change after World War II; thirty years later it reached a symbolic end when USIA, against faint protests from Fulbright's presumed heir Claiborne Pell, announced that its foreign service officers would be recruited not as substantive specialists but as generalists. In the authorization hearings of 1974, one can see the precise turning point: Pell suggested that scholars were required for CAO positions; USIA chief James Keogh, without explanation, asserted the contrary: "It is in the national interest, and we are better off, to produce our own cultural officers in our own system rather than depend upon recruiting them in a lateral sense from the academic world." Pell, rarely persistent in his questioning, inquired about quality and substance: how will USIA acquire CAOs with the credentials of "a university professor or writer or painter"? Keogh ducked and restated his position that USIA needs "cultural generalists," covering a "broad cultural spectrum." USIA can ship out all the visiting experts it needs, but on-the-ground CAOs must be generalist-administrators. Pell came back for a third try: is it possible to acquire a scholarly reputation in government? He said, "If you get to a high level, I think you need a man with his own reputation; . . . to be a guest at the Académie Française or be accepted in the Royal Academy, you have to be a man who has a reputation of his own, and this is what we want to see in the cultural officer ranks." Keogh, eager to escape from Pell and his colleagues, mumbled agreement, closing off the discussion. Pell, summing up, warned Keogh that the question would remain open. In fact, it remained closed and nothing was done by either side.[4]

As a distracted Congress looked the other way, USIA pursued the generalist path, recruiting only one "super-CAO" after 1974 until its end in 1999. The sole super-CAO case was an exception brought about by an insistent ambassador and frustrated by an unsupportive USIA, with the result that the incumbent declined to stay for a planned second year.

The design of formal cultural diplomacy in 1938 was built on the university model. Scholars on loan were its building blocks; in the field all positions were staffed by intellectuals with secure academic positions; and its supervisory bodies sparkled with intellect. No one questioned the presence of academics; on the contrary they were deemed indispensable, if only because they were able to relate to and manage other scholars, American and foreign. But there were rough edges to this design, from the beginning. Scholar CAOs could be intimidating, or challenging, or at the very least unfamiliar to those unused to the university world. When the academic CAO Charles Stevens in Mexico, after two brilliant years, was placed under the supervision of Guy Ray, disaster came quickly; when John Brown irritated his information colleague, the threat of fisticuffs was the answer. The academic cultural officers, in USIA's standard excuse, "did not always work out."

In the U.S. intellectuals can be intimidating—especially when they, in their wisdom, feel intimidated themselves among practiced professionals. The world's cultural services depend on intellectuals, but in the US case men like Morey—who could showcase American intellect, display the depth of US interest in a host country, criticize existing scholarship in that country, and help foster and guide future research—were objects of fear, even when, like Morey, they were incapable of threatening anyone. Like Ricci and Valignano, the early US cultural diplomatic theorists knew that scholars were better at sustaining discourse with other scholars than with non-scholars.

Scholars are difficult by nature because they jealously protect their first priority, dedication to their field and their research. But there is more: scholarship is a mindset. Scholars practice skepticism, they question accepted realities, they are relatively certain about what they know and open to provocative hypotheses about what they do not. The natural tensions between scholars and diplomats are obvious. Embassies manage relations from day to day, through development of flexible policy and practice; they live in a different knowledge-culture from the slower-paced research-oriented university dwellers, for whom ample time is a given. Diplomats report and make decisions on the basis of the best information they can get. At staff meetings, the master of the fifteen-second sound bite wins the day. The gap between these two modes of learning can be managed, more or less skillfully, but insecurity inhibits both sides. The scholar's attitude can be unnerving in an embassy world facing the need for answers in real time, while the practitioners' decisiveness can raise different problems.

When they serve as cultural officers, scholars specializing in the host country encourage, evaluate, contribute to, and interpret research. Those whose scholarship focuses elsewhere, like South Asian scholar Wayne Wilcox in London or labor-economist Robert Brooks in New Delhi, soon found colleagues in their fields and were certified as "university people"—*universitaires*, as the French call them. The easygoing Wilcox, a broad-gauged South Asianist political scientist who knew British politics, was rare in earning the respect of the embassy's political section. More often scholars, in one degree or another, are not easily assimilated into embassies.

In contrast to the reductionism of diplomatic reporting, intellectuals are more interested in complicating things. They can seem obstructionist; their style—intended as irony—can be confused with sarcasm; their bearing can seem arrogant, distant, or patronizing—adjectives regularly found in their personnel evaluations. The Wellesean founders, in the early design of American cultural relations, were not blind to the risk, but they accepted it as a necessary cost, trusting that in time the CAOs would learn the new culture as well as the embassies and that modes of operation would be devised.

In early 1945 MacLeish pondered the wisdom of absorbing OSS into the Division of Cultural Relations and decided to go slow. As Librarian of Congress and director of OFF, he knew William Langer's brilliant stable of researchers; he himself was comfortable with intellect and in time he might have decided to absorb that shop and turn his office into a university department of high quality. But his successor William Benton, from a different world, had few doubts: he declined the invitation to integrate the Langer shop. Instead of a university, Benton built a public relations firm. In the decision not to integrate OSS CU lost brains. Most of the intellectuals gathered by Donovan, finding no interest in Washington, returned to their universities, and the CIA had to build around those who remained.

In field posts the academic CAOs were often skillfully handled—or manipulated—by USIA's senior PAOs. Some were channeled into the role of high-gloss windowdressing, showcase figures who were relieved of paperwork, delivered lectures, and stayed out of the way. Cleanth Brooks, in London, remembered delivering hundreds of lectures, answering puzzler research questions, chairing the Fulbright Commission, sitting on boards, and leaving administrative work to others. But while Brooks was on the road, Washington managed to do what it could not do before—close the pathfinding USIS library in London. Other scholar-diplomats saw the dilemma clearly and lost interest after returning to their campuses—only Winks, James Roach, and Wilcox insisted on managing their portion of the post's administration. Winks and Roach, after their field assignments, followed cultural diplomacy closely and contributed over the years. Wilcox, at the moment of his untimely death, was negotiating to stay in London for a second tour—and was open to a longer-range career.

Beginning in 1942, cultural field staffing went through four phases. First, through the 1940s, it was all academic. Then came a mix of academics who became committed insiders, toiling alongside officers who felt at home in cultural work; this group manned CAO jobs through the 1950s and into the early 1970s, bonding in a committed foreign-service CAO corps, with occasional outsider super-CAOs. In the third phase, beginning around 1973, generalists began their slow and final takeover: suggesting in 1965 that scholars should fill all CAO positions, Frankel was told that scholars would not take such positions—like every CAO, he knew better. During the third phase distinguished intellectuals remained in the cultural office in London until they too were discontinued in 1976. The London CAOs had long been the obvious homage USIA paid to an idea it denied in theory: the indispensability of intellect in the world's major capitals. In the fourth phase, when USIA acquired complete control—especially after Fulbright left the Senate—the academics faded away. London's last outsider, aside from an unqualified Reagan appointee, left in 1976.

In the Fulbright world things were different. On the urging of people like Morey and the BFS over time, research was a formal function of the Fulbright Program. When Smith-Mundt opened the doors for two-way flow, the program outgrew the Senator's original Rhodes-derived vision. The best cultural diplomats, and especially the scholar-diplomats, were surrounded by field researchers from the universities, and interchange with them provided the two-way revitalization that the cultural diplomat needed. The academic CAOs helped foreign and US scholars, and the scholars, in turn, served as informal instructors to the cultural office and to embassy colleagues who wanted to learn.

All this was obvious to Frankel, even if he understated the difficulties of mastering the chaos, but USIA's leaders closed their minds to the advantages his ideas might have brought to USIA. Focused instead on the eternal circular search for language to wring budgets out of a reluctant Congress, in support of policy and news transmission, USIA's top officers were thrown off balance by cutting-edge research that suggested change. USIS informationists were skilled journalists—first-drafters of history—who worked with other journalists. But they were uneasy among scholars, witness Guy Ray's discomfort with Mexican intellectuals in the 1940s. In fairness, scholars are often no less comfortable dealing with skilled press and media professionals.

Ironically, USIA had a "research" division, with regional research officers scattered around the world. But "research" in this context meant only "market research" i.e., polling, the research of George Gallup rather than the humanistic cultural studies of William Langer. USIA's research arm circulated public-opinion poll results widely in Washington—domestic politics were sometimes known to shape the questions USIA asked—and these poll results had a way of filtering into presidential electoral campaigns. The polls were part of USIA's luster in Washington. News about the poor position of the U.S. in one or another country, weapons gaps, or global attitudes toward the "space race"—all this could be useful to politicians.

Frankel had another kind of research in mind. He wanted a means of looking more closely at other political cultures and the processes of international intellectual and educational interchange. In 1967, in joint talks with the Yugoslav foreign and education ministers, he broached the idea of a binational research survey, built around scholars chosen by learned societies, to "review the entire range of Yugoslav-American educational relations." At the same time, Japanese-U.S. talks were struggling to apply outside intellect to understanding problems in the Japan-U.S. relationship. Both of these were slow-moving efforts, and Frankel, frustrated by Washington resistance, wanted something quicker. He turned to short-term visits by scholar-friends, realizing that the funds going into a single USIA public opinon survey would permit three or four American scholars to spend four months each abroad. He asked his Columbia colleague Fritz Stern to look at Germany; then he invited his colleague, Middle East scholar Jacob C. Hurewitz, to visit Iran and Turkey in the summer of 1967.

Hurewitz, a self-starting scholar with deep area experience, including a stint with government, interviewed friends and various embassy officers, including the CAO teams. A dialogue on research remains in the mind of the then-CAO in Iran: the Fulbright Program was sending Iranian "researchers" to the U.S. and bringing American "researchers" to Iran, so he asked how one involved in the exchange defined "research" and then pressed for means of assessing its quality. The post had naturally relied on IIE and CIES peer panels to review Fulbright work and took their word as to quality; in Iran they were flying blind. Hurewitz reminded them that the scholarly world judged research by peer review and publication, and he suggested new ways of evaluating research in and on Iran. From these discussions came the US research institute in Tehran, the American Institute of Iranian Studies. In Iran's growing universities, a valid research dimension was the indispensable next step. Hurewitz's report to Frankel has never been made public.[5]

Deprived of academic cultural officers, CU under Frankel and his successor John Richardson set aside funding for short exploratory visits like Hurewitz's and for evaluative research into existing programs. Richardson also initiated a history project in CU, inviting reflection on the past. While budgets were small, the bureau chiefs knew that research is not expensive. Much of this internal or "operations" research was in-house work for the CU family. To no one's surprise, CU's history project and research capacity vanished when USIA absorbed CU in 1978.

Individual ambassadors, professional and political, had also noted the need for depth and substance in their work. Since USIA ignored this kind of research, several ambassadors took matters into their own hands. When Richard Holbrooke went as ambassador to Germany, a country about which he admittedly knew little, he insisted on bringing along historian Fritz Stern for a few months to help him get started. Earlier, ambassador to Germany and economist Arthur Burns borrowed political scientist William Griffith from MIT. Harvard's Edwin O. Reischauer, a major Japan scholar who was named Kennedy's ambassador to Japan, arranged to have his colleague Charles Burton Fahs assigned to his embassy as CAO. In Delhi Chester Bowles did the same for his friend the labor economist Robert Brooks. Arthur Hartman in Paris hinted to Nicholas Wahl, New York University political historian of France, that a post might be arranged for a special assistant. Daniel Patrick Moynihan, as ambassador to India, brought along his educationist friend Chester Finn, then pressed USIA hard to send out his favorite American political and social scientists for short stints—USIA insiders called them Moynihan's "Star Series," or "Pat's Pals."

What little self-study USIA funded was done at the urging of its advisory bodies, alert senior staff, or outside groups. Inside USIA a field post inspection process occasionally undertook critical inquiries at specific posts, but the inspection process was hobbled. In 1972 a retired USIA veteran and former ambassador who had moved into university administration was called back for an inspection of a post in Europe and tried to prepare himself. A fine senior officer, he had no language skills for the country in question. Over lunch with a well-informed friend, he confessed that the USIS Country Plan seemed to him irrelevant to what was going on. The discussion led to the idea that he turn his inspection into a pilot research project involving three or four of the best American scholars of that country who, representing different disciplines, would establish parameters, criteria, and work division, then spend six weeks looking at the USIS program in the country's capital and provincial cities, then regroup in Washington to agree on final recommendations. The cost of the idea at the time was estimated at $40,000—far less than a routine inspection. But the idea went nowhere. A wise senior USIA friend said of the episode, "That is precisely the kind of advice USIA does *not* want to hear."[6] In another European capital, a former USIA great headed an inspection in 1974. In the middle of the process, he took the post's CAO out for a stroll in a nearby park, warning the officer to watch his step: "Inspections have changed since you last knew one; today their sole purpose is to help the PAO run his post."

USIA never lamented its absence of intellect, to my knowledge. Two exceptions come to mind: when CAO Theodore A. Wertime headed a VOA program called the Forum, he was able to collect remarkable teams of intellectuals and guided the otherwise humdrum program into an exciting publishing event, which produced several publications by Basic Books. And when Nathan Glick was asked to put out an "intellectual" magazine for world distribution, he assembled a fine team and, reprinting articles from national periodicals, produced for a decade or more a splendid quarterly called *Dialogue*.[7] Though dotted with highly educated people, the USIA culture itself was nonintellectual—of course, if one said as much, the response was to list the agency greats who were opera lovers, Sunday artists, readers of books, or musicians.

USIA distinguished itself indeed by its failure to recruit the very Fulbrights it was handling abroad. At the time I left USIA in 1985, I knew of only two other Fulbright alumni in the agency.[8] Fulbright's name, of course, was part of the problem; USIA director Frank Shakespeare, returning from an unusually tough grilling by Fulbright and his committee, exploded at a staff meeting: "What does Fulbright want me to do, learn to play the violin?" Not only did Shakespeare miss the point, he also fell into the great American semantic trap: for him, "culture"—a major component of the agency he managed—meant "the arts."

Among the many kinds of intellect, high skill in government is certainly one of them. But nonintellectualism was part of government culture, and it could harden into unwritten rules. Entering the foreign service, I was advised to downplay my Ph.D., in deference to an unwritten rule. Only on arriving in Sri Lanka, where it was deemed useful, did the post insist on using the title doctor—a practice as unthinkable on campuses of research universities as it is in UNESCO. Surprisingly, the anti-Ph.D. culture changed overnight in 1981, when a flood of new appointees with variegated doctorates insisted on being called doctor, a habit that persisted through the 1990s.

Fine foreign service officers were themselves baffled by the nonintellectual climate of diplomacy. The most intellectually curious American senior diplomat I know was constantly baffled by his colleagues' mind-numbing "lack of curiosity"; another, after forty years in service, is still amazed at the absence of "intellectual integrity" in the service. Diplomatic work in fact generates incuriosity. Overwork makes it impossible to read many books, and overseas duty deprives one of access to a regular supply of English-language periodicals. Besides, the patient and polite social habits of diplomacy require suffering many fools gladly, not to mention living with inadequate language ability. This said, intellectuals can also underestimate the special brand of intellect which characterizes the best foreign service officers.

Length-of-tour and language policy help dumb down diplomacy. Lyndon Johnson's USIA director Leonard Marks, in testimony before John Brademas in the House, admitted that short tours made for superficiality and reassured the Greek American Ph.D. that USIA planned to lengthen overseas tours. To do this he had to reverse deep-seated attitudes toward "localitis" or "going native"—phrases the foreign service uses for officers who stay too long in a single society, allegedly losing objectivity and a clear sense of US interests. In the end Marks's pledge to prolong tours caused a minor ripple and was soon forgotten. Most CAOs, like Frankel, would argue for tours of five years; some, given the nature of their work, saw that term as a minimum. Albert Giesecke, after fifty years in Peru, probably irritated US ambassadors less sure of themselves than Ellis Briggs—i.e., most of them. To Briggs, he was priceless.

Inadequate language policy is another factor of nonintellect. High skills in language, as Valignano instructed Ricci, at a level permitting engagement with the intellectual class of a country, are defined as they are in one's home country—by the degree of literacy in the language and learning. Literacy, in the sense not of knowing how to read but of being literate, is not easy to acquire in a foreign language; those who have not achieved such language competence can be embarrassed by those who have. The classic case of this was Ben Jackson, whose spoken and written Greek was so close to perfect that he was able to keep close company with all the important poets in Greece; he was rewarded for this achievement by a transfer to Bangladesh, where he dutifully began learning Bengali—which has its own poetic tradition. His new PAO said of Jackson, "He was speaking fluent Bengali within six months. He's really an incredible guy." When a close friend, a major Greek poet, died in Athens, Jackson was invited by the Greek writers' association to take charge of publishing the poet's collected works. Jackson requested a temporary USIS assignment to Athens, where his Bangladesh PAO was now in charge but his request was refused; he renewed his request, offering to take leave without pay and do the job on his own funds, to honor his friend's memory. This too was denied so he went to Athens anyway. His host PAO in Athens told Ludovic Kennedy of the BBC: "He could speak Greek like a Greek. But this did have its disadvantages. . . . I guess Ben Jackson got a little too identified with the other side."[9]

Other than foreign-born Madeleine Albright and Henry Kissinger, the last skilled foreign-language speaker to serve as Secretary of State was the francophone Christian Herter. The US foreign service stands almost alone among the nations of the world today in not requiring fluency in a foreign language for entrance, even though sophisticated foreign language training has been available in high schools and colleges everywhere in the U.S. since 1945. State still recruits the foreign language-challenged, despite what linguists know: the second language is easier than the first, et seq. This decision ripples outward: Since new entrants do not have at least one language solidly planted, language training is taught for coping purposes, designed for low-common-denominator beginners—under-motivated spouses, Marine guards, and code clerks sit in the same classes with fine linguists, so that the gifted are alienated from the first day. In the field minimal language requirements, spelled out in the regulations, are only loosely enforced; investment in further training in the field is sporadic and niggardly. Credit for language ability or achievement is proclaimed but rarely shows up on the record, except perhaps as a one-time step increase in pay. The best officers—because they know they need language and know how to learn—pick up language skills by themselves; but even these paragons know they'll never achieve the level of excellence they could have with a small investment in training.

In key countries of high political priority, like China or the USSR, language was required and the quality of speakers was fairly impressive, if one overlooked the question of literacy. Even so, language requirements were often squandered by assignment policy. Fine Arabists, speaking one of the world's most difficult languages, found themselves in Hong Kong or the Philippines. One fine speaker of Russian and French began her career in Athens and Cyprus, where she learned Greek; her second post was Colombia, where she learned Spanish; her third was Brazil, where she learned Portuguese; her fourth was Portugal and then came Chile. She never served in a French- or Russian-speaking country or returned to Greece. On the other side of the question, dozens of officers rose to top levels in USIA and State without ever having learned a single language. Such linguistic inadequacy blunts the usefulness of field officers and contributes to the nonintellectual climate of foreign service life. And the image projected by the stunted intellectual and linguistic growth of key US embassy officers borders on a national disgrace. Despite the exception of extraordinary linguists, the foreign service's language-challenged are legion, and the foreign perception remains what it was in 1940: Americans are monolingual.

The foreign service, in general, and USIA in particular, failed as well to utilize past investments in university area studies programs. Fulbright's dream of "educating these goddam ignorant Americans" ran into the same dilemmas. Designed to exchange US and foreign intellectuals, with research as a core function, the Fulbright program managed to ride out the built-in contradictions of government, thanks to strong academic defenses at the start. But its products rarely had a chance to strengthen diplomacy.

• • •

It is time to look again at the flagship Fulbright Program. Despite its strong defenses, even this central piece of cultural diplomacy began to weaken in the 1970s. Over time more and more insider complaints about Fulbrighters were being heard—from its less educated foreign service administrators—about the low quality of US Fulbright grantees. The complaint, commonplace by the 1970s, focused primarily on the senior professorial lecturers. The burst of superb senior Fulbrighters in the 1950s eager to return to Europe after the war, including scholars like Frankel, Henry Nash Smith, Oscar Handlin, Leo Marx, Daniel Boorstin, Frank Friedel, Leslie Fiedler, and dozens of others, had raised expectations. But declining field stipends could not continue to attract that level of excellence. In the early years, when it was still unusual to reside abroad, when stipends were adequate, when universities encouraged their young scholars to take leaves for foreign travel, only the best applied for Fulbright giants. But these stars had vanished by the 1970s, under the whiplash of fading stipends and the demands of tenure-track politics. Replacing them were senior lecturers of a different kind, perhaps no less valuable but less spectacular.

By 1970 the decline of BFS, the defeat of Frankel, the sudden halt in new Fulbright agreements, and factors like the new kind of nonintellectual political leadership in USIA and CU meant that the Fulbright Program was drifting. The handling of science is one of many cases in point. A mysterious step by John Richardson, still puzzling to the science community, transferred the location of CIES and the responsibility for the senior or postdoctoral Fulbright Program away from its thirty-year home in the National Academy of Sciences (NAS), to the American Council of Education (ACE). The CIES move probably had no more serious reason behind it than a desire for renewal, but there was anger among scientists, to whom the move was never explained. Later USIA wanted Fulbright to drop science altogether, on grounds it was irrelevant to foreign policy support. Not surprisingly, the science community responded with suspicion. The overseas world had always wanted to draw on American science, and binational commissions had pressed the Fulbright Program to include a scientific component; left to market flows, the perceived academic needs abroad would easily have turned the program fully to science exchanges. But eliminating science was out of the question. The BFS accepted science but had long resisted the rush to science, in the interests of balance. They had eliminated the *applied* sciences, i.e., engineering and medicine, but kept basic science, arguing that funding for applied science exchange was plentiful; AID in particular was investing heavily in engineering and public health. The scientists understood this logic and went along.

As the years moved on, even basic science came under attack. Former BFS chair, distinguished physicist, and MIT provost Walter Rosenblith was stunned in 1984 to learn that USIA's Latin America area office had instructed all field posts, without consultation, to eliminate science from their Fulbright plans. Later recalled, the clumsy message laid bare USIA's unswerving bias: since science could not "support foreign policy," science was useless, in USIA's definition of its goals. The scientists' response was brutal. If science was irrelevant to Fulbright, then Fulbright was irrelevant to science. The alienation of the scientific community was exacerbated by Richardson's moving CIES out of NAS.

Fulbright was also failing elsewhere. The patient Richardson's eight Battle-style years did not lower the pressures on the program, or revitalize the field posts, or put fine CAOs in the field, or reverse long-standing budgetary stagnation. After the father of the program left the Senate in 1975, no leader stepped forward to take charge. No one in Congress, other than a few dogged staffers, tried to curb USIA's growing control over cultural operations or brake the growing tendency toward the tactical shorter-term use of "cultural" programs.[10]

Still, the game remained a level above the Washington fray. With growing foreign funding, the Fulbright Program chugged forward, each year adding alumni, deepening experience, and growing in its foreign reputation, despite declining budgets. At home Fulbright was on hold; abroad, it was living up to its promise, but on borrowed time. Budget losses, despite heroic efforts to stretch funds in the overseas commissions, were beginning to show. Inflation—most visibly in transportation costs—was raging.

Cost-sharing was the logical destination of a binational cultural policy and had always been Fulbright's long-range hope, one reason the Senator insisted on the necessity of independent commissions, Boxer-style. But in 1948 it was too early to write joint-funding into the legislation or the bilateral agreements: direct foreign contributions to Fulbright were only authorized by the Fulbright-Hays Act of 1961. To permit foreign contributions, the next step was to adjust or rewrite various binational agreements. Soon enough foreign contributions began to flow, then to grow. It was a deeply radical and very American idea; foreign countries were not in the habit of paying for other nations' "propaganda," as the left called the Fulbright program. Yet it began to happen in the 1960s and 1970s because the designers built Fulbright as a genuine binational ideal, and over time foreign governments had begun to understand that the Americans meant it.

Private donations were controversial and lay much farther down the road. In 1963, in the West German commission, an enthusiastic Commission member from the German Ford Motor Company proposed that Fulbright send selected candidates from its German student pool for interviews in Cologne; then Ford would cover the US travel costs of those that impressed them most. The board member pledged that the selected candidates would not be committed to accept future employment. Young commission-staffer Ulrich Littman, later a legend of the German Fulbright Program, was astonished to see the idea collapse under Washington skepticism. CU stopped the arrangement, perhaps at BFS insistence, and the Ford representative resigned, to protest the obvious lack of US trust. Later, when private support looked like the only hope for Fulbright survival, Littman recalled the episode with a bitter smile.[11]

Cost-sharing by foreign governments required adjusting Fulbright agreements. As they pressed for this radical new idea, the CAOs saw how difficult it was to adjust foreign law to the binational principle. On the political left, the USIS connection drew the usual accusations of propaganda and espionage. To realist foreign government lawyers, the binational partnership idea, perfectly natural to Americans, looked idealistic and perhaps useless. Skeptical Europeans dragged their feet. CAOs were suddenly deep into complicated negotiations touching on delicate financial and legal arrangements aimed at amendments or more often totally new agreements.

The French case is an extreme example of these difficulties. Negotiations with France began immediately after Fulbright-Hays in 1962. In the great tradition of French-U.S. cooperation since Franklin, at the time of the French love affair with the Kennedys, France agreed to match the US annual contribution. But in Washington, the unreliability vested in the Founders' checks and balances was at a peak. While Coombs was boosting the idea of joint-financing, Rooney was slashing Coombs's budget, unaware—or pretending to be unaware—of the cost-sharing idea. Coombs's budget took its first major hit. To France, this looked like an ingenious but devious plot. At the moment French funding for Fulbright was scheduled to flow, the U.S. cut its contribution, leaving France to contribute much more than half the cost. The skeptical French concluded that the wily Americans had tricked them into making up for a budget shortfall. For two decades, no one was able to dispel the idea and France's annual contribution remained low, even after US budgets began to rise. Only in the late 1980s did the French finally agree to match the US contribution.

Germany, in contrast, was deeply satisfied with Fulbright. It raised its contribution sharply and soon was paying over 80 percent of all costs. Japan went in a different direction. The Fulbright Commission there organized impressive private contributions, raising funds through its alumni by such devices as an annual golf tournament. Spain, from impressive funds generated by US rent for Spanish military bases, set aside an even greater share than Germany's, while encouraging private contributions; pressures on the Spanish Fulbright Commission to go beyond its normally stern academic values, justified by a burst of new needs in the post-Franco era, were skillfully absorbed by the commission's thoughtful directors Ramón Bella and was successor María-Jesus Pablos.

These two Spaniards typified a new breed of commission director. The days of the great American executives had passed, and by 1960 national directors were starting to fall into place, some on their way to legendary status. After the generation of Alan Pifer in London, Richard Downar in

Rome, Gene Horsfall and George Wickes in Brussels, and the indomitable Olive Reddick in Delhi came Littman in Germany, Cipriana Scelba in Italy, Bella and Pablos in Spain, Tony Pourhansl in Austria, Daniel Krauskopf in Israel, Dorothy Deflandre in Belgium, Barbara Petersen in Norway, and Nisei-American Caroline Yang in Japan. In the renewed binational spirit—often after renegotiating agreements—board chairmanships as well began to rotate annually between the two countries.

New agreements, grinding to a halt in 1963, picked up again after Morocco in 1983. With no new commissions in the interim years, the disappearance of seven earlier programs in the 1960s and 1970s, prompted by political crisis, had slowed the pace of growth. Iraq, Paraguay, South Africa, and Tunisia folded, and were joined later by Ethiopia, Ghana, and Iran after its 1978 revolution. Senior USIA officers, who loved to grouse about commission costs, sluggishness, irrelevance, and unruly executive directors, began to face the deeper paradox of binationalism, which brought costs as well as benefits. Without foreign contributions, the commissions and the Fulbright programs would stall; with them, the partner country—not unreasonably—expected a greater say in program design.

Commissions had many more functions beyond grant-making than most understood. Their most important non-grant undertaking in the 1970s was the consuming work of counseling foreign student applicants to American universities, part of the global structure that CU had been building since 1942. The murky admissions process of US postsecondary education, for a foreign student, was defeating; each college or university played its own game. In response to CU's urging, a minor counseling industry had been created in embassies abroad by the 1960s. Then, in the 1970s, USIA pushed counseling offices into Fulbright commissions; these offices were funded by both CU and USIA. But the temptation was too great for USIA's budget-makers; having transferred student counseling to the commissions, USIA began to shave its support. The battle would last for a decade, with USIA holding all the cards.

In Italy, for example, student counseling moved through three steps. First, it grew up inside USIS. Then USIS and CU asked the Fulbright Commission to absorb student counseling, with ample funding. With CU help in training the counselors, the work was handled with growing professionalism. The third step, once counseling was comfortably anchored in the commission, was to reduce counseling budgets in USIA. After USIA absorbed CU, the commission could not resist. Soon the commission was asked to absorb full costs of counseling, even if it meant reducing the number of exchange grants. The commissions were being whipsawed. The PAO in Rome and the Washington accountants—having caused the problem—howled about the rise in Fulbright's administrative overhead, fretted over the smaller number of grants, and groused about the quality of underpaid US grantees. In fact, it was unthinkable to cut counseling in Italy, where hundreds of student applicants haunted each of the six provincial consulates. At home foreign students in US higher education were a growth industry, ranked fifth among export of US services and earning perhaps $13 billion a year. Fulbright counselors, after thirty years of US investment in improving foreign-student flow, were indispensable to the educational process, vital to consulates for helping handle visa applications, and a boon to American universities. But who would pay the costs when USIA, containing CU, declined to do so?

Worldwide, ways were sought to lower the cost of the labor-intensive counseling process, e.g., charging fees—counseling, after all, was a professional service rendered. But counseling was seen by foreigners as a service of embassies and their dependencies, a tradition that could not be dispelled. As costs kept mounting and grant budgets kept falling, Cipriana Scelba in the Rome commission struggled to keep a visible and balanced program alive. She reduced grants, lowered stipends, issued partial grants, and artificially depressed her salary and her staff's for a decade. Exchanging people for high-quality educational experiences, if professionally done, is labor-intensive and costly. Doing it on the cheap can work for a few years, but soon it does its own damage.

It was particularly galling that more than one USIS post manipulated its commission's budget for financial flexibility. Posts were deplorably short of money for entertainment, and one major USIS post in Europe in the 1980s had the ingenious but perhaps criminal idea of shifting some of its funding, which Congress had declared off-limits for entertainment, to the Fulbright Commission, which the PAO chaired. When the PAO then asked the commission to fund a reception or dinner, it did so—money-laundering, by any definition. The particular case to which I refer had a sour ending: a CAO blew the whistle and an ad hoc inspection brought the practice to an end. The PAO was rewarded by transfer to a more important post where he spoke the host language fluently, and the disheartened CAO, seeing his career at an end, took early retirement.

By the 1970s, the same academic defenses built into Fulbright process, which had so impressed US and foreign universities and foreign governments, were beginning to look to PAOs like irksome impediments. In truth, Fulbright was no different from any serious education program, it was slow. But the USIA informationists did not see why and champed at the bit. In 1984, a decade after Fulbright left the Senate, USIA's European area director, in an unguarded moment over an extra glass of wine, exploded: if he had his way, he said, he would eliminate all the European commissions as an unnecessary cost. His lunch partner asked what he would do about the jointly-funded commissions in Spain and Germany, where the area director had cut his teeth and would soon take over as PAO. He had no answer.[12] By the time he made this pronouncement, all but a few European commissions were, in fact, binationally funded, Germany and Spain were getting more than three-quarters of their budgets from host governments, and six new commissions, under USIA urging, were soon to arise from the ashes of the Soviet system in the Newly

Independent States of the former USSR. Worldwide, 20 percent of Fulbright funds came from foreign governments.

As for field staffing, the cultural corps continued its steady decline in academic profile. CAOs no longer assumed they would chair Fulbright commissions: in 1968 the PAO took over in Turkey and in 1979 the PAO took the commission in Paris away from the CAO. In other posts, alleging staff cuts or more disingenuously saying that the division between culture and information was a thing of the past, PAOs spelled out the new generalist era that had begun in 1974. US cultural offices became "program offices," with assistant CAOs and occasionally a CAO becoming "Program Officers." By the end of the 1970s USIA was routinely staffing CAO positions from the generalist corps. With PAO power stronger than ever and with the mounting exodus, in protest, of experienced and committed CAOs, major CAO jobs were filled by officers—even in centers like Rome and Paris—who had never managed a cultural program or a Fulbright Commission. As the cultural corps declined, the inexperienced PAOs and younger generalists found it increasingly difficult to deal with foreign board members of high caliber or with the strong commission executive directors. They reacted by replacing the commission executives. Commission and commission director morale declined steadily.

Even with rising foreign contributions, inflation and soaring travel costs took their toll; commissions pared back grant activities and shaved staff. Unpredictable budgets, allocated year-by-year by Congress, made planning at best haphazard and at worst impossible. To avoid cutting grants, commissions maneuvred ingeniously. In Italy, the commission, long faithful to BFS policy on full academic-year grants, was reduced in 1975 to giving US senior research grants in one-month slices, called *mensualità*—monthly stipends—which went by definition only to American scholars who already had partial support for their research, thus only to the "rich." Such decisions, distorting the nature of their commitments, were justified by the optimistic faith that the lean years could not last forever.

In fact, they could and did. Grants continued to dwindle and shorten. US university scholars who accepted Fulbright grants to Italy were paid anywhere from 20 to 30 percent of their university salaries. With an additional private grant, a university professor on a half-salary sabbatical might be able to make ends meet but would have to dip into savings if family was involved. BFS, after years of insisting on academic-year grants, authorized three-month grants for senior scholars, then in desperation tried a one-month grant each year for a three-year period. In the U.S. the absurdly low stipends made it steadily harder to pry academics loose from their career tracks. Science continued its decline, whipsawed by Washington and field demands for "relevance" and "training"—code words for practical and applied fields like business administration, computer science, journalism (as opposed to journalism education) and "democracy." Commission executive directors were ordered—by PAO-chairs who had never raised a penny in their lives—to practice the special US art of fund-raising in countries where the tradition and culture of private giving did not exist.

Intent on the star-quality "speakers" they might comb out of senior Fulbrights, USIS posts continued to nag about the "quality" of the American Fulbrights. The glory days of the postwar period were over. Besides, the intellectual climate had changed. In those years of decline in Italy, one could also see attitudinal changes in the US grantees. In the 1950s Americans went to a Europe grateful to its liberators, and sipped at the fount of European learning. Now, honed to a sharp edge by Vietnam and *Ramparts* and hounded by USIS officers, the Fulbrighters of the 1970s were aware of a new "political" dimension implicit in their Fulbright grants. And they were weary to the point of irritation with anti-Americanism. Where anti-Americanism had seemed to earlier generations an understandable ignorance to be tolerated and converted over time by education, the Vietnam years had nourished a sharper and more destructive kind of anti-Americanism that looked, to young Fulbrights in Italy at least, like systemic provocation. Americans who in earlier years would have felt free to criticize America in a balanced and cautious mode now became defensive and truculent; in orientation sessions, we reminded them of Fulbrighter Leslie Fiedler's memorable essay "The Good American" (1950), which had pilloried the European left for its delight in dragging unwary Americans from mild criticism of, say, McCarthyism into accusations of germ-warfare in Korea.

As a Fulbright in 1949–50, I had tried patiently, with mixed success, to educate the understandably ignorant French students around me. By the seventies fewer Fulbrights bothered; most were irritated by the pointless ragging and focused on their work. In my 1949 experience Americans went to Europe because they loved it and wanted to absorb as much as they could. By the mid-1970s I was watching a stiff-necked group of bristly young Americans, including newly liberated women no longer charmed by Italian *machismo*, who refused to tolerate the nonsense they met everywhere. This shift, not entirely bad, had a more serious side: it tended to restrict the new Fulbrighters' capacity to mix with foreign colleagues; it deprived them of the company of those who, after the test of tough teasing, might later become devoted friends. In a word, the shift limited their learning. For the first time in my experience, I was watching young American Fulbrighters become anti-European.

That same bicentennial year of 1976, a fine American historian of Italy, a senior Fulbright scholar with a deeply liberal background who had stayed on for a second year, had an epiphany: having achieved prominence through high-quality historical publications in Italy, which were pilloried by the intellectual left as right-wing, he found himself attacked regularly in the press. He and his family were harrassed by midnight phone calls, accusing him of being a CIA agent. Mugged by the doctrinaire and sloganeering left and its mindless reaction to his work, he took a significant step, and within a year had slammed the door on the university world and joined the American neoconservative movement, where he became a serious partisan protagonist. It was a new direction for the Fulbright process.

Fulbright's great program in the 1970s was still pursuing mutual understanding, even as the Senator moved toward his sad departure from the Senate in 1975. But something had changed; the defeat of Frankel had something to do with it, as would the loss of its champion in Congress. Fulbright had long argued that partial understanding was better than no understanding at all; now Americans had begun to look at the glass as half-empty and realize, to their dismay, that understanding in fact did not necessarily lead to approval, in either direction. There was no Arkansan leader, no "gentle farseeing conservative," in Tristam Coffin's phrase, to urge them to stay with the good fight, rather than ask the exchange program to deliver a quick fix. The Fulbright Program, core of US cultural diplomacy since 1948, was adrift.

CHAPTER TWENTY

Nixon and Ford, Shakespeare and Richardson

Let us build a structure of peace in the world in which the weak are as safe as the strong, in which each respects the right of the other to live by a different system, in which those who would influence others will do so by the strength of their ideas, not by the force of their arms.

—Richard M. Nixon, 1973

PICKING UP CHRONOLOGY AFTER FRANKEL, the elections of 1968 changed one factor in cultural diplomacy: the Johnson White House was the last to pay attention to the issues of cultural versus informational diplomacy. From 1933 until 1968 it had been assumed that those responsible for cultural diplomacy could call on presidential authority when needed, but Frankel was the last to benefit from presidential access. Now the buck stopped with the toilers in the vineyards and their bosses, the heads of USIA and CU, their advisory commissions and the BFS, and a few concerned members of a distracted Congress. Forward thinking fell to a few top officers in CU and USIA, a handful of legislators and staffers, and some discouraged but activist friends of cultural diplomacy in the world of the universities, the foundations, and the media.

By the 1970s a new kind of political change could be discerned. Nixon's southern strategy relied on ideology, aiming to separate the conservative voters of the South from the Democratic Party, alleged to be dominated by its "liberals." In a land governed by consensus politics, ideology-based politics was a new art form. The idea of an ill-assorted but powerful coalition of various "conservative" trends of thought had not yet occurred to the American establishment. As former political enemies were lured onto Nixon's team, they redefined American party politics and the ideas lying beneath them. Consensus politics depended on two broad-based coalition parties; ideology meant slogans and spin. American intellectual "conservatives," led by men like Irving Kristol and Norman Podhoretz, sliced out a new piece of turf, which was called neoconservative only after toying with the designation neoliberal. The language of foreign policy, wedded to large abstractions and lofty goals, was a playing field for brilliant political historians like Henry Kissinger; Nixon's second inaugural address, calling for attention to a "structure of peace," drew on Kissinger; it sounded like cultural internationalism. Below decks, the way was being paved for the victory of the "revolution" of 1980.

Nixon appointed Frank Shakespeare to head USIA, giving the unwary nation its first look at an unabashed "movement conservative." Shakespeare's background at first blush looked like that of earlier USIA directors. Like Streibert, he was a broadcasting executive; like Murrow, he came from CBS. But in fact he came from several layers down in CBS, and from sales rather than program. In 1964 he had taken leave from his job to join a Republican political campaign and returned to the network with a burning mission: to devote his passionate convictions to US electoral politics. He was no searcher for elusive truths but rather a monothematic debater with a simplistic vision. Those who encountered and worked with Shakespeare saw a man dominated by a single passion: the defeat of the evil Soviet Union. The nationalist unilateralist was as close to a total conservative ideologue as one could get; in his call for hard-hitting, one-way information flow, he bore an odd resemblance to Sorensen.

No one among his USIA associates, at least those I have polled, remembers him reflecting on what the world might become after a US victory in the cold war. Yet in 1968 that possibility looked more real than ever before. As USIA's advisory commission had begun to say, détente was clearly on the way and Soviet weaknesses were more apparent than before.[1]

Like many in Congress, he may have assumed that USIA would evaporate after victory over the Soviets. IIA-USIA leadership since Barrett had not discouraged that money-saving hope, in the search for higher budgets. In contrast, CU leadership since 1938 had never deviated: its goal, well over the horizon, remained the same: a structure of peace, through mutual understanding.

USIA veterans soon collided with the Shakespeare mindset. Those up close kept calm and began the patient process of education, leaning against his unalterable tendency to prejudge. For these would-be teachers, he was a difficult student; colleagues found he could be brought to agree on a given day but that he would then return to default to greet the next question. As Yale philosopher Paul Weiss said of his 1948 student William Buckley, he was "very mature—which means he learned little."

My single meeting with Shakespeare took place in Iran, I believe in 1969, over a leisurely briefing luncheon with senior USIS staff. Accompanied by his friend Theodore Weintal of *Newsweek*, former Polish cavalry officer and quintessential cold warrior, Shakespeare listened as the conversation followed comfortable channels in describing the post's work. During my part of the briefing, I thought he might be interested in reaching behind the clichés; I strayed a trifle, touching lightly on the rapidly changing political culture we faced, sketching various areas in which authoritarian Iran might well be encouraged to loosen up, noting for example the Shah's stern limits on the free flow of information, his discomfort with the social and political sciences, his fears of student unrest, his tendency to identify intellect with treason, and his blind eye for high-level corruption. A wise political counselor in the embassy in those years insisted that the threat to the Shah from the right, especially the clergy, was at least as serious as that from the left. Tracing cracks in the structure, I touched on the Shah's knack for turning corruption to advantage by luring lieutenants into accepting bribes. This set off an explosion from the USIA director, who said the Shah was wise, a hero, a farseeing intelligence, and more or less omniscient; his virtues, he said, were greater even than those of the Greek colonels. My colleagues and I swallowed hard, sipped our coffee and nodded, wondering what had changed at home.

On the same tour in Eastern Europe, Shakespeare and Weintal made an impact on other officers, declaring that all promotions in USIA would depend on previous service behind the Iron Curtain—an impractical idea, if only for language reasons. He yanked some of USIA's best East Europeanists, like Yale Richmond, out of their jobs on grounds they were insufficiently anticommunist; and he drove out a good number of linguistically skilled USIS staffers who happened to be naturalized Americans of East European origin. The Polish-born Weintal could not sway the director from these demoralizing decisions. Daniel Hafrey, former crack reporter for the *Minneapolis Star*, a decorated war veteran and a Ukrainian-born speaker of seven European and East European languages, was forced into early retirement a year before he was eligible for an adequate pension. Shakespeare, who spoke no foreign language, casually destroyed priceless career officers who had been fighting communism in East Europe for decades. Hafrey, to be sure, was quickly snapped up by another agency that knew how to use his extraordinary skills. But USIA was weakened.

The director's visit to Tehran revealed the fragility of the internationalist assumptions which had attracted most of us to diplomacy and to which we had dedicated our careers. From the "conservative" viewpoint, the American cultural internationalist vision and the tactics of engagement, running back to Franklin and the founders, were anathema—Mrs. Luce called it globaloney, McCarthy, treason; and Shakespeare implemented their idea. Those who worked to engage rather than confront, by the light of a binational vision with an internationalist base, through pledges of good faith, respecting the cultural integrity of other nations— these people were thrown off stride. Senator Fulbright, already savaged by Lyndon Johnson, made the new White House "enemies list."

In the NSC Kissinger, a master at balancing power, was articulate about "interdependence." Interdependence was an alternate ideology to internationalism, which at first seemed an exciting and practical new idea, but Kissinger's version of interdependence darkened with time. It was not a pluralist approach to stable relations that respected others, tolerated difference, or listened to alternative views; rather it called for confronting enemies and forging alliances managed by the U.S. It depended less on allies than on client-states.

To children of the depression and the Great War, for whom engagement and cultural internationalism were the bonding assumptions, the new mode was a shattering challenge. To those who had spent their lives resisting the USSR, to those who believed that America needed only to show its best self over time and wait for the Soviet system to crumble, to those intent on helping strengthen Iran by encouraging the evolution of a democratic society through assistance to democratic education—to these, Shakespeare turned a deaf ear. Some retired, others withdrew from the mainstream and tried to serve the U.S. *they* knew, some went into internal retirement and cultivated their distractions. In practical terms, especially in the field, little seemed to have changed—USIA still interfered minimally in day-to-day field activities, beyond budget and personnel. But in personal terms, after 1969 we lived with Voltaire's sardonic advice about the usefulness of hanging an admiral from time to time—"to encourage the others."

In the 1960s we used the word "ideology" in the sense given it by Daniel Bell and Milovan Dijilas to attack the sterility of the hard-line Soviet political culture. Suddenly we had encountered an American ideological mindset of similar tenacity, and one which from our complex experience abroad looked as simplistic as Lenin's version of Marx. The new US ideologues considered even Kissinger—long associated with the liberal internationalism of Nelson Rockefeller—as questionable. Kissinger's neo-hawkish vision, deeply nationalist but flowing from the Metternichean manipulation of geopolitics, seemed—at least at first—compatible with the pragmatic traditions of diplomacy. He professed support of CU and USIA; yet behind the scenes talk was tougher. Asked by State's chief of African affairs to approve an expansion of the Fulbright Program in Africa, he was reported to answer, "Why? So they can go back to Africa as f—ing communists?"

Shakespeare was ready to absorb CU into USIA and made no bones about saying so. For all his ignorance of details, he must have known that CU was built, irreversibly so, on internationalism. Certainly he did not understand the concept of "culture" that guided our work; for him "culture" meant "the arts." He was unaware of the thirty-year US history of "the cultural approach" or of American practice since Franklin or of world practice since the Greeks. The culturalists doubled over in laughter when he offered to take violin lessons to appease Fulbright's pleas for culture, but they also saw peril in his ignorance. Few could believe that the bipartisan internationalist consensus that had oscillated from hawk to dove since 1919 had ended.

Kissinger's hyperintelligent nationalism, couched in learned historical and analytically realistic terms, bullied all opposition. The shrewd tactician seemed to make a great deal of sense. He was welcomed enthusiastically by diplomats when he moved from the NSC to State, where, in a courtyard ceremony, looking down at the crowd from a high platform, he quipped in his naturally morose voice that, given his bad press, the scene reminded him of the Nuremberg rallies. His vision, focused sharply on the Soviet problem, quickly dazzled colleagues impressed by his intelligence, but some worried that his approach left other questions unanswered. "Never before," said one bruised ambassador, "has such a bright light been focused on any given problem in foreign affairs. But everything around it is plunged into darkest night."

In the field, with goodwill and collegiality, Americans continued pulling together, bringing moments of coherence to their work. In Washington USIA fed an uncritical Congress its familiar info-prop rhetoric. CU was invisible to all except Fulbright and the bloodthirsty Rooney. Even in the university and foundation world, CU was no longer a factor. Abroad, foreign audiences had long ago accepted the peculiar USIS mix of propaganda and culture, of official handouts and human helpfulness, of political junkets and serious academic exchanges, of tired photo shows and splendid events like *The Family of Man*, of feasts of fine performers followed by years of famine—this was how the odd Americans did things. The American image, like Whitman's self, contained multitudes. But the thin substance of the program messages flowing out of USIS posts soon led European intellectuals to conclude that USIS people and output had lost interest. Not many years later a spray-painted graffito in English at the foot of the Garibaldi bridge over Rome's Tiber summed it up: "America, we are so bored with you!"

At the end of the 1960s, thanks in part to the probing books of Coombs and Frankel, the issues that had haunted the cultural diplomatic function since 1938 had sharper edges. After Sorensen, definitions of what USIA did had softened with time, but Shakespeare quickly hardened them. As for inputs into foreign policy, only Murrow had managed occasional contributions by his reputation and personal qualities; Shakespeare made none.

Frank Stanton, former CBS chief and Johnson-appointed chair of USIA's advisory commission, was kept in place by Shakespeare's loyalty to his ex-boss. Stanton had learned a great deal in his years with the commission. In 1969 he had begun to see that USIA's advisory role in policy-making was a paradoxical dilemma: if the role indeed existed, then USIA had to move closer to the policy-makers; if it did not, then USIA needed major rethinking. His commission reports escalated this theme until 1973.[2] That year the twenty-sixth report concerned itself with informational affairs after the cold war and assumed that the momentum in the cold war had passed to the U.S.

Despite the commission's support, USIS engagers were losing their edge. The most visible fadeaway was that of the USIS library. In Washington no one had the courage to declare them history and close them as an obvious irrelevance, once anti-Soviet policy was to be the sole point of USIA's diplomacy. Because public outcry was certain, the libraries were allowed to continue and quietly wither; old readers found few new books, and new readers found less of interest.

The caliber of the CAOs continued to decline. Outsider CAOs persisted only in London. Shakespeare himself was ambivalent on this score; he liked the idea of super-CAOs. At a cocktail party, he met the critic John Aldrich and within months had installed him as CAO Bonn, where in fact Aldrich did not remain very long—the exception did not recur. Under Shakespeare, USIA closed off the lateral-entry system for enriching the cultural cadres, used extensively in the 1960s to bring people with proven talent into the agency at mid-levels. Shakespeare's successor, James Keogh of *Time-LIFE*, made the CAO decline more definite, proclaiming the era of generalists. New USIA officers, including CAO candidates, by the end of the 1970s, were recruited solely from among recent graduates in politics or international relations, at the BA and MA level, regardless of experience. Recruits were screened by a foreign service examination designed by high-powered outside management consultants who knew of cultural diplomacy only what they had been told by PAOs and ambassadors. Language proficiency in the foreign service was honored no more than usual, and the scything of the Eastern European polyglots was demoralizing to linguists.

After the CIA revelations, the agency's orphans were knocking on various doors. Frankel had realized that only USIA and CU could easily pick up these programs, but Congress did not lift a finger. It was no longer 1949. The damage to foreign perceptions of the US cultural world and to the integrity of "private" support had been done; US domestic reactions were angrier than those abroad. For CU the former CIA programs were hot potatoes. They had intrinsic problems, e.g., they rarely involved equal-to-equal "exchanges" but rather were simple and direct political action, uncomfortable in CU's mandate; moreover after generous CIA funding, CU-USIA could offer nothing comparable.

Policy-driven USIA officers in fact wanted to absorb some of the orphans, scoffing at the idea that the agency was bound by Fulbright-Hays strictures. They persuaded USIA's lawyers to build the case for aggressive political action, using the cold war confrontational side of Smith-Mundt's schizophrenia, which in fact had been explicitly and deliberately superseded by Fulbright-Hays in 1961. In Eastern Europe, USIS posts had long mingled politically activist activities with its cleaner cultural products; now Shakespeare's USIA began adding more energetic political promotion to the mix.

Definitions and concepts in USIA had always been deliberately blurred, for good reason, given a bewildered Congress; this made it easier to do what was wanted. When Coombs and Frankel clarified concepts, ideas threatened to mean more. As a defense against the new ideological cast of US thought, the culturalists in the Shakespeare years found themselves explaining that they too had long fought the Soviets, by proven means. The attack from the US right was disconcerting to the internationalists, but in an agency wedded to pragmatism and getting it done, people did not let definitions bother them.

USIA, like America itself, had run for years on a rough consensus between two broadly based centrist factions. Because its stance in foreign affairs had been defined in broadly bipartisan terms, debate had been modulated so as to reinforce the consensus; cultural diplomacy teetered on a point somewhere between nationalist and internationalist goals. But after 1969 and Shakespeare's years, a new, stronger pull toward nationalism was afoot.

With Nixon's reelection, Shakespeare returned to CBS, wearing the halo of a senior statesman, ready with opinions when needed. Kissinger moved to State, bearing Nixon's idea for a "structure of peace." CU quickly claimed the human foundations of that structure for its own. James Keogh, a mild-mannered editor from Luce's *Time-LIFE* structure, took over USIA, yet another director from the media world. Like Shakespeare, Keogh openly coveted CU.

· · ·

To the sagging CU, Nixon had appointed John Richardson, internationalist Republican of the Ripon variety, a Bostonian Brahmin lawyer out of Harvard who had jumped with the paratroops at Nijmegen. Finding life less than challenging in the Dulles brothers' law firm of Sullivan and Cromwell, Richardson involved himself with rescue activities in Eastern Europe, with Freedom House in New York, and with the CIA-funded Radio Free Europe.[3] He was a man of probity and decency—one listener at an after-dinner speech in St. Louis captured his style, saying, "The man is overwhelming in his sincerity." His steadfast eight-year service to CU permitted him to ride out Watergate, disruptions like Nixon's resignation, and the transition to Gerald Ford. He steered CU as straight as he could, but his skiff was fighting strong tides.

Richardson, no man for theory, opted for the gradualist style and relied on his professional staff. Little in his tenure looks significantly different from Battle's efforts, but he inherited a weaker institution and stayed with it a great deal longer. He gently edged budgets upward: by the beginning of 1972 CU had reached $45 million—still well below what Battle had achieved. By the beginning of 1974 CU went to $50, in 1976 to $58.5, and in Richardson's last year, to nearly $65 million. He kept CU alive, more or less healthy, and apparently growing through the confusion of Watergate, the end of Vietnam, Fulbright's departure from the Senate, and new forms of USIA unidirectionalism.

Predictably, fear of controversy reduced CU's arsenal, most immediately in the decision to turn over UNESCO responsibilities to State's Office of International Organizations, but also in lower funding for performing arts, and in slashing short-term tours abroad by prominent Americans—a favorite Rooney target. Continuing the cleanup after Frankel and Re,

Richardson set out bravely to improve relations with USIA. USIA as usual was delighted to take anything offered and give nothing in return. Soon CU would agree to a joint planning document dictated by USIA (1973).

In 1974 CU ended a four-year self-study in the guise of a drafting exercise, redefining itself in a paper called the "CU Concept."[4] It marked a revealing moment with unusual clarity. Worked out in a process designed to build consensus among CU staff and then flow outwards, the "Concept" stated CU's mission in two short pages, designed to make sense to Congress without threatening USIA. MacLeish had pondered a similar question during his tenure: how to describe the cultural function in terms compatible with OWI rhetoric and congressional inattention. Richardson's answer lay in a word not available to MacLeish: "communication." It was Richardson's bridge to USIA. Finished a year before Stanton's twenty-sixth advisory report, the two documents complement each other in ways that suggest some elements of deliberate design. Certainly both responded to change in the climate of the 1970s.

In the story of US cultural diplomacy, the "CU Concept" is a milestone. Aside from attempts by Frankel and Coombs, there had been no efforts to nail down what CU was about. The "Concept" reformulates the original 1938 goals, yet gives little indication that its drafters paid much attention to CU history; even the doughty veteran staffers, like Espinosa, who subscribed to the ideas of Hull, Cherrington, and Ralph Turner, had forgotten their forerunners. The statement of purposes and policy flowed, with guidance, from a consensus of the CU staff itself.

The "Concept" laid out three objectives: (1) enlarge the circle of those able to serve as influential interpreters between the U.S. and foreign cultures ("influentials," a nod to USIA); (2) stimulate institutional development in support of mutual comprehension and confidence (a new stress on institutions, after years of investment in individuals); (3) reduce impediments to the exchange of ideas and information (a tainted word which Cherrington would never have allowed). Two of the three key verbs—"enlarge" and "reduce"—had traveled far from 1938's "facilitate" and "coordinate," but "stimulate" survived. Enlarge and reduce tugged in opposite directions, one aimed at including more people, the other at eliminating "impediments," presumably more than people. Notwithstanding Richardson's fervent commitment to privatization, the three goals said nothing about CU's time-honored "facilitation," an idea that had sifted downward to mean no more than stimulating institutions. One other omission contradicted Richardson's personal values: coordination of other agencies, private and public, was no longer explicit.[5]

To reach these goals, five criteria would guide priority choices: (a) CU activities should be multipurpose (a new idea, denoting openness to multidisciplinary approaches and spin-off effects, probably aimed at fighting "overspecialization"); (b) they should multiply, stimulate, and reinforce other mechanisms (cooperative relationships, facilitation, helping the private world); (c) they should engage exceptional individuals (reiterating individual excellence and counterbalancing institutional stress); (d) they should reflect the two-way character of effective communication by mutual planning, participation, support, and benefit (dialogue, two-way flow, and binationalism, avoiding the word); and (e) they should facilitate intercultural communication and draw on American strengths like individual freedom, competence, pluralism, openness, and hospitality (communication, glossing US virtues).

This collectively written but fine-tuned document, in its long-mulled words, made concealed concessions in what it said and did not say. First, it reached out a tentative hand to the psychological warriors and the targeters of influence, never explicit in CU rhetoric before, and it promised positive results—the "Concept" commits CU to "favorable" influence of relations and to work with "influentials." Influence—long "favorable" only by implication—had always been an assumed by-product of cultural diplomacy; now it was a purpose.

The new CU idea was out in the open for all—including foreign audiences—to read. Once, it had seemed folly to announce to foreigners that the U.S. intended to *influence* them. In 1938 the founders tried to convince both the American universities and foreign hosts of the "integrity" of a program aimed not at propaganda but at long-range educational and cultural growth. Now instead the implied by-products, paired with building the "human foundations" of the peace structure, had become the focus.

In search of "relevance," an elusive idea, CU's overall purpose had moved a step nearer to USIA's. CU pledged *favorable* influence in short and less-short range—"favorably influence relations between the U.S. and other countries" admitted all time frames, while "help build the human foundations of the structure of peace" was as long-range as Cherrington could have wanted. CU was moving closer to USIA, with lowered hedges; significantly, there is no evidence USIA was asked to offer a return in kind. USIA officers, unless they worked in CU, never heard of the "Concept," and in 1977, when CU was absorbed into USIA, no one could find the text.

Nor did the "Concept" impress Rooney, who let his staff do the reading. In any case, CU's trade-offs with Rooney had always carried high price tags. Budget negotiation was a full-time affair for the bureau. To play the game of the agile congressman, CU trudged through a year-long budget process that absorbed the entire bureau of some 270 souls, filled every day of CU's life, and colored every element of its thinking. Each new day was another day of preparing Richardson for Rooney's unpredictable thrusts, after which the cycle began all over again. Decent and devoted bureaucrats did what they could to anticipate the congressman's caprices, in the process turning CU into an endless budget treadmill. As usual, the process focused on costs and side-stepped benefits. Despite thousands of CU hours, the annual gains were marginal; but at least they were not losses.

Rooney's procedure by now was standard. First, he would ask, say, what a basketball coach was doing for the US national interest in Liberia. A CU staffer would pull an 8-x-10 card from a box and slide it in front of Richardson to prompt his answer. By the time Richardson began to respond, Rooney had turned to a staffer for his next question. Rooney was Oscar Wilde's cynic: he knew the cost of everything but the value of nothing. CU certainly knew he could not be impressed by activities that paid off only over decades.

Richardson's achievements in CU, which deserve to be remembered, were a mix of outright success, mixed blessings, and backward steps. First came his management style. CU was run by a tight executive group, including Richardson and his five top officers. Under them, reporting to Richardson's senior deputy William Hitchcock, five strong area directors linked to field activities. In parallel, lesser offices handled specific functions. Richardson shuffled the hedgehog chiefs of functional units—like foreign students or international visitors—with the disadvantage that corporate memory was eased out. A strong Office of Policy and Plans stepped up research, self-study, and evaluation. A new Office of Private Cooperation, ignoring the Welles-Cherrington notion that the private world do 95 percent of the work, set out on a mission to solicit business contributions to CU's work. But reported contributions were few—business reminded the office that they were already paying taxes.

Along with the basic cooperating agencies in the private world, many of which Cherrington and Thomson had helped found, CU gave grants-in-aid to a variety of voluntary groups. For example, with high-school exchanges, CU helped the bellwether American Field Service (AFS) and encouraged it to extend its reach in developing countries, where high-school exchanges were by definition more expensive and difficult. Yet CU also helped the competing Youth for Understanding (YFU), which worked primarily in the wealthier nations. When succeeding administrations cut back such assistance, both organizations were damaged. AFS went international and lost its focus, while YFU finally collapsed in 2001. For women, CU supported the UN International Women's Year and stressed US and foreign women in all its programs. Priority for predominantly black colleges was given, where possible—as it had been since the president of Tuskegee had joined the first BFS. Howard University's president, later historian John Hope Franklin followed, and Mabel Smythe graced the first Fulbright-Hays CU advisory commission. CU was likewise attentive to the AFL-CIO—its worldwide network had been damaged by the events of 1968. For student counseling abroad, CU supported overseas advising, placement, and orientation for the mounting flow of private foreign students coming to the U.S. and nurtured the growth of NAFSA. For the booming IV program, help was extended to private-support groups through its national council (NCIV). For youth activists, the American Council of Young Political Leaders exchanged delegations with the Soviets and the Germans, while the US Youth Council worked with the CIA-orphaned World Assembly of Youth. By 1968 the private-public ratio had come a long way from Welles's 95–5; one might hazard a guess that government activism had brought it closer to 60–40.

The Fulbright Program had suffered damage. Its BFS rudder, with inappropriate appointments, was weakened by staff and travel cuts. Under James Roach, University of Texas political scientist, and James Billington, Princeton historian of Russia and future Librarian of Congress, BFS struggled to retain relevance. With CU planning tugged toward USIA criteria, Fulbright decisions were more easily swayed by USIS posts, especially in the hundred-odd field posts without binational Fulbright agreements or commissions. BFS tried to reassert its relevance by proclamation. A pamphlet called *BFS in the Seventies* broadcast its message and was followed by another pamphlet for the eighties. Widely distributed, both were little read. BFS reached abroad as well by sending out "Lincoln Lecturers" and in Mexico "Lincoln-Juarez Lecturers," high-prestige American academics presumably showing the BFS flag; but at field level these high-prestige lecturers melted into the USIS program and were treated like other "speakers." While BFS was trying to reassert leadership, the CU advisory commission, expanded by Fulbright-Hays in 1961, was slowly struggling back from its 1967 cry for help.

Richardson's CU looked for better congressional relations. Fulbright application forms now contained a box for candidates to specify their congressional districts, so that legislators could be notified when constituents were awarded Fulbright grants (it was a better idea than an earlier system, "State" candidates, meaning those recommended by members of Congress; these had been avoided by field posts, after several bad experiences). NGOs were asked to help CU remind Congress of the payoffs of cultural budgets. The downside to such constituency building was not long in emerging, as legislators began thinking about programs of their own. Within a decade CU's programs would be saddled with various congressionally mandated activities, and by the 1980s congressional micromanagement became a serious threat.

Reaching for a US constituency, Richardson and the BFS, after two decades of inaction, offered quiet financial support to US Fulbright alumni, in support of efforts to organize the US Fulbright returnees—over forty thousand at that time. Intimidated by language in Smith-Mundt forbidding political use of exchanges, CU had long neglected US follow-up. In contrast, the Peace Corps was not cowed by Smith-Mundt and gave generous support to an energetic alumni organization within a few years of its birth, leading to today's flourishing and involved alumni body.

Decline in the academic caliber of BFS and advisory commission members continued. While CU's advisory commission fought back from *Is Anybody Listening?*, the golden years under John Gardner would never return. Fulbright-Hays's precise stipulations about the caliber and the categories of members of both bodies were ignored by the White House. By

Richardson's time, the commission was chaired by a remarkable man with unpromising qualifications: Leo Cherne. A Richardson friend from his days with the International Rescue Committee and Radio Free Europe, Cherne had chaired the Foreign Intelligence Advisory Board under President Ford and joined the first Intelligence Oversight Board. He was succeeded on CU's commission by an even more surprising name: former USIA director Leonard Marks, lawyer and friend to Lyndon Johnson, now a Nixon-Ford Democrat. As good a director as USIA had had after George Allen, Marks was still an odd choice to head CU's advisory commission. A fair-minded man, he nonetheless saw no problem with the one-agency-one-mission view of CU-USIA. His chairmanship was another small step toward CU's absorption by USIA in 1978.

Richardson signed no new Fulbright agreements; negotiations with Morocco began in his last year and bore fruit only after his departure. Meanwhile, China, Egypt, and India signed "cultural treaties," in the new Kissinger mode, bypassing a century or more of US diplomatic tradition, not to mention the flexible Fulbright vehicle that might easily have accommodated the new needs. With Mexico, longstanding cultural tensions were eased by amending the creaking Cultural Cooperation Agreement of 1949—neither USIS nor CU seized the moment to press for a Fulbright agreement (USIS Mexico insisted the Mexicans did not want one). Only in 1990 would an unusual but recognizable Fulbright agreement at last be put in place, thanks to the vigor of PAO Robert Earle with commitments of private support. In sub-Saharan Africa, the South African commission disappeared, by US choice; it was a slap at apartheid—a rare example of a US withdrawal of a commission for political purposes. No other African Fulbright agreements were in place. Eight annual cultural agreements were signed with the high-priority USSR during Richardson's tenure, with "Fulbright" activities handled by the independent Soviet-oriented IREX. Richardson and his first deputy Frederick Irving did not share Benton's or Frankel's vision of UNESCO's relevance to CU and saw the organization as a red flag for Rooney; supervision for UNESCO was reassigned to State's Office of International Organizations.

Richardson, with Peter Solmssen as his surrogate, persuaded Congress to pass the far-reaching Indemnity Act, insuring all formal loans of art objects to and from the U.S. against loss. Looking far ahead, he also established the CU History Project, which produced three indispensable sourcebooks—on China, Latin America, and Germany—before being scrapped by USIA in 1978.

Overseas performances were troubled as usual, but the bearish Congress could not avoid commitments to Soviet treaties. Mark Lewis, with a paltry budget of $1 million, stretched blocked currencies and permitted some events to visit other European cities. With such ramshackle improvisations, CU was barely able to keep performing artists flowing to a few major cities in Europe let alone the developing world; and the poor-mouth bargaining with the performance community left a bad taste—arts administrators likened CU negotiations to the Damascus bazaar.

Abroad, the idea of foreign contributions to binational Fulbright programs was catching on. In 1971 foreign contributions totaled around $2.5 million; by 1976 they stood at $3.6 million, with West Germany as the highest contributor. The Germans soon quadrupled the US contribution, and post-Franco Spain, with funds from military-base leases, eventually quintupled US funding. By the end of the century foreign contributions would total close to $50 million worldwide, 20 percent of total Fulbright cost. Historically it was an unprecedented vote of approval for US binationalism. But privately PAOs continued to grumble about the independent-minded commissions.

In Richardson's years Europe and Japan, perhaps aware of CU's dilemma, began paying back their literal and moral debts to the U.S. These countries, after twenty years, had understood that binational partnership in the American style served their interests. The Finland Trust, on the Boxer model, channeled loan repayments from two wars into an expanded Fulbright Program. In 1972 West Germany covered more than 80 percent of Fulbright costs and launched the freestanding German Marshall Fund for social science research and study in both countries. Norway created its Marshall Fund in 1977, similarly ignoring the Fulbright Commission. With advice from the Ford Foundation, Japan launched two private foundations to cooperate with the private US world, again bypassing Fulbright.

The Fulbright commissions in Germany, Norway, Japan, and Finland might easily have met the needs through binational partnership; instead they watched as independent—and in some cases countervailing—institutions came to life. From the quantitative viewpoint, US cultural relations took a step forward in all four countries, but in terms of overall coordinated efforts, another tiny slice was cut from US bilateral cultural diplomacy, and more uncoordinated competition was in play. The commissions took note of the sociopolitical agendas of these new entities and reduced their own commitment to social and policy studies, a point not lost on USIA and Congress, which saw fading CU relevance.

For the US bicentennial in 1976, CU worked with USIA in American studies, a field Smith-Mundt had agreed fit into both CU and USIA. Five regional conferences gathered around the world, focused on university-level study of the U.S. Yale's Robin Winks, former CAO London, coordinated the meetings from New Haven. Both agencies celebrated Fulbright's thirtieth anniversary in 1976 as well, with ten regional meetings and a publication called *A Process of Global Enlightenment*—a title that showed Louis XIV's metaphor had crossed the Atlantic for good.

On interagency coordination, Richardson hesitated, remembering Coombs's defeat; the "Concept" paper was silent on the topic. In early 1974 he formed an interagency subcommittee for the purpose of coordination. Under his delegated chairmanship the committee offered an overdue attempt to revive Welles's ICC; Richardson had no time to make it work before he was swamped with new responsibilities for public affairs. Without presidential muscle, other agencies paid no attention. Richardson was not Sumner Welles; he was not deputy secretary but the least of a dozen assistant secretaries at State's third level. The interagency committee made a persuasive case in writing and agencies subscribed to the words, but tiny CU could not command the attention of behemoths like AID, HEW, and the military's IMET, nor could they afford to staff an active office. As for the new president Gerald Ford, he had other matters on his mind.

In a pale follow-up to the 1958 Morrill report, Richardson and ACE published five task force reports on "education in an interdependent world," focused on diffusion, professional skills, collaborative research, language competencies, and libraries. The underfunded task forces were heavily staffed by government agencies and, since the government was reluctant to criticize itself, the results were tepid.

Richardson had no control whatsoever over field staffing. But in CU's Washington personnel, change was significant, even if too late to make a difference. To upgrade CU staff from the top down, senior deputy William Hitchcock made a full-court effort to raise the quality of CU's State officers by drawing on the foreign service. The bureau's born-again motto—"in the mainstream of foreign policy"—proclaimed energy and policy relevance. Talented younger foreign service officers went through CU in Richardson's time, under the shrewd eye of Hitchcock. Many later moved on to ambassadorships or to deputy assistant secretary positions. Naturally the backwash hit the Civil Service staff inside CU—more and more hedgehogs retired and collective memory shrank. Newcomers also filled positions normally reserved for field-experienced CAOs from USIA, who found a cooler reception in CU than in the 1950s and for the most part had no choice but to spend their Washington assignments in USIA.

To ease out senior veterans, Richardson's team used various methods. Two old-line greats were reassigned to the History Project. Others were layered over, like the feisty officer who had created CU assistance to foreign students in the U.S. Mistrust swept the domestic staffers. Hitchcock's predecessor, resolving to reverse the 4–1 ratio of civil servants to foreign service officers, had aimed too high—foreign service officers were not ready to serve more than two or three years, and the hedgehogs were outraged to see their value denigrated. In fact, CU depended on the expertise of its longtime staff to cover the US educational and intellectual world; foreign service officers, living abroad, could not be expected to meet this need. After vigorous efforts, the percentage of foreign service officers in CU rose from 25 percent to 30 percent, then stabilized. Cherrington had seen that CU would rise or fall by its US expertise, and he had recruited and nurtured permanent expertise from the universities. Thirty years later, some of these people had become timeservers, but CU still needed a dozen top-ranked permanent civil servants who were totally informed about questions like foreign students, who knew Congress, and who could deal with US educational leadership eye-to-eye. Their absence could already be felt in the mid-seventies.

While he moved forward, Richardson's dialogue with Shakespeare and Keogh was one-way. Inside CU, he warned firebrand CAOs not to get him into war with USIA, with which relations, for once, were better than ever—or at least there were no knives. But USIA had already gotten most of what it wanted from CU and saw more ahead. The "Rube Goldberg" CU-USIA arrangement, as Richardson called it, was never far from his mind, but he could do little more than slow its collapse.

Nixon's USIA director Keogh was a relief after Shakespeare, but the quiet Keogh was an unshakable one-agency man with his own tough views. The word "communication" began to appear more often in CU's thinking and writing; Richardson and Keogh, probably encouraged by Stanton, used it as a conceptual bridge. Soon, perhaps with hints from Stanton's commission as well as Marks's CU body, the two agency chiefs decided on a dramatic step. They asked the two commissions to cosponsor a joint report. USIA's top woman officer, Barbara White, was assigned to the job. At first things seemed to go well.

When Richardson let himself be dragooned into acting as head of State's public relations office, on top of his main job, forward motion stopped. In 1976 he became Assistant Secretary for Public Affairs and immediately rediscovered the dilemma faced by Benton, Barrett, and George Allen in the 1940s. Hitchcock filled in as acting head of CU.

The bureau was noticeably stronger. Its officers in the geographic area offices stood behind their CAOs and supported them on the right issues. CU continued trying to play a role in assignments and promotions but was ultimately powerless to support cultural officers on career questions—administrative status, promotion, assignments, American staff, and USIA budgets; CU had no way of stopping USIA from tightening its hold over CAO careers. A CU role in recruiting new officers was out of the question; as for training, CU's impact was negligible and declining. True, CU contributed to annual personnel evaluations, but its comments were disregarded or reshaped by the USIA writers and carried little weight. In fact, CU's help could do more harm than good. In the field, USIA made all CAO assignments; CU "approved," but rarely disagreed with the agency's decisions because they knew the alternative would be worse. Lateral entry of new talents was long gone; and outside appointments to CAO positions, even in London, ended in 1976.

Political appointments were growing in number. In the 1970s pressure for political appointments in CU had been resisted and minimized. When the 1973 White House–cleaning exercise after Nixon's victory sent a dozen young White House staffers knocking on CU's doors, bearing warm recommendations from Robert Haldeman, only one was accepted, a capable woman with useful experience and connections. She was apprenticed as deputy to the director of the IV Program.

After the 1973 USIA decision to go generalist, the quality of USIA cultural staff was falling faster than usual. Political scientist Wayne Wilcox, CAO London on leave from Columbia University, testified before the CU advisory commission on the disastrous closing off of lateral entry and its impact on the CAO corps. Of twenty-three promotions from Class 3 to Class 2 that year, only five—just over 20 percent—were committed cultural officers. And that was a marked improvement over the past. The CAO educational profile, he said, was declining, in contrast to other agencies' staff.[6]

The decision to shift UNESCO to State's Office of International Organizations Office was having its effect. UNESCO was the last face on IO's totem pole. Low-caliber appointments of US ambassador to UNESCO showed that the White House did not care. UNESCO oversight languished and with it the US capacity for reversing worrisome trends in Paris. American frustration with the organization, hobbled by Soviet obstructionism and hindered by its administrative culture of 180 member-states, was growing. UNESCO, the baby of the UN family, was a magnificent American idea which had turned into a complex and frustrating US chore—CU had wrought no miracles in its service. While other nations were sending their finest intellectuals to UNESCO as ambassadors—poets, scholars, philosophers, scientists, and writers—the U.S. sent party loyalists who wanted to live in Paris. UNESCO, integral to the founders' vision, was drifting toward US withdrawal and Richardson was unwilling to help. UNESCO was no more exasperating than any multilateral organization with one hundred or more member-states and intransigent Soviet tactics. Inadequate US ambassadors, when in Washington, carried no weight in Congress.

Still, hundreds of US private groups and universities that worked with UNESCO in its five fields (education, science, culture, communications, and social science) were dismayed when UNESCO was moved out of CU. The bilateral-multilateral continuum seen by MacLeish and Fulbright was shattered. When the U.S. quit UNESCO in 1984, accompanied only by the UK and Singapore, the protests of a dozen federal agencies were ignored.[7]

Under Richardson, Fulbright's program remained relatively stable; at least its budget did not decline. The interlocking defenses put in place by the founders, though weakened, were still firm. But Richardson's decision to move the postdoctoral Fulbright Program out of the NAS ruffled the scientific community.

In all, there seemed to be dozens of large and small patient victories, good and less good, in the Richardson years. But they concealed illusions. Two decades later we can see that Richardson's efforts did little more than retard the general erosion of cultural affairs and CU. Beneath CU's apparent stability and gradual growth, the chipping away of its defenses had not relented. Richardson's eight years warrant a look at the negative side.

In fact, the war had probably been lost before Richardson came to

Washington, before, during, and after the Frankel period. The moderate internationalist Richardson, while a fervent believer in CU's mission, stood at a political distance from the White House and from his State superiors, and their inattention to his ideas thwarted high-level discussion of a grand design. Testifying before his friend Dante Fascell's House committee in 1977, Richardson confessed he had never once been able to speak with a superior in State about Public Diplomacy—Fascell pride, the new euphemism for information-propaganda cum culture. Ready access to the president or the Secretary of State, which Welles, MacLeish, Benton, Allen, Thayer, and Battle took for granted, while damaged by the assumption of access by Coombs and Frankel, had permitted broader thinking and encouraged innovation. Coombs's CU, for example, still had something to say about appointments to CU's two advisory bodies and its academic CAOs. By Richardson's time, such appointments lay far beyond his control.

Most serious were budgets. In real dollars, CU budgets, while rising from Frankel's low to nearly $65 million on paper, actually fell *behind* inflation. In constant dollars, Richardson's last CU budget stood a third *below* the high-water mark of 1967, even taking into account the 20 percent supplement squeezed out of foreign currencies. To make matters worse, the 1972 oil shock sharply inflated the transportation costs by which exchanges lived.

BFS had slowly lost its bite after Lyndon Johnson turned its appointments over to domestic politics. In its first two decades, perhaps four BFS members came from outside the university world; in its third and fourth decades, this bridge to the universities counted twenty-four nonacademics, some of them indeed quietly antiacademic, thanks to the divisive Vietnam era. Among CU's suggested nominations for oversight commissions, only occasionally was one accepted by the White House. While the integrity of Fulbright's exchanges survived, there were warning signs.

For IV, the long-slumbering risk of politicization was still a threat. Battle's geographic restructuring of the program brought it closer to State's geographic bureaus and raised temptations to use it for closer policy support. CU's slogan about swimming in foreign policy's mainstream fed the short-range trend as USIA cheered from the sidelines. IV grants still served educational and cultural needs on occasion, but the mix was changing; a cultural program with political utility had reversed itself and was now a political program with an occasional cultural dimension. This was no secret to foreign observers. Pressures from the embassies, from USIA, from Congress, from powerful constituents, from AFL-CIO, and from State for shorter-range political impact—these met negligible resistance in CU and even less in the field. CU sent no strong guidelines restraining embassy political and economic sections, and so the powerful embassy sections easily coopted the program. In 1982 a survey of ambassadors—queried and advised by their PAOs—ranked the IV grant as the prime exchange tool of embassies, well ahead of Fulbright.

Frankel had argued that overtly political IV grants were desirable but should be identified as a special political action program, leaving most of IV for education. He believed cultural channels, overused for political action, lost their educational character. He knew that, to foreigners, an IV grant could easily look like an expenses-paid boondoggle, perhaps with invisible strings attached. The learning process of the IV grantee and his or her ability to share it after return were affected by the grantee's self-image and public persona. In one European capital, an exasperated CAO disengaged from IV, which had become a service station for the political and economic sections; he was roundly criticized by USIA for losing control over a program that he never had. Legitimizing the political-action quality of IV, CU and USIA began compiling annual lists of world leaders who were IV alumni to impress Congress; while the lengthy lists made a powerful statement, they skewed selection; now embassies competed in spotting future heads of state. In Washington the professional escort-interpreters who accompanied visitors around the U.S. regularly asked briefers in retraining sessions, "How on earth do they choose these guys?"

Another step toward politicization was Kissinger's decision to use the cultural treaty, brushing aside a century of US diplomatic efforts to avoid them. Until 1970 cultural agreements had been seen by early diplomacy and by CU as restrictive, difficult to respect, and wasteful; they had been used only in cases of absolute necessity, notably in the Soviet countries. Kissinger, without consulting CU, decreed that cultural treaties were desirable. The Shanghai Communique—the guiding document for Nixon's opening to China—included cultural elements, which CU had to absorb, administer, and fund. A revived Fulbright agreement, reopening the old Chinese commission or even the Boxer structure, would have served as well; but no one remembered. Joint cultural agreements, signed with India and Egypt, were rewards for helping stabilize their regions. These agreements required expensive annual binational meetings, rotating from country to country, and considerable staff time; Fulbright instead kept a small team on the ground all year long and solved problems as they arose. A more compatible treaty with Japan, on the other hand, expanded the annual Japan-U.S. dialogue known as CULCON, which helped Japan think about its own cultural investments and generated more US-Japanese exchange. Since 1938 CU had rejected attempts to negotiate cultural agreements; and now it had no choice but to cope with costly treaties imposed by those outside CU's value-structure. For Kissinger, cultural treaties were harmless sugarcoating for hard-earned bilateral agreements; for CU, they cut into meager field resources and reduced the relevance of embassy CAOs.

CU's control over field programs steadily declined under Richardson. In 1973 CU threw away its annual planning process, first generated by Coombs. The plan designed the annual program, shaped the cultural program's identity, and helped maintain an independent cultural identity within USIS posts. When Richardson agreed to discuss joint-planning with USIA, the agency rejoiced and assigned its most genteel and persuasive officer, fresh from the painful task of inflicting a Program Budgeting System on USIS's protesting field posts, to the task. To negotiate with this officer, CU sent the weakest member of its management team to the table, a man openly hostile to CU and its staff. The result: CU's plan was absorbed into the unchanged USIA plan, built not on education but on delivering policy messages to target audiences. CAOs now had to fit their programs into USIA's system of themes, audience categories, influentials to be reached, and messages to be conveyed.

For the career CAOs, CU's efforts to attract high-caliber foreign service officers reduced the number of positions open to them in Washington. CU, in theory, retained the right to approve CAO field assignments and contribute to personnel evaluations—but USIA had long ago learned how to circumvent both. Jacob Canter's itinerary, beginning in Nicaragua and ending as acting head of CU, would never be replicated.

While the IV Program moved in a shorter-term political-action direction, American specialists, prominent Americans sent abroad for dialogue and discussion, became far too political an issue—they were Rooney's favorite target. In exasperation, CU threw in the towel and closed the specialist program, except for a residual fragment concealed under the meretricious name of Short-term American grantees (STAGs). The officer handling STAGs in 1973 remembers his briefing by his CU chief. Rooney, he was told, had a long, elastic list of no-nos, reliably culled from past hearings; it began with Ivy League graduates and university professors (the incumbent was both), then moved to poets, sports figures, economists, women, Easterners, historians, scientists, and so forth. In fact there was no pattern: Rooney had attacked virtually at random every profession, every region of the country, every gender, race, or religion, and every academic discipline. Asked if any category remained, the supervisor answered, "Probably not."

As CU's ability to send out prominent Americans all but vanished, USIA eagerly picked up this "people" tool—which Fulbright-Hays had explicitly excluded. Field-post demand for "speakers," as part of telling the story, was insatiable. In fact, CU's specialists had always tried to maintain a deeply two-way cultural function, learning as well as teaching, helping CAOs engage dialogue at upper levels, establishing US links, locating other US experts, and placing foreign researchers or students in the right US universities; they lifted the level of dialogue, provided good teaching when needed, brought authoritative experiential interchange, increased the CAO's reach, and expanded networks. USIS and its PAOs instead tended to focus on single public events, stressing name recognition and star quality. "Speakers" was USIA's name for them; they fed the show-biz side of cultural exchanges, whereas specialists for years had deepened dialogue. They were the US-bound counterpart to the IV Program.

Step by step USIA sneaked "speakers" into its field posts. In 1968, perhaps with an exhausted wink and weary nod from CU, USIA began sending out performer-speakers with heavy equipment needs—a print-maker with a complete print shop, an experimental filmmaker with equipment, or a woodwind ensemble with elaborate lighting and electronic gear. Next, USIA offered to carry forward any "speaker" who was already abroad—e.g., borrowing Fulbright scholars from one country for work in another. But "abroad" was soon defined to mean Montreal or London, and "speakers" were asked to pay their way to one of those cities, where they would be given forward air-ticketing, then reimbursement for the first leg of the trip at some embassy along the itinerary where local currencies could be converted into dollars. Soon dozens of USIA-provided speakers were reaching the field, unnoticed—or at least unmentioned—by Rooney.

Having established de facto ownership of Americans abroad by stealth, USIA exercised the right to choose them and guide their performance. Until then, visitors had been asked only to lay out US policy fairly, then argue any alternative position they chose. By 1981 USIA was looking for authoritative speakers who agreed to support US policy. Soon USIA, on its funds, was sending out spokesmen from other government agencies including State. "Speakers" from State had always traveled at State expense, but they now drew down on USIA-CU's thin budgets. While their authority to speak on policy questions was impressive, they were often out of their depth when the subject moved away—as it usually did—from their narrow expertise. They were also constrained by their position as US government staff. CAOs like Duke Ryan complained that the flood of speakers on policy rapidly exhausted audience interest. As policy support grew, USIS audiences narrowed, delighting the targeteers in Washington, but impoverishing the field cultural program.[8]

A later administration took the next step, inevitable as now seems. For hard-hitting message delivery, it chose American speakers by litmus tests, focusing on those who supported current policies most compellingly. The famous "blacklisting" scandals of 1983–84 grew from those rejected by this orthodoxy. As Ryan relates the story for which he had a ringside seat, USIA staffers had compiled, in self-defense, lists of Americans their bosses did *not* want. When the press learned about this practice, it labeled the episode "blacklisting," and the name stuck. The issue for a CAO went far beyond blacklists. Visitors had once served as discussion tools, by which the U.S. displayed its openness to responsible criticism, but now critical thinkers were weeded out before the fact, and dialogue was replaced by unidirectional messages. USIA had essentially turned its attention away from dialogue and engagement to winning confrontational debates.

After the blacklist came to light, the selection process went underground, not changing but hiding. The USIA of the 1980s was not concerned that "speakers" were no longer either cultural nor exchangees;

rather they allowed the policy message to take over the cultural medium and become the only purpose. Sorensen would have been pleased.

In sum, USIA, with Rooney's help, had sliced another function out of CU and diluted a major element of substance and dialogue. Foreign audiences learned to expect the party line from a new breed of American apparatchiks. In the name of fighting the USSR, the U.S. had adopted Soviet tactics.

The greatest loss resulted from Richardson's acceptance of a second job. At its potential height, his gradualist leadership was diverted. He had made CU into a functioning bureau and devoted five years to learning the ropes. He had earned the right to address the bigger questions, to work things out with USIA, to seek White House help, and to educate Congress. At this point, he was diverted from his CU focus. For example, he might have worked with Kissinger, whose geopolitical chess games concentrated on present and predictable power and who disdained as idealism the remote possibility of changing attitudes over any reasonable time frame. Instead of dealing directly with this central issue, Richardson spent half his time in another office. Eight patient years with CU neither lowered the pressures, nor bolstered the defenses, nor revitalized the field, nor kept USIA at bay, nor reversed declining budgetary trends. He had inherited a shambles, tidied things up slowly until they approached seeming strength, while juggling the seeming madness of a maverick congressman. In the end the steadfast Richardson, achieving much, gave much away. His CU years were a classic victory of the kind won by Pyrrhus.

After Fulbright's departure in 1975, no congressional leader stepped forward to slow USIA's growing control over cultural operations or to restrain State's tendency toward tactical use of "culture." In 1978 Richardson left CU, accepting a leading role in the founding of NED and the US Institute of Peace, moving as well into the directorship of the high-school exchange program YFU. Meanwhile, CU was left to face its worst disaster since 1938.

CHAPTER TWENTY-ONE

Six Intellectual CAOs

In the changing of attitudes or the deepening of understanding, there is little certainty, no continuity and impossible institutionalization. So one simply tries, while not committing perjury, to communicate a little of the national style, grace and genius.

—Wayne A. Wilcox, 1973

RICHARDSON'S EIGHT YEARS covered most of a crucial decade for cultural diplomacy. Before examining some of the details, it may be useful to reflect on the central issue he could not touch: the quality of staff in the field, at "the point of contact," said the Fairbanks. If intellect and government intersect in the individual, cultural diplomacy in particular begins and ends with people. Nearing the end of our tortuous itinerary, veering back and forth from enlightenment to ignorance, it is a good time to turn back to the one constant in US cultural diplomacy: its occasional and repeated capacity to put marvelous people in the field and let them do amazing things, as it were, in spite of the patchwork of institutions that sheltered them from the mini-tempests of Washington.

We have visited early academic field officers, like Fairbank and Morey, and other academic figures, like Canter and Brown, who remained with the good fight. We have watched Londoners Carl Bode and Cleanth Brooks at work. Now it is time to look at a few other toilers in the field. First, two academic CAOs in London from a younger generation, men who beyond their London years devoted special energies to improving cultural diplomacy and the lot of its servants: Robin Winks and Wayne Wilcox. Sandwiched between these two short-term intellectuals, we shall observe in varying degrees of depth four of USIA's specially bred corps of CAO-intellectuals, who managed to keep their values intact while serving in USIA's world of nonintellect: Alan Dodds, Yale Richmond, Duke Ryan, and Lois Roth. All were committed CAOs, career professionals, and intellectuals by any definition.[1]

ROBIN WINKS

In 1969 Winks, Yale historian of empires, was lured to London for two years. There he deepened a permanent relationship with cultural diplomacy that had begun in New Zealand, where he studied as a Fulbright in 1952. He never wrote comprehensively about his two-year stint as

CAO—or his fifty-year experience of cultural diplomacy—before his death in the spring of 2003. But he touched on it in various writings and perhaps, in a deep sense, in all of them. Pieced together with correspondence, these fragments permit a glimpse of his sense of what cultural diplomats do.[2]

Raised on the western slope of Colorado, a student of the university in Boulder and at Johns Hopkins—where he did his dissertation on US-Canadian history—Winks went as a Fulbright student to New Zealand in 1951–52, and later as a university lecturer to then-Malaya in 1962. These were the beginnings of a lifelong commitment to international travel, teaching, and observation of how humankind has used and abused the natural resources of this world, through the study of "empires." Well before London, he had been studying the interaction of political cultures in history, with particular emphasis on the British empire and, ultimately, on the idea of an American empire. In Colorado, long before his trip to London, he had embarked on a path that would lead him into long-term service with the advisory council of the US National Park Service, in which role he became one of the first in history to visit every one of the nearly four hundred parks in that system. After London he served CU and the Fulbright Program as consultant and advisor and traveled widely as speaker and teacher, never neglecting the students at Yale whose lives he shaped and inspired. In 2002 he took a count of his service abroad: he had taught for a full academic year in nine foreign universities and was planning a tenth, held short-term visiting lectureships in fifty other universities, visited 154 countries in unusual depth, held both Eastman and Harmsworth chairs at Oxford, and was headed for the Pitt chair at Cambridge. In his scholarship on the history of empires, he never strayed far from the role of culture in international relations, in its more subtle imperial, non-imperial, and neo-imperial forms.

In New Zealand he found his life-mate Avril. He also learned, in that least typical of islands, that all history is incomplete if it is not comparative—"he who knows only his own country's history does not know his own country" was a Winks mantra. Joining with C. Vann Woodward to produce an important book on comparative history, he became a leader in the movement to internationalize the study of history, arguing that no question can be studied in any depth without reference to broad human experience as manifested in other cultures. Similarly, he was a leader in the effort to build expertise on the U.S. in foreign universities, most often called "American Studies" but more accurately, as he called it, the Study of the U.S.[3]

His commitment to cultural interchange began with his Fulbright year and never ended. He viewed cultural diplomacy with the critical love of a scholar: "In London," he wrote, "an annual task descended upon the Cultural Office from Washington, the preparation of a report called 'Evidence of Effectiveness.' I was and am an educator and I argued then, as I do now, that in the life of the mind one cannot provide . . . evidence that is conclusive that any given action produced any given direct result. Education, we know, is diffuse, slow and intangible; it is a process." From this, he concluded that cultural diplomacy "is based, as all education must be based, on the non-quantifiable belief that knowing about other societies increases understanding and that understanding at the very least lessens the likelihood of preemptive judgments."

In London the former Fulbrighter learned the intricacies of Fulbright process, in its many analogies with the practices of the university world: "The Chairmanship of the U.S.-UK Binational Fulbright Commission went with the [CAO's] territory. . . . I learned Fulbright from the other side: about what Washington hoped for, about the desperately depleted funding, about the relative values attached by different societies and bureaucracies to different academic disciplines." Regading the centrality of education as the guiding model for the Fulbright Program, he never budged: "Either we believe that [education] will inform and broaden or we do not. And since we do, we ought not to devote much time to arguing the obvious. The reply that the effectiveness of educational exchange is not so obvious to our Congressmen is best met by the simple injunction to elect Congressmen who understand."

His years in London coincided with the worst period of protest about the Vietnam War. When demonstrators—including a future US president and gifted former students—crowded Grosvenor Square, Winks—who never forgot a student and was in turn the recipient of their admiration and affection—was the embassy officer delegated to meet them: "From across the square came the announcement, by bull horn, that a delegation from Oxford University was passing through to deliver its petition. As they mounted the steps of the embassy, I realized that three of the five students in that delegation had been my own students at Yale and elsewhere. We went inside and, with the press officer, sat for an hour, debating American policy. No one shouted; no one left with a changed opinion; no one in the embassy complained when I took the students' position."

His faith in the ultimate outcomes of education and in the civility of educated political discourse was a constant theme; it marked him as a strong cultural conservative, in both domestic and foreign affairs. Studying the Fulbright Program and its problems in 1977, he wrote: "Cecil Rhodes wrote in his will that 'educational relations make the strongest tie.' I believe this to be true. I also believe that it is not possible to provide quantified evidence or fully documented data for such a view." Elsewhere, he was less guarded about the two-way payoffs of cultural diplomacy and the capacity of foreign intellectual experience to shape American minds, as it had his: "Teaching and doing research outside the U.S. have helped me internalize time, to grasp how, although sun and sand may not change, lives do change." Again, the comparatist emerges as he looks at the U.S.: "I could never understand this country if I were not able to stand outside it from time to time." But there is more—a profound understanding of teaching: "Teaching about America abroad is not missionary work or cultural imperialism, it is a form of acceptance, of one's self and of others."

In Kuala Lumpur in 1962, the subject was colonialism—at Malayan request. There he had the only experience of USIS interference he ever reported: "A somewhat obtrusive cultural affairs officer reminded me that it was against Malayan law to have students read Marx and asked to see the outlines to my lectures. But when I refused to give up my lecture notes, the ambassador sided with me." He found similar tolerance in his Washington interview, when under consideration for the London CAO job. He was frankly astonished—and reassured for his country—that no one asked about his party affilliation. The same noninterventionist stance by government officials pleased him when, for the US bicentennial in 1975–77, he was asked by USIA to organize five regional seminars overseas on the impact of America and American studies abroad. Again he was impressed "with how little interference there was from the American government, with how seldom those who provided the funds tried to influence the outcome." Winks, who once was teased into labeling himself a "Burkean liberal," kept his political affiliations to himself; the America that left such questions unasked was the America in which he believed, the America of intellectual pluralism.

Pluralism for Winks ruled out any danger of elitism, even in teaching—which he recognized as a specific tool designed to form elites. In 1977 he wrote: "If, as Senator Fulbright said in his farewell speech, cultural exchange is an alternative to traditional foreign policy, then cultural—and especially educational—exchange, indeed cultural diplomacy, must continue to champion pluralism based on excellence."

Yet his years abroad taught him "how little we are, in fact, understood." He learned as well about trust and its role as the base without which mutual understanding cannot be built. At a seminar in Kenya on US racial tensions in the unhappy year 1969, surrounded by European scholars who blandly denied any such problems in *their* countries, he was taken aside by the cultural attaché of an Eastern European Bloc nation, who told him, "You American academics have one wonderful thing going for you. You tell the truth."

Leaving London in 1971, he was regularly consulted by USIA or CU or its successor, informally, formally, and extensively. Yet something had begun to change in American political life. He signaled to two administrations, in 1974 and 1980, that he might be available for appointive office, in USIA or elsewhere, at home or abroad. In the first case, he declined to answer his interviewer's question about his party affiliation and was declined on grounds that he had neither participated in the campaign nor made a major donation. In the second case, this erudite but civilized man was rejected by USIA's director, with an expletive attached—as USIA staff quickly learned. These two experiences challenged Winks's fundamental values. Instead of serving his country twice more, he stayed in the university world and vigorously pursued his several careers—teacher, scholar, pseudonymous mystery writer, environmental consultant, travel writer, and food critic. He died in the spring of 2003, with two major books left unfinished; a much-needed memoir about cultural diplomacy died with him.

•   •   •

Winks was the traveler's traveler. A frequent visitor to USIS posts, he stayed in officers' homes and welcomed them into his farmhouse north of New Haven. He was in continual touch with a dozen or more USIA colleagues long after London. Four of those he admired—all committed insider CAOs and long-serving professionals—were intellectuals by any definition. These four have shared their own memories with me.

ALAN DODDS

Dodds was CAO Vienna when Winks was in London. After military service in the Second World War, Dodds cut his teeth in the German reorientation program in a German *Kreis* or "county." He became a McCarthy victim when he ventured to defend the contents of the USIS libraries in West Germany against the ludicrous accusations of Cohn and Schine. He resigned from the service after that episode but was quickly rehired, in part because of his fine German and Italian. He spent the rest of his career as a CAO in Europe, in Germany, Italy, and Austria. Dodds is a gifted and memorable raconteur who never commits himself to paper. What follows is my reconstruction of three revealing tales from his CAO years in Vienna in the early 1970s.[4] These three overheard stories focus on his years in Vienna; they leave a clear sense of the perils and joys of a CAO.

First, the Case of the Hovering Ambassador. Assigned to Vienna, Dodds was surprised to learn that his future chief of mission had made an unusual request, insisting on meeting and approving him. Arranging the meeting in Washington was not easy. Finally and to his amazement, Dodds was asked to appear at a given time on the large grassy oval just south of the White House. At the appointed hour, he found himself standing alone. Soon a US Army helicopter chugged overhead and, in the usual windstorm, landed on the oval. Out stepped the ambassador: "Are you Dodds?" "Yes, sir." "Service record?" Dodds recited his military affiliations. "You'll do," said the ambassador, turning back to the chopper and lifting away.

Second, the Case of the Mysterious Lunch Companion. Dodds in Vienna took to lunching alone once a week at a private club near the embassy. One day an unknown Austrian fellow diner, whom he had noticed before, approached his table; with exquisite politeness, the Austrian said he had been observing Dodds for several weeks and invited him to share lunch with him there every week—the Austrian knew that Dodds was American but had no idea where he worked; Dodds, in turn, had no idea who the Austrian was. He agreed and accepted the stranger's two requirements: that they never exchange names and that they never discuss politics. For the next year he enjoyed an extraordinary, informed, and stimulating experience, talking weekly with this intelligent and cultured European intellectual about all manner of things.

As his second year in Vienna began, a sharp change in government catapulted an unheralded new cabinet into office. At the ambassador's staff meeting the next morning, the embassy team pooled its sparse knowledge of the new government faces, and the ambassador was irritated to learn that, despite the embassy's vaunted efforts to be in touch with Austria's successor generations, no one in his embassy knew the new prime minister. No one, that is, except Dodds, who had read the morning papers and recognized his lunch companion.

Third, the Case of the Lone Supporter. As CAO, Dodds sometimes filled in for the PAO at the ambassador's smaller meetings. At one of these, the embassy team was hotly debating a tricky question of timing: when to report a given Austrian development to Washington. The discussion moved back and forth, and the staff consensus, against the ambassador's judgment, was that the news needed to be reported immediately. Contrary to his staff, the ambassador wanted to delay, get more details, and see how it played out. Dodds, knowing that the story would change significantly in a few days, thought a delay would do no harm. The exasperated ambassador finally polled the table and to his amazement found that only Dodds supported him. "Fantastic!" the ambassador exploded, "I have to come all the way to Vienna to find out that the only man who agrees with me is the f—ing CAO!"

YALE RICHMOND

Providence-born Richmond, unlike Dodds, has no writer's block; he has written a great deal about his experiences in Russia and Poland in various useful books, most notably his diligent and studious *Cultural Exchange and the Cold War: Raising the Iron Curtain*. Like Dodds a veteran of German reorientation but a far more adventurous linguist, he was another kind of intellectual, USIA-style. His career included half a dozen field assignments, largely in cultural work, in Laos, Poland, Austria, and the USSR. He was CAO Warsaw in 1958–61 and PAO-CAO Moscow in 1967–69. After that he headed Eastern European affairs in CU, moved with CU to the new ICA, then retired to various freelance activities and writing; he was on the team creating the National Endowment for Democracy (NED).

Richmond is blessed with a thoughtful mindset, a superb command of German, Russian, and Polish, an acute memory, and a spare writing style that avoids sentiment. His memories are rich. In insurgent Laos, for example, he remembers a baseball episode akin to Canter's. His ambassador, a political appointee from the advertising world, wanted to "distribute baseball caps with logos supporting the Lao government." Richmond talked him out of it.

In 1952, as "Resident Officer" in Munich, he was urged to get out and "buy a burgermeister a beer." He combed the region, meeting everyone he could, speaking wherever invited: "Germany was now independent and our job was to encourage its transition to democracy." He learned that any such discussion, or cultural exchange with the U.S., meant implicit instruction in democracy, whatever the subject of conversation or the field the grant was intended to cover; he understood that in such circumstances cultural diplomacy was never "pure" but rather an effective, noninterventionist, and durable form of long-range political action that rode alongside genuine targetted learning.

Then came the USSR. USIA Soviet area specialists had two characteristics: they made a heavy investment in language training to achieve a respectable qualitative level of proficiency; and they operated in a context in which the Russian press and media were out of reach and thus dealt mainly with "cultural affairs." But it was cultural affairs in an explicit and highly political environment. In the USSR, the word "culture" was held in reverence; to be called *nye-kulturni*, "uncultured," was a serious insult. Thus USIS did culture in a supercharged political context where every sigh had meaning. As Richmond wrote in 1988, "In the Soviet bloc, the linkage between politics and culture is so total that the dividing line between them blurs. A cultural officer finds that the work is overwhelmingly political and highly visible. . . . It is a long-range agenda, one in which cultural officers will always play a central but quiet role."

Like many East European hands, Richmond in his career with USIA was savaged by director Shakespeare's famous visit in 1969. In his hawkish vigor, with no evidence and less area experience, he pulled Richmond out of Moscow; worse, he inserted a note into Richmond's personnel file saying that this officer "did not understand the difference between communism and the free world." Since such notes remain in personnel files for five years, Richmond's promotion was long delayed—one more admiral had been hanged to encourage the others. After that same trip, Shakespeare declared that skilled foreign-born Slavic linguists were "second-class Americans," hence superfluous in USIA.

In light of this clownish but lethal behavior, it was the more ominous when Shakespeare declared that henceforth the supercharged politics of East Europe were the context for the agency he wanted to build. He concocted and decreed the totally impractical idea that all senior USIA appointments would be decided on the basis of the officer's experience behind the Iron Curtain. In effect, all promotions beyond the midpoint would be held up until candidates had served in Eastern Europe. Meeting this requirement would have cost millions in language training, bloated the eastern European posts, and starved the rest of the world for a decade or two. USIA administrators wisely dragged their feet.

Richmond's Soviet experience exemplifies his "mindset for a time of war," as he put it in 1988, just before the Soviet implosion. In both Poland and the USSR, he wrote, "governments have found it useful to have cultural relations with the U.S., a necessary element in bilateral relations. The objectives on both sides are not dissimilar. . . . Each country wants to 'tell its story,' promote its cultural achievements, and encourage study of its language, all with the hope of improving mutual understanding. . . . Improvements in political and economic relations will follow." One factor in Russian culture held promise for engaging with the Soviets: the USSR shared and remembered more history with the U.S. than Americans knew. "They know that neither Russia nor the USSR has ever had a war with the U.S.; they know that we were allies against a common enemy, Germany, in two world wars; they recall the aid sent by the U.S.—in the early 1920s to alleviate famine, in the 1930s to help industrialize, and in the 1940s to help defeat the Nazis. US cultural programs have built on this base of popular goodwill." In the most impossible conditions, it was engagement at its best.

Life behind the Curtain was not easy. Moscow "is considered a good assignment for cultural officers but only a few make it. The staffs in Moscow and Leningrad are small, there are few positions, and a deep working knowledge of the language is required. . . . Living conditions are difficult, as in 1987 when all Soviet employees left the embassy and all housekeeping and administration at the Moscow embassy had to be done by American officers—including floor-scrubbing, snow-shoveling, truck-loading and toilet-cleaning."

Outside the embassy, eager Soviet audiences were hungry and could not get enough information: "The Soviet people have an insatiable curiosity about the U.S. and it can be fun to try to assuage it." Understanding Soviet society is difficult from afar: "The best way to understand Soviet 'communism' is to live there. . . . Contact with Soviet citizens was possible even in the years before Gorbachev's *glasnost*. One of the ways of conversing with ordinary Russians, I discovered, was to open the hood of my American car and start tinkering with the engine. A crowd would immediately gather . . . and we would soon move to discussions of anything and everything, with no inhibitions." Such ingenuity was easier after hours: "The most interesting part of a cultural officer's workday came after 6 P.M., when we left Fortress America and entered Moscow's rich cultural world. . . . Evenings at the Bolshoi, with salami sandwiches and strong tea in lieu of supper."

Administering cultural programs, both exports and imports, was infuriating and laborious because of Soviet insistence on respecting every letter and comma of cultural treaties: "The main activity is exchanges . . . under intergovernmental agreement." But it is not so simple: "Exchanges have to be continually monitored because the USSR is not a very efficient place. Things are rarely done as planned, on time, or in some cases at all." Thanks to the embassy cultural office, "student exchange became a growth industry. By 1987–88 there were about 700 American students, teachers and scholars in the USSR and 400 Soviets in the U.S." Perform-ing arts were almost too abundant: they "required a great deal of nurse-maiding. In recent years we helped artists like Vladimir Horowitz, in his long-delayed return, Yo Yo Ma, the New York Philharmonic and the Dance Theatre of Harlem. In 1967 we had an American circus!" Top-level visitors from the U.S. periodically made life interesting: "Historian James McGregor Burns was planning a visit to Moscow in 1969," but Richmond missed him, called instead to Novosibirsk "for the first US event there ever, a performance by the University of Minnesota Symphonic Band." Another visitor: "In 1968 a Harvard scholar requested 'appropriate cour-tesies' . . . Henry Kissinger."

In Poland, the rules were different. Its "'revolution' of 1956 had pro-duced a 'national communist' government, seeking to restore some part of Poland's long friendly relationship with the U.S." There was chaos but opportunity: "The Party was in disarray and the intelligentsia were look-ing to the West. Ford and Rockefeller had begun large fellowship pro-grams and the government had given the green light for more." The first task was to open a Fulbright program. "The first Polish Fulbrighters went to the U.S. in 1959 and the first US lecturer arrived in 1960. Eventually there were as many as 17 Americans lecturing at Polish universities, mostly in American Studies." There was more than people exchanges; next came an American library. "The postwar USIS library had been closed by the Poles in 1950. In 1960 we opened a library in the embassy, focused on American Studies and on rich reference tools, the only library of its kind in Poland." To the library came "American 'Specialists' for short-term visits—Saul Bellow and Mary McCarthy, for example."

In Poland too, American performers were frequent: "Bernstein and the New York Philharmonic, Artur Rubinstein for his return home, Isaac Stern, Leopold Stokowski, and the Juilliard Quartet." Interuniversity rela-tions were taking root. Indiana University set up an American Studies Center at Warsaw University, and Poland supported a Polish Studies Cen-ter in Bloomington.

Overall, in 1988, there was little doubt in Richmond's mind that the work was indispensable, hugely effective, and change-provoking. Over time it stimulated change in Poland and the USSR—at suprisingly low cost. "What did we accomplish? It is always hard to measure the impact of 'cultural factors.' There is little doubt that US and other western cul-tural exchanges helped prepare the groundwork for *glasnost* and *peres-troika*." Between 1958 and 1986, "an entire generation of Soviet intellectuals visited the U.S. and Western Europe," thanks to the opening of exchanges. "They learned that their government and media had not been truthful. They understood how far behind the USSR lagged in every field. . . . The Soviet media lost their monopoly on information about the West [and] were forced to be more honest with their own people." In Richmond's life, "the USSR and Poland, two countries with communist governments opposed to the U.S., brought me the greatest satisfactions as a cultural officer. It is there I believe I made my greatest contribution to the US national interest. Every day there was another challenge, every day brought unforgettable rewards."

His book in 2003, a summation, is a rich tribute to the indirect style of US cultural affairs, pressing for engagement rather than confrontation. Ultimately, Richmond believes, it was an obvious factor in lifting—or tearing—the Curtain. In East Europe officers like Richmond reached instinctively for the tools of high culture, having understood that diplomacy cannot succeed without them. The total focus on the politics of the USSR, for the Soviet specialists, helped them understand what culture meant to USIA's overall mission. Richmond, on return to Washington, insisted on moving into CU, where he served with distinction for six years, then was absorbed with CU into USIA in 1977; he stayed briefly in USIA as additional deputy area director for Europe but finally resigned in frustration at the agency's lack of support and underutilization of his talents. After retirement, he spent eight years helping launch the new NED, created to make explicit what cultural programs had done implicitly since 1938 and perhaps since Jefferson, Franklin, and Paine—project the light of democracy into nondemocratic political cultures. Sophisticated enough to know that American democracy was not the only kind available, Richmond saw no harm in describing the US approach as an interesting option about which he could explain a few things.

"DUKE" RYAN

While Richmond was thriving behind the Curtain, Henry Butterfield Ryan, known universally as Duke, sailed calmer waters. In his twenty-five years with USIA with his wife Patty, he was a generalist inclined to information work, but his CAO friends knew that he understood their values and goals. A mid-career fellowship at Harvard polished his gift for policy analysis, and he took a year's leave at the other Cambridge to finish an M.A. Ryan served as CAO twice, in Norway in the early 1970s and later in Australia. In Brazil he was information officer. Then he worked at the NSC and finally served as deputy USIA spokesman, before retiring into a long association with Georgetown University.

In 1988 Ryan looked back on his CAO years in Oslo. The embassy, when he arrived, had no facilities for the visual arts, so he made his own: "There was a large space in a corner, . . . the lighting was not bad, and the walls were already equipped for hanging pictures." He managed to exclude embassy painters and soon had a flourishing schedule in place: "We showed local artists and used exhibits from USIA, an American painter living in Italy, an Austrian-born sculptor, an expatriate American photographer, an expatriate Indian painter, a printmaker on a Fulbright grant, and a succession of Norwegian artists." USIA exhausted his patience by repeatedly asking him to justify showing Norwegian and other non-American artists. His answer, refined over the years, was simple:

"Non-US art . . . helped maintain interest in the gallery when we had no Americans, and it helped demonstrate American and US government interest in Norway's art."

He ran a major international conference on immigration and on Norwegians in America, he gave dozens of public lectures on aspects of US life, he provided US participants for the Bergen Festival for performing artists, and he shepherded the sculptor Harry Bertoia around Norway. "A cultural officer had to be an impresario, he or she had to scratch up talent. Neighboring CAOs were a great help—we bargained to share costs. . . . Strictly speaking we should have cleared some of this with Washington, but they never complained and we never asked. The Pitt and Harmsworth professorships at Oxbridge brought us Oscar Handlin and Carl Degler."

In Norway he pushed forward a daring extension of the Fulbright Program to shorter-term purposes, something a traditionalist CAO might have skirted, even in the penurious 1970s. The extension provided, he said, "short-term grants for Norwegians, . . . people who rarely could be away for an academic year, as Fulbright required." He advertised eight such grants, eighty applied. Without a word to the BFS, he had quietly opened an alternative longer-term IV Program, controllably oriented to education and culture. It was the kind of ingenious idea that under a less scrupulous officer, in another country, might have been seen to damage Fulbright, but the Norwegian commission kept things honest. The temptation came from the funding dilemma: eight short-term grants cost the same as one full-year US grant for a Norwegian scholar.

Ryan shared the CAO's general hunger for "speakers." This "mainstay of US cultural diplomacy . . . has been a subject of confusion and disagreement for years. What is it for? And should it be 'political'?" Ryan wanted nothing more than "to show the diversity and quality of the intellectual and artistic sectors of US life, to create binational links." He slyly deflected USIA's insistence that activities must bear on current policy: "It was almost impossible to have more than a handful of speakers who could support specific policy, whatever the policy might be. . . . We could of course bring out administration officials, one or two supportive journalists, and the rare academic who will go all the way, but . . . our audiences would be quickly saturated."

Ryan, USIA's deputy spokesman during the famous "blacklisting" episode in 1983, got at the root of the story, in cultural terms, five years later. There were "charges from potential speakers that a 'political litmus test' was being applied. It was, in fact, true. . . . All were alarmed because what they saw as an impartial program to present America from all viewpoints was being raped. . . . [It was] objectivity vs advocacy, a fundamental issue in USIA's work, especially in VOA." He hit the center of the familiar issue: "This running argument in USIA . . . reflects the tensions between information and cultural affairs. . . . If they hate us for Vietnam, what good will the New York City Ballet do? . . . It was this reasoning that led Reagan administration officials to plan to slash exchanges. . . .

They were urged on, it must be said, by top-ranking USIA career officers with information backgrounds. . . . What Senator Fulbright feared when he wanted these programs kept out of USIA seemed about to happen."

Ryan sees culture as an indispensable long-range political tool, reminding us that its budgets were pitiful. In 1988, the total USIA budget for all aspects of cultural work was $297 million; in 2001 he noted, "This year the Pentagon will budget nearly half that amount for military bands alone." Of the value of cultural diplomacy, there is no doubt whatever in his mind. But, as for Robin Winks, what seems perfectly obvious to him, and to much of the world, is almost impossible to prove: "If anyone has any empirical evidence that cultural diplomacy furthers our national political objectives overseas, even the most general or long-term objectives, I have never seen it. Yet we believe." He went on to define the real question, for him: "What does one do to create understanding . . . and avoid international misconceptions? The cultural affairs community operates on the assumption that knowledge is the vital ingredient; it will bring the other virtues in its train." He added: "Cultural officers believe that they are creating a climate which over the long term will produce in their host countries a deeper understanding of our society and politics. CAOs live and work in a special state of mind. Just under the surface of the cultural affairs community runs a vein of international realism. Of course, no one in USIA would dare to say so. Just as better-world idealism is eschewed, so is the slightest hint of extra-national purpose."

In 1988 he sketched a three-part theory: "First, information programs can do little and cultural programs almost nothing to make up for unpopular policies. Second, cultural programs can help keep good relations good. Third, they can build a climate in which we can work things out over time."

After retirement, Ryan in 1988 could more openly take a strong position on the PAO job he had never wanted: "Neither theory nor practice convince me that there is any powerful logic in the structure of our information and cultural affairs staffs overseas. Each staff is commonly headed by an American officer who in turn reports to yet a third, the Public Affairs Officer or PAO. Media and cultural work abroad, the mainstays of the USIA mission, do not necessarily belong together. They can certainly coexist in one organization, as they do now, and more or less harmoniously, but there is no compelling reason for them to do so." Does the PAO in fact *coordinate* information and culture? "The two staffs seldom have occasion to work in closer cooperation than either has with other elements of the embassy. Unquestionably they support each other . . . and they always work for the same national objectives, usually in a spirit of friendly collegiality. However they do not function in the kind of intermeshed, highly cooperative, mutually reinforcing way people in USIA management proclaim. I never saw it happen in 25 years of service and I have a hard time imagining how it could, except marginally and fleetingly. Explanations of its advantages . . . defend an organizational status quo and ward off any notions, always in the wings in Washington, that USIA should be reshuffled or redistributed."

Like Stanton, Ryan in his prescriptive thinking eliminated the top field position and the title of PAO. It was "a superfluous job overseas. . . . The PAO is an administrator, a policy interpreter, and a combination buffer and conduit between his or her subordinates and the embassy. They are busy and often harried, but that does not mean they are necessary. . . . Energetic and creative PAOs tend to take over the work, or at least its highlights, of the cultural officer and the information officer."

In Oslo a well-intentioned PAO cramped his work. Ryan tried to "convince members of the intelligentsia that . . . there was a great deal in the U.S. with which they could identify . . . and be allied with unashamedly. In short, I wanted them to see the U.S. as something besides a 900-pound gorilla." Sharing his views, the enthusiastic PAO took over his work: "I had to pry the PAO away from some of those things that I could do better than he—not easy because he was an energetic and talented individual."

In Australia a Laborite parliamentarian, after a one-month IV visit to the U.S., summed up Ryan's thinking: "There's a lot wrong with your country. But . . . we are natural allies."[5]

LOIS ROTH

One of Ryan's admirers, after she discovered him and his wife on a working visit to Oslo in 1974, was Lois Roth. She came late to USIA in 1967 and quickly drifted toward the top; she was managing USIA's fine and performing arts when she died unexpectedly in 1986. In her nineteen-year stay with USIA, this striking woman never held, nor wanted, a job outside cultural affairs. She learned the CAO trade in Tehran, after ten years with the American Scandinavian Foundation in New York. In March 1967 five days before the Iranian New Year, during Frankel's CU tenure, the thirty-six-year-old New Yorker arrived at her first USIS post, as assistant CAO. She would remain in Iran until 1972, first as deputy to the CAO, then as director of the immense Iran America Society (IAS).

Before USIA, she had been shaped by the internationalist Fieldston School, by Barnard, and by Columbia's world-famous department of sociology, supporting herself by working in Columbia College student affairs. A Swedish-American second mother motivated her to begin learning Swedish, and in 1956 she spent a Fulbright year at Uppsala University, where she perfected her Swedish and ultimately came to the conclusion that she was not cut out for scholarship itself but rather for providing support to scholars. Back in New York, at the Scandinavian foundation, she was special assistant to three presidents during the next decade and set up programs for Scandinavian visitors and UN officials. With Ford Foundation assistance, she added Finland to her foundation's reach. In 1961 she tried to join USIA, but women recruits were not yet being accepted. By 1966 the hiring policy had changed, her file was unearthed, and she went to Tehran. Before her death, she had moved near the top of USIA's cultural activities, heading the division of fine and performing arts.

In Iran, she learned her trade. She discovered a country that had finally shaken off its US proconsuls, yet in it the US presence remained strong. AID was leaving and would bequeath some of its programs and staff to the cultural office. A flourishing and cooperative Peace Corps in Iran had creative and original ideas. UNESCO assisted various activities, notably an important national literacy program. USIS and the British Council were cooperating in teaching English. At surviving US missionary schools, gifted young American teachers were eager to help the cultural office. In the tradition of educator-scholars Samuel Jordan and Arthur Upham Pope, she would soon help weave many such private and public strands into a total cultural program.

Regular letters to her parents, with carbon copies to friends, kept all informed.[6] Her first year, in particular, was a constant adventure; reading her letters, we find an accidental snapshot of the cultural program she joined and helped shape a decade before the Ayatollah. "Although working hours run from 8 to 4:30 P.M., no one pays any attention. Everyone seems to work on an around-the-clock basis that combines work and social life. . . . The office is well located in the central northern part of the city—a seven-story building with our own print shop, photographer, and the Library on the ground floor."

She handled a visit by the Georgia State College Brass Ensemble, then a visit by political theorist and historian Saul Padover. She wondered how to use Padover in Iran, "where political science makes people nervous," and geared his three-lecture visit to the US constitutional experience, "not a subject discussed much in this allegedly constitutional monarchy." Without delivering a single policy message, Padover sparkled: "I think we made a dent, if only through the force of Saul's great humanism."

The IAS Student Center at the University of Tehran was funded by USIS: "Imagine, we run a student center, the only one in Iran, right across the street from the University of Tehran!" By now she had taken over administration and freed the CAO to move around Iran, using slide lectures to stimulate discussion. The dean of UCLA's School of Social Work visited and introduced her to Iranian social work education, where politics intersect education. Fulbright lecturers helped staff at "the new and exciting but terribly problem-ridden School of Social Work." A screening of the classic feature film *The Oxbow Incident* triggered thoughtful Iranian discussion of "due process—another short suit here." She reported that "we are doing a lot, with poor staff and external frustrations. Travel arrangements, communications are no longer crises, just constant and predictable everyday frustrations we learn to live with." She shepherded a visiting USIA dignitary: "He did not want to go to Isfahan so we went instead to Karaj Dam, about 40 miles from here, and it was splendid. The

VIP did not enjoy it. Poor soul, he is a genuine bore. . . . We stopped and had tea with the Dean of the Forestry School in Karaj: water, trees, flowers, a real oasis in the desert."

Musicologist Alexander Ringer of the University of Illinois visited from Tel Aviv: "He ties Persian music into the history of Western music and helps us make an important point, that the U.S. cares about more in Iran than its oil." Ringer helped her open up dialogue with Tehran University's Faculty of Arts and Sciences about university education in music.

She quickly discovered embassy collegiality, including occasional all-American parties: "The camaraderie and togetherness have their reasons; this little band of colleagues, in a very foreign society, sticks together for a kind of support which I have to admit is vital." She dined with a US couple: "He works for UNESCO on the literacy campaign here, on which we pin high hopes—better *they* do it than us."

In the June War of 1967 Tehran became a "safe-haven" for people all over the Near East. Planes unloaded US refugees at the airport and two car caravans drove over the mountains from Baghdad. She jammed four US refugee correspondents into her tiny house, wisely stocking her refrigerator beforehand. And the work went on: Near East turmoil brought a rescheduling opportunity and, with thirty-six hours notice, she found a way to stage the Gettysburg College Choir. She worked with the new university Library School: "Last night a reception given by the Iran Library Association, 14 members lured by our USIS librarian, Fulbright lecturers in Library Science [a Fulbright focus], and their common experience of US training. It was held at the new Faculty of Education of the University, the most exciting university group in town [a Fulbright project]. Their library actually has open stacks! . . . We *can* do something useful here!"

Fulbright graduate students from other countries also found refuge in Iran in 1967–68, the Fulbright Commission absorbed them, and the American graduate student and research program doubled overnight, with a heavy stress on social science research—the underbudgeted commission, with surplus capacity, easily absorbed them. When the US Fulbright director retired to a university vice presidency in Wisconsin, ex-Fulbrighter Roth took over his desk in the mornings and kept the commission moving for a month while awaiting a successor. She was busy skimming US periodicals and culling selections so as to upgrade a sad newsletter the cultural section had been publishing, in cooperation with Iranian "returnees" from US universities.

Nervous about speaking in public, she swallowed hard, knowing that "all good Cultural Types sing for their supper." In July she forced herself to speak on women in the U.S. to a women's club: "I used women as a starting point and drifted into a talk on voluntary associations, more relevant here." In women's affairs, she had discovered a theme she would pursue for the rest of her life, in a low-pressure style based first on setting an example. Beginning with the missionary-educators, American women had been reaching out to their sisters abroad; the point never made the

USIS country plan, but women officers and wives did it everywhere. Her CAO friend Mary Jo Furgal, trained as a librarian, described one episode in India's Madras in the early 1980s. Combining forces with Zonta International and the Fulbright Commission, she mounted a one-day seminar on women's rights for the area's women leaders. The seminar turned into the Joint Action Council for Women, which fought discrimination, unmasked degrading advertising, and created a shelter for battered women, helping women help themselves.[7]

By now she had produced a totally new returnee newsletter, retitled *ReNew* (Persian: *No Saz*). At the student center, she met weekly with a conversation class of twenty university students. Frankel's Columbia colleague Near East specialist "Jay" Hurewitz was in town with his wife and daughter, asking "thought-provoking" questions. A round-trip flight to Mashad in the northeast left her exhausted, having coped with both program demands and those of the local "jet-setters" who danced through the night. A trip to the Caspian Sea lifted her spirits. A sold-out piano recital by a young Iranian woman, who included Gershwin thanks to USIS-provided scores, warranted a flight to Tabriz alongside the piano-technician-tuner from Tehran. Tabriz, early center of European liberalism in Iran and site of early American and British mission schools, was definitely not Tehran. The people "seem healthier and more open-looking, seem to enjoy life more than the Tehranis. They are near the Russian border and have not forgotten the 1947 war."

She visited a five-week Fulbright-assisted management seminar for "top-level Iranians from private industry, government and the universities, all in English, sparked by a brilliant lecture from the Iranian Deputy Director of the Ford-initiated Plan Organization." The Vietnam conflict worried her but was of no concern to Tehran—"this society is little interested in the outside world." Back home, she gave a formal lunch for ten, "five shy young Iranian District Governors we are sending on a 60-day visit to the U.S., plus embassy colleagues" launching "an important project in local and self-government, designed to show young Iranian local administrators how much people can do for themselves with proper attitudes and backing." At a UNESCO-sponsored conference on music, with Yehudi Menuhin as its centerpiece, she encountered an old friend, a Finnish musicologist, and half a dozen delegates invaded her home for an improvised dinner. In Shiraz she met art historians Arthur Upham Pope and Phyllis Ackerman, who had moved there from New York with their Asia Institute, as guests of the Shah.

Her colleague Barbara Spring had married and, by law, had to resign as a USIA officer. For her farewell, Spring assembled a pathfinding show of Iranian "coffee-house" paintings: "This has become Barbara's parting gift to a country she loves, an effort to show through American eyes the colossal beauty in Iran that resides in seemingly ordinary things—like these naive paintings, by itinerant artists, which decorate the humble coffee-shops along the Iranian roads."

For the Shah's Coronation in 1967, State sent out the Los Angeles Symphony, and Roth was dazzled by teenager André Watts: "Two LA performances, alongside a French ballet, a German orchestra, an Italian orchestra and the new Iranian ballet. . . . A mess, but we'll survive!"

She greeted the returning district governors at the airport and found them "jabbering away in English, and with an apparently deep understanding of what they saw. All are said to be in line for early promotion." With the CAO away on home leave, she ran the cultural office and handled a string of people and events: a US delegation including Joan Ganz Cooley to the International Children's Film Festival, supported by Empress Farah; writer Wallace Stegner, who put her in touch with important dissident women writers; an Iran scholar from McGill University; a grant offer from the World Youth Forum in New York; harpist Mildred Dilling; Columbia University's John Badeau, former ambassador to Egypt and past-president of the American University in Cairo; and a major exhibit with a small nuclear reactor, called Atoms in Action. After eight months, she was managing the CAO office and redecorating it with furniture left over from Atoms in Action, as a surprise for the CAO's return from home leave: "The CAO in the U.S. is trying to get Iran specialists to establish an American institute for Persian Studies, to help coordinate the proliferation of research activities—one of the cultural office's most onerous functions is to help scholars get research permits."

She suffered through a time-consuming and pointless attempt to apply program budgeting to USIS Tehran. She bristled when the Ministry of Education sent only one candidate for a grant from the World Youth Forum and insisted that the ministry send several others. A Washington visitor spent a week at the embassy; years after her death, the visitor said he would never forget her because she alone made something original out of his tried-and-true stickler question: how do officers see their career futures? She said she saw her future in terms of growth—if USIA provided it, then she would be happy. In 1968 opportunities for growth were crossing her path every day.

Two more educational consultants arrived, "an engineering curriculum specialist and an international law research and education specialist. Both are helping us help the Iranians work on curriculum reform at the University—a subtle assignment in both cases. The legal opening in particular could reach far out into this society." The engineering education consultant, from Brown University, was a unique gentleman: he "is as different as he is interesting. . . . A Polish refugee, he is the perfect man to help bridge the gap between the U.S. and—not Iran but Europe!" A Fulbrighter following up on Alexander Ringer's visit was also at work building a music department at the university.

Staff cuts announced by Washington made sense to her; she believed the embassy was overstaffed and was even willing to tighten the cultural belt. Not replacing Barbara Spring would mean more work, and the CAO reminded her that "our section, not counting the Library, has 8 staff compared to 95 in the information section.'

Ten days into her second year, a four-person dinner at home brought together the newly returned American-trained rector of the new Iranian technologies university and the Brown engineering curriculum consultant, to talk over approaches to manpower-training for technological growth. The talk went on until after midnight, when, with the CAO, "we had to go, one more time, to the airport." That night, she coined Roth's Law, to the effect that an Iranian's understanding of democracy was directly proportional to the years spent in US *undergraduate* education. The next day lunch with a Fulbright library scientist raised an idea ahead of its time: "to start a major documentation center here, with computer links to the U.S." Next came the Manhattan Percussion Ensemble, "arriving for a week at the wrong time."

These glimpses into the rich life of an eager, energetic, and talented apprentice CAO show her excitement at discovering a targetted, relevant, and constantly growing cultural program, in a fast developing nation vitally important to the U.S.—and it was only her first year of five.

WAYNE WILCOX

Leaving Iran we return to London, to touch on the life of Wayne Wilcox. He left a comfortable chair in political science at Columbia University to succeed Robin Winks as CAO in 1971.[8] From North Liberty, Indiana, Wilcox was a Midwesterner and a Hoosier to the core. He studied engineering, labor economics, and politics at Purdue, traveled to the South Pole courtesy of the US Navy, and landed at Columbia, where he soon emerged as one of the nation's leading scholars of South Asia. A fine administrator, he steered his department through the aftermath of 1968.

Encountering US CAOs during his travels in South Asia, he was intrigued by the problem of cultural diplomacy. He rejoiced in his move to London, in part because he felt the academic grind had taken a toll on his wife and four children and they needed "re-potting," as he said. Like Lois Roth, Wilcox was a passionate letter writer who commented widely to his friends on his work. One cultural officer in South Asia remembered an earlier visit by Wilcox in 1965, about the time his Columbia colleague Frankel was digesting his survey of CAOs. Wilcox urged the officer to develop his knowledge of the ideological basis of that country's many-hued labor movement; he believed it would open many intellectual doors. "Of course," he added—without the slightest irony—"to do that properly you have to know at least as much about them and their world as they know about themselves." For Wilcox, the cultural officer and the scholar were a continuum; CAOs invariably recognized in him a companion searcher for similar kinds of truth.

At Columbia before London, Wilcox handled a stream of South Asian visitors and worked hard to place South Asian scholars in research roles.

His historian colleague Ainslie Embree soon would go to New Delhi as an academic CAO. Wilcox, transiting Tehran in 1967 after a visit to Pakistan, lectured at the cultural office's suggestion on a pertinent theme: a modern society's need to face the downside risks of research in order to grow in technology. In Iran new truths were feared as a threat to stability. This was a central problem in the cultural office, as young US-trained and research-minded Iranians returned in droves, only to find that the Shah's advisors found existing truths to be adequate, hence that alternative truths could be kept bottled up and parceled out later, to suit the Shah's sense of the developmental pace. Wilcox later wrote to the CAO that exchange with sophisticated Iranians about research had completely shifted his approach to the same problem in Pakistan—he complimented the team, including Roth, on its ability "to make operational use of the values we share." In his dealings with CAOs, this was a recurrent theme.

In June 1971 this broad-gauged liberal internationalist was interviewed for the London post. He met USIA director Frank Shakespeare, a hard-line movement conservative, and his tough-minded, conservative but pragmatic deputy Henry Loomis; whatever was discussed, Wilcox was in London by September. Reviewing the meeting later, he commented on the US version of ideology, 1971-style, and its impact on executive decision-making: "The field's view of the Director and his Deputy is based more on the declaratory policy of their management than on their convictions, [which are] addressed to Washington as much as to the field." This insight, *pace* Yale Richmond's dilemma, led him to a conclusion: "Should that be the case, there may be more room for subtlety in cultural-educational exchange planning." He looked forward to his two years in London as a chance to be part of a diplomatic effort "in which the USIA role is to make possible and structure . . . the exchange business."

He dug in deep. He was dismayed to learn that CU chief John Richardson had been saddled with a second job, heading State's Public Affairs. He was appalled to learn that Congressman Rooney had insisted on a "slush fund" to bring foreign labor leaders to an AFL-CIO convention, buried under the rubric of "educational and cultural exchange." His admiration for his London boss, Columbia Ph.D. William Weld, increased by the day, but he did not confuse Weld with USIA—he realized Weld was great in spite of USIA, not because of it. "Alas," he wrote to a friend, "USIA is a s— agency, and I suppose you have to be grateful for the good guys who somehow stick it out."

In the historic tradition of London CAOs, he lectured everywhere, twenty times in November 1971 alone. In London he was perhaps more probing than his predecessors: "The CAO job is pretty much what *you* can do. . . . so one simply tries, while not comitting perjury, to communicate a little of the national style, grace and genius, and tries not to be too dismayed when it comes back with the venom of a society that refracts as well as reflects." Wilcox insisted on total administrative and budgetary control of his cultural office—because he thought it wise "to exercise power commensurate with the title." His assistant Juliet Antunes admired his gift for "letting people get on with their work when he thought they were on the right track." When another assistant disappointed Wilcox, the CAO let him know it as gently as he could. This administrative stance, supporting the good and leaning on the others, made him the more impatient with Washington whenever one of its offices tried to manage *him*. In March 1972, caught in a phase of gadgetomania about fancy audiovisual equipment, USIA proudly called a conference for field staff in Europe to demonstrate new techniques. From Wilcox, the conference elicited an uncharacteristic outburst: "It was intellectually insulting, programmatically irrelevant, and technically incompetent. . . . There were assembled in Cologne some of the most senior, talented and sophisticated guys in USIA!" They included Vienna CAO Alan Dodds.

Wilcox knew there were deeper issues hiding under PAO Weld's humanity: "The agency ought to understand that its recruitment strategy and its program strategy cannot be divorced. . . . Super-CAOs are a way to build constituencies and supplement staff, but they are not substitutes for it." European area director Jay Gildner, a man Wilcox generally admired, was trying to translate his version of Tokyo's targetted library idea for Europe. Again the idea provoked a high but thoughtful dudgeon: "The greater the degree of Washington control without field input, the greater the alienation of staff. . . . It may give way later to deliberate sabotage and anarchy. The real mission of USIS is to be the embassy's outreach to the cultural and intellectual elite of that country, and the mode for doing it is not the same as for conveying substantive information." One thing was clear: people were central. He wrote, "USIA ought to be spending its money on recruitment and training. USIA today has 50% of the PhDs it had fifteen years ago. Few other agencies in government have a diminishing educational profile."

For the American Bicentennial in 1976, he floated an idea that would have delighted Rufus Morey: persuade the UK to give USIS a historic building to house Fulbright, a serious American library, American studies specialists for the University of London, and a resource center for American studies in general. He was clear on his model for this idea—Lois Roth's IAS as he had seen it in 1967. As it turned out, the idea needed more nurture than he had time to give.

In May 1973 a member of the CU advisory commission visited. At his request, Wilcox wrote him at length about the CAO dilemma, arguing that something was dead wrong. "First and foremost, this is an absolutely wonderful job. It offers an active intellectual stimulation and opportunities for [growth]; it offers a welcome respite from being an American in favor of interpreting America for the doubting Thomases of Britain." He then moved to definitions: "Cultural and educational programs are those long-term aspects of our foreign relations that are directed to the intelligentsia and the artistic community of other nations. The outreach is both altruistic—the search for truth and beauty are universal human goals and are furthered by international cooperation—and nationalistic. Foreign intellectuals and artists shape their nation's prejudices and preferences, and if they have an empathy for America then the opinion environment in which foreign governments work will be pro-American in the long run. While these observations strike me as self-evident, they lack explicit recognition in the *structure* of the foreign service."

He knew the CAO dilemma had been studied *ad nauseam*: "USIA has struggled with integrating information and culture-education. . . . Organizing the interface between aspects of our foreign life as complicated as education and culture ought to be entrusted to people with the values, talents and tastes necessary to build empathy regardless of the political environment. This suggests that the personnel system and Washington backup should be explicitly designed to reward and nourish them. . . . Most cultural officers feel like stepchildren in a large family fathered by a press baron. . . . It is unnatural for the top management of any agency to be chosen on the basis of experience in only one of its functions."

From the political scientist's angle, "it seems to me that any workable system has to fit into three quite different structures: Congress, bureaucratic Washington, and the field. Most operating officers can adjust to almost any bureaucratic thicket, but one that encourages perjury or establishes contradictory or dysfunctional personnel policies carries a high internal cost. What USIA-CU has now is maximal Congressional support, dysfunctional bureaucratic relationships in Washington, and some measure of adaptation in the field." Thus, three options: "(1) improve the present system by committing to autonomous educational and cultural work, by developing a personnel system which validates such experience, and by using good officers at maximal value; or (2) separate culture-education from information, recruiting in part from the universities; or (3) separate culture-education and transfer it to a new public corporation like the British Council."

His letter circulated in the commission and among trusted friends. It was a factor in the process leading to the Stanton commission's 1975 report. But he would not live to see it. In March 1974 Wilcox, his wife Ouida, and two of their four children were killed in the crash of a Turkish airliner fifteen minutes north of Paris.

• • •

Whatever the sins of USIA and the US political process, there is much to be said for a system which, beginning in 1942, created contexts and microworlds to shelter Americans like Robin Winks, Wayne Wilcox, and their USIA friends Dodds, Richmond, Roth, and Ryan. Put in place by decades of much error and more trial—without corporate memory—by a jerry-rigged system, the agency sometimes got lucky and enabled them, as Wilcox wrote, to show "the national style, grace and genius." The US CAOs were among those that postimperialist BBC reporter Ludovic Kennedy honored in the title of his book on empire-tending Americans around the world, *Very Lovely People.* Like these six pillars of the US educational and cultural world, many Americans—after visiting a cultural office in a US embassy here or there—have been tempted to proclaim, with Shakespeare's Miranda, "O brave new world, that has such people in't." When the rest has disappeared, perhaps this is what we shall remember.

CHAPTER TWENTY-TWO

Stanton's Challenge: Status Quo or Change?

> I would have liked to call it "propaganda." It seemed the nearest thing in the pure interpretation of the word to what we were doing. But "propaganda" has always had a pejorative connotation in this country. To describe the whole range of communications, information and propaganda, we hit upon "public diplomacy."
>
> —Edmund Gullion, 1967

THE DREAM EMBODIED IN CU, the legatee of those who tried to build a decent educational and cultural dimension into US foreign policy in the 1930s, was over. Before returning to the sequence of our story, it is appropriate to review the state of affairs for cultural diplomacy in the 1970s, in the decade just after the peak years of an American cultural diplomacy that was imperfectly yet resolutely insulated from the subtler forms of propaganda, "information," and storytelling. All this, after 1967, came more and more to be jumbled together under Public Diplomacy, a phrase that Edmund Gullion's historical vignette illuminates but in which he somehow managed to overlook culture and education.

The need for this ill-defined portemanteau phrase, in the minds of the informationists, was dictated by Washington's changing climate in the 1970s. Identifying these changes may help assess their impact on the cultural diplomatic dilemma. For one thing, the intellectual sector of US life in the 1970s was still clouded by the war in Vietnam, which had opened a chasm between government and the universities. In 1969 Robin Winks in London was assigned to meet student demonstrators; engaging in dialogue with them, he watched the gap widen. In the same year, a university-sensitive CAO visiting friends at the University of Illinois was flayed by a tipsy humanist branding him with the heinous sin of being employed by the US government. The mood of the moment did not encourage the universities to rise in defense of cultural diplomacy; on the government side, it aggravated government's mistrust of intellect.

A CAO in 1976 Italy watched a different shift, a sea change in Fulbright students that year suddenly more inclined to confront than engage. They were products of a new America, struggling with the early phases of the culture wars and the unfamiliar ideological style in US thought. The old attacks from the right led by the bumbling McCarthy were now more sophisticated. McCarthy had demonized the New Deal, polarized consensus politics, and destroyed bipartisanship. Reaching office in 1968, Richard Nixon looked at first like his mentor Eisenhower, a Republican internationalist, but his southern strategy was based on rejecting consensus politics, polarizing conservatives and liberals, and declaring the war of ideologies. Longstanding cultural internationalist values, for students born after the depression and the Second World War, growing up in a country wedded to pragmatism, tolerance, and deeply rooted cultural internationalism, were not enough. In Italy, US students were living in the most cynical of countries, where every student was trained to perform instant analyses of texts and problems from any of several conflicting ideological viewpoints. The class of 1976, at least in Italy, reflected a new American mindset of truculent defensiveness.

USIA was interested in getting it done, whatever "it" was and in whatever way worked; it was an agency wedded to serving any administration without questioning what it did. There was no time for political theory, except in its impressive anti-Soviet publication *Problems of Communism*. The U.S. had operated for a century on the basis of a rough consensus between two broadly based centrist political parties. Since 1945 its foreign affairs had been handled most often as a bipartisan question; debate in foreign policy aimed at building consensus, not delegitimizing the past. Cultural diplomacy had always swiveled back and forth, in the space between nationalist and internationalist goals. But an ideological cast of thought demanded revised definitions of everything.

In the Fulbright Program, the flagship for US cultural diplomacy, the signs of change were clear and yet its defensive foundations had been built to last. It continued to absorb about half of CU's cultural budgets.[1] Yet Fulbright by the early 1970s was fraying. Out of reach of the spinning Washington wheels, the field process trudged on, each year adding alumni and deepening experience. But with weakened oversight by a diminished BFS, with raging inflation and sagging budgets, the flagship role of Fulbright was tarnished. The program's champion left the Senate in 1975, and USIA was freed to impose its values more firmly on the once-independent program. In the field, the declining intellectual qualifications of the CAOs were beginning to show the impact of USIA's 1973 decisions to assign generalists to the job.

As Fulbright exchanges moved through the years, other changes blurred the original binationalist university-to-university design. Inflation and reduced funding forced commissions to award shorter-term grants. Direct foreign contributions to Fulbright would have made a difference had USIA pledged to match them, but they evoked ambivalence from USIA leadership, like the European area director who, after two drinks, admitted he would close all Fulbright commissions if he could. After Fulbright-Hays (1961), foreign contributions grew, but slowly. Foreign funding demanded a great deal of concerted and persuasive diplomacy by an embassy over time, but many embassies pleaded they could not afford the time. The binational agreements had been written for another era, and the example of Rooney's sabotaging the budget in 1962 at the very moment France decided to contribute was on every CAOs mind. Foreign nations still did not quite believe the American claim of binationalism; they found it odd to pay for another nation's "propaganda," as the skeptics saw it. Indeed, had the idea been proposed out of the blue by a foreign power to State or Congress, it might have received an equally cool reception. Even Americans were not comfortable with the idea, accusing it of the do-gooder sin of "idealism." Of greater concern to the tipsy USIA area director, countries investing in Fulbright expected more say in the program's operations than USIA veterans found comfortable.

Private donations lay even further in the future and had long been discouraged—in 1963 Washington rejected German Ford's offer to contribute to Fulbright. In overseas cultures where private giving and tax deductibility were not encouraged by laws, the idea needed time and, in the interim, ingenious lawyers. Today foreign private contributions flourish in the unusual case of Japan but sporadically elsewhere.

Fulbright joint-financing raised political questions as well. USIS influence over Fulbright was obvious, and USIS was the embassy's propaganda arm for most audiences abroad. Moreover, USIS ownership of the commissions had grown firmer after Fulbright. What had seemed in the past to be acts of generosity now seemed far too often to serve US interests, and the CIA disclosures made things far worse. Only West Germany, Japan, and Spain, each for its own reasons, surpassed the US contribution.

Administratively, binational administration had made steady progress in the commissions. Foreign commission executives were in charge in most countries; board chairmanships began rotating between nations. But with money short at home and abroad, tough decisions had to be made. Unsympathetic PAOs complained about commission costs, endless lead time, sluggishness, programmatic irrelevance, and the so-called Clearinghouse Clutter—by which commissions accepted a partial coordinative role for US public and private education or for foreign student counseling, none of which "supported foreign policy" in any sense hardline PAOs recognized. In a word, these PAOs wanted more control over the independent commissions. At a conference of Fulbright commission executives in Milan in the mid-1980s, the PAO veteran in charge of USIA's division of cultural affairs was seen to hammer on an implicit message: "It's *our* money, and *we* will tell *you* how to spend it."

Commissions coped, pared back grants, shaved staff and salaries, and maneuvered ingeniously, at the expense of program quality. Other commissions took on outside work. In Japan today, for example, the commission, on contract from the Japanese government, administers six hundred two-week familiarization visits by US school teachers every year—a valuable program, but one that traditional Fulbright policies in other times might have steered into other hands.

The caliber of the cultural corps lost its luster, as the early wave of academic outsiders disappeared and the first wave of talented professional USIA CAOs drifted away. Foreign friends found less interest in the cultural offices than before. The lateral-entry system, enriching USIA cadres by hiring officers like Lois Roth, had vanished. US laws on nondiscrimination for age played strange tricks on recruitment and brought in an occasional interesting newcomer, but most new officers were recruited from among recent graduates in politics or international relations at the B.A. and M.A. level. Language proficiency, either at entrance or later, was no higher and continued to earn few rewards. Super-CAO appointments were rare, unpredictable, and of little interest for the idea of a career cultural corps. The one exception, London, welcomed academic CAOs until 1976.[2]

It takes time to discourage committed cultural officers. In 1972 committed CAO Carl Bartz, whose career had developed in the Far East, found no country CAO position on the horizon. He took a branch CAO job in Karachi, serving that gigantic city and the region around it. Despite Washington informationist rhetoric and shrinking budgets, he reported to his surprise that the field was coping. In his case, he managed two cultural centers, a self-sustaining BNC teaching English with a faculty of thirty, a student counseling service handling ten thousand students a year, and a blocked-rupee account for Pakistan, providing support of $1 million annually for USIS and for researchers from HEW, Smithsonian, and the National Science Foundation.[3] That same year newcomer Lois Roth, after five years, left her monumental achievement in Tehran. Offered the post of PAO in Stockholm, she chose to return to Washington as desk officer for Scandinavia, under Jay Gildner, who confessed he hoped it would be her first step away from the CAO world; she did not see it that way.

A subtler factor of change inside USIA was the rise to top positions of the Eastern European veterans, after some had been pried out of the Soviet area by Shakespeare. They had had special success with the cultural elements of diplomacy, implicit in Yale Richmond's story because, behind the Iron Curtain, culture had done the heavy lifting from the beginning.[4] Eastern European hands, with the most highly political goals in the world, were working a quiet *cultural* miracle that would culminate in the implosion of the Soviet empire; they knew exchanges had profound political effect over time, and they understood why it was not useful to say so in their host countries. CU-USIA's highly political activities in the Soviet bloc were, in fact, its most culture-centered programs. In Moscow the Soviets forced deconstruction of the name "USIS" and accepted a more honest name, "P&C," for the separate functions of press and culture.

Mysteriously USIA's great Soviet hands, when they moved out of Eastern Europe, had no impact on redesigning USIA's overall strategies. None of my Soviet specialist friends has been able to explain this peculiar disconnect. One hypothesis flows from the special circumstances of Fulbright activity in the Soviet area, where even the purest of CU activities was suspect. When cultural relations with the paranoid USSR opened in 1958, even the Fulbright idea looked devious to the hosts. To assuage doubts, a separate academic exchange channel called the International Research and Exchanges Board (IREX) was opened. IREX did its work precisely in the university-to-university style the early BFS would have wished, except that it was far more careful to set the highest scholarly standards. Ford for several years had been investing through its ITR program in the growth of Eastern European studies in US universities, so an entire generation of young scholars was ready. Analogous to CIES, IREX administered academic exchanges for the Soviet countries only. The high requirement for language proficiency meant it drew heavily on Soviet area scholars who had high motivation to take up residence in East Europe; their home departments were highly motivated to allow them generous leaves of absence. IREX also selected high-quality scholars in English-dependent disciplines when requested by the Soviets.

IREX had high visibility in Washington. It could move swiftly—delays came not from Americans but from the Soviets. IREX was even more strongly protected against extrauniversity pressures than the Fulbright process was. But IREX, by definition, could not function in the binational style, and it operated without the advantages—and constraints—of a binational commission. Where a "Fulbright" program without a commission raised questions in other countries, IREX was itself a guarantor. Scholars and students began flowing to and from Eastern Europe. For university exchanges with the bloc, the US response was patient, sensitive, tough, and even more tightly "pure" and committed to university values than that of the BFS—which exercised loose supervision over IREX. Thus US field officers in the bloc expected more from Fulbright; when they moved to other countries, they chafed at the slow binational process, the academic calendar, and the apparent non-relevance of various academic disciplines.

The American Soviet hands, leaving Eastern Europe, were baffled by binationalism. From the Soviet viewpoint, educational relations with the U.S. amounted to the cultural equivalent of war—binationalism lay beyond Soviet comprehension. The integrity that Welles had demanded and the academic values that Fulbright had cemented into his program proved especially valuable in the USSR. But binationalism was not feasible.

The Eastern European hands had also fallen into the habit of generous funding, which disappeared when they left the area. Eastern Europe's high priority, as in the occupied nations, had taught them to expect the moon. Further, their exhilarating experience of educating immovable ideologues, trapped in towering ignorance and wearing dark blinders, fed USIA's intrinsic unidirectionalism. When the Soviet specialists entered

USIA's "real" world, their skepticism about binationalism and their yearning for tighter US control were understandable. So was their stunned realization about budget realities.

Finally Soviet hands were confirmed in their impatience by Department of State regulations and its old-line diplomatic culture. To take one example, the Congress imposed tight US security regulations on all grantees, but in the Soviet countries, it was hard to find a grant candidate who was not a "communist." A system of waivers was devised and flexibly administered, and methods of supervision for grantees in the U.S. were put in place. Outside the Soviet area, things were less flexible. Insistence on "name checks," waxing and waning with the times, had always raised problems for BFS, the Fulbright Program, and CAOs, but the waiver as a way out of the dilemma even in exceptional cases was not easy to obtain.

An example will show why this mattered. In 1975, in an allied Western European country, the Fulbright Commission learned that the host-country police had turned down its two top-ranked foreign student nominees, for unspecified reasons. A US visa could not be issued without police approval. The CAO chair, in three developing countries, had seen the waiver used on occasion to lure the non-communist left into US study visits. In this case, the embassy's request for waivers was declined. In a closely allied nation, in a transparent binational program, the turndown presented a serious dilemma. The open student competition had moved through three levels of selection; dozens of academics knew who the top two students were. Turning them down would reveal the political criteria hovering over Fulbright; it would embarrass both countries; and it would threaten the existence of the Fulbright Program in that country, with a history of twenty-six years and seven thousand alumni. At this dramatic point, the situation turned comic: the commission director learned that both students had walked into a nearby US consulate, been given visas, and were in fact already comfortably installed at a prestigious West Coast university, making it no longer a question of a visa but of *deporting* two foreign Fulbright students from the U.S. To reverse State's rigidity, CU chief John Richardson was forced to take the matter personally to the top. His meeting with Secretary Kissinger and Counselor Helmut Sonnenfeld won agreement to let the students keep their Fulbright grants, provided it did not happen again, so the matter was resolved—for 1975. To no one's surprise, a similar situation arose the following year. This time a wiser embassy opened the police files, determined the information to be trivial, and granted the visa. The case was closed—in that country, at that time—only because a dogged CAO and strong CU support had averted an ugly diplomatic episode. The sequel: the CAO survived an attempt at a punitive transfer, and both students did brilliantly—one today heads a giant world organization for the protection of cultural monuments. As for the Secretary's fear of foreigners learning to be communists in the U.S., both students, parlor Marxians from the soft Left, learned democracy in the U.S.

All this may help explain why the cultural warriors from Eastern Europe saw no reason to change the USIA that they later led, specifically in opening the door to a broader USIA role in cultural diplomacy. The impossible Soviet countries demanded great flexibility and superb follow-through. But when Soviet hands served elsewhere, their impatience at State's bureaucracy, the binational process, and fragile funding clouded the contribution they might have made to a richer and perhaps more resistent USIA. Few lessons from the strong cultural imperatives of Eastern Europe filtered into USIA's overall vision of what it did. CU—with its cultural values intact—was better informed, and frontline officers like Guy Corriden and Richmond, who began running the bureau's Eastern European division in 1973, strengthened CU understanding. But CU was drawing to its end.

•   •   •

In Washington the turmoil was as dreary as usual for the cultural diplomats. To some, Richardson's stabilizing years in CU had given cause for silent jubilation, after the Frankel debacle. But the more politicized CU he bequeathed to his successors would soon be taken over, surgically crippled, and molded to new purposes, first by a jaunty and triumphant USIA, and later by a nationalist "revolution."

The idea of a CU-USIA merger was not new; it went back to the Senator's Pyrrhic 1953 victory over Streibert and the Jackson committee. CU had survived the failure of the concerted moves of 1958–59 and the savaging of Coombs and Frankel in the 1960s. Now the beleaguered bureau, ever hopeful, took new heart because of a flurry of interest in restructuring in 1973–74, triggered by détente.

The first of course was the "CU Concept," finalized in 1974 after four years of internal CU debate. Far more important was the USIA advisory commission's 26th annual report in 1973. The idea of an independent cultural agency had in fact come back to life the year before in Richardson's good-faith dialogue with USIA's Keogh, under mild pressure from CU's advisory commission. But Frank Stanton's extended chairmanship of the USIA advisory commission was a more decisive factor. In contrast with efforts since 1952, this time there was little outsider pressure from the battle-weary foundations and universities. The thinking that began in 1973 was unusual in that it was largely internal to the government and indeed to the USIA family.

Most of the founding legislators had disappeared, and the unsuspecting Fulbright was two years away from his departure. Florida congressman Dante Fascell, despite his growing friendship with Richardson, had trouble stretching his mind around anything but one-agency advocacy, when it came to USIA. In this he was not alone: one-agency unidirectionalism had grown, even in CU. The intransigent USIA under Shakespeare had forgotten how to question its values, and Keogh was not a man to raise questions. Beginning in 1953, USIA had absorbed every CU effort to build bridges, giving nothing in return. From birth, USIA had behaved like a paranoid status quo agency, in a mode of perpetual defensiveness. But within USIA a new generation was growing into leadership positions. Stanton, with his active commission-colleague the novelist James Michener, had been hearing from some of these younger leaders that the substance of USIA had thinned down and that a richer cultural dimension would help the agency grow into the post-détente years. They saw, as Murrow had suspected at the end of his life, that reductionist "storytelling" was no longer enough.

The central issue Stanton's commission faced was USIA's longstanding claim to a policy-advisory role. To bolster this hollow claim, sharper definitions of what USIA and USIS supposedly did had been put in place in Murrow's years by men like Sorensen, with the goal of a hypothetical participatory role for USIA in policy-formation in the field and in Washington. This led to a major push inside the agency, requiring a new breed of policy-oriented officers and, in the field, a strong PAO focusing both information and education-culture to policy message delivery. Sorensen believed such tactics would earn USIA a prominent seat at the policy-making tables.

The USIA advisory commission finally had the courage to hint that the advisory role might be a pipe dream. If so, too great a proximity to day-to-day policy warped the very principles on which the agency's cultural elements had been built. If so, a new kind of agency was needed to carry out these basic values. Coombs had had the same argument with Sorensen; Frankel, with Burnett Anderson; Sorensen, with George Allen; and farther back Allen, with Benton over the showcase versus the mirror.

Only Murrow, as an individual, had succeeded in getting anywhere near the foreign policy-making process, but by 1973 Murrow was long forgotten. The White House continued to read USIA's daily compilation of foreign press reactions with interest and found interesting tidbits in USIA's public-opinion research, and USIS posts were helpful in arranging presidential or congressional visits abroad. But it was obvious that foreign policy was hammered out with no help from USIA, institutionally at least. In fact, even embassies and their heads had less and less to say about policy as years passed, so no one should have been surprised that USIA was left out.

Inside an embassy, everything USIA contributed at the Country Team level depended on the caliber of the PAO (and exceptionally the CAO, as Alan Dodds related) and the ambassador's ability to use such untraditional talents. But few PAOs shaped policy. In 1961 Sorensen had dreamed of a USIA that would affect policy, and he pressed to obtain ambassadorial postings for the better PAOs. The first success—and a dozen or more would follow over time—was William Handley, sent to a dead-end posting in Mali. He was the first to realize that USIA officers, when they became ambassadors, accepted a devil's bargain that led no-

where. Yet the temptation motivated ambitious officers who were thinking ahead to retirement, hence shaped their thinking about what USIA
and its USIS posts did.

As part of its effort to shape policy, USIA was systematically decapitat-
ing its officer corps, giving away its best officers to insignificant ambassadorships. Implicitly the agency was telling its finest talents that a career
in information and culture was less valuable than heading a small embassy in an unimportant country. Ambassadorships turned out to be
more of a booby trap for USIA than it seemed at first. Few went on to
second embassies, and former ambassadors were difficult to bring back
into USIA's assignment planning; some found outright resentment when
they returned. In the forty-odd years since USIA first won an embassy for
a senior officer, no senior USIA ambassador to my knowledge has gone
on to a second embassy. (William Weathersby went from acting ambassador Delhi to Sudan.) The CAOs may have been wiser; few had any interest in being ambassadors. Of the few committed CAOs who did, only
two or three made it. Most said, "Why would I want to be an ambassador
when I already have the best job in the embassy?"

Still the advisory role remained the issue for the informationists. The
USIA advisory commission zeroed in on the question at the very moment
when Director Keogh had decided to eliminate cultural specialists. Stanton's commission, after interviews with dozens of officers, was beginning
to see that, if the policy advisory role did *not* exist, pretending it did was
dangerous. Those who argued that USIA alone could provide a mix of
culture and propaganda, with no harm done to either function, had
begun to suspect that damage was being done to both.

The major factor prodding the USIA advisory commission's thinking
in early 1973 was the impending end of the cold war. Americans were
practicing their French with the word "détente," and it was predictable
that a few farsighted members of the USIA family might begin to think
about what USIA and CU might mean after the cold war. In 1973 the
USIA's advisory commission, still the small group of five defined by
Smith-Mundt in 1948, took up cudgels precisely on these two points:
détente and the advisory role. Its 26th annual report that year would
trigger the line of studies and thought that resulted in the Carter reorganization of 1977 and reiterated a subtheme it had first announced in 1964:
USIA's increasing lack of substance. Stanton had been the commission
chair for six years, assisted by men like Michener, because the loyalty of
his former CBS employee Frank Shakespeare kept him in place in 1969.
His report that year—and it was very much his because, as his executive
director Louis Olom relates, he fretted over every comma[5]—restated concern for the CAO career. It reported only ten to twelve positions worldwide in which committed cultural officers could work at the top rank of
the foreign service (then FS-1). Only one cultural officer, in personal
rank, had achieved that level, two had reached the second level, and fifty
others were stuck in the third rank. The commission's recommendations

for upgrading the CAO corps produced a flurry of activity; a few cultural jobs were raised in grade and a few promotions made. But it was cosmetic legerdemain. In USIA the imbalance persisted, few CAOs moved ahead, and the USIA culture did not change.

Leonard Marks, LBJ's USIA director and a Nixon Democrat, was now chair of CU's advisory commission. Once Richardson's CU adopted "communications" as its password, it built a rickety bridge between cultural relations and propaganda. CU's concept paper, it seems clearer today, stretched hard to bring the two agencies closer in theoretical terms. USIA commissioner Michener had traveled extensively with his Chinese-born wife, engaging in deep dialogue with cultural officers everywhere. Michener's role cannot be documented, but CAOs remember probing discussions during which he pressed them to speak their minds.[6]

Stanton held a Ph.D. in industrial relations—the discipline that had shaped Coombs. Invited by Kennedy to head USIA after the debates, he had declined, accepting the USIA commission chair only under Lyndon Johnson's insistence that it would represent a gesture to his departed friend Ed Murrow.

The commission's 26th report in 1973 may have been the year's most important study, but it was not alone. By Lois Roth's count, at least six different studies of USIA-CU were in process, despite the Nixon administration's cool indifference and the unlikelihood of early political change. In March 1973 Stanton's was the first to reach Keogh's desk, setting off a sequence of thoughts and actions that would not end until 1978.

Olom remembers drafting the 26th report, from his notes on the commission's deliberations, and turning it over to Stanton's tireless editing. Their single disagreement had high significance. While Stanton wanted to treat State as a viable potential partner, Olom rolled out his strong bias against State. Stanton won the point and partnership was kept in. The 26th report, an early attempt to look at the agency in the context of the cold war's end, rested on the "long-range goal of genuine and lasting détente." At the same time, it advised USIA to seek to extend "conditions in which atmosphere and substance coincide." This was not a new idea; the commission's complaints about USIA's thin substance had been reiterated for nine years. It had first urged better balance between culture and information, better treatment of CAOs, and more libraries in 1964. Coming from inside the USIA family, the report carried weight.

The 26th report rose to a new level of impatience, the product of years of futility. It said a great deal more in support of cultural diplomacy and the substance on which it depended. In contrast to Sorensen, Shakespeare, and Keogh—and perhaps in an effort to limit their impact—the report openly discussed USIA's *two* fields and called for better balance between them. Cultural programs were "at least as important in the long run" as hard news; USIA needed a permanent high-level position, a prestigious cultural director, at a level just below the director; microscopic audience selection was self-defeating; USIA had to reach out to the "average citizen or those 'natural audiences' disposed to use USIS libraries abroad"—a slap at the Tokyo library experiment. The report underlined Smith-Mundt's call for understanding the U.S. and its *people*, not solely US foreign policy; it asked for more USIA self-study; it called for an outside survey of the entire agency; and it suggested new approaches to evaluating field programs and appraising performance.

It was not surprising to find USIA's would-be advisory role at the crux. Acknowledging Murrow's brave but unreplicable try, the report called the question: did the president and Congress want USIA to advise on foreign policy or not? If policy advice was desired, then USIA had to be strengthened for that purpose; if not, then the pretense of an advisory role could not impede USIA's evolution into a different kind of agency in the years ahead. Without the advisory role, USIA had to be redirected and restructured. Among the structural alternatives USIA and all its functions could return to State, as recommended by Field Haviland in 1960, with a "Super-Secretary of State" administering three coordinate subdivisions: political affairs, economics, and the two USIA missions of information and culture. Or else *informational* and *policy* functions could return to State, in which case the rest of USIA should be allowed to mutate into "a new agency [to] consolidate and absorb all of the foreign cultural and educational programs" of USIA, State, and other government agencies, including the two Endowments, USOE, and the Smithsonian (wisely, AID was not mentioned). In either case, VOA had to become an independent government agency. The report referred with respect to the British and Canadian models but preferred a design based on the distinctive US style.

This startling prescription, from a friendly source, could not be handled like an attack by Frankel. Instead, it was treated like all internal USIA dissension: it sank from view in the defensive and self-absorbed agency. Few echoes reached the field posts. Working in CU at the time, I was not aware of the 26th report.

A third study, after the CU statement and the 26th commission report, came from a less friendly source—the Senate. Fulbright, still chairing foreign relations, was increasingly vexed. His long committee report on USIA's 1972 authorization hearing suggested USIA had become a cold war anachronism; it noted the need for a "more mature, confident approach to the world, making information about ourselves available but not trying to foist it off on people." He added: "We may be far better served if we remove our information and cultural efforts from the realm of sales and return them to the realm of diplomacy." Fulbright, looking past the cold war, called for redistributing USIA functions, perhaps returning USIA's cultural responsibilities for "objects"—like libraries—to State. VOA might do better as a quasi-independent government agency. Press, television, and motion picture services should be downsized.

Fulbright's attack on the informationists was supported by a fourth report, a giant piece of research from the Legislative Reference Division of the Library of Congress. It was a three-volume report in 1975 called "The U.S. Communicates with the World," by Joel Woldman—a USIA officer who had been pressed into early retirement. The study made no recommendations, holding true to Legislative Reference tradition. When it appeared, Fulbright was no longer in the Senate to follow up, and thus the extraordinary and compendious Woldman report was never printed.

In the House Dante Fascell's advocacy of a single agency produced a fifth report, *The Future of Public Diplomacy* (1968), a compendium of starry-eyed testimonials to USIA in which any advocate could find support for any position. Documents like Fascell's, coming out of Congress, were hard to challenge—there are no critical analyses or peer-review comments. Unchallenged, Fascell's catalog was used to put the House squarely behind USIA; it became USIA's beacon. The phrase "Public Diplomacy" had begun its trek toward the lexicons.

In 1973 Richardson and USIA director Keogh banded together to provoke a sixth report. They agreed on an in-house survey and assigned it to the single authorship of respected USIA officer Barbara White, the highest-ranking woman professional in USIA, elevated to PAO Chile by Murrow. After a year's work, her findings caught USIA leadership short. She had the audacity to concur with the 26th report; worse, this prestigious top-level USIA officer carried weighty joint USIA-CU advisory commission sponsorship. Vast changes in communications technology were on the way, she said. Political change was stirring in Eastern Europe. A modern agency, she said, must take a longer-range view of US foreign policy. White sketched out the idea of an "overseas communication program," comprising both CU and USIA, which in the coming era she believed would be able to go beyond propaganda. US foreign relations in the 1970s, she said, were leading to an era when "mutuality," meaning mutual interests and bidirectionalism, but not quite Fulbright's binationalism, could only increase. To her, this demanded greater substance in international dialogue.

White made one mistake, which she later tried to repair: her original recommendations were couched in two time frames. First, for the last six years of the 1970s, she recommended only minor changes in USIA. Then, for the 1980s, she moved to the radical conclusion that USIA's advisory role should move into State. She reasoned that policy and information were collegial, she believed that the agency providing "information" for the new world situation needed to produce less quick news and more deep information about the U.S. and its institutions, and she joined the 26th report in calling for an independent VOA. Structurally, two separate entities were essential: a stronger Public Affairs Office in State to support and advise policymakers and a new agency dedicated solely to educational, cultural, and scientific affairs. She went further than Stanton, insisting that the new agency must oversee everything: "AID educational and communications programs; State Department's science attachés; and principal educational, cultural and scientific exchange programs of other government agencies such as [Education and the] National Science Foundation." She had reinvented Coombs.

White's in-house study was potent medicine with no sugarcoating. Its resemblance to Coombs-Frankel was striking, but by 1973 the basic ideas had been knocking about in Washington for thirty-five years. Her report annoyed the standpat agency that had expected a "loyal" riposte to the 26th commission report. The White report was never released to the public; even inside USIA its circulation was limited. Senior USIA officers accused White of apostasy, rejecting her formula for USIA greatness. Corridor talk accused her of "going soft"—a phrase used of cultural officers and, at the time, of women. The "soft" White would soon retire to a distinguished decade as president of Mills College.

A year later, freed of USIA inhibitions, she recognized that she had in fact gone soft. In testimony before Fascell's committee, she retracted her six-year delay and said her recommendations for the 1980s should be implemented *immediately*. The world was moving faster than she had seen. But this footnote was buried with her report.

As the turmoil bubbled up to his level, Keogh seems to have shifted his views on CU relations. The consensus may have looked conspiratorial. His relations with Richardson cooled and he reverted to the old refrain: only one change was needed, to absorb CU into USIA. In October 1973 Keogh told Ambassador Robert Murphy's blue-ribbon commission on reorganizing foreign affairs—at a moment when he already knew what his advisory commission and White were saying—that CU should be moved into USIA. Ignoring agency history, overlooking what key advisors were telling him, he had reverted to the simplistic one-agency idea of Streibert and Shakespeare, i.e., that two programs together in the field are better managed in one Washington agency. Keogh may have been throwing out a smoke screen, or attempting to discredit White's study, or trying to nullify the 26th report, or yielding to VOA and USIA loyalists, or expressing his nationalist ideology, or all of the above. Possibly he was sending a signal, e.g., from Ford's White House or from Fascell. That so many plausible hypotheses arise, with no evidence for any, suggests the usual muddy Potomac waters.

Dismissing both USIA's advisory commission report and senior-advisor White's study under the joint sponsorship of both USA and CU advisory commissions, Keogh trashed both. CU's advisory commission under Marks saw a duty to stand by its sister commission and called for a reexamination. In May 1973 a commission member visiting London met CAO Wilcox, well known to the CU commission's director Margaret Twyman. Impressed by the vibrant, affable, articulate, flexible, but strongminded Indianan, the commissioner drew from him a long and responsive letter, which in turn led to a long discussion during a Washington visit.

Wilcox was an unusually broad-gauged political scientist. The commission did not know that he had been following the CAO question since the early sixties, when he dealt with a variety of CAOs in South Asia. He also knew a great deal about the lengthening list of discarded studies. When the CU commission invited him to undertake its study, he was prepared and bargained on two points: that the request come from *both* USIA and CU commissions, and that he conduct the survey by himself, in a time frame no longer than three months. His London PAO—ex-CAO and Columbia Ph.D. William Weld—supported him. In personnel terms, he and Wilcox stipulated that USIA send a temporary replacement of their choosing to London, and the candidate was discreetly alerted.

Wilcox already knew precisely what he wanted to say but not quite how to say it. Having roved South Asia for decades and touched base with USIS friends around the world, having watched the failure of his Columbia colleague Frankel, he intended to make a difference or else not waste his time. Friends on the staff of the Senate Foreign Relations Committee, including Chief of Staff Carl Marcy, another Columbia Ph.D., welcomed his help in cutting through the dilemma. Wilcox was a quick study. In London, succeeding Robin Winks and working with the legendary Weld, he had good teachers; he was in constant correspondence with friends around the world, and he had traveled out from his London base for lectures. Wilcox had come to believe that an internal USIA consensus lay within reach. After decades of dealing with the insoluble India-Pakistan question, the dilemma struck him as somewhat less daunting.

He planned what he called a "consultative study," by which he meant consulting with enough key figures and reflecting enough of their thinking that, when his conclusions appeared, they would be recognizable and acceptable to all. His goal was to help USIA grow by bringing CU's strengths into its structure, mission, and staffing. Somewhere in his mind lay a precooked solution—but he was a political scientist and believed in getting everyone on board first. Congress, he knew, would be relieved to accept a consensus agreed to by the professionals, and leaders like Fulbright were ready to fight one more battle.

At this promising moment, the Wilcox trail ended. Olom has no memory of the USIA commission's support ever being sought. One insider said the foundations refused to fund a study by a US government official still in service—an insignificant argument because funding was not needed (his three-month study would have cost a few air tickets, a little per diem, and time diverted from two officers' work). Wilcox's ingenious low-cost plan was worth a try, but the invitation never arrived. He stayed in London. In March, when he had planned to deliver his report to Washington, he was returning from a ski trip in Europe with his wife and two of his four children when all four were killed in a plane crash.[7]

The idea of a one-man joint CU-USIA advisory commission report had probably died months earlier. Meanwhile, a major change had taken place in USIA's advisory commission: hard-nosed *Reader's Digest* conservative Hobart Lewis had taken over the chair from Stanton, a move surely arranged by Keogh. Lewis moved quickly in the opposite direction. Still, he had to respect the 26th report's call for a prestigious outside survey. The two commissions agreed to set up an independent panel on "International Information, Education, and Cultural Relations." Richardson's friend Leo Cherne, Marks's predecessor as chair of the CU commission, ran into Frank Stanton in an airport by a fortuitous accident. It did not occur to anyone that Stanton was an interested party and perhaps the wrong man for the job, nor for that matter did it occur to Stanton. Then chairing the Red Cross, he agreed to lead the independent study of a subject he understood better than most.

Things took shape rapidly. A USIA officer, Austrian-born Walter Roberts, resigned from the agency to direct the study under Stanton. All members of both advisory commissions, five for USIA and nine for CU, joined the panel. Dean Peter Krogh of Georgetown's School of Foreign Service accepted the vice chairmanship; Georgetown's Center for Strategic and International Studies agreed to host the study; funding was patched together from Ford, Rockefeller, Lilly, and a West Coast newcomer, the Ahmanson Foundation.

Roberts was a determinant choice. With a sharp and philosophically trained mind, this son of a medieval historian at the University of Graz had left Austria in time to avoid the Nazi disaster, studied at Trinity College, Cambridge, then at Harvard, went on to Washington in 1942 to join his Harvard mentor William Langer under "Coordinator of Information" Donovan. When COI was divided into OSS and OWI, he moved to OWI and began a long career with USIA. After the Stanton report, he joined the Georgetown Center and the Board of International Broadcasting, while teaching at George Washington University.

Roberts believes he was chosen because of earlier testimony he had given before USIA's advisory commission, where he had first defined the idea of a "spokesman function," suggesting that it belonged in State. The idea lay at the core of the 26th report. In choosing Roberts, Stanton knew precisely where he wanted to go.

Less biased than it might have been, the panel was weighted to the information side. CU's nine-person commission had a balanced membership of cultural and informational representatives and USIA's had four informationists plus Michener. Krogh was a realist political scientist; Andrew Berding had been deputy director of IIA; W. Philips Davidson at Columbia was professor of journalism and, with his partner Lloyd Free, a partisan of a single—albeit more cultural—USIA; George Gallup was the famous public-opinion pollster who did contract work for USIA's research division; and Edmund Gullion was a former foreign service officer already serving as dean of Tufts, founder of the Murrow School, and author of the phrase "Public Diplomacy." Defending the educational side, political scientist Kenneth Thompson of the Rockefeller Foundation had long supported cultural independence. From CU's commission came two academic political scientists, businessmen, lawyers, and a former congressman from Missouri, but no scientist, humanist, woman, nor American of color. There was certainly no Frankel or Coombs.

The haphazard collection of policy-oriented Americans making up the Stanton panel, brought together for the most part by the vagaries of political appointment to the commissions, was honestly united, it would seem, in its concern for the well-being of both CU and USIA. Though it found an ingenious consensus of the work done in the period 1973–75, the panel reached "the most controversial conclusions of the decade," as Lois Roth put it. As it turned out, Stanton was to be the culturalists' last hurrah.

Panel members first fanned out for a series of meetings with field officers in Europe and other areas, a process which failed in its intention of calming CAO suspicions of one-agency bias. The participants in the Vienna meeting were chosen by USIA, with an eye toward minimizing CAO dissent. In Rome the cultural officer, more vocal about separate functions than most, was not informed about the Vienna meetings until they were over; and his impression of having been deliberately overlooked was understandable—the Rome PAO went to Vienna, and the deputy PAO was interviewed separately. Other CAOs who missed the conference knew they had been deliberately ignored. The printed version of the report lists ninety-eight interviewees, including Coombs and Frankel.[8] Only fourteen CAOs were interviewed; of these only four— including Lois Roth and Robin Winks—were committed and distinguished, albeit in different ways. In contrast twenty-five interviewees were identified as PAOs.

When the Stanton Commission's report appeared in March 1975, it was immediately endorsed by the powerful Murphy Commission, which had been meeting in parallel to review the entire structure of US diplomacy and had chosen to await Stanton's work before dealing with information and cultural affairs. Murphy explicitly endorsed and supported Stanton in strongly worded testimony before Fascell in 1977.

Despite the noticeable one-agency and anti-State tilt of its membership and its interviewees, the Stanton report is a shrewd, pointed, balanced, and sophisticated extension of the 26th advisory commission report. Instead of wondering whether USIA would ever earn an advisory role in foreign policy formation, it redefined the question by positing a "spokesman function," a phrase that assumed policy can only be communicated to the world at large by the agency that makes the policy. Stanton asserted such communication can only flow from State. The originality of the approach lay in recognizing the unavoidable clash of two separate functions: on the one hand, the formulation, execution, and publication of daily tactical foreign policy questions and their delivery to appropriate audiences, i.e., the spokesman function; and on the other hand, the longer-range strategies of educational and cultural relations. Of four ongoing functions (policy information, policy advice, general information—USIA's euphemism for culture—and exchange of persons), policy information and policy advice belonged in State, where policy was made. The other two functions belonged in a "cultural relations" agency. With policy in State, USIA and CU would be freed to grow together in a natural way, with the potential of becoming in time a major world-scale cultural diplomatic agency. By Stanton's functional criteria, the VOA problem fell simply into place. It could not avoid being both spokesman for US policy and an "educational broadcaster." It should therefore follow its own destinies in juggling these two functions as an independent body within government. While this VOA solution followed from Stanton's thinking, it might have been wiser to leave it for another report and focus solely on the main problem of information and cultural relations.

Paralleling White, the Stanton panel called for: (1) the creation, in place of USIA, of a quasi-independent Informational and Cultural Affairs Agency, combining CU and USIA's cultural programs, with better balance between them; (2) an Office of Policy Information in State, headed by a Deputy Undersecretary and involving some USIA positions and sub-functions; and (3) an independent governmental VOA. Stanton had achieved what MacLeish had not had time to do: reconcile policy advice and policy support with "true" propaganda. As Lois Roth noted, "the originality of the Stanton Report lay in a single idea on which the entire structure rests: that policy information, i.e. the whitewashed American version of overt propaganda, should not be disseminated by the same institution which handles general information and cultural affairs."

The Annexes to the Stanton document were as interesting as the report itself. First came a list of eleven prescient questions raised by the 24th advisory commission in May 1969, asking for example whether informational and cultural objectives were "compatible" within a single agency. Then came an excerpt from a USIA appropriations hearing in the Senate, dated 22 May 1973, with a classic statement of the dilemma by Chairman Fulbright. Next, the lengthy Annex IV traced the origin of USIA in the reports of Fulbright-Hickenlooper, Rockefeller, and Jackson, all in 1953, and followed the idea through reports by Fleming (1958), Sprague, Haviland, Free-Davison (1960), the Republican Coordinating Committee (1968), and a Senate report plus the Murphy Commission in 1973. Next, a two-page note on the "origin of CU" betrayed a biased and underinformed USIA author, who has CU coming to birth sometime after 1953, fifteen years after it actually took place.

The most dramatic annex was a tart exchange of letters between Gullion and Stanton. Gullion on 7 March, *after* advance copies of the report had been released, accused Stanton of "parcelling out" USIA to different parts of State. Stanton on 15 March answered that the report recommended "nothing of the sort," only the "spokesman function" would go to State, in return for which USIA would receive all of CU; he told Gullion icily that Gullion was "dissenting from something we are not proposing."

The defensive info-warriors of USIA were already in action. For them, the report contained three heresies. First, since ideas mattered less in USIA than staffing details, the worst heresy lay in transferring an undefined number of USIA officers to the hated State. Second, lurking in Stanton's slim forty-seven pages plus annexes was a cost-saving idea that drove a stake through the heart of USIA orthodoxy: Stanton quietly noted that, once there were separate branches in each embassy for information and for culture, there would be no need for a PAO—the cultural and information sections could stand alongside their political and economic colleagues. The third heresy was to suggest removing VOA from USIA, unthinkable for the USIA loyalists—VOA played well in Congress and deflected lightning.

Stanton's report was quickly submerged. Its sad post-publication history bordered on tragedy. First, the commission's plan for a public education campaign was inadequate and underfunded. One visit did take place: Stanton and a few colleagues visited the Carter White House to discuss the program; they were received politely but turned aside curtly by NSC advisor Brzezinski.

Second, the initial report was undermined by its own authors. Even at publication, it was endorsed by only eighteen of the panels's twenty-one members—one CU commissioner resigned to accept an embassy abroad, and Gullion pleaded insufficient time.[9] The major blow, in the first stage, was the abstention of Leonard Marks, member not only of the panel but of its executive group. The effect of Marks's move, correctly or not, was widely perceived as a veto. In 1977 Marks explained that his disagreement had focused specifically on cutting VOA loose. Just as USIA's single vote of dissent had capsized Frankel's task force, this single abstention hamstrung the Stanton report. A second level of nonsupport was stealthier. By the time of the Fascell hearings, Hobart Lewis and George Gallup had recanted. Even if only supported by sixteen members, Stanton's report was a high-caliber piece of work. For the culturalists, it was one more moment of hope.

The USIA culture, with VOA wagging the dog, had in fact no intention of changing; it had welcomed Stanton only as a putative step toward absorbing CU—even the president was not strong enough to command USIA to do anything else, unless he planned a sensitive educational campaign lasting over several years. USIA however overlooked a call to greatness. The Stanton Commission's mistakes were harder to read, especially from a chairman of such distinction. Perhaps, as hypothesized by Gifford Malone, they arose from having relied too heavily on persuasive, clear thinking, common sense, and the panel's prestige. An allied error lay in not involving Congress, most crucially Fascell, whose intransigence ultimately carried the day.

Stanton's report was the last attempt in cold print, within the USIA-

CU family, to argue that a separate and integrated cultural diplomacy, insulated from information-propaganda, was not only feasible but could help USIA grow into a better and richer agency for the years ahead. It was the most compelling and comprehensive of the many thoughtful attempts in the mid-1970s by serious people, the culmination of three decades of consistent thought, to find a common future in which the values and the contributions of both CU and USIA could flourish, support each other, and help each other grow.

One more report dropped in the trash would have mattered little. But a new administration had taken office, pledged to reorganize government. The well-intentioned efforts of Jimmy Carter's staff would brush aside the truth of what Stanton said in pursuit of their version of superior wisdom. As the Soviet world moved to its imminent and inevitable end, the stubborn USIA, supported by a handful of congressmen with little understanding of the issues, had frustrated efforts to think clearly about the ideas inherent in a decent American cultural diplomacy. It was the last chance Americans would have until the 1990s to build from the ground up, design a new structure with clear functional mandates, and thereby maximize the towering strengths America could bring to bear in projecting its soft power.

Instead, defying the cluster of studies that reached consensus in the mid-1970s, the single-agency concept had roared back to life. After Streibert, Shakespeare, and Keogh, the idea was identified with the nationalist and confrontationist view that propaganda came first and the rest did not matter. When Fulbright left the Senate in 1975, no one was ready to carry forward his powerful commitment to a decent cultural diplomacy with its own kind of integrity. No one was there to resist the encroachments of "propaganda" under the new banners of "Public Diplomacy." In the House the underinformed Florida Democrat Fascell had emerged as the proud champion of what he had helped to brand name. No one was left to call a halt to the impetuous enthusiasm and the shallow vision of the young and inexperienced Carter team. In 1978 a shotgun wedding was arranged; CU, after thirty years of resistance, finally slipped into the awaiting arms of USIA.

CHAPTER TWENTY-THREE

Paved with Good Intentions:
Carter's Reorganization

The Agency will undertake no activities which are covert, manipulative or propagandistic. The Agency can assume—as our founding fathers did—that a great and free society is its own best witness, and can put its faith in the power of ideas.

—Jimmy Carter, 1977

WHILE STANTON'S OPPONENTS were husbanding their forces, the campaign of Jimmy Carter, pledging to reorganize Big Government, was under way. A self-proclaimed outsider, Carter was a small-state Southern governor whose antigovernment campaign sought to outflank the Republicans' newfound conservative appeal in the South. He played on America's mistrust of government and its power. Gerald Ford's more traditional campaign, weakened by Watergate, his pardon of Nixon, and the ignominious end in Vietnam, lost out to Carter's promises of change.

Cultural diplomacy was scarcely a campaign issue. Carter had no position on the matter, only a sense that foreign policy should listen to foreigners more closely; but his reorganizational pledges set off a chain reaction. They would lead to the revolutionary merger of CU and USIA, a union that had been fought off for more than a quarter of a century. John Richardson, in moving CU conceptually closer to USIA through the idea of "communication," had inadvertently helped USIA leadership blur the distinction between information and culture. With Fulbright's departure, CU struggling, and BFS weakened, the old distinctions faded even more rapidly. With "flexibility" in "communication" as its highest value, USIA's defenders forgot why the cultural founders had insisted on protecting academic integrity in the first place. By 1987 USIA's director of Educational and Cultural Affairs (ECA)—Richardson's sucessor a decade later—said without apology that he used the word "Fulbright" to cover any function listed by the Fulbright-Hays Act of 1961—including libraries and the short-term, political-action IV Program.[1]

As the nation approached the elections of November 1976, Stanton's costly report was gathering dust; its outreach efforts had died. Inside USIA, outrage with Stanton was maintained at fever pitch and ricocheted around the corridors. A petition with 165 signatures, including fine com-

mitted culturalists, denounced what it said were Stanton's recommendations, misstating them in spirit and letter as Gullion had done.[2] The fears
motivating the petition looked far beyond the questions of culture and
focused on the threat of breaking up USIA. In fact, Stanton had laid out
a road map for USIA's growth and survival. But USIA's leadership was
blind to any solution but the status quo, admitting of course that it would
accept CU's unconditional surrender.

Carter owed a minor debt to Stanton for fund-raising in New York.[3]
He knew about, but probably did not read, his report. The same was true
of Stanton's neighbor Cyrus Vance, Secretary of State designate. Energetic
campaign staffers like Barry Jagoda, rapid-response shaper of campaign
themes, viewed USIA as any public relations professional might, thinking
a stronger agency would produce better public relations. One new attitude filtered into diplomatic thinking from the top; Carter's opinion that
US foreign policy talked more than it listened. This idea would be seized
upon by loyal staffers and stirred vigorously into the USIA stew that the
anti-Stanton forces were preparing.

US political transitions always cause chaos—Frederick Mosher once
noted that an enemy power intent upon attacking the U.S. should time
the event for just after an election.[4] In recent years the process had begun
to lengthen because of the cumbersome FBI clearance process. Like all
bureaucracies facing sharp change, the government was deferring decisions; and like all new administrations, Carter focused first on filling
jobs, and only later—if at all—on ideas. Carter's transition teams proved
no more capable than others of making uniformly outstanding political
appointments. In 1977 US cultural diplomacy, the long-forgotten issue,
suffered from transitional confusion, whatever the quality of individual
appointments. And its tireless champion in the Senate had now been
gone for two years, a victim of out-of-state funding provided by ideological enemies.

For committed culturalists, Carter raised hopes high by appointing
John Reinhardt to lead USIA.[5] Reinhardt was not only the first USIA director to rise from the USIA ranks, he was the first Ph.D., the first university educator, the first USIA director since George Allen to have served as
ambassador (in Nigeria), and the first top-level USIA official who had
served all his USIS postings in cultural offices. He was the real thing, a
genuine, practicing cultural diplomat. The Knoxville College graduate,
with a doctorate from the University of Wisconsin in American studies
and a thesis on James Russell Lowell, had been specially recruited from
the Virginia State College faculty during the Allen years. Assigned to
India, he was diverted to the Philippines when the PAO in New Delhi
insisted that a black American could not succeed in Lucknow. Instead he
apprenticed in the Philippines, then served in Kyoto and in Tokyo before
a truncated tour in Iran. When he was called to Washington in 1966, he

had graced four cultural offices in three countries. Back in USIA he was director for East Asia, then Africa. After Nigeria he returned to Washington to relieve Richardson of the burdens of public affairs.

For reasons explained later, USIA had changed its name to the International Communications Agency. At his ICA swearing-in in April 1977, Reinhardt called for an agency of ideas and substance: "I believe in the power of ideas," he said. "Ideas are what the ICA is all about—the generation of ideas, the exchange of ideas, the refinement of ideas." In contrast to "those who place their trust in military might, those who lean to economic determinism, those whose ultimate regard is for scientific and technological innovation," he said, "I turn to ideas."[6] The bold language of Carter's executive letter covering the merger of CU and USIA, had no precedent in USIA history, and it would prove difficult to implement.

Like any foreign service officer, Reinhardt saw the issues through the lenses of his field experience. He recognized one prejudgment in himself: CU, in particular, and State, in general, were stodgy. Believing this, he brought to USIA a deputy from State, Charles Bray, a cautious maverick, one of the "young Turk" dissenters on foreign affairs in 1973–74, who had served as his deputy in PA. A faculty son at Princeton, Bray had spent a Fulbright year in Bordeaux—lending further cultural luster to the academic caliber of Reinhardt's office. Sharing daily transportation to the office, Bray and Reinhardt became inseparable.

Reinhardt's expansive vision of USIA was shaped in post-occupation Japan, where there were cultural centers and libraries in fifteen cities. In the Philippines too he had seen a post with many USIS branch offices, engaged in nation-building and early forms of counterinsurgency. Even in Iran, disappointing to a Japan-hand more used to compliant audiences and disciplined staff, he was in a country of 25 million souls that had undergone a different but no less real kind of US occupation. There he managed a central library, the huge Tehran IAS cultural center with two extensions in Tehran, five branch posts—four with centers and libraries—and BNCs left over from other times.

A defender of the developing world, he could seem anti-European. Budgets for Europe were in fact disproportionately high because of the Soviet bloc priorities, the commitment to emerging democracy in Germany, growing European union, the structure of twenty-odd allied nations in Western Europe (some in NATO), and large European immigrant populations in the U.S. Beyond budget imbalance, he believed all USIA's area offices were too strong; he had headed two of them, including malnourished Africa. Since he placed high value on giving the field posts what they needed, he squeezed Europe. USIA's area baronies, intended to channel and defend field autonomy, seemed to Reinhardt a countervailing force resistant to his struggle for better balance.

By nature he was cautious, courteous, intelligent, and quietly modest; he spoke little but with strength. He put a high value on honesty and friendship. Beneath these sterling qualities, there were understandable uncertainties. Trained as an intellectual and a humanist, he knew too much to be dogmatic about anything. As a successful American black, he was aware of the sluggish pace of social progress in the U.S. He also understood—and perhaps in his realism accepted too readily—the gridlock of US political life. With regard to nonintellectualism in political life, he was as aware of it as anyone. All this discouraged the kind of leadership that might have cut through some of the knots. He was not a politician but a professional diplomat trained as a literary scholar. With no independent political link to the White House and with little support outside it, his only lifeline was thin—the Congressional Black Caucus. USIA colleagues admired his capacity for maintaining Buddha-like inscrutablity and mastering complexity; some feared that, mistrusting his own judgment, he replaced wisdom by rigid regulations.

In January 1977 rethinking USIA had been thrust onto the Carter agenda by Barbara White and the Stanton report; in the background was the thawing Soviet war. Reinhardt's appointment and his early directorial messages lifted the spirits of the culturalists. The game, for once, seemed open. True, there was no White House or congressional plan to anyone's knowledge, but the impression that the White House was ready to invest in change was widespread. Carter was content to leave the matter to Reinhardt's team and to his campaign advisors, now installed in the White House.

For CU, Carter asked Joseph Duffey to succeed Richardson, another apparent boost for the culturalists. For the first time, both CU and USIA were headed by Ph.D.s, and USIA had a Fulbright alumnus as deputy director.[7] Duffey, from humble beginnings in West Virginia, had gone through Marshall College in history and held a doctorate in theology from the Hartford Seminary. As a northern Baptist minister from West Virginia, he had taught urban studies at Hartford, then at Yale, organized anti-Vietnam teach-ins, served as national chair of Americans for Democratic Action, directed the Association of University Professors, and run for the Senate from Connecticut, where political deals managed to split the Democratic vote and turn over the seat to Republican Lowell Weicker (Duffey's campaign team included two Yale law students named Clinton and Rodham). In 1973 he went to Paris to try out the directorship of the post-*Ramparts* Congress for Cultural Freedom, which was struggling to survive, but decided to decline the job.[8] He and his political consultant wife Anne Wexler, who joined the White House staff, worked in Carter's campaign.

In retrospect, some have imagined that Duffey was the designated hatchet for chopping CU out of State, but all the evidence runs in the opposite direction—the Carter White House was certainly not thinking that far ahead. Duffey wanted the CU job and actively sought it. Once aboard, he had to face a hard fact: he learned that it had already been decided to merge CU with USIA.[9] Carter had apparently turned over to his staff the means of paying his debt to Stanton, but he did not realize he was feeding the CU canary to the USIA cat.

Duffey's CU colleagues, Richardson's team, persuaded him to fight the merger. But when Duffey took the matter to State's tough negotiator Undersecretary for Administration Philip Habib and his deputy Ben Reed, Duffey's nonconfrontational style could not sway the opposition; they convinced him the issue was closed. Discussion between Duffey and Habib took place before the task force on merging USIA and CU convened, so it is clear that Carter's team had made up its mind whatever the task force's findings. Aware of the White House position, Duffey was thus not entirely surprised when Carter in late May asked him to help out by taking the chair of the National Endowment for the Humanities (NEH), after his first choice for the position had fallen through. Duffey was led to understand he had no choice but NEH.

It is strange that Duffey, a recognized academic figure, saw then and still seems to see USIA and CU plowing the same furrow. He seems today never to have seen the advantages of separating information from culture. If he had a vision of how the two functions might flow together, he has never articulated it; instead he has tended to project culture and information as two unequal tools of Public Diplomacy. Knowing that the movement toward a single agency for Public Diplomacy could not be stopped, he was perhaps trying to help it, while minimizing damage to cultural diplomacy. Hypothetically, a strong active proponent of culture in the Public Diplomacy debate might have enriched the thinking of the merger-minded, especially those grouped around the shallow Dante Fascell. Had Duffey played the role of a strong advocate and insisted on staying with CU after it joined USIA, or if he had bargained for a replacement of his approximate caliber and closeness to Carter, he might in fact have made a great difference, especially after a year of learning under good CU teachers. Instead he obeyed Carter, resigned his CU job in May, and stayed in his CU office while awaiting his confirmation for NEH.

Close observers do not understand his choice to remain in CU until November. Senior deputy Hitchcock, a fine foreign service officer with six years in CU as deputy to Richardson, was ostensibly in charge during the last six months of Duffey's tenure, but he served under the presence of an absentee.

The Carter campaign had attacked so-called professionals in government, on grounds that they did not always serve citizens' interests. Without a strong leader in CU, this antigovernment mindset opened the door more widely to political appointments than ever before in CU history.

As background, the Pendleton Act (1885) had ended the famous Spoils System and political appointees dwindled in government. By 1960 fewer than five hundred appointees led a largely professional US government staff. But the number of appointments crept up under Johnson and Nixon. In CU, appointments had always been minimal—limited to the Assistant Secretary, one deputy, and one or two others. In the second

Nixon administration, with three previous Republican appointees at the top remaining in place, a single White House spin-off joined them, a highly skilled woman placed in a learning position as deputy director of the IV office.

Without Duffey's political connections, Hitchcock found it difficult to resist White House pressures. By the middle of 1977, Carter's staff had made nine new appointments to CU, more than doubling the past high. Amounting to 3 percent of the bureau staff, the newcomers were manageable, and all but one were under strong supervising chiefs, in jobs where they could learn. But one exception set a difficult precedent: to direct IV, the White House team chose a hard-charging woman not yet twenty-five years of age, with no governmental experience. Her considerable talents notwithstanding, this appointment to head a key office, not as an apprentice but as chief, unleashed immediate and longer-range consequences. In the near term, she revved up the program, climbing a notch too high by raising numbers, lifting costs, lowering quality, and provoking a major review in the fall of 1981. In the longer range, her name would become the battle flag under which the Reagan team tripled the number of Carter's appointments to CU-ECA, occupying all positions of command except deputy to the chief.[10]

The consequences for CU, even in the near term, were serious. The anti-professionalism epitomized by the political appointments aggravated the perennial problem of balancing field wisdom and domestic expertise, and further narrowed CU assignments for committed CAOs in their Washington tours. In the longer reach, the appointments were crippling. Lois Roth, after brilliant field work as a CAO in three countries and in a USIA desk officer job, was assigned in 1981 to direct the IV Program, then was demoted to another office as deputy to an appointee fifteen years her junior, with no experience at all. A veteran CAO, assigned to a senior job in educational and cultural affairs, was overriden and marginalized by the new appointees, cutting off his career at its apex. Another senior CAO was assigned to the IV office when Roth was moved aside, but then was layered over by a political appointee, left for a field posting, and retired early.

Carter had respected sacred practices and not touched field posts, reserved for foreign service officers and occasional academic professionals; but USIA's director in the 1980s, Charles Z. Wick, would appoint young underqualified outsiders, including a well-intentioned dental hygienist, to the more glamorous cities of Western Europe. Because some of these overseas appointments were offspring of prominent political figures, the press called the issue "Kiddiegate." Wick provoked stifled guffaws from USIA staff when he announced that he would never condone "discrimination against children of the rich."

With Duffey's in-house absence in 1977, there was no one to restrain the White House from pushing appointees further down into the organization. At the same time, another threat was mounting from below that had little to do with partisan politics and everything to do with the political life of the new America. Egalitarian pressures, in the unexceptionable cause of equal opportunity, were accelerating intake and promotions for women and minorities. Had the promotions been contingent upon acquiring further university qualifications, the move might have strengthened the staff, but this belated rush to justice raised younger staff to levels beyond their competence. The promotions neglected the indispensable factor of education. Once initiated, the upward movement of these "mustangs," as they were first called, was inexorable, for reasons Parkinson has articulated. Inside CU, the damage had a particular edge. Since CU was committed to interchange between the cultural elites of the U.S. and those of other nations, it depended on sophisticated staff and language skills. The newly upward-mobile were not given time off for educational upgrading and so rose in rank without attendant growth. The skilled CU professionals were squeezed between the influx of ill-prepared people from top and bottom. CU's educational profile was declining even faster than Wayne Wilcox had warned in 1973.

Duffey finally moved to NEH in November and was not replaced until February 1978, more than a year after Carter's inauguration. In the interim CU's top managers, committed to reversing the merger, put career interests aside, fought the move, and paid the price of defeat. Through March 1978, the CU team took principal guidance from the capable Hitchcock, who could only watch helplessly as USIA sharks circled CU's school of herring.

Carter was anything but a radical, yet in his handling of USIA-CU reorganization he was responsible for the single most radical moment in the story of US cultural diplomacy. Fulbright no longer barred the way; Fascell was hounding Congress with the idea of a single agency, and USIA waited with open arms. The "USIA issue," in fact, was a tempting target for reorganization because for three decades it had been studied, it was said, to death.

Carter did the obvious; he appointed a task force to study the problem, even though the decision had been made. The task force was composed not of experts but of Carter campaigners working in the frantic White House climate. The group based its thinking on three documents: the lucid functional analysis found in Stanton's forty-seven pages,[11] the unreadable heap of testimonials that Fascell had compiled in 1967 and, even more casually, another volume in June 1978. No one could have the two Fascell tomes, but there is no evidence either that anyone read Stanton. Instead, the task force began from the premise, guided by White House hints, that the decision had already been made, that Stanton's carefully hedged suggestion of a single agency coincided with Fascell's simplistic idea of sticking CU into USIA, willy-nilly. Carter's team could reassure itself that the heavy lifting had been done, but no one could possibly have read the records.

Despite the campaign rhetoric about reorganizing, the task force began work in April as a complete afterthought. When, three months into Carter's administration, no specific governmental reorganization had been announced, a questioner prodded the West Wing about the solution. The Carter team flashed into action, at the warp speed typifying young White House staff. A sizable group of aides assembled in the White House; Stanton's and Fascell's texts were to be the working documents. Thus the USIA-CU question, after four harrowing decades of anguished analysis and discussion by the best minds in America, fell to the perusal of a platoon of random eyes, preoccupied with other work, united by their ignorance of the issues, and "ten years too young for the job," as one of them later admitted.

The task force has been remarkably reticent, by Washington standards. Only two of the team have spoken to me about it. In the words of one of these, who prefers anonymity, looking back a decade later, the task force members were inexperienced. The late Rick Neustadt spoke more openly about the study to his close friends, reporting that questions of substance never arose, that meetings were aimless and meandering, that agency structure, not function, was the only constant theme, and that more time was spent on the new agency's name than on any other subject. Typical of the climate, he said, was the caustic laughter greeting his proposal that the name of the new agency reflect the legislation: the Agency for International Understanding.[12] One possible explanation for the impression of aimlessness: top members of the task force already knew what conclusions they were expected to reach. By October the Carter staffers, with no apparent inputs from recognized experts other than those selected by Fascell, came to their radical decision to merge CU into USIA, precisely what the hard-liners and nationalists since Streibert had been urging.

If few understood the enormity of what they were doing, all were aware of the prominent names who had labored for Stanton and Fascell. The White House, in announcing its decision, covered it with an unusually long and detailed executive letter, bristling with inspirational rhetoric and earnest promises—none of which could of course be kept. The task force had missed the sophisticated analysis and balance of Stanton's report and the tightly interwoven quality of its thought; instead Stanton, like Fascell, was treated like an à la carte menu, from which to choose this or that. Stanton had given them a brilliant functional blueprint for solving a forty-year-old dilemma. In it, they saw only structural hints. Fascell in contrast had given them a marvelous grab-bag. With bravado, they took a step that the professionals and the political leadership of both parties had studiously avoided for three decades.

The committed cultural diplomats saw another missed opportunity, the more so in that a sensible solution had once again seemed possible. Historians who look more deeply into the USIA-CU task force may learn more about its thinking, but twenty years later there is little evidence that it was much more than window dressing for a foregone conclusion.

Members saw themselves as courageously facing "the USIA issue"—few understood the issue, and fewer had heard of CU. In truth, reforming government is easier to announce than to do; and it is always costlier than foreseen; it is, as Woodrow Wilson said of changing a university curriculum, "no more difficult than moving a cemetery."

In June, to influence the task force's work, Fascell had spawned a second weighty volume of USIA advocacy, to outweigh Stanton's slim pamphlet. Hasty organization marked the so-called hearings that produced the ponderous compilation *Public Diplomacy and the Future*, seven hundred pages alleging to report on the task force's "discussion." In contrast to the eight months that Fulbright and Hickenlooper had spent (1952–53), the two years that went into Smith-Mundt (1947–48), the years consumed in producing the Morrill report or Coombs's Slater Exercises, this was a nine-day ramble. The safely seated Florida Democrat, chair of the seven-member Subcommittee on International Operations of the House Committee on Foreign Affairs, had claimed the role of Congress's ranking expert on USIA, which gratefully fed him its views and those of its friends. Fascell was totally committed to Public Diplomacy, or to what he thought Public Diplomacy meant—which, in fact boiled down simply to what USIA had always done.

Fascell's nine-day hearings look obese beside the historic founding debates on the subject. The 1977 volume was at least as contradictory as Smith-Mundt, with the difference that Smith-Mundt recognized two sides, clearly defined each, and accepted the fatal conflict between them. In 1977, instead, no one was questioning or listening. Even Fascell's own committee stayed away. Three members came and went; three others did not bother.

Fascell's questioning was limp. He confessed to impatience with the tenacious problem—and with Fulbright's "prejudice," as he called it. He invited all witnesses, framed all questions, and controled the discussion. His collection of ill-matched pearls seemed to have a single purpose: to fill a volume large enough to outweigh Stanton and to replace USIA-CU with a single agency. Witnesses supported the one-agency view by about three to one. Duffey declined to appear.

Fascell's volume, with an occasional gem, was a record of intellectual chaos, a dialogue of the deaf led by a distracted enthusiast. It looked first at USIA, then at VOA—with CU a distant third. "Public Diplomacy" was eulogized but never defined. Educational and cultural relations were praised, but the idea that education needed insulation from information was never aired—once again, information and culture were declared to be the same thing. Previous USIA directors "agreed with Stanton" that absorbing CU was a fine idea, although Stanton recommended nothing of the kind. On three separate occasions, Fascell sniped at the absent Fulbright. A committee member from New Jersey, attending only once, asked a series of bizarre questions, before finally understanding that "culture" did *not* mean the performing arts. The chair of BFS made a powerful statement, which was shredded by inexcusably ignorant, irrelevant, and unanswerable questioning. Leonard Marks explained his abstention from Stanton as a "personal disagreement," probably over the separation of VOA. Two other Stanton commissioners—Hobart Lewis and George Gallup—took the occasion to register their recantations, hinting that other members would join—a notion that Stanton immediately scotched. Lawyer Marks, by clever semantics, proved that policy information was the same as "general information"—his phrase for cultural affairs. VOA's friends carried on their longstanding war with State; they already had all the independence they needed inside USIA and liked it that way. Undersecretary of State Robert Ingersoll accepted the idea of a USIA-CU merger—but only on the Murphy Commission's condition that USIA move into State. He was ignored, as was Deputy Secretary Warren Christopher, who said the same. Veteran Ambassador Robert Murphy, whose probing two-year study of US foreign affairs had just appeared, supported Stanton firmly, putting the unanimous support of his prestigious twelve-person panel behind Stanton; he too was overlooked.

Participant-analyst Gifford Malone, in a perceptive book a decade later (1988), argued that Stanton's fatal mistake lay in pleading clearly from function and from basic assumptions.[13] He noted that, while some "critics understood and sincerely disagreed, . . . many neither understood nor cared, preferring to see the issue in terms of whose interests were threatened or advanced. In the end a consensus developed for . . . the lowest common denominator." Today, the mountain of Fascell's June 1977 testimony reads as a hopeless tangle of contradictions. Its purpose is clear: not to enlighten Fascell nor his congressional colleagues but to press for a single agency, at any cost. In Fascell's volumes and these hearings, one can find a quotation to justify anything.

Typical of the low intellectual caliber, semantic fog, and historical amnesia of the Fascell "hearings," and reflecting the way it was understood by preoccupied legislators and bureacrats, was an early exchange, cited by Lois Roth under the tart heading, "The Debate Dozes Off."[14] A well-informed top official of the General Accounting Office (GAO) raised the key question of propaganda versus culture, but his chief Elmer Staats, comptroller general and head of the GAO—who in 1958 had killed Douglas Dillon's Undersecretaries' proposal, stimulated by Morrill and Thayer, to return both functions to State—cut him short. "USIA has been carrying on cultural programs ever since it was set up," Staats said, "and no one has found anything incompatible with the carrying-on of those activities." No one? Anything? The veteran administrator had not read the several reports of his own staff. His proclamation of ignorance was warmly welcomed by Fascell, whose comment should shine forever among the ironies of US cultural diplomatic history: "It would be useful if we just dropped from our lexicon the word 'propaganda' and I don't know that you need persuasion. Is pure news propaganda? Is pure news persuasion? . . . I don't make an independent investigation, so I don't know that we should get hung up on the semantics of what the thing is. I think we need to say what we need to do and just do it." In these words, Fascell and Staats swept away forty years of patient elucidation, explanation, study, and advocacy by hundreds of concerned and informed Americans.

After 1977 the debate went silent, doubtless in disgust. In the newly merged USIA-CU, we were instructed to "give the new arrangement a chance." The committed cultural toilers however knew the world they had tried to build was coming to an end.

White House Plan number two, the USIA-CU reorganization, was announced and released in October 1977. Inspired by Carter's pledge to save money and eliminate waste, it did neither—the planners themselves admitted reorganization would save no money; and in fact, it opened doors to new kinds of waste, especially for Carter's successors; above all it accelerated the decline of traditional cultural diplomacy.

The task force knew their decisions were toying with sacred fire. Carter's executive covering letter aimed at reassuring the academic-intellectual world and proclaiming a golden era for an entirely new agency; his drafters knew who would be unhappy and why. From a president who had promised Americans that he would never lie, the letter was as overwhelming in its sincerity as Richardson's speeches, rolling out apologies and assurances to the world about maintaining the "integrity" of educational and cultural programs. It was not a lie, only wishful thinking.

The letter, doubtless drafted in Reinhardt's office, said ideas matter; it proclaimed good faith; and it appealed to men of good will.[15] "Public Diplomacy" was not mentioned, and the word "information" appeared only three times, while "culture" and "cultural" appear nine times. The word "propaganda" "is eschewed as bluntly as it can be, with the new agency enjoined from undertaking any activities which are 'covert, manipulative or propagandistic,'" noted Roth.

Carter's convictions regarding preaching versus listening pervaded his executive letter. He emphasized listening and, by implication, two-way learning—an issue neither CU nor USIA wanted center stage. The idea of USIA's responsibility for American learning about other nations, soon to be known—by attackers—as USIA's Second Mandate, reflected Carter's personal conviction that US foreign policy was deaf; it also counterbalanced the agency's long-standing motto: "telling America's story." Under other circumstances, a focus on listening might have laid the groundwork for a different agency, but in the climate of the late 1970s, it provoked derision from die-hard insiders, unidirectionalists, and hard-line storytellers in USIA. It would evoke worse scorn from Carter's successors.

The task force, reporting on 11 October, called a special White House press conference to announce its three conclusions.[16] First, the new name, Agency for International Communication (AIC)—specifically *not* USAIC—was intended to underline a clear break with the past, an entirely new agency, not a mix of two old ones. Second, presenters James McIntyre and Peter Szanton elaborated the nature of the new agency in response to sharp questioning. Said McIntyre, "the emphasis of the new agency will be upon mutuality, . . . bridges of understanding between the people of our Nation and the peoples of other nations." In short, "we have departed from the 'we-talk-you-listen' approach." Admitting the merger would save no money, he stressed US learning: "As the President said, the agency is going to be independent, its programs will be controled by . . . professionals, and it will be non-political." Szanton made the same point with more historic depth, still yielding to the exuberance of the moment: "If this were 1953 and the Cold War was continuing unabated or the new entity were to be a hard, Cold War propaganda agency, putting CU together with [USIA] would make no more sense than it did in 1953. We are in a different era. We are in a posture of less direct confrontation with most of the rest of the world." An interesting thought . . . but true? And relevant?

The third point turned out to be a pipe dream, an inexcusable but revealing piece of wishful thinking, quickly withdrawn twenty days later without apology or embarrassment. The two presenters announced that a single advisory commission would replace the two older ones. McIntyre further asserted that since AIC would be "non-political," the advisory commission would be so as well. The proposed seven-person advisory commission[17] would consist of members appointed without regard to party and would elect its own chair—a return to the original design of BFS. USIA's lawyers—decidedly not CU's—immediately took over and the fine intentions promised by the president's men vanished overnight. The lawyers insisted that the commission reflect Smith-Mundt's all-political rather than Fulbright's nonpolitical BFS or Fulbright-Hays's semipolitical commissions. At a follow-up press conference on 4 November, the planners casually reversed themselves, without explanation announcing a fully politicized commission. CU's semipoliticized advisory function had been absorbed into a larger, fully politicized body. No one in the press corps asked about 11 October. No one pointed out the detailed specifications of Fulbright-Hays regarding the caliber and fields of members and the scope of their responsibilities. Anyone betting that half—three or more members—of the new commission would come from the cultural-educational world and half from the informational would have lost the bet.

For USIA, the decisions announced on 11 October and 4 November boiled down to absorbing CU, a long-awaited victory. For a frustrated Fulbright in retirement, it was the long-resisted defeat of much that he held dear, even though Carter's words may have aimed to comfort him. Within USIA, reactions varied. Some like Reinhardt hoped and believed that a stronger cultural dimension might transform and enrich USIA. USIA's informational hard-liners saw problems the minute any scent of soft idealism entered their realist world. Wiser informationists welcomed an apparent injection of substance. The committed cultural officers split. Some found it hard to abandon the dream of a separate cultural function and counted the days until retirement, but others believed that a USIA-CU merger could be made to work over time and set about helping it happen.

One risk was completely overlooked: Carter, like any president, might serve only four years, one of which had already elapsed. But no one let such humdrum facts interfere with celebrating a victory and reorganizing two vital functions of US diplomacy into one agency. The danger of turning over a weakened office in the throes of a radical transition to a Republican successor, of bequeathing to the next team a defenseless bureau in a weakened agency—this seems to have occurred to no one in 1977–78. In the context of the history of the idea of cultural diplomacy, Reorganization Plan Two of October 1977, with jubilation, overlooked forty years of thoughtful discussion and wise judgment. Left to themselves, keeping their distance in State, culture's defenses had stood the test, but pruned, slashed, bruised, and transplanted, CU resistance was lowered. Still, "Why not give it a chance?"

By February 1978 Reinhardt was ready to announce that the new agency would come into being—on April Fool's Day. Like its advisory commission, the "new agency's" name had already flip-flopped. Reinhardt, content with AIC, received a phone call from Carter himself, focusing on nothing more weighty than that AIC spelled CIA backward. Reinhardt edited the name and informed field posts of the new improved version: "the International Communication Agency, United States of America." The brass plaques of USIS around the world came down, but wise veterans stored them for easy retrieval.

The press announcements of 1 April were printed on brand new stationery, not in governmental blue but in a handsome brown ink. International Communication Agency stood in bold fourteen-point type; beneath it United States of America was set in nine-point italics. But change had not ended. The agency's name would soon drift from ICA (USA) to USICA—and in two years, back to USIA. Agency officers griped, joked, and coped. USIS Bangkok slyly noted that the work "ica" in Thai meant brothel. A classically educated Italian staffer in Rome, evoking the princess who sheltered Ulysses, suggested the name NAUSICA. The optimists among cultural veterans, who knew optimism was the only path to survival, overlooked the nominal elasticity. For them, *any* new name meant difference from USIA and proclaimed change; they hoped it would prove to be a covenant as sacred as Noah's rainbow.

On 19 April, the chair of the new advisory commission was announced: Olin Robison, president of Middlebury College. Robison, ex-provost of Bowdoin College, chaired a commission without members, who would not be appointed for a year. He was not an unknown factor. A student of Eastern Europe with direct connections to Robert Kennedy and White House staffer Bill Moyers, he had occupied a gadfly pre-*Ram-*

parts office in State supporting political action by youth leaders around the world, funded in ways that were not always apparent. A youth-action enthusiast and cold warrior, he had been known to express impatience with the pace of traditional cultural diplomacy. As his new commission moved ahead at tortoise speed, he made a startling decision on his own. Staff director Louis Olom remembers long talk sessions in the office during which Robison fretted about the commission's clumsy name—which had to cover information, culture, and education. When Olom mentioned the phrase "Public Diplomacy," Robison leapt and the Advisory Commission on Public Diplomacy was born, on a whim. After a year membership was complete, but the first "annual" report of the commission did not appear until three years later, under another administration.

The naming of the advisory commission was the third significant step for the phrase "Public Diplomacy," on its way to lexicological glory, replacing Creel's time-honored "information" and further dimming the light of culture and education with the bright illusions it fostered. Public Diplomacy had come out in the open as a formal title in 1967, when former ambassador Edmund Gullion, dean of Tufts and erstwhile Stanton commissioner, devised it as a name for his university's new Murrow School. He recalled that he "would have liked to call it 'propaganda' . . . the nearest thing in the pure interpretation of the word to what we were doing." But knowing "propaganda's" pejorative connotation in the U.S., he "hit upon" Public Diplomacy, "to describe the whole range of communications, information and propaganda."[18] That neither "culture" nor "education" appeared in Gullion's formulation underlines the distance the discussion had come since 1938.

"Public Diplomacy," in fact, was a phrase devised to cover the nontraditional diplomacy practiced by USIA. What USIA did was Public Diplomacy and vice versa. As a title for the new commission, it all but excluded the cultural-educational dimension of the agency's work, despite Fulbright-Hays's mandated fields to be represented. And the phrase continues to have the same useful flaw: no one can define it. Worse—or better, depending on the viewpoint—everybody *thought* they could. For USIA's informationists, it meant reaching audiences over the heads of their governments. For diplomats, it was the opposite of *private* diplomacy—the idea Woodrow Wilson, and perhaps Creel, had implied with his "open covenants, openly arrived at." For most Americans, "Public Diplomacy" evoked the diplomatic version of public relations. In the 1980s it was twisted to another use as the name of the office in State that tried through overt and less-overt means to convince Americans that US foreign policy in Central America was justified—i.e., it meant domestic propaganda. Finally, in the 1990s it came to mean, in some thoughtful minds, an effort to deal with the communications revolution and the challenge of "citizen diplomacy," where governments could no longer make decisions without the consent of those they governed—as though they ever had. For John Richardson, testifying before Fascell in 1977, it meant helping the great

US private sector reach out to the world—a version of Welles's 5 percent bargain. In all, "Public Diplomacy" meant what one wanted it to mean, as words had in Alice's Wonderland. Just as Nelson Rockefeller had used "culture" whenever he felt like it, "Public Diplomacy" rapidly filled available semantic space.

In Carter's plan two, both gods and devils lay in the details to be spelled out later. With no follow-up task force assigned, Reinhardt was on his own. Absorbing 270 people into USIA was only a space problem—a big one, be it said—but inventing a new agency was a higher challenge. Soon the hard realities of money and people took up everyone's full attention. Carter's shiny rhetoric drifted up the airshafts of 1776 Pennsylvania Avenue.

Reinhardt had as good a chance as anyone—and a better one than most—of achieving something unique. Given five years, with bold, informed, and supportive leadership in the White House and Congress, he might have built a great new agency. But a year of Carter's administration had already provided other distractions, and his first order of priority was to help ICA survive, while absorbing CU. By the spring of 1978 Carter had nothing but Iran on his mind.

In CU everyone awaited the grim eventualities. They knew the beckoning USIA could threaten the very essence of their work. Duffey had not been entirely inactive during his hundred days in office. Wisely he pulled academic exchanges, i.e. the Fulbright Program, out of CU's geographical offices and into a single office for academic exchanges, headed by the tough-minded former European area director Richard Strauss and his bulldog deputy Jean Lashly. More questionable, as it turned out, was Duffey's decision to centralize CU's grant-making authority, its essential link to the private world. This capacity had always been divided up between individual offices—the Near East office for example helped organizations like Amideast specializing in that region. Centralization of grants seemed a harmless idea, to people of good will. No one could foresee that in 1981 the office would attract appointees with different values who would exult in running the equivalent of a small foundation disbursing $9 million annually. By 1982 a suspicious Congress, jealous of the funds the office distributed, began saddling the private-sector office with cumbersome controls.

In personnel, Duffey had made a thoughtful appointment. He brought into CU the splendid Mildred Marcy, wife of Fulbright's chief of staff and a 1961 Murrow import into USIA, where she had created and headed the agency's Office of Women's Affairs. Less wise was his decision to put the gifted twenty-five-year-old at the head of IV.

Reinhardt took office in February 1977. A full year later Carter appointed Alice Stone Ilchman to head CU in its last month in State. By any standards a superb choice, she was the first woman to head CU and in USIA the first woman to go beyond Barbara White's rank.[19] But she inherited a demoralized bureau with a destiny already spelled out by irreversible decisions. She followed a man who had abandoned the fight nine months earlier; she had no previous experience of CU or USIA or government; she could not stop the relentless reorganizational juggernaut rolling toward CU; she lost Hitchcock, who resigned rather than face the demeaning journey from State to USIA; she had to deal with invisible enemies concealed in various dark corners of USIA; and she faced a Congress which had been induced by Dante Fascell to demote the work of her bureau to that of a tool of Public Diplomacy. In all she held few cards, other than her engaging personality, her matchless optimism and energy, her thoughtul mind, and her abiding commitment to the deep values of education.

Ilchman, dean of Wellesley College, presided over CU's move to USIA and its new incarnation as ICA/E, soon to be known as ECA. Reinhardt had never met her but was impressed by her credentials as an educational economist, a teacher, a South Asianist with two years in Delhi, a daughter of a State Department great, and a university administrator squarely in the tradition of Cherrington, Coombs, and Frankel. On paper, the political process could scarcely have chosen a better qualified person, even if—like all the heroes of CU's past—she had little experience of cultural diplomacy and less of government.

In Ilchman, the White House had a rare find, showing awareness of the dangers its reorganizers had unleashed. But the clock was running fast; more than a year of the Carter administration had elapsed by the time she stepped aboard. Worse, that year had not been constructive but rather consumed months in idle nattering about a new structure and name. She spent the first month amidst State's comforts, before moving to the dingy corridors of USICA; she committed herself to doing her job as though she would live forever, while she was wise enough to remember that political death in Washington could come tomorrow. Major administrative decisions about CU, now called the E Bureau or ECA (for Educational and Cultural Affairs) had already been made; all but five top staff had left in frustration—two of those wandered in limbo and two of the other three would leave in a matter of months. In Mildred Marcy, she found a kindred spirit, whom she designated senior advisor.

Like any appointee, Ilchman had to rely on the permanent staff, but unlike her predecessors, she found fewer people than she needed. CU's corporate memory evaporated with its disappearing Senior Staff, most importantly senior deputy William K. Hitchcock.[20] Virtually without help, she had the job of managing 270 demoralized people, a few hundred distant and estranged field staff struggling to survive within a multi-tasked federal agency with competing mandates, and a host of private-sector organizations that for years had helped CU carry out its mission but recently had felt the chill of neglect. She had to fight for funding against skilled and sharp elbowed colleagues, while trying to build back relations with hundreds of American and foreign universities, NGOs, foundations, and voluntary associations. Meanwhile her weary staff spent its time grinding out ongoing program activities, from which there was no vacation.

Ilchman knew her central priority was field-staff quality. But installing talent abroad had slipped beyond sight, far under the rug. Defining ECA's job, defending its budget, regaining the confidence of American intellect, communicating a new vision to the field—each of these tasks required five years of continuity, high-caliber assistance, and exceptional political backing. She was given none of these.

To take foreign service officer Hitchcock's place as deputy, Reinhardt and Ilchman agreed on one of USIA's finest generalist officers, veteran of the Middle East and Moscow and scholar of Central Asia north and south of the Hindu Kush—the thoughtful and soft-spoken David Nalle. He and Ilchman set off Battle-style in an organic rebuilding, first digging into a group of specific issues like libraries, the while reminding USICA colleagues that "telling America's story" was no longer the only point of the agency's work.

Ilchman tried upgrading staff by special recruitment, but adding a single academic Africanist took more time than she had. For Coombs's coordinative dream, she managed to bring the colorful, gifted, dynamic, center-stage Rose Hayden from ACE. A third fine recruit, Ford's Stanley Nicholson, came at a heavy price, replacing a vital officer she might usefully have kept, Richard Strauss, who with his deputy Jean Lashly headed Duffey's new Office of Academic Programs and moved that office into USICA. The German-born foreign service officer, with deep Old World values, was made of stern material; he was a fierce defender of Fulbright values. He knew the State Department culture from the inside, and veterans considered him indispensable to CU and to the field. He was the first to tackle Congress's idea of a memorial to Hubert Humphrey, which he and Nicholson turned into a Fulbright-style one-year mid-career experience, with supervised work internships, for mid-career officials from developing countries. But USICA saw his stolid defense of CU values as "sour-puss" negativism. Realizing that his new chiefs were uncomfortable with his deeply informed obduracy, he gracefully withdrew. Asked who would succeed him, he gave a famous answer—"a certain M. Déluge."[21]

Succeeding Strauss, Stanley Nicholson, a sunny educational economist with strong Latin American experience from the Ford staff, set about learning the Fulbright ropes. He would have only two years, during which time he could do little more than finalize the Humphrey Program. He left to serve Bates College as vice president for administration and finally retired to his ranch in Montana. Nicholson, like Ilchman, arrived in the new E Bureau after the most important decisions had been made.

The USIA hard-liners dismissed CU fears as crybaby stuff. Even those who should have understood there was trouble ahead had long denied the deep disaffection of the CU staff and of USIA's cultural corps. The committed culturalists in USIA, swallowing skepticism, pumped up their faith on the basis of Carter's pledges and Reinhardt's appointment. But Reinhardt was already drowning in the daily management of USIA's far-flung empire. The CU merger was the least of his problems.

Understandably, he delegated the details of the merger; it was too late for him to master the intricacies of administration, budget, and personnel law. He rehired the best man he knew, recently retired long-time USIA administrative chief Ben Posner. Posner had spent his entire career with USIA and risen to head its management. He had never served in the field, knew nothing about CU, and was untrained in foreign affairs, but he knew every chapter of USIA's history, every penny of its budget, every regulation, every piece of legislation, every personnel policy, and every USIA staffer.[22] He was USIA's administrative memory, and he had friends in Congress.

The potential drawbacks of Posner's assignment were obvious. The White House had proclaimed the idea of a completely *new* agency; a committed CU veteran as co-chair for Posner, to defend CU's interests, would have been easy to find. Instead Reinhardt concentrated the whole job in a man who knew only USIA. Posner could have had no sense of the alternatives suggested by history, no understanding of the CU issues as they had evolved since 1938, no feel for universities and the world of intellect, and no great imaginative ability to see things from CU's viewpoint. His history, like USIA's, reached back only to 1953. And so, while it was not out of malice that he fed the tiny CU to the hungry USIA, that is what happened.

Negotiation between USIA and CU was pro forma and one-sided. Those who were wary had little voice. One young CU administrative officer bravely warned CU leadership that it was "giving away the store" to Posner; unheeded, he left for another office in State. Posner, too skillful for the CU team, went uninterrupted in doing what he honestly thought best. CU was given a new identity, as the E Bureau or ECA, and integrated into USIA as one of five bureaus, including VOA. But CU-E was not quite intact. Its performing arts were combined with visual arts and moved into another bureau; the office took the glamorous name of Arts America.

Inside USIA, an odd counterrevolution was taking shape. The hard-liners alleged that CU coddling by Reinhardt and the idealism of Carter were destroying the five thousand-person USIA. They paid the tiny 270-person implant the ultimate compliment of fear. They complained about the softer mode, about ICA's blurred focus, about the unreliable CAOs, the "foreign" CU-E staff, the State style, the Second Mandate, and E's drain on the USIA budget.

CU, despite USIA mythology, had not been a cripple through its previous decades. It had, in fact, survived serious opposition, through ups and downs, in forty years of existence—fifteen more than USIA. Its strength, rebuilt by Battle and Richardson in the 1960s and 1970s, resided in a six-man management group. Beneath, strong sinews held CU together. An alert executive office handled budget and personnel and prepared the annual budget request. Six well-staffed area offices—including a separate office for Eastern Europe—covered the globe and linked to the powerful geographical bureaus of State. A thoughtful and productive Office of Policy, Planning, and Evaluation permitted self-study, research, and troubleshooting. And healthy offices ran separate functions: academic exchanges, the IV Program, performing arts, private-sector relations, and foreign student affairs. Its top professional staff, admittedly of mixed quality after years of grinding frustration, was dedicated and hardworking; corporate memory extended back to the 1940s. Over these offices presided a dozen experienced and skilled foreign service officers, including at least three fine USIA officers. CU management was easily the equal of USIA's, and its output—close to seven thousand grants per year—was impressive. Properly used, its two advisory bodies had great political utility. And a growing Fulbright alumni body at home and abroad offered a potential constituency.

Almost as if by design, Posner managed to slit every one of CU's sinews.[23] The Assistant Secretary and three deputies were reduced to a single political Associate Director with a foreign service deputy from USIA. The executive office's personnel function and most of its budget functions were absorbed by USIA, so that the E Bureau no longer defended its own budgets or controled domestic personnel assignments. It had less administrative control than before over field staff. Its supervisory body was Robison's memberless advisory commission dedicated to Public Diplomacy; only the weakened BFS remained as a valid countervailing force. The Office of Policy and Plans was cut in half and assigned time-consuming liaison work relating E's functions to ICA's geographic bureaus. CU's geographical offices, instead of joining ICA's area offices, with their director as a second deputy area director, were eliminated—supposedly because Reinhardt believed USIA's area offices were already too strong. Only Yale Richmond, CU director for East Europe and indispensable to the multiagency coordination of Soviet exchanges, was brought into the European area office as a second deputy but soon resigned for more interesting work outside USIA. University exchanges and Fulbright were relatively untouched, with Strauss and Lashly sturdily in charge and the BFS watching.

The structure of the vital and well-run IV office, slightly overextended, went through three revealing organizational phases. First, five geographical teams joined USIA area offices. Next, IV staff were reassigned to an IV office built around USIA's thematic fads—economics, military-security problems, and so forth. Finally IV was rebuilt again, this time around geography, like academic exchanges.

Some CU officers left for the field and others retired; those who remained found no comparable positions in USICA. CU's head of policy, a veteran of the US Office of Management and Budget, floated free in the administrative office until he came to earth as supervisor of the agency's move into a new building. CU's executive officer resigned and was replaced by an outsider from the Small Business Agency. The BFS office, further reduced in staff and budget, was crammed into smaller space. The foreign service officer heading Foreign Student Affairs resigned and his hedgehog CU veteran deputy rose to fill the gap, again with reduced staff. The CU history and archives project, meaningless to USIA, was exiled to a dusty, windowless office across the Potomac with what remained of CU's archives; its two veteran staffers soon joined the retirees and the remains of CU's records were transferred to the University of Arkansas's Fulbright Archives. Without space, other CU files and archives were violently weeded and large amounts of data were irretrievably lost—most tellingly, records of American Fulbright alumni. ECA added libraries, centers, and ELT to its responsibilities. Mysteriously, CU's Office of Performing Arts, merged with USIA's Visual Arts Office, was lodged not in ECA but in the bureau known as P, for Policy and Programs, where USIA's "thematic programming" and visual arts had been housed. Visual and performing arts were together for the first time since 1953, but they were no longer part of cultural affairs. Nor surprisingly, their budgets drifted downward.

In short, Reinhardt's dream of a tranquil new agency ended before it began. In the end Posner pulled off the classic administrative nightmare. The new whole, USIA plus CU, added up to less than the sum of its parts. All this was put in place so quickly that few, including Ilchman, knew what was happening, had time to mull alternatives, or fully understood the consequences. It was the more unpleasant for the CU staff in that their new home in the ancient USIA building was cramped, run-down, roach-infested, with window ledges encrusted with pigeon droppings, looking out on grim airshafts. OWI and USIA had lived there since the 1940s, with two advantages: proximity to the White House and the adman's dream address, 1776 Pennsylvania Avenue. Cracking at its seams, the dreary USIA building was a comedown from the immaculate color-coded corridors of State and the building's attendant human perks: various food facilities, post office, bank, credit union, library, barbershop, dry-cleaning, and the rarest of Washington commodities, subsidized parking.

Still, Reinhardt seemed to be taking charge. Counting more than twenty-five "assistant directors" in USIA, he decided to curb these "barons" by creating "a few earls," in his words. He divided ICA into four divisions: Education and Cultural Affairs (E or ECA), Policy and Programs (P), Management (M), and VOA. Cribbing from the university world, he called the four division chiefs Associate Directors. The six area chiefs, Assistant Directors, sat below these four in theory; even so they continued to wag the agency and soon would acquire a champion in the form of a Counselor, an office added in 1981 to cap the professional service and help guide the inexperienced new director in foreign policy.

Whatever Carter and Reinhardt had preached from October through March was soon forgotten. USIA had swallowed CU in a single gulp, and the familiar agency dominated the enfeebled cultural bureau. In the structure of the ICA country plan design, the closest document USIA produced to a self-definition, cultural elements—including the mighty Fulbright Program—were listed as ICA's "tools" or as its "media."

The vision of the founders in 1938 had finally disappeared. The American effort to distill and refocus the human traditions of cultural diplomacy, as practiced by nation-states throughout recorded history, as improvised informally for 150 years without government help by Americans of all stripes from the Founders to the philanthropists, as put in place in 1938 and purloined by other government agencies from AID to the Peace Corps—all this had ended in a shapeless jumble, without definition or coordination. In the 1940s visionary architects, like Welles, the Duggans, Cherrington, MacLeish, and Fulbright, had designed an honest cultural function for US diplomacy, standing aside from day-to-day politics, aiming at the longer range, resisting the showy temptations of a Rockefeller, eschewing propaganda and the covert, dealing in truth by exchanging people, books, and ideas; channeling the work of dozens of government agencies, and helping them flow together with the private foundations and universities. They left behind an ethos that for four decades kept its self-protective distance from propaganda. But unrelenting erosion and an ill-considered reorganization had sapped the structure beyond the point of return.

By the time Reinhardt took charge of USIA, by the time Ilchman took her CU chair in Feburary 1978, their energies and commitment notwithstanding, neither could afford to admit that it was too late. But it was.

CHAPTER TWENTY-FOUR

Two Decades of Decline

> Exchanges? There is no greater bulwark against the winds of fragility.
>
> —Charles Z. Wick, 1982

> At its best, the Fulbright program does nothing and therefore no harm; at its worst, it damages the national interest.
>
> —Mark Blitz, 1986

IT WAS ARGUABLY THE LAST CHANCE, but in the strange world of US politics there is always one more chance for an idea whose time may yet come. In 1938 the founders opened an independent office to do 5 percent to facilitate the private sector's leadership over US cultural relations with other nations. Their thinking embodied a more than decent respect to the practices of humankind over millennia and an understanding of the ways in which humans have handled the dialogue of ideas. Their thought rested on the conviction that intellectual relations are best carried on by denizens of the world of intellect. State's original Division of Cultural Relations was designed to facilitate and coordinate, not execute. It helped private US activities by lending communications and field staff; its leadership style was quiet advice. Supporting the foundations of foreign relations, cultural affairs stood at arm's length from the tactics of the short run.

Erosion of the cultural vision was relentless. By 1973 in USIA it had become obvious to insiders like Barbara White that USIA had lost its substantive depth. Frank Stanton outlined an ingenious way to incorporate cultural diplomacy into the information agency's mandate, deepening substance and building American values into the core of what might have become the world's finest agency for *both* culture-education and information. Instead, rejecting Stanton's sensible approach, USIA surely hastened its death two decades later.

The betrayal of the Stanton idea by the well-intentioned but inept Carter reorganization vested hope in John Reinhardt and Alice Ilchman, presiding over the shotgun wedding that Carter's team and Ben Posner had arranged. They set to work with the gritty optimism of the convinced.[1]

Inexplicably, Reinhardt decided to order David Nalle, the perfect Ilchman deputy, to New Delhi as PAO. Powerless before the argument that he had been "too long" in Washington, where his wife assisted a prominent senator, he declined the transfer. Reinhardt's commitment to USIA discipline forced him to rule against his friend and Nalle retired.

He was replaced in ECA by master PAO Jay Gildner, returning from Delhi. Gildner, a Minnesotan internationalized by a junior-year summer in Germany, had served his time with the family business then joined USIA as press officer in late-occupation Germany, then went as PAO to Ottawa, and served as White House aide to Pierre Salinger under Kennedy. He then served as PAO Tel Aviv, Tehran, and Delhi, and as European area director. CAOs differed on Gildner. Like all occupation veterans, he wanted big and costly programs; he set special value on vibrant BNCs like the Tehran IAS he had helped Lois Roth build. On the other hand, this devotee of libraries lauded the Tokyo idea of two thousand tightly themed books, to the dismay of wary admirers like Wayne Wilcox.

A one-agency advocate socialized by the rich German program, Gildner had never served in a cultural office, but he knew better than many what CAOs did. CAOs like Lois Roth appreciated his open mind and the leeway he gave the cultural cogs in his intricately designed field operation; others felt like cultural cogs. His policy-advocacy skills were among the best, and like the East Europe hands he knew the value of a cultural-education base under his public affairs program. Still, he wanted control over his post. Close CAO friends notwithstanding, he was surprisingly blind to their disaffection. Nor did he see in 1981 the untended wounded, including some of his best friends, left by the rout of CU.

Ilchman reveled in government work. She teased her once-and-future university colleagues about the joys of having a staff dedicated to helping rather than sabotaging her. Still, she was a novice in government, and she knew she was walking a tightrope stretched over forty years of ill-understood terrain, jostled by skeptical veterans of the old USIA, and observed warily by a historically hostile Congress, budget axe at the ready. She saw the tattered remnants of CU, with the help of the NGOs, running a collection of sophisticated programs, producing more every day than could be expected and perhaps more than they could handle well. She saw outworn CU traditions. She saw too that CU-ECA was trapped in a surrounding ICA culture of thinly veiled impatience tending toward hostility. Gildner was a useful balance; Gildner with blindspots was better than a clearsighted unidirectionalist.

At least E had it all together, or most of it—the loss of performing arts to another bureau was a nagging anomaly. The old USIA "objects"— books, libraries, ELT, and cultural centers—had rejoined CU's "people." Under the new structure, impressive on paper, the realities were sadder. A shopworn domestic and foreign-service staff was stretched thin and the quality of the cultural field specialists was in steady decline. Ilchman today is too elegant-minded to contrast the caliber of her colleagues in the university world with the downtrodden domestic bureaucrats and field officers who managed E's programs. Working with what she had in Washington, she looked to education. She knew people could only grow over time, with guidance and careful education, and then only if they *chose* to learn. As for her field agents, once uniquely university people, they suffered from three decades of neglect. The saplings grown from Keogh's generalist seeds of 1973, all-purpose officers socialized to USIA purposes as defined by USIA's perception of its twenty-five-year history, were beginning to outnumber the specialized CAOs. Some were very good, but not all.

Ilchman pressed for field-staff reeducation in incremental ways. To Fascell, at budget hearings, she noted that overseas CAOs by definition lost touch with American life and suggested regular updating seminars in the field—an idea, had it happened, that would have amounted to the old CAO conferences which terrorized Sorensen. Her proposal was a thin tactical wedge—no educator believed that an inadequate field officer could be made adequate by a single seminar, but a three-day field retreat of CAOs provided a chance for encouragement. She was putting a foot in the door, hoping to commit Congress to upgrade the CAOs over time. Fascell expressed sympathy, but nothing was done.

In August, after six months in the job, she was invited by Fascell to another set of hearings on the subject of international education. Fulbright himself was invited. More bluntly than was his habit, the retired Senator—aware that Fascell had been sniping at him for years—read into the record a trenchant letter from Charles Frankel, analyzing the mistakes of the USIA-CU merger. Ilchman, in her appearance, took a loyalist tack and pleaded for a central ECA role in US education—enhancing sophistication in foreign languages and area studies to help reshape US society and meet global challenges. Without waving USICA's so-called Second Mandate, already a red flag, she noted that one US job in eight depended on exports and talked searchingly about political and economic interdependency, the internationalization of US university curricula, and ECA's unexploited potential to help US growth. Echoing Stephen Duggan on "sharing a common destiny," she called for ECA staff growth through education. Rose Hayden's new coordinative office stood ready to inventory the US government's total educational activities abroad and to share data with twenty or more contributing agencies. Ilchman was reaching for the ICC touchstone in the founders' design.

Fascell fished for complaints but she loyally dodged the invitation. He asked again about the "integrity" of her program, a code for the USIA-CU merger. The loyal Ilchman slipped away: "It's a serious and continuing job." Fascell again invited her to talk freely—"before the academic community does." Loyalty won out that day, and no gloves-off talk with Fascell is on record.

Little energy was flowing from a White House distracted by the Tehran hostages. Ilchman began moving. With IV Program quality weakening, she initiated a task-force study. She made sure UNESCO got a superb ambassador, Wellesley president Barbara Newell. She overturned history since 1967 and shepherded outstanding academic names onto the BFS. With Hayden, she tried to revitalize the ECA coordinating function. She tried but failed to convince USICA's "research" office to go beyond public-opinion surveys, market research, and media analysis. She pressed for greater ECA independence in USICA's country plan process. She looked to the restoration of other tattered elements. But each mini-victory reminded her, and the veterans, of how much had been lost.

Posner had removed CU's geographical base. Rebuilding it was a cautious priority. First, the strong CU area offices were put into USIA's, but—alleged to be clumsy and overstaffed—the CU staffers were then expelled. The IV office mirrored the academic office in a geographic structure, so that ECA had two sets of mini–area offices. The final step would have been to create an overall area structure akin to CU's, but Ilchman's time ran out. Yale Richmond, additional deputy area director for Europe, threw in his towel and retired. She tried to persuade USICA's Policy Office that E's work needed its own plan, but the negotiation got no further than changing the designation of ECA products from "tools" to "programs." Later a separate section for ECA was opened, still couched in USIA terms as "audiences" and "influentials" to be "targetted" or "reached."

From the status quo hard-liners, Reinhardt was fielding mendacious flak about the threat of ECA power, complaints about an alien insurgency, and the trouble-making potential of the irksome cultural province in his middle-size kingdom. One senior officer argued that exchanges should *not* be considered "acts of social science," a mysterious remark which probably targetted social scientist Ilchman. Another senior officer gained immortality by branding the CU-ECA loyalists as "artsy-f—sy."[2] Informationists piously noted that USICA's Second Mandate flaunted Smith-Mundt restrictions on propagandizing US publics, as though learning could be separated from teaching. With her USICA friends, Ilchman needed no enemies.

Recuperation from Posner's surgery was slow, noticeably so in the case of Fulbright. ECA staff and the CAOs in subordinate positions in ICA began to articulate what they had always known: the educational-cultural program, especially Fulbright, was a tool of nothing but rather an end in itself. ECA rhetoric branded the Fulbright Program "a national treasure and a public trust," a battle-cry for the long war ahead. Fulbright exchanges, partially funded by participating nations, touched a broad constituency in the U.S. and abroad. In an interdependent world, academic exchanges fed invisible but vital national needs for fostering internationalist growth, for minimizing cultural clash, and for projecting America's soft power. With Fulbright decisions vested in airtight peer-review structures, the program continued its course. Scholar Ilchman's university-bred values were boldly restated by the reinvigorated BFS.

In Ilchman's eyes, Fulbright was ECA's foundation. Outstanding academic appointees, which the White House had declined to provide since Frankel, joined BFS: MIT Provost, physicist Walter Rosenblith; South

Asianist Suzanne Rudolph, University of Chicago; and world-class NYU mathematician Monroe Donsker. Rosenblith was elected chairman. The universities took note, as did their mediating extensions, IIE, CIES, the overseas commissions, and NAFSA.

In October 1980 Ilchman called a major conference on Fulbright's future, staged in the Smithsonian's turreted red sandstone castle. The meeting was designed to reassure the world—and remind USICA—that Fulbright was alive and well, that ECA retained a measure of independence, and that its relations with the intellectual world were healthy, open, and bidirectional. For the USIA veterans, it was a rare event: few offices in the self-satisfied agency sought outside advice. In the Smithsonian encounter, Ilchman, Nicholson, and Rosenblith radiated optimism, banished doubt, and preached faith in the future. Senator Fulbright's participation lifted spirits. ECA was declaring that it had its own friends and that together they could work modest miracles.

The hamstrung ECA, trapped in an agency in which even the best elements did not fully understand the bureau's values and needs, was slowly healing; but it still walked on crutches. The Fulbright Program ground out five thousand new grants each year; IV handled over two thousand annual international and "voluntary" visitors—those traveling on their own funds and helped by the IV network; libraries persisted around the world; a great deal of English was being taught under USICA auspices; fine and performing arts were exported, albeit at a modest level still driven by Eastern Europe; BNCs and cultural centers endured and some flourished; and translations of US books appeared regularly. In the field, USIS posts still provided attractive open sites where thoughtful foreigners could ponder the meaning of America and where CAOs willing to overlook Washington contradictions could introduce relevant US visitors. Energetic, committed, and lucky individuals still performed mini-prodigies in the field.

The superb BFS appointments found a parallel in the appointment of Olin Robison, and John Hope Franklin a year later, to USICA's seven-person advisory commission, converted to Public Diplomacy by Robison's unilateral decision. Three years later, neither Robison nor Franklin would be replaced by an academic of repute, nor would White House appointments by either party respect the fields the Fulbright-Hays legislation mandated for representation, or the scope of the oversight assigned.

Abroad, the Iranian Fulbright Commission and the IAS had been expropriated and the sizable Fulbright bank account confiscated; the hostages were ending the first year of their humiliating captivity, as Walter Cronkite reminded the nation nightly. The week of the Smithsonian conference, Carter debated Reagan. Ilchman had been in office only thirty months. She and Reinhardt had arrived too late to establish ECA's indispensability to USICA, to demonstrate how it could nourish USICA programs and staff, or to demonstrate the advantages to the former USIA of cultural diplomacy's independence, either in planning, interagency coordination, or budgets. She was no less ill-prepared for her moment than the best of her predecessors; yet she was a heroic, gracious, and tireless fighter against USICA's single-interest unidirectional informationists. Today, she confides her sense of exhilaration in a losing cause. Contrasted with the sixteen years she would spend building Sarah Lawrence College and her years with the Rockefeller Foundation board, the time history allotted her in ECA was sadly short.

• • •

In 1981 cultural diplomacy coped with an entirely different kind of erosion. Beginning with the so-called Reagan "revolution," the attacks came from unexpected angles. ECA had needed a longer period of slow recovery from Posner's surgery than Ilchman's two years. Now aprioristic newcomers, even more ignorant than their predecessors about the history of cultural diplomacy, CU, and the E Bureau, invaded the convalescent office, waving their banners. Instead of ministering to ECA's open wounds, the appointees—as it seemed from inside—found proof of the very incapacities and incompetence prophesied by their field manual, the Heritage Foundation's agenda for change. The newcomers had in mind a new role for ECA as the high-ground from which to "fight the Cold War of ideas." ECA veterans, who thought they had been doing just that for forty years, were dismayed by the confrontational language. Cultural diplomacy's quiet victories of the past—the reorientation of Germany and Japan and the seeding of the imminent Soviet implosion—were ignored, as was its role in inspiring and pioneering spin-offs like AID's technical assistance, Education's international programs, the CIA's experiment with intellect and ideas, Smithsonian and Library of Congress outreach, a dozen research centers in the Middle East and South Asia, the Peace Corps, and the international arms of NEH and NEA. While each of these spin-offs diminished CU and weakened its claim to be the natural coordinating center for US overseas educational work, each was a contribution to US dialogue with the world. Meanwhile Fulbright's flagship program, firmly defending its original ideals, trod its familiar paths and continued fulfilling its promise.

Ilchman's successor was a Notre Dame Ph.D. in political philosophy and intellectual history, an adjunct at New Rochelle College, and founder of a "conservative" book club. Richard Bishirjian, after an unusually long clearance process, inherited the demoralized remains of CU, including caretaker Gildner, policy deputy Alan Dodds, and an ECA staff hungry for some kind of leadership. Compared to Richardson's CU, the office was unrecognizable, but its doughty staff was ready to try.

The director-designate, awaiting confirmation, took shelter in an unmarked ECA office, while younger appointees streamed into the bureau.

The newcomers entertained their revolutionary colleagues with sardonic comments about what they found. For example, word quickly spread among E staff that the top appointee, at a cocktail party, had boasted of his "270 incompetents." Such perceptions fed the White House in its attempt to force-feed more appointees into all directorial jobs. When challenged, they pointed to the precedent of Duffey's IV chief. During its first two years, the new administration jammed three times more appointments than Carter had into ECA, or ten times more than Richardson had absorbed. The new team showed no curiosity about the past; some claimed to have read Ninkovich on the 1940s, but their reading seemed selective and sifted through ideological filters.[3] In the two-volume Heritage agenda, few sectors of government were so carefully targeted, and few swallowed a deeper draught of the revolutionary brew than ECA.

The USICA director, chosen over respected newsman David Gergen, was the colorful Charles Z. Wick, who had little idea what was going on in ECA and showed no interest. His approach to USICA overall was clear. For him, the agency was the nation's public relations office. Television and VOA mattered; universities and education did not. Confrontation was the point; there was no time for engagement. From the first day, he pledged a return to the name USIA: "I have yet to meet anyone who likes the name USICA," he would say—in fact, he had met no one at all from ECA, nor anyone in USIA ready to brave his thin-skinned irascibility.

A free-spirited Cleveland-born lawyer, Wick had tried careers in jazz piano, big-band arranging, and performance management—before discovering a way to make money for his friends in venture capital. Neighbors in Pacific Palisades, the Wicks and the Reagans had become inseparable car-poolers and child-minders. Wick was the court jester of the so-called "Kitchen Cabinet"; the wives formed their own club.

Having lived by his not-inconsiderable wits, Wick was impatient with challenges to his centrality. His trademark was the one-liner, and he took pride in entertaining dinner parties with stand-up comedy routines, California-style. In staff meetings humor clouded clarity. With no experience of journalism, foreign affairs, or diplomacy, he practiced what he knew best. His deputy was a New York public relations man, but lone-operator Wick had little use for a deputy, especially one like Abbott Washburn, who might have quietly managed the operation below. To fill the gaping intellectual vacuum in foreign affairs, Wick elevated the multilingual East and West European area director to a newly created position as counselor of USIA. John W. Shirley, aka Jock, advised Wick and chaired a powerful new countervailing committee of five area directors.

Even before the agency formally renamed itself USIA, the old plaques at USIS posts and the one in Washington about "telling America's story" were back in place. Public relations and storytelling were metaphors that busy legislators could grasp, and Wick used them. In State, a new office dedicated to Public Diplomacy—USIA had neglected to patent the phrase—tried to provide the media with canned and sometimes unattributed information justifying US policy in Central America. Wick, like Nelson Rockefeller, found it natural to extend relations with the NSC and CIA.

The long-standing culture-information split in USIA, papered over repeatedly since 1953, had certainly not been healed by the 1977 merger. The issues remained: advocacy versus cultural communication, direct confrontation versus indirect engagement, hard sell versus soft, and propaganda versus cultural-educational relations. Carter and Reinhardt had both tried to shift the mix toward engagement without damaging policy support; now a sharp lurch to aggressively confrontational policy advocacy reopened all the old questions and shook the frail cultural skiff. One principle was etched into Wick's mind: the nationalist mantra since McCarthy of the demonic Soviet Union. Speechwriter Patrick Buchanan had caught the Manichean mood in his phrase "the evil empire."

Looking back, Gifford Malone, a State officer who spent two tours at upper levels of USICA-USIA in the Wick years, put the best face possible on the period. In his thin critical volume, written after a sturdy career in East European affairs, he praised the return of policy advocacy and admired Project Truth, Wick's aggressive attempt to unmask Soviet disinformation as it appeared.[4] Above all, he reported, budgets rose. Like all those who praised Wick for "getting the money," Malone's analysis of how the money was spent was less thorough.

The new funds in fact went into a range of informational activities, skewing priorities even further to activist propaganda and neglecting longer-range elements like Fulbright and libraries. A film done on the cheap, with a suspiciously familiar over-voice, was entitled "Let Poland Be Poland"; it tried to support Lech Walensa's Solidarnosc. Although the ambitious, farseeing, and costly scheme called Worldnet permitted two-way policy discussions between US officials and officials of other nations via satellite, field staff questioned its usefulness.[5] For Cuba, bypassing VOA's existing broadcasting, Wick initiated Radio Martí, later inflated to TV Martí, with unevaluated effect on the hardy perennial Fidel Castro. For VOA and TV, Wick pressed for costly technological modernization.

In ECA new funding became available, in spite of Wick. He arrived in his job to find that David Stockman's Budget Office had mandated a general cut of 8 percent for USICA. With ambitious media plans, Wick proposed to focus the entire cut on ECA—which would have caused a 50 percent cut in exchanges and closed half the world's Fulbright programs. He justified the risk by explaining that his friend the president would reinstate the funding, sooner or later. ECA's Bishirjian, building his launching platform for the war of ideas, told staff of his brave efforts "to save E's ass."

USIA veterans divide on how Wick arrived at this astonishing decision to slash ECA. One school argues he did it on his own, overriding professional advice, and another claims the decision was a maneuver—career advisors allegedly persuaded Wick to target exchanges, knowing that public outcry from USIA's only real constituency would reverse the decision. The culturalists who heard the latter version were pleased to learn that USIA leadership knew about the exchange constituency, but they were appalled by the potential damage; even hardened Machiavellians admitted that a great deal was being taken for granted at high risk.

The decision to slash exchanges alarmed ECA's wearied staff. To reassure them, Wick called a special meeting and rambled on in a conciliatory mode. Exchanges, he preached to the amused faithful, would resist "the winds of fragility." Beneath the flow of velvet words, his iron hand was implicit. He reminded staff that, if they held the expertise, he held the money. In ECA, acting chief Gildner gathered top advisers and ordered them to keep news of the threatened cuts inside the house. More than one saw a wink, or perhaps a nod, or perhaps an ironic tone, and disobeyed. Word spread like brushfire, especially through the Fulbright and IV networks. Congress was deluged with mail, and the cuts were soon rescinded. For the first time since 1948, the exchanges community had stood up massively to be counted. Wick sent out fence-mending feelers to Fulbright, but the Senator's calendar was full.

If ECA staffers were unhappy, so was Congress and its staff. In the Senate, Rhode Island's Claiborne Pell, Fulbright's putative successor in foreign relations, reacted with uncharacteristic strength and persuaded Congress to double funds for "exchanges" over the next four years. Wick, in response, downplayed the opening, asserting his need to "balance" USIA's program, or so ECA staff were told. USIA's budget office, defining "exchanges"—for the first time—as a separate category, minimized the base to be doubled. The not-quite-doubled funding was quickly absorbed by inflationary increases and diverted into "initiatives"—like marginally useful "orientation" sessions for foreign Fulbrighters in the U.S. The number of grants rose very slightly and today remains at more or less the level of 1981.

Wick had awakened a major constituency and turned it against himself. Confidence in the administration's good faith sagged, among intellectuals. In Congress, staffers who knew more about exchanges than Wick were not fooled; they made sure that future exchange funds could not be reallocated to other functions of USIA, by earmarking. Congress imposed a "charter" on ECA, modeled on the VOA Charter of 1958: it ordered USIA to keep its hands off ECA funding and functions. The loose-fitting charter said nothing that had not been said before, but it provided an overdue pat on the back for the culturalists. Earmarking, as a reaction to Wick's cuts, slowed down budgetary zig-zags, but it was the first step in a new game: congressional earmarking soon led to micromanagement of grants, as members of Congress proposed pet ideas and hog-tied USIA into administering them out of existing funds.

Beyond inflationary costs, the new "exchanges" money went into expensive initiatives of questionable priority. "Orientation" sessions, for example, cost close to $1 million each. They held particular interest for the newcomers, for reasons worth exploring. Since 1938 it had been customary for USIS field posts and commissions to brief foreign Fulbrights before they left home; then, on US campuses, foreign-student staff, faculty, and student colleagues took over, with IIE or CIES supervising from a distance. In the new mode, foreign students and senior scholars were asked to convene for a week in Washington. In hindsight, the stress on orientation seems to have been designed to counteract the political bias the newcomers saw in the US universities. Their mantra was "balance." Traditional E programs and the universities that administered them seemed to them to reflect only the "liberal" viewpoint, thus any means to inject "conservative" thought into the Fulbright Program had high value.

Like Fulbright, the IV Program for forty years had in fact boasted of its balance, proud that it never told visitors what to do or see. Now, in the interests of the new semantics, a foreign notable who asked to talk with a specific journalist was induced to meet as well with a journalist of ECA's choosing. "Balance" in the earlier sense meant that visitors, shaping their own programs, were put in touch with balanced people who presented both sides of any issue fairly and fully; only if asked did they declare their own opinions. An ECA staffer defined the new meaning: "For every one of *your* kooks, they must meet one of *ours*." Foreign Fulbrighters and IVs, already far too inclined to suspect political brainwashing, found their fears vindicated; the more sophisticated minds, accustomed to skillful ideological theorizing from right and left, were intrigued and ultimately dismayed by the poverty of US conservative thought and the thin-spun quality of American political theory. Some senior foreign researchers, off the record, admitted to outrage; others resented being treated like children, but most were good-humored and chalked it up to the odd "Americans," while enjoying Washington.[6]

Wick believed the private sector should take over much of ECA's responsibility. He rounded up his friends. A dozen citizen committees, at unrecorded cost, supported his efforts in various fields, for example, trying to move more US films abroad for TV broadcasting or encouraging more sports exports. None of this activity, which was not free, did any visible harm, but only self-fulfilling reports argued for its value.

Wick was especially proud of his youth initiative, a rare venture into his version of "education." He spoke often of "youth," uninformed about the word's history since 1938. In the counterinsurgent 1960s, "youth" programs involved working with youth-wings of political parties; a decade later the same programs sought to reach the Successor Generation. Wick had another idea, springing from his particular definition of "youth" and "students," by which it turned out he meant high-school students. His idea was to import foreign teenagers for a year before their political attitudes hardened.

Private-sector zeal inspired his vision: he asserted this could be done at no cost. For travel, he knew airlines would be delighted to offer free space. For hospitality, he believed that thousands of US families would eagerly open their homes and pocketbooks. For recruiting, he waved aside concerns that a foreign country—or parents—might worry about deculturated youth or brainwashing; and he pooh-poohed foreign reservations about sending children to American high schools of unknown quality, at a vulnerable point in their careers, with no guarantee of readmittance to the tight conveyor belts of their own education systems. For tuition, Wick insisted that high schools would be eager to waive out-of-area fees. He was poorly informed on all counts.

To mobilize the private world for youth exchanges, Wick threw a party in the form of a glittering White House meeting, with a touching ECA-drafted address by the president. Alliances were forged with the Advertising Council and the Business Roundtable, and soon TV commercials, produced at no cost, were airing free of charge. A Williamsburg conference with European leaders solicited foreign cooperation and contributions.

All this produced little. Still, the youth-initiative had two unanticipated silver linings. First, saved from fiasco by dogged ECA professionals, an office emerged and survives today, as a productive center for teenage exchanges. Second, it later became clear that organizations like AFS, after forty years of pioneering, had begun at about that time to see their welcome wearing thin, reflecting national skepticism about overseas outreach and security; host families, volunteers, and cash contributions had begun to fade, and state governments were thinking about raising out-of-state tuition fees. The initiative may have helped counter this trend and gave high-school exchanges a lift at a critical moment. Even so, the stalwart YFU a decade or so later would finally fold, while the great AFS program turned international and moved on to other purposes. About $4 milllion in cash contributions trickled into the youth office in the enthusiasm of the first two years. To raise these funds, the office—headed successively by three senior USIA officers with the full time of half a dozen staffers—cost USIA perhaps $2 million, disregarding opportunity costs. The surviving youth office, under the steadfast Robert Persiko, still keeps attention focused on younger foreign audiences—all of whom have a way of growing older by the year.

Wick's optimism about private-sector capabilities resembled Welles's 95 percent assumption, adjusted for the 1980s and for the California style. The difference: in 1981 there were five times more nations with which to deal, and expectations had been raised around the world by past US programs. Across the Mall from USIA, a presidential committee on the arts and humanities, chaired by Chicago industrialistist Daniel Terra, was preaching private funding for the arts, with the purpose, insiders reported, of providing a private alternative to NEH and NEA once the administration had dismantled them. The theory overlooked the scope of the problem. Privatizing cultural diplomacy, in the expected American style, would have cost the private sector several hundred million dollars every year, forever.

Skepticism about multilateral agencies was another tenet of the 1980s. Previous administrations had looked on international organizations like UNESCO and the International Labor Organization, inspired by neo-Wilsonian Americans like Fulbright and MacLeish, as frustrating but indispensable. They assumed that the multilateral international system needed patient US engagement, over a very long run, if it was to find its way to usefulness. For the Heritage theorists, it was simpler. The UN experiment had failed and the UN system should be put out of its misery.

UNESCO, CU's responsibility until the end of the 1960s, was the element of the UN system most open to attack. US attitudes toward this dream of Fulbright, MacLeish, Milton Eisenhower, Benton, and George Allen, had always been underinformed and skeptical.[7] US staff was underrepresented in UNESCO—when US staff in UNESCO were hounded out of their jobs by McCarthy's team, other countries gladly filled the slots. In the meantime, Soviet obstructionism had flared. By the 1970s both political parties in the U.S. had lost interest, and Washington was paying little attention to the world's capstone multilateral organization for education and intellect. Political appointees had never been able to fill Milton Eisenhower's shoes in managing the clumsy one hundred-member US national advisory commission. UNESCO, lodged in State's Office of International Organizations, got less attention than it had in CU. State never managed to apply the right mix of strong leadership and diplomatic sensitivity to US engagement with UNESCO.

While all in fact was not perfect, UNESCO was vital. When the U.S. was fully engaged in its work, America was a natural leader, both in substance and in its gifts at finding consensus. An example of US leadership was the World Heritage Convention, the child of environmentalist Russell Train, which watched over more than seven hundred monuments around the world. But without vigorous US leadership UNESCO had become a forum for shrill sloganeering and posturing about alleged US global dominance of culture and communications.

Knowing that Margaret Thatcher's government would follow its lead, the U.S. targetted Senegalese Director General Amadou Mahtar M'bow. He had benightedly wandered into the minefield of press freedom under the peculiar banner of a New World Information Order, designed in his mind to restrain the globalization of information and protect the smaller nations. Once the American media went into high gear about this alleged assault on press freedom, US public opinion accepted withdrawal without a murmur. The protests of a dozen or more concerned federal agencies were ignored by an administration that had made up its mind.

UNESCO, with its 180 member-nations (today, 190), was stunned. The abrupt loss of a quarter of its budget brought it close to collapse. In the U.S. private connections with UNESCO, especially in science and engineering, went on with little loss—except for US leadership. Predictably, the US savings of $60 million—half the cost of a fighter plane—were not reallocated to bilateral cultural diplomacy.

In the bustling USIA, the 1981 appointees found much in common with veteran hard-line USIA hawks on the old issues, for example, in deriding the Second Mandate. USIA veterans who had become sufficiently "realist" to welcome more funding for USIA, whatever the purpose, rejoiced that Wick had the president's ear. In ECA the new team defined its agenda; since USIA was a propaganda agency and a key weapon in the cold war, ECA was by definition the means to unite the intellectuals of the world in common struggle against the evil empire—in effect, it was to be a governmental version of the Congress for Cultural Freedom, without the world-class intellectuals. The new revolutionaries sent out feelers for networking with the right side of the foreign political spectrum all over the world; they came uncomfortably close to neo-Fascist elements in Italy and Germany.

For interagency coordination, ECA leadership seemed to believe it was enough to meet privately after work with other revolutionaries, behind locked doors. The natural we-they clash between newcomers and veterans reached a high ebb; transparency was gone. After initial attempts at civility and patient education were rebuffed, staff settled in for a cold winter.

Carter's reassurances about the "integrity" of the exchange programs were brushed aside overnight. He had not anticipated an assault from the right, any more than he anticipated a one-term presidency. Program integrity was redefined—where the universities once anchored the defenses of cultural diplomacy, now they were part of the problem, seedbeds of dangerous liberalism. For forty years, Fulbright's concentric circles of university-based defenses had held firm against propaganda. Now the neopropagandists unapologetically saw culture as "propaganda by other means," as one said. Four decades of thought and experience went into history's dustbins.

An enduring Wick contribution was USIA's move from the shabby building with the memorable address to a mass-produced modern building in the southwestern part of the city. Wick said the move would bring the several buildings of USIA together into one place. After two years, at unreported cost in money and time, USIA occupied one more building than before. The new main building, near VOA, was miles away from everything else—thirty minutes by shuttle bus service from State—and had thin partition walls and bargain-basement wall-to-wall carpeting, soon speckled with snags from passing footwear.

In ECA political appointees, with career professional deputies, led every division. The newcomers came from conservative marshaling centers like Heritage, the Claremont Institute in California, and the Intercollegiate Studies Institute in Bryn Mawr. Wick was no ideologue, only a nationalist businessman friend of the president who agreed with the other appointees on the USSR and the need for a confrontational stance. While various intellectual strands comprised the conservative coalition that backed Reagan, Wick had little to do with them or with the fact that ECA appointments were dominated by so-called movement conservatives and the disciples, sometimes at one remove, of allegedly conservative political philosopher Leo Strauss.

Like secrecy, security was a high value. Wick never went abroad without his comical bulletproof raincoat; the new ECA chief anguished over security, amusing E staffers by changing the locks on his door and bringing in his personal shredder. This flew in the face of the CAO adage adapted from Ben Franklin: if a cultural officer had secrets, he or she was probably doing something wrong.

The career professionals tried to help the new team understand the rules of the game, as they were taught to do, but concluded that the appointees thought they had nothing to learn. Some had a more practical idea, believing simply that liberals had run things for too long, badly and perhaps even treasonously, and that now it was their turn. Both attitudes discouraged continuity, healing, creativity, and sound administration.

The professionals posed the greatest threat to the newcomers. CU-ECA careerists like Yale Richmond, a consummate cultural diplomat who had fought the Soviet empire for three decades, were eased aside; two fine career officers in sequence were moved out of the IV Program; others were shuffled around ECA or sent into internal exile. The CAOs and CU veterans, who had been helping appointees for decades to understand how to do what they wanted and to warn them when it might be difficult, were replaced by yes-men unencumbered by history. Wick's piano teacher was imposed on the bureau, which turned him to relatively—if cost-inefficient—good use. Elsewhere in ECA, veterans struggled to keep moving forward.

Various failed proposals amused the veterans. One was the idea of spending a quarter of a million dollars in shipping a Folger Theatre production of *Romeo and Juliet* to Tel Aviv and Cairo, to remind the Near East of the cost of blood feuds. Another would have added Shakespeare to all USIS library shelves, on the grounds that Shakespeare—and the Bible— were the most common books on the US frontier; advisors quietly noted that USIS library shelves were closed to foreign authors. Such ideas flowed naturally from the exuberant youth and inexperience of this first genuinely radical moment in US cultural diplomatic history. The tone, as Elliott Richardson hinted in 1982 with reference to the entire administration, was "ignorant zeal."

For the committed cultural diplomats, it was not fun. They had always been squared off against the informationists, but now they were caught in a cross fire from an unanticipated direction. Career staff, domestic and foreign, arranged transfers to the safety of the field or took early retirement.

In the field the damage at first was slight; the hard-line rhetoric of confrontation permitted some PAOs to overlook time-honored gentlemen's agreements. In the "Kiddiegate" episode, a handful of unprecedented political field appointments—children of prominent administration figures—went to glamorous cities in Europe. Past erosion continued. The deliberate depletion of dedicated CAO talents, begun a decade earlier, meant that by now "generalists" were assigned as CAOs without earlier cultural experience, even to showcase posts. With thinning professional ranks, the defenseless cultural program was redefined. Libraries, in particular, suffered as generalists like Wick failed to understand how they supported US policy. Some had already closed and more were converting to Information Resource Centers (IRCs), loaded with electronic gear, hidden behind security guards and open to visitors by appointment.

Bishirjian was replaced by a teacher of freshman English from a four-year Midwestern campus which he proudly insisted was eclectic in teaching everything "except John Maynard Keynes." Following him came the gifted Straussian political theorist and Heidegger specialist Mark Blitz, who had studied abroad and taught at the University of Pennsylvania. First, he headed ECA's private-sector programs; then he moved to the Senate Foreign Relations Committee staff; then he went to the Peace Corps; then he returned to head ECA; and finally he left government for the Hudson Institute before taking off to a West Coast university. Supremely intelligent, imposingly learned, and an unchallenged master of Trivial Pursuit, he worked closely with an outstanding former-CAO foreign service deputy. A recognizable figure in the intellectual constituency of ECA, he still pressed steadily for new agendas. Despite his oft-cited opinion that the Fulbright Program could damage US interests, he did little to change it.

Beneath these top-level appointments, a collection of ideological friends and brothers took their places. One, a historian of esoteric thought from a Florida campus, took over academic programs, sized up its defensive advisory bodies, private contract agencies, and academic screening committees, and decided to leave things to his superb CAO deputy, while he became the most-traveled CU-ECA office-director in history. Another newcomer, who had grown up on foreign military bases as an Army son, displaced a fine CAO professional to head the IV Program. Lois Roth was made deputy to a Texan Libertarian fifteen years her junior who had previously held no job outside graduate teaching assistantships; with the versatile Roth, he worked out a modus lavorandi by which she ran three of the office's four divisions—libraries, ELT, and cultural centers—while he managed books with a staff of three. Admitting inexperience, he engagingly reminded colleagues of Lenin's dictum that, in a well-ordered system, "any housewife can govern."

Another appointee, inseparable crony of the first ECA director, took over the private-sector "foundation" created by Duffey in CU. Through the thin walls of his office, staff swore they overheard him telling friends how to win sizable grants from his office with an impressive letterhead. The selective generosity of this enthusiast finally forced Congress to step in.[8] A new grants process was established: advertising in the Federal Register, fielding ungainly formal proposals, running through a time-consuming process of sifting competitive bids, setting up screening committees within the bureau, getting Wick's signature on all grants, and awaiting approval by a Senate committee. The ponderous process, restraining the zealous grantmaker, limited traditional CU flexibility. And questionable grants still slipped through.

A letter dated September 1983 to Wick from Senator Zorinsky (D-Nebraska) of the Foreign Relations Committee shows how the system could be outfoxed. At issue was a proposal to grant $58,883 (just under the $60,000 limit) to an *ad hoc* organization called the International Youth Year Commission (IYYC), to help guide US participation in UNESCO's International Youth Year (the U.S. was months away from withdrawing from UNESCO). Zorinsky saw a disguised pass-through, intended for the National Strategy Information Center (NSIC), which he said had previously channeled funds to the controversial Rockford Institute. NSIC's director was a consultant to ECA, and Zorinsky saw conflict of interest. The activist political purpose of the grant ignored Fulbright-Hays's insistence on nonpolitical activities. IYYC's president had earlier run a program for European journalists that its participants had complained was "disastrous" and "completely unbalanced." In two single-spaced pages, Zorinsky advised Wick to curb such "abuses." The zealous grant maker was slowed but not stopped.

With such distracting "initiatives," few noticed that other ECA responsibilities, sanctified by four decades of CU history, were being neglected. For example, America's dialogue on world education was slowly breaking down, and without UNESCO the damage would worsen. In 1944 Fulbright chaired the Allied Council of Ministers of Education; in the 1970s Stephen Bailey of Syracuse University, working with ACE on CU funding, made sure that US universities were appropriately represented at meetings of the European Council of University Rectors; CU's Richard Strauss, with Sanford Jameson of the College Boards, labored for years on academic equivalencies. The new Europe was coming together in culture and education and new systems for university interchange like ERASMUS were evolving, but the U.S. was paying no attention. A letter from Frankel to Fascell warned that, after the merger, dialogue was breaking down because USIA had no interest in education. In Saudi Arabia, Wahhabi control over education was ending its first decade without reaction from State or USIA; the attitudes of Saudi youth were already changing.[9]

• • •

Reagan passed his torch in 1988 to the senior George Bush, who during his campaign proclaimed himself "the Education President." Succeeding Wick at USIA was Bruce Gelb, one of three brothers who had inherited the Bristol-Meyers empire. In Europe the Soviet empire was rapidly dissolving, and its long-awaited implosion might have raised new questions and challenges for American cultural diplomacy. But a divided Congress was unwilling to augment USIA's budgets, as it had done in a similar moment of opportunity four decades earlier when it helped finance German and Japanese reorientation. No one in USIA urged the Education President to change minds. Gelb, learning his job, was paralyzed by we-they mistrust. He neglected to initiate planning for a new USIA attuned to the post-Soviet era.

Congress seemed to have abandoned the very notion of bipartisanship, let alone nonpartisan interest in cultural diplomacy. USIA's "new" ideas looked all too familiar, and they earned no new funding. Twenty-six new posts opened in the former Soviet Union, as twenty-nine had in postwar Germany. They looked like mini-versions of every USIS post in the world. To expand massively without new money, the agency reordered its priorities. A mistrustful Congress stepped up micromanagement with a string of earmarked programs mandated for financing from existing funds. Some were named for favorite heroes of the past: e.g., the John Marshall Fellowships, helping train lawyers and political administrators, and the Alexander Hamilton Fellowships, assisting young managers, educators, and graduate students. SEED (Support for East European Democracy) promoted exchanges in economics and business, educational reform, social sciences, and journalism, and occasionally attracted funding from AID, less well equipped than USIA to work in the former Newly Independent States (NIS).

Gelb avoided changing things he barely understood. His connection with Bush was distant, he had few contacts in Congress, and he had little background in foreign affairs. While modest about his intellect, he did not see fit to appoint a strong advisor to link USIA with the scholarly world. For ECA, he was given William Glade, a quiet and gentlemanly University of Texas economic historian of Latin America, who managed to stay ahead of E's day-to-day problems but was wise enough to change little. After rainmaker Wick, USIA's budgets were dry. There were signs that Americans were eager to extend a helping hand to Eastern Europe in self-governance, civic responsibility, education, democratization, institutional linkages, and educational development, but neither USIA nor Congress seized the initiative—there was no interagency coordinating memo like MacLeish's 1945–46 plan for Germany. Without coordination or planning, private and public activities sprouted in every corner of the East European landscape. But they were doing less than they might and far less than was needed.

AID moved into the vacuum, drawing large appropriations from Congress for "democracy building." With little experience in that art, AID channeled part of its funds to USIS field offices in Eastern Europe—the best disciplined staff available at the time and the best USIA had to offer, given its long investment in excellence for Eastern Europe. Instead of seeking supplemental funding to support these expenditures, USIA took funds for the AID programs out of its other programs. Instead of actively seeking to coordinate all government and private activities, as Welles and MacLeish had done, USIA became a pass-through and staffing operation.

In ELT, the USIA of ten to fifteen years earlier would have been the obvious choice for central coordinator—as it was all over the world in the late 1960s—but again the agency had lost interest. Redefining its traditional idea of "developing countries" to meet the new challenge, Peace Corps stepped into the NIS. Meanwhile USIA's direct ELT programs, in their untended vineyard, continued to wither.

Gelb was replaced in 1990 by Henry Catto, a man with considerable diplomatic experience, who understood USIA in its time-honored self-definition. With a vision of cultural diplomacy left over from another era, he maintained existing overseas posts and worked closely with Secretary of State Baker to help define USIA's contribution. But he could not convince Congress to fund new cultural centers in the NIS. In the Senate, USIA was paying the price of having passed for three decades as an anti-Soviet weapon and, ignoring Stanton and Barbara White, for neglecting to plan for the new era. Meanwhile a single senator from North Carolina was topping all of John Rooney's records for capricious obstuctionism.

Cultural diplomacy, since 1977 a reluctant full-time guest of its ambivalent USIA host, was caught in the trap; at the precise moment when it should have swung into independent action, it could take no initiative. USIA's advisory commission on Public Diplomacy, still unsure of what its name meant, declared in its first report after the Soviet demise that things had changed—but instead of analyzing that change and suggesting responses, it raved about how well the U.S. was telling its story. Content-analysis of the commission's glossy annual reports from the 1980s shows that by 1990 "exchanges," including Fulbright, were already only one of many tools of Public Diplomacy. From then on, the words "culture" and "education," year by year, appeared less frequently and finally disappeared. It occurred to no commissioner to spend a day at Harvard, where Huntington already suspected the central issues lying ahead would be cultural and where Joseph Nye was exploring the implications of the softer varieties of US power.

• • •

The Clinton campaign in 1992 turned on the US economy and staked out a surprisingly conservative position, reflecting the rightward tug of the powerful Democratic Leadership Council. Once elected, Clinton would focus, laser-style, on balancing the national budget. In USIA, leadership decided that costs outweighed impact. Understanding of the uses of cultural diplomacy in the new Congress was at a new low. CAO Juliet Antunes Sablosky cites an unnamed, uninformed, but honest congressman who said of exchanges, "Wonderful programs; the US government cannot afford them. It will burden my children with national debt." Yet total foreign affairs spending dropped from 4 percent of the national budget in 1964 to 1 percent in 1998—a decline of 75 percent in thirty years. Disappointed by the government's refusal to help, US universities struggled to keep international student flows high. Foreign governments were helping: by 2000 they covered more than 20 percent of total Fulbright costs. No one in political leadership set to work to remind Americans that foreign relations were central to their lives and their welfare, that foreign "assistance" rather than bankrupting the nation was priming the pump for US prosperity.

Clinton, a Rhodes scholar, Yale law graduate, and acolyte of Senator Fulbright, was a cautious FDR liberal who moved to the right to offset the second wave of Nixon's southern strategy. As an early disciple of Fulbright, he was an internationalist, but he was mugged by his own campaign and then tied in knots by a single maverick senator.

In his first quadrennium, foreign affairs took a back seat to the economy. Despite several gestures toward reentering UNESCO, nothing happened. In his second quandrennium, the style persisted. After eight years the U.S. had done nothing about UNESCO, revitalization of the Fulbright Program, preserving fine and performing arts exports, salvaging selected USIS libraries, reopening field posts, restoring cultural staffing, or coordinating government overseas efforts in education so that the U.S. with one voice might speak knowledgeably and act persuasively. "Cultural" diplomacy popped up on his agenda just before his departure, when the White House held a splashy conference on the subject, replete with Hollywood stars, but the focus of the event was arts diplomacy.

It was a time for large-bore thinking. By the 1990s Huntington had put cultural issues on the agenda; "soft power" was a Washington cliché waiting to go operational. Around the globe, the postcolonial drive for self-determination and national identity, freed from the bipolarity of the cold war, brought deep cultural issues to the surface; in counter-tension, the world was moving rapidly toward a globalized economy, more dominated by the U.S. than Americans understood.

For the committed culturalists, the selection as USIA director of the same Joseph Duffey who had briefly stopped by CU in a wintry 1977, seemed to make sense. In the interim he had presided over two major universities, and on paper, he was eminently qualified for innovative strategic thinking. But as USIA director, he soon found himself embroiled in dozens of problems without answers. For example, the decision to make VOA an independent body, responding to the semi-private Board of International Broadcasting, had already been made. He might have delegated the VOA debate to his deputy and the VOA chief.

On appointive staffing, Duffey was swept away by the wave Carter had set in motion and Reagan had exploited. By the time he took office, many key appointments, including his own deputy, had already been made—like Murrow he could have reversed them but instead chose loyalty. His defining appointment was the same woman to whom he had entrusted leadership of the IV Program in 1977. On board long before him, she served as shadow chief of staff, playing a hip-shooting, underinformed, and censorious role. Foreign service officers were convinced she nurtured special animus toward them, alleging earlier persecution at their hands. Wielding iron control over USIA appointments, she poured salt into the we-they wounds. Rumor said she in fact had chosen Duffey.

In total numbers, Clinton's appointments surpassed Reagan's, but they brought a qualitative difference: some brought highly appropriate experience, e.g., a young staffer assigned to congressional relations who had served in USIS Rome and London in the 1970s. However, Clinton's unrestrained political appointments primarily favored women and minorities over experience, as part of "making the administration look like America"— which created a stress on appearance over excellence that did not encourage the professionals. Nothing was done to replenish the depleted ECA staff, except in the academic division, which had persistently brought in area studies scholars since Ilchman began the practice and had built a critical mass.

Duffey's nonconfrontational style was swamped by the energetic White House. His background as a Baptist minister had trained him in consensus building and peacemaking. He prided himself on his ability to spark "conversations," although staff noted that these conversations rarely reached conclusions or produced decisions. His ECA director was a party worker who had served Duffey at several levels down in the NEH in the late 1970s. The deputy imposed on Duffey, as a reward it was said for bringing the "neo-conservatives" to the polls for Clinton, had no experience in managing a large bureaucracy. An experienced take-charge deputy might have made Duffey's philosopher-king style effective; instead he was given a philosopher-prince, with an opposite viewpoint. Six years later the deputy addressed a gathering of PAOs in Mexico City and said of USIA, "I have yet to find out what it does." His example provided a new definition of leadership.

Clinton's vow to balance the budget at all costs plunged a USIA with unfocused leadership into continuous cutting. While savvy Clinton cabinet and sub-cabinet appointees managed to move their agencies forward even as they appeared to tighten belts, Duffey with convincing sincerity took the mandated cuts as an order and complied. Close associates say he regularly confused domestic and foreign affairs priorities. For example, visited by a group of congressional staffers eager to help boost USIA funding, he was impressive until the last minutes, when he concluded the meeting by confessing that he had trouble justifying USIA's budgets when there were people starving in Los Angeles. Not surprisingly, new money never came.

Skirting internal problems and doing a little reinvention here and there, USIA's leadership in the 1990s aggravated the confusion. Two US conferences, in St. Louis and Atlanta, purported to link USIA to expanded trade and commerce in the former USSR, and gave the world another semantic innovation: "multilateral" approaches to foreign policy referred not to UN agencies but to private-public US-foreign bilateralism. As it had in 1938, the private sector was looking for leadership from State and USIA; instead it got undirected cheerleading. There was no MacLeish.

The NIS was a half-missed opportunity; so were Bosnia and other parts of the former Yugoslavia, Somalia, and Africa. And the Middle East, even after the putative pacification of the Gulf War, was rumbling more loudly than usual. No one thought to dispose of surplus war material Fulbright-style, by launching more exchanges with the Arabian peninsula. Late in the Clinton years, an ECA task force took a serious look, for the first time since 1974, at interagency coordination, in a well-staffed but quixotic effort that came decades too late. The agency had grown no new enforcement teeth; even if the White House had ordered compliance, USIA was unequipped to do the weighty job.

Around the world, the number and size of USIS posts continued to shrink, with the greatest losses in the cultural components. By 1998 USIA had lost a third of its 1993 funding and staff, and field officers had declined from twelve hundred (in the 1960s) to less than 750. ECA, already trimmed to the bone, lost less budget than other parts of USIA, but the field team delivering products at the "point of contact" was decimated. By 2003 60 percent of the world's USIS posts were staffed by a single American officer. Arts America closed in 1997. In 1994 the final phase of converting USIS libraries to closed-access electronic IRCs began. Direct ELT in the nineties was a thing of the past. Field staff, resembling Jacob Canter in Nicaragua in 1947, had to do everything, and as flexible generalists, everything was expected of them; if they took their work seriously, they were either exhausted or cynical. The rare committed CAO who remained in service had to practice press and media skills along with his or her educational activities; specializing in cultural work was impossible.

Serious time and energy went into "reinventing government," the Clinton campaign's analog to Carter's reorganization.[10] Vice President Gore had untried ideas about putting the new electronic media to work streamlining government, via the "information highway." This added one more burden to USIA, which had already gone through twelve years of aimless tinkering. Juliet Sablosky, a fine CAO who had served in London under both Winks and Wilcox and served as deputy director of academic programs in ECA, described reinvention with loyalist sympathy: "New technology to connect posts to the Internet to give them immediate access to foreign affairs documents and policy statements, putting library resources on-line to give the public access to information about the U.S. via Websites and through overseas 'information resource centers,' using electronic journals instead of printed magazines and pamphlets, and expanding the use of teleconferences and digital video conferences to extend the reach of its speakers' programs . . . these innovations meant revolutionizing the way in which USIA would be 'telling America's story to the world.'" As good a CAO as USIA ever produced, she was describing the new storytelling and its hi-tech informational tools.

Juggling timeless clichés with signficant silences had a purpose—it tried to attune USIA to the so-called new diplomacy for the post–cold war period. Since diplomacy could no longer be managed by elites talking to elites—as if it ever could—it required broad-scale private participation and modern technologies—as it always had. The new words polished up an old idea: reaching people over the heads, and under the feet, of their governments.

At the end of the cutting, USIA's weakened ECA remained relatively intact. In contrast to ECA, USIA's Information Bureau (I) gave up 30 percent of its staff, earning the I Bureau a Gore "hammer award." But the field posts, where E's programs were administered, had deteriorated. What was achieved by reinvention and electronification, other than cutting costs at the expense of quality, is not clear. Beyond services to a few sophisticated European countries, the idea of relying on electronics was ten years ahead of the semi-industrialized world, twenty years ahead of the developing countries, and eons beyond ordinary people everywhere. What foreigners saw was clear: a declining US presence.

Searching for ideas, the best statement USIA could produce glazed many an eye. The *1996–2002 Strategic Plan* identified USIA's "new" mission: to "promote the national interest and national security of the U.S. through understanding, informing and influencing foreign publics and broadening dialogue between between American citizens and institutions and their counterparts abroad." This was new? All the old words were there, in a different order, with the usual things left unsaid. The plan pledged to increase "*acceptance* of US strategic goals" and promised to broaden "cooperation"—with no means adduced—and to do "research"—defined, as usual, as market studies of "foreign publics and media opinion." In all, the plan rehashed five decades of USIA rhetoric, with the faintest possible nod to CU-ECA. Cultural diplomacy was never mentioned, nor were culture and education.

In fairness, the Clinton administration had to keep one eye on Senator Helms, holding the illustrious chair of foreign relations that Fulbright had graced for two decades. Helms led those who believed USIA was an obsolete weapon of the cold war. In 1919 Creel's operation had been abruptly slashed, but in 1945 the Congress and doughty bureaucrats made sure the reduced Division of Cultural Relations and OWI continued to function. In the aftermath of a third world-scale war, Helms reverted to 1919. Pressing for "consolidation," meaning absorbing USIA into State, he pushed as well for State's absorption of AID and the Arms Control Agency. Clinton opposed all three moves in principle, but in practice his team was no match for Helms's hardball. The senator held hostage important initiatives like the Chemical Weapons Treaty and dozens of ambassadorial appointments. Taking office as Secretary of State at the beginning of Clinton's second administration, Madeleine Albright struck her celebrated bargain with Helms—a closed covenant secretly arrived at. Events soon suggested that it contained a pledge to return USIA to State.

After years of creative foot-dragging by Duffey, a task force met to plan consolidation in 1998. The joint State-USIA team was headed by a fine foreign service administrative officer, who keynoted the team's first meeting by declaring that the discussion was "not about ideas but about people and money." Wise insiders understood then and there that the parceling-out of USIA had begun.

The team agreed that ECA, with its congressional charter, its BFS-supervised Fulbright Program, and its earmarked budget, would move into the State structure relatively intact but remain in place in southwest Washington. VOA would take administrative shelter under the semi-private Board of International Broadcasting. The informationists would be scattered around State's regional bureaus; some moved to the field, a few as ambassadors. USIA's administrative functions would sift into State offices. In State's personnel system, a new "cone" for Public Diplomacy was added to those for political, economic, consular, and administrative affairs. In the rush, USIA's advisory commission was forgotten.

Public Diplomacy would be headed *de jure* by an Undersecretary for Public Diplomacy. But an undersecretary was not, in fact, as in Welles's day, the deputy secretary but rather one of six at the third level down. As their offices had developed over the last thirty years, the undersecretaries commanded no bureaus comparable to those of the assistant secretaries. In the first proposal, three assistant secretaries (for public affairs, overseas information, and educational and cultural affairs) reported to the new undersecretary. Information soon fell away, reporting directly to the undersecretary, because as it was explained, there were not enough assistant secretary slots to go around. But ECA's constituency was quietly pleased that a separate bureau of education and culture, under its own assistant secretary, had survived.

The administration submitted its reorganization plan, and after seven years of delaying tactics and forty-six years of life, USIA came to an end on 1 October 1999. The most optimistic estimates of money saved by the reorganization, beyond the savings already sacrified by the dutiful Duffey, approximated zero. As soon as reorganization was announced, Duffey resigned to become vice president of a private for-profit corporation delivering education to needy sectors of society in the U.S. and abroad.

He had inherited a confused USIA and a demoralized ECA, with a renegade senator nipping at his heels. Facing huge world opportunities, the USIA team could find neither vision nor direction to justify expanding its activities; a sophisticated but resolutely ambivalent leader did not notice that the tools were slipping from his hands. Continuity was interrupted and historical memory was fading. In southwest Washington, the photo display of USIA directors from Creel forward was replaced by CU and ECA directors, including Sumner Welles but omitting Laurence Duggan, Ben Cherrington, and Charles Thomson.

The second Bush in the White House appointed a brilliant advertising executive as Undersecretary for Public Diplomacy, who wasted two years trying to apply US advertising techniques to foreign policy, "brand-naming" the U.S. as her Madison Avenue years had taught her. The failure was particularly painful in the Near East, where mushrooming impatience with the U.S. capped by the mind-numbing events of 11 September 2001 had raised the stakes. It was too late for Madison Avenue slogans.

In ECA an independent-minded assistant secretary, the gifted and tenacious Italian-American public relations professional and party official Patricia Harrison, set about making ECA work. Insiders admired her style, courage, open-mindedness, and energy. When, like George Allen in 1947, she was called upstairs to act in place of the Undersecretary, she left ECA in the hands of a gifted and caring team of career professionals. She kept her eye on E and made no effort to revitalize the Public Diplomats, instead awaiting the return from Morocco and Iraq of old Bush friend Margaret Tutweiler in 2003. In office for less than a year after her return, Tutweiler announced her departure for higher office in New York."

ECA was potentially involved when, in September 2002, the president announced the US return to UNESCO. On 1 October of the following year Mrs. Bush presided over the reentry ceremony in Paris, after which ECA staged an evening of American performances at the Louvre auditorium. But responsibility for UNESCO affairs, abandoned by CU in 1968 and never considered a USIA responsibility, remained with International Organizations.

•   •   •

While progress in cultural diplomacy today is possible, without dramatic action it will be slow and barely discernible. The distance to be covered, as this sixty-five-year survey has shown, is daunting. The future holds only questions. But good questions may produce more than did a past built on unreliable assertions and doubtful certainties.

Sunset or New Dawn?

> Probably nothing separates the West and the Islamic world more than
> cultural misunderstanding. This may not be new, but it can no longer
> be ignored. And it is too much to expect "public diplomacy," today's
> euphemism for cultural propaganda, to provide a quick fix.
>
> —Alan Riding, 1 April 2004

TWO DECADES DISTANT from my mole burrow in government, after ten years
in two fine universities, I see the story of American cultural diplomacy in
the twentieth century with despair and hope. If a cultural critic as sensitive as the *International Herald Tribune*'s Alan Riding can casually equate
"cultural propaganda" with "Public Diplomacy" while recognizing the
profound cultural dilemma of the Near East and the impossibility of
quick fixes, then one may wonder what less astute Americans may hold
in their minds.

The pundits say the world of the 1950s and 1960s has passed, yet in
the context of the enduring values of culture and education such speculation may be overstated. It is argued that the horrifying attack on the Twin
Towers, a convenient milestone and handy mythic turning point, triggered permanent and radical change. While time may temper that judgment, it is today's mantra. Among many reactions, the attack on the
towers set off a frenzied national search for remedies against foreign hatred, swamping the quieter search for deeper causes.

Most of the reactive inquiry has focused on the US image, hence on
Public Diplomacy. By this writing, one can count eighteen surveys and
studies of Public Diplomacy's failures, plus panel discussions without
number. Even stalwart CAO veterans buy into the discussion, ponder the
undefinable Public Diplomacy, and in so doing weaken their claim to
defend the unique quality of the work they did. Cultural diplomacy, as
an independent entity akin to Stanford or Boston's Museum of Fine Arts,
is discussed nowhere; even Nye's most recent statement on soft power
(2004), enumerating a goodly list of cultural issues and programs, calls
for more and better *Public* Diplomacy. More fundamental questions remain unasked. What drained the reservoirs of good will? Why do Americans, having discovered the appalling damage to America's image and,
beneath that thin crust, to US credibility and trust, overlook our rich
history of cultural diplomacy? Why do they turn so instinctively and so

exclusively to public relations, advertising, and propaganda? Does a great corporation blame its public relations or its ad agency for an inferior product?

The most probing of the eighteen reports, chaired by distinguished Middle East diplomat Edward Djerejian, begins in valiant optimism under the culturalist's dream title: *Changing Minds, Winning Peace*. At four different points, the report leads up to, then scurries away from US foreign policy—beyond their mandate, the authors explain. They admit repeatedly that clever spin cannot make a bad policy good and that there are no quick fixes. Since the real point of their inquiry has been placed off-limits, the Djerejian report has to settle for image. Its authors know image decay did not happen overnight, yet they call for an implausible crash assembly-line approach to some very long-range cultural solutions, e.g., creating four hundred Arabic-speakers and a thousand Arabic book translations yearly (Arabic is ranked by the Foreign Service Institute as one of the world's three most difficult languages). With such impractical prescriptions, it seems not yet to have crossed even enlightened American minds that no amount of ingenuity in "getting the story out" can paper over a bad story, or that cultural channels once destroyed cannot be easily rebuilt. All these reports, looking to the panacea of propaganda, forget that image is a surface manifestation of what lies beneath, in this case trust and reliability.

Decently applied over the last six decades, in continuity with the past, and at some reasonable level of quantity, a decent cultural diplomacy might have made a difference, at little cost. It is surely the only element of foreign diplomatic activity which over that time frame might have slowed and perhaps softened the relentless US slide to pariah-dom. It might even have helped bring Israel and the Arabs a step or two closer instead of today's desperate face-to-face confrontation. I have underlined in these pages a few of the quiet cultural miracles of the last century, successor to a century and a half of victories beginning with Franklin in Paris. Such victories might have helped, had they been continued. But they became increasingly difficult after 1953 and even more difficult after the 1978 surrender of CU to USIA's tough mercies. I have left these last decades for younger students and practitioners to explore, but from the outside it seems to me that the decline of trust in the U.S. began its steep decline in that year.

Still, after six decades of gentle erosion and almost thirty of steep decline, cultural diplomacy is a hardy survivor. Its very tenacity proves its worth. One marvels that the Fulbright Program and the IVP have remained as healthy as they have, when all else has declined or disappeared. Nevertheless, the daily news makes it ever clearer that the world today sees little evidence that America cares.

William Carlos Williams wrote:

> It is difficult
> to get the news from poems
> yet men die miserably every day
> for lack
> of what is found there.

In Williams's sense, cultural and educational affairs are the poetry of diplomacy—a serious problem in a country that overlooks poetry. Diplomacy is not different from life: it needs a balance of prose and poetry if it is to be worth living.

In the preceding pages I have been more descriptive than prescriptive; it is time to be more explicit in my conclusions. First, in the form of a functional definition; then, as a few recurrent themes.

• • •

What, in the end, does a cultural diplomat *do*? This innocent yet provocative question finds no ready-made answers in the foregoing pages. Over the years each US cultural officer has done what he or she can, in the time available, using the means afforded, with the people at hand, in the host-country situation of the moment, to project the US national culture and values and to share US intellectual wealth. Yet no CAO experience can speak for all. These pages skim the surface of one man's experience, in his time.

Defining what a CAO does *is* a way of theorizing. But no one, extrapolating theory from actual practice, can improve on Frankel and Coombs, even if their brilliant work has vanished from American memory. We need a paradigm to explain a cultural diplomacy that might fit the new century. I envy the discipline of the social scientists or the historian, who begin their books by confessing the methodological biases underpinning their work. But that is not the humanist's way.

A field theory of cultural diplomacy reaching beyond Frankel has not been tried, partly because of the variety of CAO experiences, partly because of the distortions of working within the context of the USIA culture, partly because of semantic confusion, partly because of CAO burnout and postretirement lethargy, partly because Frankel did the job so well in the first instance. Drawing on the preceding pages however, I believe a *functional* definition may serve to supplement Frankel's. A commonsense reduction of this tangled story-history to its separate kinds of action, on the assumption that deeds matter more than words, boils down to five functions. Any CAO will recognize them, and generalist diplomats will see them as common to all diplomacy.

They are: Representation (showing the flag); Research and Advice (acquiring and applying knowledge); Negotiation and Administration (making it come out right); Networking (bringing friends to bear); and Programming (guiding change). These functions mark all diplomacy. But the cultural officer builds on two major differences. First, CAOs operate in different ways, with different tools, with different audiences, in different time frames, and at a different pace. Second, the CAO's audience is not only different in the quality of its individuals, but relations with individuals in that audience may reach greater depth than is granted to the generalist diplomat.

Obviously all diplomats represent, advise, negotiate, administer, and network; and they even program, for example, every time they give a dinner party. But it is equally obvious that the CAO—seen by most foreigners as politically less constrained by policy and therefore open to alternative kinds of dialogue—will relate to intellectuals, artists, scientists, university and secondary educators, deans and university presidents, students, researchers, ministry officials in education and culture, and specialized educational institutions principally—but not only—in the law, administration and policy sciences, in medicine, engineering, architecture, and agriculture. CAOs deal at greater length and depth with their audiences than can traditional diplomats for the simple reason that this is their job, not a diversion. They can afford more time than most harried embassy officers—good CAOs expect to average as much as half of each day outside their offices.

The nature of their knowledge, in principle, should also be different. If a cultural diplomat is an intellectual, then like all intellectuals he or she will approach knowledge not as fixed facts but as an ever-growing and changing body of uncertain information, unrestricted by real-time demands. Scholar-CAOs like Fairbank, Cuyler Young, Morey, Cleanth Brooks, Winks, and Wilcox already knew a lot about their countries; new learning was stored away neatly in thier orderly minds. But *applying* such knowledge inside an embassy was more difficult. For one thing, the CAOs were obliged to report to the embassies through the PAO, who may or may not have conveyed the message in its full depth to levels above. Individuals like Wilcox who could reach around these protocols were rare.

The best cultural diplomats do what other diplomats do, but they do it in a different style, with a broader range of people, on a more persistent basis, and usually with a deeper historical knowledge base. Their networking is invariably extensive: a CAO carries his or her Rolodex from country to country and draws on a growing list of academic and intellectual friends in the U.S. and around the world. Since reverence for culture is high in most countries, the CAO often has unusual access; "cultural" neutrality and frequent public appearances in turn mean they can be more visible than their ambassadors.

Good ambassadors welcome CAO independence. Arriving in Ceylon–Sri Lanka in 1963, six months after the US Congress forced a suspension of AID programs when Ceylon nationalized the island's rusting gasoline distribution system, a newly arrived CAO was briefed by his ambassador. US-Ceylon relations had been all but destroyed, she said. He was to show his face everywhere, accepting all invitations even if there was nothing to say or if the company was politically objectionable: "At this point, *you* are all we have."

In one specific function, programming, the CAO's role is different to the point of uniqueness. A CAO has a near-exclusive claim on and special tools for fostering and perhaps planning continual growth and change. Embassies observe, report, and react, but forward-looking action to change minds over time is rarely an embassy's main business. Cultural diplomats instead assume that mind-changing action is precisely their job and in the best case their *only* job. They apply the CAO's various exchange tools to guiding their activities toward constructive change in the bilateral relationship over time. The educational activities of an embassy cultural program, properly planned, will stimulate then guide change. AID's similar projective capability is better funded but stringently limited by self-restricting definitions. The unidirectional Peace Corps can also foster change through education and example in the host country. But the two programs rarely work closely together and more rarely look for guidance to the CAO. In short-lived episodes in India and Iran, both AID and the Corps accepted gentle advice from the cultural office, but the moments were finite and rare. In any case, AID and the Corps are not present in every embassy; the CAO is often all embassies have.

Until two decades ago, when there were still US cultural officers in every embassy, the CAO was the only officer designated, budgeted, and staffed to invest in human growth. The CAO's tools were educational but not interventionist—CAOs know that education, in fact, *invariably* intrudes, as it does in American life, but they believe, and foreign audiences accept, that it is helpful intrusion, leaving ample room for choice, in the service of growth; only sloganeers or enemies call it brainwashing. CAOs work with the private US educational world and educators abroad to focus the change that can be fostered by available resources, never losing sight of the broad purposes of US foreign policy over time.

How does a CAO plan such a program? First, by consulting on arrival educators and foreign diplomats who may be plowing the same furrow. Second, he or she looks for situations that are ready to change. Third, seeds are planted and carefully tended. We have seen in these pages that educational work goes beyond schools; overall it is perhaps more telling to say that CAOs are adult educators, reflecting the American conviction that learning must be continuous throughout a lifetime if humans are to keep abreast of rapid change. The CAO as adult educator can also carry public information to great depth—libraries teach more than press releases. In the 1950s and 1960s a CAO with a sound plan, even with limited resources, could with patience transfer knowledge to virtually any individual or group, at any age, in almost any situation. With embassy concurrence, he or she could send almost any category of host-country national to the U.S. and bring remarkable Americans to the field.

Bilateral cultural relations are shaped by context. In rare cases, existing bilateral cultural relations are already flourishing, hence need little more than occasional attention, a touch of maintenance, and ongoing encouragement. But two other cases are more common: either what is going on is less effective than it might be, requiring gentle adjustments here and there; or else important things are not taking place at all or are taking place in negative ways, requiring more radical initiatives. In all three cases, the goal is change, not only of individual minds but ultimately of institutions—e.g., a stronger department in a university or a new university department reflecting technological advances or a computerized cataloging system for the national library or a different approach to a traditional discipline like history. Learning is the primary objective, and learning means growth and change.

The best cultural planning is approximate and flexible—educational outcomes are rarely predictable, and local circumstances and CAO resources never permit doing precisely what one wants at precisely the right time. Goals are never fixed. American universities openly boast of changing their students, but they would never dare predict where change will lead. CAOs similarly have no crystal ball and they learn to promise nothing, even if Congress demands it. Natural discretion, a factor of cultural sensitivity, leads them to see the folly of telling an IV grantee that a precise change of mind is the program's goal, even if the CAO knows it will happen. Grant maker and grantee are aware that some kind of unspecified change of outlook will naturally take place—without this, the grant has been wasted.

In cultural and educational programming, as in education itself, change is unruly. There may be no change at all; sometimes the learning may be selective and may reinforce prejudices; and sometimes the change that takes place is not what was foreseen, either for better (the Serendipity Syndrome) or for worse (the Frankenstein Factor). Gaps between design and results may be wider than expected by shortsighted PAOs, overimaginative ambassadors, State Department inspectors, evaluators, distracted congressmen, walk-in citizen enthusiasts, skeptical journalists, and the GAO. The CAO must keep all these constituents informed and make them understand that more good things than bad will happen.

Inflated expectations, either their own or others', plague CAOs. On the US side, it is foolish to expect that sending Ms. X to visit the U.S. will induce her to vote "our way"—this is "buying" people or "renting" them, a much more expensive game than an IV grant and emphatically not the business of cultural diplomats. Converting no one to specific causes, education most certainly does not make the learners love or even like their sponsors, their teachers, or their institutions. All Senator Fulbright wanted was to raise the level of *understanding*, clearly a lot better—even when inconvenient—than *mis-* or *non-*understanding. At best, education exposes its participants to alternative ways of thinking, to different ways of doing things, to other ways of analyzing situations, and to new visions of the world. It can remind participants that slogans or ideologies always short-change realities, that so-called realities may look different from another viewpoint, and that most realities can and do change. Education, in the cultural diplomat's sense, is neither brainwashing, reeducating, nor reprogramming, but only a means of bringing out the best in people by showing them how to handle alternate truths.

Two examples, again from Sri Lanka. A prominent Trotskyite party leader sadly admitted that a CAO had destroyed his lifetime idol by giving him Herbert Deane's superb book on the political thought of Harold Laski, hero to South Asians of the socialist stripe. For the Trotskyite, Deane's work—suggested to the CAO by Daniel Bell—had permanently tarnished his hero moving him from simplistic hero worship to a sadder level of reality. In the same country a vibrant and talented young marxian labor leader, sent by the Asia Foundation in the mid-1960s to visit Southeast Asia, shifted his priorities drastically. Departing, his principal *casus belli* was the early Vietnam War; but on return Vietnam had slipped to third place on his list, behind hunger, as in Calcutta, and corruption, as in Indonesia and the Philippines.

The more a CAO stays out of the way, the sooner a good grantee will sort out the learning. The key for the CAO, for both students and IV participants, lies in locating bright people unfettered by too many prejudices and equipped with decent English; a good grantee is open-minded, ready and motivated to learn. Some ask if a nation can justify funding for unpredictable goals. Of course it can, just as society justifies funding Cornell, however its graduates behave. The art of cultural diplomacy consists in providing educational experiences that will maximize the chances of bettering the lives of others and the futures of their countries, while minimizing the dangers of making things worse.

Educative programming means more than importing and exporting talented people. It means books and performers and paintings and exhibits and film-videos and English language and exposure to world civilization beyond the US variety. All this takes place thanks to events as trivial as luncheon chit-chat. CAO work may require delicate human services. In 1960s Iran we spent a great deal of energy helping US-trained returnees, some seriously disoriented, to re-insert themselves after years abroad. As returning emigrants streamed back in the late 1960s, the cultural office did discreet job searches when appropriate and sensitive trouble-shooting when a returnee collided with the Old Guard. Such work assumes networks—CAOs play to their networks, as they network with their returned grantees. Networks are the means; people and their growth remain the ends.

In all, cultural diplomacy is the art of getting the right people together at the right time under the right circumstances with the right supporting materials. At their best, CAOs meet people, learn who they are, ascertain their interests, remember them, stay in touch, and, when someone or something comes up—a visitor or a book—make the right connection.

Meanwhile, as Lois Roth reminded us, the best CAOs never cease growing themselves.

• • •

I have tried to clarify the functions of a cultural diplomat, in the hope of helping Americans understand what we have squandered. It may be similarly useful to look at cultural diplomacy not as functions but as themes. In our examination of its early design and its tenacious implementation in the U.S. before 1978, the alert reader will have detected various interlaced themes and lessons, perhaps more than I do myself. Let me list those that I see:

- Cultural and educational diplomacy flows from a historical continuity that the U.S., in its first 150 years, understood and used remarkably well, filling "reservoirs of good will" everywhere. Corollary: reservoirs take decades to fill and minutes to empty but can be replenished.
- Cultural *relations* happen naturally in all bilateral relationships, for better or worse; cultural *diplomacy* takes place when diplomats, i.e., governments, try to shape the flow of cultural relations between two or more countries in the interests of all. Corollary: good diplomats track natural trends in ongoing cultural relations, encourage positive elements, and redirect the rest.
- State's cultural designers in the 1930s recognized that facilitating, enhancing, adjusting, and extending ongoing cultural relations was the objective; formal cultural diplomacy was designed as the enlightened handmaiden of private energies.
- Cultural diplomacy requires cultured agents. The great cultural diplomatic victories of history have been won by individuals, rarely by institutions. In the mosaic of US history, hundreds of *tessera* lie buried in the unreported lives of field veterans, for some of whom the ramshackle USIA-CU structure provided enough freedom for ingenious improvisations.
- The individuals recruited to serve formal cultural diplomacy in 1938–46, and sporadically thereafter, reflected an initial consensus of political leadership, foreign affairs agencies, and American intellect. Their principal qualification, along with the teacher's gift, was deep knowledge and even scholarship about the host country. Corollary: America's formal generalist ambassadors from 1776 on were citizen-diplomats from the tiny American educated class. When cultured professional diplomats began taking over in 1924, political appointees, some superbly qualified, remained and today manage about one-third of US embassies. They too must be the best.
- The new republic's least-government approach long overlooked educational and cultural policy, at home and abroad, yet persistently

allowed private efforts to flourish and discreetly helped when appropriate.

- The rise of US world leadership created an unprecedented US economic and cultural hegemony, unanticipated by the citizenry; an unsuspecting nation was dragged out of its false dream of isolationist minimalism, for better or worse. Today, the U.S. has become, without willing it, without understanding its costs or its responsibilities, the world's hegemon.
- Before 1945, few imagined that government could ever be more than a benign helpmate to the private world. Since then, the key to US success has been public-private cooperation. Public-private conflict as in the post-Vietnam era has brought problems.
- Wartime needs distort cultural diplomacy. In 1917, in 1942, in the forty-year struggle with the USSR, in Korea, in Vietnam, and twice in the Gulf, America's declared and undeclared wars have blurred the first purpose of cultural diplomacy—to build the structures of peace over time, in fair weather and foul. England and France made the same adjustments to wartime adaptations but reverted to traditional values when conflict ended. In the U.S. since 1917, nine decades of cold and hot war have shaped entirely new habits of mind.
- Cultural diplomacy means education; perhaps 90 percent of sound cultural diplomacy as practiced by CAOs abroad was secondary, undergraduate, graduate, and adult education, by any definition.
- Cultural diplomacy is an instrument of engagement, not confrontation.
- The U.S., instead of tailoring field structures to each foreign cultural reality, put in place a rigid worldwide USIS model beginning in 1917. Since cultural diplomacy, by definition, relates to idiosyncratic foreign cultures, the rigid field structure seriously impeded its work.
- The CAO's capacity to educate, thus to foster and guide change over time, permits embassies to reach beyond their traditional roles of negotiation and reporting to provide a "fourth dimension" for diplomacy, in Coombs's phrase. A good cultural office, an activist tool for changing realities, can initiate and shape change in foreign—and American—minds over time.
- From 1908 forward, binationalism was the hallmark of the US approach to cultural diplomacy. Education is done *with* people, not *to* them; decent nations do not impose their cultures on others but work together for common purposes and agreed-upon mutual interests.
- With obvious exceptions, process outweighs product; in McLuhan's terms, the medium often tends to matter at least as much as the message.
- The long-range payoffs of cultural and educational exchange are unpredictable and unmeasurable but inevitable.

- Americans detest propaganda, whatever Public Diplomacy theorists may argue; they irreversibly equate it with lying. But they also live with propaganda's less noxious offspring, advertising, public relations, and spin. Creel's heirs brought to US life an amiable mishmash of public purpose and private goals, intellect and press releases, truths and half-truths, straight talk and spin, education and sales pitches, all staffed by well-meaning Americans. Fighting the Big Lie with truth, few anticipated the permutations the elusive concept of "truth" would open to the gifted spinners of the present era.
- Since 1917 the unrelenting tug-of-war between culture-education and propaganda has been a lamentable mismatch. The management of the late USIA, in the hands of gifted and often well-intentioned PAOs, communicated a propagandistic vision to Congress and enforced propaganda's values on USIA staff. All but the best of USIA's leaders, notably George Allen, considered culture a minor tool; and even the best were unwilling to discuss more independence.

• • •

After theory and themes, we are ready to risk a few tentative prescriptions. Over the years I have found three categories of people who never have to ask what is meant by "cultural diplomacy": historians, anthropologists, and foreigners. For a European, new or old, cultural diplomacy means the deliberate projection of a nation's culture and values, as an undisputed dimension of their foreign affairs.

Reflecting on the permanence of what Americans did suggests what might still be done. From a cultural viewpoint, the world has changed less than the pundits say. It is still torn between two interlocked and conflicting tensions reaching back half a century or more. On the one hand, the breakup of the great colonial empires, the loosening of national authority, the rise of regional and subnational cultural entities, and the loss of mission by the former Great Powers—all this has set off a quest for national identities, invariably taking the form of a deep historical and predictably antiforeign inquiry into factors like culture, language, and religion that shape societal values, goals, and prospects. Tugging in the opposite direction is the homogenizing force of globalization, a convenient foreign slogan for Americanization, offering vast benefits but seeming to threaten these same emergent cultures. The Communications Revolution, now in its third millennium, has steadily bound humankind ever more closely into one gigantic English-speaking and technology-driven cultural unit. But the seekers of identity see ominous flotsam in the wake of its apparent bounty. In the last decades a new noncommunist anti-Americanism has arisen, as the omnipotent US mastermind is seen to exploit globalization for its own purposes.

Faced with such a set of definable cultural tensions abroad, the American political process has thrown up its hands. Obsessed with domestic concerns, paralyzed by political gridlock, and dragged down by know-nothings, US politics has surrendered the high ground long held by the cultural diplomats and discarded America's only tool for dealing affirmatively with such global paradoxes.

After decades of neglect and erosion, the end for formal and focused cultural diplomacy seemed to draw closer by the day. Long-dormant seeds of reform came once again to life in the final gasp of Stanton's Report in 1975, but they were trashed in 1978 by Carter's well-intentioned reorganization, up-ending two decades of heroic efforts to clarify the culture-information muddle. Two years later the naive and zealous nationalist psy-warriors of the Reagan Revolution, admitting few restraints, turned the clock back to Creel. Clinton's budget slashers, obsessed with domestic priorities, counted costs but neglected benefits; they saw no way but surrender to deal with the know-nothing Senator Helms. In 2001 it was the turn of the advertising industry, boasting about turning the U.S. into a brand name and Public Diplomacy into a spin-control operation. The subsidiary cultural affairs budgets, in real dollars, continued to sag; key functions like libraries disappeared. And the best field officers continued to take early retirement. USIA was dismantled in 1999, its parts scattered back into State; the revival of a healthy US cultural component or, more ambitiously, the restoration of a positive US cultural presence in the world, was on hold. Even with high leadership, it will take decades to rebuild. There is still no quick fix.

If it were in fact too late to change all this, the subject would be "academic"—a word hinting at US anti-intellectualism. Cultural diplomacy might be no more than a question for the ironies of thoughtful historians, in which case this volume would hold little interest. But it is not too late. Cultural diplomacy was built quickly in 1938–42, and its structures can be rebuilt, quickly and with more modest funding than it cost in the past. Once in place cultural diplomats can begin the long task of refilling of reservoirs.

One major change will make things easier: where the endless half-century debate on reorganization always focused on structure, now USIA is gone. Structure today is a dependent detail. A decent cultural diplomacy can flourish under State, under the Smithsonian, under the Library of Congress, under a semipublic "foundation," under AID, or in some revived version of USIA—each of these options is possible and plausible. But structure matters less than people. To rebuild cultural diplomacy, the U.S. need only build a corps of authentic cultural diplomats.

True, we would have to recruit such people at competitive salary levels, train them, retrain them periodically, assign and reassign them, reward them, set work priorities in keeping with their status, promote them to ever-higher responsibilities, praise them from time to time, and—most difficult of all—allow them to govern themselves by their own criteria. This would mean a self-directed cultural corps, based on the fact that intellectuals manage intellectuals best and scholars scholars, hence that cultural diplomats are the best managers of cultural diplomats. In a decade or less the U.S. could build a body of perhaps two hundred people of excellence, drawn largely from the universities and the most appropriate officers already in State. It would be like building a small university. The corps would by definition be insulated from the demands of propaganda and short-term foreign policy. And it would scrupulously and systematically maintain deep contact with the private educational and cultural world, making it clear to the US and foreign academic and intellectual worlds that the CAOs were its special envoys, its extension agents, and its overseas interlocutors.

Ellis Briggs in the 1930s scoffed at the idea that self-respecting intellectuals might accept the discipline of diplomacy, but he was wrong. Over forty years I have worked alongside intellectuals in government, and I have talked with hundreds of university people about service as a CAO. Their answer is always the same: "Where do I sign up?" Recruitment is not the problem. What matters more is the absolute need to establish, to be *seen* to have established, and to maintain over time the appropriate working and governance conditions for a Corps of this kind, while giving the CAOs the resources they need to do their job.

It requires nothing more than resolution and heart. George Kennan in 1993 noted that vision, if humans cared to cultivate it, could alleviate any world dilemma; the challenge was "to see what could be done, and then to have the heart and the resolution to attempt it." Heart and resolution are matters for US political process. Without a renewed and lasting commitment from an understanding Congress, from both political parties, from the universities, and from a broad spectrum of American citizens, the idea of a decent US cultural diplomacy might better be put to sleep, to await the kiss of some Prince Charming in decades to come. Alternately, Americans might resolve now to put together a strong bipartisan—or nonpartisan—agreement of principle, designed to resist pressures over time, override electoral zig-zags, and survive through changes of administrations.

The idea could not be made simpler. First, recognize the importance of cultural diplomacy, its exceptional nature and its indispensability to present and future US relations with the world, and agree that the dialogue of American culture and education with the rest of the world is neither frill nor domestic political football but rather the deepest element of a positive, forward-looking US role in the world of tomorrow. Second, admit that cultural diplomacy is too important to leave to the vagaries of contemporary US political process or to ordinary bureaucracy, just as we would not expect Congress to interfere in the selection of a university department chair, the commander of an aircraft carrier, or a heart surgeon. Americans need only resolve to make US cultural diplomacy flow from American culture.

Americans, pondering the nature of the reluctant US hegemony into which they have strayed without national discussion or referendum, are ready for such a commitment. They know that education costs less than policing the world; they know that educational diplomacy nurtures US growth and strength. They know that cultural diplomacy, more than a means of building the US image abroad, builds trust and confidence in the U.S. as a respectful partner. Rebuilding cultural diplomacy is not an impossible dream, only a long task requiring steady hands and an unusual kind of total US national commitment, inspired by the kind of bipartisan friendship which Fulbright and Taft forged in 1945. No diplomatic tool is more vital, be it to head off the clash of cultures or as the obvious banner under which to deploy America's soft power.

Our nation needs help to cope with today's extraordinary challenges and opportunities, help of a new kind and quality. If, in the history that will be written fifty years from now, the new American "hegemony" is remembered as an empire of education and sharing, of mutual respect and trust, of service to humankind and the survival of our planet, then our grandchildren may be proud of what we did.

NOTES

INTRODUCTION

1. Personal letter to author, 1980. Kennan is among the most cultured of diplomatic thinkers.

2. Marcel Mauss in *The Gift: Forms and Functions of Exchange in Archaic Studies* explored the metaphor of gift exchange as early as 1925. The Smithsonian's Wilton Dillon helped me link this idea to cultural diplomacy (see his *Gifts and Nations: The Obligation to Give, Receive and Repay*, 1968). Natalie Zemon Davis developed the idea in *The Gift in Seventeenth-Century France* (2000). For details on French cannonry I am indebted to Mme Sylvie Leluc of Musée de l'Armée in Paris.

3. Three kinds of writers have dealt with cultural diplomacy: culture-dedicated State Department veterans, USIA loyalists, and a few scholars who may have labored in the vineyards. (A fourth group, focusing on the CIA's cultural work and the Congress for Cultural Freedom, is noted in Chapter 10.) The first group began with the pioneering MacLeish-inspired volume by Ruth McMurry and Muna Lee, *The Cultural Approach: Another Way in International Relations* (1947). Three volumes were produced by the defunct history series launched in 1972 by the State Department, dropped by USIA in 1978: Wilma Fairbank, *America's Cultural Experiment in China 1942–49* (1976); J. M. Espinosa, *Inter-American Beginnings of US Cultural Diplomacy 1936–48* (1976); and Henry J. Kellermann, *Cultural Relations as an Instrument of US Foreign Policy: The Educational Exchange Program between the U.S. and Germany 1945–54* (1978). Yale Richmond, another cultural practitioner, has written about his experience of cultural diplomacy in the USSR in *Cultural Exchanges and the Cold War: Raising the Iron Curtain* (2003). H. B. Ryan did a simple but complete statement of function in the *Newsletter* of the Society for Historians of American Foreign Relations in his article "What does a Cultural Attaché Really Do?"

Loyalist servants of USIA have produced a small library of books, of which the most readable is Thomas C. Sorensen's *The Word War* (1968). Hans J. Tuch's *Communicating with the World: US Public Diplomacy Overseas* (1990) is less amusing but cuts a truer line in describing "propaganda" or "Public Diplomacy" in a whitewashed American style. The loyalists tend to laud an agency under attack and after 1999 plead more or less openly for the revival of USIA. These writers treat cultural relations unapologetically as a tool of propaganda or as one of USIA's "media," downplaying the distinctive nature of cultural affairs and melding it into USIA's unilateralist mission of "telling America's story to the world."

Outside the small world of practitioners, one finds two kinds of study. On the one hand, the historical mainstream has paid little attention to cultural diplomacy. Biographers of key players like Sumner Welles, Nelson Rockefeller, William Benton, Archibald MacLeish, Dean Acheson, and even Fulbright rarely mention the subject. Three biographies of Edward R. Murrow already in existence (Sperber, Kendrick, Persico) are rich in implications but oriented to USIA. Except for insider historians like Walter Johnson with Francis Colligan (*The Fulbright Program:*

A History, 1965) and Walter Laves with Charles Thomson (*Cultural Relations and US Foreign Policy*, 1963), few historians have turned their attention to US cultural diplomacy. For this reason Frank Ninkovich's ground-breaking critical history stands all the taller: *The Diplomacy of Ideas: US Foreign Policy and Cultural Relations 1938–50* (1981) is the point from which all must begin. His teacher Akira Iriye has written extensively on US Far East policy, with deep sensitivity to its cultural aspects; his slim and thoughtful volume on Cultural Internationalism lays the best cultural-historical framework for the US approach (*Cultural Internationalism and World Order*, 1997). Historians, like John Dower in *War without Mercy* (1986), have begun exploring the cultural dimension of foreign interactions. Richard Pells spent a year with USIA as a resident intellectual, and more than one Fulbright year teaching American studies abroad; his wide-ranging but Eurocentric reflections and insights were published in 1997 under a misleading title (*Not Like Us: How Europeans Have Loved, Hated, and Transformed American Culture since World War II*). Burgeoning studies by the next generation of historians seem to be looking more carefully at the American cultural presence abroad, moving from diplomatic history to cultural history (see the recent work of historians like Emily Rosenberg, or Gilbert Joseph and his Latin Americanist colleagues).

The second group of of scholarly writers consists of those who participated briefly but deeply in cultural affairs: Ben Cherrington, Charles Thomson, Howard Lee Nostrand, Walter Laves, Philip Coombs, and Charles Frankel. A range of academic CAOs or observers—like Carl Bode, Cleanth Brooks, John Hope Franklin, Stanley Katz, Laurence Wylie, Wayne Wilcox, Gordon Wright, Roger Masters, and Robin Winks—have so far published little beyond notes. The university-based in-and-outers, especially Frankel, deal in depth with cultural diplomacy as a discipline commanded by an ethos of its own. Two volumes by Fulbright alumni writing about their experience—Arthur Dudden and Russell Dynes, *The Fulbright Experience* (1987) and Richard Arndt and David Rubin, *The Fulbright Difference* (1993)—fall into this category, although, or perhaps because, few Fulbright alumni seem to have been aware of the embassy cultural office during their stay abroad. This useful series was discontinued after 1993. Some of the academics moved easily between universities, foundations, and government. Of these, Coombs and Frankel, with three volumes between them, produced the best collection of thinking about cultural diplomacy ever compiled in any country.

4. Jacques Barzun, *The House of Intellect* (New York: Harper Collins 1959).
5. Louis Menand, *The New Yorker*, 24 March 2003, 80–81.
6. From MacLeish's brief note in *The Nation* (1940) and his introduction to McMurray and Lee, *Cultural Approach*, 3.
7. In Charles Frankel, *The Neglected Aspect of Foreign Affairs: American Educational and Cultural Policy Abroad* (1965).
8. Samuel Huntington, *The Clash of Civilizations and the Remaking of World Order* (1996). Huntington's edited volume, with AID veteran Lawrence Harrison, *Culture Matters: How Values Shape Human Progress* (2000), reveals broader acceptance of culture, but dwells primarily on culture as an impediment to development.
9. In European posts like London, the embassy cultural offices established after World War II divided from the start into Education (the Fulbright Program, other exchanges, American studies, and the library) and Culture—the arts. In State, what began in 1938 as the Division of Cultural Relations soon shifted to Educational and Cultural Affairs and remains so today. Significantly, Education still comes first.
10. The diplomatic culture has changed radically in the last decades. George Kennan caught the ethos which drove his generation, and to a great extent this book, in remarks to the American Foreign Service Association—the diplomats' "union"—in 1961 (reprinted in *Foreign Service Journal*, February 2004, 47–49).

11. Cited in the report of the Smithsonian Conference on "The Future of Fulbright," October 1980.

CHAPTER 1

1. See Mauss, *The Gift*.
2. The vast literature on early human history and prehistory, of which I have read too little, refers only implicitly to cultural diplomacy; but the records might be usefully questioned from this viewpoint. A decade of residence in the Near East and South Asia, other visits since then, and seven years of residence in Rome and Tuscany brought me into contact with historians and archeologists of antiquity, as did friendships with scholars at various institutes and academies in Rome, Paris, New York, and Washington, principally the American Academy in Rome and the Center for Advanced Study in the Visual Arts at the National Gallery in Washington. The written record lacks up-to-date syntheses, suggested world historian William H. McNeill in the *New York Review of Books* (29 June 2000); he thought it time to "patch together," from new-found evidence, a picture of the pre- and proto-history of human civilization, offering his own gloss of 100,000 years in a "short history of humanity." Tel Aviv political scientist Raymond L. Cohen and international associates have analyzed the diplomacy of the Bronze Age Amarna letters and other early sources. Friends and acquaintances like Arthur Upham Pope, Roman Ghirshman, Richard Fry, Theodore A. Wertime, Ezat Negahban, and other historians and archeologists, have enriched my understanding of Persia. For my knowledge of the eastern Mediterranean, I owe much to American, French, and Lebanese scholars encountered in Beirut and to Mahmad Fantar in Tunisia. John Clarke of the University of Texas helped me turn a corner regarding the trade in art objects around the early Mediterranean. Marian Feldman of Berkeley generously shared aspects of her work on luxury gifts in the late Bronze Age. For information about the pre-Roman period, I am indebted to Sybille Haynes for her monumental *Etruscan Civilization, A Cultural History* (2000) and for numerous personal communications, to Erkinger Schwartzenberg for thoughtful contextual suggestions, to Frank E. Brown for two thorough visits to his excavation at Cosa, to Malcolm Bell of the University of Virginia for several extended treatments of Morgantina, to Henry A. Millon of MIT and the National Gallery, and to the late John D'Arms of the University of Michigan and ACLS.
3. Raymond Cohen and Raymond Westbrook, eds., *Amarna Diplomacy* (2000), 22.
4. Cohen and Westbrook, *Amarna Diplomacy*, pp. 5, 7.
5. Richard N. Fry, *The Heritage of Persia* (1963), 111.
6. See Edward Schafer, *The Golden Peaches of Samarkand* (1953); also W. M. Thackston, *A Century of Princes* (1989), and Wilfrid Blunt, *The Golden Road to Samarkand* (1973).
7. Lionel Casson's engaging *Libraries in the Ancient World* (2001) provides unique insights into the export of libraries by nations.
8. My generation owes an unredeemable debt to Werner Jaeger and his translator Gilbert Highet for *Paideia: The Ideals of Greek Culture* (1945).
9. To Malcolm Bell, I owe information about the Greek poets Gorgias (d. c. 380), Pindar (d. 438), and Simonides (d. 468?) among many who took up residence abroad, Pindar and Simonides at the court of Hiero I of Sicily and Gorgias as Sicilian ambassador to Athens. All composed spectacles, on commission, to celebrate political and military events, while playing their diplomatic roles.
10. My thanks to Sybille Haynes for this example.
11. The late John D'Arms shared with me his unpublished insights into the public use of private gardens in Rome.
12. The history of philanthropy is closely linked with cultural policy and diplomacy. See Robert H. Bremner, *Giving: Charity and Philanthropy in History* (1996).

13. On Augustus and the imagery of power, see Paul Zanker, *Augusto e il potere delle imagini* (1989), in particular his last chapter, "La Diffusione del mito imperiale."

14. David Nalle underlined for me the importance and role of Bayt al-Hikmat. See also Casson, *Libraries*.

15. The literature on this fascinating figure is extensive, first of all Ernst Kantorowicz's monumental volumes. My gleanings reflect more generalist sources.

16. Two remarkable books, each in its way, bring Ricci to life. First is the narrative biography by Vincent Cronin, *The Wise Man of the West* (1955); later came the extraordinary scientific and cultural history by Jonathan Spence, *The Memory Palace of Matteo Ricci* (1984).

17. Mary J. Carruthers, *The Book of Memory: A Study of Memory in Medieval Culture* (1990), is an eye-opening insight into the mnemonic techniques and skills of pre-print scholars.

18. Ricci's clock is pictured in Daniel Boorstin's *The Age of Exploration*.

19. Friends at the National Gallery's Center for Advanced Study have enriched this page in French history. Most useful has been director Elizabeth Cropper's fertile *The Diplomacy of Art* (2000), in which Anthony Colantuono's fine essay "The Mute Diplomat" (51–76), an analysis of Holbein's *Ambassadors*, is especially valuable. Both scholars recognize their debt, as do I, to Garrett Mattingly's *Renaissance Diplomacy* (1955).

20. Marc Fumaroli, in a series of lectures in Rome in 1996, illuminated this period for me. The Quai d'Orsay's *Histoires de diplomatie culturelle des origines à 1995* (1995), by François Roche and Bernard Pigniau, is an indispensable survey of French cultural diplomacy since its beginnings; pp. 9–11 skim its history before the Revolution. Significantly, the authors chose the unusual plural *Histoires* for their title, suggesting they share my concern that it is too soon to write "history"; for now, "stories" will have to do.

21. An imaginative evocation of Diderot's life in St. Petersburg and Catherine's relations with Voltaire and other French intellectuals may be found in Malcolm Bradbury's amusing novel *To the Hermitage* (2001).

22. My readings in early US history, all too sporadic and implemental, have leaned to the biographical. Joyce Appleby's *Inheriting the Revolution: The First Generation of Americans* (2000) develops themes central to my question, as does Jill Lepore's search for the origins of American identity, including language as a tool to unite the new nation, in her *A Is for American* (2002). The contribution of particular ethnicities is another part of the picture, for example, Frank Trommler and Elliott Shore, eds., *The German-American Encounter: Conflict and Cooperation Between Two Cultures, 1800–2000* (2001), especially Kathleen N. Conzen, "Phantom Landscapes of Colonization: Germans in the Making of a Pluralist America," 7–21. Michael Kammen's *In the Past Lane: Historical Perspectives on American Culture* (1997) helped me synthesize.

23. The bibliography on Franklin has no end. Most useful was David Schoenbrun's *Triumph in Paris* (1976). David McCullough, in *John Adams* (2001), lets his enthusiasm for Adams diminish Franklin more than needed; and Claude-Anne Lopez, *My Life with Benjamin Franklin* (2000) and *Mon Cher Papa: Franklin and the Ladies of Paris* (1990) lend color. Edmund Morgan's concise meditation on Franklin came too late to be of use, but various of his reviews have nourished my view of Franklin over the years.

24. See Robert Illing's article, "The Envoy and the Cleric," *Foreign Service Journal* (November 1997).

25. Fitzhugh Green, USIA veteran, completely missed this point in his unfortunate *American Propaganda Abroad from Benjamin Franklin to Ronald Reagan* (1988), depicting Franklin and Jefferson as propagandists. Perhaps they had that strategic impact, but tactically they were both culturalists.

26. Preceding citations from Schoenbrun, *Triumph*.

27. I am indebted for this citation to the late Robin Winks, passed on as a hint from Edmund Morgan.

28. Joseph Ellis, *American Sphinx* (1995), 82–84. Ellis pays close attention to cultural factors. My sense of Jefferson has many roots: having spent four years at his university, my sense of the man is a seamless affair, picked up from students, historians like Merrill Peterson, Norman Graebner, and Dumas Malone. I record my basic debt to Saul K. Padover, who began instructing me on Jefferson in Sri Lanka in 1964, and Richard B. Morris, in a dialogue which began in 1970 in Iran and lasted until his death.

29. Malone, *Jefferson and His Time* (1948), 93.

30. In the ample literature on Paine, the indispensable source is David Freeman Hawke, *Paine* (1974), for which I thank my colleague Robert Morgan at Mr. Jefferson's University.

31. Hawke, *Paine*, 401.

32. This anecdote comes from Professor Norman Birnbaum; neither he nor I have found its source.

33. James Field's indispensable book is rich in evidence of cultural and educational interchange: *America and the Mediterranean World, 1776–1882* (1969). Richard B. Parker's *Uncle Sam in Barbary* (2004) explores the culture gap with the Barbary pirates and the role of poet Joel Barlow as envoy.

34. Initially alerted to Giesecke by an article in the *Reader's Digest* in 1947 and then by the tribute paid him by Ellis O. Briggs in *Proud Servant: The Memoirs of a Career Ambassador* (1998), I am indebted to Giesecke's late granddaughter Margareta, who before her death shared material from the family archives in Lima.

35. J. M. Espinosa, *Inter-American, Beginnings*. 8–12.

36. See Emily Rosenberg's chapter on Millspaugh's two missions in *Financial Missionaries to the World* (1999), 183–86 and footnotes.

37. See Philip M. Katz, *From Appomattox to Montmartre: Americans and the Paris Commune* (1998).

39. I am indebted to Professor Raimondo Luraghi of the University of Genoa for this anecdote.

40. Reginald Belknap's delightful but rare book on this episode—*American House-Building in Messina and Reggio* (1910)—can be found in the Library of the US Navy in Washington. Through the kindness of USIA archivist Martin Manning, I was able to read it on an inter-library loan.

41. The literature on the rise of US philanthropy is extensive. It begins with Merle Curti's *American Philanthropy Abroad*, reedited with new material (1988). Of particular interest for the idea of stewardship is Albert Schenkel's book, pointed out by Robin Winks, on John D. Rockefeller Jr.: *The Rich Man and the Kingdom* (1995).

CHAPTER 2

1. Cited by Paul Kramer in "Princeton and the Spanish-American War," *Princeton Alumni Weekly* (10 June 1998), 12.

2. Rosenberg's *Financial Missionaries* is especially rich in its analysis of the intellectual background of "missionaries" like Millspaugh in Persia. See chapter I, "Gold-Standard Visions: International Currency Reforms, 1898–1905."

3. Zimmerman, Warren, *First Great Triumph: How Five Americans Made Their Country a World Power* (2002). Recent historical literature on Wilson suggests a different picture from that which the young Fulbright would have put together at the feet of his Pembroke master Ronald B. McCallum; see for example the review by Ronald Steel of five recent volumes on Wilson in *The New York Review* (20 November 2003), 26–35.

4. See especially the grisly pictures painted by Paul Fussell in *The Great War and Modern Memory* (2000).

5. See Tyler Stovall, *Paris Noir* (1996); the US contribution to France's romance with

jazz and "the black other" is a theme of Brent Berliner's *Ambivalent Desire: The Exotic Black Other in Jazz-Age France* (2002).

6. Roche and Bernard, *Histoires*, 36–39.
7. James Mock and Cedric Larsen, *Words That Won the War: The Story of the Committee on Public Information, 1917–19* (1939). My debt to this dense and farseeing book is obvious.
8. Emily S. Rosenberg, *Spreading the American Dream, 1890–1945* (1982).
9. The indispensable source is Espinosa's *Inter-American Beginnings*.
10. Cited by the scholarly British Council veteran Roderick E. Cavaliero, in "Cultural Diplomacy: The Diplomacy of Influence," in *The Round Table* 298 (1986), 139–44.
11. Larry Tye, *The Father of Spin: Edward L. Bernays and the Birth of Public Relations* (1998).
12. Iriye, *Cultural Internationalism* (1997), 59.
13. Anders Stephanson, *Manifest Destiny* (1996). See also Dower, *War Without Mercy*.
14. Roche and Bernard, *Histoires*.
15. Harvey Levenstein's history of US tourism in France is useful: *Seductive Journey: American Tourists in France from Jefferson to the Jazz Age* (1998).
16. See Henri Peyre's autobiographical remarks in *The Cultural Migration* (1953), 27–81. The volume was edited by pioneer sociologist Rex Crawford of the University of Pennsylvania, a first-generation CAO in Chile and Brazil. Peyre bypasses his relations with the French cultural services in his first US seven-year tour (1925–32).
17. Roche and Bernard, *Histoires*, 40–55.
18. Frances Donaldson, *The British Council: The First Fifty Years* (1984), 11–12.
19. See, among other works by J. M. Lee, "British Cultural Dipomacy and the Cold War: 1946–61," *Diplomacy and Statecraft* 9, no. 1 (1998), 112–34.
20. To Ulrich Littman, for three decades director of the US-German Fulbright Commission, we owe a thorough compendium: *Partners Distant and Close: Notes and Footnotes on Academic Mobility Between Germany and the U.S., 1923–93* (1997). Manuela Aguilar, in *Cultural Diplomacy and Foreign Policy: German-American Relations, 1955–68* (1996) is less focused and will confuse readers because she accepts USIA's definition of cultural diplomacy as a minor tool of Public Diplomacy.
21. Fritz Stern, *Einstein's German World* (1999), 36 and 145.
22. Merle Curti in *American Philanthropy* documents this burst of activity.
23. John King Fairbank, *Chinabound: A Fifty-Year Memoir* (1982), 39.
24. Johnson and Colligan, *Fulbright Program*.
25. Johnson and Colligan, *Fulbright Program*, 14.
26. Of three extant biographies of Murrow, the most interesting is A. M. Sperber's *Murrow: His Life and Times* (1986).
27. Iriye, *Cultural Internationalism*, 111.
28. His late son, Benjamin Welles, captured the prescient element in Welles's thinking in his courageous biography *Sumner Welles: FDR's Global Strategist* (1997).
29. To denote this unique American mix of public and private activity, I shall use the word "corporatism," in the hope of rescuing it from Mussolini's euphemism for Fascism.
30. All examples from Curti, *American Philanthropy*.
31. Curti, *American Philanthropy*, 321.

CHAPTER 3

1. The reference is to Rosenberg's carefully balanced revisionism in *Spreading*. This chapter draws heavily on Ninkovich's *Diplomacy of Ideas*, a ground-breaking critical history of the period 1938–50. Ninkovich's conceptual framework and mine were shaped by Iriye whose views are developed in *Cultural Internationalism*. J. M. Espinosa's *Inter-American Beginnings* nourishes every page of this chapter. Bio-

graphies, including *Sumner Welles* by Benjamin Welles, *Murrow* by A. M. Sperber, *The Life of Nelson A. Rockefeller* (1996) by Cary Reich, *Archibald MacLeish* (1992) by Donaldson and Winnick, and *George Messersmith* by Jesse Stiller, as well as memoirs, including George Kennan's and *Proud Servant* and *Farewell to Foggy Bottom* by Ellis O. Briggs, have provided human background. The Cherrington Archives at the University of Denver were opened to me during a visit some years ago; the archives of the former USIA, skillfully managed and preserved despite insuperable obstacles by Martin Manning, have been indispensable.

2. Welles, *Sumner Welles*, 139–40.
3. Sperber, *Murrow*, 47, and Briggs, *Proud Servant*.
4. Murray Lawson, for a brief moment before his death, served in an unprecedented and unreplaced job as USIA historian; he left notes and uncollated materials in the USIA Archives, where this comment by Welles was found.
5. Cited by Espinosa, *Inter-American*, 68.
6. Lawson, USIA Archives, 10.
7. Cited by Espinosa, *Inter-American*, 71 et seq.
8. Lawson, USIA Archives, 65.
9. Lawson, USIA Archives, 6 and 13.
10. Ninkovich, *Diplomacy of Ideas*, 24.
11. Lawson, USIA Archives, 10.
12. Espinosa, *Inter-American*, 85.
13. Letter from Pattee to Espinosa, *Inter-American*, 92.
14. Lawson, USIA Archives, 28.
15. Personal communication from Giesecke family archives, Lima.
16. Espinosa, *Inter-American*, 96.
17. Cited Espinosa, *Inter-American*, 102.
18. Philip H. Coombs, *The Fourth Dimension of Foreign Policy* (1963), 27.
19. MacLeish's words originally appeared in *The Nation*; I am indebted to the late Anthony Hecht for this prescient article, reprinted in *Archibald MacLeish, A Time to Speak* (1941).
20. As recollected in Ben Cherrington's unpublished memoirs, cited by Espinosa, *Inter-American*, 113.
21. Briggs, *Proud Servant*, 125.
22. Briggs, *Proud Servant*, 130.
23. "Communist Romantics: The Reluctant Laurence Duggan," Weinstein and Vassiliev, *The Haunted Wood: Soviet Espionage in America—the Stalin Era* (1999), 3–21.
24. Weinstein and Vassiliev, *Haunted*, 20.
25. Welles, *Sumner Welles*, 363.
26. Interview with Paul Nitze, June 1999.
27. The author, a Fulbright student in France in 1949, hereby acknowledges his deep personal debt to Duggan and IIE.
28. Lawson, USIA Archives.
29. I am indebted to Dean William C. Olson for his recollections of Cherrington, for whom he was a graduate student, instructor, and assistant in the early postwar years.
30. Cited by Espinosa, *Inter-American*, 113.
31. Espinosa gists the defining Hull letter, *Inter-American*.
32. Cited by Espinosa, *Inter-American*, 114.
33. Cherrington's unpublished memoirs, cited by Espinosa, *Inter-American*, 115.
34. Hull, Welles and Wallace cited by Espinosa, *Inter-American*, 141–42.
35. Ninkovich, *Diplomacy of Ideas*, 35–60.
36. Coombs, *Fourth Dimension*, 28.
37. State Department *Bulletin*, 3 January 1942.

CHAPTER 4

1. For this chapter, the two indispensable works remain Espinosa, *Inter-American Beginnings* and the critical historical perspectives of Ninkovich in *Diplomacy of Ideas*, especially his chapter on "wartime departures from tradition." Ninkovich and Espinosa do not always agree. My experiential viewpoint often gives the nod to Espinosa. The incomplete and uncatalogued papers by USIA historian Murray Lawson in the USIA Archives are revealing; Lawson combined access to materials with the historian's critical stance. In my search to bring life to this story, I have relied on biographies; the most important of these is the late Cary Reich's splendid first volume on Nelson Rockefeller. Townsend Hoopes and David Brinckley, in their biography of Forrestal, shed light on this tortured man. For Fulbright, there are three biographies so far, with Seth Tillman's yet to come; conversations with Tillman, a former special assistant to Fulbright who is now at Georgetown University, have helped put things in perspective. To the previously cited biographies of Murrow, Welles, and MacLeish, I should add James Chace on Acheson, George Baer's edited volume on Loy Henderson, Jesse Stiller's work on George Messersmith, and Arthur Schlesinger's autobiography, *A Life in the Twentieth Century* (2000) as well as Ellis O. Briggs's memorable posthumous *Proud Servant*. As we move closer to our times, I note that in relying and more on personal discussions, participants will be identified only when their contributions pass the level of conversation.
2. My debt to the late Cary Reich will be obvious throughout.
3. Reich, *Rockefeller*, 169.
4. Reich, *Rockefeller*, 178.
5. Reich, *Rockefeller*, 184.
6. Lawson, USIA Archives, 1–4–5.
7. Espinosa, *Inter-American*, 159–60.
8. Briggs, *Proud Servant*, 132–33.
9. Reich, *Rockefeller*, 201.
10. Briggs, *Proud Servant*, 133.
11. See Seth Fein, "Transnationalization and Cultural Collaboration: Mexican Film Propaganda During World War II," *Studies in Latin American Popular Culture* 17 (1998), 105–28.
12. Reich, *Rockefeller*, 220–22.
13. Curious scholars will find extraordinary rewards in the wartime papers of these academic cultural officers, as they turn up in the public domain, if we may judge by Fairbank's *Chinabound*, a key source in every respect. Cuyler Young's papers are in the care of Dr. James Bill of the Reve Center at William & Mary University. Howard Lee Nostrand's pamphlet "The Cultural Attaché" (1947) suggests there may be more material available on his work.
14. See David Reynolds, *Rich Relations* (1995), especially pp. 175–77 and 180–81.
15. Haldore Hanson, *The Cultural Cooperation Program, 1938–44* (1944).
16. Espinosa, *Inter-American*, 319.
17. Ninkovich, *Diplomacy of Ideas*, 37, 41.
18. The Wilder letter is preserved in the USIA archives. In our readings, Ninkovich and I focus on different elements in this unusual document.
19. After the war *Washington Post* journalist Ferdinand Kuhn used this demeaning phrase to denote cultural officers in his highly influential recommendations on the future shape of USIS posts. Kuhn, heading the British affairs section of OWI during the war, enlisted the help of scholars like Margaret Mead, Allan Nevins, and Henry Steele Commager in writing pamphlets and books to explain the U.S. to the British—obviously he knew that intellectuals were more than "contact men," but his report betrays them. See Reynolds, *Rich Relations*, especially his chapter "Hearts and Minds."

20. For the playful side of culture and its projection abroad, see John L. Brown's classic article, "But what do you DO?" *Foreign Service Journal*, vol. 41, no. 6 (1964).
21. Ninkovich, *Diplomacy of Ideas*, 44.
22. Ninkovich, *Diplomacy of Ideas*, 39–40.
23. Lawson, USIA Archives, 1-3-39.
24. Espinosa, *Inter-American*, 196.

CHAPTER 5

1. For the mid-1940s Ninkovich's *Diplomacy of Ideas* remains indispensable, as does Espinosa, *Inter-American Beginnings*. To these must be added two other invaluable studies of early cultural affairs triggered by John Richardson during his eight years with State's cultural relations: Kellermann on Germany, *Cultural Relations* (1978) and Wilma Fairbank, *America's Cultural Experiment in China, 1942–49* (1976). Among biographies and autobiographers of particular interest to this period are Chace's *Acheson*, Schlesinger's *A Life*, Donaldson and Winnick's *MacLeish*, Cary Reich's *Rockefeller*, and Joseph E. Persico's and Sperber's *Murrow*.
2. Espinosa, *Inter-American*, 226.
3. See Donaldson's *Archibald MacLeish*, a rich and literate source.
4. Ninkovich, *Diplomacy of Ideas*, 116.
5. See Persico, *Murrow*, 191–92.
6. See Reich, *Rockefeller*.
7. Schlesinger, *A Life*, 290.
8. Reprinted in MacLeish, *A Time to Speak*, 1941.
9. State-War-Navy Coordinating Committee (SWNCC), Policy Statement 269/5, June 1946, cited by Kellermann, *Cultural Relations*.
10. Kellermann, *Cultural Relations*, 20–21.
11. The "B" in Wells's name, like the "S" in Harry Truman's, was a name, not an abbreviation, and takes no period.
12. See Volker Berghahn, *America and the Intellectual Cold Wars in Europe: Shepard Stone Between Philanthropy, Academy, and Diplomacy* (2001).
13. A copy of state's review was found in USIA Archives, courtesy of Martin Manning.
14. Letter from Chace to author, 15 November 1998.
15. Roche and Bernard, *Histoires* 58–89.
16. Roche and Bernard, *Histoires*, 69.
17. Interview, 1996 (name withheld on request).
18. Curti, *American Philanthropy*.
19. Interviews, over time, with the late John Howard and Margot Betz Howard, former special assistant to Charles Frankel, cultural diplomat, and former Ford staff in Iran, helped me understand ITR.
20. McCaughey, in *International Studies and Academic Enterprise* (1984), critically evaluates the ITR effort, especially in chapter 8, "The Fruits of Philanthropy."

CHAPTER 6

1. It is a sad fact that few cultural diplomats have left memoirs, with the noteworthy exception of the early sections of Fairbank's *Chinabound*. This chapter thus depends upon forty years of conversations, discussions, and correspondance with American and foreign colleagues. In 1988, at the University of Virginia, I began assembling a collection of manuscripts extracted from friends by dint of relentless and doubtless annoying questioning and requestioning. At the same time, I was beginning to collect the essays which make up Arndt and Rubin, *The Fulbright Difference*. Since no one expressed interest in the "CAO book," the matter

dropped. Some of the material in this chapter (Canter and Harkness) and some in later chapters is distilled from that experiment.

2. See Jesse H. Stiller, *George S. Messersmith, Diplomat of Democracy* (1987), a workmanlike and balanced picture of this difficult man.

3. His fatuous remark is cited by both Ninkovich, *Diplomacy of Ideas,* and Espinosa, *Inter-American.*

4. Both Fairbanks touch on the impressive career of Dr. Greene, in *Chinabound* and *Cultural Experiment.*

5. Espinosa, *Inter-American,* 242.

6. See Espinosa's thorough chart listing all the early Latin American cultural officers, *Inter-American,* Appendix II, 334–38.

7. Howard Lee Nostrand's *Cultural Attaché* is less a memoir than a partial attempt to conceptualize the work of the cultural officer. It remains nonetheless a unique document and insight into the mindset of the period. In this relatively abstract treatment, Nostrand does not mention his colleague Albert Giesecke.

8. From Canter's memoir, produced by extended correspondence (1988).

9. Conversation with Brown, 1988.

10. See Frankel's *Neglected Aspect.*

11. Laves and Thomson, *Cultural Relations,* 45.

12. Cited by Espinosa, *Inter-American.*

13. Wilson Dizard, *The Strategy of Truth* (1961), 58.

14. It goes without saying that the following vignettes are highly accidental, reflecting lucky encounters. In 1988 in corresponding with ex-CAOs. I found it surprisingly difficult to break into circles of reticence, augmented by the fading of memory.

15. Canter memoir, 1988.

16. Excerpted from an unpublished memoir worked out with Harkness (1988).

17. The material on Young, whose papers are preserved at the College of William & Mary, comes from conversations with him beginning in 1971 until his death, supported by the graceful memoir of Nesta Ramazani on her Tehran girlhood, *The Rose and the Nightingale* (1999).

18. From several extended conversations with Oram (1998).

19. An insight triggered by Ninkovich, *Diplomacy of Ideas,* 117.

20. A copy of Smith's unpublished thesis is preserved in the USIA archives. Reading Smith's version of events in Stevens's tour in Mexico, I found myself puzzled enough to ask two experienced USIA officers, one a CAO and the other a highly literate IO with special experience in personnel management, to read through Smith's recital. The three of us agreed that it told a special story between its lines; I have tried to suggest that interlinear story.

CHAPTER 7

1. Jane C. Loeffler, *The Architecture of Diplomacy: Building America's Embassies* (1998). Her thorough treatment provides the basis for this section.

2. See Frederic Spotts, *Hitler and the Power of Aesthetics* (2002). Spotts argues that professional artist Hitler's long-range goal was to create, at any cost, a "supreme cultural state."

3. It is useful to remember that in architecture time-lags of years and decades are the norm, so what emerged in 1948 had been long in the planning.

4. Extended conversations with Masey began in 1961. See Conway Lloyd Morgan's article on Masey, "Master Mind," *Grafik* 109 (September 2003, 30–31).

5. Ben Forgey, *Washington Post,* 27 May 2000.

6. Conversation with Professor Emeritus David A. Johnson, University of Tennssee.

7. Thomas Friedman, "Birds Don't Fly There," *New York Times,* 21 December 2003.

8. Casson, *Libraries.* I note that my experience with USIS libraries began in Beirut in 1961 and continues to this day. What follows will reflect forty-odd years of

observation, discussion, and visits to dozens of overseas libraries in various states of glory or decline. There are several partial books on the libraries, like Gary Traske's *Missionaries of the Book: The American Library Profession and the Origins of US Cultural Diplomacy* (1985). Some treat USIS libraries, including Paxton Price's sparse collection of documents, *International Book and Library Activities: The History of a US Foreign Policy* (1982). Numerous internal USIA studies, only some of which are in USIA's archives, have not been made public.

9. In Joyce Appleby, *Inheriting the Revolution: The First Generation of Americans* (2000).
10. Kennan, "International Exchange" (1956).
11. Interview in 2000 with Hans J. Tuch, CAO Frankfurt in 1949.
12. Discussions with the late Mark Lewis took place over the years; two episodic memoirs were provided by him before his death in 2002.

CHAPTER 8

1. This chapter leans on the previously cited works of Espinosa, Ninkovich, and Iriye, as well as on Laves and Thomson's reminiscenses in *Cultural Relations* (1963) and the unfinished work of USIA historian Murray Lawson. For UNESCO Luther H. Evans's rapporteur notes *The U.S. and UNESCO* on the 1945 delegation's meetings are revealing (1971). The chapter draws importantly on a group of biographies, most particularly *Acheson* by Chace, *The Lives of William Benton* (1969) by Sydney Hyman, *Archibald MacLeish* by Donaldson and Winnick, *Murrow* by Sperber, and *Rockefeller* by Reich.
2. A copy of the Kuhn Report is in the USIA Archives.
3. Hyman, *Benton*, 333.
4. In the bound volume of these hearings which Carl Marcy left to his family, the comment is on 795.
5. Hyman, *Benton*, 306–307.
6. Hyman, *Benton*, 323.
7. Hyman, *Benton*, 349.
8. Hyman, *Benton*, 349.
9. Ninkovich, *Diplomacy of Ideas*, 119.
10. Laves and Thomson, *Cultural Relations*, 59.
11. Ninkovich, *Diplomacy of Ideas*, 121.
12. Ninkovich, *Diplomacy of Ideas*, with Laves and Thomson, *Cultural Relations*, is especially useful on the history of the founding of UNESCO. See also L. H. Evans, *The U.S. and UNESCO*. Discussions over the years with participant and later deputy DG of UNESCO John E. Fobes have filled out my views.
13. The delegation included: Dean Mildred Thompson of Vassar, member of Fulbright's 1944 delegation to London and friend of Eleanor Roosevelt; Arthur Compton, Nobel physicist and Benton friend from Chicago, now presiding over Washington University in St. Louis; George N. Shuster, president of Hunter College in New York and long-time GAC member; and two congressmen, a Republican from the House Foreign Affairs Committee and a Democrat from the Senate Foreign Relations Committee.
14. Biographer Hyman believed Biddle was Benton's choice, perhaps in the illusion that the U.S. was *entitled* to the job; but inadequate communication with the White House seems more likely—Benton needed help to make such a mess.
15. Richard B. Parker wrote of this episode in *Prospects & Retrospects* (I, 1, 24–25), the magazine of Americans for UNESCO, in the spring of 2004.
16. Dean William C. Olson unearthed a copy of this course outline, for which the assigned textbook was McMurry and Lee, *Cultural Approach*, from the course archives of the University of Denver. The document provides a stark insight into the central role that UNESCO occupied at that moment in Cherrington's thought.

17. Fulbright's biographers, understandably fascinated by political aspects of his life, are at the beginning of their labors; they have not yet attacked the defining dimension in his life as he saw it: his struggle to create a decent cultural and educational diplomacy for his nation. Iriye mentions this ultimate cultural internationalist only once, in reference to the UNESCO resolution; Ninkovich devotes several pages to the international politics of establishing overseas Fulbright Commissions but ignores the man; Welles's biographer-son mentions him only in connection with the UN resolution, MacLeish's not at all, Acheson's once; Tristram Coffin, in focusing on the Senator (*Senator Fulbright: Portrait of a Public Philosopher*, 1966), spends six sound pages describing the exchange program; and Fulbright's own most important biographer to date, Randall Woods (*Fulbright: A Biography*, 1995), dwells on Arkansas politics and Fulbright's doubts about Vietnam, slipping past cultural internationalism, university exchanges, and the celebrated program bearing his name. The long-awaited biography by Senate staffer Seth Tillman will clarify many of these points; he has been generous in sharing insights that have sharpened my view of the man I knew in the last decade of his life.
18. See William Friday, et. al., *Fulbright at Fifty: Meeting the Challenge of the Next Fifty Years* (1998).
19. I owe the phrase to Woods, *Fulbright*, 24.
20. Woods, *Fulbright*, 77.
21. Coffin, *Senator Fulbright*, 57.
22. Other members: MacLeish, Ralph Turner, US Commissioner of Education John Studebaker, Eleanor Roosevelt's surrogate Dean Mildred Thompson of Vassar, and Dean Grayson Kefauver of Stanford University's School of Education.
23. Woods, *Fulbright*, 83.
24. Iriye covers this rich moment succinctly in *Cultural Internationalism*, 143.
25. Laves and Thomson, *Cultural Relations*, 67.
26. Laves and Thomson, *Cultural Relations*, 66.
27. Ninkovich, *Diplomacy of Ideas*, 125.
28. Copies of the three letters are in the Cherrington Archives, University of Denver.

CHAPTER 9

1. Comparable materials from other countries' textbooks show the Americans to have been less inclined to national travelogues.
2. TESL later gave birth to the more general TESOL, teaching of English to speakers of other languages.
3. As a former teacher of language, I have paid close attention to the teaching of English and other languages around the world and in the U.S. for half a century. Books on the subject of ELT all seem to be written for professionals in the field. Endless statistical reports were compiled by USIA's English-Teaching Branch for decades; they were geared to impressing Congress with numbers and low costs. This section reflects personal experience, unless otherwise noted. Special gratitude is owed to colleagues like Edward Bernier, Mary Finocchiaro, Susan Fitzgerald, Robert Gosende, Gloria Kreisher, Robert Murphy, Dennis Shaw, Richard Yorkey, and dozens of others, including British Council staff and *mutatis mutandis* French cultural diplomats.
4. Interviews with Ms. Kreisher, beginning in 1977.
5. During my two years in Beirut (1961–63), Ms. Fitzgerald was at the height of her powers. I am indebted to her for years of discussion beginning then and more particularly for a discussion in 2001.
6. The Iran case study is a fragment of my five-year tour there (1966–71) and a sixth year of observation reported by IAS director Lois Roth (1967–72).

7. Report on the Iranian Language Institute provided by letter from a friend in to-day's Tehran.

8. This summary of USIA's book programs is based on personal observations and reports by friends and colleages over forty years. I confess to having been less involved in book programs than with other elements after working alongside George Thompson, Audrey Hendricksen, and Don McNeil in Washington. A deeper study based on the documents and focusing on impacts and evaluations is overdue.

9. Gene D. Overton and Marshall Windmiller, *Communism in India* (1960).

10. Two veterans of USIA Eastern Europe related these details about the Paris ware-house; significantly, I was unaware of it during my many years in Paris.

11. See John K. Fairbank's "fifty-year memoir" *Chinabound* and Wilma Fairbank's CU history *Cultural Experiment in China.*

12. Fairbank, *Chinabound,* 195–97.

13. This and preceding citation from Fairbank, *Chinabound,* 310–12.

14. Ninkovich, *Diplomacy of Ideas,* 117.

15. I first learned about the Italian work of Morey when I began my tour in Rome in 1974. At that time I began collecting information about an illustrious predeces-sor. For this composite portrait, I am indebted to conversations and correspon-dence with a dozen or more of his friends, colleagues, and students, among them: Frank Brown, Margo Cutter, Lorenz Eitner, Albert Elsen, Frederick Hart, Norman Kogan, Irving Lavin, Rensselaer Lee, Henry Millon, Isabella Panzini, Cipriana Scelba, Craig Smyth, and Martha Lou Stohlman.

16. The title of the engaging book by Joseph La Palombara, *Democracy, Italian Style* (1987).

17. A faded copy of Morey's "squawk" can be found in the Fulbright Archives at the University of Arkansas in Fayetteville.

Chapter 10

1. This chapter too draws heavily on Espinosa, Ninkovich, and Iriye, as well as on Laves and Thomson and USIA historian Murray Lawson, all cited earlier. The biographies of Acheson, Benton, Briggs, MacLeish, Messersmith, Murrow, Nelson Rockefeller, and Welles, also undergird this section.

2. See Walter Isaacson and Evan Thomas, *The Wise Men* (1997), short biographies of six key players including John J. McCloy, High Commissioner in West Germany.

3. To avoid the dizzying sequence of its historical names, we shall refer to this func-tion by the name it acquired in 1961, AID (the Agency for International Develop-ment).

4. See Richard F. Kuisel, *Seducing the French: The Dilemma of Americanization* (1996).

5. For these insights into the AID function, I am grateful to colleagues over the years in Lebanon, Sri Lanka, and Iran, and more specifically to Mark Ward and to AID oral-historian Havens North. On productivity, see Kuisel, *Seducing.* Needless to say, interpretations are my own.

6. Books about clandestine activity are unreliable by definition. Most useful in un-derstanding the extent of Soviet activity is the workmanlike Clive Rose, *The Soviet Propaganda Network* (1988).

7. Interview with the NSA officer (name withheld by request) and Cassandra Pyle in 2001.

8. The CCF is well covered by Peter Coleman, under his revealing title *The Liberal Conspiracy* (1989). Cord Meyer's discreet memoir *Facing Reality* (1980) is helpful, if read between the lines. Ninkovich touches on the CCF with his usual acumen in *Diplomacy of Ideas* and the Congress is covered in considerable detail by Volker Berghahn in *America.* Frances Stonor Saunders's *The Cultural Cold War* (1999) is less reliable.

9. Cord Meyer, *Facing Reality.*

10. Charles Frankel tells this story in his postmortem *High on Foggy Bottom* (1968). Citations from pp. 161 and 193.
11. Coleman, *Liberal Conspiracy*, xiii.
12. Evan Thomas's book *The Very Best Men, Four Who Dared* (1996) is a lively evocation, considering source limitations.
13. Robin Winks in *Cloak and Gown* (1990) succeeded in bringing to life the spirit of patriotism and adventure, along with trenchant illusions, which motivated the OSS and the early CIA. Ending his book in 1960, he only hinted at the growth of the anti-CIA myth, as published evidence of various covert interventions in the 1950s, and especially of the Bay of Pigs in 1961, mounted higher.
14. The history of the Fulbright Program, an enormous task, has barely begun to be written. A crucial volume for the early years of the Fulbright Program is the two-decade history by Johnson and Colligan, *Fulbright Program*. Their work initiated the historical quest for the US side of the story, but a program operating in 150 or more countries, each with its individual character, will need take a massive descriptive effort and may fall beyond the reach of scholars. Yet there is nothing more revealing of the American mindset, forged by the missionary-educators and reconstituted in the 1940s, than Fulbright's unique creation and its tenacious survival. Ninkovich, *Diplomacy of Ideas*, is helpful on the period before 1950. Two of the three volumes issued by State in the CU years of John Richardson are keystones: Kellermann's *Cultural Relations* and Fairbank's *Cultural Experiment*. Two books produced by the US Fulbright Alumni Association, collecting individual episodes, are stimulating: Dudden and Dynes's *Fulbright Experience* and Arndt and Rubin's *Fulbright Difference*. In the latter the introductions to each decade of Fulbright activity, taken together, providethe outline of a useful historical forty-five-year sketch.
15. The decision to create CIES underscores the academic intentions of the BFS. BFS asked State to turn to the Conference Board of Associated Research Councils, a consortium formed in 1944 by the ACLS (for the humanities) with the National Research Council (for science), and the Social Science Research Council, then joined in 1945 by ACE. BFS invited the Conference Board to handle the senior Fulbright Program and, with $40,000 in start-up funding from the Rockefeller Foundation, CIES began its work. The story is told by Espinosa in *Inter-American Beginnings*, citing an unpublished history written by Elizabeth P. Lam in 1971 which I have not been able to find.
16. Kellermann, *Cultural Relations*, 7.
17. The question disappeared when the Freedom of Information Act of the 1970s made security checks for Americans inadmissible.
18. Interview with Jean Lashly, May 2001. She proudly recalled that State had the "guts" to recommend the second victim to CIES, where she served senior Fulbright candidates for half a century with high distinction.
19. Winks tells the story in his afterword to Arndt and Rubin, *Fulbright Difference*; Pells tells his in *Not Like Us*. Both stories have been amplified in discussion with the authors.

CHAPTER 11

1. The burst of internationalist activities in the immediate post–World War II period is richly documented by Merle Curti in *American Philanthropy*. Insights into this period and the context of earlier exchanges can be found in the dense book by long-time German Fulbright Commission director Ulrich Littman, *Partners*. A less helpful book is Aguilar, *Cultural Diplomacy*, in which the author unfortunately follows USIA in confusing cultural and Public Diplomacy. Of dozens of CAOs and other participants from this period who shared their memories with me, I must pay special homage to the late Carl Marcy, chief counsel of the Senate For-

eign Relations Committee, and to his wife Mildred, colleague and friend since 1961.

2. On international student flows, the publications of NAFSA and *Open Doors*, the annual census conducted by IIE, trace the rise of interchange over the years, as well as the flattening off and decline beginning post-9/11 in the years 2001–2004.

3. For the German reorientation program, the indispensable guide is Kellermann, *Cultural Relations*.

4. Kellermann, *Cultural Relations*, 30.

5. Daniel Costelle in *Les Prisonniers* (1975) gives a French journalist's version of the POWs. A more serious treatment, limited to German prisoners, is Ron Robin's *The Barbed-Wire College: Reeducating Germans POWs in the U.S. during World War II* (1995). Conversations with Professors Inis Claude and Norman Kogan took place over the years.

6. I am indebted to Craig Smyth, both for his *Repatriation of Art from the Collecting Point in Munich after World War II* (1988) and for two decades of enlightening discussion. Other discussions over time have taken place with various art-historian-participants who knew the MFA&A.

7. Curti, in *American Philanthropy*, documents this extensive activity.

8. I am indebted to Jean Edward Smith and his fine biography *Lucius D. Clay: An American Life* (1990), completed when we were colleagues at the University of Virginia. His book provides a remarkably clear view of this broad-gauged soldier of many parts.

9. Kellermann, *Cultural Relations*, 35.

10. Smith, *Lucius D. Clay*, 376.

11. Kellermann, *Cultural Relations*, 33.

12. Walter Laves and Charles Thomson, *Cultural Relations*, 74.

13. The return of the Kaiser Wilhelm paintings is covered by Smith, *Lucius D. Clay*, 309–22.

14. Kellermann, *Cultural Relations*, 30.

15. Volker Berghahn's access to Stone's papers, the basis for his pathfinding book on America and the intellectual cold wars (2002), has produced an indispensable biography of the man and guide to this period, viewed through the eyes of one central participant. With time, historians may better be able to place Stone's contribution in a broader world context.

16. One of many conversations with Tuch, this one in 1999.

17. Laves and Thomson, *Cultural Relations*, 74.

18. To my knowledge, the Japanese case has been less clearly studied. What follows draws heavily instead on the memories of participant Leon Picon, on a memoir by Carl Bartz, and on the delightful book of Beate Sirota, *The Only Woman in the Room: A Memoir* (1999), drawn to my attention by Japan-hand Robert Immerman. The memoir by Bartz, a unique copy, is in my possession; it will be cited in later chapters.

19. The best critical analysis I have read on the US approach to exporting democracy is Robert C. Orr's unpublished dissertation "Paradigm Lost? US Approaches to Democracy Promotion in Developing Countries" (1996).

20. Sirota, *Only Woman*, 120.

21. The episode took place at the Miller Center in Charlottesville, Virginia, after a three-man Hungarian delegation had spent three weeks on an IV grant working on a revision of the Hungarian Constitution, in dialogue with Professor A. E. Dick Howard of the University of Virginia Law School.

22. Laves and Thomson, *Cultural Relations*, 76.

23. In 1988 Bartz collected his memories for a projected but unpublished book on the CAOs.

24. Dozens of conversations with Picon took place over the years beginning in 1968,

but the capstone took place just before his death, over lunch in a Chinese restaurant where he went regularly to practice the Mandarin Chinese he was busily teaching himself at the end of his life.

25. Edward Barrett's *Truth Is Our Weapon* appeared in 1953.

26. Roth's article was printed on three different occasions, with changes in the latter two. The best of these, because of useful appendices, is "Public Diplomacy and the Past: The Search for an American Style of Propaganda" in *The Fletcher Forum* 8 (Summer 1984). The final version, prepared with my help just before her death, brought matters roughly up to 1985; it appears in Walter Brasch and Dana Ulloth, *The Press and the State* (1986).

27. Through the kindness of Mildred Marcy, I consulted at length the personal leather-bound record of these hearings preserved by Carl Marcy, the Fulbright committee's chief counsel during the hearings and for more than two decades thereafter.

CHAPTER 12

1. As we advance in our story, personal experiences begin to crowd out the printed literature. This chapter, for example, reflects years of personal dealings with hundreds of participants from these years. As ever, books like Ninkovich's *Diplomacy of Ideas* are essential, as are Kellermann's *Cultural Relations*, Laves and Thomson's *Cultural Relations*, Reich's biography of Nelson Rockefeller, and Johnson and Colligan's *Fulbright Program*, among others previously cited. Martin Merson's slim memoir of his trying year at the side of Robert L. Johnson, *The Private Diary of a Public Servant* (1955), is compelling in its emotion, the more so in that he came only gradually—like Johnson—to see the high value of cultural diplomacy. The Fulbright-Hickenlooper hearings are a rich trove, as is Lois Roth's work on the studies of the question, especially those undertaken in anticipation of the Republican victory in 1952. Future participants like Philip Coombs, Charles Frankel, and Thomas Sorensen shed different light in their memoirs.

2. Martin Merson's story of Johnson's sad stay in Washington is narrated in *Private Diary*.

3. Merson, *Private Diary*, 7.

4. Fulbright-Hickenlooper hearings, 1439.

5. See Lois Roth, "Public Diplomacy."

6. Reich's *Rockefeller* is indispensably rich for these years of Rockefeller's life.

7. Personal communication from Hoopes, 2001.

8. Merson, *Private Diary*, 80–81.

9. Philip H. Coombs, *Fourth Dimension*, 33–34.

10. Conversation with Lawrence Norrie in Tehran, 1968.

11. Thomas C. Sorensen, *Word War*, 50.

12. Both Coombs and Frankel later headed State's cultural office and produced perceptive books, not only about cultural affairs, but about bureaucratic culture.

13. Copy in USIA Archives.

14. Conversation with John Howard, father of ITR at Ford, and Margot Betz Howard, former Ford staff in New York and Tehran, assistant to Charles Frankel, and CU program officer.

15. McCaughey, *International Studies.*

16. Richard D. Lambert, "Durable Academic Linkages Overseas: A National Agenda," in *The Annals* 491, May 1987, 140–53.

CHAPTER 13

1. Documentation on the 1950s is scattered through dozens of ephemeral publications, reports, government reports, and personal memories. Lois Roth's study of

the various reports of the 1950s underlines key moments in the intellectual history of the period.

2. Washburn during this writing was preoccupied with illness; he died in December 2003, and his wife a month later. Two phone conversations and a letter giving his general reaction to an early version of this chapter are all that time allowed me to draw from him. The "Golden Age" remark came in a phone conversation about George Allen.

3. The USIA Archives contain an impressive number of Allen's speeches, drawn to my attention by Joseph Duffey. Excerpts have obviously been selected to shed light on his views of USIA's cultural dimension. I have unfortunately been unable to consult Allen's papers in the Eisenhower Library in Abilene.

4. A copy of this speech is in the ACE library.

5. The North Carolinian, who smoked heavily and would soon die of it, had gone to work for the Tobacco Institute.

6. A copy of the *Tribune* article is in the USIA Archives.

7. Both statements from introduction to Morrill et al., *The Universities and World Affairs.*

8. By a cautious estimate, the entire federal government outlay on international educational and cultural programs at that time amounted to less than 1 percent of the military budget. It is much less now.

9. Lois Roth, "Public Diplomacy," 734, in Brasch and Ulloth version.

10. Marx, before Fascell committee, 1977.

11. Conversations with Francis X. Sutton and follow-up letter dated 5 March 1999.

12. Charles Frankel, "The Man in the Middle," in *Neglected Aspect.*

13. The vignettes of Carl Bode and Cleanth Brooks are extracted from longer portraits written by them in 1988 for an unpublished book.

CHAPTER 14

1. Three generous Murrow biographies are so far in print: Alexander Kendrick's *Prime Time: The Life of Edward R. Murrow* (1969), Persico's *Edward R. Murrow*, and Sperber's *Murrow*. Of these, Sperber's is the most complete, especially for the early years, while Kendrick's has the special insights of long friendship. From the viewpoint of cultural diplomacy, the biographers complement each other and, taken together, reveal parallels and divergences the authors do not always see; I have tried to be attentive to footnoting their work; from a focused reading of the three, a Murrow differing from any of the three monographic portraits emerges. In contrast, see Robert A. Lincoln, *"The U.S.—Warts and All": Edward R. Murrow as Director of USIA, Presenting the U.S. to the World*, reporting a commemorative symposium at which fifteen USIA colleagues spoke (1992). In the booklet's sixty-one hagiographic pages, educational and cultural affairs are not mentioned.

2. Persico, *Edward R. Murrow*, 57.

3. Persico, *Edward R. Murrow*, 79.

4. Kendrick, *Prime Time*, 113.

5. J. Edgar Hoover attempted to block Murrow's appointment in 1961.

6. Kendrick, *Prime Time*, 238–39.

7. Sperber, *Murrow*, 634.

8. Kendrick, *Prime Time*, 481 and 486.

9. Sperber, *Murrow*, 620.

10. Sperber, *Murrow*, 614.

11. See Sperber's interpretation of the transition, *Murrow*, 624–25.

12. This and the following quote come from a letter to the author from Don Wilson, 2 Oct 2003.

13. Sorensen, *Word War.*

14. Sperber, *Murrow*, 625.

15. Sperber, *Murrow*, 634.

16. Sperber, *Murrow*, 634.
17. Sorensen, *Word War*, 127.
18. Sperber, *Murrow*, 679.
19. Robert E. Elder, *The Information Machine: The US Information Agency and US Foreign Policy* (1968).
20. Sperber, *Murrow*, 635.
21. Sperber, quoting Sorensen, *Murrow*, 677.
22. Wilson's speech is in the USIA Archives.
23. Kendrick, *Prime Time*, 492.
24. Kendrick, *Prime Time*, 497.
25. Coombs's post-mortem, *Fourth Dimension*, is silent on personal details but vital for cultural diplomatic thinking. More details and an interpretation of Coombs's five hundred days can be found in Randolph Wieck, *Ignorance Abroad: American Educational and Cultural Foreign Policy and the Office of the Assistant Secretary of State* (1992), drawn from Wieck's more extensive thesis, done for the Sorbonne under the direction of André Kaspi, *Philip Coombs: Secrétaire d'Etat à l'Education et aux Affaires Culturelles* (1989).
26. Kendrick, *Prime Time*, 465.
27. Half of the Corps's first-year volunteers were classroom teachers.
28. I attended CAO conferences in Beirut in January 1962 and Delhi in 1965. In retrospect, I learned more about the CAO profession and its supporting organizational structure in those two meetings than in six weeks of Washington training, home-leave consultation, and four years in my first two posts.
29. From Bartz's 1988 unpublished memoir.
30. Coombs's personal investment in *Beacon* is suggested by a footnote in his book. He calls it "required reading" (Coombs, *Fourth Dimension*, 97).
31. For this and following citation, "the common theme . . . ," see Coombs, *Fourth Dimension*, 44.
32. Coombs, *Fourth Dimension*, 45.
33. Wieck, in *Ignorance Abroad*, devotes three convincing pages to the value of the Slater Exercises, 56–58.

CHAPTER 15

1. I am grateful to Lucius D. Battle for confidence since 1963 and especially for a long luncheon interview in 1998, from which many details in the following material were drawn. More of the Battle style was experienced in my work—I was in field posts in Beirut and Colombo during his tenure, with a memorable first meeting at a CAO conference in Beirut.
2. For the story from Adams's viewpoint, see his unrelentingly trivial account of the trip, *On the Road for Uncle Sam* (1963).
3. The history of the Fulbright Program has only begun to be written. For its first two decades, beyond Ninkovich's *Diplomacy of Ideas*, Johnson and Colligan's *Fulbright Program*, Laves and Thomson's *Cultural Relations*, the annual reports of BFS, and the two collections of individual memoirs and contextual commentary (Dudden and Dynes, *Fulbright Experience*, and Arndt and Rubin, *Fulbright Difference*), there is little in print. As a Fulbright alumnus from 1949, as an administrator of Fulbright exchanges in five countries, as past president of the US Fulbright Association, I write as a participant-observer.
4. From Bartz's unpublished 1988 memoir. See also Robert L. Clifford, "Burma Beginnings: Fulbright and Point Four," in Arndt and Rubin, *Fulbright Difference*. Clifford's memoir underlines the heavy technical-assistance thrust of the first year of the Burmese Fulbright Program and takes some responsibility for it; his article meshes with Bartz's and Lelyveld's perception of overemphasis on development in Burma.

5. I am indebted to Ulrich Littman, longtime director of the German Fulbright Commission, for decades of friendship and for this detail and the insight it provides into the importance Adenauer gave the program.

6. The annual reports of the cultural advisory commission are essential documents, most completely collected at the Fulbright Archives of the University of Arkansas in Fayetteville.

7. Espinosa, *Inter-American*, is the best source for information on the GAC, especially p. 163.

8. Humphrey's sister Frances Humphrey Howard insisted until the end of her life that her brother conceived the idea of the Peace Corps and scoffed at the idea it might have owed something to the missionary-educators.

9. From Ms. Ruppé's essay, "The Third Goal: Uncovering America's Hidden Heart," in *International Education: The Unfinished Agenda*, eds. William Olson and Llewellyn D. Howell (1984), 40–55.

10. *The Washington Post*, 16 March 1999.

11. Noel Riley Fitch, *Appetite for Life: The Biography of Julia Child* (1997).

12. I first met Brown in 1974 at a luncheon arranged by former Brussels CAO Edwin Kennedy to help prepare me for my assignment in Rome; Brown and I met regularly until the end of his life. In 1988, after extended exchanges, he adapted an earlier publication to nourish a book on the American cultural attachés. All citations come from that manuscript.

CHAPTER 16

1. A cultural attaché need make little effort to be plunged into the art scene of his or her host country or to befriend its artists and art historians. In Morey's phrase, the artists and scholars are the "humanists-at-large" who stand in the front line of the natural cultural dialogue between any two countries. This chapter dwells on one of the many consequences of the US decision not to keep people like Morey and the two Fairbanks at the point of contact.

2. To list the hundreds of US and foreign artists, art historians, and archeologists I have known in a dozen nations abroad and in the U.S., plus a dozen art-sensitive USIA colleagues like Ed McBride and Lois Roth, would serve no purpose. Much of what follows comes from living in proximity to the world of the visual and performing artists, more actively in the four decades since I arrived in Beirut. Specially focused insights have come from association with the American University of Beirut, Arthur C. Danto, John Ferren, the artists of Lebanon, Sri Lanka, and Iran, the American Academy in Rome, Danny Berger, numerous American artists in Rome and Paris, Hélène Baltrusaitis in Paris, and Malcolm Bell at the University of Virginia, as well as from a decade of informal fellowship with the scholars of the Center for Advanced Study in the Visual Arts of the National Gallery in Washington. To the center and its first two directors, Henry A. Millon and Elizabeth Cropper, and deputy director Teresa O'Malley and so many others—to all these, I owe thanks for tolerating of my inadequate education.

3. Conversation with Dr. Landais, April 1992.

4. Copious details on Nelson Rockefeller are provided by Reich in the first volume of his biography, *Rockefeller*. For a critical review of the tensions between art and diplomacy in the 1940s Washington, see Frank Ninkovich, "The Currents of Cultural Diplomacy: Art and the State Department, 1938–47," *Diplomatic History* 1 (Summer 1977).

5. See Jean Smith's biography of soldier-diplomat Clay, *Lucius D. Clay*.

6. Interviews with McBride, Cogswell, Masey, and Joshua Taylor, among others, have taken place over the years. Special thanks to Lois Roth, Barbara Spring, Mary Gawronski, Ted Kennedy, Frances Switt, Douglas James Johnson, David Galloway, and many others impossible to enumerate.

7. The story is related in fine detail by Fitch in her biography of Julia Child, *Appetite*.
8. The catalog is available in Clervaux but may also be found in dozens of USIS posts where it gathers dust on cultural office bookshelves and in storerooms. In my years, it was the CAO's favorite gift.
9. From 1963 until his death, I was privileged to correspond with and have frequent meetings with Ferren and his wife Rae. Both described the impact of Beirut on his work as transfiguring. Conversations with Schehadé, Carswell, both Fricks, and Lebanese and Syrian artists nourish my sense of his stay in Lebanon.

CHAPTER 17

1. For biographical materials on Frankel and the Frankel moment in CU history, *Foggy Bottom* is indispensable; because he wrote fluently and personally on cultural diplomacy, insights into his views can be found throughout his bibliography. I draw as well on a personal acquaintance begun in 1960 and picking up speed after 1965.
2. Most of the books on cultural diplomacy, beginning with McMurry and Lee in 1947, Laves and Thomson in 1963, and Johnson and Colligan also in 1963, were hard going, although incomparably better than the work ground out by the informationists, which tended to be inward-looking and self-referential. Coombs was markedly better, but his informing discipline, manpower economics, was complex. All this made dull reading and seemed confused. Frankel's first goal instead was to be readable, especially in *Foggy Bottom*, after the weight of government service had lifted.
3. Frankel, *Neglected Aspect*. On Calkins's call for a "more thorough analysis" than *Beacon*, see p. viii. For Frankel's idea of a handbook or manual, see p. 132.
4. McPherson declined my invitation to discuss this historic moment, other than by a short telephone converation and a graceful letter, with a few clues like this one.
5. Frankel, *Foggy Bottom*, 11.
6. Frankel, *Foggy Bottom*, 13.
7. For what happened inside the task force, I can only adduce two partial but anonymous sources; but its operations were a fairly open matter even while taking place.
8. Frankel, *Foggy Bottom*, 98.
9. Frankel, *Foggy Bottom*, 19.
10. Conversation with Ford officer, who prefers anonymity.
11. The reference title is to Harrison and Huntington, *Culture Matters* (2000).

CHAPTER 18

1. See Berliner's *Ambivalent Desire*.
2. Naima Prevots made an initial stab at getting the remarkable and manifold outreach of American dance onto paper, in her *Dance for Export: Cultural Diplomacy and the Cold War* (1999). Unfortunately David Caute's *The Dancer Defects: The Struggle for Cultural Supremacy During the Cold War* (2003) was published too late to be of use in this study; Michael Kimmelman's long review in the *New York Review of Books* (27 May 2004) suggests that Caute's is a sophisticated treatment.
3. See Stovall's *Paris Noir*.
4. I remind the reader that much of what I write draws on experience and a peculiar memory for trivia, hence cannot be footnoted. The gloss of performances in Lebanon, Sri Lanka, and Iran in the 1960s is from memories, reinforced by occasional file materials.

5. Letter from Kenneth Bloomquist, 2002.
6. I am indebted to "Mim" Johnson Hallock for some of these details, conveyed in a long e-mail in the spring of 2003.
7. See Tim Page, "From Baghdad, A Classical Opportunity," *The Washington Post*, 10 December 2003.
8. Adams told his own version of this story, *On the Road*.
9. Michael Kimmelman, *NYRB*, in reviewing David Caute's book about the ballet wars, laments the days when the arts were believed to have power "in shaping politics and society in the postwar years." He expresses "nostalgia for this dangerous time when the high arts were treated as germane to world affairs and celebrated as nationalist propaganda." At the same time, he wonders about the arts as weapons of war. He is right on all counts.

CHAPTER 19

1. Cited by Woods in *Fulbright*, 77.
2. Former Undersecretary of State David Newsom devotes a chapter to "Academia" in *The Public Dimension of Diplomacy* (1996), 121–39.
3. If I dwell on university *scholars* or *intellectuals*, it is to avoid the pointless game of defining intellect in the idiosyncratic American case. Scholars may be intellectuals, but intellectuals—like Herschel Brickell and Morill Cody, Paul Child and John Brown—are not always scholars. Cultural diplomacy has always needed cultivated persons familiar with human history and thought, people with a learned turn of mind—and the language skills—to deal on an equal footing with host-country intellects, as Valignano taught Matteo Ricci.
4. Authorization hearings, Senate Foreign Relations Committee, 1974.
5. Margot Betz Howard, special assistant to Frankel, recruited Hurewitz and heard his report on return; my memories and hers and Lois Roth's correspondence are the source of this episode.
6. Related by William H. Weathersby, then vice president of Princeton University.
7. These are the only two exceptions of high-caliber intellectual publishing that I can report, in a quarter-century of service with USIA, overlooking the special case of Abraham Brumberg's *Problems of Communism*. Like all exceptions, they confirm the rule of the non-substantive quality of USIA's work.
8. During CU's move into USIA, because of space problems, records of American Fulbright alumni were destroyed. The Fulbright Association has spent twenty years patiently trying to reassemble these records for their mailing lists.
9. Ludovic Kennedy, *Very Lovely People: A Personal Look at Some Americans Living Abroad* (1969), 263.
10. Two heroic Foreign Relations Committee staffers did their best—John Rich and Peter Galbraith—before leaving the committee for ambassadorships.
11. Conversation with Ulrich Littman, Bonn, 1996.
12. Conversation with Terence Catherman, European Area Director for USIA, 1984.

CHAPTER 20

1. In our movement through chronology, we have entered the period when it is impossible to separate personal experience from documentation. In 1968, when Nixon was elected, I was CAO in Tehran; it was there that my single meeting with Frank Shakespeare took place. In 1972–74 I worked in Richardson's CU. From 1974 I was CAO in Rome and Paris, an agent of Richardson's CU and to a lesser extent of Shakespeare's, Keogh's, and briefly Reinhardt's USIA. Where possible, I shall try to refer the reader to other sources, but for the most part what follows is a personal memoir, with generous help from dozens of other participants in these years.

2.   I am indebted to Dr. Stanton for a probing luncheon conversation, as well as to Walter Roberts and Louis Olom, former executive director of the USIA advisory commission, for information on the unusual tenor of the commission reports of the early 1970s.

3.   I am indebted to John Richardson for years of collegiality, friendship, for various generous interviews over lunch, and for reviewing some of these pages in an early state. Richard K. Fox, executive office of CU under Richardson, also reviewed an early draft, as did William K. Hitchcock. All three reshaped some of my perceptions and helped smooth rough edges. None of them is responsible in any way for the views expressed here.

4.   The "CU Concept Paper" can most easily be found in an appendix to the version of Lois Roth's paper on the US style of propaganda reprinted in the *Fletcher Forum* (1984).

5.   Richardson did appoint an ineffective task force on interagency coordination in the spring of 1974, which I chaired. It will be discussed below.

6.   Personal communication.

7.   My interpretation of the UNESCO story has been reinforced by discussions over twenty-five years with such UNESCO veterans as John E. Fobes, Thomas Forstenzer, Richard K. Nobbe, André Varchaver, and Raymond E. Wanner, plus a dozen others, to whom my gratitude is extended. None of them is responsible for any of the views expressed here.

8.   When USIA was gently purloining "speakers" from CU, I was the CU officer in charge of the STAG program; my counterpart in USIA was the late Leon Picon. Between us, we tracked the stages of the slow takeover, which we both accepted as a *fait accompli* and an unavoidable necessity, in view of CU's abandonment of authority and USIA's voracious appetite for speakers.

CHAPTER 21

1.   Some of the materials for these vignettes were collected in 1988 but have been updated since then. Others have been collected more recently. They all rely heavily on conversation and correspondence; some texts have been checked at various stages with the subjects. In the case of these six, wherever possible, I have used the words they wrote or spoke.

2.   The principal insights into Robin Winks's thought, in addition to letters and constant dialogue over three decades, are his two essays for Dudden and Dynes, *Fulbright Experience*, and Arndt and Rubin, *Fulbright Difference*. His essay "Imperialism" in C. Vann Woodward's *Comparative Approach to American History* (1968) and his inaugural lecture at Oxford *The Imperial Revolution* (1994) are also fertile sources. It should be noted that Winks, more than any other of my virtual teachers, followed sections of this manuscript until his death. Among the compliments I have received in my life, one of the greatest was his silent acceptance of what I was doing and his occasional gift of a word, an idea, an article or a book.

3.   A deliberate omission from this book is a discussion of "American Studies"—a world primarily inhabited by academic specialists in US literature and history that has been documented and redocumented by its participants, among them Winks. The principal vehicle for their reflections, and a treasure trove for the subject, is *American Studies International*, published for four decades from an office at the University of Pennsylvania. On occasion, it has produced thoughtful retrospective treatments of its own history, e.g., "The Fulbright Program: Retrospect and Prospect" in the winter of 1982, as well as other collections in 1988 and 1998. Richard P. Horwitz edited a useful volume, *Exporting America: Essays on*

American Studies Abroad, in 1993. The Dutch Americanist Rob Kroes edited *Predecessors: Intellectual Lineages in American Studies* in 1999. The picture that emerges from ASI over the years is not as bad as Charles Boewe indicates in his memoir, "American Studies in India," where he describes the discipline as "laudatory when not homiletic and sentimental when not maudlin" (*ASI,* vol. 42, no. 1, 2004, 91). But *ASI,* over its forty-year-plus span, relentlessly conveys, often in the acerbic style of the disgruntled American humanist, the broad disaffection of the US academic community with the ramshackle structure that the US political process, with help from USIA, put in place and maintained for forty-six years to add a cultural and intellectual dimension to US diplomacy. In USIS terms, "American Studies," with or without the capital "s," was the means of reaching into university departments other than English (e.g. history, politics, law) where English was not the common language.

4. Dodds read an early version of this vignette at his home in Bologna; true to his style he sent no comment, which I have accepted as silent consent.
5. All quotations but one come from Ryan's 1988 memoir, reinforced by discussions since that time. His comment about the budgets for military music comes from his article "What does."
6. Letters by Lois Roth underlie this portrait. A longer version of this memoir appears in Arndt and Rubin, *Fulbright Difference.*
7. Communication from Mary Jo Furgal, February 2004, recalling Roth's enthusiasm about the episode in Madras.
8. All excerpts and quotations come from letters and copies of letters and reports from Wilcox to the author and others, as well as dozens of personal encounters.

CHAPTER 22

1. A convenient way of glossing Fulbright history is to peruse the two-page introductions to the five decades covered by Arndt and Rubin, *Fulbright Difference.*
2. In 1976, as if to make the very point it was discarding, USIA assigned one of its finest professional CAOs, Irving Sablosky, former music critic for a Chicago newspaper, to the London cultural office. After Sablosky came a political appointment.
3. From Bartz's unpublished 1988 memoir.
4. The predominant impact of USIA-CU's cultural tools in the Eastern European countries is particularly visible in Yale Richmond's most comprehensive book *Raising the Iron Curtain* (2003).
5. Olom was a graduate student at Chicago of the great Charles E. Merriam, who had headed USIS Italy for CPI during the First World War, and of Harold Lasswell. At the beginning of World War II, he joined a Rockefeller-funded group analyzing foreign propaganda, lodged in MacLeish's Library of Congress; he then moved into Rockefeller's office. He directed USIA's advisory commission for more than two decades. I am indebted to him for numerous frank conversations and discussions about the 1940s and about Stanton's chairmanship of the commission; like Olom and Stanton, he and I disagree on State but on little else.
6. Olom remembers commission colleagues as impatient with Michener's wisdom. In 1970 Michener returned from a year-long trip centered on the Islamic world. At the first meeting after his return, he was invited to report. In his quiet and understated manner, he concluded with a troubling assertion, to the effect that Islam was about to explode. No commisioner followed up with a question. No one asked how his report related to USIA's mission.
7. From 1964 until his death, I was one of Wilcox's regular correspondents; in particular, Lois Roth and I watched this little-known episode closely. There were also

frank discussions and exchanges of documents with the late Margaret Twyman, then executive director of the CU advisory commission.

8. See Stanton, et al., *International Information, Education, and Cultural Relations: Recommendations for the Future* (1975).

9. This exchange appeared as an annex to the report, suggesting Stanton's irritation.

CHAPTER 23

1. Author's interview with Mark Blitz, director of the E Bureau, spring 1989.

2. A copy of this signed petition can be found in the USIA Archives.

3. Discussion with Frank Stanton, New York, 1992, revealed this detail and many others that have helped understand this period.

4. Mosher made this remark at a seminar for mid-career fellows at the University of Virginia in 1989. I am not aware whether the celebrated public administration educator ever developed this off-the-cuff thought.

5. I first met Reinhardt in Tehran in August 1966, and we have grown closer over the years. I am indebted to him for two long interview discussions and advice on part of an early draft.

6. From Reinhardt's first letter to USIA staff. The USIA Archives are especially rich in documents from the Reinhardt period.

7. I am indebted to Dr. Duffey for extended interviews, as well as other help since 1978.

8. A footnote in Berghahn's book, *America*, based on the papers of Shepard Stone, conveys another view of Duffey's short stays in Paris.

9. Duffey was not alone in knowing by May that the decision to merge CU into USIA had already been made. At least one member of the White House task force, which spent four more months pondering the question as though it were still open, knew it.

10. These numbers are difficult to pin down. As an officer of the American Foreign Service Association at the time, I kept a fairly careful count, working with the representative of the American Federation of Government Employees. If the number is not precise, the order of magnitude is.

11. Stanton, *International Information.*

12. Interview with Rick Neustadt, Paris, January 1978.

13. Gifford D. Malone, *Political Advocacy and Cultural Communication: Organizing the Nation's Public Diplomacy* (1988).

14. In Roth, "Public Diplomacy and the Past: The Search for an American Style of Propaganda, 1952–77" (1984), 353–96.

15. Copies of this letter can be found in the USIA archives.

16. The transcript of this press conference can be found in the USIA Archives. The ignorance in the founding legislation, in the task force, and to some extent in the USIA legal office suggest how little the details mattered. It would soon become an unshakable tenet of USIA's legal office that the Smith-Mundt Act of 1948 authorized USIA while Fulbright-Hays authorized educational and cultural affairs. In fact, Fulbright-Hays, according to two of its drafters Carl Marcy and Michael Cardozo, was explicitly designed to supersede all previous legislation, including Smith-Mundt. In the 1980s and 1990s, when a tougher and more confrontational stance required it, the two distinct sides of Smith-Mundt and its explicit effort to protect and provide for both information and culture were conveniently forgotten.

17. The number seven was improvised by Leonard Marks, before Fascell's committee, splitting the difference between the USIA commission's five and the CU commission's nine. It is another example of the slapdash thinking behind the merger.

18. I am indebted to my CAO colleague John H. Brown of Georgetown University for this citation.
19. My debt to Dr. Ilchman, whom I first met in Paris in 1979, covers a quarter century of friendship, several long interviews, thoughtful correspondence, and a review of an early draft of this section.
20. My friendship with Hitchcock dates to 1961, but discussion of the late 1970s have been veiled in professional reticence and restrained by his disappointment.
21. After E, Strauss eked out a living advising the West German embassy on US educational relations, monitoring an ongoing US-German textbook-renewal project, counseling the International Baccalaureate movement, helping the College Boards negotiate European-US university equivalences, and writing a weekly column about the U.S. for a Jewish newspaper in Frankfurt. In 1991, driving with his wife to their synagogue in Chevy Chase late on a Saturday morning, he was killed by a drunken driver.
22. Curiously, I never had a chance to meet Posner.
23. See Richard Arndt, "Public Diplomacy, Cultural Diplomacy: The Stanton Commission Revisited," in *The Stanton Report Revisited*, ed. Kenneth W. Thompson (1987), where space permitted greater detail about this ill-considered moment.

CHAPTER 24

1. This chapter glosses the last two decades of decline when, in effect, the die had been cast for cultural diplomacy by the reorganization of 1977. A rapid summary of twenty years, this chapter has the advantage and weakness of relying on personal observation at one remove. To take two examples from the head of this chapter, Wick's words were heard by the entire staff of the E Bureau. Blitz's remark on Fulbright was made to several staff, two of whom reported it to me.

   Leaving USIA in the fall of 1985, I followed events as closely as possible, relying on a small group of trusted friends for information and documents, but these last years have inevitably produced a declining knowledge curve. My version of these years therefore pretends to nothing more than a first draft, to guide or mislead historians looking more closely at this period.
2. The same officer, as deputy director of E some years later, would bring the fine and performing arts back under E's jurisdiction.
3. See Ninkovich's indispensable critical history, *Diplomacy of Ideas*.
4. See Malone, *Political Advocacy*.
5. A cabled poll of European PAOs reported unanimous support, but Wick was not told that the area office had phoned all PAOs beforehand to insist that only positive results be reported.
6. By one estimate, the roughly $2 million going into US orientation for foreign students and senior scholars, with foreign contributions and foreign-currency support, would have increased the total annual number of the world's foreign Fulbrights by 4 to 5 percent.
7. In the spring of 1949 Ben Cherrington and graduate student William C. Olson at the University of Denver gave a course entitled "UNESCO in World Affairs." The syllabus discussed the UNESCO program in the U.S., with a section on operations in the various states. The final section of the syllabus debated unilateral versus multilateral cultural programs and suggested that Cherrington, after trying his experience with bilateral cultural operations, saw multilateralism as the best path to the future.
8. CU-ECA grants had rarely been questioned by Congress over the years. They were decentralized, i.e., administered by the various divisions in areas of their professional competence; they went in many cases to private bodies spun off by CU, a device now called out-sourcing; and they were monitored within CU by a no-nonsense executive office.

9. Lecture and two articles by, and followup conversation with William Rugh, former Arab Peninsula diplomat then heading Amideast (2001).
10. See Ezra Suleiman's disturbing analysis of the trend to de-professionalize government bureaucracies in Europe and the U.S., in his *Dismantling Democratic States* (2003).
11. As of this writing, no replacement as undersecretary has been named.

BIBLIOGRAPHY

Adams, Joey. *On the Road for Uncle Sam.* New York: Geis, 1963.

Aguilar, Manuela. *Cultural Diplomacy and Foreign Policy: German-American Relations, 1955–68.* New York: Peter Lang, 1996.

Appleby, Joyce. *Inheriting the Revolution: The First Generation of Americans.* Cambridge, Mass.: Belknap, 2000.

Arndt, Richard T. "Cultural Diplomacy: Nurturing Critical Junctures." In *Psychodynamics of International Relationships*, eds. Vamik D. Volkan, Demetrios A. Julian, and Joseph V. Montville. Lexington Mass.: Lexington Books, 1988.

———. "El primer agregado cultural noteamericano: Albert A. Giesecke." *Colección documental y bibliográfica: Albert A. Giesecke Parttey Müller*, Instituto Riva-Agüero and Catholic University of Peru, 5–12. Lima, November 2003.

———. "The Precarious Balance: US Information and Cultural Policy." In *The Theory and Practice of International Relations*, ed. William C. Olson, 8th ed. Englewood Cliffs, N.J.: Prentice-Hall, 1990.

———. "Public Diplomacy, Cultural Diplomacy: The Stanton Commission Revisited." In *The Stanton Report Revisited*, ed. Kenneth W. Thompson, 85–104. *Rhetoric and Public Diplomacy*, vol. 7. Lanham, Md.: University Press of America, 1987.

———. "Revolutionary Projections: French and American Cultural Diplomacy." In *le Discours sur les révolutions* II, 375–97. Paris: Economica, 1988.

———. "Saving Art: Some Early American Rescuers," *The Yale Review* 87, no. 3 (July 1999), 85–105.

Arndt, Richard T., David Bame, and Steven A. Blodgett. "Fulbright's Fortieth: Culture and Power Revisited." Review of "The Fulbright Program and Academic Exchanges," ed. Nathan Glazer, in *The Annals* (May 1987). *Bulletin of International Interchange* 27 (February 1988): 6–25

———. "Public Diplomacy, Cultural Diplomacy: Why no End to the USIA Debate?" *Bulletin of International Interchange* 29 (October 1988): 19–30

Arndt, Richard T., and David L. Rubin. *The Fulbright Difference, 1948–92.* New Brunswick, N.J.: Transaction, 1993.

Arndt, Richard T., and Lois W. Roth, "Information, Culture and Public Diplomacy: Searching for an American Style of Propaganda," In *The Press and the State: Sociohistorical and Contemporary Interpretations*, eds. Walter M. Brasch and Dana R. Ulloth. Lanham, Md.: University Press of America, 1986.

Avery, Peter, *Modern Iran.* New York: Praeger, 1965.

Baer, George W., ed. *A Question of Trust: The Origins of US-Soviet Diplomatic Relations: The Memoirs of Loy W. Henderson.* Stanford: Hoover Institution Press, 1986.

Baldwin, Deborah. "Broken Traditions: Mexican Revolutionaries and Protestant Allegiances." *The Americas* 40, no. 2 (October 1983): 229–58.

Barrett, Edward. *Truth Is Our Weapon.* New York: Funk and Wagnalls, 1953.

Barzun, Jacques. *The House of Intellect.* New York: Harper Collins, 1959.

Beevor, Antony, and Artemis Cooper. *Paris after the Liberation, 1944–49.* London: Hamish Hamilton, 1994.

Belknap, Reginald. *American House-Building in Messina and Reggio.* New York and London: Putnam, 1910.

Benfey, Christopher. *The Great Wave: Gilded Age Misfits, Japanese Eccentrics, and the Opening of Old Japan.* New York: Random House, 2003.

Berghahn, Volker R. *America and the Intellectual Cold Wars in Europe: Shepard Stone Between Philanthropy, Academy, and Diplomacy.* Princeton: Princeton University Press, 2001.

Berliner, Brett, *Ambivalent Desire: The Exotic Black Other in Jazz-Age France.* Amherst: University of Massachusetts Press, 2002.

Bernays, Edward L., and Burnet Hershey. *The Case for Reappraisal of US Overseas Informational Policies and Programs.* New York: Praeger, 1970.

Bingham, Alfred M. *Portrait of an Explorer: Hiram Bingham, Discoverer of Machu Picchu.* Ames: Iowa State University Press, 1989.

Blum, Robert, ed. *Cultural Affairs and Foreign Relations.* New York: Prentice-Hall, 1963.

Blunt, Wilfrid, *The Golden Road to Samarkand.* London: Hamish Hamilton, 1973.

Boewe, Charles. "American Studies in India, A Personal Memoir." *American Studies International,* vol. 42, no. 1 (2004).

Braistead, Paul J., ed. *Cultural Affairs and Foreign Relations.* Washington, D.C.: Columbia, 1968.

Brasch, Walter M., and Ulloth, Dana R. *The Press and the State: Sociohistorical and Contemporary Interpretations.* Lanham, Md.: University Press of America, 1986.

Bremner, Robert H. *Giving: Charity and Philanthropy in History.* New Brunswick, N.J.: Transaction, 1996.

Briggs, Ellis O. *Farewell to Foggy Bottom: The Recollections of a Career Diplomat.* New York: McKay, 1964.

———. *Proud Servant: The Memoirs of a Career Ambassador.* Kent, Ohio: Kent State University Press, 1998.

Brinton, Jasper Yeates. *The American Effort in Egypt: A Chapter in Diplomatic History in the Nineteenth Century.* Alexandria, 1972.

Brooks, Van Wyck. Title essay in *Fenollosa and His Circle,* 1–68. New York: Dutton, 1962.

———. *Literature in New England.* New York: Garden City, 1944.

Brown, John L. "But what do you DO?" *Foreign Service Journal,* vol. 41, no. 6 (1964).

Byrnes, Robert F. *Awakening American Education to the World: The Role of Archibald Cary Coolidge.* South Bend, Indiana: Notre Dame Press, 1982.

Carruthers, Mary J. *The Book of Memory: A Study of Memory in Medieval Culture.* Cambridge: Cambridge University Press, 1990.

Casson, Lionel. *Libraries in the Ancient World.* New Haven: Yale University Press, 2001.

Cavaliero, Roderick E. "Cultural Diplomacy: The Diplomacy of Influence." *The Round Table,* 1986, 298, 139–44. Butterworth: London, 1986.

Chace, James. *Acheson: The Secretary of State Who Created the Modern World.* New York: Simon & Schuster, 1998.

Chisom, Lawrence. *Fenollosa: The Far East and American Culture.* New Haven: Yale University Press, 1983.

Clarke, John R. *Looking at Lovemaking: Constructions of Sexuality in Roman Arts 100 B.C.–250 A.D.* Berkeley: University of California Press, 1998.

Coffin, Tristram. *Senator Fulbright: Portrait of a Public Philosopher.* New York: Dutton, 1966.

Cohen, Raymond, and Raymond Westbrook, eds. *Amarna Diplomacy: The Beginnings of International Relations.* Baltimore: Johns Hopkins Press, 2000.

Coleman, Peter, *The Liberal Conspiracy: The Congress for Cultural Freedom and the Struggle for the Mind of Postwar Europe.* New York: Macmillan, 1989.

Colligan, Francis J. *Twenty Years After: Two Decades of Government-Sponsored Cultural Relations.* Washington, D.C.: Department of State International Information and Cultural Series, Series 59, 1958.

Committee on Culture and Intellectual Exchange, National Citizens' Commission on International Cooperation. Report prepared for the White House Conference on International Cooperation, 28 November–1 December 1965. Mimeographed.

Conzen, Kathleen Neils. "Phantom Landscapes of Colonization: Germans in the Making of a Pluralist America." In *German-American Encounter*, eds. Frank Trommler and Elliot Shore, 7–21.

Coombs, Philip H. *The Fourth Dimension of Foreign Policy: Educational and Cultural Affairs*. New York: Harper & Row, 1964.

———. "The Past and the Future in Perspective." In *Cultural Affairs and Foreign Relations*, ed. Robert Blum, 139–71. New York: Prentice-Hall, 1963.

Copeland, William, et al., eds. *Finnish-American Academic and Professional Exchanges: Analyses and Reminiscences*. Helsinki: US Educational Foundation in Finland, 1983.

Costelle, Daniel. *Les Prisonniers*. Paris: Flammarion, 1975.

Crawford, W. Rex, ed. *The Cultural Migration: The European Scholar in America*. New York: Barnes, 1953.

Cronin, Vincent. *The Wise Man from the West: Matteo Ricci and His Mission to China*. London: Hart-Davis, 1955.

Cropper, Elizabeth, ed. *The Diplomacy of Art: Artistic Creation and Politics in Seicento Italy*. Milan: Nuova Alta Editionale, 2000.

Curti, Merle. *American Philanthropy Abroad*. 1963. Reprint, with new introduction by the author, New Brunswick, N.J.: Transaction, 1988.

David, Ralph Rogers. "The Development of Activities and Policies of the US Government in Inter-American Cultural Relations." Master's thesis, University of Denver, 1951.

Davis, Natalie Zemon. *The Gift in Seventeenth-Century France*. Madison: University of Wisconsin Press, 2000.

Delaney, Robert F., and John S. Gibson, eds., *American Public Diplomacy: The Perspective of Fifty Years*, Medford Mass.: Murrow Center, Fletcher School and Filene Center, Tufts University, 1967.

Diebel, Terry L., and Walter R. Roberts, *Culture and Information: Two Foreign Policy Functions*. Beverly Hills and London: Sage Washington Papers IV, 1976.

Dillon, Wilton. *Gifts and Nations: The Obligation to Give, Receive, and Repay*. The Hague: Mouton, 1968.

Dizard, Wilson P. *The Strategy of Truth: The Story of the US Information Service*. Washington, D.C.: Public Affairs, 1961.

Donaldson, Frances. *The British Council: The First 50 Years*. Jonathan Cape: London, 1984.

Dower, John W. *War without Mercy: Race and Power in the Pacific War*. New York: Pantheon, 1986.

Dudden, Arthur P., and Russell R. Dynes, eds., *The Fulbright Experience, 1946–86*. New Brunswick, N.J.: Transaction, 1987.

Dunne, Michael. "American Judicial Internationalism in the Twentieth Century." In *Proceedings of the 90th Annual Meeting of the American Society of International Law*, 27–30 March 1996.

Elder, Robert E. *The Information Machine: The US Information Agency and US Foreign Policy*. Syracuse: Syracuse University Press, 1968.

Ellis, Joseph J. *American Sphinx: The Character of Thomas Jefferson*. New York: Knopf, 1995.

Espinosa, J. Manuel. *Inter-American Beginnings of US Cultural Diplomacy 1936–48*. Washington, D.C.: Department of State, 1976.

Evans, Luther H. *The United States and UNESCO*. Dobbs-Ferry: Oceana, 1971.

Fairbank, John King. *Chinabound: A Fifty-Year Memoir*. New York: Harper, 1982.

Fairbank, Wilma. *America's Cultural Experiment in China, 1942–49*. Washington, D.C.: Department of State, 1976.

Fallon, Daniel. "German Influences on American Education." In *German-American Encounter*, eds. Frank Trommler and Elliott Shore, 77–87. New York: Berghahn, 2001.

Farquharson, John E., and Stephen C. Holt. *Europe from Below: An Assessment of Franco-German Popular Contacts*. London: Allen & Unwin, 1975.

Fein, Seth. "Transnationalization and Cultural Collaboration: Mexican Film Propaganda During World War II." *Studies in Latin American Popular Culture* 17 (1998): 105–28.

Field, James A., Jr. *America and the Mediterranean World, 1776–1882*. Princeton: Princeton University Press, 1969.

Finn, Helena Kane. "The Case for Cultural Diplomacy: Engaging Foreign Audiences." *Foreign Affairs* 82, no. 6 (November 2003): 15–20.

Fitch, Noel Riley. *Appetite for Life: The Biography of Julia Child*. New York: Doubleday, 1997.

Flack, Michael J. *Five Studies in International Cultural and Educational Exchange*. School of Public and International Affairs, Pittsburgh, 1964. Typescript.

Frankel, Charles. *Controversies and Decisions: The Social Sciences and Public Policy*. New York: Sage, 1976.

———. "The Era of Educational and Cultural Relations,"*Department of State Bulletin* (June 1966).

———. *High on Foggy Bottom: An Outsider's Insider View of the Government*. New York: Harper & Row, 1968.

———. *The Neglected Aspect of Foreign Affairs: American Educational and Cultural Policy Abroad*. Washington, D.C.: Brookings, 1965.

———. "The Scribblers and Foreign Affairs." *Foreign Affairs* 44. October 1995: 1–14

———. *The Faith of Reason: The Idea of Progress in the French Enlightenment*. New York: Octagon, 1969.

———. *A Stubborn Case*. New York: Norton, 1972.

Friday, William, et al. *Fulbright at Fifty: Meeting the Challenge of the Next Fifty Years*. Research Triangle Park, N.C.: National Humanities Center, 1998.

Fry, Richard N. *The Heritage of Persia*. New York: World, 1963.

Fulbright, J. William and Bourke Hickenlooper, Hearings of the Senate Foreign Relations Committee, 1952–53 (bound copy of more than 2000 pages in the possession of Mildred Marcy).

Fussell, Paul. *The Great War and Modern Memory*. New York: Oxford, 1975.

Gardner, John, et al., *A Beacon of Hope: The Exchange of Persons Program*. A Report from the US Advisory Commission on International Educational and Cultural Affairs. Washington, D.C.: GPO, 1963.

Glazer, Nathan, ed. *The Fulbright Experience and Academic Exchanges*. *The Annals* 491 (May 1987).

Gluck, Jay, Noel Siver, Sumi Hiramoto Gluck, eds. *Surveyors of Persian Art: A Documentary Portrait of Arthur Upham Pope and Phyllis Ackerman*. Ashiya, Japan: SoPA, 1996.

Gordon, David C. *Images of the West: Third World Perspectives*. Savage, Md.: Rowman and Littlefield, 1989.

Grant, Michael. *From Alexander to Cleopatra*. New York: Scribner, 1982.

Green, Fitzhugh. *American Propaganda Abroad from Benjamin Frankin to Ronald Reagan*. New York: Hippocrene, 1988.

Greenwood, Douglas McCreary. *Art in Embassies*. Washington: Friends of Art and Preservation in Embassies, 1989.

Guruge, Ananda W. P. *Free at Last in Paradise*. Bryn Mawr, Pa.: Books on the Web, 1999.

———. *The Serendipity of Andrew George*. Berkeley: First Books, 2003.

Gwama, Bitrus Paul. "Multi-Cultural Programming as a Strategy in Public Diplomacy: Leo Sarkisian and VOA's 'Music Time in America.'" Unpublished dissertation, Ohio State University College of Communication, 1992.

Haddow, Robert H. *Pavilions of Plenty: Exhibiting American Culture Abroad in the 1950s.* Washington: Smithsonian, 1997.

Hanson, Haldore. *The Cultural Cooperation Program, 1938–43.* Department of State publication 2137, 1944, updated in 1948.

Harrison, Lawrence E., and Samuel P. Huntington, eds. *Culture Matters: How Values Shape Human Progress.* New York: Basic, 2000.

Hawke, David Freeman. *Paine.* New York: Harper & Row, 1974.

Haynes, Sybille. *Etruscan Citilization: A Cultural History.* Los Angeles: Getty Museum, 2000.

Heger, Kenneth H. "Race Relations in the U.S. and American Cultural and Informational Programs in Ghana, 1957–66." *Prologue,* vol. 31, no. 4 (1999).

Heindel, Richard H. "The American Library Abroad: A Medium of International Intellectual Exchange." *The Library Quarterly* 16 no. 2 (1946): 93–107.

Hixson, Walter L. *Parting the Curtain: Propaganda, Culture, and the Cold War, 1945–61.* New York: St. Martin's Press, 1997.

Hocking, Elton. *Experiment in Education: What We Can Learn From Teaching Germany.* Chicago: Regnery, 1954.

Holland, Kenneth, ed. *International Exchange of Persons: A Reassessment. The Annals* 424 (March 1976).

Hoopes, Townsend and Douglas Brinkley. *Driven Patriot: The Life and Times of James Forrestal.* New York: Vintage Books, 1993.

Hoover, Herbert, et. al. *The Hoover Commission Report.* New York: McGraw-Hill, 1949.

Horwitz, Richard P., ed. *Exporting America: Essays on American Studies Abroad.* New York: Garland, 1993.

Hughes, Thomas L. "Two Decades in the Front Office: Reflections on How the Carnegie Endowment for International Peace Operated in Cold War Washington." In *Beyond Government: Extending the Public Policy Debate in Emerging Democracies.* Boulder, Colo.: Westview, 1995.

Huntington, Samuel P. *The Clash of Civilizations and the Remaking of World Order.* New York: Simon & Schuster, 1996. First sketched in *Foreign Affairs,* 1992.

Hyman, Sidney. *The Lives of William Benton.* Chicago: Chicago University Press, 1969.

Illing, Robert F. "The Envoy and the Cleric." *Foreign Service Journal* (November 1997).

Iriye, Akire. *Across the Pacific: An Inner History of American-East Asian Relations.* New York: Harcourt, Brace, 1967.

———. *Cultural Internationalism and World Order.* Baltimore: Johns Hopkins Press, 1997.

———. "Culture and International History." In *Explaining the History of American Foreign Relations* eds. Michael Hogan and Thomas G. Paterson. New York: Cambridge University Press, 1991.

———. "Culture and Power: International Relations as Intercultural Relations." *Diplomatic History* 3, no. 2 (Spring 1979): 115–28

———. *Power and Culture: The Japanese-American War, 1941–45.* Cambridge: Harvard University Press, 1981.

Isaacson, Walter and Evan Thomas. *The Wise Men: Six Friends and the World They Made.* 1986. Reissue. New York: Simon & Schuster, 1997.

Issawi, Charles. *Cross-Cultural Encounters and Conflicts.* New York: Oxford, 1998.

Jaeger, Werner. *Paideia: The Ideals of Greek Culture,* 3 vols. New York: Oxford, 1944.

Johnson, Haynes, and B. M. Gwertzman, *Fulbright the Dissenter.* New York: Modern Library, 1968.

Johnson, Robert Davis, ed. *On Cultural Ground: Essays in International History.* Chicago: Imprint, 1994.

Johnson, Walter, and Francis J. Colligan. *The Fulbright Program: A History.* Chicago: Chicago University Press, 1965.

Joseph, Gilbert M., Catherine C. LeGrand, and Ricardo D. Salvatore, eds. *Close Encoun-*

ters of Empire: Writing the Cultural History of U.S.-Latin American Relations. Durham: Duke University Press, 1998.

Kallen, Horace. Culture and Democracy. New York: Boni and Liveright, 1924.

Kammen, Michael. In the Past Lane: Historical Perspectives on American Culture. New York: Oxford, 1997.

Kaplan, Amy, and Donald E. Pease, eds. Cultures of US Imperialism. Durham, N.C.: Duke University Press, 1993.

Katz, Philip M. From Appomattox to Montmartre: Americans and the Paris Commune. Cambridge: Harvard University Press, 1998.

Kellermann, Henry J. Cultural Relations as an Instrument of US Foreign Policy: The Educational Exchange Program Between the U.S. and Germany, 1945–54. Washington, D.C.: Department of State, 1978.

Kendall, Harry H. A Farm Boy in the Foreign Service. Berkeley: First Books, 2003.

Kendrick, Alexander. Prime Time: The Life of Edward R. Murrow. New York: Little, Brown, 1969.

Kennan, George F. International Exchange in the Arts. New York: International Council, Museum of Modern Art, 1956.

———. "George Kennan in the FSJ: A Compilation of his Writings," in special issue of Foreign Service Journal, "At a Century's Ending: Diplomat Extraordinaire George Kennan Turns 100," 81, 2. February 2004.

Kennedy, Ludovic. Very Lovely People: A Personal Look at Some Americans Living Abroad. New York: Simon & Schuster, 1969.

Keohane, Robert O. After Hegemony: Cooperation and Discord in the World Political Economy. Princeton: Princeton University Press, 1984.

Kramer, Paul. "Princeton and the Spanish-American War." Princeton Alumni Weekly (10 June 1998): 12–16.

Kraske, Gary E. Missionaries of the Book: the American Library Profession and the Origins of US Cultural Diplomacy. Westport, Conn.: Greenwood Press, 1985.

Kuisel, Richard F. Seducing the French: The Dilemma of Americanization. Berkeley: University of California Press, 1996.

Lambert, Richard. "Durable Academic Linkages Overseas: A National Agenda," in The Annals 491, May 1987, 140–53.

La Palombara, Joseph. Democracy, Italian Style. New Haven: Yale University Press, 1987.

Laves, Walter H. C. and Francis O. Wilcox. "Organizing the Government for Participation in World Affairs." American Political Science Review, vol. 38, no. 5 (1944).

Laves, Walter H. C. and Charles A. Thomson. Cultural Relations and US Foreign Policy. Bloomington: Indiana University Press, 1963.

———. UNESCO: Purposes, Progress, Prospects. Bloomington: Indiana University Press, 1957.

Lawson, Murray. The United States Information Agency: A History. USIA archives, 1970. Unfinished manuscript, notes, and unbound papers.

Lee, J. M. "British Cultural Dipomacy and the Cold War: 1946–61." Diplomacy and Statecraft 9, no. 1 (1998); 112–34.

Lepore, Jill. A is for American: Letters and Other Characters in the Newly United States. New York: Knopf, 2002.

Levenstein, Harvey. Seductive Journey: American Tourists in France from Jefferson to the Jazz Age. Chicago: University of Chicago Press, 1998.

Lewis, Mark B. "Shelving Access for USIA Libraries Lies Ahead." American Libraries 28, no. 2 (1997): 49–53.

Lincoln, Robert A., et al. "The U.S.—Warts and All": Edward R. Murrow as Director of USIA, Presenting the U.S. to the World. Commemorative symposium by the USIA Alumni Association and the Public Diplomacy Foundation. McLean, Va.: The Public Diplomacy Foundation, 1992.

Littman, Ulrich. Partners Distant and Close: Notes and Footnotes on Academic Mobility

Between Germany and the U.S., 1923–93. DAAD-Forum, 19. Bonn: Deutscher Akademischer Austauschdienst, 1997.

Loeffler, Jane C. *The Architecture of Diplomacy: Building America's Embassies.* Princeton: Princeton Architectural Press, 1998.

Lopez, Claude-Anne. *Mon Cher Papa: Franklin and the Ladies of Paris.* New Haven: Yale University Press, 1990.

Lui, Elizabeth Gill. *Building Diplomacy: The Architecture of American Embassies.* Ithaca, N.Y.: Cornell University Press, 2004.

———. *My Life with Benjamin Franklin.* New Haven: Yale University Press, 2000.

Mack, Rosamund. *Bazaar to Piazza: Islamic Trade and Italian Art.* Berkeley: University of California Press, 2002.

MacLeish, Archibald. *A Time to Speak.* New York: Houghton Mifflin, 1941.

Malone, Dumas. *Jefferson and His Time.* Boston: Little, Brown, 1948.

Malone, Gifford D. *Political Advocacy and Cultural Communication: Organizing the Nation's Public Diplomacy.* Series on Rhetoric and Political Discourse, ed. Kenneth W. Thompson, vol. 11. Charlottesville, Va.: Miller Center, 1988.

Manguel, Alberto. *A History of Reading.* London: HarperCollins, 1996.

Manheim, Jarol B. *Strategic Public Diplomacy and American Foreign Policy: The Evolution of Influence.* New York: Oxford, 1994.

Mattingly, Garrett. *Renaissance Diplomacy.* Baltimore: Penguin, 1964; first published 1955.

Mauss, Marcel. *The Gift: Forms and Functions of Exchange in Archaic Societies, 1954.* Rev. with introduction by Mary Douglas. London: Routledge, 1990.

McCaughey, Robert A. *International Studies and Academic Enterprise: A Chapter in the Enclosure of American Learning.* New York: Columbia University Press, 1984.

McCullough, David. *John Adams.* New York: Simon & Schuster, 2001.

McDougal, Walter A. *Promised Land, Crusader State: The American Encounter with the World Since 1776.* New York: Houghton Mifflin, 1997.

McMurry, Ruth, and Muna Lee. *The Cultural Approach: Another Way in International Relations.* Chapel Hill: University of North Carolina Press, 1947.

Menand, Louis. *The Metaphysical Club.* New York: Farrar, Straus, and Giroux, 2001.

Mendras, Henri, and Laurence Duboys Fresney. *la Seconde Révolution française, 1965–84.* Paris: Gallimard, 1988.

Merson, Martin. *The Private Diary of a Public Servant.* New York: Macmillan, 1955.

Meyer, Cord. *Facing Reality: From World Federalism to the CIA.* New York: Harper and Row, 1980.

Millspaugh, Arthur C. *Americans in Persia.* Washington, D.C.: Brookings, 1946.

———. *The American Task in Persia.* New York and London: The Century, 1925.

———. *The Financial and Economic Situation of Persia.* Boston: Pinkham Press, 1926.

Mitchell, J. M. *International Cultural Relations.* London: Allen & Unwin, 1986.

Mock, James R., and Cedric Larsen. *Words That Won the War: The Story of the Committee on Public Information, 1917–19.* Princeton: Princeton University Press, 1939.

Morgan, Conway Lloyd. "Master Mind." *Grafik* 109 (September 2003): 30–31.

Morris, Edmund. *Theodore Rex.* New York: Random House, 2001.

Mulcahy, Kevin V. "Cultural Diplomacy and the Exchange Programs: 1938–78." *The Journal of Arts, Management, Law, and Society,* vol. 29, no. 1, (1999).

Mylonas, Denis. *la Genèse de l'UNESCO: la conférence des ministres alliés de l'éducation, 1942–45.* Brussels: E. Bruyland, 1976.

Newsom, David D. *The Public Dimension of Diplomacy.* Bloomington: Indiana University Press, 1996.

Ninkovich, Frank A. "The Currents of Cultural Diplomacy: Art and the State Department, 1938–47." *Diplomatic History* I (Summer 1977): 215–37.

———. *The Diplomacy of Ideas: US Foreign Policy and Cultural Relations, 1938–50.* Cambridge: Cambridge University Press, 1981.

————. *Modernity and Power: A History of the Domino Theory in the Twentieth Century.* Chicago: University of Chicago Press, 1994.

————. *US Information Policy and Cultural Diplomacy.* New York: World Affairs Council, 1966.

Nostrand, Howard Lee. *The Cultural Attaché.* Hazen Foundation Pamphlet No. 17, 1947.

Olson, William C. and Llewellyn D. Howell. *International Education: The Unfinished Agenda.* ITT Key Issues Lecture Series. Indianapolis: White River Press, 1984.

Orr, Robert C., "Paradigm Lost? US Approaches to Democracy Promotion in Developing Countries." Ph.D. diss., Wilson School, 1996.

Parker, Richard B. *Uncle Sam in Barbary, A Diplomatic History.* Gainesville: University of Florida Press, 2004.

Pells, Richard. *Not Like Us: How Europeans Have Loved, Hated, and Transformed American Culture since World War II.* New York: Basic, 1997.

Persico, Joseph E. *Edward R. Murrow: An American Original.* New York: McGraw-Hill, 1988.

Prevots, Naima. *Dance for Export: Cultural Diplomacy and the Cold War.* With introduction by Eric Foner. Hanover, N.H.: Wesleyan University Press, 1999.

Price, Paxton P., ed. *International Book and Library Activities: The History of a US Foreign Policy.* Metuchen, N.J.: Scarecrow, 1982.

Prothero, Stephen. *The White Buddhist: The Asian Odyssey of Henry Steele Olcott.* Bloomington: Indiana University Press, 1996.

Putnam, Robert D. *Making Democracy Work: Civic Traditions in Modern Italy.* Princeton: Princeton University Press, 1993.

Ramazani, Nesta. *The Rose and the Nightingale.* Syracuse: Syracuse University Press, 1999.

Reich, Cary. *The Life of Nelson A. Rockefeller: Worlds to Conquer, 1908–58.* New York: Doubleday, 1996.

Reichard, John F., ed. *International Educator,* vol. 7, no. 2–3. (1998).

Reynolds, David. *Rich Relations: The American Occupation of Britain, 1942–45.* New York: Random House, 1995.

Richmond, Yale. *Cultural Exchange and the Cold War: Raising the Iron Curtain.* University Park: Pennsylvania State University Press, 2003.

Robin, Ron. *The Barbed-Wire College: Reeducating German POWs in the U.S. during World War II.* Princeton: Princeton University Press, 1995.

Roche, François, and Bernard Pigniau. *Histoires de diplomatie culturelle des origines à 1995.* Paris: Documentation française, 1995.

Roger, Philippe. *L'Ennemi américain: Généologie de l'antiamericanisme français.* Paris: Le Seuil, 2002.

Rose, Clive. *The Soviet Propaganda Network: A Directory of Organizations Serving Soviet Foreign Policy.* New York: St. Martin's, 1988.

Rosen, Seymour N. *The Preparation and Education of Foreign Students in the USSR.* Department of Health, Education, and Welfare series on Information on Education around the World, no. 44. 1960.

Rosenberg, Emily. *Financial Missionaries to the World: The Politics and Culture of Dollar Diplomacy, 1900–30.* Cambridge, Mass., and London: Harvard University Press, 1999.

————. *Spreading the American Dream, 1890–1945.* New York: Hill and Wang, 1982.

Roth, Lois W. "Public Diplomacy and the Past: The Search for an American Style of Propaganda, 1952–77." *The Fletcher Forum* 8 (Summer 1984): 353–96. Rev. ed. Walter M. Brasch and Dana R. Ulloth. *The Press and the State.* Lanham, Md.: University Press of America, 1986.

Ryan, Henry Butterfield. "What Does a Cultural Attaché Really Do?" *Newsletter,* Society for Historians of American Foreign Relations, vol. 20, no. 3 (1989).

Sablosky, Juliet Antunes. "Reinvention, Reorganization, Retreat: American Cultural

Diplomacy at Century's End." *The Journal of Arts, Management, Law, and Society*, vol. 29, no. 1 (1999).

Saunders, Frances Stonor. *The Cultural Cold War: The CIA and the World of Arts and Letters*. New York: The New Press, 1999.

Schafer, Edward H. *The Golden Peaches of Samarkand: A Study of T'ang Exotics*. Berkeley: University of California Press, 1953.

Schenkel, Albert F. *The Rich Man and the Kingdon: John D. Rockefeller Jr. and the Protestant Establishment*. Minneapolis: Fortress, 1995.

Schlesinger, Arthur M., Jr. *A Life in the Twentieth Century: Innocent Beginnings, 1917–50*. New York: Houghton Mifflin, 2000.

Schoenbrun, David. *Triumph in Paris: The Exploits of Benjamin Franklin*. New York: Harper & Row, 1976.

Schwantes, Robert. *Japanese and Americans: A Century of Cultural Relations*. New York: Harper, 1955.

Shuster, W. Morgan. *The Strangling of Persia*. 1912. Reprint. New York: Greenwood, 1968.

Sirota (Gordon), Beate. *The Only Woman in the Room: A Memoir*. New York and Tokyo: Kodansha International, 1999.

Smith, Jean Edward. *Lucius D. Clay: An American Life*. New York: Holt, 1990.

Smith, Paul A. *On Political War*. Washington, D.C.: National Defense University Press, 1989.

Smyth, Craig Hugh. *Repatriation of Art from the Collecting Point in Munich after World War II*. Marsden-The Hague: Schwartz-SDU, 1988.

Sorensen, Thomas C. *The Word War*. New York: Harper & Row, 1968.

Spence, Jonathan. *The Memory Palace of Matteo Ricci*. New York: Viking Penguin, 1984.

Sperber, A. M. *Murrow: His Life and Times*. New York: Freundlich, 1986.

Spotts, Frederic. *Hitler and the Power of Aesthetics*. New York: Overlook, 2002.

Stanton, Frank, et al. *International Information, Education, and Cultural Relations: Recommendations for the Future*. Washington, D.C.: CSIS, 1975.

Starr, Richard F., ed. *Public Diplomacy: USA Versus USSR*. Stanford: Hoover Press, 1986.

Steichen, Edward. *The Family of Man: Témoignages et documents*. 1955. Reprint. Luxembourg: Ministry of Cultural Affairs, 1994.

Stephanson, Anders. *Manifest Destiny: American Expansion and the Empire of Right*. New York: Hill and Wang, 1995.

Stephens, John Lloyd. *Incidents of Travel in Central America, Chiapas and Yucatan*, ill. by Frederick Catherwood. 2 vols. 1841. Reprint. New York: Dover, 1969.

Stephens, Oren. *Facts to a Candid World: the American Overseas Information Program*. Stanford: Stanford University Press, 1955.

———. *Incidents of Travel in Yucatan*. 2 vols. 1843. Reprint. New York: Dover, 1963.

Stern, Fritz. *Einstein's German World*. Princeton: Princeton University Press, 1999.

Stiller, Jesse H. *George S. Messersmith, Diplomat of Democracy*. Chapel Hill: University of North Carolina Press, 1987.

Stovall, Tyler. *Paris Noir: African-Americans in the City of Light*. New York: Houghton Mifflin, 1996.

Strauss, David. *Menace in the West: The Rise of French Anti-Americanism in Modern Times*. Westport, Conn.: Greenwood, 1978.

Strouse, Jean. *Morgan: An American Financier*. New York: Random House, 1999.

Suleiman, Ezra. *Dismantling Democratic States*. Princeton: Princeton University Press, 2003.

Susman, Warren. *Culture as History: The Transformation of American Society in the Twentieth Century*. New York, Pantheon Books, 1984.

Sussman, Leonard R. *The Culture of Freedom: The Small World of Fulbright Scholars*. Lanham. Md.: Rowman & Littlefield, 1992.

Thackston, W. M. *A Century of Princes: Sources on Timurid History and Art*. Cambridge, Mass.: Aga Khan Program, 1989.

Thomas, Evan. *The Very Best Men, Four Who Dared: The Early Years of the CIA*. New York: Simon & Schuster, 1996.

Thompson, Kenneth W., ed. *The Stanton Commission Revisited, Rhetoric and Public Diplomacy*, vol. 7. Lanham, Md.: University Press of America, 1988.

Thomson, Charles A. H. *The Overseas Cultural Service of the US Government*. Washington, D.C.: Brookings, 1948.

———. *See also* Laves, W. H. C.

Tomlinson, John. *Cultural Imperialsm: A Critical Introduction*. London: Pinter, 1991.

Trommler, Frank, and Elliott Shore, eds. *The German-American Encounter: Conflict and Cooperation Between Two Cultures, 1800–2000*. New York: Berghahn, 2001.

Tuch, Hans J. *Communicating with the World: US Public Diplomacy Overseas*. With foreword by Marvin Kalb. Washington, D.C.: Institute for the Study of Diplomacy, Georgetown University, 1990.

———, ed. *USIA: Communicating with the World in the 1990s*. Washington, D.C.: Public Diplomacy Foundation, 1994.

Tye, Larry. *The Father of Spin: Edward L. Bernays and the Birth of Public Relations*. New York: Crown, 1998.

Wagnleiter, Reinhold. *Coca-Colonization and the Cold War: The Cultural Mission of the U.S. in Austria after the Second World War*. Chapel Hill: University of North Carolina Press, 1995.

Webb, James H., Jr. "Cultural Attaché: Scholar, Propagandist or Bureaucrat?" *South Atlantic Quarterly*, vol. 71 (Summer 1972).

Weinstein, Allen, and Alexander Vassiliev. *The Haunted Wood: Soviet Espionage in America—The Stalin Era*. New York: Random House, 1999.

Welles, Benjamin. *Sumner Welles: FDR's Global Strategist*. New York: St. Martin's, 1997.

Wieck, Randolph R. *Ignorance Abroad: American Educational and Cultural Foreign Policy-and the Office of the Assistant Secretary of State*. Westport: Praeger, 1992.

———. *Philip Coombs: Secrétaire d'Etat à l'Education et aux Affaires Culturelles*. Thesis, Paris, Sorbonne Nouvelle, 1989.

Wilson, Donald M. *USIA Rhetoric and Persuasion: An Insider's View*. USIA Archives. Mimeograph.

Wilson, Howard E. "National Programs of International Cultural Relations." *International Conciliation* 42 (Carnegie Endowment: New York, June 1950).

Winks, Robin W. *Cloak and Gown: Scholars in the Secret War, 1939–61*. New York: Morrow, 1987.

———. *The Imperial Revolution: Yesterday and Today*. Oxford: Clarendon, 1994.

———. "Imperialism." In *The Comparative Approach to American History*, ed. C. Vann Woodward, 253–70. New York: Basic, 1968.

Wolper, Green. "Ghosts, Balloons and a Pocket of Venom: US and Allied Foreign Propaganda Services in World War I." In *On Cultural Ground*, ed. Robert Davis Johnson, 111–22. Chicago: Imprint, 1994.

Woods, Randall Bennett. *Fulbright: A Biography*. Cambridge: Cambridge University Press, 1995.

Woolf, Leonard. *International Government*. Westminster: Fabian Society, 1916.

———. *Village in the Jungle*. London: Arnold, 1913.

Wright, Louis B., and Julia H. MacLeod. *The First Americans in North Africa*. Princeton: Princeton University Press, 1945.

Zanker, Paul. *Augusto e il potere delle imagini*. Einaudi: Turin, 1989, esp. final chapter, "La Diffusione del mito imperiale."

Zimmerman, Warren. *First Great Triumph: How Five Americans Made Their Country a World Power*. New York: Farrar, Straus and Giroux, 2002.

INDEX